Contemporary Security Studies

Contemporary Security Studies

SECOND EDITION

Edited by Alan Collins

OXFORD
UNIVERSITY PRESS

OXFORD
UNIVERSITY PRESS

Great Clarendon Street, Oxford ox2 6DP

Oxford University Press is a department of the University of Oxford.
It furthers the University's objective of excellence in research, scholarship,
and education by publishing worldwide in

Oxford New York

Auckland Cape Town Dar es Salaam Hong Kong Karachi
Kuala Lumpur Madrid Melbourne Mexico City Nairobi
New Delhi Shanghai Taipei Toronto

With offices in

Argentina Austria Brazil Chile Czech Republic France Greece
Guatemala Hungary Italy Japan Poland Portugal Singapore
South Korea Switzerland Thailand Turkey Ukraine Vietnam

Oxford is a registered trade mark of Oxford University Press
in the UK and in certain other countries

Published in the United States
by Oxford University Press Inc., New York

© Oxford University Press 2010

British Library Cataloguing in Publication Data
Data available

Library of Congress Cataloging in Publication Data
Data available

Typeset by MPS Limited, A Macmillan Company
Printed in Italy by L.E.G.O S.p.A

ISBN   978–0–19–954885–9

10 9 8 7 6 5 4 3 2 1

Preface

The genesis of the first edition was the need to provide a wide coverage of a discipline that had, and is still, undergoing significant changes—changes not only in what Security Studies was concerned with, but also in what it means to be secure and how something actually becomes a security issue. The dynamic nature of this field of enquiry has ensured that since the first edition appeared more topics have emerged on the security agenda and new approaches to studying security have evolved.

The second edition maintains the structure of the first edition: the Approaches section is followed by the Deepening and Broadening of the subject before we finish by looking at a range of Traditional and Non-Traditional security issues. The second edition is, though, significantly larger than the first; in all, seven chapters have been added. The section to benefit the most from this enlargement is the first. Rather than explaining the traditional approach to studying security in one chapter, this has now been divided into two ('Realism' and 'Liberalism'). The book thus provides a more detailed explanation of these two traditional approaches, enabling a greater appreciation of their breadth. In addition, another two chapters have been added to this section: 'Social Constructivism' and 'Historical Materialism'. All the other approaches from the first edition remain. The chapters have been updated, with 'Critical Security Studies' and 'Gender and Security' in particular receiving significant adjustments. In all, the Approaches section boasts nine chapters, an increase of three chapters from the first edition.

The second section embraces the Deepening and Broadening of what Security Studies examines and here there are two changes to the first edition. First, the 'Military Security' chapter has a new author and thus appears as an entirely new chapter from the first edition. Secondly, the section has an additional chapter, 'Globalization, Development, and Security'. The other chapters have been updated to reflect changes in the world; for example, the 'Economic Security' chapter has a new case study on the current global recession.

The final section on Traditional and Non-Traditional security has two new chapters: 'Humanitarian Intervention' and 'Energy Security'. It maintains the same coverage as the first edition on the other security issues, but the chapter on HIV/AIDS has been broadened to encompass other diseases and is retitled 'Health', while the chapter on children and war is more narrowly focused on the issue of 'Child Soldiers'.

Acknowledgements

With all projects there are many people to thank, and this is no exception, for without their support this book could not have been produced. First and foremost thanks must be given to the contributors first for agreeing to write their chapters and then for diligently submitting them on schedule, complete with pedagogic features. Thanks must also be given to those reviewers who commented in detail on the first edition; the second edition has benefited from, and been adjusted in the light of, their useful thoughts. Special thanks also go to Gillian Rollason, who was responsible for preparing and producing the resource centre that supports the book. I am also grateful to Professor John Baylis for originally encouraging me to take on this task. Finally, thanks also go to Ruth Anderson and Claire Brewer at OUP for their professionalism and assistance during the preparation of this book.

Brief Contents

Detailed Contents

---

1   Introduction: What is Security Studies?   1

Alan Collins

Part 1   Approaches to Security   13

---

2   Realism   15

Charles L. Glaser

---

3   Liberalism   34

Patrick Morgan

Liberalism and democracy   42

Conclusion   44

Questions   47

Further reading   47

Important website   48

4   Social Constructivism   49
    Christine Agius

    Introduction   50

    Definitions and key concepts   53

    Wendt's three cultures of anarchy   60

    Conventional and critical constructivism   61

    Critiques of constructivism   64

    Conclusion   66

    Questions   67

    Further reading   67

    Important websites   67

5   Peace Studies   69
    Paul Rogers

    Introduction   70

    The early years   70

    Evolution amidst controversy   72

    What is peace studies now?   75

    Responding to the new security challenges   78

    Conclusion   81

    Questions   82

    Further reading   82

    Important websites   83

6   Critical Security Studies: A Schismatic History   84
    David Mutimer

    Introduction: 'Follow the sign of the gourd'   85

    Toronto desire: *Critical Security Studies*   87

    Copenhagen distinctions   91

    Aberystwyth exclusions   92

    Constructing security   95

    Everyone's Other: poststructuralism and security   97

    Conclusion   102

    Questions   103

    Further reading   104

    Important websites   105

Part 2   Deepening and Broadening Security   167

11   Military Security   169
Michael Sheehan

12   Regime Security   185
Richard Jackson

13   Societal Security   202
Paul Roe

17   Coercive Diplomacy   277
     Peter Viggo Jakobsen

     Introduction   278
     What is coercive diplomacy?   279
     Theories and requirements for success   281
     The challenge of defining success   285
     Western use of coercive diplomacy 1990–2008   286
     Why coercive diplomacy is hard   292
     Conclusion   296
     Questions   297
     Further reading   297
     Important websites   298

18   The Role of Intelligence in National Security   299
     Stan A. Taylor

     Introduction   300
     Definitions and theory of intelligence   300
     Intelligence services of different nations   301
     Intelligence collection disciplines   304
     The intelligence process   306
     Intelligence and security since the Second World War   308
     Legal and ethical issues involving intelligence   310
     Covert action   311
     Terrorism, Iraq, and the post 9/11 security environment   313
     Conclusion   315
     Questions   317
     Further reading   318
     Important websites   319

19   Weapons of Mass Destruction   320
     James J. Wirtz

     Introduction   321
     Nuclear weapons   322
     Chemical weapons   327
     Biological weapons   331
     Conclusion   335
     Questions   336
     Further reading   337
     Important websites   337

Notes on Contributors

Christine Agius. Lecturer in International Relations and Politics in the School of English, Sociology, Politics and Contemporary History (ESPACH) at the University of Salford. She is the author of *The Social Construction of Swedish Neutrality: Challenges to Swedish Identity and Sovereignty* (Manchester: Manchester University Press, 2006).

Jon Barnett. Australian Research Council Fellow in the Department of Resource Management and Geography at the University of Melbourne, Australia. He is the author of *The Meaning of Environmental Security: Ecological Politics and Policy in the New Security Era* (London: Zed Books, 2001).

Alex J. Bellamy. Professor of International Relations and Executive Director of the Asia-Pacific Centre for the Responsibility to Protect at the University of Queensland, Australia. Recent books include, with Paul D. Williams, *Understanding Peacekeeping* (2nd edn., Cambridge: Polity, 2009) and *Responsibility to Protect: The Global Effort to End Mass Atrocities* (Cambridge: Polity, 2009).

Helen Brocklehurst. Lecturer in International Relations in the School of Arts and Humanities at Swansea University, UK. She is the author of *Who's Afraid of Children? Children, Conflict and International Relations* (Aldershot: Ashgate, 2006).

Barry Buzan. Montague Burton Professor of International Relations at the London School of Economics, UK. His latest books include *The United States and the Great Powers: World Politics in the Twenty-First Century* (Cambridge: Polity, 2004), and, with Lene Hansen, *The Evolution of International Security Studies* (Cambridge: Cambridge University Press, 2009).

Alan Collins. Senior Lecturer in International Relations in the School of Arts and Humanities at Swansea University, UK. He is the author of *Security Dilemmas of Southeast Asia* (London: Macmillan, 2000) and *Security and Southeast Asia: Domestic, Regional and Global Issues* (Boulder, CO: Lynne Rienner, 2003).

Neil Cooper. Senior Lecturer in International Relations and Security in the Department of Peace Studies at the University of Bradford, UK. His most recent publications include the co-authored book *War Economies in their Regional Context: The Challenges of Transformation* (Boulder, CO: Lynne Rienner, 2004) and the co-edited book *Whose Peace? Critical Perspectives on the Political Economy of Peacebuilding* (Basingstoke: Palgrave Macmillan 2008).

Christopher M. Dent. Professor in East Asia's International Political Economy at the University of Leeds, UK. His latest books include *East Asian Regionalism* (London: Routledge, 2008) and *China, Japan and Regional Leadership in East Asia* (Cheltenham: Edward Elgar, 2008).

Stefan Elbe. Reader (Associate Professor) in International Relations in the Department of International Relations at the University of Sussex, UK. He is the author of *Virus Alert: Security, Governmentality and the AIDS Pandemic* (New York: Columbia University Press, 2009) and *Security and Global Health* (Cambridge: Polity, forthcoming 2010).

Ralf Emmers. Associate Professor at the S. Rajaratnam School of International Studies (RSIS), Nanyang Technological University, Singapore. He is the author of *Cooperative Security and the Balance of Power in ASEAN and the ARF* (London: Routledge Curzon 2003) and *Geopolitics and Maritime Territorial Disputes in East Asia* (Abingdon: Routledge, 2009).

Jeanne Giraldo. Lecturer in the Department of National Security Affairs at the Naval Postgraduate School, Monterey, USA, and Program Manager of the Defense Institution Reform Initiative for the Office of the Secretary of Defense, USA. She is co-editor of *Terrorism Finance and State Responses: A Comparative Perspective* (Palo Alto, CA: Stanford University Press, 2007) and of a forthcoming volume on Central American gangs to be published by the University of Texas Press.

Charles L. Glaser. Professor of Political Science and International Affairs, Elliott School of International Affairs, the George Washington University, USA. He is the author of *Analyzing Strategic Nuclear Policy* (Princeton: Princeton University Press, 1991) and *Rational Theory of International Politics* (Princeton: Princeton University Press, forthcoming 2010).

Eric Herring. Reader in the Department of Politics, University of Bristol, UK. He is co-author with Glen Rangwala of *Iraq in Fragments: The Occupation and its Legacy* (London: Hurst and Cornell University Press, 2006) and co-author with Barry Buzan of *The Arms Dynamic in World Politics* (Boulder, CO: Lynne Rienner Publishers, 1998).

Richard Jackson. Reader in International Politics, Aberystwyth University, UK. He is the co-author (with Jacob Bercovitch) of *Conflict Resolution in the Twenty-First Century: Principles, Methods, and Approaches* (Ann Arbor: University of Michigan Press, 2009) and co-editor (with Marie Breen Smyth and Jeroen Gunning) of *Critical Terrorism Studies: A New Research Agenda* (Abingdon: Routledge, 2009).

Peter Viggo Jakobsen. Associate Professor in the Department of Political Science, University of Copenhagen, Denmark. He is the author of *Western Use of Coercive Diplomacy after the Cold War: A Challenge for Theory and Practice* (Basingstoke: Macmillan Press, 1998) and *Nordic Approaches to Peace Operations: A New Model in the Making?* (London: Routledge, 2006).

Caroline Kennedy-Pipe. Professor of War Studies and Director of the Centre for Security Studies, University of Hull, UK. Her publications include *Russia and the World* (London: Edward Arnold, 1998) and *The Origins of the Cold War* (Houndmills, Basingstoke: Palgrave, 2007).

Pauline Kerr. Director of Studies in the Asia-Pacific College of Diplomacy (APCD) at the Australian National University, Australia. She is the co-editor (with Stuart Harris and

Qin Yaqing) of *China's 'New' Diplomacy: Tactical or Fundamental Change?* (New York: Palgrave Macmillan, 2008).

Brenda Lutz. Ph.D. candidate, Department of Politics, University of Dundee, UK, and Research Associate, Decision Sciences and Theory Institute, Indiana University-Purdue University, USA. She is the co-author of *Global Terrorism* (2nd edn., London: Routledge, 2008) and *Terrorism in America* (New York: Palgrave, 2007).

James Lutz. Professor in the Department of Political Science at the Indiana University-Purdue University, USA. He is the co-author of *Global Terrorism* (2nd edn., London: Routledge, 2008) and *Terrorism in America* (New York: Palgrave, 2007).

Patrick Morgan. Professor of Political Science and holds the Thomas and Elizabeth Tierney Chair in Global Peace and Conflict Studies at the University of California, Irvine, USA. He is the author of *Deterrence Now* (Cambridge: Cambridge University Press, 2003) and *International Security: Problems and Solutions* (Washington: CQ Press, 2006).

David Mutimer. Associate Professor in the Department of Political Science and Deputy Director of the Centre for International and Security Studies at York University, Canada. He is the author of *The Weapon State: Proliferation and the Framing of Security* (Boulder, CO: Lynne Rienner Publishers, 2000).

Nana K. Poku. John Ferguson Professorial Chair in the Department of Peace Studies at the University of Bradford, UK. He is the author of *AIDS in Africa: How the Poor are Dying* (Cambridge: Polity Press, 2006) and is the co-author of *Globalisation, Development and Human Security* (Cambridge: Polity Press, 2007).

Paul Roe. Associate Professor in the Department of International Relations and European Studies at the Central European University, Budapest, Hungary. He is the author of *Ethnic Violence and the Societal Security Dilemma* (London: Routledge, 2005).

Paul Rogers. Professor of Peace Studies in the Department of Peace Studies at the University of Bradford, UK. He is the author of *Losing Control: Global Security in the 21st Century* (2nd edn., London: Pluto Press, 2002) and *Global Security and the War on Terror: Elite Power and the Illusion of Control* (London and New York: Routledge, 2008).

Sam Raphael. Lecturer in Politics and International Relations at Kingston University, UK. His publications include, with Doug Stokes, *Imperial Logics: US Hegemony and Global Energy Security* (Baltimore, MD: Johns Hopkins University Press, forthcoming 2010).

Michael Sheehan. Professor of International Relations in the School of Arts and Humanities at Swansea University, UK. He is the author of *International Security: An Analytical Survey* (Boulder, CO: Lynne Rienner, 2005) and *The International Politics of Space* (London and New York: Routledge, 2007).

Joanna Spear. Director of the Security Policy Studies Program, The Elliott School of International Affairs, George Washington University, USA. She is the author of *Carter and Arms Sales: Implementing the Carter Administration's Arms Transfer Restraint Policy* (London: Macmillan, 1995).

Doug Stokes. A Senior Lecturer in International Politics at Kent University, UK. His publications include *America's Other War: Terrorizing Colombia* (London: Zed Books, 2004), he is the co-editor of *US Foreign Policy* (Oxford: Oxford University Press, 2008) and the co-author, with Sam Raphael, of *Imperial Logics: US Hegemony and Global Energy Security* (Baltimore, MD: Johns Hopkins University Press, forthcoming 2010).

Stan A. Taylor. Emeritus Professor of Political Science and Research Fellow at the David M. Kennedy Center for International Studies at Brigham Young University, Utah, USA. He is the co-author of *America the Vincible: US Foreign Policy for the 21st Century* (3rd edn., New York: Prentice-Hall, 2005).

Harold Trinkunas. Associate Professor in the Department of National Security Affairs at the Naval Postgraduate School, Monterey, USA. He is the co-editor of *Global Politics of Defense Reform* (New York: Palgrave Macmillan, 2008).

Ole Wæver. Professor of International Relations in the Department of Political Science at the University of Copenhagen, Denmark, and director of CAST, Centre for Advanced Security Theory. He is the co-author, with Barry Buzan, of *Regions and Powers: The Structure of International Security* (Cambridge: Cambridge University Press, 2003) and co-editor, with Arlene B. Tickner, of *International Relations Scholarship Around the World* (London: Routledge, 2009).

James J. Wirtz. Dean of the School of International Studies and Professor in the Department of National Security Affairs at the Naval Postgraduate School, Monterey, USA. He is the author of *The Tet Offensive: Intelligence Failure in War* (Ithaca, NY: Cornell University Press, 1991, 1994) and co-editor of *Complex Deterrence: Strategy in the Global Age* (Chicago: University of Chicago Press, 2009).

List of Figures

List of Tables

List of Boxes

KEY QUOTES

Guided Tour of Learning Features

This book is enriched with a range of learning tools to help you navigate the text and reinforce your knowledge of Security Studies. This guided tour shows you how to get the most out of your textbook package.

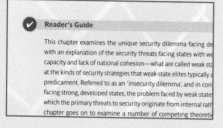

Reader's Guides

Reader's Guides at the beginning of every chapter set the scene for upcoming themes and issues to be discussed, and indicate the scope of coverage within each chapter.

Boxes

A number of topics benefit from further explanation or exploration in a manner that does not disrupt the flow of the main text. Throughout the book, boxes provide you with extra information on particular topics that complement your understanding of the main chapter text. There are five types of box:

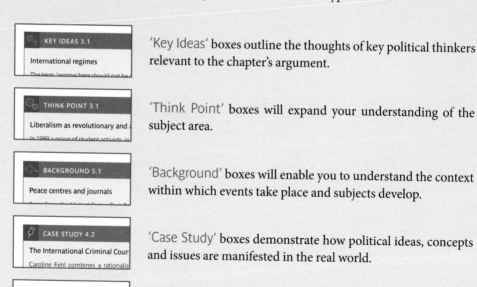

'Key Ideas' boxes outline the thoughts of key political thinkers relevant to the chapter's argument.

'Think Point' boxes will expand your understanding of the subject area.

'Background' boxes will enable you to understand the context within which events take place and subjects develop.

'Case Study' boxes demonstrate how political ideas, concepts and issues are manifested in the real world.

'Key Quotes' boxes include memorable quotes from scholars, politicians and others to help bring ideas and concepts to life.

tary conflict or of militarization in general. The
Discursive aspects are exemplified by the connections made between **militarism** and **masculinity**
and between nurturing, peace, and **femininity**.

This distinction is wedded to two further developments that reinforce the central relationship
between gender and security. The first involves the
acceptance of a broader concept of security than
has been traditional. A number of terms have been
used to describe this process, **'human security'** or
'soft security' being the most common. Up until

Glossary Terms

Key terms appear in blue in the text and are defined in a glos-
sary at the end of the book to aid you in exam revision.

KEY POINTS

- Realism's basic shared assumptions include that the
  international system is anarchic, power is a defining
  feature of the international system, and states are
  rational, unitary actors.

- A key divide within realism is between theories that
  focus on the structure of the international system and
  those that focus on states' motives.

Key Points

Each main chapter section ends with a set of key points that
summarize the most important arguments developed.

QUESTIONS

1. Why are some issues considered as security questions while
2. How is a process of securitization completed?
3. Is an act of securitization generally dominated by powerful a
4. Is securitization more likely to succeed in authoritarian state
5. What are the benefits of securitizing or desecuritizing an iss
6. Assess the dangers of securitization.
7. What are some of the shortcomings of the securitization mo

Questions

A set of carefully devised questions has been provided to help
you assess your understanding of core themes, and may also be
used as the basis of seminar discussion or coursework.

FURTHER READING

■ Copeland, D. (2000), *The Origins of Major War*, Ithaca, NY: C
  realist theory of preventive war.

■ Glaser, C. (forthcoming 2010), *Rational Theory of Internation*
  Press. Presents a general rational theory that integrates str
  states' information about motives as a key dimension of their

■ Jervis, R. (1978), 'Cooperation under the Security Dilemma',
  classic discussion of how offence – defence variables influence

Further Reading

Reading lists have been provided as a guide to finding out more
about the issues raised within each chapter and to help you
locate the key academic literature in the field.

IMPORTANT WEBSITES

- http://www.upeace.org   The UN University for Peace, centre
  world.

- http://www.sipri.org   The Stockholm International Peace Re
  centres for the analysis of arms and disarmament.

- http://prio.no   The Peace Research Institute of Oslo (PRIO) is

- http://www.brad.ac.uk/acad/peace/   Currently the world's lar

Important Websites

At the end of every chapter you will find an annotated summary of useful websites that are central to Security Studies and
that will be instrumental in further research.

Guided Tour of the Online Resource Centre

www.oxfordtextbooks.co.uk/orc/collins2e/

The Online Resource Centre that accompanies this book provides students and instructors with ready-to-use teaching and learning materials. These resources are free of charge and designed to maximize the learning experience.

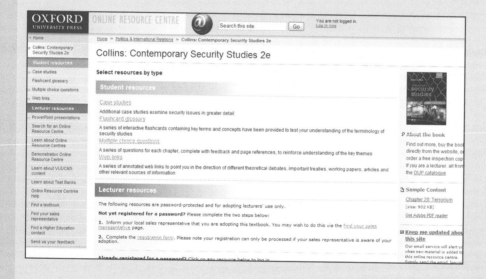

Case Studies

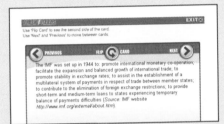

Four additional case studies on women and war, terrorism, securitization of communicable disease, and water resources examine pressing security issues in greater detail.

Flashcard Glossary

A series of interactive flashcards containing key terms and concepts have been provided to test your understanding of the terminology of Security Studies.

Multiple Choice Questions

A bank of self-marking multiple-choice questions has been provided for each chapter of the text to reinforce your understanding and to act as an aid to revision.

Web Links

A series of annotated web links have been provided to point you in the direction of different theoretical debates, important treaties, working papers, articles and other relevant sources of information.

FOR INSTRUCTORS:

PowerPoint® Presentations

These complement each chapter of the book and are a useful resource for preparing lectures and handouts. They allow lecturers to guide students through the key concepts and can be fully customized to meet the needs of the course.

1

Introduction: What is Security Studies?

ALAN COLLINS

> **→ Chapter Contents**
>
> - Introduction
> - Definition of security
> - Structure
> - Conclusion

Introduction

Welcome to Security Studies: *the* sub-discipline of International Relations. It is the study of security that lies at the heart of International Relations. It was the carnage of the First World War, and the desire to avoid its horrors again, that gave birth to the discipline of International Relations in 1919 at Aberystwyth, United Kingdom. This concern with the origins of war and its conduct enabled International Relations to 'distinguish itself from related disciplines such as history, economics, geography, and international law'

(Sheehan 2005: 1). It is the survival of agents, which for much of the discipline has meant sovereign states, that has become accepted as the dominant explanatory tool for understanding their behaviour. Security is a matter of high politics; central to government debates and pivotal to the priorities they establish. Quite simply, 'no other concept in international relations packs the metaphysical punch, nor commands the disciplinary power of "security" ' (Der Derian 1995: 24–5).

Definition of security

Welcome, then, to a subject of great importance and, since you are about to embark upon the study of this subject, no doubt you would like to start with a definition of security. Or, what it means to be secure? You will see in Key Quotes 1.1 that many scholars have done so. The good news is that a consensus has emerged on what security studies entails—it is to do with threats to survival—and the even better news is that hidden within that simple definition lies the complexity that you are about to delve into. What is most striking about the definitions in Key Quotes 1.1 is that, while war and the threat to use force is part of the security equation, it is not exclusively so. The absence of threats is sufficiently far-reaching for Security Studies to encompass dangers that range from pandemics, such as HIV/AIDS, and environmental degradation through to the more readily associated security concerns of direct violence, such as terrorism and inter-state armed conflict. The latter, which so dominated the discipline that during the Cold War it became synonymous with Security Studies, is actually a sub-field of Security Studies and is known as Strategic Studies. Oxford University Press publishes a textbook that is concerned with Strategic Studies: it is called *Strategy in the Contemporary World*.

With the Cold War over, Security Studies has re-emerged, and core assumptions about what is to be secured, and how, have come to occupy our thoughts. Traditionally the state has been the thing to be secured, what is known as the **referent object**, and it has sought security through military might. In the chapters that follow you will find alternative approaches to security; approaches that offer different referent objects, different means of achieving security, and that indicate that past practice, far from enhancing security, has been the cause of insecurity. You are, then, about to study a subject that is undergoing great change as it questions its past assumptions, deepens its understanding of what should be secured, and broadens its remit to encompass a diverse range of threats and dangers. Of course, this broadening of the subject matter creates a blurring in the distinction between Security Studies and the study of International Relations more generally. In this sense the broadening of Security Studies mirrors the wider blurring between International Relations and Political Science. The process of globalization has led to internal issues becoming externalized and external issues internalized. The role of domestic agents and policy concerns appear prominently on global agendas, whether it is the future political structure of Iraq or deforestation in the Amazon. This blurring of the demarcation between International Relations, Political Science, and Security Studies can be seen in the breadth of topics covered in this book and the centrality of security in theories of international relations (for more on this see Chapter 27). This is to be welcomed. I know it can appear confusing and it would be much easier to categorize topics neatly, but this is to misunderstand the nature of the social sciences. These disciplines are sub-disciplines precisely because they overlap and have 'something to say' about the same topics. Instead of looking for different subject matters, it is better to think about different approaches. Despite the contested nature of security, you know that ultimately we are interested in how referent objects are threatened and what they can do to survive. With that thought in mind, examining this diverse range of topics might seem rather less daunting.

KEY QUOTES 1.1

Definitions of security

'Security itself is a relative freedom from war, coupled with a relatively high expectation that defeat will not be a consequence of any war that should occur.'

Bellamy (1981: 102).

'A nation is secure to the extent to which it is not in danger of having to sacrifice core values if it wishes to avoid war, and is able, if challenged, to maintain them by victory in such a war.'

Walter Lippman, cited in Buzan (1991a: 16).

'National security may be defined as the ability to withstand aggression from abroad.'

Luciani (1989: 151).

'A threat to national security is an action or sequence of events that (1) threatens drastically and over a relatively brief span of time to degrade the quality of life for the inhabitants of a state, or (2) threatens significantly to narrow the range of policy choices available to the government of a state or to private, nongovernmental entities (persons, groups, corporations) within the state.'

Ullman (1983: 133).

'Security, in any objective sense, measures the absence of threats to acquired values, in a subjective sense, the absence of threats to acquired values, in a subjective sense, the absence of fear that such values will be attacked.'

Wolfers (1962: 150).

'Security-insecurity is defined in relation to vulnerabilities—*both internal and external*—that threaten or have the potential to bring down or weaken state structures, both territorial and institutional, and governing regimes.'

Ayoob (1995: 9; emphasis in original).

'Emancipation is the freeing of people (as individuals and groups) from the physical and human constraints which stop them carrying out what they would freely choose to do . . . Security and emancipation are two sides of the same coin. Emancipation, not power or order, produces true security. Emancipation, theoretically, is security.'

Booth (1991: 319).

'If people, be they government ministers or private individuals, perceive an issue to threaten their lives in some way and respond politically to this, then that issue should be deemed to be a security issue.'

Hough (2004: 9) (emphasis in original).

'Security . . . implies both coercive means to check an aggressor and all manner of persuasion, bolstered by the prospect of mutually shared benefits, to transform hostility into cooperation.'

Kolodziej (2005: 25).

Structure

The book is not designed to be read from start (Chapter 1) to finish (Chapter 27) because that is not the way to read an academic text. If this seems a peculiar thing for me to write, then let me explain. You are not reading a novel in which the aim is to keep you in suspense until the final pages where you discover who committed the crime or whether the lovers live happily ever after. You want to know the questions and the answers as soon as possible, and then, because, as important as the answers are, they are not the most important thing, you should want to know why these are the answers and how they were reached. Think of it as a complicated maths question in which the mathematician has scribbled furiously on the blackboard (or more likely today the whiteboard) a series of, to a layperson, unintelligible equations that eventually lead to an answer. It is the bit in between the question and the answer (the bit in between is those impenetrable equations) that reveals why the answer was found and found in that particular way. It is like this with your studies too. You should want to know, and your tutor will certainly want to know, why you believe in the answers you have found: to know your thought processes. Knowing why you think about a subject the way that you do, so that these thought processes can be convincingly articulated in oral and written form, is what reading for a degree is all about.

Therefore in this book, when reading the chapters, it is perfectly fine to read the introduction and then the conclusion, but you then have to read the bits in between to know why the answers found in the conclusion were reached. To understand the author's thought processes will help you develop yours. So, having read what this book contains, which you will find in this chapter, then read the conclusion. Chapter 27 will present you with the state of Security Studies, and the theorizing that has taken place in the discipline. It provides you with the context of why we, students and tutors (scholars of the subject), think about the subject the way that we do. In particular, the chapter reveals the differences between American and European approaches to theorizing about security, as it traces past, present, and possible future trends in how security is studied by today's scholars. For those new to Security Studies and/or International Relations, it will be a testing read, but stick with it, because it will be a chapter that you will want to read more than once as you increase your knowledge of this subject; in each read you will discover something new. Once Chapters 1 and 27 have been read, the book becomes a pick 'n' mix, so if you want to start with weapons of mass destruction (Chapter 19) or terrorism (Chapter 20) then go right ahead. That is not to say that the structure has no meaning, and I would strongly advise that you at least begin with the approaches section and especially Chapters 2 and 3 in order to appreciate the primary role that states and power have had in the study of security. By beginning with the approaches section you will be able to appreciate just how hugely important different approaches are in establishing what constitutes security; a point that will be evident once you have read Chapter 27.

The book is divided into three sections: differing approaches to the study of security; the deepening and broadening of security; and, finally, a range of traditional and non-traditional issues that have emerged on the security agenda. The authors come from a range of countries, and their examples are global in scope. Nevertheless, the field of Security Studies, as with International Relations more generally, is dominated by Western thought and approaches. One of the refreshing changes in post-Cold War Security Studies is that the security problems of the developing world are no longer either ignored or seen through the prism of the East–West conflict. We are therefore examining these security problems and, perhaps, in doing so, we will witness the emergence of specifically African or Asian approaches to the study of security that will force us to rethink core assumptions and gain a greater understanding of the Security Studies field.

In the meantime the field, while global in scope, remains dominated by Western thought.

Approaches

In the book's first substantive chapter, Chapter 2, Charles Glaser introduces the first of the two dominant explanations of why and how states have sought security: realism. Realism is not one approach but rather a set of approaches, and in this chapter you will be introduced to the divisions within this explanation of why states behave the way they do as they seek security in an anarchic international environment. One such division concerns debates within structural realism, but there is also a more fundamental division within realism: structural realism versus motivational realism. Utilizing the emergence of China as a great power, this chapter explains the key concepts realism brings to the study of security as well as the breadth of approaches that fall within its framework. The second dominant explanation of why and how states have sought security is the focus for Chapter 3. Here, Patrick Morgan will introduce you to liberalism. Whereas realism seeks an explanation for state behaviour in the international system, liberalism looks to the state as the unit of analysis and places importance on domestic actors' power and preferences and the nature of their political systems. Since behaviour is a product of domestic circumstances for liberalists, states are not alike, and this means that international relations are determined by the choices people make; the world can operate in a realist manner, but for liberalists it does not have to. The recognition among state leaders that they have common, shared, values means that they can establish agreements on a range of issues from trade to human rights that will benefit them all and thus create a secure environment. Liberalism, while recognizing that cooperation can be difficult, is nevertheless an optimistic approach that posits lasting security as a possibility.

We can think of these opening chapters as covering traditional approaches to understanding the search for security because they have underpinned much of our thinking during the previous century; they remain hugely influential, and just because they are traditional does not mean they have been replaced by more recent thinking. New thinking about security has emerged, especially in the post-Cold War period, and such approaches are explained and examined in the other chapters in the Approaches section. You should think of these new approaches as challenging the dominance of the traditional insights offered by realism and liberalism. It may be that you find the traditional explanations of how security can be conceived of and achieved convincing. This is fine so long as you reach that conclusion with an understanding of the other approaches—in other words, that you find an approach to understanding security convincing based not on ignorance of other approaches but with a full understanding of them.

The first alternative approach is relatively new; first coined in 1989, social constructivism has rapidly emerged as providing a third explanation for state behaviour. As with realism and liberalism, it is not one approach, and in Chapter 4 Christine Agius introduces us to two broad camps: conventional and critical constructivism. For constructivists identities matter in explaining the search for security, and identities are constituted through interaction. Since state identities are malleable and can change as a consequence of interaction, this means we create the world in which we live. Conceiving of relations as a product of how we think of them—as opposed to them being something independent from us—enables us to think of threats as socially constructed. This can, as Chapter 4 reveals, provide important insights into topics such as NATO enlargement and the War on Terror.

The next alternative approach, and one that shares with realism and liberalism a long tradition, is peace studies, although as a formal field of study its origins are found in the post-1945 period. Here the approach to security is distinctively broad based, both in the nature of threats that the field covers and also in its approaches to finding solutions. Thus, although initially concerned with the arrival of nuclear weapons, peace studies, long before the post-Cold War era, were noting the security implications of environmental degradation and poverty. With its wide agenda, it is not perhaps surprising to learn that academics working in peace studies come not just from politics and international relations but other disciplines in the social sciences, notably anthropology and sociology, as well as the natural sciences, such as physics and mathematics; it is a truly interdisciplinary field. In Chapter 5 a leading authority, Paul Rogers, provides a historical account of how peace studies developed, highlighting its characteristics and revealing its continued relevancy to contemporary security studies.

The following chapter captures the reflections that took place by some scholars studying security in the immediate post-Cold War period. Labelled Critical Security Studies (CSS), these reflections pre-date the end of the Cold War, but they have flourished since the removal of the nuclear sword of Damocles that hung over the study of security. David Mutimer provides an explanation of the different approaches that have developed since CSS first arrived on the scene in 1994. For those new to critical thinking it is a demanding read, but thoroughly worthwhile, because, amongst many of the things on which it will give you pause to ponder, it unashamedly forces you to think through your assumptions, and it reconnects security with its normative origins.

A criticism aimed not just at security studies but at the wider field of international relations is the failure to appreciate the important insights that gender provides. Caroline Kennedy-Pipe reveals two elements that gender can provide in our understanding of security: a practical appreciation of the role women have been ascribed in the security field and a discursive element that reveals the implicit link between militarism and masculinity. The latter highlights how the notions of honour, nobleness, and valour are associated with masculinity and war, implicitly therefore leaving femininity devoid of such positive attributes. The former notes how women, if they are mentioned at all, are portrayed in a secondary, supporting role to men, whereas the reality is that in many ways (rape, prostitution, breeders) women are victims and their plight has remained a silence in the study of security.

One of the new 'buzz words' in the security literature is human security. It shares much in common with critical approaches to security, the most notable being its critique of the state-centrism of the traditional approach. As the name suggests, the referents for security are humans, but, as Pauline Kerr explains in Chapter 8, while this change of referent object reveals the close connection between development and security, it also brings many challenges to maintaining analytical rigour. Dividing human-security proponents into narrow and broad schools makes it possible for you to appreciate the vast arrays of threats that exist to humans and their livelihoods and thus enables you to make your own judgement about what constitutes security. The chapter also compares the state-centrism of realism with human security to reveal both of their strengths and weaknesses.

The penultimate chapter in the Approaches section, Chapter 9, examines a process known as 'securitization' that was introduced to the literature by scholars working at the Conflict and Peace Research Institute (COPRI) in Copenhagen. Known collectively as the Copenhagen School, these scholars place primary importance on determining how an issue becomes a security issue, by how it is articulated. That is, we think of something as a security issue because the elite, such as political leaders, have convinced us that it represents a threat to our very survival. They are, therefore, interested in the 'speech acts' that the elite use in order to convince an audience that, in order to counter a threat, they require emergency powers. It is then a subjective approach to determining what constitutes security. A threat exists because an audience has been convinced it exists by the elite and it has granted the elite the authority to use emergency powers to counter the threat. The threat therefore is not something that simply exists; it has to be articulated as a threat for it to become a matter of security. Ralf Emmers explains this process, notes limitations with the concept of securitization, and uses case studies ranging from

Australian reaction to undocumented migration to the invasion of Iraq in 2003.

The final chapter in the Approaches section discusses historical materialism; written by Eric Herring, it provides both an explanation of what historical materialism is (it is a version of **Marxism**) and how it relates to the other approaches in this book's first section. The exploitative nature of **capitalism** and the insecurities this generates form the focal point for this approach to understanding what constitutes security, and this is explained with reference to the arms trade industry.

Deepening and broadening

The middle section of the book examines the deepening and broadening that has taken place in Security Studies. As will have become evident from the Approaches section, the theoretical approach you take towards examining security will determine the type of subject matter that you consider constitutes security. This part of the book contains six sectors of security; these are the recognizable sectors that you will find in the Security Studies literature. The exception is **regime security**, which I have included instead of political security, first because political security has a tendency to become a miscellaneous section in which security issues that cannot fit in the other sectors end up, and secondly because, while political security is concerned with external threats (concern with recognition), its greater utility lies in internal threats (concern with legitimacy) to the regime. Labelling the chapter 'regime' therefore clarifies what the referent object is and also highlights the internal dimension of this security sector. Whether these sectors do constitute security is contentious, so, as with all your reading, adopt a critical, enquiring mind, and see if you are persuaded.

We begin with military security because it is the home of our traditional understanding of what constitutes security; the use or threat to use force. In Chapter 11 Michael Sheehan provides a clear exposition of the issues that are the staple diet of military security: war, **deterrence, alliances, arms control,**

and so on; but, while these can be explained by traditional approaches, this chapter reveals that the alternative approaches have something to say about these issues as well, and, in so doing, shed new light on the subjects. Military security used to be the *sine qua non* of security studies, and, while it no longer dominates the discipline as it once did, it remains very much part of the security agenda and remains an indispensable component. What has changed is what constitutes military security, and this chapter reveals the breadth and depth of the subject in a concise and accessible fashion.

Turning our attention to the security concerns within states enables us to appreciate that life in the developed world is far from indicative of that lived by most of the planet's inhabitants. The majority of people living in the developing world face a vast range of insecurities, from half a million people dying each year from the use of light weapons to 40,000 dying each day from hunger. There is, as Richard Jackson writes in Chapter 12 on regime security, 'a profound disjuncture between the kinds of security enjoyed by a small group of developed nations and the kind of security environment inhabited by the majority of the world's population'. In this chapter you will have the opportunity to understand the underlying causes of the developing world's inherent insecurity and why it is that, far from being the providers of security, governing regimes become the main source of their peoples' insecurity. It is a bleak picture that is portrayed, but after reading the chapter you will appreciate the complexities that make bringing security to these millions of people both urgent and yet extremely difficult. The notion of an **insecurity dilemma** captures not only the spiralling nature of the violence but also how problematic finding a solution is.

The broadening of security so that it means more than a preoccupation with the state and military defence should have been appreciated by now. In Chapter 13 on societal security, an alternative to the state, and indeed the individual, is posited. In this instance you will be introduced to the notion of a collective of people becoming the thing to be secured. In recent times the term 'ethnic' has become a popular label for describing conflict between groups within states. In this chapter Paul Roe introduces you to a means of examining the dynamics behind those ethnic conflicts where identity lies at the conflict's core. Importantly he does so by focusing on non-military issues that can give rise to insecurity and thereby shows how ambiguity in such seemingly non-threatening issues, such as education, can indeed become matters of great concern. If you have an interest in the nexus between security and identity, this is a must-read chapter.

Although it pre-dates the end of the Cold War it was in the 1990s, and especially because of concern over ozone depletion and global warming, that environmental change began to be thought of as a 'new' security threat. In Chapter 14, while you will be exposed to the vast array of environmental degradation that is occurring in today's world, the question of interest is what makes environmental change a matter of security. Jon Barnett provides an explanation of why the environment emerged on the security agenda before providing six interpretations of environmental security. You will, therefore, have the opportunity to consider whether the environment really is a security issue and whether labelling it as a matter of security helps or hinders attempts to reverse environmental degradation. For those with a normative interest in studying international security, this is an important chapter to read.

The final two chapters in this section are concerned with economics; in the first the referent object is the state and in the second it is the individual. In Chapter 15 a state's economy and its access to resources are presented as essential components in determining its ability to protect itself in an anarchical self-help environment. This, though, is only part of the equation and actually tells us little of what economic security is. In this chapter Christopher Dent uses the term **economics-security nexus** to describe the above. The chapter will use a specific definition of economic security to highlight that what is being secured is not just the economy but also its ability to provide prosperity in the future. In this sense economic security concerns promoting activities that enhance a state's, or region's, economic growth. You will be introduced

to eight types, or typologies, of economic security, including accessing markets and finance; transborder economic cooperation; and the ideologies that underpin economic activity. You will also be able to note the role institutions such as the International Monetary Fund and the World Trade Organization play, as well as appreciate the economic-security issues raised by such crises as the East Asian financial crisis of 1997–8.

The final chapter of the deepening and broadening part of the book, Chapter 16, continues the economy theme, but here the focus is on individuals in the developing world and specifically on the range of insecurities presented by the globalized world. With the focus on individuals, it will not be a surprise to discover that human security is the approach adopted as Nana Poku reveals the development problems of Africa and the threats that blight people's lives on that continent.

Traditional and non-traditional

The final section of the book highlights a series of traditional and non-traditional security issues that have emerged on the Security Studies agenda. The section begins with traditional security concerns and then moves to the non-traditional issues that have emerged as the subject area has expanded. We begin by addressing the traditional security concern of the threat and use of force. This is examined by looking at how Western strategy has evolved post-Cold War away from deterrence to compellence and in particular to the use of coercive diplomacy. This captures the logic behind Western, and in particular US, strategic thinking.

The Bush administration's willingness to talk of 'pre-emptive' use of force, and indeed to implement it, has revealed a significant change in strategic thinking in the West. It is no longer simply enough to deter opponents from taking action; it is now necessary to persuade, coerce, and, on occasion, force them to change their behaviour. This, as Peter Viggo Jakobsen writes, has led to the post-Cold War era witnessing the pursuit of **coercive diplomacy**. Coercive diplomacy is the threat, and if necessary the limited use of force, designed to make an opponent comply with the coercer's wishes. It is action short of brutal force and thus an attempt to achieve a political objective as cheaply as possible. It has been used to respond to acts of aggression, halt WMD programmes, and stop terrorism. Chapter 17 provides you with the criteria for what constitutes coercive diplomacy and the obstacles to its success, and concludes that Western efforts have largely failed. If you want to understand the strategy that underpins Western, and specifically US, policy on the use of force since the end of the Cold War, this is a chapter for you.

The role of intelligence in determining security concerns and outcomes has never been more prominent than in today's security environment. Chapter 18 explains the different types of intelligence agencies that exist and how they collect information. Stan Taylor explains the intelligence cycle so that you can appreciate what a lengthy process it is, and more importantly how errors can occur. Covert action is examined, and, with reference to the 2003 invasion of Iraq, intelligence failure, or what might more properly be called policy failure, is examined. This chapter ties in closely with coercive diplomacy, since the threat to use force in order successfully to compel an opponent requires knowledge about his goals. In a world of pre-emption, good intelligence is a necessary condition for success.

Since the tragic events of 9/11, the acronym WMD has been catapulted into everyday usage. Weapons of mass destruction, and the fear that rogue states or terrorists will target the USA or Europe with such weapons, has become a central concern for Western states. The belief that Iraq had an undisclosed arsenal of WMD provided the justification for the USA's decision to remove Saddam Hussein's regime, and it was the nuclear programmes of both North Korea and Iran (the former a declared weapons programme; the latter a potential and feared possibility) that earned them membership of Bush's 'Axis of Evil'. What, though, are WMD, why are they considered so different from conventional

weapons, how easy are they to use, and what has been their impact on international relations? These are the questions that James Wirtz addresses in Chapter 19.

Terrorism, perhaps even more than WMD, has come to occupy a top spot on the security agendas of states. In Chapter 20 Brenda and Jim Lutz provide a definition of terrorism and explain the various types (religious, ethnic, ideological) and causes of terrorism. Using a typology that sees terrorism as either a form of war, or crime, or disease, they are able to explain why certain countermeasures are adopted by states and their implications for civil liberties. The chapter will provide you with details of terrorists ranging from the Ku Klux Klan to al-Qaeda and reveal the incidence of terrorism that has occurred throughout the world in recent times.

After the end of the Cold War but prior to 9/11 the subject that came to prominence in the field of international security concerned the use of (primarily Western) military force to intervene in cases of severe human suffering; it has not gone away, and in Chapter 21 Alex Bellamy charts the arguments for and against humanitarian intervention. The atrocities committed in Bosnia and the genocide of Rwanda heralded the arrival of the **responsibility to protect** (R2P). What R2P means, what it means for coercive state intervention, and what future R2P has in a world where mass atrocities continue—as witnessed in Darfur—are the subjects the chapter examines.

We then turn our attentions to the increasing demands for energy coupled to the declining pool of available resources; in the light of this, it is not surprising that energy security has become a critical issue for states (and people). Chapter 22 on energy security provides both a detailed coverage of the topic, specifically related to oil demand, and a link to previous chapters in the approaches and the deepening/broadening sections. You will, for example, have an opportunity to look at what historical materialism argues about the state of energy security, and at the connections that energy security has to economic and regime security, as well as thinking about energy security as an issue not just for states but for human security as well. The United States figures prominently, and reading this chapter will enable you to appreciate that energy security involves a complex nexus of geopolitical, economic, and strategic concerns, which link together distant regions of the globe, and disparate security concerns.

Chapter 23 examines the last of the traditional security issues in this book: the arms trade, or what Joanna Spear and Neil Cooper call the defence trade. In this chapter they examine the reasons why states procure weapon systems, ranging from the **action–reaction model** to technological determinism, before providing details of trends in defence expenditure, the state of the market, and the different types of goods and services that constitute today's defence trade.

In Chapter 24 we turn to our first non-traditional security issue, health, and here Stefan Elbe examines how diseases such as **AIDS** and SARS are a threat to both human and national security. AIDS is a **pandemic**; it is estimated that in 2007 thirty-three million people were living with **HIV** and on average almost three times as many people die from **AIDS-related** illnesses *every day* as died during the terrorist attacks on 9/11. This chapter shows how diseases can be thought of as a security issue, ranging from peacekeeping operations spreading AIDS/HIV to terrorists deliberately using a biological agent to spread terror. While ill health is an exacerbating factor for national security, it is in itself a direct threat when individuals are the referent object.

In 1999 Thailand identified the narcotics trade as the country's number one threat to national security.

Drug trafficking, along with, among others, human trafficking and money laundering across national frontiers, are all forms of **transnational crime,** and, as the Thai experience reveals, this non-traditional security issue has risen rapidly up the national-security agendas of states in the post-Cold War era. In Chapter 25 Jeanne Giraldo and Harold Trinkunas reveal the multiple ways in which transnational crime impacts directly, and indirectly, on human and national security. They explain why it has become more prevalent since the 1990s, the links between **organized crime** and terrorism, and the various responses that states have taken to curb its operation. If you want to appreciate a 'dark side' of globalization and how transnational criminal activity has impacted on international security, this is a must-read chapter.

The examination of what non-traditional issues constitute Security Studies today concludes by examining the concept of child soldiers. This is a topic that has recently gained prominence, but it is not new; children have been agents in conflict for centuries. They are an undertheorized and underutilized political agent, and in Chapter 26 Helen Brocklehurst brings to the fore their recruitment and role and the implications these have for our thinking about war and security. The legal dimension is examined and the difficulties of demobilization and reintegration are highlighted. Throughout the chapter provides a critical analysis, challenging preconceptions and revealing the complexities the topic of child soldiers encapsulates.

Conclusion

You are, as I am sure you appreciate having read the above, about to embark upon a whirlwind tour of a fascinating subject—a subject that has undergone, and continues to undergo, a thorough introspection of its core assumptions. It is a wonderful

time to be a scholar of the discipline—and by scholar I mean students and tutors—because there is so much new and innovative thinking taking place that it is impossible for it not to open your mind. Listen to the ideas contained in the chapters that follow and if, by the end of it, you are more confused than you are now, then it has been a worthwhile enterprise. A caveat should, though, be added: that your confusion is not a reflection of ignorance but an appreciation of how complicated and complex the subject is and how challenging it is therefore to be a scholar of security studies. The chapter began with the question: what is Security Studies? It is all the above and more. Happy reading.

 Visit the Online Resource Centre that accompanies this book for lots of interesting additional material: www.oxfordtextbooks.co.uk/orc/collins2e/

PART 1

Approaches to Security

2

Realism

CHARLES L. GLASER

Chapter Contents

- Introduction
- What is realism?
- Waltz's structural realism
- Offensive realism
- Defensive realism
- Motivational realism
- Realism and war
- Conclusion

Reader's Guide

This chapter describes the basic features of realist theory, including its emphasis on the implications of international anarchy and the importance of power. The chapter then explores major divisions within the realist family, and their implications for states' security policies and war. The most fundamental division is between structural realism—which focuses on the impact of the international system on states' decisions—and motivational realism—which focuses on the impact of variation in states' motives. Also important is the ongoing debate within structural realism—between Kenneth Waltz's structural realism, offensive realism, and defensive realism. The first two of these find that international structure generates a strong tendency towards competitive policies, while defensive realism finds that cooperation is under some conditions a state's best strategy for achieving security. The chapter illustrates how these different arguments result in divergent predictions for how China's continuing economic growth is likely to influence international security.

Introduction

Virtually all states place great value on maintaining their international security—remaining free from attack and coercion by other states. Realism is a theory of international relations that addresses how states achieve security and possibly other goals. Realism attempts to explain the security strategy a state should choose. In the broadest terms, realism asks whether a state should choose a competitive or a cooperative strategy. Competitive approaches for achieving security include building up arms, searching for allies, and using military force. In contrast, cooperative approaches include negotiating arms-control agreements and exercising unilateral restraint in the acquisition and use of force. Closely related, realism attempts to explain a variety of international outcomes—war and peace, arms races and arms control agreements, alliances and their dissolution.

Realist theories attempt to understand states' choices and international outcomes by employing a general framework that abstracts away from the details of specific states and the international system.

Realism is therefore considered a high-level or grand theory of international relations theory. States are typically characterized in terms of their basic motives and interests, most prominently security. The international system is characterized in terms of states' potential to achieve their objectives, most prominently their power. Realism gives little or no weight to individual states' political systems, their leaders, and other specific attributes of their domestic political systems.

Realism is widely accepted as the dominant theory of international politics. While many scholars reject at least some of its arguments, most acknowledge the importance of key elements of realist theory. Realism's central place in international-relations theory should hardly be surprising. Its enquiry is driven by the most consequential international issues—states' security, war, and peace. And realism focuses on the elements of the international system—states, power, and international anarchy—that are clearly essential for understanding international security.

What is realism?

Given its central place in debates over international relations theory and states' security strategies, it may be unexpected that realism is not a single, well-defined theory, but instead a broad family of theories and arguments. Within the realist family we find disagreements about such key issues as the factors that drive international politics; the implications of key assumptions; and the possibilities for international cooperation and for peace between states. This section begins with a description of the elements that are shared by most realist theories; it then describes the key divides within the realist family.

Basic shared elements

There are a few basic features that characterize the realist family. First, realism emphasizes that the international system is anarchic—there is not an international authority that can enforce agreements and prevent the use of force. In this context, anarchy does not refer to state behaviour; it does not mean that international relations are chaotic. Instead, anarchy simply describes the lack of authority in the international system.

Second, realism views power as a defining feature of the international environment that states face. In fact, for most realists power is *the* defining feature. Although a more complicated concept than it might initially appear, for our purposes it is adequate to understand power as the resources available to a state for building military forces. Key elements of power include a state's wealth, population, and technological sophistication. More powerful states can build larger and more sophisticated military forces.

The importance of power and military capabilities follows closely from the anarchic nature of the international system. Without an international authority to protect them, states need to rely on their own capabilities to achieve their international goals. Power plays a central role in enabling states to acquire these capabilities.

Third, realism envisions states as essentially unitary actors. This is clearly not an accurate assumption—states are made up of leaders, governing institutions, interest groups, and populations. Realist theories make this assumption because it is analytically productive—helpful for understanding the key features of the choices states face and, closely related, for understanding their strategic interactions.

Fourth, realism sees states as rational actors: states make decisions that are well matched to the achievement of their interests, given the constraints imposed by their capabilities and the uncertainties they face about other states' capabilities and motives. In making these decisions states are strategic—that is, they take into consideration how other states will react to their policies. Although there are realists who do not adopt this rational actor assumption and question its importance, and others who are not clear about the rationality of states, the rationality assumption is employed sufficiently widely for it to provide a reasonable characterization of this overall body of theory.

Fifth, realist analysis 'black-boxes' opposing states: states assess each other in terms of their power and capabilities, not in terms of the variation that exists within states, including such domestic characteristics as regime type, nature of leadership, ideology, and so on. Some realists do use the information provided by opposing states' observable international actions to help assess their motives, but others do not.

Sixth, realists tend to see states as the key actors in the international system. The primary alternative is international institutions. Realists argue that international institutions play a less important role than states; many argue that they play a relatively unimportant role. Some realists take the key role of states as an assumption; others argue that the limited role for institutions follows deductively from the theory's basic assumptions. Either way, the dominant importance of states is a common strand that runs across the realist family.

Finally, realism is maybe most frequently associated with its bottom line—states exist in an international system that is characterized by competition and war. Although the following section makes clear that this characterization is no longer fully deserved, being aware that realism is commonly characterized this way is helpful for appreciating its role both in the debate over international relations theory and in debates over foreign and national security policy.

Map of the realist family

Beyond these important similarities, to get a fuller understanding of the realist family requires distinguishing between its key members.

International structure versus states' motives

The most fundamental divide within realism is between the strand that emphasizes the impact of the international system and the strand that emphasizes the impact of states' motives and fundamental goals. The former, which is termed **structural realism** or **neorealism**, argues that the constraints and opportunities created by a state's international environment are the key to understanding its behaviour. States that are interested only in maintaining sovereign control of their territory can end up in arms races and war because of the pressures created by the anarchic international system. These states—which I term 'security seekers'—want only to be secure in the status quo. Nevertheless, competition and conflict can occur between rational security seekers because the international system generates insecurity and drives them into competition.

In contrast, the latter strand of realism, which I term 'motivational realism' (and which includes some of classical realism and neo-classical realism) emphasizes the importance of states that have an inherent desire to expand for explaining international competition and conflict.[1] These states—which I term 'greedy states'—are interested in territorial expansion even when they are secure in the status quo. From this perspective, the international environment is not unimportant—it will constrain these states and provide opportunities for them to expand. But, in contrast to the structural-realist argument, for motivational realism the international environment is not the source of these states' desire to take territory and, in turn, of conflict between states.[2]

Classifying states according to their motives often turns out to be more difficult than might be suggested by the analytically neat categories of security-seeker and greedy. In practice, there is often serious debate over states' motives. There are, however, some relatively clear historical examples. Hitler's Germany is widely considered to have been a greedy state—motivated to expand primarily by a toxic mix of racial and ideological beliefs that called for territorial expansion. In contrast, pre-First World War Germany is commonly characterized as a state motivated by insecurity, which reflected Germany's belief that it was surrounded by hostile major powers and that it was becoming weaker relative to Russia.

Divides within structural realism: Waltz versus offensive versus defensive realism

There are a number of competing theories within structural realism. While less fundamental than the state versus structure divide, understanding the divides within structural realism is important for two reasons. First, structural realism has been extremely influential since the 1970s, which makes the intra-structural-realist debate important. Second, the divergent strands focus attention on different logics of interaction and result in quite different assessments of the likelihood of international competition and the prospects for cooperation; consequently, structural realism's key conclusions about states' prospects for achieving security depend on which version of the theory is most compelling.

Kenneth Waltz (1979), who established the foundation of structural realism, finds that international structure generates a general tendency towards competition between security-seeking states. The pressures and incentives created by the international system greatly limit the potential benefits of cooperation. Waltz does, however, also argue that states recognize the importance of limiting their pursuit of power. Power is a means to achieving security. A state's acquisition of excessive power convinces other states to align against it, thereby undermining this strategy. Recognition of this dynamic moderates the competitive nature of the international system.

By comparison, offensive realism sees a still more competitive world. John Mearsheimer (2001), whose formulation defines offensive realism, agrees that states pursue power as a means, not an end, but finds that states try to maximize their power and pursue **hegemony** when possible. Consequently, offensive realism understands international politics to be still more competitive than does Waltz's neorealism.

In contrast to both Waltz and offensive realism, defensive realism finds that international structure does not create a general tendency towards competition. Under a range of conditions, states can best achieve security by cooperating. The security dilemma lies at the core of the defensive realist argument—competitive policies that a state pursues to increase its own security can reduce its adversary's security. Decreasing the adversary's security is a potential danger, because the adversary may react to this insecurity by pursuing policies that then reduce the state's own security. As a result, under some conditions a state's best option can be cooperation or restraint, not competition. And, under some conditions, even though the international system is anarchic, states can be highly secure.

---

[1]'Neo-classical realism' is sometimes used to cover the theory that I am referring to as motivational realism. As I explain below, neo-classical realism is a broader theory that incorporates a number of domestic-level factors. For earlier use of the term motivational realism see Kydd (1997).

[2]States can be motivated by both security and greed. In fact, we expect that most, if not all, greedy states are also interested in security. To simplify the discussion and analysis, I refer to these mixed-motive states simply as greedy states.

The following sections explore these versions of structural realism, laying out their basic arguments and assessing how they reach their divergent conclusions.

Realism and suboptimality

Before turning to that task, one further distinction is important to make. Starting in the 1980s, a number of theories that address states that are pursuing suboptimal policies—that is, states that are not acting rationally—have been classified as realist. Some theories commonly considered to be defensive realist have this feature. For example, one set of arguments focuses on states that misevaluate the international environment they face because their militaries have a biased view of the feasibility of offensive military missions, believing that they are easier than is actually the case. According to this strand of analysis, Germany exaggerated both its insecurity and the prospects that war could solve its security problems because a 'cult of the offensive' led Germany's leaders to exaggerate the feasibility of strategic offensive missions. Combining this theory of militaries with a defensive-realist foundation leads to the conclusion that competition and war have been more frequent than required by international structure alone (Van Evera 1999). Another theory of this broad type that is built on a rational defensive realist foundation makes a related argument, holding that certain types of domestic regimes are likely to be captured by narrow interests groups, including militaries, which leads these states to pursue overly competitive and expansionist policies. Jack Snyder (1991: 113) identifies Japan as a prime example, arguing that 'the overexpansion of the late 1930s was due to logrolling between the army and navy elites and to blowback from their self-serving imperial ideologies'.

Another grouping of theories that addresses states that make suboptimal choices is termed neo-classical realism. These theories are built on a motivational-realist foundation, which emphasizes the importance of greedy motives, and, like other realist theories, sees power having a large impact on states' interactions. However, these theories also stress that the international environment that states face is quite complex, and, as a result, their assessments of power are influenced by domestic variables. Moreover, states' abilities to extract resources and convert them into military capabilities also vary. As a result, power does not translate as directly into outcomes as is suggested by structural and motivational realism, and states' policies may be flawed when judged against these theories.[3]

---

[3] Rose (1998) assesses a number of works that helped define this category.

Figure 2.1 Types of realist theories and multi-level theories built on realist foundations

		Theory emphasizes	
		States' motives	International structure
States act rationally/ optimally	Yes	Motivational realism	Structural realism, including offensive and defensive realism
	No	Neo-classical realism = motivational realism + unit-level misperception of complexity, limits on state's extraction capability, etc.	Defensive realism + unit-level theories of military bias, flawed state decision-making, etc.

Although these arguments contain major elements that are included in realist theories, classifying them as realist is potentially misleading, because the states they explore are not acting rationally, or at least are constrained domestically in ways that significantly influence their behaviour. At a minimum, we need to draw a sharp line between theories of states that pursue rational policies and those that adopt suboptimal ones. At the risk of rejecting widely used terminology, it might not be going too far to exclude these theories from the realist family. They are instead multi-level theories that combine a rational realist foundation with a theory of suboptimal state behaviour. Figure 2.1 captures some of the key distinctions made above.

> **KEY POINTS**
>
> - Realism's basic shared assumptions include that the international system is anarchic, power is a defining feature of the international system, and states are rational, unitary actors.
>
> - A key divide within realism is between theories that focus on the structure of the international system and those that focus on states' motives.
>
> - There is debate within structural realism over whether the international system creates a general tendency towards competition or whether instead cooperation is under some conditions a state's best strategy.

Waltz's structural realism

Kenneth Waltz's *Theory of International Politics* (1979) transformed realist theory, shifting the focus of explanation towards the international environment that states face and away from states themselves. Waltz begins with the simple, minimal assumption that all states give priority to ensuring their own survival; although states may have other goals, we can understand their interactions by focusing on the survival motive alone.

Survival is a benign motive—the goal is not to take what other states have, but simply to protect what one already has. Maybe the most striking finding of Waltz's structural realism, therefore, is the seemingly counter-intuitive conclusion that international politics will have a strong tendency towards competition. The international system will drive states into competition, even though they lack fundamental conflicts of interest. Waltz (1989: 43) argues that, 'their individual intentions aside, collectively their actions will yield arms races and alliances'.

Competition

What explains the competitive nature of the international system? Waltz explains that international anarchy puts states into a condition of 'self-help'—without an international authority capable of protecting them, major powers must look out for themselves. Self-help is usually understood to mean that states will pursue unilateral competitive policies to protect their own interests. Waltz (1979: 111) argues that a 'self-help situation is one of high risk—of bankruptcy in the economic realm and of war in the world of free states'.

Facing these dire possibilities, states have a strong inclination to pursue policies that will increase their ability to defend themselves and are especially reluctant to adopt policies that could result in reductions of this capability. 'The possibility that force may be used by some states to weaken or destroy others does, however, make it difficult for them to break out of the competitive system' (Waltz 1979: 118–19). The possibility that an adversary will cheat on an agreement is also a major barrier. Even an agreement that would initially increase a state's ability to defend itself could be too risky if the adversary might cheat on the agreement, leaving the state more vulnerable to attack.

This inclination towards competition is reinforced by uncertainty about states' future motives and intentions. Even if confident today that other states have benign intentions, a state cannot be confident about others' future intentions. Uncertainty about others' intentions makes cooperation difficult. When uncertain about the opposing state's intentions, a state must worry not only about whether cooperation will make it better off—increasing its security or prosperity—but also about which state will gain more. Even if cooperation would make the state better off—that is, provide absolute gains—the state might reject cooperation because its adversary would gain more. This is because allowing its adversary to achieve these *relative* gains could leave the state worse off, because in the future its adversary might use its increased capability to attack or coerce the state.

Balancing

How do states go about achieving security? The key to security is for the state to possess the ability to protect itself from attack. States value power—manifested in some combination of territory, population, economic resources, and military capabilities—because it enables them to protect against attack. Power is, therefore, the essential means for achieving security. Economic resources provide the state with the option of building military capabilities and can deter attack by indicating a state's potential to win a long war. Military capabilities provide the state with the immediate ability to fight and defend, and therefore play an essential role in protecting the state against the possibility that its adversary will attack with the expectation of being able to win a war quickly and decisively.

Waltz argues that states have two basic options for acquiring power and the capability to defend. The first is external balancing—forming alliances with other states, thereby enabling the state to draw on other states' resources. The second is internal balancing—increasing the state's own economic capability and building larger and/or better military forces. Although balancing behaviour is commonly envisioned as possible only in

a system of three or more major powers, in fact balancing is possible when there are only two major powers. In this bipolar case, major power alliances are not an option, leaving internal balancing as the key form of balancing. States' efforts to offset others' advantages (and possibly to acquire their own) generate arms races, instead of alliances. According to this argument, although NATO and the Warsaw Pact were important alliances during the Cold War, internal balancing and the arms race that resulted were the key means by which two superpowers—the United States and the Soviet Union—pursued security. Although the major West European states contributed significantly to NATO's overall power, these states were disproportionately dependent on the United States; they had little prospect of providing for their own security against the Soviet Union, whereas the United States had reasonable prospects of defending itself without its alliance partners. The relative importance of the United States was reflected in its ability largely to determine the contours of alliance military policy.

When there are three or more major powers, states have a choice between searching for allies and building up arms. Major powers will tend to do some of both. Alliances have the advantage of reducing the resources the state needs to devote to security, because the state gets to rely on its allies' resources. But alliances also bring risks—a state's allies might fail to meet their commitment to defend the state, leaving it vulnerable to attack; and the state's commitments to the alliance might result in being drawn into wars that it would otherwise have been able to avoid (Snyder 1997).

The key alternative to a balancing alliance is a **bandwagoning** alliance. In a balancing alliance a state joins the weaker side to offset the power advantage of the stronger side. In contrast, in a bandwagoning alliance a state joins the stronger side. Why does structural realism see states balancing instead of bandwagoning? It is not immediately obvious—would not the state be more secure on the stronger side? The problem with bandwagoning is that on the stronger side there is the danger that the state will be attacked by one of its allies, because on the stronger side the state is not essential to the alliance's security. By comparison, on the weaker side the state is more secure because its allies need its contribution to offset the power of the stronger side.

If, on the other hand, a state were trying to maximize its power to satisfy its greedy motives, bandwagoning could be more attractive than balancing. The more powerful alliance would have better prospects for conquering territory, which it could then divide among its members. The Soviet Union's decision to ally with Hitler's Germany provides an example of this type of behaviour—although Stalin was motivated partly by security concerns, he also desired the territory that the alliance would yield, because it satisfied his non-security expansionist goals (Schweller 1998: 137–9). In contrast to a greedy state, a state that values only its security would be less willing to run the risks of being vulnerable within the alliance.

Waltz emphasizes that balances of power tend to form not because states necessarily desire balance, but rather because states try to offset others' power advantages and to gain advantages of their own to protect themselves. With states acting and reacting to offset advantages in power, balances of power tend to form.

> **KEY POINTS**
>
> - Power is a means for achieving survival, not an end in itself.
> - Structural incentives—the necessity of self-help, the importance of preventing adversaries from acquiring military advantages, and concern about relative gains—lead states to adopt competitive policies.
> - States can acquire power via internal and external balancing.
> - States tend to balance instead of bandwagon.

Offensive realism

Power maximization

A still more competitive version of structural realism is offered by offensive realism. John Mearsheimer argues not only that states face uncertainty about others' intentions, but in addition that states should assume the worst about these intentions. Consequently, states focus solely on other states' capabilities; they compete for power, attempting to increase it whenever feasible.

According to offensive realists, therefore, states attempt to maximize their power. The reason is straightforward—the more powerful a state is, the better its prospects for defending itself if attacked. A state would be most secure if it were the dominant, hegemonic power; states will pursue competitive policies to achieve this position, if they have a reasonable probability of success.

It is important to emphasize that for offensive realism power maximization is a means, not an end. As with Waltz, survival is the end that all states give priority to achieving. According to offensive realism, the best way for states to ensure their survival is to maximize their power.

In contrast to offensive realism, Waltz argues that states do not maximize power. This is a key disagreement, so it is worthwhile to consider how it arises. From Waltz's perspective, the most obvious reason a state should not try to maximize its power is that these efforts are likely to fail: balancing coalitions will form to offset advantages in power and to defeat states that go to war to take territory and increase their power. Recognizing the likelihood of effective opposition, states work to protect the power they have, while tending to forgo major efforts to acquire more. Waltz's point here is not that more power would be undesirable, but rather that other states' reactions make acquiring it infeasible. This argument is reinforced by Waltz's argument, noted above, about why states balance instead of bandwagon—because states give priority to survival, they forgo the power maximization that might be achieved by joining the stronger side in an alliance. Thus, with respect to alliance behaviour, Waltz is arguing that, even if feasible, power-maximizing behaviour could reduce a state's security and therefore is not its best option.

Inefficient balancing and buckpassing

In contrast, offensive realism holds that balancing is often insufficiently effective to make clear that territorial expansion is infeasible. Potential allies are sometimes geographically separated, which reduces their ability to come to each other's aid, thereby reducing the value of balancing. In addition, states may be slow to balance, because they disagree about how to coordinate their efforts and how to share the costs of fighting. Moreover, states may choose not to balance against an expansionist state, hoping that the state that is immediately threatened will be able to defend itself and/or that other allies will come to its aid. In other words, a state may *buckpass* instead of balance. Major powers that have been slow to balance are not hard to find—for example, both the United States and the UK were slow to throw their full weight into opposing Germany during the Second World War. The possibility that balancing will be ineffective, and may not even occur at all, increases the probability that a state's efforts to increase its power will succeed, thereby opening the door to rational power-maximizing behaviour.

This discussion points to another difference between Waltz and offensive realism. Waltz emphasizes the constraining implications of the tendency of states to balance, although he recognizes that states have incentives not to balance. In

contrast, offensive realism argues that states prefer to buckpass than to balance and holds that buckpassing is the more common behaviour. As explained above, the result is that the international system fuels behaviour that is more competitive (see Case Study 2.1).

It is worth noting, however, that the gap between Waltz and offensive realism may be still smaller than it first appears: both see a world in which the anarchic international system consistently produces competition between states; both provide arguments that lead to important qualifications regarding power maximization; and, the more competitive world explained by offensive realism seems to be quite possible for Waltz. Waltz (1979: 125, 164–5, 170–2) acknowledges that balances are sometimes slow to form, that states have incentives to pass the buck, and that states sometimes make mistakes that could lead them not to balance when they should. Given the benefits of gaining power, a state that recognizes these possibilities will be more inclined to maximize its power as a means of maximizing its prospects for survival. On the other hand, Mearsheimer (2001: 37) argues that, although major powers always desire more power, they recognize the constraints imposed by the international system and therefore do not always pursue it: 'before great powers take offensive actions, they think carefully about the **balance of power** and how other states will react to their moves . . . If the benefits do not outweigh the risks, they sit tight and wait for a more propitious moment.'

KEY POINTS

- In the face of uncertainty, states should assume the worst about others' intentions.

- Although power is a means, not an end, states try to maximize their power, because this is the best way to ensure their survival.

- There are many reasons that effective balances may not occur, which create the possibility for successful power maximization.

Defensive realism

Although it starts with essentially the same assumptions as Waltz and offensive realism, defensive realism finds that cooperation and restraint will be a state's best options under a range of conditions. In sharp contrast to the other structural realist theories, defensive realism argues that the international system does not generate a general tendency towards competitive behaviour; under some conditions states can be highly secure (Glaser 1994–5) (see Case Study 2.1).

The **security dilemma** plays a central role in defensive realism. A security dilemma can exist when the military forces that a state deploys to increase its security are also useful for attacking

---

CASE STUDY 2.1

China's rise

Will China's continuing economic growth lead to international competition and insecurity? Since the end of the Cold War, there has been little security competition between the world's major powers. During this period, the United States has been the world's dominant power. China's growth has the potential to challenge America's dominance. China has recently become a major regional power in Northeast Asia. If it continues to grow successfully, China will become as powerful, or more powerful, than the United States.

The different realist theories provide a range of views on the implications of this change in the balance of power. Offensive realism sees China striving to become the hegemonic power in its region. Regional hegemony would require China to build military forces capable of defeating its neighbours, thereby gaining tremendous political influence. In addition, China would attempt to push the United States out of Northeast Asia, because, if America remains active in its region, China would fail to achieve the influence and security provided by hegemony. The United States, however, would be threatened by Chinese hegemony and would therefore respond. One option would be to form a balancing coalition—including Japan, Russia, and South Korea—to contain China.

Competition would intensify as China tried to split the American-centred alliance and the United States worked to hold it together. Both sides would build up their arms to offset, if not overwhelm, the other, and both sides would be insecure because they would lack confidence in the adequacy of their forces.

Defence realism sees greater potential for a relatively calm region. China need not pursue regional hegemony, because security does not require it. China's power—its size, large population, and wealth—would provide the resources necessary for effective defence. In addition, China's separation by water from Japan makes defence easier. Maybe most important, nuclear weapons would provide China with an excellent deterrent capability. These defensive capabilities would not threaten the United States. China's nuclear deterrent could be designed to avoid threatening America's nuclear deterrent. Moreover, even if China does pursue a more threatening nuclear force, the United States would have little difficulty reacting and preserving its deterrent capabilities. The United States would not be directly threatened by China's conventional military capabilities because the two countries are separated by a vast ocean. Finally, because it can be secure with the United States still actively involved in its region, China would probably not press the United States to leave; and the United States would probably stay, providing Japan and other allies with insurance via security guarantees.

Motivational realism focuses on whether China turns out to be a greedy state, determined to expand even though it is secure. If it does, then the region will be competitive and dangerous. Power will play a central role in determining China's success. If it becomes as powerful as the United States, China will have significant military advantages within its region. If China is a very greedy state—willing to run large risks to expand—then the prospects for deterrence will be poor. A less expansionist China might be deterred, especially given the risks of conventional war in a nuclear world. Even in this case, however, China and the United States and its allies will all engage in intense military competition.

a potential adversary. In such a case, the state's efforts will reduce the adversary's ability to defend itself, which can make the adversary less secure.

Before we look at why the adversary's insecurity is a problem, two features of the security dilemma deserve to be highlighted. First, uncertainty about the adversary's type—whether it is a security-seeking state or a greedy state—is an essential element of the security dilemma. If states were confident that other states were security-seekers (and were also confident that they would remain so), then other states' capabilities to attack would not make them insecure.[4] In contrast, a state will be insecure when it is uncertain about its adversary's motives and the adversary possesses capabilities for attacking it. Second, the security dilemma is the key to explaining competition between states that are security-seekers. If states could build forces that provided the capability to defend, but not to attack, then security-seekers could increase their security without making other states insecure. In this case, the international system would not produce insecurity or competition.

Risks of competition

The adversary's insecurity is a potential problem, not because the state places inherent value on its adversary's security, but instead because the adversary's insecurity may in turn reduce the state's own security. This interaction can proceed through three key mechanisms. First, in response to the state's acquisition of new military capabilities, the adversary could respond by building up its own forces to increase its security. The adversary's build-up could leave the state less secure than it was before its own build-up because the adversary's build-up might more than offset the state's build-up. These build-ups could also leave both states less secure, because their new forces add more to their ability to attack than to defend, leaving both states more vulnerable to attack.

---

[4]This actually requires an additional condition: for a state to be secure it would also have to know that the opposing state knew that it was a security-seeker.

Second, the adversary's insecurity can lead it to pursue policies that increase the probability of crises and war. Under some conditions, expansion would increase the adversary's security—for example, by increasing its power, or by reducing the state's power, or by providing strategically valuable territory that improves its prospects for defence. Because it is now more insecure, the adversary is more willing to pursue these dangerous, risky policies to regain its security. Consequently, the state is also more insecure.

Third, the adversary's build-up can convince the state that it is more likely that it faces a greedy state—one that values taking territory for reasons other than increasing its security. Because a greedy state is willing to pay greater costs to expand and is therefore harder to deter, the state concludes that it is more insecure, which, as described above, can call for more competitive policies. Moreover, as a state increases its assessment that its adversary is greedy, cooperation becomes riskier, making competitive policies still more attractive. These interactions can lead to a continuing deterioration of political relations, fuelling a negative political spiral (Jervis 1976; Glaser 1997; Kydd 2005).

Benefits of cooperation

Because competitive policies can have these negative effects, a state needs to consider the risks and benefits of cooperative policies. In terms of military forces, cooperative policies could include arms control and unilateral restraint. An arms control agreement that limits the size of deployed forces can provide protection against losing an arms race. An arms control agreement that limits forces that are especially effective for attacking can enhance both states' abilities to defend and deter, leaving both more secure than if they had competed in that type of offensive weaponry.

In addition to enhancing states' military capabilities, cooperative policies can improve their political relations, and in turn increase their security. By cooperating, a state may be able to communicate information about its motives, leading the adversary to conclude that the state is more likely to be a security-seeker. Cooperative policies have the potential to generate a positive spiral—as a state finds its adversary more likely to be a security-seeker, cooperation become less risky, so states adopt cooperative policies that make cooperation still more attractive.

Sending this information requires the state to send a 'costly signal'—an action that is less costly for a security-seeker than for a greedy state. Communicating information requires a costly signal because a greedy state has incentives to mislead its adversaries into believing that it is a security-seeker, because its adversaries would then be more likely to adopt policies that leave them vulnerable, improving the greedy state's prospects for achieving its expansionist objectives. An arms control agreement can serve as a costly signal because forgoing the possibility of winning an arms race is more costly for a greedy state than a security-seeker. Similarly, an agreement that limits both sides' offensive capabilities is more costly for a greedy state, because offence is more valuable for it than for a security-seeker. A state can also send a costly signal by unilaterally limiting the size or type of forces it deploys. However, unilateral restraint will often be riskier than arms control, because the adversary may continue its build-up, thereby undermining the state's defensive capabilities. Consequently, unilateral restraint is less likely to increase the state's security.

Cooperating, however, is not without risks of its own. Most obvious, an adversary may cheat on an agreement, increasing the state's vulnerability to attack. The challenge, therefore, is for states to design and agree to monitoring arrangements that provide timely information on violations. If effective, the risks posed by the adversary's cheating can be smaller than the risks of losing an arms race. Another danger lies in the possibility that the adversary is a greedy state and that cooperation will lead it to question the state's resolve. If facing a greedy adversary, the state should worry less about the adversary's insecurity and more about whether cooperating would lead the adversary to question the state's determination to protect its interests. Thus cooperation under uncertainty about motives is risky.

Defensive realism does not find that states should in general cooperate or compete. Instead, the benefits and risks of both types of policies need to be compared. There is not a general answer, because the benefits and risks will vary, depending on the international situation a state faces. Much of the relevant variation is in the magnitude and nature of the security dilemma.

Variation in the security dilemma

Unlike versions of structural realism that define the international situation entirely in terms of the distribution of power, defensive realism includes an additional variable; the security dilemma. When the security dilemma is severe, security will be harder to achieve, states will find competition more attractive, and war will be likely. When the security dilemma is mild, the opposite will result.

The intensity of the security dilemma depends on two material variables (Jervis 1978). The offence–defence balance reflects the relative difficulty of offensive and defensive missions. The more an adversary needs to invest in military forces to defeat a state's defence, the larger the advantages of defence. In other words, the larger the advantage of defence, the easier it is to defend.

When defence has the advantage, the security dilemma is less severe, because a state can increase its ability to defend while posing a relatively small threat to its adversary's ability to defend. Thus, arms races should not be intense. Moreover, arms control agreements will be less risky, because cheating on an agreement will pose a smaller danger, so cooperation should be still safer. War will be less likely for a variety of reasons. Negative political spirals will be less likely and less intense. Defence advantage not only makes expansion more difficult, but also makes it less valuable, because states can be secure without acquiring more territory and greater wealth.

In contrast, offence advantage has the opposite effects. Arms races are more intense; arms control agreements are harder to achieve because cheating

Figure 2.2 Implications of offence – defence variables

		Advantage	
		Offence	Defence
Offence and defence can be distinguished	No	Arms races are intense Expansion is easy War is frequent	Arms races are mild Expansion is difficult War is infrequent
	Yes	Qualitative arms control is feasible and valuable, but risky Signalling is feasible and valuable, but risky	Qualitative arms control is feasible, but less valuable, because security is high Signalling is feasible, but less valuable

has greater potential to leave a state vulnerable to attack. Territorial expansion is more valuable, which fuels insecurity, and in turn competition and efforts to expand.

The offence–defence balance can be influenced by a variety of factors, maybe most importantly by technology and geography. Distance makes attacking more difficult and therefore tends to favour defence. The same is true for terrain and water that are difficult to cross because they slow or expose attackers. Nuclear weapons favour defence because survivable retaliatory capabilities, which are the key to deterrence, are much easier to maintain than are the forces required to deny nuclear retaliation.

The security dilemma also depends on whether the forces that are useful for defensive missions are also useful for offensive missions. If offence and defence can be distinguished, then states can choose to build only defence and can negotiate qualitative arms control agreements that limit forces that support offensive missions. This distinguishability of offence and defence reduces the severity of the security dilemma (see Figure 2.2).

Offensive realists have challenged defensive realism over the importance of these offence–defence variables. Common criticisms hold that the concept of the offence–defence balance is not well defined and that states are incapable of measuring it. If correct, then states would focus on power, not on the combined effect of the offence–defence balance and power, and the cooperative possibilities identified by defensive realism would be reduced or eliminated.

Threats and balancing

Defensive realism also offers a different analysis of the conditions under which states form balancing alliances. Instead of focusing entirely on power, defensive realism focuses on the danger (or threat) posed by potential adversaries (Walt 1987). Threat reflects the combination of the adversary's offensive capabilities and its motives. Threat increases with increases in the adversary's offensive capabilities, in the probability that the adversary is greedy, and in the extent of its greed. An opposing state's offensive capabilities reflect its power and the offence–defence balance: greater power and greater offence advantage make greater offensive capability possible.

This different assessment of balancing flows from key differences between defensive realism and the other structural realisms. Defensive realism emphasizes states' abilities to perform military missions, not power alone. This follows from the theory's core logic because a state's security depends on its ability to acquire defensive capabilities. We see this distinction reflected in the emphasis that the theory places on variation in the security dilemma and in offence–defence variables.

Defensive realism also places much greater weight on states' assessments of others' motives and, closely related, their political relationships. Instead of assuming the worst about others' motives, or essentially neglecting them altogether, defensive realism argues that states that ignore the information they have about others' motives are failing to

make rational decisions. While there are risks in cooperating with a state that might be greedy, there are also costs in competing with a state that might be a security-seeker. States need to consider both types of dangers in choosing between competitive and cooperative policies.

> ### KEY POINTS
>
> - In contrast to Waltz and offensive realism, defensive realism finds that the risks of competition can make cooperation a state's best strategy.
>
> - Cooperation can under some conditions increase a state's prospects for avoiding military disadvantages and enable it to signal its benign motives, thereby increasing its security.
>
> - Variation in the security dilemma influences the pressures for competition, and the feasibility and risks of cooperation.
>
> - States balance against threats, not power.

Motivational realism

In contrast to structural realism, which essentially assumes that states are security-seekers, what I am terming 'motivational realism' emphasizes the importance of variation in states' motives and goals. More specifically, motivational realism argues that the key to understanding competitive and conflictual international behaviour lies in the nature of individual states—specifically their greedy motives—not in international structure. On the one hand, in a world in which all major powers are security-seekers, cooperation and peace are likely; on the other hand, in a world in which one or more major powers are greedy states, competition and war are likely (see Case Study 2.1).

The motivational realist argument is not that international structure does not matter, but rather that structure is not itself a cause of competitive

behaviour. Instead, structure influences the ability of states to expand, but does not cause their desire to expand. This argument stands in stark contrast to structural realism—including the Waltzian, offensive, and defensive varieties—which focuses on whether and how international structure causes security-seeking states to pursue competitive policies.

In fact, in significant ways the theoretical importance of motivational realism depends on one's conclusions about the divide within structural realism. If Waltz is correct that the international system consistently produces competition, then variation in states' motives would matter relatively little. Across the full range of international conditions, pure security-seekers and greedy states would adopt competitive policies, forgoing opportunities for cooperation and unilateral restraint.

As a result, explanations that focus on differences in states' motives would be less important. The more purely structural theory would be preferable, offering much greater parsimony at little cost in explanatory power. In contrast, by explaining that security-seekers should sometimes pursue cooperative policies, defensive realism gives motivational realism something to explain. Under those international conditions that defensive realism argues should lead states to cooperate, motivational realism would be required to explain why rational states pursued competitive policies.

Motivational realism need not provide an explanation for states' greedy motives. Instead, it can simply posit greedy states and ask what strategies they should choose, given the international situation they face. This said, some well-established realist theories that are at least partially consistent with motivational realism do provide such explanations. Maybe best known is Han Morgenthau's argument that states' pursuit of power is rooted in human nature, which is characterized by 'an essential and universal lust for power as an end in itself that knows no limits' (Smith 1986: 136). State greed could, however, reflect a wide range of other sources, including a state's desire to increase its wealth and prosperity, and to spread its political ideology or religion.

There are conditions under which a greedy state should choose competitive policies, but security-seekers would choose cooperation. Recall that this is why defensive realism is insufficient on its own to explain or prescribe strategy for all types of states. Unlike the case of security-seekers, understanding why greedy states choose competitive policies is not a puzzle: their basic motives cannot be satisfied without competition, requiring threats or actual use of force. For example, whereas a security-seeker could prefer to cooperate when it had an even chance of winning (and losing) an arms race, a greedy state would be more likely to prefer to compete. The greedy state would see greater value in the military advantages provided by winning the race, because these advantages would be necessary to achieve its expansionist objectives. In addition, the greedy state might also see smaller costs in the negative political impact of arms racing, because it understands that its goals are necessarily incompatible with good political relations. Similarly, a greedy state might start a war when a security-seeker would not. Assuming it places greater value on territory than does the security-seeker, the greedy state will be prepared to pay higher costs in fighting the war and therefore will be harder to deter. Closely related, the greedy state will bargain with more determination to acquire the territory, increasing the probability that coercion would lead to a crisis that would escalate to war.

This said, it is important to note that greedy states will not always pursue competitive policies. A greedy state will be deterred from expanding if it anticipates that the costs of acquiring territory are too high and/or the probability of success is too low. Put another way, under some conditions balancing against a greedy state can succeed. Similarly, the less likely a greedy state is to win an arms race, the lower the probability that it will initiate one. As these comparisons suggest, the power of opposing states should play an important role in a greedy state's choice of strategy.

Greedy states may also make different alliance choices than security-seekers (Schweller 1998). They have a greater incentive to bandwagon, because they place greater value on gaining power. A key factor pushing security-seekers away from bandwagoning is the danger presented by other states on the more powerful side. Greedy states are more willing to run this risk because they place greater value on the potential gains that the stronger side may be able to provide. A prevalence of bandwagoning creates the possibility of a still more competitive and dangerous world. Instead of states balancing to offset advantages in power, or buckpassing and thereby neglecting potential imbalances of power, in a bandwagoning world states actively join together to create imbalances of power in their favour. Possibilities for war and for hegemony therefore increase.

In response to these motivational realist arguments, structural realists argue that at a minimum the motivational realist argument underestimates the potential impact of international structure. Specifically, the combined impact of anarchy and the security dilemma can be the driving force behind states' decisions to compete. Essentially, structure can by itself drive states into competition. However, structural realism can (and, as I argue in the Conclusion, should) concede that greedy motives can also matter for whether states decide to engage in military competition and war and therefore need to be factored into assessments of states' security policies.

> **KEY POINTS**
>
> - Greedy states, not international structure, are the driving force behind competitive international policies.
>
> - Greedy states can be deterred, so the balance of power plays an important role in determining whether they will attempt to expand.
>
> - Greedy states will be inclined to bandwagon instead of balance.

Realism and war

The preceding discussion has been cast in the broad categories of competition and cooperation, with the most immediate logic applying to arms competition and alliance choices. Realism also offers a more specific set of arguments about the causes of war. Because of space limitations, only a brief review of these arguments, all of which are contested, is possible here.

An unresolved debate is over whether war is more likely in **bipolar** or **multipolar** systems. Bipolar systems have two major powers; multipolar systems contain three or more major powers. Some realists argue that war is less likely in bipolar systems. In a multipolar system states have incentives to buckpass, which can undermine effective balancing and create opportunities for expansion. Relatedly, in multipolar systems there is greater uncertainty about the size and commitment of opposing coalitions. Even if opposing states are going to balance, a potential attacker can underestimate the true likelihood of balancing, which makes war look more attractive. In addition, war can be more likely in multipolar systems simply because there are more major-power dyads across which war could occur.

The standard counterargument is that balancing in multipolar systems can provide large power advantages to states joining together to defend the status quo. In contrast, in bipolarity the balance of power between the major powers is roughly equal, making war more attractive than in multipolarity in which states balance effectively. Moreover, in multipolarity, even if balancing fails to occur, a major power attacking an equal major power has prospects that are no better than in bipolarity.

A second important argument about war focuses on the impact of changes in states' power. A state that is declining can have incentives to start a war before it becomes significantly more vulnerable to attack and coercion (Copeland 2000). This type of war is commonly termed preventive war. A state that prefers peace to war could nevertheless prefer war sooner (while it is stronger) both to war later (when it is weaker) and to the political concessions it would have to make to avoid war once it is weaker.

In deciding whether to launch a preventive war, a state needs to consider not only shifts in power, but also the probability that the rising power would attack or coerce it. Uncertainty about the rising state's future motives makes this a complicated calculation and may tend to lead states towards war. The inability of a state to promise credibly that it will not use its increased power against the declining state is an unavoidable result of international anarchy and contributes to the incentives for preventive war.

A third set of arguments focuses on the offence–defence balance and the security dilemma, in addition to power. As described above, when offence has the advantage, competition will be more intense and political relations will be worse, which will increase the probability of crises. Offence advantage also increases the instrumental value of territory, because it increases the prospects for successful expansion, which makes war more attractive. Offence advantage also increases incentives to strike first in a crisis, thereby increasing the probability of pre-emptive war (Van Evera 1999). Defence advantage has the opposite effects, making peace more likely.

KEY POINTS

- Debate over whether war is more likely in bipolar or multipolar systems remains unresolved.

- A state whose power is declining will have incentives to launch a preventive war.

- War is more likely when the offence – defence balance favours offence.

Conclusion

The preceding discussion makes clear that realism, while sharing a number of key assumptions, is a broad family of arguments that diverges on some important issues. Some of this divergence reflects disagreement over the deductive logic of the structural-realist arguments. A sign of progress will be the eventual resolution of these disputes.

Other disagreements are more reconcilable and suggest the possibility of a more general realist theory. There are two reasons for merging structural realism and motivational realism. First, their assumptions are compatible and complementary. Both see an important role for international structure, although the theories do emphasize quite different implications. The theories focus on different types of state motives—with structural realism focusing on security-seekers and motivational realism focusing on greedy states—but there is nothing inconsistent about considering the interactions of both types of states fully.

Second, we lack a strong theoretical rationale for giving special weight to one theory over the other. Defensive realism shows that international structure does not consistently and intensely drive competition; greedy states could matter. It also shows that structure can by itself drive competition and, therefore, cannot be reduced to a factor that simply constrains states' choices.

This more general theory has the advantage of spanning both basic types of states. As a result, it eliminates a key debate within the realist family and refocuses attention to a range of empirical issues, including the types of states that are interacting, and the severity of the security dilemma they face. The more general theory makes clear that a state's choice of security policy should depend both on its motives and goals, and on the international situation it faces; neither is generally sufficient on its own for explaining or prescribing a state's strategy.

QUESTIONS

1. Why is realism better understood as a family of theories than a single theory?

2. What assumptions are shared by most realist theories?

3. What is the key divide between structural and motivational realism?

4. Why does Waltz believe that the international system tends to generate competition?

5. Why does offensive realism believe that states maximize power?

6. Why does defensive realism believe states should attempt to signal their benign motives?

7. What variables influence the severity of the security dilemma and how do they matter?

8. How can a state's declining power create incentives for preventive war?

9. How does defence advantage reduce incentives for war?

 FURTHER READING

■ Copeland, D. (2000), *The Origins of Major War*, Ithaca, NY: Cornell University Press. Provides a nuanced realist theory of preventive war.

■ Glaser, C. (forthcoming 2010), *Rational Theory of International Politics*, Princeton: Princeton University Press. Presents a general rational theory that integrates structural and motivational realism, and adds states' information about motives as a key dimension of their international environment.

■ Jervis, R. (1978), 'Cooperation under the Security Dilemma', *World Politics*, 30/1: 167–214. Provides the classic discussion of how offence–defence variables influence the security dilemma.

■ Mearsheimer, J. (2001), *The Tragedy of Great Power Politics*, New York: Norton. The definitive statement of offensive realism.

■ Smith, M. (1986), *Realist Thought from Weber to Kissinger*, Baton Rouge, LA: Louisiana State University Press. Provides an analysis and comparison of key classical realists.

■ Schweller, R. (1998), *Deadly Imbalances: Tripolarity and Hitler's Strategy of World Conquest*, New York: Columbia University Press. A motivational realist analysis that emphasizes the importance of greedy states and variations in the balance of power.

■ Snyder, J. (1991), *Myths of Empire: Domestic Politics and International Ambition*, Ithaca, NY: Cornell University Press. Combines realist and domestic-politics arguments to explain why states over-expand.

■ Van Evera, S. (1999), *Causes of War: Power and the Roots of Conflict*, Ithaca, NY: Cornell University Press. Explores the many ways in which military opportunities and pressures can lead to war, and how military biases can exacerbate these causes.

■ Walt, S. (1987), *The Origin of Alliances*, Ithaca, NY: Cornell University Press. Analyses alliance formation, moving beyond power by bringing in intentions and offence – defence variables.

■ Waltz, K. N. (1979), *Theory of International Politics*, New York: McGraw Hill. The seminal statement of structural realism.

 Visit the Online Resource Centre that accompanies this book for lots of interesting additional material: www.oxfordtextbooks.co.uk/orc/collins2e/

3

Liberalism

PATRICK MORGAN

 Chapter Contents

- Introduction
- Characteristic features of the liberalist approach
- Central elements in liberalist thinking; commercial liberalism
- The pursuit of human rights
- Liberalism and international organizations
- Liberalism and democracy
- Conclusion

 Reader's Guide

In this chapter the liberalist approach to the theory and practice of international politics is presented. As one of the two classic conceptions, along with realism, of international politics, its chief characteristics are identified and the major liberalist schools of thought are described and briefly examined, particularly with reference to how they overlap with, yet depart in significant ways from, the realist perspective. There is a brief discussion of how the liberalist perspective dominates contemporary international politics, and the ways in which critics attack it for its alleged intellectual weaknesses and the adverse effects of liberalism in practice.

Introduction

The liberalist tradition is usually traced back to the Enlightenment, particularly to the philosopher John Locke and, on certain matters, to the philosopher Immanuel Kant. In the field of international politics it is considered to have reached a high point in the initial years after the First World War, particularly under the intellectual and political leadership of President Woodrow Wilson, who sought to make it the basis for radically transforming international politics so as to do away with major warfare. In his efforts, Wilson highlighted all the main themes that have been displayed in the liberalist approach ever since (Kegley 1995). It was then somewhat eclipsed, particularly in the academic study of international politics, by the rise of Fascism and the Second World War followed by the emergence of the Cold War, but it still played an important role in the development of international relations among the Western countries throughout the Cold War years. It blossomed when the Cold War ended, the East–West conflict dissolved, and the Soviet Union disappeared.

Characteristic features of the liberalist approach

There are several characteristics that, taken together, are associated with liberalism and define its distinctive approach to international politics. Perhaps the most obvious is that it is fundamentally optimistic, now more than ever. It is optimistic about politics, economics, and the broad prospects for international politics, including cooperation among international actors and our chances for a peaceful world. It holds that international politics is not inherently full of conflict and violence and that peace and security are plausibly attainable and getting more so. Cooperation among states and societies need not be limited and difficult. There is no inherent security dilemma in international politics. In short, international politics need not be as doleful as much of its history has been, and therefore the study of international politics is not a modern-day dismal science.

A second notable characteristic is that, while the liberalist approach offers elements of a theory, it is not one. It is a broad analytical approach with a family of related ideas and preferred practices. While it offers guidelines, advice, conclusions, and orientations for the better conduct of international affairs, it is a bit short of well-developed theoretical explanations of why those things work. Analysts cite similar deficiencies in other theoretical approaches in the field, but liberalism seems to display this more than most. Nevertheless, it has a strong appeal and robust vigour. It is the dominant conception in the *practice* of international politics today and is influential in the *study* of international politics as well.

Next, it is old enough to be a classical approach and overlaps a good deal with the other great classical perspective, the realist approach, while discarding central realist contentions. It identifies nation states as the most important actors in international politics, the ones who's behaviour we most care about and most wish to explain, but then gives considerable attention to other actors as well: international organizations (IGOs), international regimes, non-governmental international organizations (NGOs), multinational corporations, and domestic actors such as interest groups, elites, political parties, and government bureaucracies. In the same way, liberalism accepts the idea that the international system, its nature and its structure, can have important effects on the behaviour of the actors, yet rests on the contrary view that the system is ultimately not as important in determining states' behaviour as (1) domestic actors' power and preferences and (2) the nature of states' domestic political systems.

Pulling all this together, we can say that a liberalist approach insists nation states are not basically alike, and how international politics operates tends to reflect their differences in character. With the 'right' sorts of (liberal) political systems and the right sorts of domestic (liberalist-oriented) groups running them, states can arrange to have international cooperation flourish and can tolerate the vigorous participation of international organizations and numerous sorts of non-state actors, with the resulting constraints on state behaviour that those non-state elements impose. Thus international politics is not the same everywhere; it is 'realist' only in some places and at certain times. Its nature is not always dictated by how anarchy and the resulting international system shape the members' behaviour. Instead, international politics is also shaped by the political, economic, and social choices people in the member states make, choices not necessarily driven by the international system. Thus liberalists agree with realists that international politics can be highly realist in character, but not on whether it *must* be.

This is an 'inside-out' approach to describing and explaining why governments do what they do, in contrast to a realist approach in which the external environment is crucial. States make important choices in conducting their foreign interactions, and, like domestic policies and actions, foreign policies and resulting acts are shaped in the end by domestic factors, particularly the *political* factors that determine who rules, who crafts decisions, who's perspectives and preferences are in charge. Domestic political struggles and competing bureaucratic interests and perspectives are important, plus the pressures from elites, interest groups, and others in the society, not just the pulling and hauling between states. Domestic politics is itself a competition among perspectives and interests, with elites and leaders who represent them competing for power, office, and influence. The shifting results of the competition eventually determine foreign policy. External pressures and opportunities, especially threats, are certainly important but seldom decisive. Hence it is sometimes suggested,

especially with regard to very powerful states, that foreign policy is an effort by domestic political elements also to pursue their domestic preferences and policies abroad—foreign policy is domestic preferences projected outwards. Whether this is the case or not, the state's national interests and its policies on pursuing them are not semi-automatic or predetermined; somebody has to decide what they are.

This makes the state as an entity, apart from its society, an important component of foreign policy making but, in comparison with realism, less as a semi-autonomous actor and more often as an agent of the dominant interests and coalitions. States as states have some interests and concerns of their own, but the controlling factor is more often who rules, which involves a constant struggle inside the government and major elites and among important interest groups. Hence states are not unitary actors, and domestic forces, values, interests, and perspectives must also be considered significant factors in international politics. For instance, in seeking to maintain state security, what influential domestic elements think is good for *their* concerns and interests can be quite different from what the state's military officials would like, and the policies preferred by those domestic groups might well be adopted.

KEY POINTS

- Liberalism is basically optimistic about improving international politics and making it safer.

- It describes international politics as evolving, becoming more imbued with interdependence, cooperation, peace, and security.

- While seeing states as the most important actors it also highlights other kinds of actors—IGOs, NGOs, major private economic entities, and international regimes.

- It depicts states' behaviour as mainly the result of the perceptions, preferences, and decisions of elites and officials, which are related to the nature of each state's political system.

- Thus the character of international politics changes depending on the nature of its members, their objectives, and their decisions on what to do, how to interact.

Central elements in liberalist thinking; commercial liberalism

Politically, liberalism prefers certain perceptions, values, and interests- and favours-related policies. While there is controversy on details, liberalism is associated with: strong support for democracy, which is considered vital for the legitimacy of a government; strong support for private property and free enterprise—a market economy—at home and abroad; a belief in open relationships among societies—not only in trade and investment but in flows of information and ideas, people, and culture; strong support for cooperation in international affairs; and strong support for human rights based on the importance of the individual.

Adherents differ a good deal about which of these should receive the most attention or how to rank them in priority, leading to a somewhat confusing array of analytical claims and policies. Analysts sort all this out by classifying the factions via the following categories: *commercial* or *economic* liberalism, *human rights* liberalism, *international organization* or institutions liberalism, and *democratic* liberalism.

The oldest may well be *commercial* or *economic* liberalism. It descends from the free-trade ideas that emerged and grew steadily more influential in the eighteenth and early nineteenth centuries, particularly in Great Britain. The term 'free trade' encompassed flows not just of goods but also of capital, and the proponents had both domestic and international economic activities in mind. The general idea is that the production and accumulation of wealth are most rapid and efficient if economic activities are largely in the hands of private owners/actors who interact largely in accordance with the dictates of markets. This is in contrast with having economic activities, domestic and international, operated, organized, or tightly regulated by governments, as owners or through laws, regulations, and other restraints. It is, therefore, opposed to restrictions on transnational flows. After 1945 the United States became the main proponent of this kind of economic system, at home and abroad, and it continues in this role today. The contemporary global economic system is basically the US-led one constructed among non-communist countries during the Cold War. It is characterized by vast flows of capital (well over a trillion dollars daily), constantly expanding trade, considerable transfers of technology, and notable movement of workers across national boundaries, legally and illegally. In degree of interdependence it is roughly equivalent to the international economic system before 1914, which was disrupted by the two world wars, but on a much larger scale.

A regular contention about such domestic economies and this kind of international economic system is that rising economic interdependence ultimately brings about peace and security. Prior to the First World War it was often said that wars would decline because they were bad for business—too costly, disruptive, and expensive for societies to put up with. After the Second World War this view of interdependence was an important influence in the creation of the European Common Market, forerunner of the EU, with integration undertaken not just for greater economic well-being but to promote better political relations among the members so that warfare among them would disappear.

A current version of the benefits of an open international economy contends that, when the main governments in a region are controlled by liberalism-oriented elites strongly interested in economic growth plus greater domestic freedom and mobility, those governments will promote export-led national development, including seeking foreign investment to help develop productive capacities for exporting. To maintain the right environment for this, they reduce their conflicts and expand their economic contacts while expanding other kinds of cooperation better to manage their rising interactions. As a result, chances of war among them decline, as does the likelihood they will develop nuclear weapons, while the prospects for successful arms control rise (Solingen 1998; 2007).

Thus one reason for liberalism's optimism is the continuing expansion of capitalism in the belief that this approach brings wealth and higher living standards in such a way that war is typically irrelevant or counterproductive, curbing the influence of elites historically devoted to war, conquest, and the national power and glory associated with them. Instead there is a rising *common* interest in

international cooperation to facilitate these developments and manage their complex effects.

This interest in the potentially pacifying results of rising economic interdependence took on greater prominence after the Cold War as most former members of the communist world joined the liberal international economic system and **globalization** surged. Globalization is a powerful contemporary symbol of the liberalist view, especially in economic activities. Proponents see it further eroding national boundaries, knitting the world together in a global community.

KEY POINTS

- Adherents of liberalism strongly support democracy, private property, and free enterprise, widespread international interactions, international cooperation, and human rights.

- Commercial or economic liberalism stresses the benefits of open-market economies and widespread international trade and investment.

- The benefits include greater cooperation plus less conflict and war, an important motivation behind the European integration effort.

- In other regions governments with open economic systems relying on exports for national development have been highly likely to pursue conflict reduction and greater cooperation with neighbours.

- A reason for optimism is that the world has been developing along these lines for decades, including the globalization of today.

The pursuit of human rights

A second, and very striking, school of liberalist thought and action today is preoccupied with *human rights*. In a sense its roots lie in the concerns, from early in the **Westphalian** international system, that states have often had about how religious and ethnic groups of great interest to them were treated by their neighbours. In the beginning these concerns were expressed in diplomatic pressures, military interventions, and peace agreements (Krasner 1999). However, for several centuries the concern was due not to liberalist sentiments but to members of ethnic and religious groups caring about compatriots abroad. This began to change in the nineteenth century, especially

with the movement in Britain and elsewhere to end the slave trade, espousing not a specific national concern but a universal human right. Such thinking was readily extended to support for national self-determination, targeting empires and particularly colonial empires. This was quite intense after the First World War at the peace negotiations and a source of bitter recrimination by nationalities not favoured in the agreements. It was even greater after the Second World War.

Modern human rights oriented liberalism is still concerned with self-determination. It does not widely support separatism, because most countries are multi-ethnic and supporting separatism would invite chaotic dissolutions, but will endorse it when separation looks unavoidable and serious fighting and other bloodshed seem certain without it. This is illustrated by the slow evolution of the Kosovo problem towards an independent Kosovo, or the way a liberalist view holds that the former Soviet republics are entitled to reject membership in a Russian sphere of influence and are not to be subjected to a forcible Russian takeover. Religious persecution also remains a broad liberalist concern. In all these matters the goal is protecting an inherent human right, not to advance underlying national interests of a different sort.

Liberalism's adherents today, private and governmental, support a broad list of human rights pertaining to economic, medical, political, sexual, and other forms of deprivation and discrimination. The democracies regularly pressure other governments, and each other, to become more supportive of and sensitive to human rights concerns. They take actions in support of political prisoners, rights and opportunities for women, religious freedom, civil rights, victims of famine, and so on.

Those efforts are influenced by domestic groups devoted to human rights concerns, and groups that reinforce the policies internationally through a huge network of private organizations (NGOs) often referred to as **international civil society**, another aspect of globalization. These organizations campaign for human rights, and often actively promote them in **peace-building** efforts and other activities abroad, drawing on their extensive private resources and on funding from governments, foundations, and international organizations.

> **KEY POINTS**
>
> - Liberalism's interest in human rights in the nineteenth century is notable for the focus on slavery and national self-determination, including anticolonialism.
>
> - Added in the twentieth century, particularly since the Cold War, were campaigns on behalf of persons subject to economic, sexual, gender, religious, and political persecution, discrimination, or deprivation.
>
> - Much of the impetus on these matters now comes from potent private organizations operating both inside their societies and internationally.

Liberalism and international organizations

Adherents of liberalism have long sought to enhance international cooperation and bolster national and international security by international organizations. Early in the twentieth century interest was high in forming a league or alliance of governments to prevent wars. Woodrow Wilson put great emphasis on inserting this into the agreements signed at the peace conference after the First World War and in his campaign after that to get the USA to join the new League of Nations, reasoning that, once it was in place and operating, many other improvements in international politics would become possible.

Of course, the USA did not join, and the League was a failure in preventing wars in the 1930s and the coming of the Second World War. But the idea was revived after the Second World War with the creation of the United Nations, the World Bank, the International Monetary Fund, and other institutions for managing international affairs. In the ensuing decades many additional organizations have been created. This contributed to a continued emphasis on cooperation as desirable and possible.

This has been reinforced by two additional developments. One, mentioned above, is the surge in the numbers and activities of NGOs, adding an impressive additional dimension to the concept of international cooperation. The other is the concept of 'international regimes', which expanded the concept of international cooperation even further (see Key Ideas 3.1). Cooperation was often taking the form of norms and understandings as to appropriate behaviour on important, often sensitive matters (such as non-proliferation or the continuing non-use of nuclear weapons). Regimes can exist not only in connection with international treaties and formal international organizations but even without them. This made it apparent that there was a good deal more cooperation, more management, in international politics than previously understood. Today all the forms it takes are referred to as international 'institutions'.

The liberalist view of international institutions runs along three different lines. One is neoliberal institutionalism—sometimes called rational-choice liberalism. It accepts the realist view that anarchy makes cooperation very difficult—the temptation to cheat is too great and fear of being cheated is pervasive. Then, using a kind of analysis developed by economists, it explains how regimes and international organizations can nevertheless facilitate it (Oye 1986). For instance, the cooperation needed for agreements can be inhibited if governments have too little information about the problem cooperation is designed to solve and about its likely effects; international organizations may be able to generate that information. Cooperation often requires extensive interaction and bargaining; international organization can provide forums for this along with expert advice. Governments will fear that, if they follow agreements, others will free ride—gaining the benefits without doing their share—or simply cheat; international organizations can monitor compliance to discourage free-riding and cheating and reassure governments it is not taking place, or provide procedures to resolve disagreements on compliance. They can also administer agreements and report on their effectiveness. In other words, international organizations and regimes are *practical* in that they

---

🔑 KEY IDEAS 3.1

International regimes

The term 'regime' here should not be confused with its use as a substitute for 'government' or 'state' or 'ruler' in domestic politics. Here it is a term for an international institution that contains principles, rules, norms, and procedures for decision making that international actors use to plan and carry out actions pertaining to some specified subject matter. The principles, rules, and norms may be written into a formal treaty or other international agreement to which governments officially subscribe—like the Kyoto Protocol—or they may be informal—like the tradition or taboo that has grown up on the non-use of nuclear weapons. In the same way, the procedures for decision making may involve setting up a formal international organization with rules of procedure and a clear definition of what it is to decide. Or the decisions might be made by governments independently; for instance, under the non-proliferation regime non-nuclear powers promise not to try to develop nuclear weapons, but the decision actually not to do so also has to be made when opportunities arise to start a nuclear weapons programme or to continue it, decisions that would be made by each government on its own—the regime would simply lead governments to expect that the decisions will always be negative.

Regimes are attractive not only for what they do but because they can be so flexible. For instance, they can emerge gradually, and very slowly, even be unnoticed for quite a while. The democratic peace is, in fact, such a regime. This means a regime can emerge partially and then develop over time, something harder to do with a formal agreement, which normally sets a minimum number of signatories for it to go into operation. Sometimes, regimes emerge because that number is not met, so the formal agreement does not go into effect, but those who signed decide to adhere to it anyway—being up and operating, the regime can put pressure on non-signatories to join after all, especially if it is having a noticeable effect without them. Sometimes such states will join unofficially, living up to the regime's requirements but not formally signing it. This kind of flexibility is often useful.

reduce transaction costs. Being useful makes them valuable, thus hard to do without once they are up and running, which is why cooperation in international politics is often durable. This analysis has been influential, in part because it bridges realist and liberalist thinking.

Another view is that international institutions are 'natural', an obvious recourse for an increasingly interdependent world. As cooperation grows, so does everyone's stake in it, giving rise to increased support for organizations, rules, and even laws. Like demand for a traffic light at a busy intersection, the magnitude of the interaction incites coordination arrangements. This is a *functionalist* view—rising interactions generate important functions that need to be performed; international organizations are either created to meet them or flourish because they turn out to meet them. The Law of the Sea Treaty is an example of the former, and the World Health Organization's growing role in dealing with threats of global epidemics embodies the latter.

Finally, there is the argument that governments can be induced to part with sovereignty to create governing international institutions. They may want more efficient decision making, or less domination by the most powerful or wealthiest members, or greater legitimacy for a norm, or some other compelling need. Examples include the development of the EU and, more recently, the European Central Bank, or the recent emergence of international criminal courts. The permanent members' veto power in the UN Security Council is often cited to illustrate how devoted to sovereignty nations are, but the Council's power to order military action to deal with threats to peace and security is quite impressive and shows how far international governance can be carried. The World Trade Organization settles major issues as a potent actor, not just as an agent of the members.

Still, parting with elements of sovereignty and autonomy is a drastic step. Is something else needed to induce governments to accept it? One argument is that it takes a hegemon—a dominant state that provides leadership, organizes the cooperative effort, provides necessary enforcement, and so on. The establishment of the Bretton Woods system after the Second World War for the international economy is often considered the supreme example. Another argument is that, if cooperation is important enough, nations redefine national interests to embrace the necessary shrinking of national autonomy—the national interest then transcends sovereignty and autonomy.

Finally, one liberalist conception of international cooperation is shared with constructivism. This is the idea that international politics develops elements of community, one indication being the emergence of international institutions with a network of norms and rules to which leaders, governments, and societies are expected to adhere. Liberalism has consistently promoted 'higher-order' norms and principles, sometimes advocating forcible steps to enforce them. Examples include avoiding advocacy of secession, non-use of nuclear weapons, and, inside society, avoidance of genocide. An example of a slowly emerging norm is the idea that sovereignty is not simply a right to national autonomy; it is also an obligation of a government in charge of a society to treat the society with reasonable decency, and that failure to do so can be rectified by international intervention. It is not that international politics must eventually embrace and inculcate these particular norms, but that, as an elaborate social activity, international politics needs elements of community including a structure of norms. Liberalists are busy pushing their preferred norms with this in mind.

From a liberalist perspective, therefore, states are not rigid about sovereignty and autonomy, and not averse to cooperation. A final aspect of this is that all liberalism adherents see cooperation as encouraged and reinforced when participants expect it to be reiterated along with its benefits, which is technically referred to as the influence of the shadow of the future. Under these conditions it is easier to get cooperation, trust others, and make agreements in the present.

KEY POINTS

- Liberalism has been interested for at least a century in building international organizations. To this it has more recently added advocacy of the use of NGOs and international regimes, enlarging the arsenal of cooperative arrangements.

- Explanations of the contributions of organizations range from neoliberalism's elucidation of their facilitative contributions, to functional analyses, to claims that organizations can meet certain political needs.

- Elaborate cooperation is apt to require something else: perhaps a hegemon, or an innovative redefinition of the national interest.

- International cooperation represents, and benefits from, the development of community, and is enhanced by a significant likelihood that it will be recurring.

Liberalism and democracy

Not surprisingly, liberalism rejects the idea that warfare is all but inevitable, and has a strong preference for non-violent methods in pursuing national objectives. The main evidence cited now on this is the 'democratic-peace' thesis, which brings us to *democratic liberalism*. The thesis treats a notable statistical pattern in relations among modern liberal democracies as a virtual law: modern liberal democracies never go to war with each other. In fact, they spend no effort preparing even for possible wars with each other. Despite often being amply armed—frequently with significant *offensive* military forces that might be expected to produce great insecurity in others—democracies display no signs of a security dilemma in their relations, and coexist peacefully even when they have serious disagreements. Technically, the democracies constitute a **pluralistic security community**: even with no superior ruling authority, these states have no fear of being attacked by each other.

Liberalism champions the spread of democracy to achieve security—'if you want peace promote democracy', so to speak. The goal is a universal pluralistic security community. That spreading democracy will have this effect is not a new idea (Kant suggested it; Woodrow Wilson endorsed it), but it is the democratic peace thesis that has made it so prominent now. It is an extension of Liberalism's inside-out approach and the belief that the nature of an international system is significantly shaped by the character of its members. It contends that a system composed of democracies will be a sharp departure from much of the history of international politics.

Sceptics cite the fact that democracies that are new, not deeply rooted, often display aggressive, expansionist behaviour and national pugnacity (Mansfield and Snyder 1989; Snyder 1998). And analysts agree that democracies readily go to war with non-democracies, so it cannot be their pacifism that creates the democratic peace. Critics also note that liberalist analysts lack a consensus as to what generates the democratic peace—they have no accepted theory to explain it (see Key Ideas 3.2).

This has not slowed the promotion of democracy. It is now integral to the liberal democracies' foreign policies. In response to the 9/11 attacks President Bush proposed a war to end terrorism by, in large part, promoting democracy in the Middle East. Many commentators have concluded that this called liberal internationalism into ill repute and that it is dying out, but that is not the case. Western countries have vigorously encouraged democracy throughout the former Soviet empire in Eastern Europe to help ensure the area will be peaceful. The Western approach to peace building in societies torn by civil war is intervening to, in part, promote rule of law, political parties, elections, an active media, and civil rights as the proper recipe for creating stable societies and responsible governments.

As noted earlier, a related aspect of this is the rise of 'international civil society.' A pervasive element in liberalism is respect for the private sector, not just in economic activities but in intellectual, cultural, social, and political spheres. Individuals and groups are expected to make important contributions to society on their own, apart from (as well as in cooperation with) the government. This is viewed as an essential component of democracy. International civil society is reproducing the activism and non-governmental character of domestic activities characteristic of civil societies in liberal democracies, for the purpose of containing threats to peace and security. These activities reflect a profound belief in both the existence of a global community and the need to expand it.

 KEY IDEAS 3.2

Explaining the democratic peace

Here are examples of how varied the explanations for the democratic peace are, drawn from items on the list of suggested readings or sources cited in the chapter. One explanation is that democracies have a unique ability to get along without fighting because they see democracy as legitimizing a government and therefore treat other democracies as deserving of respect and trust—limiting how far they will carry conflicts with them. A related argument is that democracies are devoted to resolving issues through compromise, so they trust and respect each other to use that to avoid a war.

Another is that democracies make leaders accountable to many groups, some of which oppose wars, and this makes it hard to secure the broad support leaders want in a war, or will want in the next election—so leaders are reluctant to have to build that support. A related explanation is that democracies are full of restraints on governments—constitutions, legal restrictions, public opinion, separation of powers, opposition parties, and so on—making it difficult for a democratic government to go to war. A variation on this is that the restraints make it hard to get into a war *quickly*, allowing more time for negotiations or other approaches to work. A classic view is that republics are particularly sensitive about concentrating too much power in the government's hands and wars have that effect, so republics are wary about taking on wars.

It is possible that, since democracies are more transparent than other kinds of political systems, they more readily interact with confidence and with less concern about hidden motives. It is also the case that democracies are more open to opinions, pressures, and so on from outside, particularly from other democracies, and that this makes them more responsive to other democracies points of view in conflicts. And the oldest argument is that citizens hate to bear the costs of war, so that makes it harder for democratic governments to get into one.

Finally, it is argued that democracies more readily develop a wide range of interactions and a higher level of interdependence with each other, and more readily set up international institutions as a result. This allows analysts to argue that liberalism's emphasis on those things as good for reducing warfare applies particularly strongly to democracies, making the various facets of liberalism interactive and reinforcing in keeping democracies from fighting each other.

Naturally, there are many ways to disparage these arguments. And, while there are ways to test many of them, there are strenuous debates about whether those tests are properly done. There is not even agreement on just when a government is a democracy in building lists of democracies over time, or is enough of a democracy.

KEY POINTS

- Democratic liberalism has long promoted democracy to change international politics. Now that is reinforced by the democratic peace thesis: democracies do not go to war with each other – they constitute a pluralistic security community.

- However adherents of this view lack consensus on why democracy has this effect, especially since democracies are quite capable of making war on non-democracies.

- Spreading democracy is now a major part of the foreign policies of democracies.

- This is reinforced by the pro-democracy orientation and activities of much of international civil society.

Conclusion

Liberalism is optimistic and with good reason. For the first time in history, all the world's richest, most economically and militarily potent nations are part of the liberalist camp or (Russia, China, India) significantly interacting with it. Wars between governments have sharply declined. Internal wars that pose threats to international peace and security have begun to decline in recent years and many are targets of moderate to vigorous international efforts to end them and establish conditions that discourage their return. International outcries over even modest collateral damage in warfare have grown. The total number of democracies is higher than it has ever been. Efforts at expanding international cooperation continue, especially on environmental management, in international economic matters, and on international crime and terrorism. There is more cooperation on non-proliferation of weapons of mass destruction than in the past.

Thus far, at least, opposition to the liberalist vision since the Cold War remains fragmented. It is customary to disparage Fukuyama's declaration (1992) of the end of history after the Cold War; his argument was that the major challenges to democracy have been defeated, so contention as to which is the ultimate form of social and political organization is at an end. Saying that no further challenges would appear was premature in view of the opposition from the Islamic world and particularly Islamic fundamentalist-inspired terrorism. But the terrorists may be a frantic response to the continued spreading of the liberalist vision, not another great challenge like Fascism and Communism, the sort of challenge Fukuyama had in mind.

However, the liberalist perspective and liberalism in practice certainly have critics. Some are analytical, lamenting aspects of liberalism in theory. As noted, some analysts remain suspicious of democratic peace theory, believing the correlation and the absence of war is spurious, that some third factor is responsible for the absence of war among democracies (Rosato 2003). Since wars among all states have significantly declined, maybe the democratic peace is just a reflection of the growing obsolescence of war (Mueller 1989). Or maybe democracies have long had identical or overlapping national interests so they make natural allies and their difficulties are not serious enough to fight about. This, not democracy or their special regard for each other as democracies, could be the key variable. This criticism is hard to refute, because the liberal democracies do indeed have many important interests in common, and only time will tell if it is accurate.

Constructivist and postmodernist approaches, which reject some or all of liberalism's methodologies and theoretical explanations, have grown in influence. Their adherents find liberalism out of touch, failing to appreciate the inherent limitations of trying to develop a somewhat 'scientific' theory of international politics and not readily appreciating how liberalist impulses are often, to much of the world, part of the problem of international politics.

Consider the possibility that the current liberalist influence merely reflects Western dominance. What if, as some analysts suspect, that dominance is finally coming to an end with the rapid development of non-Western states and societies that encompass well over half the world's population? If the sun sets on the West's pre-eminence, will it also set on the liberalist perspective? If so, the implications might include a clash of regions or civilizations, perhaps the return of a very realist world.

When it comes to putting liberalism into practice, there are annoying limitations on using it as a guide, because it is often internally inconsistent. For peace and security purposes, is it vital to cooperate with autocratic governments (such as China, Iran, Russia), such as on arms control agreements, or to sanction and isolate them because they reject democracy and violate human rights? Is the best approach to a difficult government like North Korea an honest and sincere engagement effort—economic assistance, normal relations, even foreign investment—or a sustained effort to undermine the regime? Which should come first in peace-building priorities, a stable, effective, reasonably democratic government or installing better economic policies and practices (a good tax system, cuts in bloated government spending)? Putting democracy first may cancel the economic improvements—why would desperately poor citizens vote for better tax collection and cuts in government jobs? Should it be democracy first or decent human-rights improvements (like equal treatment for women)? Why should citizens approve greater rights to women if that is disparaged in their religion and culture? On the other hand, how will economic, human rights, and other reforms take hold without a reasonably strong democracy to make them legitimate?

The oldest such inconsistency is the tension between self-determination and the need for viable states. Creating a state for a disaffected minority often alarms other minorities within its boundaries. Their fears of being mistreated are often well founded. The problem has arisen repeatedly in new states carved out of the old Soviet Union (like Georgia). Liberalism offers no ready way to resolve these inconsistencies and little help for governments in making the relevant decisions.

There is also great difficulty in sorting out when to use force. In one form of this problem governments disagree about when force is justified, or how to determine the will of the international community—that is, how to 'legitimize' using force. This was the issue between the USA and others over the invasion of Iraq in 2003. Should action always be suspended when there is serious disagreement? The other form of the problem is when there is unhappiness with a particular situation and a willingness to see force used to deal with it but widespread reluctance to bear the costs—typical in serious security problems in Africa. The moral and analytical justifications for force often conflict with the political, financial, and other considerations involved.

Critics were given a boost when the USA, unable to obtain Security Council approval for its war on Iraq in 2003, went ahead anyway. This seemed to confirm realist assertions that national power and selfish state interests still regularly trump international norms and the general welfare. The Bush administration was lacerated by contrasting criticisms. On the one hand, it was wide open to the charge that it had abandoned many of liberalism's central tenets: it expressed disdain for various multilateral agreements and international organizations, it ignored many human rights concerns in the war on terrorism, it stressed putting American 'interests' ahead of international cooperation on several matters. On the other hand, it was seen as 'Wilsonian internationalism [liberalism] on steroids' in wanting to bring democracy and a respect for human rights to Iraq (and perhaps other rogue states) at the point of a gun.

A weightier criticism is that liberalism, particularly in its more forceful version, is an updated expression of Western imperialism, a rationalization of what is basically a hegemonic effort to spread Western values to make the global environment more congenial for the West. Subscribers to this view see Western practices as provocative and subversive, undermining many established ways of life. They reject the West's claim that it is promoting universal values (Johnson 2006).

This is certainly debatable. After all, liberalism helped undermine Western colonialism and now promotes efforts to enhance development and raise living standards around the world. Future historians may see international politics today as still being uplifted by the continued unfolding of the eighteenth century's democratic revolution and its attendant values. Liberalism may be on the cutting edge. On the other hand, this means liberalism is revolutionary; advocates of the democratic peace, for instance, are hardly status quo oriented and this is not comfortable in much of the world. Western governments and their peoples are always ready, even eager, to see many of the world's political systems overturned and many of its existing social and economic systems radically altered. No wonder many see the liberalist effort as imperialistic (see Think Point 3.1).

This is reinforced by the way globalization often produces short- or long-run effects at odds with

---

THINK POINT 3.1

Liberalism as revolutionary and a threat

In 1989 a group of student activists, in connection with the death of a former leader who had sought reforms in China's political system and had been removed from high office as a result, began demonstrating on behalf of democracy in the leading public square in Beijing, Tiananmen Square. The demonstration quickly grew in size and took over the square, with thousands of students sitting/sleeping in, and similar demonstrations began to appear in other cities. Although the demonstration remained peaceful, the government eventually suppressed it violently.

The important elements for observing liberalism in action were these. The demonstration attracted enormous Western media coverage almost totally in support of the students. The Chinese Communist Party leadership acted out of fear that the regime would begin to lose support and dissolve, and chaos would ensue. The Western response was to condemn the suppression and institute significant sanctions on China. This was despite the fact that China had enjoyed close cooperative relations with the Western countries, was moving to participate more normally in international institutions, and was actively introducing capitalism and a wide open relationship (by Chinese standards) with the international economic system. Western governments were supporting an effort markedly to alter the Chinese political system anyway, with hostility towards the regime because it *was still at variance with Western liberalism*—on democracy, on human rights. It was therefore somewhat illegitimate.

That incident has made the Chinese ruling elite much more wary ever since about introducing any Western political practices and ideals, treating such steps as a threat to the regime's survival. It invited Chinese leaders to see Western attitudes as imperialist and revolutionary, as interference in China's internal affairs intended to transform the political system. This spills over into other issues. For instance, it helps lead Chinese leaders to see the US position on Taiwan as yet another way of trying to disrupt or weaken China. It cripples China's leaders on taking the West's liberalism seriously on its own terms. For instance, the key to the American position on Taiwan today is that Taiwan is a vigorous democracy; an open effort by China to invade would be opposed by the USA for this reason and condemned by democracies around the world. Instead, Chinese leaders are prone, in good realist fashion, to see the West trying to contain China's power or to prevent its rapid rise in the international system. Thus both sides have an insufficient understanding of what the other's perspective is and why.

---

liberalism's values. This is true of contemporary environmental degradation from rampant economic growth. It is true of the way in which whole ways of life are being rudely uprooted by land seizures and other economically driven dislocations, or the rapid erosion of sovereignty and national autonomy for many countries, on many levels. This has contributed to a reaction against global free-trade efforts, in favour of regional trade arrangements and **free-trade agreements** limited to only a few countries. Thus the latest attempt at global negotiations to further liberalism's international economic agenda has been an abysmal failure. Leftist rejections of modern capitalism are evident in Latin America.

There is plenty of evidence that nationalism and states remain powerfully attractive. They continue to be vehicles for evoking and conveying the most intense human feelings now in play in international politics, yet liberalism often seems to suggest that all this should be dying out, is passé. Maybe, as with Mark Twain, the reports of their demise are greatly exaggerated.

Also disturbing is that the leading states in the North Atlantic–European region actively promoted democracy, capitalism, an open international economy, and rising interdependence several times in the past. After the first such era, the military savagery of the First World War ensued. The second attempt occurred after that war, highlighted by Wilsonian internationalism, and did not prevent the Great Depression, the rise of Fascism, and the Second World War. The third effort was mounted in the first decades of the Cold War, a part of Western efforts to woo developing countries by offering rapid progress towards modernization. Broadly speaking, that effort also failed, despite the immense efforts and resources applied. Things went better when governments and societies worked out for themselves why and how to introduce Western values and methods. Nevertheless, the USA plunged into a post-Cold War campaign rapidly to Westernize Russia. It was so unsuccessful it created a political backlash; Russians condemned the campaign, based on its effects, as an American plot to ruin the country! Thus we have been down this road before. What if elements of the Western world cannot be readily transferred but must be absorbed by others only when they wish and only at their own pace?

The best conclusion for now is taking refuge in ambiguity. It is too soon to say that liberalism in international politics has run its course and is on the decline. It is also too soon to say with confidence that it is not headed that way.

KEY POINTS

- There are good reasons for optimism by adherents of liberalism—many developments are going in the preferred direction.

- However, liberalism faces challenges intellectually, with critics complaining that it is theoretically thin and out of date.

- There are annoying internal inconsistencies in liberalism that limit its utility.

- It is also criticized as just Western imperialism, or the latest attempt to remake societies from the outside, something that has failed too often.

- The future of liberalism is therefore unclear.

? QUESTIONS

1. What are the main characteristics of the liberalist orientation?

2. What are the main categories or types of liberalism in the study and conduct of international politics?

3. In what sense can liberalism be considered the dominant perspective in international politics today?

4. How do NGOs now play a role in international politics in the pursuit of liberalist objectives and values?

5. Why is liberalism relatively optimistic about the possibilities for cooperation, and for cooperation leading to significant improvements in international politics?

6. What are the main components of commercial or economic liberalism?

7. What is the democratic peace thesis and what are its implications for understanding and trying to improve international politics?

8. In what ways is liberalism often inconsistent on dealing with important issues in international politics?

9. Why do some critics see liberalism as a form of Western imperialism?

10. In what sense is liberalism revolutionary in international politics and, as such, a serious threat?

FURTHER READING

■ Adler, Emanual, and Barnett, Michael (1998), *Security Communities*, Cambridge: Cambridge University Press. Valuable on pluralistic security communities and other cooperative arrangements in international politics.

■ Doyle, Michael (1997), *Ways of War and Peace*, London: Norton. Contains an excellent review of the foundations of democratic peace theory.

■ Brown, M. E., Lynn-Jones, S. M., and Miller, S.E. (1996) (eds.), *Debating the Democratic Peace,* Cambridge, MA: MIT Press. Good coverage of many elements of democratic peace theory and its alleged deficiencies.

■ Keohane, Robert O. (1984), *After Hegemony: Cooperation and Discord in the World Political Economy,* Princeton: Princeton University Press. A good introduction to theory on hegemony in international politics, and the foundation volume on neoliberal institutionalism on cooperation in international politics.

■ Ikenberry, John, G. (2000), *After Victory,* Princeton: Princeton University Press. How the USA led the way in constructing the Western community along liberalist lines during the Cold War.

■ Moravcsik, A. (1997). 'Taking Preferences Seriously: A Liberal Theory of International Politics', *International Organization,* 51/4: 513–53. One of the most interesting efforts to develop a theory of liberalism for international politics.

■ Smith, Tony (1994), *America's Mission: The United States and the Worldwide Struggle for Democracy in the Twentieth Century,* Princeton: Princeton University Press. The US effort to promote democracy traced in detail. A strong case offered for liberal internationalism.

■ Zacher, Mark W., and Matthew, Richard A. (1995), 'Liberal International Theory: Common Threads, Divergent Strands', in Charles Kegley, Jr. (ed.), *Controversies in International Relations Theory,* New York: St Martins Press, 107–50. Pulls together many aspects of the liberalist perspective.

IMPORTANT WEBSITE

● http:nobelprize.org/nobel_prizes/peace/articles/doyle/index.html   This is a link to Michael Doyle's essay on 'Liberal Internationalism: Peace, War and Democracy'.

Visit the Online Resource Centre that accompanies this book for lots of interesting additional material: www.oxfordtextbooks.co.uk/orc/collins2e/

4

Social Constructivism

CHRISTINE AGIUS

Chapter Contents

Reader's Guide

Since the late 1980s, social constructivism has emerged as an influential approach in international relations theory and international politics. This chapter examines its impact on security studies and how it calls into question the assumed orthodoxy of rationalist approaches to security and the international system by asking how security and security threats are 'socially constructed'. It focuses on the importance of social relations and why identity, norms, and culture matter. Whereas rationalist approaches focus on material forces to understand and theorize security, social constructivism argues that ideational as well as material factors construct the world around us and the meanings we give to it. Therefore, its significance for security studies is crucial in terms not only of conceptualizing security but of providing alternative readings of security. However, constructivism is not a uniform approach. As this chapter demonstrates, it is broadly divided into two camps, which differ on questions of methodology and particular aspects of how knowledge and identity are interrogated. Throughout this chapter case studies of constructivist approaches to security questions will be discussed, and the chapter concludes with a consideration of the critiques of constructivism.

Introduction

Social constructivism (henceforth shortened to 'constructivism') brings to the fore the importance of ideas, identity, and interaction in the international system, revealing how 'the human world is not simply given and/or natural but that, on the contrary, the human world is one of artifice; that it is "constructed" through the actions of the actors themselves' (Kratochwil 2001: 17). Since Nicholas Onuf coined the term in 1989, constructivism has risen rapidly, reshaping debates in International Relations (IR) and challenging the dominance of rationalist theories such as neorealism and neoliberalism[1]. Many of its core concepts have been inspired by sociological theory (see Key Ideas 4.1). With the emergence of Critical Security Studies (see Chapter 6), the constructivist approach[2] forms part of the post-Cold War transformation in security studies, and argues that 'security' can be socially constructed. It therefore offers the possibility of alternative readings of security that go beyond rationalist theorizing that neglects ideational forces in favour of material ones. The world is social, and not purely material. This has implications for thinking about security and security relations internationally. Constructivism puts into context the actions, beliefs, and interests of actors and understands that the world they inhabit has been created by them and impacts on them.

Constructivism has three basic ontological positions. First, normative or ideational structures are important and matter as much as, if not more than, material structures. This means that ideas are centre stage and are privileged. This presents a different picture compared to dominant theories such as neorealism and neoliberalism. For neorealists, the key to understanding state behaviour has been the anarchic international system and the importance of the distribution of material capabilities in the international system; for neoliberals, even though cooperation and international institutions are the focus, state interests are also defined in material terms.

The second ontological claim of constructivism is that identities matter. Identities give us interests and those interests tell us something about how actors act/behave and the goals they pursue. Quite simply, actors cannot act without an identity and identity explains the actions of actors. Since neorealists see all units (states) as similar, it is difficult to make sense of why a state such as the USA may have conflictual relations with one state (for instance, Iran), and friendly relations with another (say, Australia). Identity is therefore crucial to constructivists—as Alexander Wendt (1996: 50) puts it: 'A gun in the hands of a friend is a different thing from one in the hands of an enemy, and enmity is a social, not material, relation.' For neorealists and neoliberals, actors such as states are rational, unitary actors, pursuing their interests in the international arena. However, we understand only the material interests of such actors in these two accounts. Material forces, which Wendt (1999: 371) defines as 'power and interest', do not readily tell us where ideas, values, beliefs, and norms come from; the trick is to examine how their content and meaning are made up by ideas and culture. By focusing on how interests are obtained and developed, constructivists argue that we get a better picture of identity and relations as social. Identity is not given but is constituted through interaction.

---

[1] For some, its impact has been so great that constructivism is seen to form the 'fourth debate' in IR theorizing (constructivists versus rationalists), usurping older debates between realists and liberals (Fierke and Jørgensen 2001: 3).

[2] Debate still exists over whether constructivism is a theory or an approach. Wendt's *Social Theory of International Politics* (1999) is widely regarded as an attempt to elevate constructivism as a theory, or a form of systemic theorizing. However, constructivists themselves have maintained that it is not a substantive theory of politics but rather 'a social theory that makes claims about the nature of social life and social change' (Finnemore and Sikkink 2001: 393). Ruggie (1998: 879) also contends that it is not an IR theory in the same manner that the balance-of-power theory is; rather it should be seen as 'a theoretically informed approach to the study of international relations'.

Third, agents and structures are mutually constituted. This attention to how actors shape the world and how the world shapes actors means that human relations are inherently social and we create the world that we live in and it influences us as well. International politics is not something that is independent from us; if the world 'out there' is a *World of our Making* (as the title of Onuf's book suggests), it means that different understandings of security may be possible. As part of the agency–structure debate, constructivism's appreciation of the mutual constitution of both agents and structures is important. When Alexander Wendt (1992) states that 'anarchy is what states make of it', he means precisely this. If we exist in a world of anarchy (the absence of an authority above the state), it is because we have come to believe that is how the world is, and our actions correspond to that reading of an 'anarchic world'. Thus, if we find ourselves in an anarchic system, it is because we believe it is anarchic. Anarchy is not a given feature of the international system; it is an idea that states buy into, and, because they buy into it and understand the world as 'anarchic', they act accordingly. Therefore, anarchy is not a natural part of the international system; actors who believe it to be so construct it.

 KEY IDEAS 4.1

Origins of constructivist thought

Constructivism owes its origins to earlier philosophical and sociological modes of thought. From Kant, constructivists gain an appreciation that our knowledge about the world may never be objective because we process that knowledge through our own structures of understanding. Social facts, such as 'money', rely on common agreement about their meaning. Money in itself has no intrinsic meaning apart from our common understanding of it. We use it to buy things, it has a function in the market, and we may associate it with our own security. Sovereignty is a social fact because states and citizens understand its principles of non-interference and recognition in the international system. From Searle, constructivists understand that social facts differ from 'brute' facts such as a lake or a mountain; they are common understandings not only about the object but about its broader meaning. This implies that the world 'out there' is not given but constructed by those who inhabit it. Giddens's structuration theory has been influential here with regard to how structure has a dual nature, constraining human actions but also altered by it (Ruggie 1998: 875). Weber regarded humans as 'cultural beings', 'endowed with the capacity and the will to take a deliberate attitude towards the world and to lend it significance' (Weber cited in Ruggie 1998: 856). His concept of *verstehen* ('understanding' the meaning that someone intends or expresses) relates to analysing individualized experiences in a broader collective framework (Fierke, 2001: 117; Ruggie 1998: 860). Social ideas and beliefs frame our understanding of the world. Durkheim proposed that different relations in a particular social order could influence social outcomes. In explaining why suicide was less likely to be prevalent in Catholic societies than in Protestant, he looked to the social bonds and belief systems that constructed Catholic society and the belief that suicide was a 'sin' as an explanation (Ruggie 1998: 856–8). Berger and Luckmann (1991), by developing a sociology of knowledge, sought to understand how everyday life and practice relate to ideas about reality—the 'social construction of reality'. Through our actions and shared beliefs, our reality becomes 'institutionalized', sedimented, and habitual.

The more critical form of constructivism draws its influences from ideas about the power of language and speech. Wittgenstein's notion that language is a form of action that is constitutive of the world and Habermas's theory of communicative action add insights into how language games, argumentation, speech acts, and the social nature of language construct our reality. The idea that speech is a form of action is crucial in this regard, and constructivists working along these lines draw inspiration from Searle, John Austin (who distinguished between different types of speech acts), Foucault on discourse and its relationship to power and knowledge, and Derrida's deconstruction and the idea that text matters (Fierke and Jørgensen 2001: 4–5).

Social constructivism has contributed to understanding 'security' by focusing on the agenda above. It has lent new insights to topics such as European integration, NATO's persistence and enlargement since the end of the Cold War, national-security policy, the social construction of threat (such as Islamic fundamentalism and immigration), the impact of norms and values in the international system (such as respect for human rights), and, also, the possibility for change in the international system. (For how the 'war on terror' has been socially constructed, see Think Point 4.1.) An important part of the constructivist agenda is to show how identity and interests are not fixed over time and space and are open to change and revision. This has important implications for security studies, offering the possibility of moving beyond the logic of anarchy and the 'timeless wisdom' of realist theorizing. The identity and interests of states (or any other kind of actors) differs over time and place. States also have more than one identity—the UK is a member of the European Union (EU), but it also has a history and relationship with other states (such as the USA or the Commonwealth and former colonies) and international organizations (such as NATO, the UN, and the Organization for Security and Cooperation in Europe (OSCE)).

THINK POINT 4.1

Security as 'socially constructed': the war on terror

The terrorist attacks of 9/11 were defined by former US President George W. Bush as an attack on freedom and democracy on a global scale, requiring a new response to a new kind of war. When framing the attacks, Bush drew on shared values and collective meanings in both the international and the domestic context. For the international community, the attacks represented a threat to freedom, security, and modern ways of life. Equating the ideologies and methods of al-Qaeda and fundamentalist terrorism with 'Fascism, Nazism and totalitarianism,' Bush (2001) claimed that this is 'the world's fight . . . civilization's fight. This is the fight of all who believe in progress and pluralism, tolerance and freedom'. Fierke (2002: 342) observed that the initial characterization of the attacks as a 'clash' or 'crusade' (which could alienate Muslim populations and states) shifted to an emphasis on bringing together a global coalition of states to 'fight terrorism'. Domestically, Bush drew comparisons with the attack on Pearl Harbor in 1941, which remains a significant event in the American collective memory, where America was caught by surprise, leading to massive losses. Bush argued that the attacks represented a new kind of war that requires new strategies, resources, and tools, such as deploying intelligence, diplomacy, force, cutting off the financial resources and support of terrorist groups, and other methods. The Office of Homeland Security, established in 2002, coordinates security responses to threats to US security. It brings together a number of government agencies, such as immigration and emergency planning. In its first five years, the Office of Homeland Security claimed to have increased border security, screened millions of travellers, increased the number of agents in the field, enforced immigration laws, and protected vital infrastructure. The impact of the war on terror has affected not only international relations but also everyday life. At the international level, states coordinate information and policy more closely in order to combat terrorism. Notions of pre-emptive action and the treatment of 'enemy combatants' at sites such as Guantanamo Bay, where normal legal codes do not apply, are also some of the ways in which the regular norms of security have changed. In terms of our daily practices, the war on terror is deemed to affect us in numerous ways, such as identity fraud, heightened surveillance, and conditions on our free movement (airports use technology to scan us, its personal to frisk us and tell us what we cannot take on board a flight, and so on). In the USA, threat levels are monitored daily, ranging from green ('low') to red ('severe').

But this is one dominant 'story' about the war on terror. Constructivism's task is to show how security is a socially constructed idea. The meaning that actors give to such constructions of security differs. For the hijackers, the suicide mission was a 'rational act' within their own structures of meaning (perhaps self-sacrifice for the greater good of Allah). For those outside—and even within—this structure of meaning, this act was seen as 'irrational' (Fierke 2002: 342). Terrorism studies tend to be dominated by an unquestioning focus on 'terrorists' and on policy issues in terms largely defined as threat and response. Richard Jackson (2005: 50–1) claims that the events of 9/11 could have been interpreted in a number of different ways (such as the North–South divide or movements against the state and revolutionary actors), but the story that dominated was that of the threat of barbarism versus civility. Both Jackson (2005) and Hülsse (2008) suggest that terrorism needs to be interrogated more critically and that we need to understand how it is socially constructed by discourses and categories that are broadly accepted.

Definitions and key concepts

In order to delve a bit deeper into constructivist understandings of phenomena and security, some of its key concepts require elaboration. By focusing on identity and interests, and how they inform each other, constructivists pay more attention to a dynamic that goes beyond causation. Considering how things are 'put together' or socially constructed implies interpretation, and seeing how certain types of political behaviour and outcomes are possible (Finnemore and Sikkink 2001: 394). This also applies to understanding identity change. Frederking (2003: 365) puts identity, beliefs, and norms together in his example of the merger of all three: 'Global security arrangements include beliefs about the world (e.g., the nature of security), norms about social relationships (e.g., the appropriateness of the use of force), and identities about self and other (e.g., enemy, rival, citizen, or friend).' The Introduction above gives a snapshot of the ideas that animate constructivists, and, in order to help you grasp the meaning of identity, collective or shared knowledge and culture, and norms, this section explores them further and contrasts them with rationalist positions on the questions constructivists pursue.

Identity

Identity is central to constructivist research for a basic reason: identity tells us who actors are, what their preferences and interests are, and how those preferences might inform their actions.

Quite simply, interests cannot be pursued without a particular identity, and 'the identities, interests and behaviour of political agents are socially constructed by collective meaning, interpretations and assumptions about the world' (Adler 1997: 324). Shared ideas construct identity and interests and are not given by nature. Why does the USA consider five North Korean nuclear weapons to be more of a threat to its security and interests compared to five hundred British nuclear weapons? Wendt (1999: 1, 255) argues that it is because of 'shared understandings'. The UK is an ally of the USA, but, furthermore, it shares similar ideas, beliefs, and a liberal democratic identity. It also has a historical 'special relationship' with the USA, one that former Prime Minister Tony Blair (2000) claimed was 'about bonds of kinship and history. It is about a shared language and most of all it is about shared values.' **Intersubjective** meanings are ideas and concepts that are shared and held in common, and from these we can understand action and behaviour (Hopf 1998: 173). This differs from rationalist thinking, which relies on **causality** (that one thing impacts on another in a straight line of 'action–reaction'). Intersubjective meanings involve a different type of relationship, where practices and meanings come from interaction (Fierke and Jørgensen 2001: 117).

For rationalists, identity is either given (assumed to already exist and therefore unchangeable) or negligible as a factor in relation to security. For neorealists, states are 'like units', all seeking security in an anarchic world. The anarchic system 'tells' states what they want and what they should do to get it. Variants of liberalism generally agree on this aspect—states have certain goals to secure in the international realm. They may try and secure those goals via cooperation, but the same assumption is the rule—states have material interests. If states cooperate in the international system, they do so for their own (pre-given and assumed) interests, and do not cooperate on the basis of how they interact with other states. Interaction for rationalists is largely for strategic reasons. If neoliberals look to identity and interests, they may examine the domestic realm or ignore interest formation, assuming it to be **exogenous** (relating to or caused by external factors) rather than **endogenous** (having internal cause or origin) (Wendt 1994: 384; Ruggie 1998: 879). The problem with this, however, is that constructivists think more deeply about identity and argue that the process of acquiring identity is *interaction*; actors form their identity when they meet and interact with others,

and this can set up friendly, conflictual, or other types of relations. Constructivists owe this idea of identity formation to earlier social theories. Berger and Luckmann (1991: 194) provided the notion that 'identity is formed by social processes'. The behaviour of states is not simply the result of exogenous forces. Germany and France have historically been enemies, but, through their cooperation in the context of European integration, their relationship has evolved into a different one. War between the two is now considered impossible, because their relationship has evolved through interaction and the development of shared understandings to one of friendship. In another example of how security is not determined solely by the structure of the international system, some have examined the social construction of neutrality, explaining its persistence after the Cold War and the meanings it contains for domestic identity (see Case Study 4.1).

CASE STUDY 4.1

Neutrality

Realists on the whole argue that neutral states' security policies are conditioned by the international system and exogenously given—if a state is neutral it is because it is weak, geographically unfortunate, or isolationist. However, the end of the Cold War saw this logic challenged. With the end of bipolarity, rationalists expected neutrality to be consigned to the dustbin of history—after all, there was nothing to be neutral between. Neutral states were expected to 'get with the programme' and join NATO. However, that logic did not readily translate into reality. In Western Europe, neutrals such as Sweden, Austria, Finland, and Ireland did not rush to join NATO, and, even if political leaders wanted to ditch neutrality and sign up to European security initiatives, such a move was on the whole unpopular with the public, which came to associate neutrality with the identity of that state. A constructivist reading of neutrality examines the norms and values attached to neutrality over time. Constructivists argue that 'neutrality is what states make of it'—neutrality need not be interpreted in one way (isolationist and self-interested states not dirtying their hands in the ugly business of war) but can also contain other meanings (neutral states can promote change and peaceful initiatives in the international arena and are not part of power

politics). Sweden is a case in point here. Its neutrality has existed for over 200 years and it has influenced the way in which Sweden sees security and itself. The hegemonic Social Democratic Party also saw neutrality as part of Sweden's domestic and international profile—concepts of solidarity, which had meaning domestically, were associated with Sweden's foreign policy. Sweden practised an 'active neutrality policy' and bucked the assumption that neutral states were isolationist and self-interested. It promoted peaceful initiatives such as dialogue and cooperation, disarmament, mediation, and peacekeeping, and took a deeper view of security in terms of inequalities in the international system in the North–South divide. It was also a vocal critic of superpower politics, defying the idea that neutral states are isolationist, keeping their heads down to protect their own interests (Agius 2006).

When Sweden joined the EU, it, along with Finland, 'exported' the core ideals associated with neutrality to the Amsterdam Treaty of the EU via the 'Petersberg Tasks', suggesting a less militaristic approach to the EU's security profile. These tasks included the areas where active neutral states had great experience: crisis management, peacekeeping, humanitarian and rescue tasks, and peacemaking. This is an example of small states being norm entrepreneurs.

However, identities are malleable and subject to change. As Sweden interacts with the EU, it takes on its norms and values too. Sweden now defines its security in the context of European security. Although militarily non-aligned, Sweden contributes to European security cooperation. Laurent Goetschel (1999) has also applied constructivist ideas and themes to the relationship between EU security policy and neutral member states of the EU. Other works that adopt constructivist rather than rationalist readings of neutrality include Mlada Bukovansky's work on the importance of domestic and international processes with regard to identity and US neutrality in the early nineteenth century. She argues that, rather than isolationism, US neutrality was connected to a specific reading of US identity, Jeffersonian ideals, and republicanism (Bukovansky 1997). Karen Devine's work on Irish neutrality takes a critical constructivist position, deconstructing the 'Unneutral Ireland' discourse that drives the idea that Irish neutrality is a 'myth' (a device used by those who advocate dropping neutrality). Devine (2006) shows that competing meanings attached to neutrality are mired in a political struggle over its meaning and status.

Wendt distinguishes between different types of identity. In an early work he contrasted between corporate and social identity. Corporate identity refers to the intrinsic, self-realized identity of an actor. The interests of a corporate actor exist before interaction with others, and an actor can have only one corporate identity, which is the basis for developing other identities. Social identity refers to 'sets of meanings that an actor attributes to itself while taking the perspective of others'. Actors can have multiple social identities that vary in importance (Wendt 1994: 385). He later adds 'type', 'role', and 'collective' identity to this. Type identities are multiple, intrinsic to actors, and self-organizing, and, in the international system, capitalist states and monarchical states are examples of type identities (in that we can classify them according to their 'type'). Wendt (1999: 226) claims that these do not rely on other states for their existence. Role identities exist only in relation to others. The example Wendt provides is that of professor and student—this is an institutionalized role, part of our 'stocks of collective knowledge'. One cannot be a student without a teacher and vice versa. Collective identity 'takes the relationship between Self and Other to its logical conclusion, identification'. This is where self and other becomes blurred. It is a mix of role and type identities (Wendt 1999: 226–9). As we will see below, many scholars are critical of this categorization of identity, but this provides some basis for thinking about how identity differs and how it is formed in terms of process and interaction.

Beliefs, collective ideas, and culture

Identity does not simply emerge but is part of a historical process of interaction, made up of beliefs, which, according to Frederking (2003: 364–5), are 'social rules that primarily make truth claims about the world … Beliefs are shared understandings of the world.' Shared knowledge is important in identity formation, as it sets up shared understandings between individuals, communities, states, and the system of states. Collective meanings and shared knowledge constitute how we understand the world and respond to it. When humans and Martians encounter each other for the first time in Tim Burton's film *Mars Attacks!*, the gesture of releasing a dove is interpreted by the Martians in a completely different way from how we, as humans, might ordinarily understand it. We know that releasing a dove is a gesture of peace and goodwill. The Martians, however, interpret this as hostile and zap it with their ray guns. Ignoring for the moment that the Martians had intended all along to destroy Earth—and happily get down to the business of completing this task for most of the film—how would they have known the symbolic significance of the act of 'releasing a dove'? We, as humans, are aware of the significance and meaning of this act (because it forms part of our collective knowledge), but its construction and associations may be unknown to the aliens.

In this respect, constructivism gives more attention to culture (see Key Quotes 4.1). Most constructivists regard culture as a set of practices that give some sort of meaning to shared experiences and actions. Katzenstein's edited volume *The Culture of National Security* (1996) contains chapters linking national culture to security beliefs and practices. Berger's study of German and Japanese post-war anti-militarism makes the argument that, instead of considering explanations of international structure, we can further understand both states' defence policies by examining the domestic cultural–institutional context. Berger argues that the impact of their defeat in the Second World War affected domestic societal and political actors. Their reluctance to use military force became institutionalized, changing their approach to national security in ways that other states may not contemplate (Berger 1996: 318). These studies of strategic culture examine the impact that the culture of a nation may have on grand strategy, military organization, security and defence policy, and political and societal actors. Wendt (1996: 49) described the Cold War as a 'cultural rather than material structure', and Huntington's (much criticized) idea of 'cultural clashes' or 'civilizational clashes' demonstrates growing attention to this category. Culture can have an impact on how states see security, but it is also crucial in terms of constructing the values and rules that inform identity. Whether it be fear of immigrants and refugees as a 'threat' to security, or fear of the cultures of others that are drastically different from our own, culture can be an important underlying reason when defining security problems that affect the state and other agents. That human rights are considered an important issue to individual and societal security also has cultural influences, because culture refers to standards that we set as acceptable to us.

Norms

Shared knowledge and practices produce norms, which are the 'collective expectations about proper

> ❝❞ **KEY QUOTES 4.1**
>
> ### Culture
>
> 'Culture refers to both a set of evaluative standards (such as norms and values) and a set of cognitive standards (such as rules and models) that define what social actors exist in a system, how they operate, and how they relate to one another.'
>
> Katzenstein (1996a: 6).
>
> Clifford Geertz (1973: 89) defined culture as 'an historically transmitted pattern of meanings embodied in symbols, a system of inherited conceptions expressed in symbolic form by means of which men communicate, perpetuate, and develop their knowledge about and attitudes towards life'.

behaviour for a given identity' (Katzenstein 1996: 5). Norms are vital to identity formation; the norms that we adhere to (or choose not to adhere to) are part of how we define ourselves. Norms can be seen as good or bad, but they contain specific meanings for actors and provide a social guide to behaviour. Norms do not appear out of nowhere but are constructed by actors who have strong ideas about appropriate or desirable behaviour (see Key Quotes 4.2). Finnemore and Sikkink (1998) examine the cycle of norms, which start when cognitive frames are set, normally against existing norms. They illustrate this in their work on women's suffrage, and how this confronted traditional ideas about women and the appropriate role for women. New ideas about appropriate behaviour compete with existing norms, then cascade (or spill over) and become institutionalized. Berger and Luckmann (1991: 70–2) see institutionalization as habitualized human activity, from the individual to the collective.

Constructivists distinguish between *constitutive* and *regulatory* norms. Constitutive norms define the identity of an actor, constituting their behaviour and interests. Regulatory norms tell us what to do; they are the standards that tell a given identity how to act. A common illustration is that of sovereignty. The regulative norm of sovereignty is

> ## KEY QUOTES 4.2

Norms

'Norms are the intersubjective beliefs about the social and natural world that define actors, their situations, and the possibilities of action. Norms are intersubjective in that they are beliefs rooted in and reproduced through social practice.' Norms constitute actors and meaningful action by situating both in social roles.

Farrell (2002: 49).

'Norms do not determine outcomes, they shape realms of possibility. They influence (increase or decrease) the probability of occurrence of certain courses of action.' Norms are 'a shared expectation about behavior, a standard of right or wrong. Norms are prescriptions or proscriptions for behavior.'

Tannenwald (1999: 435–6).

'Norms are social rules that primarily make appropriateness claims about relationships.'

Frederking (2003: 364).

that it tells actors how to behave in order to be identified as 'sovereign' and sets out the rules of the game. The constitutive effect is that, as 'sovereign states' behave according to these precepts, they 'become' sovereign—their interests and preferences are shaped by sovereignty and others recognize *this actor as sovereign* (Katzenstein 1996: 5; Hopf 1998; Ruggie 1998: 71). Nina Tannenwald's work (1999) has examined the norm of the nuclear 'taboo', arguing that it represents both a regulative and a constitutive norm. She argues that realism's reliance on deterrence to explain the non-use of nuclear weapons since 1945 is incorrect and lacking in empirical evidence. She asks the following questions:

- When the threat of retaliation was absent, why have nuclear weapons not been used? The USA had the opportunity to attack its enemies when its nuclear programme was in the ascendancy.

- Why have nuclear weapons not failed to deter attacks by non-nuclear states against states that possess nuclear weapons?

- If deterrence matters, then why have many states chosen not to develop nuclear weapons, particularly if they have not been included under the 'nuclear umbrella' of a larger nuclear state? And, if the 'nuclear security dilemma' exists, then why do non-nuclear states fail to conform to its logic?

Tannenwald argues that the nuclear taboo delegitimizes nuclear weapons as weapons that can be used in war. The norms (both regulative and constitutive) surrounding nuclear weapons both stabilize and restrain states from acting in a self-help manner on this issue. Furthermore, the taboo is international and systemic. Public opinion, international organizations, and other types of multilateral fora all reinforce the taboo, the notion that this weapon should not be used. International agreements and regimes exist (such as the Nuclear **Non-Proliferation Treaty** (NNPT), arms-control agreements, and nuclear weapon-free zones, as well as general laws of armed conflict) to control and restrict the use of nuclear weapons. Taking US policy as a case study, she examines how norms surrounding the use of nuclear weapons shifted in decisive contexts. When the USA used nuclear weapons against Japan in 1945, there was no nuclear 'taboo', even though some forms of constraint, such as just war theory, codes of military conduct, ethical issues, and international law, were well established. It was during the **Korean War** when the norm against non-use emerged, growing in strength by the time of the Vietnam War. By the time of the Gulf War in 1991 the norm against use was taken for granted and institutionalized. Central to the taboo were ideas of 'civilized states', which set the boundaries for identity and behaviour. States that possessed nuclear weapons were judged by their restraint in using them. Restraint was associated with 'being civilized'. The taboo was both a regulative and a constitutive norm. It proscribed behaviour (non-use, thus *regulative*), but it also had constitutive effects (relating its non-use to civilizational associations of the Self and Others).

CASE STUDY 4.2

The International Criminal Court

Caroline Fehl combines a rationalist and constructivist examination of the establishment of the International Criminal Court (ICC), which came into existence in 2002 despite US opposition to it. The US government rejected the implications that its own troops would be held accountable and tried outside US jurisdiction with respect to war crimes. However, the ICC came into being without the USA, largely because the norms of human rights and the need for international criminal justice was held not only by the states that signed up to the ICC but by international NGOs actively lobbying for its creation. Even though some regarded the influence of NGOs as problematic, signalling a 'new diplomacy' where non-state actors have greater power, there were those who would have preferred an effective ICC rather than one that would

have been watered down if the USA signed up to it. These 'norm entrepreneurs' argued that problems of legitimacy existed when it came to effective criminal justice in national and international courts (such as the UN international criminal tribunals for Rwanda and the former Yugoslavia). Fehl is interested in the constitutive effects of norms, how human rights norms and the problem of effective international justice were of increasing concern. Since the 1970s, more human rights conventions were adopted and ratified by more and more states, resulting in an almost universal acceptance of this norm (Fehl 2004: 371). Furthermore, human rights norms are more than just 'institutional rules'; they also define the identity of the members who are part of it. Even though some states might not comply, the norm has a constitutive effect in that it represents a *standard* for states.

Norms have been central to the work of many constructivists. Finnemore (1996) shows that humanitarian norms have influenced patterns of humanitarian military intervention since the mid-nineteenth century. Decolonization and the abolition of slavery are amongst her examples and she demonstrates that unilateral and multilateral interventions on the basis of humanitarianism, whilst not entirely new, are important and are related to what is considered appropriate over time. Newman (2001) also looks at humanitarian intervention as part of norm change, where the individual is the referent object of security. Intervention to protect against human rights abuses is emerging as a stable norm in the international arena. Constructivism posits that collective meanings can change over time and affect norms. Audie Klotz (1995) argued that transnational anti-apartheid activists influenced the USA to instigate sanctions against South Africa. The norm operating here was a normative view of racial equality, and the activist groups linked the issue of civil rights in the USA with apartheid. To discriminate on racial grounds was considered by these activists to be a 'bad thing', even though the USA had material strategic and economic interests in South Africa, and the norm of sovereignty (non-interference in domestic affairs)

was strong. Rationalist approaches relying on explanations of material interest, Klotz argues, do not fit this change in US policy. Fehl also suggests that non-state actors had an important role to play in the establishment of the International Criminal Court (see Case Study 4.2).

Constructivists also examine 'epistemic communities' and 'norm entrepreneurs'. The former refers to groups with specialized expert knowledge, who share norms and create new norms informed by their expertise. Constructivists see epistemic communities playing an important role, transmitting shared ideas and causal belief with respect to policy problems. This form of 'evolutionary epistemology' (inspired by Habermas's notion of communicative action) sees actors alter how they deal with problems and their notions of problem solving. Rather than adapting to the constraints of the international system (Ruggie 1998: 868), the 'learning' that takes place in epistemic communities has implications for security, as Adler (1992) demonstrates in relation to international arms control. He argues that the high level of socialization and shared ideas amongst those forming this epistemic community (made up of individuals from the RAND corporation, Harvard, and MIT) imparted essential norms about the necessity of arms control via their scientific expertise. The diffusion of American arms-control ideas to the USSR was important with regard to creating the Anti-Ballistic Missile (ABM) regime.

Mutual constitution

For Alexander Wendt—one of constructivism's leading figures and the one who generates most debates animating constructivism (more on this below)—'anarchy is what states make of it'. He argued that neorealism has given anarchy a privileged position in explaining international relations. For neorealists, anarchy produces a self-help world. The lack of a power above the state means that the 'logic' of self-help produces competition in the international system, creating security dilemmas and problematizing the possibilities for collective action. Interaction never affects this process, and interests and identities are ignored. Wendt argues that self-help and power politics are not a logical or causal aspect of anarchy. Anarchy contains no logic in itself. Instead, practices matter: 'Self-help and power politics are institutions, not essential features of anarchy. *Anarchy is what states make of it*' (Wendt 1992: 394–5). Wendt defines institutions as 'a relatively stable set or "structure" of identities and interests'. These structures can take the form of rules and norms but are dependent on collective knowledge. Institutions might be conflictual or cooperative. Wendt (1992: 399–401) sees self-help as just one kind of anarchy, an institution.

By thinking about anarchy in this way, Wendt highlights two important critiques of the rationalist dependency on anarchy as structuring the world. Wendt suggests that the structure is not given but rather constituted by the actions and practices of actors, whose identities and interests have a role to play. This relates to the agency-structure debate in IR theorizing, and here Wendt is influenced by Anthony Giddens's structuration theory, which stresses the duality of structures. His ideas about identity are informed by the symbolic interactionism of Herbert Blumer and George Herbert Mead, who examine how the self is constituted by and reflects processes of socialization (Wendt 1992).

The actions of states and how they interact with each other constitutes international relations, and this can produce cooperation or mistrust. Once again this reinforces the idea that the world is made up of social relations and is not simply *given*.

Many constructivists refer back to Karl Deutsch's idea (1957: 36) of a security community, the idea that integrated interests produce a 'we-feeling'. Security communities represent common interests and a preference for peaceful conflict resolution. Deutsch suggested that two forms of security communities existed: amalgamated, which refers to a unified security community where government is shared, and a pluralistic one, where integration is deep but states retain their political independence. The Nordic region was seen as a pluralistic security community, where a shared sense of culture, history, and economic links strengthened consensus and cooperation (Deutsch 1957: 6). Adler and Barnett (1988) have developed Deutsch's ideas along constructivist lines, placing emphasis on shared values, identities, and meanings when they consider how security communities emerge. They identify how conditions, process, structure, trust and collective identity are important for the emergence and development of security communities, from 'nascent' to 'ascendant' to 'mature'.

If the world is not given, then this provides some scope for thinking about its dynamism and the potential for change. This is the distinction between rationalist and constructivist approaches (Hopf 1998: 172). Neorealist theorizing pays little attention to the possibility of change in the international system. It seeks to identify 'regularities' and patterns of behaviour, but moreover neorealism tends to argue that its account of international relations provides a 'timeless wisdom'—its rules and regularities can be observed and are repeated across space and time. As Wendt points out, for neorealists, the 'logic of anarchy is constant'. Although neorealism acknowledges structural change, it accounts for change only with regard to the shift from one distribution of power to another. Social change—for instance, moving from feudalism to a system of sovereign states—is not considered to be structural, because anarchy still exists and the distribution of power remains unchanged (Wendt 1999: 17). The following section examines Wendt's consideration of the types of anarchy that characterize the international system, and then explores the critiques directed at his conceptualizations.

KEY POINTS

- Relations are social, not material, and identity determines interest. Identity is formed via interaction and shared meanings.

- The norms that actors hold guide their choices in the international arena, and norms are both regulative and constitutive.

- Actors and the social world they inhabit are mutually constitutive. Therefore, if we live in an anarchic international system, it is because we make it so.

- However, there is possibility for change. Norms and ideas can change, pushing actors to alter their relationships and understandings, potentially from antagonistic to cooperative. Norm entrepreneurs, epistemic communities, and other forms of shared ideas can create security communities or more cooperative forms of security collaboration.

Wendt's three cultures of anarchy

If 'anarchy is what states make of it', then this opens up the possibility to explore different types of international security worlds that go beyond neorealist configurations. Wendt develops this idea further in *Social Theory of International Politics* (1999), where he proposes three cultures of anarchy: Hobbesian, Lockean, and Kantian. Neorealists are limited to viewing anarchy as producing one type of system based on war, military competition, and the balance of power (Wendt 1999: 247). Wendt does not stray far from Waltz's idea of anarchy—he simply suggests that there can be more than one culture of anarchy, and anarchy does not have to lead to a self-help system.

Wendt suggests that at the centre of each type of anarchy there exists a particular posture: in Hobbesian cultures, the relationship between states is that of 'enemies'. The logic of Hobbesian anarchy is that of a 'true' self-help system, where no self-restraint exists and actors cannot rely on each other for help. Survival relies on military power, security dilemmas abound, and security is a zero-sum game. Wendt (1999: 265) argues that a Hobbesian culture has characterized the international system over time, but not all the time.

A Lockean culture is characterized by rivalry, and Wendt sees this culture dominating since the Treaty of Westphalia and the beginning of the modern system of states. In a Lockean culture, actors regard each other as rivals but exercise some restraint in violence; warfare is accepted but at the same time contained (Wendt 1999: 283). A Kantian culture is characterized by friendship, where force and violence is eschewed in favour of cooperation in matters of security. Here, friendship is a 'role structure' where states resolve disputes in a non-violent manner and protect each other (collective security). There exist three levels or degrees of cultural internalization: coercion, interest, and legitimacy. When an actor is forced to comply with a norm (because non-compliance would result in some form of punishment), this is first-degree internalization. Second-degree internalization is different, in that states will comply with a norm because of self-interest. When states comply with and internalize a norm as legitimate, this represents third-degree internalization. Why does this matter? It matters because Wendt suggests that shared ideas may not lead to cooperation. It is possible to have a Hobbesian culture that is deeply underlined by shared ideas (that war is good) or a weak Kantian culture where ideas about security cooperation are only weakly shared by actors (Wendt 1999: 254). Wendt is adamant that there is no such thing as a 'logic of anarchy': 'What gives anarchy meaning are the kinds of people who live there and the structure of their relationships' (Wendt 1999: 308–9). Structural change occurs when actors redefine who they are and what they want. The shift from one culture to another and structural change is propelled by four 'master variables': interdependence, common fate, homogenization, and self-restraint, which affect collective identity formation. The first three are active causes, and the more actors engage in these 'prosocial' forms of behaviour the further the egotistic Self erodes, bringing in Others. However, identifying with Others might pose a threat to the Self or survival; Wendt (1999: 336–66) suggests that the problem of being 'engulfed' by Others we identify with can be managed through self-restraint. Wendt's view (1999: 314) is that in the West structural change signifies the move from a Lockean to a Kantian culture in the late twentieth century, compared to most of international history resembling a Hobbesian culture, 'where the logic of anarchy was kill or be killed'.

Wendt's constructivism has generated much debate, largely because he accepts a number of neorealist tenets, such as states being the main actors in the international system and a commitment to a particular scientific understanding of phenomena, which jars with many of his critics. In this sense he is a 'conventional' constructivist because he sees similarities between constructivism and **rationalism**. Critical constructivists are more sceptical of this link, and the following section explores the differences between these two brands before moving on to the critiques of rationalists and post-structuralists.

KEY POINTS

- There is not one type of anarchy that is understood only in terms of self-help, and Wendt suggests three cultures of anarchy: Hobbesian (where actors see each other as enemies), Lockean (as rivals), and Kantian (as friends).

- Each 'culture' does not produce a definitive structure of anarchy; this depends on how deeply certain shared ideas are internalized.

- The possibility for change in the international system exists, and Wendt believes we are moving towards a Kantian culture.

Conventional and critical constructivism

Wendtian constructivism tends to generate the most debate, but it is important to note that constructivism is not a uniform approach; rather it houses a number of different ways of thinking about identity and social relations. United as they may be about the point that the *ideational* matters, constructivists have been broadly divided into two camps: conventional

and critical.[3] What separates the two tends to revolve around questions of methodology and how identity is interrogated. Conventional constructivists tend to accept key aspects of neorealist systemic theorizing, such as the centrality of the state and the importance of a scientific or positivist approach to comprehend phenomena. Constructivists such as Wendt,

---

[3]In the literature on constructivism, different authors label these distinctions in different ways, such as 'modern' and 'postmodern' (Reus-Smit 1996: 187–8), 'conventional' and 'radical' (Fierke and Jørgensen 2001: 5), or 'thick' and 'thin'. For the sake of simplicity I label these divisions in the same way as Hopf (1998: 171), into 'conventional' and 'critical'.

Ruggie (1998: 880–2) distifnguishes between three variants of constructivism: neo-classical, postmodernist, and a third category that merges the two with an emphasis on scientific realism. He adds Wendt to this third category but all three categories in Ruggie's description relate to questions of scientific method and the degree to which its proponents differ.

NATO's persistence after the Cold War and its expansion

A number of constructivist explanations have emerged over NATO's persistence since the end of the Cold War (despite realist predictions that it would fold) and its enlargement to include new members. Adler (2008) claims that NATO recognized the shifting nature of security in the post-Cold War where borders between East and West blurred, and new security threats emerged, adjusting its rationale to include NATO's Strategic Concept of 1999 repositioned it from a Cold War defence pact to a 'security community' based on the common values of democracy, human rights, and the rule of law. It created the institutions (such as Partnerships for Peace) to prepare applicant countries for membership through 'social learning' (that is, 'teaching' newcomers to adapt to NATO norms and practices, such as training and assistance). Gheciu (2005a) also notes that 'teaching and persuasion' were crucial for NATO in terms of projecting liberal democratic norms to the former Eastern bloc states. NATO was able to shape ideas about appropriate action (peaceful dispute settlement, multilateralism, and the promotion of human rights). This in turn impacted on the national identities of the former

Soviet states. Many of these states were seeking a new 'home' in the international system, a 'return to Europe'. The Czech Republic, Poland, and Hungary were the first to join, because they made significant advances in internalizing Western democratic norms and values (Schimmelfennig 1998). Networks emerged to promote cooperation in both military and civilian circles, focusing on self-restraint and security cooperation, which in turn provided NATO with a new purpose—transforming it into a different security community.

However, others see this change in more complex terms. Fierke and Wiener (1999) argue that speech acts and language are important in understanding the enlargement process, and that we cannot assume that socialization happens unproblematically. For instance, what of Russia's problems with NATO expansion? How did these discourses affect the applicant countries and NATO itself? Williams and Neumann (2000) also point to the importance of narratives and recognizing different discourses that exist in this context, arguing that NATO represented a symbolically powerful civilizational entity that had cultural commonalities. NATO's enlargement also had implications for Russia, framing its options in specific ways.

Katzenstein, and Adler see constructivism as a bridge between rationalist and reflectivist approaches, enabling both to benefit from the insights of the other. In *Social Theory of International Politics*, Wendt (1999: 39–40) declares he is a positivist, because he thinks what really matters is what there is to know (ontology) rather than how we know it (epistemology) and that science should be question-driven, not method-driven.

Critical constructivists find this reliance on positivism problematic and argue that the distinction between the ideational and the material world simply reproduces the binary distinctions that characterize positivist methodology (such as strong/weak, man/woman, and, in this case, ideational/material) (Fierke 2001: 116). Inspired by Foucault, Derrida, and Lyotard, critical constructivists query the power of discourse, language, reality, and meaning, adopting a more cautious approach to truth claims and power relations (Fierke and Jørgensen 2001: 5). Critical explorations

of identity can also be found in the works of Doty (1996: 2), who explores civilizing discourses in North–South relations and how they established 'regimes of truth and knowledge'. Weldes's work (1999a) on the Cuban missile crisis presents an image of social construction in terms of US identity and its claims to being a global power. Works such as these are important because they remind us that 'many of the categories we treat as natural are in fact products of past social construction processes, processes in which power is often deeply implicated' (Finnemore and Sikkink 2001: 398). In this respect, critical constructivists problematize identity more so than their conventional counterparts do, preferring to see identity as more complex than stable, less solid and given, and more reliant on power and representation (see Case Study 4.3). For instance, when we think of American or Australian identity, we see only the dominant interpretations, not voices that have been silenced. These omissions are dangerous, because we privilege one construction of identity over possible others, such as sub-national groups. There is also the assumption that domestic politics is consistent at all times (McSweeney 1999: 126–9).

Critical constructivists also pay deeper attention to language and point to its role in constructing reality. The works of Onuf, Kratochwil, and Fierke focus on how language is crucial in terms of comprehending meaning and interpreting the relationship between word and world. Onuf relates rules to language, taking Wittgenstein's notion of language as similar to the rules of a game. Speech acts, which relate language to action, and rules, constitute actors. Onuf (1998: 66–8) identifies three types of speech acts: assertions, directives, and commitments. Assertions relate to knowledge about the world (for instance, 'democracies do not fight each other'). Directives give us instructions: what to do, what will happen if we fail to do something (we may be threatened with a punishment for failing to comply). Commitments entail promises (such as signing up to a treaty). By examining the meanings that speech acts invoke, we gain a stronger sense of how language structures our world and relations, and a more complex sense of communication between actors. Language is constitutive and does not simply represent the world as it is: 'By speaking, we make the world what it is.' Speech *produces* (for instance, rules and policies) and *expresses* our goals and intentions (Onuf 2002: 126–7; see also Fierke 2002). Fierke's focus on 'games' also highlights a different way of seeing security (see Case Study 4.4). Language and speech acts have enormous importance because they can 'securitize', as Huysmans (2002: 44–5) observes: 'Language is not just a communicative instrument used to talk about a real world outside of language; it is a defining force, integrating social relations.' Security language can create a different picture about a social problem or a source of insecurity, and Huysmans draws attention to the role of language in constituting a link between migration and security problems (such as drug trafficking, terrorism, and fundamentalism, as a threat to the economy or the welfare state, to name some). The 'security knowledge' produced by police agencies and the military, the media and other official bodies, are powerful in that they can articulate threat or danger; speaking and writing can construct security problems. Those who deploy language when examining the construction of threat, danger, and identities claim that we gain a better understanding of the complexity and construction itself.

CASE STUDY 4.4

Cold War endings

Understanding how the Cold War ended is crucial with regard to thinking about dominating ideas of how the demise of bipolarity was evidence of a 'triumph of the West' and liberal capitalist democracy. However, constructivists and others read this change in different ways, and saw it as linked to Soviet foreign and domestic policies of the mid-1980s – early 1990s. Rather than the Soviet Union 'losing' the Cold War, it was Gorbachev's programme of *perestroika* and *glasnost* that set a new framework for Soviet foreign and domestic relations. For Risse-Kappen (1994: 185), structural or functional explanations for the end of the Cold War (whether realist or liberal) could not account for the change in Soviet foreign policy and the Western response to it. For Fierke (2001: 131–3), the end of the Cold War was not about a victory or end of a game; it was about the conflict between two different games of security. One game was defined by deterrence, the threat or use of force and the balance of power. The other was about the possibility of change via dialogue promoted by human rights and peace initiatives in both the East and the West, which was eventually adopted by the superpower leaders, Gorbachev and Reagan, which resulted in the breakdown of the Cold War structure.

At the core of the distinctions between conventional and critical variants of constructivism is the degree to which there is an acceptance on what is 'fixed'. Critical constructivists aim to denaturalize identity and the logic through which we comprehend the world, focusing instead on the context of interaction and intersubjective meanings. As Fierke points out, these things matter. Uttering an apology or describing a conflict as **'genocide'** has implications for meaning and action, constituting what is possible and what is not. The reluctance of the USA to describe the conflict in Rwanda as 'genocide' existed for a reason—to do so would have compelled intervention. Understanding the conflict as one of 'local tribal warfare' would not imply intervention because of the different moves and understandings invoked by sovereignty (Fierke 2002: 348).

> **KEY POINTS**
>
> - Conventional constructivism puts forward the idea that there can be a *via media* (a synergy or 'bridge') between rationalist and reflectivist approaches. Critical constructivists argue that this goal is contradictory and problematic.
>
> - Both differ in their treatment of identity. Critical constructivists argue that identity is more complex and multiple than conventional constructivists present it. The latter tend to see identity as uniform and solid, ignoring questions of power and representation.
>
> - Critical constructivists argue that language structures our reality and has a constitutive role, something that conventional constructivists tend to ignore or downplay. This has resulted in a positivist (conventional) and post-positivist (critical) divide between the two camps.

Critiques of constructivism

Critical constructivism's problems with its conventional sibling hints at a broader set of critiques that have emerged around this approach. Despite its stellar rise, constructivism faces a number of attacks and this section explores the rationalist and poststructuralist complaints. Let's start with rationalism. On a general level, rationalists claim that constructivism cannot test its claims empirically and fails to recognise that alternative theories may say essentially the same thing. When constructivists try to explain how ideas have been crucial in shaping the interests and actions of states—for instance, on what basis and for what reason would a country join the EU?—Moravcsik (2001: 177–84) argues that other theories such as liberal inter-governmentalism draw upon similar explanations (see also Kowert 2001: 165). So the questions that Moravcsik asks are: what makes constructivism different and what sort of contribution does it make to how we understand the world?

Kowert (2001: 161–5) is sceptical about the value of identity and Wendt's lack of a theory of identity formation. Wendt's three cultures of anarchy also appear to be separate worlds of their own and limited to these three images of enemy, rival, and friend. Dale C. Copeland also critiques Wendt for failing to account for an important realist category: uncertainty. Wendt does not consider that actors might deceive each other and his theory of systemic constructivism does not comment on the present and future intentions of other actors. Copeland suggests that we cannot know if another actor is acting cooperatively—they may be acting so in order to mask aggressive goals. Both Copeland and Krasner argue that there is little empirical evidence about cooperation. Krasner is also doubtful about the power of norms, particularly when interests are at stake. A norm of sovereignty is the principle of non-interference but this norm can be violated (Krasner 2000). How can we 'prove' norms exist and affect behaviour? Furthermore, how do we know which norms are at play in a given situation (Farrell 2002: 60–1)? Another common criticism is that constructivism takes the state as given and assumes it to be the most important actor, neglecting internationalization in a globalized world (Keohane, 2000). Constructivist research tends to focus on the state and 'good norms'. The centrality of the state is a point of contention for poststructuralist critiques, which argue that the reification of the state is a key problem of constructivism.

David Campbell also sees the constructivist treatment of identity as problematic. He argues that identity is always constructed as difference and we must be aware of how this creates 'insides and outsides' and the need to confront these divides when examining the construction of danger from 'evil others' outside the state. Identity has been the basis of problematic interventions by states into the outside world, defining others as inferior and relations as hierarchical. Furthermore, Campbell sees the turn to culture, norms, and ideas as problematic.

'Culture' can become a variable that is given causal qualities. These categories can be constructed as a threat, ignoring larger ethical-political issues at stake. Additionally the notion that ideas have a causal power is problematic. Campbell argues that, by privileging the ideational as causal, conventional constructivists simply replace material causality with ideas. This contradicts one of the central claims of constructivism: inter-subjectivity, which is a dialogical (relating to or in the form of dialogue) relationship where meanings and practices stem from interaction. What is more interesting is the possibility of deconstructing and denaturalizing identity, to consider alternative readings of identity (Campbell 1998a: 218–23; Fierke 2001: 116–17). Ronen Palan (2000: 598) also argues that the potential to explore the relationship between

---

THINK POINT 4.2

Contestable identities and the limits of Wendtian identity

Wendt's treatment of the state is problematic because he sees states as the most important actors and takes their identity as given. Zehfuss argues that we fail to get a sense of more complex readings of identity from Wendt's formulation of it—how do we know how it came about, what shaped it, and if it is in fact 'whole'? Zehfuss (2002: 61) also criticizes the lack of attention to the domestic level. In Wendt's reading of identity and change, we only get a sense of change coming from outside forces or influences. Zehfuss reveals the level of complexity that can be gained from a more critical reading of identity. In her examination of Germany's decision to undertake military

intervention in the 1990s, she argues that the discourses of the past ('never again war', 'never again dictatorship') made German identity contestable. The power of these discourses (never again to become an aggressive military force) competed with new challenges (what to do about ethnic cleansing in Europe's backyard?). Its military participation in these efforts also had implications for understanding Germany's future identity and its place in Europe. Hence, by failing to pay attention to language and power relations, Wendt's identity lacks these depths. Wendt (2002: 48–9) relies only on gestures and signals where interaction is concerned, meaning we only get a sense of how states communicate through their behaviour rather than through language.

KEY POINTS

- Rationalists criticize constructivism because its claims cannot be tested or observed empirically. Norms, values, and identities are something we cannot 'see'. Furthermore, intentionality is difficult to discern and rationalists argue that we cannot say for sure which norms are operating in a given situation.

- Wendt is limited in his three cultures of anarchy and cannot tell us much about domestic identity formation because his focus is the states system.

- Poststructuralist critiques point to a reification of the state and a singular or essentialized identity. Placing culture at the centre may be dangerous in itself and privilege dominant power relations.

- Furthermore, constructivism results in an uncritical and apolitical explanation of politics and security problems.

practice, theory and institutional behaviour has been lost through an inaccurate employment of social theory, which results in a problematic form of 'idealism'. Both Cynthia Weber and Maja Zehfuss put deeper concerns about the implications of constructivism forward. For Weber (1999: 439–40), constructivism is an 'evacuation' of politics,

'replumbing' neorealism through identity construction; it privileges state-centrism and resurrects the anarchy myth. Zehfuss (2002: 262) also claims that constructivism is apolitical and limits the space for critical thinking, because it takes 'reality' as given, closing off alternatives (see Think Point 4.2).

Conclusion

This chapter has explored some of the central themes of constructivism and how it relates to security. By making the claim that identity matters, constructivism presents a challenge to rationalist theorising. Neorealist theories contend that states are bound to do the same thing in the international system—seek security and power—because the anarchic international system provides the logic that this is what a state must do to survive. Wendt's suggestion that 'anarchy is what states make of it' brought the debate back to agency, arguing that it is states who make the system anarchic, not that anarchy is a natural feature of the international system. This opened up the possibility of change. New norms can enter collective understandings and recreate the international system of states. Interaction means that states do not just bump against each other as in the billiard-ball model, but through interaction states can alter their identities and establish new frameworks for cooperation and shared understandings. Social learning and communication are important in interaction, and actors learn from each other. France and Germany are now allies, not enemies, via their interaction in European integration, and, although the USA treated Iraq as an ally in the 1980s, how do we explain its shift to viewing Iraq and Saddam Hussein's regime as an enemy in the 1990s? Shared norms, values, and beliefs, constructivists argue, can explain much more than rationalist theorizing. The central point is that we construct the world according to the meanings we give it.

Constructivism has lent insights into a number of security issues such as NATO's survival and enlargement, why neutral states have not yet joined NATO, and why human rights have become a central concern in the security policies of states and international organizations such as the UN, the OSCE, and others. But the way in which we can undertake a constructivist analysis differs. Conventional forms of constructivism tend to accept that there exists some compatibility between rationalist and constructivist approaches. By highlighting identity, norms, and values, some constructivists believe that they can fill in the gaps of rationalist theories. Others remain sceptical about this possibility, arguing that we must pay attention to power, the importance of discourse, and language, and interrogate them critically. Conventional constructivists such as Wendt accept that the state is the most important actor in the international system and that the identity of a state is given. Many critical constructivists find this to be lacking and argue that we must investigate identity more rigorously in order to uncover its meaning and construction.

Constructivism now forms one of the dominant modes of analysis in international relations and security studies. Its attention to identity, norms, values, culture, and interaction have produced some alternative readings of security problems, how we frame and define them, and how our shared ideas impact on security issues. The idea that we construct the world around us and what it means suggests an escape clause from realism's 'timeless wisdom'.

QUESTIONS

1. Why does identity matter to constructivists?

2. What are norms and how do they affect security?

3. What is the difference between conventional and critical constructivism? Does it matter? If so, why?

4. How do constructivists think about agents and structures?

5. What is problematic about Wendtian constructivism?

6. How do constructivist accounts of security questions, such as the persistence and expansion of NATO after the Cold War differ from rationalist accounts?

7. Is security always about identity?

8. Do any of Wendt's three cultures of anarchy accurately reflect the international system today?

9. What is beneficial and problematic about conventional constructivism's claim to build bridges between rationalist and reflectivist approaches?

10. To what extent is culture important in terms of security?

FURTHER READING

- Biersteker, T. J., and Weber, C. (1996) (eds.), *State Sovereignty as Social Construct*, Cambridge: Cambridge University Press. An excellent edited volume that contains numerous essays exploring the social construction of sovereignty in relation to a number of topics and themes, such as colonial imperialism and national identity.

- Fierke, K. M., and Jørgensen K. E. (2001) (eds.), *Constructing International Relations: The Next Generation*, New York: M. E. Sharpe. A very good introduction to constructivism, particularly critical constructivism, with contributions from key poststructuralist scholars.

- Guzzini, S., and Leander, A. (2006) (eds.), *Constructivism and International Relations. Alexander Wendt and his Critics*, Abingdon and New York: Routledge. Contains some rather advanced essays on constructivism, all directed at Wendt's *Social Theory of International Politics*, with a reply by Wendt in the final section.

- Katzenstein, P. J. (1996) (ed.), *The Culture of National Security. Norms and Identity in World Politics*, New York: Columbia University Press. Excellent for getting to grips with conventional constructivism, strategic culture, and security questions. This edited volume contains contributions from Wendt, Finnemore, Barnett, and many other names associated with security and constructivist analysis. Focuses more on norms.

- Kubálková, V. (2001) (ed.), *Foreign Policy in a Constructed World,* New York: M. E. Sharpe. This edited collection contains essays outlining constructivism and applications of constructivism to foreign policy and security case studies.

- Weldes, J., Laffey, M., Gusterson, H., and Duvall, R. (1999) (eds.), *Cultures of Insecurity: States, Communities, and the Production of Danger*, Minneapolis: University of Minnesota Press. An extremely useful and relevant edited volume, this brings together security and culture with a great range of chapters covering various topics related to security.

IMPORTANT WEBSITES

- http://www.arena.uio.no   Arena is an interdisciplinary centre for advanced European Studies at the University of Oslo. Here you can access a number of working papers and other publications that are directly concerned with social constructivism or apply constructivist analysis to European politics and questions of security.

- http://www.allacademic.com   This website is an excellent portal for conference papers and, while most searches may only provide an abstract, you can access many conference papers here.

- http://www.opendemocracy.net/article/democracy_power/america_power_world/citizen_identity   'I Am an American': Portraits of post-9/11 US citizens. Cynthia Weber's project 'I am an American' explores different interpretations of American identity in response to the United States' Ad Council campaign to unite the nation after the 9/11 attacks. Weber's documentary problematizes these idealized images of American unity represented by the Ad Council with representations of Americans who fall outside of this ideal.

 Visit the Online Resource Centre that accompanies this book for lots of interesting additional material: www.oxfordtextbooks.co.uk/orc/collins2e/

5

Peace Studies

PAUL ROGERS

Chapter Contents

- Introduction
- The early years
- Evolution amidst controversy
- What is peace studies now?
- Responding to the new security challenges
- Conclusion

Reader's Guide

This chapter examines the origins and development of the field of peace studies after the Second World War, initially in relation to the East–West confrontation and the nuclear arms race. It analyses how peace studies responded to the issues of socio-economic disparities and environmental constraints as they became apparent in the 1970s, and explores its development as an interdisciplinary and problem-oriented field of study, often in the midst of controversy. The chapter then assesses the state of peace studies now, before concluding by examining how it is relevant to the new security challenges facing the world.

Introduction

Peace studies is a field of study that developed after the Second World War, largely because of the failure of a range of social and international-ist movements to prevent the outbreak of two world wars within twenty-five years. Its early development in the 1950s was hugely conditioned by the East–West nuclear arms race and the very real threat of a catastrophic nuclear war, but peace studies was also quick to embrace major issues of the North–South wealth/poverty divide and the potential effects of global environmental constraints. It is a field that has had more than its share of controversies—peace studies was frequently labelled 'appeasement studies' at the height of the Cold War, but has survived and thrived, especially since the early 1990s with a marked increase in interest in issues of peace-keeping, conflict resolution, and post-conflict peace building. There has been a particular interest in many parts of Latin America, Africa, the Middle East, and much of Asia, and the concern of the peace-studies community to rise above the Western ethnocentric attitudes that still dominate much of international relations (IR) has been greatly aided by this global context.

The early years

Peace studies only became established as a formal field of study, with its own institutions and jour-nals, in the post-1945 period, although earlier pioneers included Pitrim Sorokin, Quincy Wright and the British meteorologist Lewis Fry Richardson. (Sorokin 1937; Wright 1942; Richardson 1960) A more sustained interest in peace studies devel-oped after the Second World War (Galtung 1969) as the combination of the early years of the nuclear arms race, the proxy wars of the Cold War era such as Korea, and the violence in a number of colonies, all contributed to a perception of a world of profound instability, even more shocking given that this was barely a decade after the world's worst-ever conflict. It was in this pessimistic envi-ronment that the origins of peace studies are to be found.

The universities get involved

In these early years, peace studies developed pri-marily in North America and Western Europe, with some of the developments even preceding the tense years of the 1950s. Theodore Lenz's Peace Research Laboratory was founded in St Louis in 1945 and in Europe the Institut Français de Polémologie was established in the same year. One of the main European contribu-tors to the new field of peace research was the Dutch jurist Bert Rolling. He had been a judge at the Japanese war-crimes tribunal and went on to establish peace studies, or polemology, in the Netherlands.

Another key feature of peace studies was estab-lished in the early post-war era—the entry into the field of mathematicians and natural scien-tists into what was otherwise a social sciences area of study. This was later prominent both in the contribution of the **Pugwash** movement and in the publication of the *Bulletin of the Atomic Scientists*. It has been an enduring feature of peace studies since the mid-twentieth century that its interdisciplinary nature stretches well beyond the range of social science disciplines to embrace the physical and natural sciences and mathematics.

One of the earliest initiatives in the United States was the publication in the *American Psychologist* in April 1951 of a letter from two social scientists, Kelman and Gladstone, arguing for a serious and systematic study of pacifist approaches to foreign policy. Coming at a time of heightened tensions, and with anti-communism rampant in the United States, this was a courageous suggestion and it resulted in the establishment of the *Bulletin of the Research Exchange on the Prevention of War* the following year.

The middle 1950s were to see major developments on both sides of the Atlantic. In the United States a key research group came together at Stanford University's Center for Advanced Studies in the Behavioral Sciences. As well as Herb Kelman, this included Kenneth and Elise Boulding and Anatol Rapoport. Joining them was Stephen Richardson, the son of Lewis Fry Richardson, who brought with him his father's copious but largely unpublished material on microfilm. This combination produced a highly active and innovative group that was to develop the *Bulletin* into the *Journal of Conflict Resolution*, based at the newly established Center for Conflict Resolution at the University of Michigan. In the first issue of the *Journal* the editors gave two reasons for establishing it, and these give the flavour of those early years:

 The first is that by far the most important practical problem facing the human race today is that of international relations—more specifically the prevention of global war. The second is that if intellectual progress is to be made in this area, the study of international relations must be made an interdisciplinary enterprise, drawing its discourse from all the social sciences, and even further.

Journal of Conflict Resolution, 1/1 (1957), 3.

In parallel with these developments in the United States, peace studies developed apace in Europe and Japan, with the establishment of more departments, research centres, and journals (see Background 5.1).

BACKGROUND 5.1

Peace centres and journals

Away from the United States, Bert Rolling founded the Polemological Institute at the University of Groningen in the Netherlands, and the Norwegian peace researcher Johan Galtung founded the forerunner of what became the Peace Research Institute of Oslo (PRIO), which publishes two key journals, *Security Dialogue* and the *Journal of Peace Research*.

Two of the largest peace studies centres were to be established in Sweden and the United Kingdom. To celebrate 150 years of peace, the Stockholm International Peace Research Institute (SIPRI) was set up in 1966 and went on to establish a worldwide reputation for its work on arms races and arms control. Its yearbook, *Arms and Disarmament*, has long been seen as an essential source of data. Seven years after the founding of SIPRI, members of the Society of Friends (Quakers) in Britain sought to establish a British equivalent and were able to aid the University of Bradford in setting up a Department of Peace Studies.

Elsewhere, the Japanese Peace Research group was founded in 1964, the Canadian Peace Research and Education Association was established two years later, and the Tampere Peace Research Institute was founded in Finland. One of the other key journals, *Peace and Change*, was started by the US Conference on Peace Research and History, which had itself been formed in 1963. Given the global spread of this new field, the final development was the formation of the International Peace Research Association, which holds biennial conferences.

Some were essentially started at the instigation of governments and obtained most of their money from central government sources, continuing to do so successfully over many years. As such, they had a degree of financial support that was welcome, but such centres could also be subject to sudden political change. The Peace Research Centre at the Australian National University in Canberra failed to survive a change of government, and the Copenhagen Peace Research Institute was to lose its independence in a centrally directed amalgamation of institutes.

Evolution amidst controversy

In the early 1960s, there were sharp divides between the outlooks of peace researchers and those of the 'realist' school in international relations. Realist IR scholars saw the failure of the League of Nations and the intensity of the ideological division between Western liberal democracies and the totalitarian systems of the Soviet bloc as providing an urgent need to undertake research that would essentially favour the survival of the former. The standpoint was very much that of an Atlanticist outlook.

Many peace researchers, on the other hand, saw this as a narrow Western ethnocentric outlook that failed properly to analyse what they saw as the reality of two competing systems locked into a single dynamic of military confrontation and escalation. They had much in common with 'idealist' outlooks in international relations, and their work attracted particular attention at a time when the nuclear arms race was accelerating.

In late 1962, the United States and the Soviet Union came very close to an all-out nuclear confrontation over the latter's plans to deploy medium-range nuclear missiles in Cuba, close to the United States. The crisis was resolved, with difficulty, and one consequence was a new-found determination by the United States and the Soviet Union to seek progress in arms control, leading to a period of relative détente in the mid-1960s.

A new agenda: environment and poverty

Given that peace studies had developed partly in response to Cold War tensions and the risk of global nuclear war, it might have been expected that it would have gone into decline in the wake of these improvements in East–West relations. In practice this did not happen, as three other major international issues were coming to the fore that were to become central to the developing field.

One was the widely held view that former colonies had successfully achieved political independence in the 1950s and 1960s but had certainly not achieved economic independence— the anticipated progress from the much-vaunted Development Decade of the 1960s has simply not materialized. Such a view, common in the newly developing field of development studies as well as within peace research, was regarded as a radical analysis by most mainstream economists. As far as the discipline of International Relations was concerned, North–South relations were simply not important and received scant attention from most scholars, an aspect that in 2009 tends to differentiate peace researchers from most of the international relations community.

A second issue, surfacing initially in the late 1960s, was the state of the global environment. The first **UN Conference on the Human Environment**, in 1972, placed emphasis on the possible limits to economic growth if the global ecosystem was to prove to be unable to cope with rapidly increasing human impacts. This suggested that such growth alone could not meet the needs of the majority of humankind in the South. Environmental security therefore had to be linked to development aspirations, and prospects for international development were necessarily linked to the asymmetric

---

CASE STUDY 5.1

Conflicts to come: energy wars and climate change

Whether or not the termination of the Saddam Hussein regime in Iraq had much to do with the control of Iraq's oil reserves, these are one part of a regional concentration that is quite remarkable. Just five Gulf States—Saudi Arabia, Iran, Iraq, Kuwait, and the United Arab Emirates—control well over 60 per cent of known oil reserves. During the latter part of the Cold War, the United States became particularly concerned about a possible Soviet threat to Gulf oil resources, and this resulted in the establishment of the Rapid Deployment Force at the end of the 1970s. Following the 1979–80 Iranian Revolution and the start of the 1980–8 Iran–Iraq War, the Rapid Deployment Force was elevated into a full unified military command, Central Command (CENTCOM), and it was this organization that fought the 1991 Iraq War and has been responsible for operations in Afghanistan and Iraq in recent years.

The key reason for potential conflict in the region is that all the world's major industrial regions, including Western Europe, the United States, and East Asia, are becoming increasingly dependent on Gulf oil reserves as their own production decreases and demand rises. Thus, one of the core security issues for the two decades through to 2030 is whether there can be sustained international cooperation over the utilization of Gulf oil reserves, or whether the region will be a focus for conflict. Moreover, this is part of the wider problem of whether the global community can continue to rely on fossil fuels or whether the security implications of climate change will make that mode of living redundant.

Although climate change was seen as an important issue by the early 1990s, it was expected that the major effects would be felt by the richer countries of the North and South temperate latitudes, which might best be able to cope. By the mid-1990s, though, some of the climate modelling was showing a disturbing picture of much greater effects on tropical climates than had previously been thought likely. In particular, there was a growing likelihood that climate change would have a major impact on rainfall distribution across the tropics and sub-tropics, the main effect being a tendency for rainfall to decrease substantially over these land masses and increase over the world's oceans and over the Polar regions (Rind 1995).

If this does happen, and the timescale is over the thirty years through to 2040, then the effects will be profound. The majority of the world's population, well over four billion people, live in the tropical and subtropical land masses, with almost all of them dependent on locally grown food. If the tropical regions 'dry out', then there will be a substantial decrease in the 'ecological carrying-capacity' of some of the world's richest croplands. If this happens, then the effects will be massive, not just in terms of increases in famine and malnutrition, but in increased migratory pressures as many millions of people seek to move to countries where they can survive.

The phenomenon of climate change and the tropical land masses is likely to become one of the key international security issues. Countering the likely effects over the decade through to 2020, and moving more insistently towards sustainable economies, could be a great contribution to ensuring a more peaceful and stable world, and it could also markedly reduce the risk of conflict over energy resources.

---

environmental impact of industrialized states. Otherwise, a world beset with deep socio-economic divisions that also had finite limits on its economic growth potential set by environmental constraints would be a world of much potential violence, fragility, and insecurity. This debate of the early 1970s is being revisited with even greater urgency as the impact of climate change becomes rapidly more apparent, and the Persian Gulf, with its massive fossil-fuel resources, becomes a locus not just of economic competition but of open warfare (see Case Study 5.1).

The 'maximalist' agenda and structural violence

Finally, one specific conflict, the Vietnam War, was to cause deep controversy as some radical peace researchers argued that the injustices were such that there could be occasions when violence could be justified in the pursuit of justice. That brief controversy was in the context of the development of a 'maximalist' agenda emerging in European peace research, especially with Johan Galtung's conception (1969) of structural violence.

This proposed that the condition of peace required the absence not just of overt violence but also of structural violence—the persistence of economic and social exploitation in societies that might otherwise be said to be at peace. In similar vein, Herman Schmid (1968) argued that much of peace research was not critically engaged with defining peaceful societies as entities in which justice genuinely prevailed. An absence of war could obscure deep injustices that made a mockery of notions of peace. Others engaged in peace research saw this as a constant expansion of the peace research agenda 'acquiring the qualities of an intellectual black hole wherein something vital, a praxeological edge or purpose, is lost' (Lawler 1995: 237).

This dispute, sometimes described as between maximalists and minimalists, has never been fully resolved, but most peace researchers came to accept that, in addition to the original aim of seeking to prevent nuclear war, other themes were of legitimate concern for those working in the field. The primary issues were initially those of global North–South disparities and the risk of an environmental crisis, but, significantly, a concern for gender inequalities also came to prominence rather earlier than in the fields of development studies or international relations.

New goals: equality, justice, and dignity

By 1973, and as a result of such changes, the editors of the *Journal of Conflict Resolution* sought to broaden its original remit beyond its previous concentration on inter-state conflict and the nuclear issue:

> The threat of nuclear holocaust remains with us and may well continue to do so for centuries, but other problems are competing with deterrence and disarmament studies for our attention. This journal must also attend to international conflict over justice, equality, and human dignity; problems of conflict resolution for ecological balance and control are within our proper scope and especially suited for interdisciplinary attention.

Journal of Conflict Resolution, 17/1 (1973), 5.

By the end of the 1970s, this much broader focus was embedded in peace studies but was then overtaken by the development of the final and perhaps most dangerous phase of the Cold War. The Soviet invasion of Afghanistan, the Iranian Revolution and hostage crisis, the election of the Reagan and Thatcher governments, and the deployment of new generations of strategic nuclear weapons all combined to give a renewed urgency to those very issues that peace researchers had largely eschewed. For the best part of a decade, many researchers returned to issues of deterrence and disarmament, contrasting their analysis markedly with that of international relations realists and, on occasions, earning the enmity of their own governments.

Even so, issues of environment and development continued to be addressed, and there was a substantial increase in research on techniques of mediation and other forms of conflict resolution, on peacekeeping and post-conflict peace building (see Think Point 5.1). Partly because of this, a number of peace studies centres not only survived the sudden ending of the Cold War in 1989–90 but were able to adjust to the post-Cold War world much more easily than many of the international relations centres, which were, to an extent, floundering in the face of such unexpected change.

THINK POINT 5.1

Conflict resolution

The area of study and practice usually grouped under the term 'conflict resolution' has been one of the fastest-growing aspects of peace studies since the 1990s, but has not been without its controversies. Involving such processes as mediation, conflict transformation, and post-conflict peace building, it has been an active field of academic study as well as burgeoning into an 'industry' involving non-government organizations and international agencies.

Two problems have emerged, one theoretical and one practical. At the theoretical level, some critical theorists have argued that conflict resolution is palliative rather than transformative—being concerned with a 'sticking-plaster' approach that may appear to promote peace but does not address underlying reasons for conflict. In a sense this is a replay of the 'maximalist' controversy of the 1970s.

At the practical level, many of the organizations attempting to resolve conflicts, at whatever level, need to demonstrate success, not least to ensure their continuing sources of funding. There can, therefore, be a tendency to overdo their claims of progress. In practice, the best forms of mediatory intervention are those with very modest expectations of success and an ability to remain unpublicized. Some of

the 'peace churches' such as the Quakers have a good record in this respect.

As to the wider criticism, many peace researchers would argue that conflict resolution should properly be seen as a specific and integral part of the peace studies tradition. As Ramsbotham, Woodhouse, and Miall (2005) argue:

> We suggest that peace and conflict research is part of an emancipatory discourse and practice which is making a valuable and defining contribution to emerging norms of democratic, just and equitable systems of global governance. We argue that conflict resolution has a role to play in the radical negotiation of these norms, so that international conflict management is grounded in the needs of those who are the victims of conflict and who are frequently marginalized from conventional power structures.

KEY POINTS

- Peace studies sought to provide a non-state centric and more global view of major issues of conflict.
- By the 1970s it was responding to issues of socio-economic divisions and environmental constraints.
- In the 1980s, in the final period of the Cold War, there was bitter opposition to what was sometimes seen as 'appeasement studies'.

- Within peace studies, one of the later developments was a major interest in conflict prevention, conflict resolution, and peacekeeping.

What is peace studies now?

Peace studies in the early twenty-first century is an established and thriving field with a range of journals, a number of research institutes such as the Peace Research Institute of Oslo (PRIO) and the Stockholm International Peace Research Institute (SIPRI), many centres in universities and colleges, and an international body, the International Peace Research Association (IPRA). In countries of the South there has been a real increase in interest in peace studies since 2000, with a particular concern

with what peace studies can offer in countering violence and open conflict. Furthermore, since the effects of wars can be so much more long-lasting in poorer regions, there is an added impetus to work towards war termination, conflict resolution, and peace building.

What are the main characteristics of peace studies? Rogers and Ramsbotham (1999) suggests a number of features that mark it out as a defined field of study

1. *Underlying causes.* A concern to address the root causes of direct violence and to explore ways of overcoming structural inequalities and of promoting equitable and cooperative relations between and within human communities. This means that peace studies goes well beyond the absence of war to work towards societies that are intrinsically more peaceful. This means addressing a wide range of inequalities whether rooted in class, race, or gender divisions, with these analysed at a range of levels from the individual and community through to the international.

2. *Interdisciplinary approaches.* A realization that an interdisciplinary response is essential, given the multifaceted nature of violent conflict. The larger peace studies centres will have among their staff people drawn from political science, international relations, psychology, anthropology, economics, history, sociology, and other disciplines. They may well have people trained originally in mathematics, physics, or the biological sciences. This leads to conceptual enrichment, but can also cause disputes about appropriate methodologies and theoretical frameworks.

3. *Non-violent transformations.* A search for peaceful ways to settle disputes and for non-violent transformation of potentially or actually violent situations. This does not mean endorsing the status quo, since unjust and oppressive systems are seen as some of the chief causes of violence and war. It does mean the comparative study of peaceful and non-peaceful processes of social and political change; and of ways to prevent the outbreak of violence, or, if it does break out, of ways to mitigate it, bring it to an end, and prevent its recurrence thereafter. Within these parameters there is continuing debate about the efficacy and legitimacy of the use of force in certain circumstances. This is especially true in the case of humanitarian intervention in internal conflicts.

4. *Multi-level analysis.* The embracing of a multi-level analysis at individual, group, state, and inter-state levels in an attempt to overcome the institutionalized dichotomy between studies of 'internal' and 'external' dimensions that are seen to be inadequate for the prevailing patterns of conflict. This is seen as particularly significant given the relative decline of inter-state conflict and the rise of sub-state conflict. It is also seen as relevant in analysing the tendency towards 'trans-state' conflict. This may include detention without trial, across state borders, of individuals who have status neither as conventional criminals nor as prisoners of war under the terms of the Geneva conventions. This has become a feature of the Global War on Terror, as has the 'rendition' of individuals—their transfer to countries likely to use torture in extracting information.

5. *Global outlook.* The adoption of a global and multicultural approach, which locates sources of violence globally and regionally as well as locally, and draw on conceptions of peace and non-violent social transformations from all cultures. Such an approach has become even more relevant as peace studies centres have increased in number in East and South Asia, Africa, and Latin America.

6. Analytical and normative. An understanding that peace studies is both an analytic and a normative enterprise. While there has been a tendency to ground peace studies in quantitative research and comparative empirical study, the reality is that most scholars have been drawn to the field by ethical concerns and commitments. Deterministic ideas have been largely rejected, whether in realist or Marxist guises, with large-scale violence and war seen not as inevitable features of the international system, but as consequences of human actions and choices.

With ethical commitments among the core motivations of peace researchers, it can be argued that such an environment can result in

THINK POINT 5.2

The war on peace studies

In the early years of the 1980s, Cold War tensions were particularly high, and there was a strong perception of renewed danger, with a palpable risk of all-out nuclear war. This fed into a burgeoning anti-nuclear movement across Western Europe, together with a renewed interest in peace studies, especially in schools but also in universities. In Britain, political polarization was particularly evident and conservative opponents of peace studies viewed it as unpatriotic appeasement studies.

The opposition was focused very largely on politicians and rarely stretched to the armed forces—indeed the defence colleges were keen to debate the issues openly and frequently asked peace researchers to lecture to their students. The 'war on peace studies' lasted from around 1981 to 1987, but died away as the Cold War came to an end. Indeed, peace studies attracted much greater attention over the following few years, as many other areas of peace research, such as the theory and practice of peace keeping and issues of environmental security, came to the fore.

Some of the academics involved in peace research at that time now reflect that the 'war on peace studies' was very good for the emerging discipline. As well as attracting some particularly able students into the area, the constant critical scrutiny of research output, especially on areas such as armaments and arms control, meant that standards of work had to be particularly high. Peace researchers became subject to far tougher scrutiny of their work than most other scholars in international relations and many of them now think that they became better academics as a result.

---

the sloppy pursuit of causes with little concern for academic rigour. This was a particular issue in several countries in the 1980s (see Think Point 5.2), but the level of critical analysis of peace studies programmes actually helped ensure that unusually high standards had to be, and were, set.

7. *Theory and practice.* Linked to this is the close relationship between theory and practice in peace studies. While a clear distinction is persistently made between peace studies and peace activism, peace researchers very frequently engage systematically with non-government organizations (NGOs), government departments, and intergovernmental agencies. They frequently see this as part of a process of empirical testing of theoretical insights, regarding it also as a two-way process.

Many people working in the field regard the policy implications of their work as more significant than its reception among fellow academics. Given the modern era of 'research assessment' in some Western countries that is primarily geared to academic output in the conventional literature, this can be a disadvantage for the discipline. Furthermore, this 'engagement' with the policy process does not fit in with the prevailing academic culture in most Western countries, even if it is more commonly found in academic centres in the majority of the world.

KEY POINTS

- Core elements of modern peace studies include a concern with underlying causes of conflict and the search for non-violent approaches to conflict transformation.

- It remains an interdisciplinary field that embraces multi-level analysis from the individual to the international.

- It is both analytical and normative, frequently involving ethical motivations on the part of students and researchers.

- Peace studies engages persistently with opinion formers and policy-makers.

Responding to the new security challenges

Given these characteristics, how relevant is the peace studies agenda in the early twenty-first century and how valuable might it be in responding to the major issues of conflict and insecurity that might face us in the coming decades? To answer these questions we need to analyse the main security challenges likely to face us and then look at the main attributes of peace studies in terms of its possible contribution.

Global security during the forty-five years of the Cold War was dominated by the East–West confrontation but was also a period of major conflicts in many parts of the world, with over 100 wars leading directly to more than twenty million deaths and well over fifty million injuries, as well as much more suffering in post-war environments especially in impoverished communities. The ending of the Cold War, while leading to the settlement of some long-standing disputes, also increased instability, not least in the Caucasus and the Balkans, and there were also continuing tensions in the Israeli/Palestinian confrontation, the 1991 Iraq War, and the devastating conflicts of the Great Lakes region of Central Africa.

 THINK POINT 5.3

A more peaceful world?

In the years since the 9/11 attacks, most people in Western countries would probably say that the world has become distinctly more dangerous. It is not just the memory of the planes crashing into the World Trade Center followed by the collapse of the towers; it is also the impact of the subsequent wars in Afghanistan and Iraq. With 100,000 civilian deaths and the US forces mired in a violent insurgency, first in Iraq and then in Afghanistan, as well as numerous paramilitary attacks in Madrid, Bali, London, Istanbul, Mumbai, and many other cities, there is a presumption of an unstable and fragile world in which sudden violence can break out when least expected.

This may actually be an illusion, as some research suggests that the world has actually become more peaceful since the end of the Cold War. The *2005 Human Security Report*, published at the height of the Iraq War, for example, cites a 40 per cent decrease in armed conflicts overall since the early 1990s and an 80 per cent decrease in major conflicts. The study was undertaken at the Liu Institute for Global Issues at the University of British Columbia in Vancouver, and the resulting report was a powerful antidote to many common assumptions.

As well as an overall decrease in conflicts, the report pointed to a decline in the number of autocratic regimes, with their penchant for human-rights abuses, and also claimed that an expansion in UN peacekeeping operations, as well as a much greater emphasis on conflict prevention, have combined to good effect. The results may seem surprising but were supported by a number of similar studies from the Center for International Development and Conflict Management at the University of Maryland.

In addition to the impact of conflict prevention and peacekeeping operations, other factors may be at work. The Cold War era was characterized by numerous 'proxy wars' fought on an East–West axis but rarely involving the two superpowers in direct conflict. These included Korea, Vietnam, Afghanistan, and the Horn of Africa. Furthermore, the early part of the Cold War period coincided with numerous wars of decolonization, including French Indo-China, Malaya, Kenya, Cyprus, and Algeria. Almost all the colonial conflicts had ended by the 1970s.

There were also particular conflicts associated with the ending of the Cold War, especially in the Caucasus, as well as the break-up of Yugoslavia. These had reduced if not ended by the turn of the century, and even the enduring conflicts in Northern Ireland, Sri Lanka, and the Basque region of Spain seemed to be winding down. When all these factors are put together, it is easier to understand the results from the *Human Security Report*. The question remains as to whether this is a long-term trend or a welcome but potentially short-lived period of relative calm before new conflicts kick in, especially over issues such as energy resources and climate change.

By the end of the 1990s, a number of these conflicts had been transformed into an uneasy peace, and others such as Northern Ireland also showed some prospects of settlement. (see Think Point 5.3) Against this, the attacks in New York and Washington in September 2001 were to herald a vigorous military reaction from the United States, leading to the termination of regimes in Afghanistan and Iraq and the beginnings of potentially long-drawn-out conflicts in both countries.

While these were immediate issues of conflict in the early twenty-first century, they were evolving in an international context in which two much broader issues are becoming salient. The first concerns the deep and enduring inequalities in the global distribution of wealth and economic power, which are likely to ensure that, by 2040, one-seventh of the world's population will control three-quarters of the wealth, largely but not entirely on a geographical basis. While there have been immense efforts at development, almost entirely from within the poorer countries themselves, the global picture is one of enduring disempowerment and increasing socio-economic polarization. This is not just the case at the global level but is particularly marked in countries such as China and India that may be experiencing rapid economic growth but with most of the increases in wealth being concentrated among a minority of the population.

Furthermore, environmental constraints are likely to exacerbate the effects of human activity on the global ecosystem, making it increasingly difficult for human well-being to be improved by conventional economic growth. The combination of wealth–poverty disparities and limits to growth is likely to lead to a crisis of unsatisfied expectations within an increasingly informed global majority of the disempowered.

On the basis of these issues, three broad conflict trends are probable. The first arises from a greater likelihood of increased human migration through economic, social, and environmental motives. Focusing on regions of relative wealth, this is already leading to shifts in the political spectrum in recipient regions, including increased nationalist tendencies and cultural conflict, not least in Western

Europe and Australasia. Such tendencies are often most pronounced in the most vulnerable and disempowered populations within the recipient regions. If, as seems probable, climate changes induce a partial 'drying-out' of the tropical land masses (see Case Study 5.1) then the migratory pressures will be greatly accelerated.

Secondly, it is probable that environmental and resource conflict will escalate. This may be local or regional on issues such as food, land, fresh water, or marine resources, and global on issues such as fossil fuel and mineral resources. The Persian Gulf, as the repository of most of the world's remaining reserves of fossil fuels, is likely to be a particular focus for competition and conflict (see Case Study 5.1).

Finally, and probably most importantly, competitive and violent responses of the disempowered should be expected within and between states and also in the form of transnational movements. The Zapatista revolt in southern Mexico, the earlier Shining Path guerrilla movement in Peru, the neo-Maoist rebellion in Nepal, the Naxalite movement in India, social unrest in China, and disempowerment responses in North Africa and the Middle East may all be early examples of a developing trend, not infrequently exacerbated by political, religious, and nationalist fundamentalisms. This is linked to underlying historically conditioned weaknesses in many post-colonial states, struggling as they are to accommodate twin pressures of globalization and fragmentation, and a prey to sectarian and factional exploitation. Increased internal political tensions, not least secessionist movements, in populous states such as China, India, and Indonesia, would have very wide repercussions.

The key development that links with socio-economic divisions and environmental constraints is the marked improvement in education, literacy, and communications across much of the world since the 1960s. Achieved largely through indigenous efforts, primary-level education is now much more prevalent than at the end of the colonial period, and this has been accompanied by substantial improvements in levels of literacy. While male literacy levels increased first, levels of female literacy are at last starting to catch up.

Coupled with these changes, there has been an explosion of technological change in relation to radio, television, and the print media. For much of the world's 'data-poor' majority, the impact of the web, e-mail, and even DVDs are still to come, but the changes that have already taken place mean that there is a much greater awareness of world developments. The implications of this are fundamental, in that there is a much greater recognition among the disempowered majority of the world's population of that very disempowerment. The end result is not so much a revolution of rising expectations, a feature of consumerism in the 1970s, as a revolution of frustrated expectations as the levels of exclusion become more readily apparent.

Moreover, the development of non-Western satellite news channels such as al-Jazeera means that reporting of events in Iraq and other countries of the Middle East is no longer under the influence of local elites and therefore subject to censorship. Nor is it more widely dominated by transnational broadcasting organizations that may provide minimal coverage to their international audiences except in the instances of major violence.

Consequences of the effects of marginalization are legion, from the high levels of urban crime in many Southern cities, the need for heavily protected gated communities for the elite rich, the outbreak of violence in France in late 2005, through to some of the radical and extreme social movements in Nepal, India, Pakistan, and elsewhere. Although the al-Qaeda movement may be rooted in South West Asia and specific to extreme interpretations of one religious tradition, its evolution into a transnational phenomenon owes much to the persistent publicizing of the human consequences of the war on terror, not least in Iraq.

A choice of responses

Responses to socio-economic divisions and environmental constraints might best take the form of consistent cooperation for sustainable development, including debt relief, trade reform, and development assistance at a level much higher than that of recent years, coupled with a multiplicity of programmes for conflict prevention and resolution as embodied in the UN **Agenda for Peace**.

They might, on the other hand, take the form of a vigorous programme of maintaining the status quo, ensuring that the wealthy sectors of humankind maintain their privileged position by appropriate trading and financial measures, backed up by military force where necessary. Described as 'liddism', or keeping the lid on a potentially fractured international system, this would appear to be the current trend, not least in terms of the US-led response to the 9/11 attacks. The consequence of this might well be Brooks's fear, expressed over thirty-five years ago, of 'a crowded glowering planet of massive inequalities of wealth buttressed by stark force and endlessly threatened by desperate people in the global ghettoes . . .' (Brooks 1974).

By 2009, some eight years after the 9/11 attacks, the prevailing security paradigm was still very much dominated by the United States and buttressed by stark force. Two regimes had been terminated, over 100,000 civilians had been killed in the process, 120,000 people had been detained without trial and torture, and prisoner abuse had been widespread. Even so, the al-Qaeda movement remained active, with associates capable of mounting attacks across the world at a level substantially higher than in the eight years preceding 9/11, with US forces still in Iraq while deeply mired in a complex insurgency in Afghanistan and western Pakistan.

Whether this paradigm will collapse under the weight of its own inadequacies or whether it will survive and prosper will depend on the further evolution of the **global war on terror** into a 'long war', but may also depend on the degree of critical analysis of its underlying assumptions, coupled with the promotion of viable alternatives that might be undertaken by a vigorous academic community.

This is a challenge for the international relations community as a whole, and the peace studies community in particular. The short-term responses include the principal *Agenda for Peace* peace-support elements, themselves in part drawn from peace-research terminology, such as crisis prevention, peacekeeping, peacemaking, and the shorter-term elements in post-settlement peace-building. This also involves ethically involved intervention and regional and global arms control and demilitarization. They are required of an international community of states that shows little evidence of wisdom or leadership and consequently places most responsibility on an under-resourced UN system. While improvements in efficiency and capability must come from within the UN, the NGO role is substantial, especially in the more powerful states of the UN, with improved links between NGOs and the academic community an essential part of the process.

There are longer-term processes involved in conflict resolution and conflict transformation (see Think Point 5.1). This is a wide agenda, but now quite well understood and reasonably clearly focused, involving contextual, structural, relational, and cultural elements in the analysis of protracted social conflict with, beyond this, an increasing need for fundamental responses at the global level.

KEY POINTS

- Major issues for the future centre on the effects of a combination of socio-economic divisions and environmental constraints.

- The 9/11 attacks and the subsequent war on terror have yet to address the underlying reasons for current perceptions of insecurity.

- Responding to a potentially fragile and insecure international system will require sustained analysis combined with persistent efforts to suggest viable alternatives to the current security paradigm.

Conclusion

If the analysis offered in this chapter of a polarized, constrained, and potentially fragile and unstable world is correct, then the issue of rich–poor confrontation is likely to acquire a far greater saliency in future. This will demand a comprehensive rethinking of concepts of security, incorporating unprecedented cooperation for sustainable international economic development and environmental management. This needs to be paralleled by progressive demilitarization linked to the establishment of regional and global conflict prevention processes. For peace researchers there is now an even greater imperative for them to deepen their understanding of the interconnected problems of international economic relations, the possibilities of sustainable development and their relationship to security. Peace studies has developed over the past half century and has seen the rigidities and dangers of the Cold War evolve into a more uncertain and unpredictable world. In its own development it has embraced a strong interdisciplinary outlook, a consciously global orientation, and a determined linkage between theory and practice. While it has sought to respond to the problems of conflict since the 1960s, in all probability, its greatest challenges are yet to come.

QUESTIONS

1. What was the impetus for the development of peace studies in the 1950s?

2. Why did peace studies develop beyond its Cold War focus and how did it come to put an emphasis on wider issues such as socio-economic divisions and environmental constraints?

3. Why was there such bitter opposition to peace studies in the 1980s and how did it affect the subsequent development of peace studies?

4. Is it possible for peace studies to be both analytical and normative or does this produce irresolvable tensions?

5. Should students of peace studies engage with policy-makers or should they concentrate on academic discourse?

6. Should peace studies explore underlying causes of conflict or should its main emphasis be on more immediate responses to specific conflict situations?

7. Is the post-9/11 security paradigm of rigorous control of threats an adequate response?

8. Is climate change a threat to security?

9. How are 24-hour news reporting and the evolution of the Internet affecting the coverage of conflict?

10. To what extent have the conflicts in the Persian Gulf since 1980 been about the control of oil?

 FURTHER READING

■ Black, Jeremy (1998), *Why Wars Happen*, London: Reaktion Books. A deeply informed book covering five centuries and using a remarkable range of resources.

■ Booth, Ken, and Dunne, Tim (2002) (eds.), *Worlds in Collision: Terror and the Future of Global Order*, London: Palgrave. Responses of a wide range of scholars and analysts to the 9/11 attacks.

■ Curtis, Mark (2003), *Web of Deceit: Britain's Real Role in the World*, London: Vintage. One of the best examples of careful empirical research combined with critical analysis.

■ Graham, G. (1997), *Ethics and International Relations*, Oxford: Blackwell. A stimulating text raising many issues significant in peace studies.

■ Jeong, Ho-Won (2000), *Peace and Conflict Studies: An Introduction*, London: Ashgate. A good introductory text.

■ Kegley, Charles W., and Blanton, Shannon L. (2009), *World Politics: Trends and Transformations, 2009–10 Update Edition*, New York: St Martin's Press. One of the few international relations textbooks that avoids an excessively Western ethnocentric style.

■ Myrdal, Alva (1980), *The Game of Disarmament: How the United States and Russia Run the Arms Race*, Nottingham: Spokesman Books. A definitive and well-informed account of the Cold War arms race and of processes of international militarization.

■ Ramsbotham, Oliver, Woodhouse, Tom, and Miall, Hugh (2005), *Contemporary Conflict Resolution*, 2nd edn., Cambridge and Malden, MA, Polity Press. The second edition of what has rapidly become the standard work on conflict resolution.

IMPORTANT WEBSITES

- http://www.upeace.org   The UN University for Peace, centred near San Jose in Costa Rica with units across the world.

- http://www.sipri.org   The Stockholm International Peace Research Institute (SIPRI) is one of the world's main centres for the analysis of arms and disarmament.

- http://prio.no   The Peace Research Institute of Oslo (PRIO) is noted, in particular, for its work on civil wars.

- http://www.brad.ac.uk/acad/peace/   Currently the world's largest university centre for peace studies.

- http://www.incore.ulst.ac.uk   INCORE (International Conflict research) is a joint project of the University of Ulster and the UN University.

- http://humansecurityreport.info   The site for the Human Security Report Project.

- http://opendemocracy.net   One of the liveliest open source sites, especially on international issues.

- http://fpif.org   Foreign Policy in Focus is a US site providing wide-ranging analysis on international security and foreign policy themes.

- http://oxfordresearchgroup.org.uk   Oxford Research Group is a UK-based think tank working on innovative approaches to international security, especially the concept of sustainable security.

 Visit the Online Resource Centre that accompanies this book for lots of interesting additional material: www.oxfordtextbooks.co.uk/orc/collins2e/

6 Critical Security Studies: A Schismatic History

DAVID MUTIMER

Chapter Contents

- Introduction: 'follow the sign of the gourd'
- Toronto desire: *Critical Security Studies*
- Copenhagen distinctions
- Aberystwyth exclusions
- Constructing security
- Everyone's Other: poststructuralism and security
- Conclusion

Reader's Guide

This chapter provides a partial history of a label. It is partial both in that it is not, and cannot be, complete, and in that I am both the author of, and participant in, the history. It is therefore partial in the way all other history is partial. The label is 'Critical Security Studies'. The chapter tells a story of the origin of the label and the way it has developed and fragmented since the early 1990s. It sets out the primary claims of the major divisions that have emerged within the literatures to which the label has been applied: constructivism, critical theory, and post-structuralism. Ultimately, the chapter suggests that Critical Security Studies needs to foster an 'ethos of critique' in the study of security, and that the chapter is an instance of that ethos directed at Critical Security Studies itself.

Introduction: 'Follow the sign of the gourd'

Very soon after being identified as the Messiah in *Monty Python's Life of Brian*, Brian is chased by a growing crowd of would-be followers. In his haste to get away, Brian drops the gourd he has just bought and loses one of his sandals. Several of the followers remove one of their shoes and hop about on one foot, convinced this is what their newly found Messiah has told them to do. One follower picks up the shoe and shouts: follow the sign of the shoe. Another picks up the gourd, shouting: follow the sign of the gourd. Perhaps predictably, within seconds, those hopping are fighting those who are following the shoe who are fighting those who are following the gourd. Brian's 'ministry' has splintered into sects before it has even had the chance to establish itself as a ministry. The Python gang were, of course, satirizing the tendency of religious movements to fragment, as they had at the outset of the film satirized the similar tendency of political movements: 'Are you the Judean People's Front?' 'Fuck off! We're the People's Front of Judea ... Judean People's Front ... SPLITTERS!'

Sadly, perhaps, this all too human tendency to fragment into ever-smaller and more exclusive and exclusionary clubs affects academic movements every bit as much as it does religious and political. Any society of ideas is, in addition, a potential source and expression of power. It provides the intellectual resources around which to mobilize people and resources of other kinds: whether these are tithes/alms, ballots/arms, or even tenure/articles. None of this should be in any way surprising to those who work within the area covered by this chapter. While the chapter will show the divisions into which **critical Security Studies** has rapidly fallen, one of the shared commitments of the work it will discuss is to the political potency of ideas. The social world is produced in and through the ideas that make it meaningful, which are themselves necessarily social. A consequence of this observation is that study of the social

world is inextricably bound up with the world it studies; it is part of the productive set of ideas that make the world.

This chapter provides a partial history of a label. It is partial both in that it is not, and cannot be, complete, and in that I am both the author of and a participant in the history. It is therefore partial in the way all other history is partial. The label is 'Critical Security Studies'.[1] It is a label that has (one of) its origins in a conference held at York University in Canada in 1994. As a label it has been fought over rather more than it has been applied. It does not denote a coherent set of views, an 'approach' to security; rather it indicates a desire. It is a desire to move beyond the strictures of security as it was studied and practised in the Cold War, and in particular a desire to make that move in terms of some form of critique. It is a desire articulated in the first line of the first book bearing the title 'Critical Security Studies': 'This book emerged out of a desire to contribute to the development of a self-consciously critical perspective within security studies' (Williams and Krause 1997: p. vii)

The form of security studies against which Critical Security Studies was directed has been neatly captured by one of the proponents of the traditional approach:

> Security studies may be defined as the study of the threat, use, and control of military force. It explores the conditions that make the use of force more likely, the ways that the use of force affects individuals, states, and societies, and the specific policies that states adopt in order to prepare for, prevent, or engage in war.

Walt (1991: 212).

---

[1]When I refer to the label or to the 'field' of enquiry that is increasingly gathered under that label, I will capitalize Critical Security Studies. Otherwise, I leave the terms in the lower case.

KEY QUOTES 6.1

Definitions: Critical Security Studies

Critical Security Studies has proven reasonably resistant to clear definition. This has been largely intentional, as the provision of a definition is limiting in a way that those behind the *Critical Security Studies* text wished to avoid. Nevertheless, there are some definitions in the literature:

'Our appending of the term *critical* to *security studies* is meant to imply more an orientation toward the discipline than a precise theoretical label, and we adopt a small-c definition of *critical* . . . Perhaps the most straightforward way to convey our sense of how *critical* should be understood in this volume is Robert Cox's distinction between problem-solving and critical theory: the former takes "prevailing social and power relationships and the institutions into which they are organized ... as the given framework for action, while the latter calls them into question by concerning itself with their origins and how they might be in the process of changing". Our approach to security studies . . . thus begins from an analysis of the claims that make the discipline possible—not just its claims about the world but also its underlying epistemology and ontology, which prescribe what it means to *make* sensible claims about the world.'

Williams and Krause (1997: pp. x–xi).

'An emerging school of "critical security studies" (CSS) wants to challenge conventional security studies by applying postpositivist perspectives, such as critical theory and poststructuralism. Much of this work . . . deals with the social construction of security, but CSS mostly has the intent (known from poststructuralism as well as from constructivism in international relations) of showing that change is possible because things are socially constituted.'

Buzan, Wæver, and de Wilde (1998: 34–5).

'Critical security studies deal with the social construction of security. The rhetorical nature of "threat discourses" is examined and criticized ... Critical security studies consider not only threats as a construction, but the objects of security as well ... Critical security studies ... have an emancipatory goal.'

Erikkson (1999: 318).

'Critical security studies is a sub-field within the academic discipline of international politics concerned with the pursuit of critical knowledge about security. Critical knowledge implies understandings that attempt to stand outside prevailing structures, processes, ideologies, and orthodoxies while recognising that all conceptualisations of security derive from particular political/theoretical/historical perspectives. Critical theorising does not make a claim to objectivity but rather seeks to provide deeper understandings of oppressive attitudes and behaviour with a view to developing promising ideas by which human society might overcome structural and contingent human wrongs. Security is conceived comprehensively, embracing theories and practices relating to multiple referents, multiple types of threat, and multiple levels of analysis.'

Booth (2007: 30).

The focus on the threat, use, and control of military force imposed a series of important strictures on the study of security in this period. Military forces are generally the preserve of states, and, what is more, there is a normative assumption that they *should* be the preserve of states, even when they are not. Indeed, our common definition of the state is that institution which has a monopoly on the legitimate means of violence. Therefore, by studying the threat, use, and control of military force, security studies privileges the position of the state. Furthermore, such an approach implies that the state is the primary object that is to be secured—that is, the state is the **referent object** of security. Finally, and most obviously, thinking of security as the threat, use, and control of military force reduces security to *military* security, and renders other forms of security as something else.

The various scholars who followed the desire towards a critical security study were troubled by all three of these major assumptions underlying the conventional study of security. They wondered, first of all, whether our concern needed to be only on the state and its security. What of the security of people living within states? The standard assumption of security studies is that the people are secure if the state is secure, but those drawn towards Critical Security Studies wondered about those times when this was not the case: when states ignored the security of some of their people, when they actively oppressed some of their people, or when the state lacked the capacity to provide security for its people. They were therefore led to wonder whether we should be thinking about referent objects other than the state.

Questioning the referent object of security leads inexorably to questioning the exclusive focus on the threat, use, and control of military force. Large, powerful, stable states such as those in which 'security studies' tended to be practised—the United States, the United Kingdom, or Canada—may be seriously threatened only by war. On the other hand, other potential referent objects, particularly people and their collectives, can be threatened in all sorts of ways. Therefore, once you question the referent object of security, you must also question the *nature and scope* of security, and thus of security studies.

Not everyone who questioned the referent object and the nature and scope of security would be drawn to desire for a critical security study, however. That desire was driven by a recognition of the power of ideas, and thus a discomfort with the way traditional security studies focused on the state. The concern was not that there were other objects to be secured in other ways, but rather that the *effect* of studying security as the threat, use, and control of military

force tended *in and of itself* to support and legitimate the power of the state. While other scholars sought to broaden and deepen security studies to consider other referents and other threats, those whose desire ran to a 'self-consciously critical perspective' were centrally concerned with the politics of knowledge. Security studies as it had been practised provided intellectual and, ultimately, moral support to the most powerful institution in contemporary politics: the state. Those drawn to a critical security study sought a different security politics as well as a different security scholarship.

The remainder of the chapter traces what happened as scholars acted on this desire for a self-consciously critical security study. In doing so, it sets out the major fault lines that have emerged among those initially animated by this shared desire. The signs that have driven these fault lines are not simply Monty Python's signs of the shoe and the gourd, but rather represent disagreements about the nature of critique and thus of different forms of critical security study. Thus, while the chapter outlines the sects into which critical desire has fractured, it also sets out a range of answers to the question of what critical security studies might be. My history of these splits begins in 1994.

Toronto desire: *Critical Security Studies*

In May 1994, a small conference was held at York University in Toronto entitled *Strategies in Conflict: Critical Approaches to Security Studies*. It brought together from around the world a variety of scholars, both junior and senior, with interests in security and with a concern about the direction of security studies in the early post-Cold War era. It was in the course of the discussions at and around that conference that the label 'Critical Security Studies' started to be applied to the intellectual project that drew the participants to the conference, and it was used as the title of the book, edited by Keith Krause and Michael C. Williams, that the conference produced: *Critical Security Studies: Concepts and Cases* (1997).

The conference and book were an expression of the desire for self-consciously critical perspectives on security, but they both worked extremely hard to avoid articulating a single perspective in response to that desire: 'Our appending of the term *critical* to *security studies* is meant to imply more an orientation toward the discipline than a precise theoretical label . . .' (Williams and Krause 1997: pp. x–xi). The book therefore served to launch the label Critical Security Studies, but not to fill it with a precise content (see Key Quotes 6.1 for some of the ways in which Critical Security Studies *has* come to be defined). Metaphorically, it threw open the doors of the church of critical security and tried to welcome the followers of the shoe *and* the gourd, and even those hopping around on one foot.

In their contribution to that volume, Krause and Williams aimed to set out the scope of a critical security study, and it has served as a touchstone in the further development of Critical Security Studies. They began their case for Critical Security Studies from the concerns with the traditional conception of security I recounted above. In particular, Krause and Williams began by questioning the referent object of security: who or what is to be secured. The traditional answer to this question is that the referent object is the state: security refers to protecting the state from external threats, and the people living within the territory of the state are considered secure to the degree that the state is secure. As Krause and Williams put it, such a view largely reduces security for the individual to citizenship: 'Yet, while to be a people without a state often remains one of the most insecure conditions of modern life (witness the Kurds or the Palestinians), this move obscures the ways in which citizenship is also at the heart of many structures of insecurity and how security in the contemporary world may be threatened by dynamics far

beyond these parameters' (Krause and Williams 1997a: 43). If the focus on state as a referent object is insufficient, what if we adjust our focus to the individual human being, or perhaps to the community in which humans live? What, indeed, if we ask about the security of humanity as a whole, beyond rather than within the states in which most of us now find ourselves? These are the questions Krause and Williams pose as the foundation of Critical Security Studies. They argue that posing such questions opens a broad and complex agenda for security studies, an agenda that is largely hidden by the traditional focus on the state and the military. Suddenly we can ask about the ways states pose threats to their own people, as well as asking about the responsibility for providing security when the state does not. This question of the responsibility of an international community for the security of those inside a state cannot be seriously posed within traditional security studies, and yet only a few years after the Toronto conference, an International Commission on Intervention and State Sovereignty proclaimed a 'responsibility to protect' those subject to radical insecurity within their own states (see Background 6.1 and see also Chapter 21).

 BACKGROUND 6.1

The responsibility to protect

In 1999 and 2000 the UN Secretary General challenged the members of the UN to address the questions raised by recent incidents of genocide and ethnic cleansing: Somalia, Rwanda, Bosnia, and Kosovo. In particular, in a world of sovereign states, what could and should the international community do when those inside the state were subject to extreme abuses of their human rights? In response, funded largely by the Government of Canada, the International Commission on Intervention and State Sovereignty (ICISS) was formed, and in 2001 the Commission released its report, *The Responsibility to Protect*.

Synopsis of *The Responsibility to Protect*

Basic Principles

A. *State sovereignty implies responsibility,* and the primary responsibility for the protection of its people lies with the state itself.

B. Where a population is suffering serious harm, as a result of internal war, insurgency, repression, or state failure,

and the state in question is unwilling or unable to halt or avert it, the principle of non-intervention yields to the international responsibility to protect.

Elements

The responsibility to protect embraces three specific responsibilities:

A. *The responsibility to prevent*: to address both the root causes and direct causes of internal conflict and other man-made crises putting populations at risk.

B. *The responsibility to react*: to respond to situations of compelling human need with appropriate measures, which may include coercive measures like sanctions and international prosecution, and in extreme cases military intervention.

C. *The responsibility to rebuild*: to provide, particularly after a military intervention, full assistance with recovery, reconstruction and reconciliation, addressing the causes of the harm the intervention was designed to halt or avert.

ICISS (2001: XI).

While the broadening of the security agenda was an important feature of the foundations that Krause and Williams were attempting to lay, rather more significant was the **epistemological** implications they drew from the challenges to the traditional conception of security. They argue that by looking at individuals, and particularly the communities in which they live, a critical security study has to take seriously the ideas, norms, and values that constitute the communities that are to be secured. Traditional security studies treats its referent object as just that: an object. The state is a 'thing' that is found, out there in the world, and subject to objective study by security analysts. By contrast, Krause and Williams argue that thinking of the varied communities in which people live requires an interpretative shift, a recognition that ideas (at least in part) constitute communities and that therefore the ideas of analysts are not entirely separable from the objects studied.

Having opened the doors of what they hoped would be a broad church, Krause and Williams set out the agenda of what would attract scholars to the service. Critical Security Studies would:

- question the referent object of security: while states were clearly important, human beings were both secured and rendered insecure in ways other than by states and military force; Critical Security Studies would engage in research that recognized this and explored its implications;

- consider security as more than just military security: once the referent object was opened up, so too were the questions of what rendered referents insecure, and how security was to be achieved, both for the state and for any other referent objects; and

- change the way security was studied, as the objectivity assumed by traditional approaches to security is untenable; indeed, once you consider the way human communities are constituted by ideas, norms, and values, it becomes clear that this applies even to the state, and so critical security studies becomes a **post-positivist** form of scholarship. With the

Critical Security Studies text, a range of scholars responded to this invitation in a variety of different ways, laying the foundations for the variation in Critical Security Studies we continue to see.

When students and scholars discuss the breadth of the initial desire of *Critical Security Studies*, they will often make almost immediate reference to Mohammed Ayoob's contribution: 'Defining Security: A Subaltern Realist Perspective' (Ayoob 1997). Ayoob focuses on the first of Krause and Williams' challenges, and questions the assumed nature of the state in traditional security studies. He argues that the state in traditional security studies is the state of the advanced, industrial north. He seeks to expand that notion of security to account for the security concerns of the majority of the world's states, concerns that 'mirror the major security concerns evinced by most Western European state makers during the sixteenth to the nineteenth centuries' (Ayoob 1997: 121–2). Thus, while Ayoob questions the nature of the referent object of traditional security studies, he does not introduce alternative possibilities nor does he enquire very far into other means of providing security and he certainly does not contest the epistemological nature of security study.

R. B. J. Walker's contribution to the volume is exemplary of a much more radical break with the traditions of security studies understood as the threat, use, and control of military force. Walker seeks to understand the conditions that make possible certain ways of thinking and speaking about security, and in doing so explores the intimate connections between security and the history of the modern state. Ultimately, he argues that to think seriously about security in the present is to think about the reformulation of politics broadly: 'If the subject of security is the *subject* of security, it is necessary to ask, first and foremost, how the modern subject is being reconstituted and then to ask what security could possibly mean in relation to it' (Walker 1997: 78). This is a profound challenge, but one that has been taken up by a range of scholars who assemble around the label of Critical Security Studies, as we shall see below.

KEY IDEAS 6.1

Security and Ken Booth

One of the most interesting and unusual contributions to *Critical Security Studies* is Ken Booth's chapter 'Security and Self: Reflections of a fallen realist' (Booth 1997). Booth came to critical security studies as a well-established practitioner of traditional strategic studies—in his own words, a realist. That tradition trains you to keep yourself out of your research and writing, because its epistemology instructs the strict separation between the object of analysis and the analyst. Critical Security Studies emerged from a tradition that rejected that separation, and in 'Security and Self' Booth explores the consequences of that change through what he describes as 'an experiment in

autosociology'. He examines the way in which the field has functioned as a discipline, to produce students and teachers of a particular type and to create a field of questions and limit the types of answer that can be given to those questions. The conclusion he reaches is 'that there is a critical relationship between the me/I as a theorist of security and what it means to study security. The argument has been that the meaning of studying security is not simply or necessarily created by the changes out there in the world, but by the changes—or lack of them—in here (who we think we are, and what we think we are doing)'.

Booth (1997: 112).

In between the avowed realism of Mohammed Ayoob and the radical political philosophy of R. B. J. Walker, the *Critical Security Studies* text showcased a number of responses to Krause and Williams's challenges (see Key Ideas 6.1 for one of the more intriguing), which drew on a range of theoretical traditions and explored concrete problems of contemporary security. Several chapters drew on the constructivism that was making an important mark more broadly in international relations. Others were more inclined to draw theoretical inspiration from the heterogeneous products of twentieth-century continental philosophy that are often lumped together as 'poststructuralism'. In addition, Ken Booth and Peter Vale, in considering critical security in the southern African context, began a journey that would lead ultimately

to the post-Marxist, Frankfurt School (see below, the section 'Aberystwyth exclusions').

Krause and Williams expressed the desire that led first to Toronto and then to the *Critical Security Studies* volume as seeking a 'critical perspective' on security. They worked hard to ensure that this critical perspective was not monopolized by a single theoretical approach, and so opened the conference and the volume to a range of theoretical positions. Nevertheless, the desire for a (single) perspective somehow remained as scholars responded to the challenges they laid down in creating their foundation for Critical Security Studies. Thus, despite their claims to Catholicism, Krause and Williams create the conditions for schism—the schism I continue to trace. In doing so, one of the key questions I consider

---

KEY POINTS

- The Critical Security Studies label emerges from a 1994 conference in Toronto, and is then used as the title for the book that conference produced.

- The initial agenda of Critical Security Studies was set by a series of challenges to the traditional conception of security: the state was not a sufficient referent object for security; thinking more broadly about referent objects required thinking more broadly about the sources of both insecurity and security; these forms of rethinking

required an epistemological move beyond the empiricist, positivist traditions of security studies.

- *Critical Security Studies* tried to create a broad church for the critical study of security, seeing 'critical' as an orientation rather than a unique theoretical perspective.

- The desire for a critical security study initially drew scholars from a range of theoretical perspectives, including constructivism, poststructuralism, and post-Marxism.

is: if Critical Security Studies is not a perspective, not a position, what is it? The first answer to this question was given by those of the so-called Copenhagen School.

Copenhagen distinctions

The year after *Critical Security Studies* had appeared, Barry Buzan, Ole Wæver, and Jaap de Wilde published *Security: A New Framework for Analysis* (1998). This book was intended to serve as a relatively comprehensive statement of what has come to be known as 'securitization studies', or the Copenhagen School.[2] I will not discuss Copenhagen in detail, as it is treated elsewhere in this volume (see Chapter 9), but it warrants a short sideline, for it has made two important contributions to the history I am tracing.

Security: A New Framework for Analysis is built around two important conceptual developments in the study of security: Barry Buzan's notion of sectoral analysis of security and Ole Wæver's concept of 'securitization'. Both of these ideas have helped to inform the broad church of Critical Security Studies, but it is the notion of 'securitization' that has been the more theoretically important. 'Securitization' is perhaps the most significant conceptual development that has emerged specifically within security studies in response to the epistemological challenge Krause and Williams note. Essentially, Wæver suggests that we treat security as a speech act: that is, a concrete action that is performed by virtue of its being said. 'Securitization' raises a number of very interesting questions that have informed critical security study since Wæver introduced the concept.

Despite this influence on Critical Security Studies, the Copenhagen School has sought to distance itself from Critical Security Studies. In part this is a function of an incoherence inherent in the approach between the sectoral analysis of security and the concept of securitization. While securitization opens the possibility of the radical openness of social life, the sectoral approach, as it had developed before merging into the Copenhagen School, draws on a largely objectivist epistemology. In other words, the epistemological underpinnings of the concept of securitization do not cohere with those of the sectoral analysis of security. It is the epistemology of securitization, however, that does cohere with that called for by the desire to a critical security study. In *Security: A New Framework for Analysis*, the authors argue that Critical Security Studies is informed by poststructuralism and constructivism, and thus is open to the possibility of social change. By contrast, they suggest that the Copenhagen approach recognizes the social construction of social life, but contends that construction in the security realm is sufficiently stable over the long run that it can be *treated as* objective. In other words, they resolve the incoherence by assuming long-term stability and so enabling a largely positivist epistemology (Buzan, Wæver, and de Wilde 1998: 34–5).

The explicit separation of the Copenhagen School from Critical Security Studies did more than simply announce that Copenhagen is *sui generis*. One function of the text has been to create 'Critical Security Studies' as something more concrete and less heterogeneous than the original desire. The Copenhagen authors talk of Critical Security Studies an 'an emerging school', and they shorten it to CSS. What is more, they ascribe to this emerging school two specific theoretical positions, poststructuralism and constructivism. This text, then, marks an important moment in the creation of Critical Security Studies as something other than an orientation towards the discipline, and also effects conceptual exclusions that are the subject of contestation, not least by scholars at Aberystwyth University, who have considerable institutional claim to the Critical Security Studies label.

---

[2]Bill McSweeny (1996) is generally credited with coining the label 'Copenhagen School' to refer to the work of Buzan, Wæver, and a series of collaborators.

KEY POINTS

- *Security: A New Framework for Analysis* sets out a distinctive position on security studies, often known as 'the Copenhagen School', blending Buzan's 'security sectors' with Wæver's 'securitization'.

- There is an epistemological incoherence at the heart of the Copenhagen School between the epistemology of sectoral analysis and that of securitization.

- The Copenhagen School resolves its incoherence by arguing that the social production of security is sufficiently stable to be treated objectively.

- *Security: A New Framework for Analysis* seeks to distinguish between its approach and Critical Security Studies, and in doing so tends to produce Critical Security Studies as an emerging 'school'.

Aberystwyth exclusions

Rather ironically, the most aggressive attempt to produce a coherent approach for critical security studies—to marshal all adherents to the sign of the shoe or the gourd, but not both—has been made from a position largely excluded by the Copenhagen School's characterization of Critical Security Studies as being informed by constructivism and poststructuralism. The attempt has been focused around scholars based in Aberystwyth (indeed, Steve Smith (2005) calls it the Welsh School), and has found its most complete expression to date in two recent volumes: *Critical Security Studies and World Politics* (2005) and *Theory of World Security* (2007). Central to both of these books is the work of Ken Booth, who edited the first and wrote the second. Indeed, *Theory of World Security* is intended to be a fairly definitive statement of Booth's thirty-year research programme leading to a critical theory of security. (Booth 2007: pp. xvii–xviii)

In both these texts, Booth is explicit in arguing that not everyone who would consider themselves working within Critical Security Studies will accept his orientation to a critical security theory. In other words, he is making a clear case for restrictive understanding of critical security theory—he is saying to us, follow the sign of the gourd, and means it. He argues, in fact, that the formulation of a singular 'critical security theory' is the second stage of Critical Security Studies work. Booth's intervention, therefore, is an unapologetic desire for

fragmentation. As he says: 'There are times when definite lines have to be drawn' (Booth 2005a: 260). He distances himself sharply from Krause and Williams of *Critical Security Studies*, rejecting the broad church in favour of a single tradition aimed at giving rise to a coherent critical theory of security.

In his first cut at elaborating a critical theory of security in 2005, Booth followed his Aberystwyth colleague Richard Wyn Jones, who had drawn on the Frankfurt School tradition to think about security theory in his 1999 book *Security, Strategy and Critical Theory*. Both see the Frankfurt School tradition as centrally important to the development of a critical theory for security studies. In *Critical Security Studies and World Politics*, Booth throws his net slightly wider than Frankfurt in identifying the tradition, adding Gramscian, Marxist, and Critical International Relations to the Frankfurt School. In other words, Booth drew on the range of post-Marxist social theory, particularly as it has been drawn into International Relations, with pride of place to the work of the Frankfurt School in general and Jürgen Habermas in particular.

The theoretical net of Booth's critical theory of security was expanded still further with 2007's *Theory of World Security*. Here he took an explicitly eclectic approach to theory building, engaging in *Perlenfischerie* (pearl fishing), following the term of Hannah Arendt. His first set of pearls is the same set he drew from the post-Marxist oyster bed in 2005,

KEY IDEAS 6.2

Themes of post-Marxist Critical Theory

- All knowledge is a social process.

- Traditional theory promotes the flaws of naturalism and reductionism.

- Critical theory offers a basis for political and social progress.

- The test of theory is emancipation.

- Human society is its own invention.

- Regressive theories have dominated politics among nations.

- The state and other institutions must be denaturalized.

- Progressive world order values should inform the means and ends of an international politics committed to enhancing world security.

Booth (2005a: 268).

---

and still with Frankfurt School the first among them. To this he adds a second, lesser, set of ideas: world order, peace studies, feminism, historical sociology, and social idealism. He calls the whole of the string of pearls that his fishing produced *emancipatory realism*.

What would such a critical security theory look like? Booth argues that there are eight themes that can be drawn from the collection of post-Marxist theory useful to a critical security theory (the eight are summarized in Key Ideas 6.2). He begins with the central claim of the Frankfurt School, that all knowledge is a social process—that is, knowledge is not simply 'there', but rather is produced socially, and thus politically, and there are 'interests of knowledge'. Knowledge benefits some and disadvantages others; it is, in the noted words of Robert Cox in International Relations, 'always for someone and for some purpose'. A critical security theory, therefore, must reveal the politics behind seeming neutral knowledge. Such a conception of knowledge implies a critique of traditional theory, including traditional security theory, which, by not recognizing its political origins and content, tends to a naturalism, assuming the ability to maintain a rigid division between the analyst and the social world she is analysing. If Critical Theory, therefore, reveals the false naturalism of traditional theory and the political content of all knowledge, it

provides the basis for social change—indeed for progress. This third theme, of the possibility of progress, leads to a fourth: that the test of a social theory is its capacity for fostering **emancipation**. Change is possible, and progressive change is emancipatory.

The first four themes Booth derives from the broad Critical Theory tradition in social theory. To these four he adds four gathered from the specific, emergent critical tradition in International Relations. The first is that human society is its own invention. Indeed, this is a necessary condition for the operation of his earlier themes, for only if society is a social invention can knowledge serve as the basis for social change and open the possibility of emancipation. The second theme that Booth derives from critical IR is a particular claim about contemporary world politics: that regressive theories have dominated the field. If all knowledge is *for* someone and *for* some purpose, regressive theories are the ones that are *for* those presently in power with the purpose of maintaining their dominance. Critical IR theory has shown how the mainstream theories, including security studies, serve just this purpose. If this is true, then, the final two themes Booth develops are aimed at overcoming the regressive nature of world politics. The first is that the state and other international institutions must be *denaturalized*, so as to open the possibility of change, and finally that, in effecting that change to global (security) practices, politics must be governed by emancipatory values.

These themes enable Booth to argue that a critical-security theory can serve as the basis for answering three sets of crucial questions in relation to security:

- First, what is real? If we reject naturalism, which assumes that the social world can be treated as objective in the same fashion as the natural world, then we cannot assume that the social world we investigate is 'real' in the same sense as the physical. Critical Theory's focus on knowledge provides a way into understanding social **ontology**, and thus the creation of social facts.

- Second, Critical Theory of this kind provides a means of thinking about knowledge, or the epistemology of social life. It directs our attention to the interests that underlie knowledge claims, and leads us to ask: whom particular forms of knowledge are for, and what function they serve in supporting the interests of those people or groups.

- Finally, it suggests asking the old Leninist question, what is to be done? Critical Theory is a theory of praxis, a step in a process of political engagement designed to transform the world. As Marx put it: the point is not to understand the world; the point is to change it.

These reflections provide the basis for a specific critical theory of security (see Key Quotes 6.2 for Booth's definition of this theory). It draws on a relatively coherent body of social theory and its application to International Relations, and aims to inform scholarship and political practice in the future. While developed largely in parallel to the critical tradition in International Relations, Booth's critical security theory is quite clearly designed to provide a specific theory of security within critical IR. What this means is that Booth and his colleagues in the Welsh School have provided a clear answer to the question I posed at the end of the discussion of *Critical Security Studies*: critical security study *should* be guided by a single, specific theory, and

that theory should be informed by Critical Theory, with capital letters.

> **KEY QUOTES 6.2**
>
> ### Critical security theory
>
> In his recent work, Ken Booth (2007) has argued for the development of a distinctive critical theory of security, and proposed the following definition of such a theory, beginning from the Frankfurt School of Critical Theory:
>
> 'Critical security theory is both a theoretical commitment and a political orientation concerned with the construction of world security. As a theoretical commitment it is a framework of ideas deriving from a tradition of critical global theorising made up of two main strands: critical social theory and radical international relations theory . . . As a political orientation it is informed by the aim of enhancing world security through emancipatory politics and networks of communities at all levels, including the potential community of all communities—common humanity.'
>
> Booth (2007: 30–1).

In order to make the case for exclusion as forcefully as possible, once he has set out the elements of a critical security theory, Booth (2005a: 269–71; 2007: 160–81) distinguishes it from other possible sources of critical security study. He explains, in other words, what is wrong with following the sign of the gourd or with taking off our shoes and hopping around on one foot. In particular he distinguishes critical security theory from four pretenders: feminism, Copenhagen School, constructivism, and poststructuralism.

The exclusion of feminism is the most troubling to Booth's position in some ways, but in others the easiest to achieve. As most feminist writing will freely admit, there are various feminisms that draw in their turn from a wide variety of social-theory traditions in developing analyses of gender. These traditions include the Critical Theory tradition from which Booth proceeds. Therefore, gender analysis can be considered already to be within

Critical Theory, and thus within a critical security theory; however, other forms of feminist theorizing are as antithetical to critical security theory as their theoretical traditions are to critical theory more broadly. The Copenhagen School is similarly dismissed with relative ease. The near-naturalism of the Copenhagen approach to society—so stable it can be treated as objective—leaves it 'only marginally "critical"', and in Booth's eyes (2005a: 271) suffers the same forms of incoherence I noted above.

There remain two challengers to the critical security theory Booth champions, the same two that the Copenhagen School identified in *Security: A New Framework for Analysis*. The first is constructivism, which Booth (2007: 152–3) argues is not a theory at all, but rather an orientation to world politics that serves as a basis on which to reject traditional theories. While Booth's argument may be true, it ignores the possibility, which I will explore below, that there are within that orientation various constructivist theories that do have something to say about security—just as other orientations, including Booth's, contain a number of specific theories within them. For Booth (2005a: 270) that leaves only poststructuralism, which is just too dangerous with its toxic mix of obscurantism, relativism, and faux radicalism'. In other words, Booth (2007: 177–8) argues, poststructuralism provides no basis for political action.

As might be imagined, and as Booth freely admits, the dismissal of constructivism and poststructuralism as elements of Critical Security Studies is not shared by all. These two theoretical positions represent, in fact, the conceptual underpinning of most of what might be drawn under the label, understood as the broad church. But even among them the sign of the shoe is defended against those hopping around on one foot.

KEY POINTS

- Ken Booth, Richard Wyn Jones, and their Welsh School colleagues argue for a specific critical security theory.

- The tradition within which they develop this theory is the post-Marxist tradition identified with Gramscian and other Marxist International Relations and, particularly, with Frankfurt School Critical Theory.

- The elaboration of the Critical Theory tradition gives rise to eight themes and a definition of critical security theory.

- Critical security theory provides the possibility of answering three key questions: what is real, what is knowledge, and what is to be done?

- Critical Security Studies should be organized around this critical security theory, and should not include feminism, the Copenhagen School, constructivism, and particularly poststructuralism.

Constructing security

If we exclude the Copenhagen School and feminist writings on security,[3] and further if we watch those committed to a critical theory of security build a hard and fast line between themselves and the rest of what might be considered Critical Security Studies, what are we left with? Keith Krause provided an answer in a review of the research programme of Critical Security Studies

---

[3]The exclusion of feminism in the production of the Critical Security Studies label is a truly fascinating issue, worthy of complete treatment on its own. As we have seen, Ken Booth effects this exclusion through arguing that feminism is a broad church in its own right and that certain feminist analyses of gender form an important element of Critical Theory. Keith

Krause (1998: 324 n. 4) effects a similar exclusion in his review of the scholarship of Critical Security Studies: 'I have not treated the principal themes of feminist or gender scholarship on security as a separate category. These are dealt with in detail by [others].' Lene Hansen (2000) has reflected on this same exclusion in the case of the Copenhagen School.

in 1998, and it is the same answer to which Ken Booth came: constructivism and poststructuralism. Indeed, as with *Critical Security Studies*, Krause's 1998 review largely elides any difference between these two positions—the church is still broad, and so you can follow the sign of the shoe or take off your shoe and hop around on one foot if you like.

In an attempt to impose some order on the studies that compose Critical Security Studies, without resorting to the definitional strictures employed by both Booth and the Copenhagen School, Krause organizes a range of literature into a broad research programme. The effect of this move is to provide a characterization of Critical Security Studies, which, while still inclusive, clearly privileges constructivism. He organizes the scholarship of Critical Security Studies under three headings: the construction of threats and responses; the construction of the objects of security; possibilities for transforming the security dilemma. Krause explicitly does not intend these headings to capture the full range of critical security scholarship, nor does he suggest that scholars will tend to treat these issues separately. Nevertheless, the effect, particularly appearing at a time in which the Critical Security Studies label was being established, and coming from one of the editors of the *Critical Security Studies* volume, was to mark the character of Critical Security Studies as concerned with 'the social construction of security' (Eriksson 1999: 318).

There are two important features of Krause's review in the story of the creation of the Critical Security Studies label. The first is that it demonstrates the impressive array of research that is being conducted and published to which this label could be attached, countering, as Krause (1998: 316) notes, 'the oft-heard charge that critical scholarship is inevitably sloppy or unsystematic'. Secondly, he is able to derive from the review a characterization of Critical Security Studies that is far more specific than that provided by *Critical Security Studies*, and is clearly distinct from Booth's critical security theory. Krause suggests

that there are six claims that tie Critical (Security) Studies together:

1. Principal actors (states and others) are social constructs.

2. These actors are constituted through political practices.

3. The structures of world politics are neither unchanging nor determining because they too are socially constructed.

4. Knowledge of the social world is not objective, as there is no divide between the social world and knowledge of that world.

5. Natural-science methodology is not appropriate for social science, which requires an interpretative method.

6. The purpose of theory is not explanation in terms of generalizable causal claims, but contextual understanding and practical knowledge.

A pair of recent books by Alexandra Gheciu both illustrate the approach Krause sets out and demonstrate the sort of rigorous scholarship that is possible within the research programme. In *NATO in the New Europe* (2005b) Gheciu explores the socialization of former Eastern Bloc states by NATO in the years after the end of the Cold War. Socialization is an important idea in social construction, because it is the means by which actors are constructed to become members of a particular social system or community. Gheciu provides a detailed account of the way in which NATO socialized the Czech Republic and Romania to become 'Europeans' in a sense that allied with the liberal democratic notions of what it meant to be European in the 1990s. Furthermore, she shows how this socialization was an explicit security strategy, which she terms a Kantian or 'inside' approach to security—the formation of the state as a particular kind of state and thereby productive of security (Gheciu 2005b: 7–9) In the more recent *Securing Civilization* (2008), Gheciu explores the 'inside' approach to security further, by looking at the ways in which three key European security institutions—the EU, NATO, and the Organization for Security and

Cooperation in Europe (OSCE)—respond to the post-9/11 threat of international terrorism. At the heart of these responses is the constitution of members as civilized/secure and those outside as barbaric/threatening (Gheciu 2008: 5).

The focus on the social construction of agents and structures, together with a commitment to interpretative method, contextual understanding and practical knowledge, marks Krause's account of Critical Security Studies as largely rooted within the tradition of constructivism in International Relations, a tradition Gheciu (2005b), for example, then explicitly claims. Constructivism clearly shares homologies with both post-Marxist Critical Theory and poststructuralism, but it is not the same as either. Those following the sign of the gourd are welcome, as are those hopping around on one foot, but they may feel that they are then expected to join in following the sign of the shoe.

> **KEY POINTS**
>
> - Social constructivism forms an important strand within Critical Security Studies.
> - Constructivism takes agents and structures as constituted in and through political practices.
> - Constructivism denies the division between the social world and the analyst, and thus seeks an interpretative rather than a naturalist methodology.
> - While attempting to maintain the broad church, the constructive account of Critical Security Studies privileges social constructivism.

Everyone's Other: poststructuralism and security

Ken Booth's antipathy to poststructural approaches to International Relations in general and security studies in particular reflects a common, and commonly virulent, reaction. In addition to obscurantist, relativist, and faux radical, approaches labelled poststructural have been called prolix and self-indulgent (Walt 1991), and accused of having no research programme (Keohane 1988). The virulence of the rejection of poststructural work reflects, I would suggest, its radical promise. It shares with the rest of the work discussed in this chapter a pair of key commitments: a rejection of positivist epistemology and hence methodology, and commitment to social critique. However, unlike any of the other forms of critical scholarships I have thus far discussed, it does not stop short of the radical implications of these commitments. Indeed, a crucial commitment shared by poststructural scholarship but not by other forms of critical theory is a rejection of overarching grand narratives, and thus an acceptance that knowledge claims are always unstable and contingent. As a fairly sympathetic critic has put it: 'it is for this reason that most social constructivists and critical security studies writers are at such pains to establish the difference between their work and that of poststructuralists. Put simply, poststructuralists deny the form of foundations for knowledge claims that dominate the security studies debate. As can be imagined, this has led to much hostility toward poststructuralism ... (S. Smith 2005: 49)

The work that is generally labelled poststructural—and, as with the other labels we are discussing, it is more commonly applied by others than by a scholar to her own work—draws on a series of intellectual traditions largely having their roots in French philosophy (as opposed to the German philosophy that animates the Welsh School, for example). While the work draws on an eclectic collection of writing, the most common points of departure are the work of Jacques Derrida and

THINK POINT 6.1

Traditional subjects in a poststructural gaze

Poststructural writing can take on subjects that on the surface appear to be the same as those found in traditional security studies. What the poststructural traditions provide, however, is often a radically different way of asking questions and providing answers. Here are two examples: the first, 'about' nuclear weapons; and the second, Canadian policy towards missile defence.

Hugh Gusterson, *Nuclear Rites* (1998)

Gusterson is a social anthropologist whose discipline privileges a particular kind of fieldwork leading to ethnographic writing. Traditionally such ethnographies are written about others' cultures, often the cultures of indigenous populations that have been (largely) untouched by European expansion. (Fortunately for the anthropologists, such cultures are often found on south Pacific islands!) Gusterson is part of a movement in anthropology turning the ethnographic gaze on his own society. In *Nuclear Rites* he engages in an ethnographic study of the scientists at one of the US nuclear weapons laboratories. Making use of both ethnographic method and Foucault's notions of discipline, he investigates the ways in which the laboratories function to create the conditions of possibility for the building, testing,

and deployment of nuclear weapons. As the title suggests, some of what he finds is that the design, building, testing, and deployment of nuclear weapons have evolved into a ritualized culture among the scientists that has little or nothing to do with the stories we tell ourselves about the needs of deterrence and defence.

Marshall Beier, 'Postcards from the Outskirts of Security' (2001)

In his study, Beier reflects on a study trip he took with a number of other Canadian scholars to visit the North American Aerospace Defense (NORAD) headquarters. NORAD is located in the middle of a mountain, usually identified as being on the outskirts of Colorado Springs. It is actually closer to the small town of 'Security' Colorado, and Beier uses this observation as the starting point for a reflection on the ways in which semiotic markers can affect group dynamics and contribute to the disciplining of dissent. He examines the ways in which opposition to missile defence was silenced within the tour, and considers the implications for the decision the Canadian government had to take on whether and how to participate in the US missile defence programme.

Michel Foucault.[4] The rejection of grand narratives—such as those of 'progress' and 'emancipation' that inform the Welsh School—together with the varied and eclectic theoretical inspirations for poststructural work, means that there are no simple summaries or sets of bullet points that can

be adduced, as with the other approaches. Ultimately, to borrow an expression, the only way in is through, and many of the texts called poststructural demand close and careful reading.[5] Therefore, rather than providing such a summary, I will consider a number of a number of important authors and texts that are

---

[4]In his attack on poststructural IR, Booth suggests that most of those in IR who work from Foucault use his work on psychiatry, and then goes on to dismiss the IR work through criticisms of this early work of Foucault. To my knowledge, few working in poststructural security studies draw extensively on *Madness and Civilization*, an early work Foucault called 'archaeology', but rather on the later genealogical work, particularly *Discipline and Punish*, *The History of Sexuality*, and two incomplete elements of a larger programme on politics and war, *Society must be Defended* and 'Governmentality'. See, among others, Campbell (1998a), Gusterson (1998), Edkins (2003), Duffield (2007), Grayson (2008), and Dillon and Lobo-Guerrero (2008).

[5]One of the concerns with much of the criticism directed at poststructural work in IR generally is that it is not always founded on such a reading of the texts it purports to criticize. As David Campbell (1998a: 210) notes: 'What is most interesting about the conventional critics of "postmodernism" is the unvarnished vehemence that adorns their attacks. Accused of "self-righteousness", lambasted as "evil", castigated for being "bad IR" and "meta-babble", and considered congenitally irrational, "postmodernists" are regarded as little better than unwelcome asylum seekers from a distant war zone. Of course, had the critics reached their conclusions via a considered reading of what is now a considerable literature in international relations, one would repay the thought with a careful engagement of their own arguments. Sadly there is not much thought to repay.'

routinely cited, and thus form an important part of the story of the production of the Critical Security Studies label—even though few, if any, of these authors would slap the label on their own work.

One of the first of these works is Bradley Klein's 1994 book *Strategic Studies and World Order*. In terms of the history of Critical Security Studies, the importance of the text is that it took on one of the central problems that motivate the later development of the label: what are the political consequences of traditional security studies—that is, strategic studies. Klein considered strategic studies as a discourse constitutive of the global state and military system it purports to study. His approach to that discourse is informed by Foucault's work, which Foucault discusses as a history of the present, or a genealogy. Genealogical work seeks to reveal the historical trajectory that gave meaning to particular discourses and how they then function in the present. Famously, Foucault provided such genealogies—for example, of criminal punishment and Western sexuality. Klein turns this form of investigation on strategic studies, and in the process makes a compelling case for one of the founding assumptions of Critical Security Studies: that theories about the world constitute that world, and thus that theory, including security theory, has political effects. What Klein shows is that strategic studies is productive of the very system that makes contemporary global violence possible.

Simon Dalby's first book, *Creating the Second Cold War*, similarly turns the poststructural gaze on a central problem of conventional security studies: in his case, the renewed Cold War confrontation under the Reagan administration in the United States. Dalby explores the intellectual underpinnings of US security policy, or, as he puts it in his subtitle, the discourse of politics. As a geographer, Dalby (1990) is particularly concerned with the ways in which geopolitics serves as a discourse underpinning the militarism of Reagan's international policy, and it is a concern with geopolitics as discourse which has then animated much of the rest of his work. In 1998 he teamed with Gearóid Ó Tuathail to edit *Rethinking Geopolitics*, which sought 'to radicalize conventional notions of geopolitics through a series of studies of its proliferating, yet often unacknowledged and under-theorized, operation in world politics past, present and future' (Dalby and Ó Tuathail 1998: 2). More recently Dalby turned his attention to security studies more explicitly, and explored the effects of geopolitical discourse in relation to attempts to 'securitize' the environment, and the environmental effects of this discourse when it largely ignored the environment (Dalby 2002).

Perhaps the most widely cited of the scholars working within these traditions is David Campbell, and for good reason. As Steve Smith (2005: 50) notes, 'David Campbell has written some of the best empirical work in poststructuralist security studies'. The first of these works is *Writing Security*, in which Campbell explores the manner in which the United States has been produced in and through discourses of danger. He asks of US Foreign Policy some of the same questions, inspired by Foucault, that Klein used to think about Strategic Studies. In the book, he shows how Foreign Policy discourse is inseparable from what he terms foreign policy (the capitalization is the key)—that is, the production of an American self and a (dangerous) other, or a (secure) domestic and a (threatening) foreign. As with Klein's work, the contribution to Critical Security Studies thinking is clear. In the case of Campbell's work, both what Critical Security Studies will call the *referent object* and the *agent* of security (the state in both instances) is shown to be produced in its own practices.

The principal objection Ken Booth (2005a: 270) raised to poststructuralism as part of a broad Critical Security Studies church was its supposed inability to inspire a politics, and in particular its inability to '"shape up" to the test of Fascism as a serious political challenge'. This is, of course, a serious criticism of any form of critical theory that sees itself in any sense part of a politics of change, as it is difficult to imagine a politics more in need of change than Fascism. It is also an argument repeatedly raised by critics of poststructural scholarship, regardless of how many times it is answered. In Campbell's case,

THINK POINT 6.2

Researching Bosnia

The challenge of the wars in the former Yugoslavia, particularly the war in Bosnia, attracted the attention of a number of scholars in the poststructural tradition. The ethical and political challenge of the violence is central to these works, but what also emerges is a concern with the place of Western scholarship, and the nature of the research enterprise. In order to establish his argument about the political potential of deconstruction, Campbell (1998b) first provides a deconstructive reading of the violence in Bosnia. He explores the production of identities in Bosnia that enabled the violence of the wars and their attendant 'ethnic cleansing'. Making use of Derrida's notion of 'ontopology', he explores the production of identities tied to place in such a way that the other could not be allowed even to inhabit certain spaces without undermining the self. He then turns to the responses, particularly the international responses, to the violence, and shows how various Western discourses (including security studies) created the conditions that made the genocidal violence in Bosnia possible.

While critical of some of the intellectual moves Campbell makes, Elizabeth Dauphinée takes up similar themes in her recent book, *The Ethics of Researching War: Looking for Bosnia* (2008). Dauphinée too is concerned with the place of Western discourses in the violence of Bosnia, but she does not limit herself to an impersonal account of scholarly influence. Rather, she turns the scholarly gaze on her own place as researcher, asking what it means that, in the words with which she opens the text, 'I am building my career on the loss of a man named Stojan Sokolovic (and on the loss of many millions of others who may or may not resemble him)' (Dauphinée 2008: 1). Her answer takes seriously the poststructural recognition that the observer is never, and can never be, detached from what she observes, and in doing so provides a telling account of the limits of our ethics, and our research.

Questions of research are also central to Lene Hansen in her *Security as Practice: Discourse Analysis and the Bosnian War* (2006). The book also picks up the themes Campbell developed in both *Writing Security* (1992) and *National Deconstruction* (1998b), as Hansen develops a poststructural account of identity and foreign policy, and then uses that account to inform an analysis of Western policy in response to the Bosnian War. Where Campbell analyses Bosnia in part to answer the critics' challenge that poststructuralism provides no politics, Hansen analyses the same war in part to answer the challenge that poststructuralism does not engage in rigorous research. Hansen sets out a detailed method of analysis, drawing among others on Foucault and Derrida, which she then applies to Bosnia. Indeed, she concludes by comparing her analysis to Campbell's in an attempt to open an 'intra-poststructuralist debate', but holds true to her starting point by doing so not to determine who is right and wrong, but rather to explore the analytical effects of methodological choices (Hansen 2006: 217–20).

---

his most extended answer came in his 1998 book *National Deconstruction: Violence, Identity, and Justice in Bosnia*. The Yugoslav wars of the 1990s posed exactly the sort of challenge alluded to by Booth, as it appeared to mark the return to Europe of the kind of violent Fascism to which all had said 'never again' in 1945. (For a number of responses to Bosnia, see Think Point 6.2) In a sophisticated and compelling text, Campbell engages directly with the question Booth demands to be answered: what is to be done?

Campbell's answer (1998b: 196) to the question of politics demands to be read, and read closely, but centres around fostering the ethos of democracy: 'Democracy is not a substance, a fixed set of values, a particular kind of community, or a strict institutional form ... what makes democracy democratic, and what marks democracy as a singular political form, is a particular attitude or spirit, an ethos, that constantly has to be fostered.' This is not an answer that many find comfortable, because it provides no simple blueprint, no single strategy. Fostering the ethos of democracy does not mean that when you hold a competitive election and anoint a 'democratic' government your work is done, and so the politics that is demanded by Campbell's accounts of responsibility and democracy are profoundly more difficult and challenging than those found in most areas of security studies, even Critical Security Studies. The difficulty has led, in fact, to a concerted effort among a number of scholars working in a poststructural tradition to consider issues of ethics and responsibility in relation to 'the worst'. Much of their work draws its philosophical inspiration, in part, from the work of Emmanuel Levinas, as did Campbell in developing his arguments about a politics in response to Bosnia.

The idea of fostering an ethos is also central to the notion of critique in much of the writing labelled poststructural. Both Welsh School critical security theory and constructivist Critical Security Studies provide an answer to one of the questions I posed at the outset: what is meant by 'critical'. For the Welsh School, it involves revealing the interests behind knowledge claims, with a goal of social change. Similarly for the constructivists, it is reaching contextual and practical understanding to know whom knowledge claims serve. Both of these are relatively static conceptions of critique: they can be done in a finite sense. Just as Campbell argues democracy is never reached, but rather is an ethos ever to be fostered, so too is critique. Poststructural writing sees its critical purposes as fostering an ethos of critique, always working to destabilize 'truths', revealing their contingency and the nature of their production. It is not a finite project, however, but rather a process in which to be constantly engaged. As with its politics, the poststructural conception of critique is difficult for many to accept, because again it is not easy. It does not allow for finite claims and finished projects, and, as students of society, we are trained to provide 'findings' and test them in a settled fashion.

Neither Bradley Klein nor David Campbell—nor indeed a number of others often also included in a poststructural security studies list, such as James Der Derian, R. B. J. Walker, Cynthia Weber, or even Michael Dillon—applies the label 'Critical Security Studies' to his work. They are surely and avowedly engaged in critical scholarship—that is the fostering of an ethos of critique—and much of their work is centrally concerned with security. Michael Dillon (1996), for example, has written an extended political philosophy of security out of the tradition of French social theory, and his more recent work explores Foucault's notions of biopolitics in relation to the post-9/11 security strategies of the United States and other western powers (Dillon 2006; Dillon and Lobo-Guerrero 2008; Dillon and Neal 2008). Similarly, R. B. J. Walker is one of the leaders of a large research programme on 'Liberty and Security', in relation to the contemporary practices of the war on terrorism.

While most of these scholars have not entered the broad church of Critical Security Studies, their work has inspired some within it to take off a shoe and jump around on one foot. In doing so, some have hopped right back outside again, wondering what applying the label Critical Security Studies to their work adds to the project in which they are engaged. Indeed, the ethos of critique that work of this kind aims to foster demands that we turn our critical gaze on the very scholarly practices in which we are engaged. It demands that we ask about the politics of our own labelling, including the Critical Security Studies label, one of whose stories I am telling.

KEY POINTS

- 'Poststructuralism' is a marker for a diverse set of writing inspired by a number of, generally French, philosophers including Michel Foucault and Jacques Derrida.

- A number of works in this tradition within International Relations are claimed by Critical Security Studies, most notably those of Bradley Klein, David Campbell, R. B. J. Walker and Michael Dillon.

- Despite criticism to the contrary, poststructural work does provide answers to questions of political action, just not the kind of comfortable answers many are seeking.

- Central to the political and critical nature of poststructural writing is the idea of fostering an ethos of democracy and an ethos of critique. These are never finite, never reached, but for which we must constantly strive.

Conclusion

This chapter has been unlike many in a textbook of this kind. I have not provided clear and unproblematic answers to questions such as: what is critical security studies, what is meant by 'critical' and 'security', how do you 'do' critical security studies. Rather, I have tried to turn the ethos of critique that should animate a critical study of security on the very label I was asked to discuss. I have told a story of the short history of the label and its politics, a story that attempts to reveal how Critical Security Studies came to be what it is, and what the effects are of that coming. (For a recent attempt to repair some of the divisions that emerge in that history, see Background 6.2.) Questions of history and politics are the questions—though by no means the only questions—that an ethos of critique leads us to ask, and the kind of story I tell here is one of the ways—though, again, by no means the only way—that they can be answered.

 BACKGROUND 6.2

Parisian enCASEment

In 2006 a group of scholars attempted to reconstruct the broad church of Critical Security Studies that had been central to the original Toronto desire. These scholars met first in conference in Paris, and gathered together students of security from across Europe who shared a commitment to some form of critical scholarship about security, broadly conceived. Out of this meeting was produced an article later published in *Security Dialogue* as 'Critical Approaches to Security in Europe: A Networked Manifesto', with the author given as 'The CASE Collective'. The goal of the collective was explicit in aiming to overcome precisely the sorts of divisions I have outlined in this chapter: 'the aim of working and writing as a collective, a network of scholars who do not agree on everything yet share a common perspective, is based on a desire to break with the competitive dynamic of individualist research agendas and to establish a network that not only facilitates dialogue but is also able to speak with a collective voice' (CASE Collective 2006: 444). Specifically, they sought to bridge the gaps they saw between the 'Copenhagen', 'Welsh', and 'Paris' schools (with the latter a largely poststructural position centred around Didier Bigo at *Science Po* in Paris).

The near impossibility of constructing a broad church is clearly demonstrated in the responses the CASE Collective generated. In a series of rejoinders published by the journal, Andreas Bhenke, Mark Salter, and Christine Sylvester took the Collective to task for a series of exclusions they effected even in their attempts to forge and inclusive network (Bhenke 2007; Salter 2007; Sylvester 2007). Bhenke and Salter take the Collective to task for its 'European' focus, asking both what is meant by 'Europe' (Bhenke 2007: 106), and what about the critical scholars who are clearly not European in any sense, but still involved in the critical security project (Salter 2007: 114). Bhenke (2007: 108) also wonders about the exclusion of theoretical positions from this reformed church, as there seems no room for his interest in Carl Schmitt, for example. Sylvester makes a similar, and even more damning critique, in asking where the feminists are in this network—even a poststructural feminist security scholar such as Lene Hansen, who actually works in Copenhagen, but whose work is missing from this broad network (Sylvester 2007).

Since the conference in 1994 with which I began this story, the issue of 'security' has taken on a greatly renewed significance. During the Cold War, the Soviet–American rivalry and the ever-present possibility of nuclear war lent an urgency to questions of security that seemed to have been lost with the fall of the Berlin Wall. Such a decline in urgency was surely to be welcomed, and led, indeed, to the possibility of an idea like Critical Security Studies taking hold. Many of the concerns that animated the conference and the book had been articulated before the end of the Cold War, but that historical context made it impossible to follow them through. Critical Security Studies was a label ripe for reception at the moment it was spoken. Now, with the events of 9/11, security has regained its urgency.

In the context of a war on terrorism, wars in Afghanistan and Iraq, annual updates of 'anti-terror' legislation, the reorganization of government to provide 'homeland security', and stories of the brutal practices of 'extraordinary rendition', security studies has never had it better. (This thought alone should give us pause, as we recognize the close connection of security studies to such extravagant violence and the abuse of people's rights and persons.) What is the state of the label Critical Security Studies in this present context? It seems the broad church is edging toward institutionalization. There are now courses taught in universities on

Critical Security Studies, and departments advertise for specialists under this label. As you know from reading this chapter, textbooks include Critical Security Studies in their lists of approaches. Perhaps because of this, the followers of the sign of the gourd are still squabbling with those following the sign of the shoe and particularly with those holding their shoes and hopping around on one foot. The stakes in this contest over the label are now higher: jobs are at stake, as are authorships of chapters.

Nevertheless, in an age in which security is so important, and some of the practices of security so troubling to those committed to liberty and justice—to the ethos of democracy—security study demands an ethos of critique, even with the recognition that it does not provide a destination we can finally reach.

QUESTIONS

1. If you were to become a critical-security scholar, which sign would you follow and why?

2. Why did Krause and Williams aim to create a 'broad church' of Critical Security Studies? What are the advantages and disadvantages of such a conception? Who does it favour, and who does it marginalize?

3. Critical Security Studies has itself been criticized for excluding feminist approaches to security and questions relating to gender more generally. Why do you think that is, and what can be done about it?

4. What are the various understandings of the term 'critical' that are found in the literature on Critical Security Studies? Which one do you find the most convincing?

5. Should the Critical Security Studies label apply to the Copenhagen School?

6. Do you think that the 'war on terrorism' makes the claims of Critical Security Studies more or less convincing?

7. The Welsh School suggests that Critical Security Studies should be guided by Critical Theory, which is the theory developed by the Frankfurt School. This suggestion makes intuitive sense; do you agree with it?

8. What is the difference between 'constructivism' and 'poststructuralism' in security studies? Does it make a difference?

9. Do an ethos of critique and an ethos of democracy provide sufficient guidance for a progressive politics of security in the contemporary world?

10. How does the rendition of a 'partial history of a label' differ from other ways of presenting approaches to security studies? What difference does it make?

FURTHER READING

Constructing Security

- Krause, Keith, and Williams, Michael C. (1997), *Critical Security Studies: Concepts and Cases*, Minneapolis: University of Minnesota Press. This edited volume launched the label 'critical security studies' and continues to be a standard reference.

- Krause, Keith (1998), 'Critical Theory and Security Studies: The Research Programme of "Critical Security Studies"', *Cooperation and Conflict*, 33/3: 298–333. In this article, Krause provides a useful overview of the broad church of Critical Security Studies and the literature to which the label may be applied.

There are a number of good texts that apply explicitly constructivist theory to important contemporary questions of security: Alexandra Gheciu (2005b), *NATO in the New Europe: The Politics of Socialization after the Cold War*, Stanford, CA: Stanford University Press (a constructivist account of NATO enlargement); Alexandra Gheciu (2008), *Securing Civilization: The EU, NATO, and the OSCE in the Post-9/11 World*, Oxford: Oxford University Press (the re-configuration of European security to confront the 'threat' of terrorism); Jennifer Milliken (2001) *The Social Construction of the Korean War: Conflict and its Possibilities*, Manchester: Manchester University Press (an account of the decision-making around the Korean conflict); Jutta Weldes (1999b), *Constructing National Interests: The United States and the Cuban Missile Crisis* (an account of the decision-making around the Cuban Missile Crisis).

The Copenhagen School

- Buzan, B. (1992), *People, States and Fear: An Agenda for International Security. Studies in the Post-Cold War Era*, 2nd edn., Boulder, CO: Lynne Rienner. Buzan's work provided an important precursor to Critical Security Studies, and serves as one of the two strands that come together as the Copenhagen School.

- Buzan, B., Wæver, O., and de Wilde, J. (1998), *Security: A New Framework for Analysis*, Boulder, CO: Lynne Rienner. This work is the most elaborate statement of the Copenhagen School approach, and clearly distinguishes it from CSS.

The Welsh School

- Booth, Ken (2005a), *Critical Security Studies and World Politics*, Boulder, CO: Lynne Rienner, and Booth, Ken (2007), *Theory of World Security*, Cambridge: Cambridge University Press. These are the most explicit statements of a Welsh School of Critical Security Studies, with Booth's own contributions arguing for a specific critical security theory, rather than the broad church.

- Wyn Jones, Richard, *Security, Strategy and Critical Theory*, Boulder, CO: Lynne Rienner, 1999. Wyn Jones's book is the most philosophically elaborated statement of the Welsh School approach.

Poststructuralism and Security

- Dalby, Simon (1990), *Creating the Second Cold War*, New York: Guilford Press, and Klein, Bradley (1994), *Strategic Studies and World Order*, Cambridge: Cambridge University Press. These two books are among the first to draw on poststructural philosophy to think about the areas of conventional security studies, and in particular the politics of the study of security itself.

■ Campbell, David (1998a), *Writing Security: United States Foreign Policy and the Politics of Identity*, rev. edn., Minneapolis: University of Minnesota Press. Campbell's first book is a touchstone for virtually all poststructural security studies literature. The Epilogue to the second edition provides a very useful account of the distinction between poststructural IR and constructivism.

■ Campbell, David (1998b), *National Deconstruction: Violence, Identity, and Justice in Bosnia* (Minneapolis: University of Minnesota Press. In *National Deconstruction* Campbell responds to the standard criticism of poststructuralism that it cannot stand up to Fascism.

There are a number of books that use poststructural theory to consider questions of contemporary security: Hugh Gusterson (1998), Nuclear Rites: *A Weapons Laboratory at the End of the Cold War*, Berkeley and Los Angeles: University of California Press (uses Foucault to explore nuclear weapons from an unusual perspective); Simon Dalby (2002), Environmental Security, Cambridge: Cambridge University Press (looks at the relationship between the environment and security and shows how thinking about geopolitics has shaped this discussion); Elizabeth Dauphinée (2008), *The Ethics of Researching War: Looking for Bosnia*, Manchester: University of Manchester Press (considers the place of the academic and West more generally in violent conflict); Kyle Grayson (2008) *Chasing Dragons: Security, Identity, and Illicit Drugs in Canada*, Toronto: University of Toronto Press (explores the relationship of drugs and security in the making of Canadian identity).

 IMPORTANT WEBSITES

● http://www.iciss.ca/menu-en.asp   The report of the International Commission on Intervention and State Sovereignty introduced the notion of the 'responsibility to protect'. The Human Security Policy Division of the Canadian Department of Foreign Affairs maintains a site dedicated to the promotion of this notion.

● http://www.libertysecurity.org   The Liberty & Security Project is a site at the focus of a wide-ranging project looking at the intersection of security and liberty in a world characterized by a global war on terror.

● http://www.watsoninstitute.org/infopeace/index2.cfm   The Information Technology, War and Peace Project is an online portal for a project exploring the relations among information technology, contemporary media, and global security.

 Visit the Online Resource Centre that accompanies this book for lots of interesting additional material: www.oxfordtextbooks.co.uk/orc/collins2e/

7

Gender and Security

CAROLINE KENNEDY-PIPE

 Chapter Contents

- Introduction
- Discursive representations
- Practical context: soldiering
- Contradictions: biology and security
- Victims
- Women and peace
- Multiple perceptions, same realities?
- Conclusion

 Reader's Guide

This chapter examines issues of gender and security. It begins with an explanation of what we mean by gender and explains why the issue of gender is central to any understanding of security. We look at how International Relations specialists have begun to explore the ways in which men and women respond differently to both the national and international policies which govern security, conflict, and war. The chapter demonstrates that through understanding and placing notions of gender at the centre of any debate on security we unleash a series of interlocking understandings of the way people of either sex relate to fear, insecurity, violence, and the institutions of war and peace.

Introduction

Gender and security are both concepts that invite endless categorization and clarification. Security has been conceived in many different ways (Krause and Williams 1997b; Buzan et al. 1998). Much of this difference can be understood and illuminated in terms of gender. But gender too has multiple meanings and applications, as its different deployments within contemporary scholarship and politics indicate (Tickner 1992).

This chapter outlines the significance of considering gender and security together by considering two angles of vision. I distinguish between 'practical' and 'discursive' aspects of the relationship between gender and security. Practical aspects are exemplified by the concrete role of women in armed forces, or as victims, bystanders, or helpers of military conflict or of militarization in general. Discursive aspects are exemplified by the connections made between militarism and masculinity and between nurturing, peace, and femininity.

This distinction is wedded to two further developments that reinforce the central relationship between gender and security. The first involves the acceptance of a broader concept of security than has been traditional. A number of terms have been used to describe this process, 'human security' or 'soft security' being the most common. Up until

the events of 9/11 this involved a relative downgrading of the traditional focus on military matters within security, with implications both from and for the practical and the representative aspects of the gender–security relationship. A second process was in trends that allegedly meant that in the 1990s technological innovation allowed for a remote control of a virtual war such as Kosovo removing the need for 'men' in battle. Indeed arguably war and battle had been rendered gender neutral. Technology meant intervention could 'save strangers' in danger without cost. However, as we will go on to see, it was not that simple. Kosovo revealed that traditional gendered roles remained intact especially for those on the receiving end of intervention.

The deepening of interest in the gender/security nexus has if anything been deepened since the terrorist attacks of 9/11. Specifically the wars in Iraq and Afghanistan and the chronic instability in Pakistan caused by the struggle with the Taliban and al-Qaeda have highlighted how gender and issues of gender affect security locally, nationally, and globally. It is suggested that attention to this relationship continues to be illuminating and to expose the complexity of the nexus between man, the state, women, and violence/war.

Discursive representations

Perhaps one of the most general trends in recent international relations theory in general has been the growing recognition of the role of what we might loosely call 'ideas' or, perhaps better, discursive contexts in international political life (Onuf 1989; Kratochwil 1991; Walker 1993; Rengger 1999; Wendt 1999).

Perhaps the most celebrated image of the international system—that states perceive themselves as inhabiting a zero-sum and therefore dangerous inter-

national environment of self-help—is taken as evidence of that; in Alexander Wendt's famous phrase (1992) 'anarchy is what states make of it'. Traditionally and certainly according to realist accounts of international relations, states have ranked their national security or the national interest (itself always an ambiguous concept) as a priority, perhaps the very highest priority. In the interests of 'national security', large defence budgets, nuclear weapons, the military conscription of the male population (sometimes but not usually the female population), foreign invasion and intervention, and the curtailment of domestic civil liberties have all been justified, at various times. The security of the state is perceived as a fundamental duty of the government and as a task that must be supported by most if not all citizens. The events of 7/7, for example, when four British suicide bombers killed 52 citizens and injured over 700 in an attack on London's public-transport system, demonstrated quite clearly that certainly in the United Kingdom not all citizens shared similar conceptions of duty to the state. However, loyalty to the state has been apparent in periods of war and in times of national emergency. The provision of national security in most states has been and continues to be the almost exclusive province of the male. While many women support and underwrite what are considered to be legitimate calls for state military action, the primary task of defining and defending the security of the state has been seen as the work of men. Yet this male province has rested in many ways on the work, the co-option, or the exploitation of that group known as women.

Of course, historically, war and combat have represented the highest aspirations of the male members of political, social, and cultural elites, across time and culture. In the modern period, military service for one's country has long been regarded as a badge of honour. The power of the critical poetry of the First World War is made so by the widespread acceptance of the values that it was criticizing; it *was* widely thought that 'Dulce et decorum est, pro patria mori' (It is sweet and proper to die for one's country) (Owen 1995 edn.). War was and, many would argue, still is associated with masculine values such as physical strength, honour, and courage. In ancient Greece, some form of military training was regarded as a prerequisite to manhood (Dawson 1996). Shakespeare famously has Henry V declare to his troops before Agincourt that 'Gentleman in England now abed will think themselves accursed to be not here'. In more contemporary times, Doctor Johnson is often quoted as believing that 'Every man thinks meanly of himself for not having been a soldier or not having been at sea' (Keegan 1998). Even more recently, Theodore Zeldin (1998: 214) has

explained that men fight to 'kill dissatisfaction with themselves more than their foe ... but that adventure and honour have been their goals'. The idea of combat as serving a purpose of maleness and male bonding resonates from Shakespeare's 'Band of Brothers' to that of Stephen Ambrose.

In certain societies, those men who would not or could not fight might be classified as 'women': some have even been made to don dresses as a sign of their weakness (Davie 1929). Indeed we know that in recent times, as the scandal has unfolded over the treatment of terrorist suspects in Abu Ghrab or Guantanamo, male suspects were made to wear female garb as a sign of humiliation. Military training was always (and is still) designed to reinforce certain notions of masculinity. The use of boot camps, a degree of violence, and bullying associated with basic training are all designed to cultivate and construct certain notions of what it is to be a man (Steans 1998). **Misogyny** can be a useful component: males can be goaded into grinding down whatever might be regarded as womanly or feminine and thus an attribute unfit for a soldier. Norman Dixon, for example, has argued that various British military conventions were in certain periods designed to subordinate female characteristics: hence piano playing was denounced (Dixon 1976). To sacrifice one's life for one's country in war has been regarded as the highest form of patriotism, but a failure to fight is the act of a coward or evidence of some physical or mental weakness that renders the male less than he should be. Equally, to deny loyalty to the state or to inflict hurt on the state as the British suicide bombers did in the summer of 2005 is to question the very essence of what we consider to be the duty of a citizen. This noble interpretation of what it is to be a man and a soldier is somewhat at odds with the very recent accounts of the sexual abuse of female soldiers serving in the US armed services in both Iraq and Afghanistan. A percentage of female GIs now report incidents of rape by fellow officers. We will return to the idea of women as victims, but such reports highlight the complexities of the relationship between men and women under stress in war, even if both sexes are technically bonded on the 'same side'.

Women, in contrast to men, have long been regarded as the carers and the nurturers of the young. In many narratives of war, women have inhabited only the private sphere tasked with the defence of that ubiquitous feature of national life—the home front, implying that women, even in war, never really left the home (Sherry 1995). This polarization between the sexes has been described in the following terms: 'Women are excluded from war talk and men excluded from baby talk' (Elsthain 1987: 222). Yet women, although depicted historically as 'carers', such as the nurse figure embodied in Florence Nightingale, also have had other connections with war. Frequently they have been represented as the 'spoils of war'. This perception of women as 'spoils of war' was consistent historically with the legal status of women: they were regarded as the property of the male. Rape (see Think Point 7.1) was perceived as an injury to the male estate, and not to the women herself (Brownmiller 1975).

From the raping of the Sabine women in Greek mythology to the accounts of the sexual abuse and mutilation of women in the Balkan wars of the 1990s, the act of rape has been a common feature in both the representation and the realities of war. It was, though, not until the late 1990s that feminist scholars drew attention to female experiences of war: an area that hitherto had not been discussed nor indeed considered central to any discussion of international relations. The rape of women during and after war is now well documented (Nicarchos 1995), as are the examples when rape appears to have been used as a 'tactic' of war to humiliate or demoralize the enemy. We now know, thanks to the work of scholars such as Anthony Beevor, of the routine use of rape by soldiers of the Red Army as it advanced on and occupied German cities in the spring of 1945. Members of the NKVD encouraged the use of rape, not just as a tool of revenge but as a way of undermining the male population left in the city. Scholars examined the use of rape as a supposed tactic of war by Serbian and Croatian soldiers during the conflict in Kosovo (Aydelott 1993; Beevor 2002). More recently we have become used to tales of sexual humiliation perpetrated by American soldiers on Iraqi prisoners of war. Interestingly, we have also been made aware of female service personnel engaging in such behaviour and challenging notions of what it is to be female and highlighting the brutality assumed by women in positions of relative power.

Some male scholars, perhaps intent on controversy, have depicted women as the cause of war and point to the cases in which women have urged their men on to battle. The somewhat hazy representation of girls pressing white feathers into the hands of those young men reluctant to volunteer for service in the First World War is juxtaposed with the semi-mythical creatures who, according to Martin Van Crevald (2001), bared their breasts to urge warriors on. When women do appear in the literature of war, the Amazons, Boudicca, and Mrs Thatcher are all used to exemplify the war in which some women ape maleness to assert political leadership. Despite these latter characterizations, overall the female place in or rather outside war is clear. As Nietzsche said in a well-known if by now somewhat tedious formulation: 'Man should be trained for war and women for the recreation of the warrior: all else is folly' (Hollingdale 1977: 275).

These representations of women and war are important because of the connection between war, maleness, and the modern state, a connection many actors in the modern world are unashamed to acknowledge. Indeed, Dixon (1976: 218) quotes General Adna Chaffe to the effect that 'Let war cease and a nation will become effeminate'. The modern state was born in war and consolidated through war: as Charles Tilly (1990) famously put it, 'war made the state and the state made war'. In some, one might say in many, cultures, masculine attributes have traditionally been rewarded with social advancement or the holding of high political office. In Israeli society, as in a number of others, military service provides a standard for manhood. The essence of womanhood is still regarded as being fulfilled by marrying a hero—a man who has served (Lieblich 1997). This assigns to women, even in a state as security minded as Israel, a passive role—that of the hero's wife or girlfriend (Lieblich 1997).

In the contemporary literature on world politics, perhaps the most potent reflection on the interpretations of the female, the state, and war is that of

Jean Elshtain (1987). In her book *Women and War*, Elshtain claims that a distinction between 'beautiful souls' (women) and 'just warriors' (men) has been at the core of much of the theorizing about the respective role of women and men in both war and society. She also emphasizes the key role that narratives of war play in reinforcing traditional gender roles in a domestic/social context.

Histories of states are usually constructed in terms that are highly gendered. While nowadays nations might gather in support of (all-male) football, rugby, or cricket teams, within many states traditionally identities coalesce around the narration or stories or celebration of wars of independence or national liberation. Victory in battles hundreds of years ago are still revered, and statues of war heroes abound. Most villages, towns, and cities in many countries house war memorials, plaques, and expression of reverence for male sacrifice. Many nationalist movements have utilized a variety of gendered imagery that encourages men to fight for the establishment and defence of a country, and a patch of land to be protected is usually depicted in female terms. 'Mother' Russia, 'Marianne' in France, or the Statue of Liberty in America are powerful symbols of the supposed spirit of a nation. National anthems are frequently war songs, and national holidays might in some countries or regions be celebrated with military or paramilitary marches usually participated in by men (Edwards 1999).

Collective histories, therefore, are central to the way in which individuals and communities define themselves as citizens as well as the way in which political elites generate support for foreign policy decisions, particularly those for war. It is rare, although one can think of Joan of Arc, that such collective memory contains heroines. These are, as noted earlier, predominantly celebrations of men in war. According to some types of feminist account, the association of the male with war has necessarily privileged man, because of the way in which military service and, certainly during the years of the Cold War and again after 9/11, conceptions of national and nuclear security were valued in male terms. For some feminists, usually designated as liberal feminists

(see Key Points below), the gendered nature of the state is significant for the inequalities of treatment for women within society generally. Equality for women can be achieved first by gaining equal opportunities in education, in social institutions, and in the workplace and then through the gradual achievement of parity of representation in the central offices of the state: within government, the judiciary, and, of course, the military. The argument was and is a simple one: men have 'captured' the state, so women must reclaim it. Here, as Jill Steans has pointed out, the armed services and military institutions are regarded as especially important to those women trying to achieve high office. To paraphrase, the military plays a special role in the ideological structure of patriarchy, because the notion of combat plays such a central role in the construction of manhood and in the construction of the social order (Steans 1998). Therefore, by obtaining equality in this sphere, women will be able to participate in the key narratives of, to use Michael Ignatieff's phrase (1997), 'blood and belonging'.

 THINK POINT 7.1

Rape

Although we are familiar with historical cases of rape in war, the phenomenon remains with us. Tony Blair made a commitment to prevent further rape during the Kosovo conflict in the 1990s, but rape remains a weapon that can be used against enemy populations or indeed as an instrument of the state to stifle debate and dissent. In December 2008 this was manifest in the plight of Uzbek women arrested by the authorities for alleged Islamic extremism; they suffered rape as an instrument of 'torture policy' by the state. In contemporary Afghanistan in early 2009 there is concern that legislation rushed through by Hamid Karzai will lead to rape. Article 132 in the new Shia Family Law requires a woman to obey her husband's sexual demands, negating the requirement for sexual consent. Reports by international organizations such as Amnesty International highlight how directed rape is used as a tactic by warlords in Liberia to terrify local populations. Rape seems endemic, therefore, from the Balkans, through Afghanistan into Africa, where international aid agencies remain concerned by the prevalence of rape across a range of regions.

KEY POINTS

- Feminist analysts and gender analysts are not united in their views about the relationship between women, men, and security.

- Liberal feminists wish to see a complete equality of opportunity between men and women and are keen to see equal representation of women in the high offices of state and advocate the right of women to participate in combat.

- Radical feminists would prefer to see a shift in the dynamics of the state-security apparatus. This includes a rejection of masculine values and a desire to feminize institutions and conflict. Some radical feminists emphasize peace as the endpoint of changing institutions and mindsets.

- Marxist feminists work on the issue of class and gender. Their work highlights not only the subordination of women in the workplace but the general over-representation of women in the lowest socio-economic groups across the globe. They draw our attention to the links between economic deprivation, security, and vulnerability.

Practical context: soldiering

According to some female scholars, even in the contemporary era, experience in combat can still be a way of earning high office or, in a state such as America, of securing political election (Steans 1998). Just as ancient and medieval civilizations gave special respect to citizens who had proved themselves in war, it can still be a special mark of respect to be a war veteran. This is an honour that overall is denied to women. Women have traditionally been thought unfit or unsuited for the holding of high offices associated with the military or issues of national security. If women were rarely warriors, they were equally unlikely to be heads of the CIA or Strategic Air Command. If in olden times it was men who headed armies, it is predominantly men who still act as the heads of militaries, intelligence services, and nuclear industries. Women, though, have traditionally been employed as spies, special agents, and in special intelligence units (Steans 1998). There is little need to emphasize that this type of employment might fit nicely with traditional gendered views of women as perhaps devious, cunning, and able to fool men through the use of sexual favours. Not for nothing has the reputation of Mata Hari exercised such a keen fascination.

In the United States, Sheila Tobias has suggested that there are greater hurdles to those politicians,

even male politicians, seeking office who have not served in the military (Elshtain and Tobias 1990). Former generals are looked upon as prime presidential material, and some American politicians have run for office on the basis of their war records. John McCain argued that his own record in Vietnam served to make him fit to lead. It may have been thought that the election of first Bill Clinton, whose own record as a 'draft dodger' was somewhat controversial, and Barack Obama had ended the linkage between military service and electoral success, but it still seems to persist. George W. Bush, of course, despite his decision to shy away from service in Vietnam, made a virtue out of the association between strong leadership and military prowess by appearing in combat uniform and striding manfully around the deck of an aircraft carrier!

Yet, any positive view of the way in which men have been treated after serving their country in war must be contested. Veterans of the Vietnam conflict, especially those drawn from the native African community in the United States, might find it difficult to recognize their treatment as that of heroes or to find that their combat experiences advanced them socially (Sherry 1995). The recent controversies over the level of compensation for those killed and maimed in conflicts such as the First and Second

Gulf Wars also do not point to a necessary glorious post-war life for those who have served, particularly those who are not drawn from the officer class. Recent reports from both wars in Iraq have demonstrated that war, or rather occupation duty after war in a hostile environment, is proving extremely stressful for young soldiers and has longer-term psychological implications. There is a recent and worrying rise in the number of army suicides, as, for example within the UK armed forces (Keegan 1998; M. Smith 2005).

Despite the increasing evidence of the toll that soldiering exerts on the individual, to die in combat for one's country was at least in certain narratives of war regarded as an honour and was one that was revered within many cultures. Yet, death in battle or at least honourable death as a warrior was an honour for which women could not even compete (Tickner 1992). Although many women have died in times of conflict, in the service of the state, war memorials rarely carry the names of those females killed in war. In 1995, in recognition of this, the United States dedicated a memorial at **Arlington National Cemetery** for those women who had served in the military from the time of the US Civil War through to the conflict in the Gulf. Again, one must be careful with this equation of maleness, honour, privilege, and war, as one has only to think of the 326,000 unidentified corpses from the First World War to see that an unmarked grave has been the permanent resting place of many a young man serving his country.

The construction, though, of a male security state is not accidental. As Cynthia Enloe (1993: 253) points out, militarism has not been 'kept going by merely drawing on a type of civilian masculinity . . . rather it requires drill sergeants . . . and men's willingness to earn their manhood credentials by soldiering: it also requires women to accept particular assumptions about mothering, marriage and unskilled work [as well as policies, written and unwritten] to ensure certain sorts of sexual relations'. Enloe's formulation is important because arguably it helps explain why, even though women in the second part of the twentieth century were increasingly integrated into many state institutions,

the military and the capability to wage war remained predominantly the preserve of men.

It is not just at the highest levels, that of the presidents and the generals, that scholars claim that there is a linkage between man, war, and the state. The relationship between the bearing of arms and citizenship has a long history in Western political thought. Judith Hicks Stiehm argues that we in the West have traditionally held militarized conceptions of citizenship and that different categories of citizenship arise from the classes of those excluded from military service. The very young, the old, the disabled, in some societies the homosexual, are barred from combat (Hicks Stiehm 1983, 1989). This is odd in many ways, but for our purposes it has meant historically that the fittest in society were slaughtered. As Nicolai has argued:

> Children and old men are protected by Government, but besides them the blind, deaf and dumb, idiots, hunchbacks, scrofulous and impotent persons, imbeciles, paralytics, epileptics, dwarfs and abortions—all this human riff-raff and dross need have no anxiety, for no bullets will come hissing against them, and they can stay at home and dress their ulcers while the brave, strong young men are rotting on the battle-field.

(Pick 1993).

Within such a rubric, women have been excluded along with the infirm from battle. In the United States and within other NATO countries, as the women's movement grew, demands escalated from the inclusion of women into the military to an insistence on the right to participate in combat. Some feminist groups have claimed that taking part in combat will further advance the position of women in a general sense. The **National Organization for Women (NOW)** was established in the United States in 1966 to promote women in public life. One component of the campaign has been an advocacy of the 'right to fight'. Those pushing for the placement of women in combat have argued that, apart from the issue of political rights, those males who serve in the US military enjoy a range of economic benefits, such as free medical care and cheap loans, which are denied to women. Yet there is much that is culturally and socially sensitive here. In the words of one American official, 'a woman POW is the ultimate nightmare'. Those who have opposed the lifting of restrictions on women in combat have used the possibility of a female POW to justify the case against the full inclusion of women. This reflected the fear that female POWs might in captivity indeed be subjected to sexual assault or rape. When one army specialist, Melissa Rathbun-Nathy, was captured by the Iraqis during the Gulf War, there was much media speculation about how her Iraqi captors treated her and whether she had in fact been the subject of sexual assault (Nantais and Lee 1999). Stories of abuse are consistent for some female scholars with the military tactic of using the 'protected' to motivate male soldiers (Nantais and Lee 1999). More recently, of course, much was made in the American media of the capture of a young American female soldier, Jessica Lynch, taken prisoner by the Iraqis and then subsequently rescued by male soldiers. Lynch returned to a frenzy of excitement in the USA. As it turned out, Lynch's story was one that had been much embellished by the media. Even so there were some very confused messages here about women, war, and international relations. Not the least of these was what exactly we were meant to learn from the stories of female soldiers. Women can actually fight? Women can actually survive captivity? Women might actually not be heroic when captured? Or perhaps, most cynically of all, that the life of one young American female soldier was perhaps worth so much more airtime than the hundreds of young American men killed. In the United Kingdom, too, during the recent wars in Iraq and Afghanistan, much media coverage was expended on the deaths of British women in a combat zone. In fact, what both of these wars prove that there has indeed been a blurring of the lines of battle, with 99 per cent of US women serving in 'support' roles but still in the line of fire, such is the complexity and fluidity of counter-insurgency operations. Actually record numbers of female soldiers are dying on the American side, mainly as the result of improvised

explosive devices (IEDs), which do not respect gender, rank, or mission.

Let us just invert part of the feminist argument here and reflect on whether the reluctance to allow women into 'battle' and the efforts to 'save' Lynch represent a prizing, not a degradation, of the female. But there is yet another layer here too, which is that thousands of Iraqi women have been killed, wounded, or hurt by this war, but little attention has been paid to their plight. The flight of many Iraqi women from their homeland into Jordan has thrown up a story of multiple rapes by the Iraqi security forces and displacement into a life of refugee status. This, therefore, may be the paradox at the heart of the modern so-called liberal way of war: that Western women are 'celebrated' for their roles in modern war but that non-Western women still bear the brunt of the cruelty of international politics.

The issue of female soldiering, though, could be a simple extension of rights and of course duties. If women are full members of society, then there is a corresponding duty to fulfil the obligations asked by the state. Until women are thought fit for military service, they will continue to be excluded, not just from the highest offices of the armed services, but from full equality within society. It is the linkage between man, the state, and war that needs to be broken down or at least recognized and the complex, contested, contestable, and contextual structure that it is acknowledged and discussed.

KEY POINTS

- The analysis of gender is a relatively new phenomenon in international security studies.

- International relations theorists, let alone security analysts, rarely admitted that gender was an important component of thinking about the state, the international system, or international security.

- Feminist analysts introduced and answered the question of where are the women in security. They also alerted us to the idea that the experiences of women in relation to the state, state militaries, and conflict are often very different from those of men.

Contradictions: biology and security

For some, of course, women are seen (as they have always been seen) as the 'weaker'—sometimes termed the 'fairer'—sex, and so will continue to be second-class citizens dependent on men for protection in the international environment, both in a domestic context and also ironically within the armed services themselves. In many contemporary societies the state has conscripted its young men for service in the armed forces, but women have usually been excluded. The overall effect is therefore to 'arm' men and 'disarm' women. There are to the minds of some feminist scholars important consequences of the exclusion of the female from the bearing of arms: one is to render women dependent on men for their protection. To walk a woman 'home' in the dark is a metaphor for how the female must need a protector to survive outside the alleged security of home and hearth. Which is why feminists who recognize the threat posed to women (and indeed men) by violence in the street talk of the need to 'take back the night' rather than to look for a 'hero' to walk you home. Both culturally and in institutional terms this function of protection has been linked to masculinity.

There are, of course, some pragmatic reasons for this at a state level. After all, the slaughter of women on the battlefield along with men would decimate future generations. The phrase 'women and children' is one commonly used to symbolize the place of the female within the community—note a subordinate one, linking women with 'dependants'. It is an important place, because of biology and the continual demands of the state on its female and child-bearing constituencies. Women have been used by virtue of their biology to promote certain security goals. Not the least of these has been the demand to breed for empire or the national interest. Although this may seem a rather crude formulation, it is central to understanding how states and societies after war reproduce their populations and survive. Not for nothing did Stalin demand an increase in the birth rate after the Second World War (see Case Study 7.1). In the Russian population women were encouraged to have a high number of children as the Soviet state sought to recover from the ravaging of its population in the years of war (Kennedy-Pipe 2004). In certain states, women were denied access to birth control or abortion to promote and achieve a certain rate of reproduction (Buckley 1989). Arguably the most intimate of human activities for women were less important than the demands of male political and religious elites that women provide a functional and biological service to the state. This role of women as 'breeders' remains imperative for the health of many wealthy industralized societies. Security of all societies rests on women's ability to look after their health and have access to contraception and adequate maternity care. It is worth noting that President Obama has, much to the delight of feminist lobbies, revoked former President Bush's ban on contraceptive supplies to the world's largest family-planning organization, Marie Stopes International. Bush's legislation had prejudiced the healthcare of women in a number of countries, including Malawi, Ghana, Sierra Leone, Tanzania, Uganda, and Zimbabwe. The very essence of a state or a community rests upon the ability to produce the next generation safely.

CASE STUDY 7.1

Breeding for the state? The Soviet example

In 1944, as victory against Germany became apparent, the Soviet authorities turned their attention to increasing the birth rate. This was an acute pressure because of the heavy wartime losses. Some twenty-four million Soviet people had died during the war, with the result that there was a very large preponderance of women left in the population. By 1946 women outnumbered men by almost twenty-six million. Because relatively few men were available to marry, the Soviet authorities encouraged women to have illegitimate children. Small allowances were made by the state to single mothers or these women could place their children in state homes without cost. Effectively, as Mary Buckley has shown, the state took over the financial role of the father. This was designed to prevent single women who had children by married men from disrupting his existing family and to encourage them to return to work after giving birth. The state also promoted the idea of very large families, with the introduction of decorations for motherhood. Motherhood Glory went to mothers of seven, eight, and nine children. After bearing ten children, women became 'Heroine Mother'.

These measures were designed to address the population of surplus females and male population loss. Children were

needed to address gaps in the labour market. So too were women. Despite maternity leave and some state benefits, women were also expected to return to the workplace after childbirth. The so-called women question (the emancipation of women), which had been highlighted after the Revolution by both Trotsky and Lenin, was therefore subordinated to the demands of a state recovering from war and the decimation of the male population.

Buckley (1989).

Victims

In the age of professional armies, this reliance on women might not provide a crisis in the provision of military forces, though it might raise soft security issues of demographics, ethnic balance, and age profiles. Indeed, the protection of that group—women—which can provide the future of the state or the community through its biology makes sense in certain ways. However, the protected may have had little say in the terms of how they are rendered 'safe' by either the state or the military institutions that wage war on their behalf. In truth, recent work on how women are treated both in and after war demonstrates the somewhat ambiguous relationship that can exist between armed forces and civilian women. While women have often been the targets of violence by the enemy in conflict, it is also the case that they may suffer at the hands of their so-called protectors. In 2008 reports by Amnesty International, for example, provided compelling evidence of brutal behaviour by troops on all sides of the civil wars in West Africa, including brutality by those soldiers tasked with maintaining peace (Sorenson 1999; for more on this see Chapter 24). Again, this may actually strengthen the case for female soldiers to be engaged in certain types of peacekeeping work and especially to be employed in post-conflict situations, although the equation between female and peacekeeping rests on a certain reading of female soldiering and

a benign view of what experiences of war may or may not have on soldiers. So, in the current war in Afghanistan, Afghan women suspected of offences are searched by female soldiers because to use male personnel would cause massive offence to local people.

Work examining the Balkan Wars in the early 1990s and the first Gulf War has revealed a degree of violence perpetrated against women by soldiers returning home from the trauma of conflict. A claim might be made that violence against women is more prevalent both in militarized societies and within military families and that the idea that women and

KEY POINTS

- Looking at women and their place in contemporary and historical conflicts helped bring about recognition that there are specific female issues relating to control of biology and reproduction.

- Women relate differently to state policy than do men.

- Women are intimately affected by state policy on contraception, abortion, and marriage.

- States quite often use women to fulfil state politics in relation to demographic shortages.

- Biology is crucial to state security.

- Female soldiers are quite often used for tasks by virtue of their biology.

children are, as a matter of course, protected by male soldiers should be re-examined (Human Rights Watch 1999). So, too, as the number of female soldiers in combat zones increase, should we be aware that there may also be a breakdown in traditional thinking about women and domestic violence.

Women and peace

Whatever the evidence for these claims, and allegations of 'domestic' violence are difficult to substantiate, it is important therefore to be careful that we do not essentialize gender characteristics by always equating militarism with masculinity and with qualities such as strength, aggression, and violence and by suggesting that women, even female soldiers, are synonymous with the will to nourish. These stereotypical notions of men and women are to be found throughout the security studies literature. Most commonly women have been associated not with soldiering but with campaigns for peace and justice, such as that at Greenham Common during the 1980s and in Washington more recently to protest against the torture of detainees in Guantanamo. Female voices often lead those protests that are against the stationing of foreign troops or missiles in local areas.

As Elshtain's discussion of 'beautiful souls' alluded to above reminds us, of course, there is a long tradition that seemingly demonstrates that women and peace are interconnected: that females as the bearers of children or the potential bearers of children are necessarily more anti-war than men. These anti-war and now anti-torture movements have habitually treated the military apparatus of the state, especially the military component, as an expression of male aggression (Alonso 1993). Within this rubric mothers are life affirming, and biology of the female kind negates male militarism. While the 'peace' women of the 1980s can justifiably claim that they did in fact influence the military debate through their actions of 'chaining themselves to fences outside nuclear bases, dancing on missile silos and jumping into convoy jeeps as they pass by', the problem was, as Christine Sylvester points out, that all these activities can be discounted by those in power. In her words, 'peace camps

do not lead us to the edge of war. They do not stockpile weapons and hurtle us into arms races . . . They do not matter' (Sylvester 1996). It should be noted, however, that the engagement of women with the politics of peace was actually of concern to a number of those in power. During the Cold War, the CIA monitored women's groups associated with peace campaigns with a great deal of interest. Women as a constituency with no 'natural' loyalty to their state were considered to be especially vulnerable to the propaganda campaigns of other states (Laville 1997). There is no evidence that women are more prone to the betrayal of their state than a group called man, but nevertheless the engagement of women in the politics of defence seems to have aroused a great deal of state interest.

Those linkages between 'men and war' and 'women and peace' are important, even if, as we have seen, so often they are ill founded. They imply, as the American academic Bell Hooks (1995) has argued, that women by virtue of simply being women have played little or no role in supporting and upholding the militarism of the state). Women have in this one-dimensional version of historical events been merely 'observers' of and objects in war.

Women have, however, always been engaged in the business of war. For some scholars this is important, because it means that the history of war and indeed histories generally have been told in such a way that it is just that: 'his story'. Women and their stories or narratives are therefore absent from a number of textbooks or what are regarded as the important studies of war. More recently, academics have concentrated in growing numbers on the telling of female histories, and we do now have a number of works that tell some of the stories of women as victims of war—for example, monographs and scholarly works that tell the stories of mass rape in war or examine the gendered effects of war (Stiglmayer 1994).

The woman as 'victim' is, as we saw earlier, an important thread in the stories of war. Indeed, in 1990 an estimated 90 per cent of war casualties were civilians, the vast majority women and children, but contemporary scholarship has uncovered numerous examples where women have supported the role of men in war and participated in civil war and war itself. The tales of these women shed fascinating light on the work of the female in war, revealing female experiences as soldiers, special agents, nurses, surgeons, laundry women, cooks, and prostitutes (Isaksson 1988). They do not suggest that men and women are different in some absolute way. It may also be that such formulations ignore the contribution that many men have made to peace movements and to pacifism. Individual men have often sought to avoid combat and most conscript armies have been dogged by desertion and so-called cowardice brought about by the trauma of war. As we move into the twenty-first century, and know about the problems of trauma in war amongst even very brave and honourable people, it is difficult to see how long we can sustain the idea of war as either heroic or the natural place for a human regardless of gender.

KEY POINTS

- The traditional literature on security has treated women as upholders of peace.

- Women have indeed been involved in many powerful national and international movements promoting peace and disarmament.

- We need to understand the nature of men and women, and how they relate to war and peace in specific contexts.

- Recent scholarship demonstrates that war may not be heroic and that gender alone is not a determinant of bravery.

Multiple perceptions, same realities?

We in the West have had the luxury of being able to acknowledge the problems of humankind and war. Indeed, since the revolution in military affairs (RMA) there has been a gradual erosion of the state's military demands on its peoples: a trend accelerated in the Western world by the decline of Communism. In many democracies, the notion of the soldier as citizen has simply died. Even if we do not yet live in a post-heroic culture, as Edward Luttwak (1995) has claimed, war as trial by national survival is almost certainly dead. We, or certainly those in the Western world, live in a world where war is at a distance, our own casualties are minimized and controversial, and the preferred option of democratic states at war is that of aerial bombing. Wars at a distance from our civilian engagement have changed the way in which modern militaries fight and the way in which civilian populations respond. As we saw during the Kosovo conflict of the late 1990s, liberal states were able to wage a successful war against Serbia without having to suffer a single conflict fatality. The nature of this conflict led some scholars to argue that gender made little difference to the conduct of war, as soldiers of whatever gender did not now need to be placed in harm's way. This use of 'virtual war', to use Ignatieff's term, solved the problem of men, women, and war. If actual combat could be avoided, then male and female soldiers could wage war on equal terms.

As the nature of war has changed after the Cold War, however, from one of war conducted by mass armies through defence by nuclear deterrence to 'virtual war', the role of both men and women in relation to conflict has changed. We in the West can engage in mass killing through technology with few apparent costs to ourselves. This might, except at the margins, mean that debates over the relative fitness of men and women for war are irrelevant. But there is a problem here, and it is one that is raised in much of the security literature on women and war and development and security. The problem is, to put it bluntly, that, while gender and war in the West may have been about the 'right to fight' or the right to object to state policies fought in the name of national politics, in most of the rest of the world men and women have far fewer choices. In many parts of the globe campaigns for women to be allowed to fight and die in national armies would seem bizarre. While war may be sanitized for those of us living in the West, women (and indeed men and children) in war zones such as Afghanistan, Sri Lanka, Iraq, or Latin America are victims of, are witnesses of, may participate in, but almost certainly seek to remove themselves from, war and violence. Conflict in these cases is rarely about the historical contract between the individual and the central authorities but a battle for individual, familial, or communal survival in a local patch. Add into this the complexities of what are now known as soft security issues, AIDS, illegal trading of people, and economic hardship, and our understanding of gender as a divide between men and women must be elaborated upon to provide a more complex picture of what it means to a man or a women in a specific time and place.

> **KEY POINTS**
>
> - Technology has rendered the battlefield 'gender neutral' in some respects.
>
> - War takes many forms and for those in the third world still represents a battle for survival.

Conclusion

The traditional literature on security largely ignored the issue of gender. It was implicit in most of the literature on war and security that gender produced different roles for men and women. In short, boys would have 'toys' (weapons) and girls would have 'dolls' (children). Women as a category were ignored and on the whole were regarded either as unfit for service in war or as unsuited for leadership or in some cases even citizenship. While men were warriors, women were either ignored or depicted as passive in terms of security issues. Quite often even the role of women as victim was regarded as irrelevant to the business of state security. Women did, however, serve the purposes of nationalist causes, with nationalism often served up in highly gendered and female terms. Female symbols of statehood were and remain a characteristic of many modern states. The figure of the women as mother to the nation is a familiar one (see Case Study 7.1).

Feminist and critical security investigations into the state, war, and security allowed us in the 1980s and 1990s to go beyond the rather simple categories of men/warrior/protector and women/mother/protected. What the feminist literature did was to alert us to a series of consequences that state security policies had for women. The first was to alert us to the fact that war could have specific and gendered consequences, not least that not only were women likely to be victims of war as indirect casualties but that war policy itself might specifically target women in terms of genocidal rape or sexual abuse. The value attached to women might, as we saw during the Balkan Wars and more latterly in Afghanistan and in Pakistan, make them susceptible to attack and abuse. In 2009 we have seen the reintroduction of Sharia law into the territory of North West Pakistan. Women are once again been denied basic human rights such as education or health care. The reintroduction of Sharia law has reluctantly been endorsed by the US government as the quid pro quo for opposition to al-Qaeda in the region.

Feminist writings reveal other sufferings inflicted on women in terms of economic and social displacement after conflict. So, for example, women after conflict may be forced into the international sex slave trade. In a more positive fashion, we also learnt that women might organize themselves to protest against state policy and certain facets of nationalism. Feminist writers and historians also alerted us to the way in which states have historically sought to control the biology of women to construct certain state policies. Women might be coerced or persuaded to produce children for the state. They might, for example, not be allowed access to abortion or contraception depending on the whim or needs of the central authorities or indeed the US government. Perhaps more importantly, though, the feminist and gender literature allowed us to rethink notions of security that had dominated international relations. It allowed us to ask key questions. These included the questioning of core certainties of international relations such as the notion of state power. What does power actually mean for different men and different women, both within the state and outside? What might citizenship mean for men and women? What might war mean? Crucially, how do men and women define issues of security? Do they in fact define security differently?

Perhaps, though, the most telling feature of recent literature is that 'gender' is a way of unlocking security concerns, allowing us to see that gender as a category is a social construction. That is, the way men and women act or react may be a product of sexual difference but may also be a product of circumstance. We should ask, therefore, how both men and women in different contexts relate to local, regional, and international security apparatus. Is it the case that security policies, as some feminists have claimed, always privilege men and always discriminate against women? Or is it that we need to understand that men are not always or simply leaders, warriors, or the oppressors of women?

'Gender' and 'security' are terms that require, for a proper understanding of either, to be related. But, of course, this does not mean that either is reducible to the other nor that either does not have a role independent of the other. Gender—in all its forms and with all its complexities—affects many things other than security, and security—in its turn, and however it is understood—is dependent on many things other than gender. But, as I hope to have shown, trying to understand either without an appreciation of the role of the other results in an impoverished understanding of both. Understanding, of course, does not necessarily lead to any change in practice, but it is an assumption that governs any reasoned (and reasonable) politics that it must be a first step.

? QUESTIONS

1. How do we understand the term 'gender'?

2. What difference does it make to an understanding of security to ask about the place of women?

3. What are the consequences of state and international policies on contraception/abortion for the security of women?

4. Why does rape seem to accompany every war?

5. Are men natural warriors?

6. Should citizenship be linked to militarism?

7. How have the wars in Iraq and Afghanistan highlighted the complexities of the gender question in international relations?

FURTHER READING

■ Enloe, Cynthia (1989), *Bananas, Bases and Beaches: Making Feminist Sense of International Politics*, London: Pinter. This is in many ways one of the most important readings of feminist international relations. Enloe was amongst the first to pose and answer the question 'Where are the women in international politics?' Enloe alerted us to the fact that women occupy multiple roles in security, diplomacy, trade, and local and regional politics.

■ Enloe, Cynthia (2000), *Maneuvers,* Berkeley and Los Angeles: University of California Press. Professor Enloe continues her mission of uncovering the effects of militarization on women in a global context. She argues that women everywhere are affected by the presence and ethos of military institutions and the processes of militarization. Security of the female individual and community is compromised and undermined by the needs of the military.

■ Steans, Jill (1998), *Gender and International Relations: An Introduction*, Cambridge: Polity. A clearly stated analysis of how women and men have related to the state, war, and the international system. Links gender to nationalism and the construction of citizenship, and explores in detail the various arguments over whether women are fit to fight. Also looks at women and development issues.

■ Tickner, Ann (1992), *Gender in International Relations: Feminist Perspectives on Achieving Global Security*, New York: Columbia University Press. A feminist analysis of the existing major theories of international relations. Includes interesting and clear analysis of feminist thinking on subjects such as ecology. Especially useful on security.

■ Van Crevald, Martin (2001), *Men, Women and War: Do Women Belong in the Front Line?* London: Cassell. A provocative and lively account that argues against women as suited for the tasks of war. The author argues that women should not be engaged in the business of national security and war.

IMPORTANT WEBSITES

● http://www.uswc.org   Connects US women working for rights and empowerment and links them with the global women's movement.

● http://www.womenwarpeace.org   The United Nations Security Council in its October 2000 resolution on Women, Peace and Security noted the 'need to consolidate data on the impact of armed conflict on women and girls'. This website is the response to this. It is a portal that provides data on the impact of armed conflict on women and girls.

● http://www.womenwagingpeace.net   This website provides details of the Initiative for Inclusive Security, a network established in 1999 that enables women from around the world to connect with one another and have an impact on decision-makers.

● http://www.dcaf.ch/women   Women in an Insecure World is part of the Geneva Centre for the Democratic Control of Armed Forces and has as its main objective the empowerment of women as security sector actors.

Visit the Online Resource Centre that accompanies this book for lots of interesting additional material: www.oxfordtextbooks.co.uk/orc/collins2e/

8

Human Security

PAULINE KERR

 Chapter Contents

- Introduction: the concept's intellectual and empirical purpose
- Is human security a valuable analytical and policy framework?
- Reconciling tensions
- Utility for practitioners
- Conclusion

 Reader's Guide

This chapter examines the concept of human security and its role within both security studies and the policy community. It argues that the concept is a recent development of earlier human-centric arguments, which propose that people ought to be secure in their daily lives. The label 'human security' came into currency in the mid-1990s and now serves several useful purposes, the most important being to highlight some critical issues, especially intra-state political violence, that are not included in the state-centric paradigm that dominates discourse. The concept of human security does not challenge the relevance of state-centric arguments in so far as these concern the protection of the state from external military violence of a realpolitik nature. However, the human security concept does show that state-centric realism is not a sufficient security argument in that it does not adequately address the security of people inside states from political violence. Realism therefore does not deserve to be the dominant understanding of security. In the contemporary context the concept of security should encompass properly functioning states and their people. But so far attempts at conceptually reconciling or converging arguments about the security of the state and people are underdeveloped and vulnerable to criticism. From a practical perspective the concept of human security receives mixed responses from the policy community: some practitioners adopt both state and human-centric approaches, others reject the human security approach, and others misuse it to justify policies that have other motives. Nonetheless, there is a slowly evolving practical agenda for human security that is merging with other programmes for addressing internal conflict, especially those for supporting the 'responsibility-to-protect' principle. Unfortunately, though, recognition that these programmes are intellectually founded on human security is often overlooked, and the concept receives insufficient credit. The chapter concludes with a summary of the concept's likely future as a practical concept and in the conceptualization and practice of security.

Introduction: the concept's intellectual and empirical purpose

In little over a decade and a half the concept of human security has become a core component of contemporary security studies. The concept questions the dominant state-centric approach to security, which posits that the state is the referent object, or the entity to be made secure, and that its relations with other states is the proper focus of security. Human security by contrast shifts the focus to individuals, to people, as the referent object, and it gives most attention to those people suffering insecurities inside states.

Despite the concept's recent introduction into security studies, the idea that people ought to be secure in the conduct of their daily lives is not new, which should not be surprising. A human-centric focus continues to drive the very old political philosophy of liberalism, which places people and the individual at its epicentre and prescribes some necessary conditions, such as freedom and equality, for people to be secure. Likewise, the tradition of liberalism within the discipline of International Relations focuses on broad normative visions that aim to ensure that people will be secure, such as through the adoption of universal human rights. International Relations' subdiscipline, security studies, and its critical security school, often place the security of people at the centre of its critique of state-centric and military security. Indeed, these arguments by critical security scholars for deepening and broadening the idea of security are driven to a large extent by a vision of the conditions that ought to pertain for people to be secure.

This long philosophical and political human-centric tradition has only recently included a concept labelled 'human security'. The term apparently had its origins in policy statements emanating from the United Nations in the mid-1990s and in particular the 1994 United Nations Development Programme (UNDP) *Human Development Report*

1994. In this document 'human security' is described as a condition where people are given relief from the traumas that besiege human development. Human security means, 'first, safety from such chronic threats as hunger, disease and repression. And second, it means protection from sudden and hurtful disruptions in the patterns of daily life—whether in homes, in jobs or in communities' (UNDP 1994: 23). Ensuring human security requires a seven-pronged approach to address economic, food, health, environment, personal, community, and political security. This particular understanding of human security is categorized as one of the broad definitions and is the basis for division about the meaning of human security, which we will explore in the next section.

In the meantime it is useful to ask why the concept came into centre stage in the mid-1990s and what intellectual and empirical purpose it serves. The point to remember about concepts is that, like theories, they are developed to serve a purpose, or several purposes, and some do so more usefully than others. So, what purposes does the concept of human security serve and are they useful? Going back to the recent origins of the term, the UNDP coinage can be seen as a post-Cold War attempt to focus attention on the issue of development, or more precisely human development, so as to move human and financial resources towards poverty relief and away from simple GDP economic indicators of development and the all-consuming Cold War military and traditional security agenda. The extent to which this occurred is questionable.

The focus that the concept of human security puts on the nexus between conflict and development is nonetheless very useful and important. Empirical observations and several data-collection studies reveal the significance of that nexus. Conflict since the mid-1990s overwhelmingly takes place within the borders of developing states, not between states. These borders frequently surround what is often called disrupted states, where governance is inadequate often because there is conflict among armed groups—sometimes between the government and rebels, and sometimes between competing rebel or social groups. Caught in between the warring parties are countless civilians, many of whom are women and children. Disturbingly, the main perpetrator of violence against civilians is frequently the ruling regime and state actors such as the police and military. The significance of the nexus between development and conflict is not just that it raises ethical issues about human suffering but that its frequent outcome, so called state failure, has dire local, regional, and global effects.

The human security concept also serves as a reminder that many of the debates about the practical measures for managing internal conflict, such as those slowly evolving mechanisms for supporting the responsibility to protect (R2P) and its three components—the responsibility to prevent, react, and rebuild—are intellectually founded on the concept. This, as we will see, is sometimes overlooked.

The focus on the human security concept highlights the view that the threats to humans, as well as to state entities, are changing and increasing. These changes have spurred the debate about the meaning of security and the arguments for its broadening and deepening. Apart from violence within the state, there are non-military threats of environmental degradation and the effects of global warming, pandemics such as HIV/AIDS, SARS, and avian flu, and people movements (refugees and internally displaced peoples). Like internal violence, these transnational issues have serious local, regional, and global effects.

From a normative perspective the concept serves to highlight the importance of good global norms. Human security is an underlying motivation for the Universal Declaration of Human Rights, the UN Charter, the Geneva Conventions, the Ottawa Treaty, and the International Criminal Court. Human security often serves as an umbrella norm for various treaties and conventions that aim to protect vulnerable people from persecuting actors, notably the state. Developing good global norms is important not only for moral and ethical reasons but also because, as most democratic countries illustrate, they serve to enhance state and international security.

The concept of human security even serves to support some realpolitik interests. Sukhre (2004: 365) suggests that Canada and Norway were strong advocates of human security, not least because the concept could assist their lobbying efforts during the early 1990s to gain a seat as the non-permanent members of the UN Security Council. The concept can serve other types of realpolitik interests, as we will see later in the chapter.

Notwithstanding the point that human security can serve some realpolitik issues, it is apparent that human security is quite different from state-centric security. As indicated at the start of this chapter, human security challenges the state-centric approach to security by suggesting that people who are the victims of political violence, usually from state authorities, can be as insecure as those threatened by conflict between states.

KEY POINTS

- The human-centric tradition, which emphasizes the desirable human conditions for people to be secure, now includes the concept of 'human security'.

- Concepts are tools, and human security is no exception. The label of human security, developed in the mid-1990s, serves to highlight several issues in world politics: for example, political violence inside states, obstacles to human development, the nexus between development and conflict, the increasing number of transnational threats, the normative humanitarian agenda, and even realpolitik interests.

- The concept's main contribution to security studies is to focus critical attention on the approach to security offered by the traditional and dominant state-centric model.

Is human security a valuable analytical and policy framework?

The proposition in the above discussion is that the concept of human security raises issues about the security of people that are not part of the dominant state-centric argument of security. However, even if this is the case, does the concept provide a satisfactory analytical and policy framework that can challenge state-centric positions and should it be the dominant argument? Answering these questions requires an examination of the concept: its meaning according to the different schools of human security and the analytical relationship between these schools. From this analysis readers can then compare the human and state-centric arguments.

This section makes two arguments: first, that there are major differences between the schools of human security that appear to raise questions about its prospects as a framework for challenging the dominant argument; and, second, that it is possible nonetheless to reconcile these differences and develop an analytical framework.

Tensions between the schools of human security

Human security, according to its advocates, challenges the traditional state-centric view that the state is and should be the primary object, or referent, of security. For the advocates, human security is the end and state-centric security is the means to that objective. But what does human security actually mean? Putting aside differences between state-centric and human-centric positions for the moment, the meaning of human security is contested by the different schools of human security. While all the advocates agree that people are the referent object, they are divided over the type of threat that should be prioritized, or securitized. The dispute over prioritizing threats has divided advocates into the narrow and the broad schools.

The narrow school

Mack, a proponent of the narrow school, argues that the threat of political violence to people, by the state or any other organized political actor, is the proper focus for the concept of human security. The definition that Mack supports is that human security is 'the protection of individuals and communities from war and other forms of violence' (Human Security Centre 2005a). Mack (2004: 367) acknowledges there are many other threats to people apart from systematic violence. However, his emphasis on conceptual clarity and analytical rigour involves treating many of these other threats as correlates of violence; for example, violence correlates with poverty and poor governance. For Mack, there is advocacy value in expanding the security agenda to include the broad agenda below but doing so has analytical costs. This narrow definition has been simplified as 'freedom from fear' of the threat or use of political violence and is distinguished from the broad definition below, which is labelled 'freedom from want'.

The broad schools

The broad schools argue that human security means more than a concern with the threat of violence. Human security is not only freedom from fear but also freedom from want, which is the focus of human development in the UNDP Report mentioned earlier. Moreover, according to some, human security goes beyond freedom from want in underdevelopment and involves other human freedoms and values. For example, Thakur holds that 'human security is concerned with the protection of people from critical life-threatening dangers, regardless of whether the threat are rooted in anthropogenic activities or natural events, whether they lie within or outside states, and whether they are direct or structural' (2004a: 347). Human security is '"human centred" in that its principal focus is on people both as individuals and as communal groups. It is "security orientated" in that the focus is on freedom from fear, danger and threat' (2004a: 347). Thakur attempts to install some limitations to the broad schools by referring to life-threatening situations that have become crises and by putting those that are not crises onto the broader development agenda. An example of the even broader definition of human security is one proposed by Alkiri. Alkiri (2004: 360), who was a member of the 2003 Commission on Human Security, co-chaired by Amartya Sen and Sadako Ogata, argues that the objective of human security is 'to protect the vital core of all human lives in ways that advance human freedoms and human fulfilment'. Thakur defends these broad conceptualizations on the grounds that, although analytical rigour may be lost, there is value in having inclusive definitions.

The broad definitions of human security certainly receive the most criticism and often provide the grounds for critics to dismiss the entire concept. Paris, for example, claims human security 'encompasses everything from substance abuse to genocide'. From this perspective, the problem is that the number of causal hypotheses for human insecurity are so vast that frameworks for research and policy are difficult to formulate. Paris (2004: 371) dismisses the whole concept as being 'inscrutable', a strong condemnation considering that, in the *Concise Oxford Dictionary* (2006: 734), the word means 'impossible to understand or interpret'.

Differences over means

Debate about the types of threats that should be included in the definition has, of course, implications for the means for enhancing human security. The means for the development broad school are the same as those proposed in various UNDP reports—for example, the 2005 UNDP Human Development Report (UNDP 2005). However, because the broad schools also include definitions

that go beyond the development agenda to include threats to 'vital core of all human lives', and, since these can be quite subjective and variable, the means are equally variable. The broad schools, comprising threats to human development and particularly the very broad threats to 'vital core of all human lives', appear to have no common factor that connects all the different threats, except that each is perceived as a threat to people. Thus the means for the broad schools will depend on whatever the threat is perceived to be and are, therefore, limitless. However, because the narrow school is connected by the common focus on the threat of political violence to people, the means are directed at managing that threat. A wide variety of economic, social, political, and military/policing means are found in the literature on managing internal conflict and transnational violence, though there is considerable debate about which means work and when.

The means issue is further complicated by arguments over the role of the state and the appropriate agents of human security. In many situations the state is the perpetrator of violence and of other threats to its people's security and is therefore the problem, or a major part of the problem. Such behaviour by the state is often taken to be synonymous with the state-centric position on security. From this perspective, human security is hard, even impossible, to achieve if the state remains the major actor in world politics.

This perspective raises important issues about the role of the state as a means to achieve human security. It is certainly the case that some states are at the heart of human insecurity. But there are several other issues to consider. First, because some states wilfully behave badly does not mean that all states should be dismissed as actors and that all state-centric positions work against human security; second, pragmatically, states continue to have the main material assets for logistically delivering human security; third, in reality state building towards better states continues to be the objective of the major global institutions, including the UN, and many non-governmental organizations (NGOs) and civil-society groups; fourth, realistically, comprehensive normative change does not occur quickly and thus adopting a hands-off states and policy approach is not helpful in the short term, when there are many current crises in which people need immediate relief from atrocities. Hence it is necessary to deal with the immediate situation while still pursuing long-term change. For that reason it is necessary to engage in a direct way in a policy agenda for human security. It is also necessary to involve a variety of actors—institutions of global governance, non-state actors, civil society, and states—in addressing the narrow and broad agendas. Nonetheless, scepticism about the state's capacity to deliver and reform remains, and hence the division over means continues to be a divisive issue. Another major difference over the means to human security concerns the place of humanitarian intervention using military means in situations where systematic violence within a state is the cause of human insecurity (see Chapter 21).

In conclusion, the means for addressing human insecurity as violence will involve a range of measures and actors, and their roles will continue to be contested. Regardless of critics' concerns about the role of states, properly functioning states will be indispensable actors, not least because the intervening military and police force, albeit in blue berets, will have the assets and human resources to provide immediate security from violence. The key actors for reconstruction, once security is assured, will be state-based aid programmes, global institutions, local and international NGOs, and civil-society groups.

KEY POINTS

- There are tensions between the different schools of human security about the meaning of, threats to, and the means to human security.

- The narrow school focuses on threats of violence, often called freedom from fear; the broad schools focus on threats arising from underdevelopment, often called freedom from want, and on threats to other human freedoms.

- The means to human security are also contentious, with divisions over the role of the state and the justifications for humanitarian intervention using force.

Reconciling tensions

In principle the above discussion illustrating the divisions between the different schools of human security raises questions about the concept's capacity to challenge the dominant state-centric argument about security. However, this section argues two points: first that it is possible to develop analytical and policy frameworks based on both the narrow and broad schools that show that there are important connections between them; and, second, that, as Table 8.1 suggests, this framework has the potential to challenge the realist state-centric school by showing that realism is a necessary but not sufficient security argument. However, that said, human security is itself a necessary but not sufficient approach to security.

The framework that shows the possibility of reconciling the narrow and broad schools focuses upon (1) human insecurity understood as political violence and (2) the causes of human insecurity understood as political violence. To use social-science language, human insecurity as political violence (the narrow school) is the dependent variable. The many causes of human insecurity as political violence include the problems of underdevelopment (the main broad school) and these are the independent variables (see Figure 8.1).

There are several analytical advantages to this formulation. First, the connections between the two schools are quite clear. Second, the causal links can be multifactorial and interconnected: for example, threats of poverty and disease and poor governance are two interconnected causes of political violence (see Figure 8.1). Third, causality can be a circular dynamic: for example, not only can poverty and poor governance cause political violence; it can work the other way as well—that is, political violence

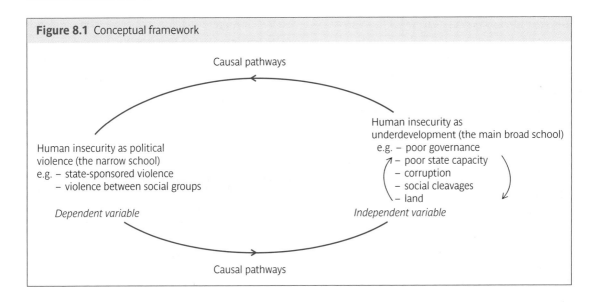

Figure 8.1 Conceptual framework

Causal pathways

Human insecurity as political
violence (the narrow school)
e.g. – state-sponsored violence
      – violence between social groups

Dependent variable

Human insecurity as
underdevelopment (the main broad school)
e.g. – poor governance
      – poor state capacity
      – corruption
      – social cleavages
      – land

Independent variable

Causal pathways

can cause poverty and bad governance (see Figure 8.1). Fourth, because this conceptual framework identifies the problem of violence and its causes, it provides a sound basis for policy (see Figure 8.2). Importantly, it shows that crisis management of violence requires both immediate action in terms of diplomacy and, failing that, intervention. Plus at the same time it requires crisis prevention measures from the broad development agenda. Proper management requires policies that address the narrow school's focus on violence and the broad schools'

focus on development. Each type of policy is equally important.

This framework helps to overcome many of the tensions between the schools, and it may satisfy some of the critics. It will not, however, please those human security advocates who want to include the very broad agenda of protecting the 'vital core of human lives' as human security. And it will frustrate those who want to include non-violent issues, such as horizontal inequality or people movements, as the dependent variable unrelated to violence.

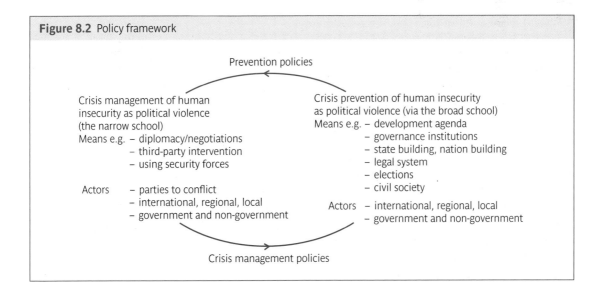

Figure 8.2 Policy framework

Prevention policies

Crisis management of human
insecurity as political violence
(the narrow school)
Means e.g. – diplomacy/negotiations
            – third-party intervention
            – using security forces

Actors   – parties to conflict
          – international, regional, local
          – government and non-government

Crisis prevention of human insecurity
as political violence (via the broad school)
Means e.g. – development agenda
            – governance institutions
            – state building, nation building
            – legal system
            – elections
            – civil society

Actors   – international, regional, local
          – government and non-government

Crisis management policies

Human-centric and state-centric security: both necessary both insufficient

Finally, there is still the question of whether or not it is a framework that can challenge the dominant state-centric security argument. Taking into account the arguments in Chapter 2 about the justification for the state-centric approach to security, not least because of the continuing occurrence of conflict between states (albeit a declining event), it is clear that this traditional approach cannot be dismissed. However, adopting a human security approach to security means that the flaws in the state-centric perspective become evident. But the shortcomings of the human security approach—the inadequate attention to continuing state-to-state conflict and a rather undifferentiated criticism of the state as a protector of human security—are problematic. Nonetheless, there is intellectual strength in the human security concept, and the possibility of reconciling its different schools makes it plausible to argue that both the human-centric and the state-centric approaches are necessary but not sufficient approaches to security.

Lodgaard helpfully draws out the conceptual dimensions of this proposition. His starting point is that both arguments provide the 'concepts that security policies will be organised around' in the future (2000: 1–2). He proposes a reconceptualization of security as a 'dual concept of state security and human security'—the former involving defence of territory and freedom to determine one's own form of government and the latter involving people being free of physical violence (2000: 1–6). Lodgaard's approach can be elaborated into a fuller proposition in which there are not only dual referent objects (people and state), but also internal and external threats to both, and in which the means to security in each case involves a variety of measures, both the use of force and non-military measures (Kerr 2003). Nonetheless, these attempts at conceptualizing security in terms of both arguments are embryonic and abstract and there is much more work to be done to make it a clear and convincing argument. But it is a step in the right direction.

KEY POINTS

- One way of reconciling the different schools of human security and developing an overall framework is to focus on the nexus between the narrow school's focus on violence and the broad schools' focus on human development. The narrow school's focus on political violence is the dependent variable and the broad schools' focus on human development is the independent variable. This framework highlights the intellectual and causal connections between the two schools and provides policy directions for crisis management and prevention.

- An examination of the tensions between the human-centric and state-centric approaches to security shows that in the contemporary context each approach is necessary but not sufficient.

- Although in principle this suggests that both state-centric and human security are needed for an understanding of security, there is much to be done to consolidate the conceptual foundations of this proposition.

Utility for practitioners

Up to this point the discussion has explored the conceptual dimensions of human security and its role within security studies. In doing so, reference has been made to the concept's capacity for policy guidance and the argument being made up to this point is that, despite the critics' claims that the concept is not useful

Table 8.1 Human-centric and state-centric security: both necessary both insufficient

	Human-centric security – the narrow school	State-centric security
Referent object	People at risk of political violence	State and territory at risk of outside military interference or invasion
Threat/s	Organized political violence: e.g. • civil war (involving the government and rebel or communal groups) • non-state conflicts (involving communal or rebel groups or warlords but not the government) One-sided violence (involving government forces or non-state armed groups against defenceless civilians)	Political violence from the military forces of other states
Practical means	Military and non-military: • prevention: diplomacy; addressing the causes of conflict; international regimes for countering small arms/light weapons trade and anti-personnel land mines; deterrent measures (e.g. ICC, war-crimes tribunals) • reaction: diplomacy; mediation; humanitarian military intervention, etc. • rebuild: diplomacy; state and nation building; law and order through policing, judicial systems; the broad school agenda The means are based on an assumption that sovereignty is a responsibility not simply a right	Military and non-military • the military power of the state • diplomacy The means are based on an assumption that sovereignty is an inviolable right
Actors	• The state: outside states and depending on the situation, domestic governments • Non-state: international, regional and domestic	• The government/state, the military forces of the state

for policy guidance, it is possible to develop a framework that is. However, the question now raised is does it offer guidance and in what way is it valuable?

Once again scholars disagree in their answers about the utility of the concept. Hubert (2004: 351) argues that empirically it was the foreign policies of some particular states that led academics to develop and elevate the concept. Canadian and Norwegian foreign policies starting in the 1990s are cited as evidence for this view. That is, the concept was a response to existing practice and moreover its mandate became a guide to many states—for example, those belonging to the Human Security Network. The 2003 report *Human Security Now* compiled by the Commission for Human Security

offers additional guidance and encouragement to states to adopt policies of human security. From this perspective human security is operationalized, providing sound guidance and being implemented. However, Suhrke (2004: 365) makes some different observations, arguing that there is a decline in interest in the concept as a foreign-policy theme in the policies of the original promoters, Canada and Norway, and other supporters. Furthermore, the Commission on Human Security had little impact, and the Human Security Network has a membership of just thirteen states (Suhrke 2004: 365), and none of them major players in world politics.

Several case studies on the utility of human security for policy-makers, undertaken by Kerr, Tow, and Hanson, suggest that the practitioners in these cases adopted the narrow human security agenda when a crisis of human insecurity in another state was perceived to be a threat to their own state's national interests. However, the means for reducing that threat in the long term often involved measures based on human security, such as law and order to protect citizens (Kerr et al. 2003: 102). For example, Australia's intervention in the Solomon Islands in 2003 took place when Australian policy-makers perceived that violence there had reached a crisis point and threatened Australia's national security interests. The Howard government, while not referring to the concept of human security, nonetheless made community policing to protect civilians and prevent violence a key focus of rebuilding the Solomon Islands. Such rebuilding had the effect of making Australia more secure in the future.

Another case study, on the US invasion of Iraq, demonstrates that, although the US intentions for invasion were always vague, when the post-invasion period descended into chaos the US elevated the human-security agenda as a justification for the war in Iraq, arguing that the US aim was to rescue the people of Iraq from the human insecurities caused by Saddam Hussein. However, tellingly, even then the USA did little to restore law and order through implementing policing and justice measures—key elements of the narrow school's policy agendas. This suggests that the rhetoric, but not the implementation, of human security was used by US policy-makers when a crisis of human insecurity was perceived to undermine their state-centric interests.

From the perspective of practitioners in many developing countries, human security is a quite subversive concept. The narrow version is often seen as an attempt to interfere in the internal affairs of decolonized states and impose Western values and changing ideas about sovereignty. In the Asia-Pacific region several states champion the broad schools' understanding in development terms and the broader non-military transnational threats of environmental degradation and diseases such as HIV/AIDS and SARS. However, there is little support for the narrow school's emphasis on violence inside the state and human rights. At the non-state

level in the Asia-Pacific, however, there is growing advocacy for the narrow school's focus on violence.

The human security framework is often adopted by UN practitioners as a diplomatic framing tool for setting normative standards and for demonstrating the connections between conflict and human development in important UN statements. Examples include the *2005 Human Development Report* (UNDP 2005) and the 2005 Secretary General's 'In Larger Freedom' (United Nations 2005b), which was his response to the High Level Panel Report, and the 'Draft Outcome Document' from the 2005 World Summit (United Nations 2005a).

Another issue that relates to the question of the utility of the concept for practitioners is the development of a practical agenda that supports human security. Krause (2007: 4) notes the evolution of a policy agenda for supporting the objectives of the narrow school—for example, through such measures as international regimes to regulate small arms and light weapons trade, and anti-personnel land mines (1997 Ottawa Treaty) as well as through deterrent measures such as specialist tribunals to address war crimes (in, for example, the former Yugoslavia, Rwanda, and Sierra Leone) and the International Criminal Court, which prosecutes perpetrators of crimes against humanity.

Another related practical agenda that supports human security is connected to the principle of the responsibility to protect (R2P) and its three practical objectives, the responsibility to prevent, react, and rebuild. The R2P principle was developed in the 2001 report *The Responsibility to Protect* produced by the Commission on Intervention and State Sovereignty (ICISS), which is discussed further in Chapter 21. Despite the valuable articulation of such responsibilities, there is still insufficient 'operationalization' and practical substance to R2P and therefore to human security. Mindful of this, the UN Secretary-General Ban Ki-moon in a speech in Berlin on 15 July 2008 foreshadowed his intention to submit proposals to the General Assembly by the end of 2008 that would help practically to achieve the R2P objectives of preventing, deterring, and responding to serious violations against people.

This development of the practical agenda for human security through the R2P agenda is a point of discussion and some contention. Luck (2008: 5) argues that 'human security offers important non-traditional way of thinking about security, but does not attempt to offer the kinds of specific policy choice and instruments that R2P does'. Luck's point is correct in a strict practical sense; however, it fails to acknowledge that the measures associated with human security mentioned above are important aspects of the responsibility to prevent violence and that the concept of human security is the intellectual justification for R2P. Human security and R2P are two sides of the same coin.

Why human security is often overlooked as the foundation of practices applied to address political violence inside states is an interesting question. Given some practitioners' concern about the implications of human security for their sovereign control of domestic affairs, there may be an inclination among those who wish to promote R2P to distance themselves from the concept. Yet, R2P obviously supports the same intervention option if states are unwilling or unable to stop genocide, war crimes, ethnic cleansing, and crimes against humanity, albeit working under the Charter of the United Nations and Chapters VI, VII, VIII. Or, it may be that as practical measures evolve they take on a life of their own, and debates that follow are about the details of which practices are appropriate.

One important question is whether, despite the shortcomings in the development of a practical agenda for pursuing human security and indeed the lack of evidence-based evaluations of measures adopted, there have been any changes in global political violence and whether the concept and its practice are causally relevant. Data from the Human Security Report Project (HSRP) at Simon Fraser University in Canada show that there has indeed been a remarkable decline in internal violence since the mid-1990s (see Think

---

THINK POINT 8.1

The decline in global political violence

- From the beginning of 2002 to the end of 2005, the number of armed conflicts being waged around the world shrank 15 per cent from 66 to 56. By far the greatest decline was in sub-Saharan Africa.

- Battle death tolls declined worldwide by almost 40 per cent between 2002 and 2005. (Battle deaths are prone to considerable error, however, so these findings should be treated with appropriate caution.)

- The steep post-Cold War decline in genocides and other mass slaughters of civilians has continued. In 2005 there was just one genocide—in Darfur. In 1989 there were ten.

- The estimated number of displaced people around the world—refugees and internally displaced persons—fell from 34.2 million to 32.1 million between 2003 and 2005, a net decline of 6 per cent.

- The number of military coups and attempted coups fell from 10 in 2004 to just 3 in 2005, continuing an uneven decline from the 1963 high point of 25.

- The number of non-state conflicts (those between communal or rebel groups or warlords, but in which the government is not a warring party) have undergone a marked and consistent decline since data were first collected in 2002. They have declined by a third—from 36 to 24 between 2002 and 2006. Reported battle deaths from these conflicts declined by 60 per cent over the same period.

- Campaigns of 'one-sided violence' (involving deadly campaigns against defenceless civilians by either governments or non-state armed groups) have dropped sharply. In 2004, the peak year, 38 campaigns of one-sided violence were being perpetrated around the world. In 2006 there were just 26—a new decline of 32 per cent from 2004. (At least 25 fatalities a year have to result to be counted as data.)

Human Security Report Project (2007).

Human Security Centre (2006).

Points 8.1 and 8.2). According to the *Human Security Brief 2006* this decline is largely explained by UN and international activism in peace operations. There can be little doubt, notwithstanding the complexity of identifying the motivations for intervention, that a major part of explanation for UN and international activism is the objective of human security.

The research produced by such organizations as the HSRP has generated important findings on internal conflict that are highly relevant to policy-makers. Apart from the data mentioned above on global trends in human insecurity, the Project has developed different types of data-sets—for example there are data on 'one-sided violence'—situations when unarmed civilian groups are the target of violence by either the government or non-state armed groups. This allows policy-makers to understand the exact nature of the violence (for example, its drivers) and develop appropriate policies. As the HSRP points out, 'such information and analysis is a necessary—though not sufficient—condition for the "evidence-based policy" that increasing numbers of international organizations and donor governments are demanding' (*Human Security Brief 2007*: 7).

KEY POINTS

- There is disagreement about the extent to which the human security concept is adopted by practitioners.

- On the one hand it appears that despite the rhetoric there is limited implementation of the human security agenda by states. On the other hand the active involvement of UN practitioners in peace operations that aim to address human insecurity is one of the reasons why there is a decrease in internal conflict.

- In general, state practitioners appear to refer to or implement the human security agenda when it serves their material interests. However, in doing so policy makers often adopt human security measures as the means for ensuring their long term national interests are enhanced.

- The development of a practical agenda for human security over the last 3–4 years has become merged with the many other programmes for addressing political violence inside states, including R2P. These programmes often overlook the fact that their intellectual foundations are based on human security and the concept frequently does not receive due credit.

- The practical agenda is slowly evolving and evidence-based research on human security is increasingly demanded by international organizations and donor governments. However, more research needs to be conducted on the processes of implementation, for example diplomacy, and on criteria for assessing which practices improve human security.

Conclusion

The final question to be asked concerns the future prospects of the human security concept in security studies and in the policy community. The argument in this chapter is that the concept contributes to understandings of security by showing that realism, the dominant state-centric security argument, is necessary but not sufficient, and should not be the dominant understanding of security. Because human security makes people the referent object, it puts the onus on realism to explain why the state is the referent object if it is not a means to people's security. Unless the ultimate purpose of state-centric security is the security of people, then the relevance of the state is questionable, and likewise state-centric security arguments. In this way the human security concept will continue usefully to highlight the point that the relationship between the people and the state and the role of sovereignty is at the centre of understandings about security.

This suggests that in the future the human security concept will continue to flourish in academic circles and in the teaching curriculum. The Tokyo University, for example, offers graduate programmes

THINK POINT 8.2

Explaining the decline in political violence

- In the early 1990s, with the Security Council no longer paralysed by Cold War politics, the UN spearheaded an explosion of conflict prevention, peacemaking, and post-conflict peace-building activities. This unprecedented surge in international activism included:

  - a sixfold increase in the number of preventive diplomacy missions (which seek to stop wars from starting) mounted by the UN between 1990 and 2002;

  - a fourfold increase in peacemaking missions (those that seek to stop ongoing conflicts) over the same period;

  - a sevenfold increase in the number of 'Friends of the Secretary-General', 'Contact Groups', and other government-initiated mechanisms to support peacemaking and peace-building missions between 1990 and 2003;

  - an elevenfold increase in the number of regimes subjected to economic sanctions between 1989 and 2001

(sanctions can be used to pressure warring parties to negotiate and help stem the flow of war resources);

  - a fourfold increase in the number of UN peace operations between 1988 and 2004.

- Peace operations in the 1990s were not only more numerous than previously; they were also far larger and more complex that those of the Cold War era.

- They also made a real difference. A recent RAND Corporation study found that two-thirds of UN peace-building missions were successful—a better success rate than that of the USA. They were also cost effective.

- The single most compelling explanation remains the upsurge of international activism that followed the end of the Cold War.

Human Security Centre (2005b).

---

in human security, as do many other universities. At the academic level, the relationship between the state, people, and sovereignty remains a robust debate, and there is a normative impetus among many academics to focus on the human condition. If the latter continues to be part of the motivation of academics and students, then the future of the concept is assured. There is a great deal of research to be done on human security: for example, on the cross-disciplinary triangular relationship between security, governance, and development; on further conceptual development of the idea, especially as there have been so few advances in the 2000s; and on the connections between the schools of human security. As Thomas (2004: 354) points out, 'the ultimate test of the utility of the concept lies in the extent to which policy makers and scholars can draw out the interconnections between these two streams of concern'. Continuing and expanding the quantitative and qualitative databases on human security are other important areas of research. Regular editions of the *Human Security Briefs* are essential to

sustain. Despite a decade and a half of human security being a key concept in contemporary security studies, there are still many textbooks dedicated to the subject yet to be written.

However, at the level of practice, despite agreement that we live in an interdependent world shared by billions of stakeholders in human security, the future of the concept is less rosy. In the first place, the USA, the key actor in world politics, under the Bush administration was preoccupied with terrorism in Afghanistan and Iraq and did not set adequate human-security standards at home or abroad. The Barack Obama administration will hopefully correct this vacuum in leadership.

In developing countries the main perpetrators of human insecurity will continue to resist changes that will enhance human security because the short-term gains from holding political and economic power are too seductive. Appeals to recalcitrant leaders will have to continue through the argument that short-term benefits are fatal for long-term survival of governing elites and the state. Diplomacy using the human security framework and hard data showing that human security and a moral conscience are in their interests should be the primary approach. Failing that, intervention following the ICISS and the UN's 2005 World Summit principles may be necessary, even though as of mid-2009 the peacekeeping intervention in Darfur is failing to provide human security.

It remains up to the United Nations to continue to provide leadership on human security. Despite the urgency for reform of the UN, the institution has nonetheless been highly instrumental in helping to reduce the incidence and scope of internal violence through peace operations. Data show that since the mid-1990s there has been a dramatic global decline in the scope and incidence of battle-related deaths from internal conflict. (See Think Point 8.1 on the decline in global political violence and Think Point 8.2 on the explanations for the decline.) Also important in reducing conflict is the continuing role of regional organizations, such as the African Union, despite many problems. NGOs and civil society groups continue to be essential actors in the decline of violence, despite the need for better accountability. Indeed, civil society's bottom-up embrace of human security is vital for

advancing the practical agenda. Finally, the role of properly functioning states will continue to be central to improving human security.

It will be critical to develop the practical agenda for human security and equally important to be able to judge which measures produce human security. Again the UN has an important leadership role, and Secretary-General Ban Ki-moon's determination to inject practical substance into R2P is critical, but it will need the support of UN member states.

The most important imperative for continuing to elevate the concept of human security is that ordinary people living in the midst of political violence naturally enough want security. Public opinion polls conducted in Afghanistan by the Asia Foundation in 2008 show that 'the biggest problems faced by Afghanistan as a whole are . . . security (36%), economic issues including unemployment (32%), high prices (22%), and poor economy (17%)' (Asia Foundation 2008: 10). Other research on people living in violence and who are also poor shows that their strongest wish is to be secure from violence. Everyday people everywhere want human security. States and other actors have the responsibility to provide it for ethical reasons and for the common good of us all.

QUESTIONS

1. What is security? Is human security important and if so why?
2. Can human security and state-centric security be reconciled conceptually and in practice? If so how?
3. Should humanitarian intervention using force for the protection of people from large-scale atrocities be conducted if it endangers international stability?
4. Is human security a concept that guides states' policies? If not, why not?
5. Is human security measured by the number of battle-related deaths?
6. What are the problems with the framework proposed in this chapter?
7. What is the relationship between governance, security, and development?
8. What are the local, regional, and global effects of human insecurity?
9. What are the advantages and disadvantages of the concept of human security?

FURTHER READING

■ Collier, P. (2003), *Breaking the Conflict Trap. Civil War and Development Policy*, Oxford: Oxford University Press. Provides an economic view of the causes of civil war and proposals for an agenda of global action.

■ Hampson, F. O., Daudelin, J., Hay, J. B., Reid, H., and Marting, T. (2002), *Madness in the Multitude*, Toronto: Oxford University Press. Presents a strong argument for understanding human security as a global good.

■ *Human Security Briefs 2005, 2006, and 2007*. These publications are important quantitative and qualitative contributions to the analysis of global trends in human insecurity. To download the *Briefs* go to www.hsrgroup.org

■ MacFarlane, N., and Khong Y. F. (2005). *Human Security and the UN: A Critical History*, Bloomington: Indiana University Press. As the title indicates, this is a critical intellectual history of the UN's approach to human security.

■ *Security Dialogue* (2004), 35/3. A special section in the journal provides a very good overview of the debate about human security from many of the main participants.

■ Thakur, R., and Newman, E. (2004) (eds.), *Broadening Asia's Security and Discourse Agenda*, Tokyo: United Nations University Press. A critique of the state-centric paradigm from the perspective of a very broad understanding of human security.

■ Thomas, C. (2000), *Global Governance, Development and Human Security*, London: Pluto Press. Focuses on the issues of governance and development that are central to human security.

■ United Nations Development Programme (2005), *UNDP Human Development Report 2005*, Oxford: Oxford University Press. Analyses of the problems of human development around the world.

 IMPORTANT WEBSITES

● http://www.hsrgroup.org *Human Security Briefs 2005, 2006 and 2007* can be downloaded from this site.

● http:// www.cidcm.umd.edu The Center for International Development and Conflict Management (CIDCM) regularly publishes a very good source, 'Peace and Conflict', which canvasses the interplay between conflict and development.

● http://www.crisisgroup.org/home/index.cfm?l=1&id=3624 International Crisis Group (ICG) regularly publishes 'Crisis Watch', a report on crises around the world.

 Visit the Online Resource Centre that accompanies this book for lots of interesting additional material: www.oxfordtextbooks.co.uk/orc/collins2e/

9

Securitization

RALF EMMERS

Chapter Contents

- Introduction
- Securitization model
- Limitations of the securitization model
- Cases of securitization
- Conclusion

Reader's Guide

The chapter introduces, assesses, and applies the Copenhagen School and its securitization model. The School widens the definition of security by encompassing five different sectors—military, political, societal, economic, and environmental security. It examines how a specific matter becomes removed from the political process to the security agenda. The chapter analyses the act of securitization by identifying the role of the securitizing actor and the importance of the 'speech act' in convincing a specific audience of the existential nature of a threat. It argues that the Copenhagen School allows for non-military matters to be included in security studies while still offering a coherent understanding of the concept of security. Yet the chapter also stresses the dangers and the negative connotations of securitizing an issue as well as some shortcomings of the model. While the chapter is conceptually driven, it relies on a series of illustrations to apply the securitization model.

Introduction

The Copenhagen School emerged at the Conflict and Peace Research Institute (COPRI) of Copenhagen and is represented by the writings of Barry Buzan, Ole Wæver, Jaap de Wilde, and others (Wæver 1995; Buzan et al. 1998; Buzan and Wæver 2003). The Copenhagen School has developed a substantial body of concepts to rethink security, most notably through its notions of securitization and desecuritization. The School has played an important role in broadening the conception of security and in providing a framework to analyse how an issue becomes securitized or desecuritized. It is part of a broader attempt to reconceptualize the notion of security and to redefine the agenda of security studies in the light of the end of the Cold War.

The Copenhagen School has developed its approach to security in numerous writings, most notably in *Security: A New Framework for Analysis* (Buzan et al. 1998). In this volume, Buzan, Wæver, and de Wilde start by defining international security in a traditional military context. 'Security', according to them, 'is about survival. It is when an issue is presented as posing an existential threat to a designated referent object (traditionally, but not necessarily, the state, incorporating government, territory, and society)' (Buzan et al. 1998: 21). With

this point in mind, the Copenhagen School identifies five general categories of security: military security as well as environmental, economic, societal, and political security. The security-survival logic is therefore maintained as well as extended beyond military security to four other categories.

The dynamics of each category of security are determined by securitizing actors and referent objects. The former are defined as 'actors who securitize issues by declaring something, a referent object, existentially threatened' (Buzan et al. 1998: 36) and can be expected to be 'political leaders, bureaucracies, governments, lobbyists, and pressure groups' (Buzan et al. 1998: 40). Referent objects are 'things that are seen to be existentially threatened and that have a legitimate claim to survival' (Buzan et al. 1998: 36). Evidently, the referent objects and the kind of existential threats that they face vary across security sectors. Referent objects can be the state (military security); national sovereignty, or an ideology (political security); national economies (economic security); collective identities (societal security); species, or habitats (environmental security) (Buzan et al. 1998).

The Copenhagen School adopts a multi-sectoral approach to security that represents a move away from

---

KEY POINTS

- A narrow interpretation of security concentrates on the state and its defence from external military attacks. In response to this narrow definition of security, other approaches to security studies have called for a widening and deepening of security to include non-military threats.

- The Copenhagen School stresses that security is about survival. A security concern must be articulated as an existential threat. The School maintains the security-survival logic found in a traditional understanding of security.

- Yet the Copenhagen School broadens the conception of security. It identifies five general categories of security:

military, environmental, economic, societal, and political security. The School thus broadens the concept of security beyond the state by including new referent objects such as societies and the environment.

- The dynamics of each security category are determined by securitizing actors and referent objects.

- It is important, however, to preserve the conceptual precision of the term security. This is where the Copenhagen School contributes to the security-studies literature. It provides a framework to define security and determine how a specific matter becomes securitized or desecuritized.

traditional security studies and its focus on the military sector. Four of the five components account for non-military threats to security. In addition to widening the definition of security beyond military issues, the Copenhagen School deepens security studies by including non-state actors. A crucial question, though, is whether the concept of security can be broadened to such an extent without losing its coherence. There is a risk of overstretching the definition of security, with the result that everything, and therefore nothing in particular, ends up being a security problem. A loose and broad conceptualization of security can lead to vagueness and a lack of conceptual and analytical coherence. In other words, the redefinition and broadening of the concept of security need to be matched by the development of new conceptual tools. This is where the Copenhagen School with its securitization and desecuritization model has sought to contribute to the debates by developing an analytical framework to study security. The Copenhagen School raises the possibility for a systematic, comparative, and coherent analysis of security.

Securitization model

Two-stage process of securitization

The Copenhagen School provides a spectrum along which issues can be plotted. It claims that any specific matter can be **non-politicized, politicized, or securitized**. An issue is non-politicized when it is not a matter for state action and is not included in public debate. An issue becomes politicized when it is managed within the standard political system.

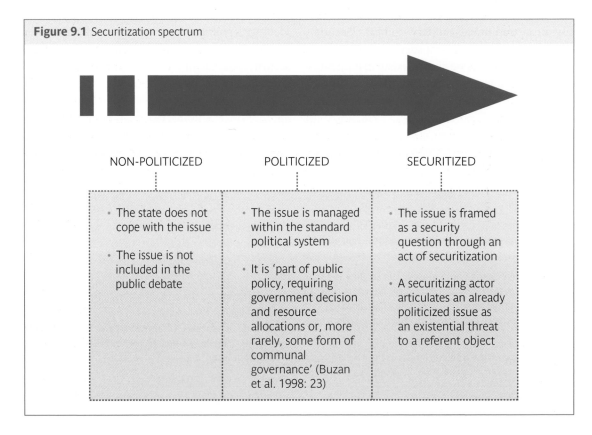

Figure 9.1 Securitization spectrum

NON-POLITICIZED

- The state does not cope with the issue

- The issue is not included in the public debate

POLITICIZED

- The issue is managed within the standard political system

- It is 'part of public policy, requiring government decision and resource allocations or, more rarely, some form of communal governance' (Buzan et al. 1998: 23)

SECURITIZED

- The issue is framed as a security question through an act of securitization

- A securitizing actor articulates an already politicized issue as an existential threat to a referent object

A politicized issue is 'part of public policy, requiring government decision and resource allocations or, more rarely, some other form of communal governance' (Buzan et al. 1998: 23). Finally, an issue is plotted at the securitized end of the spectrum when it requires emergency actions beyond the state's standard political procedures.

The Copenhagen School argues that a concern can be securitized—framed as a security issue and moved from the politicized to the securitized end of the spectrum—through an act of securitization. A securitizing actor (for example, government, political elite, military, civil society) articulates an already politicized issue as an existential threat to a referent object (for example, state, groups, national sovereignty, ideology, economy). In response to the existential nature of the threat, the securitizing actor asserts that it has to adopt extraordinary means that go beyond the ordinary norms of the political domain. Buzan, Wæver, and de Wilde argue, therefore, that securitization 'is the move that takes politics beyond the established rules of the game and frames the issue either as a special kind of politics or as above politics. Securitization can thus be seen as a more extreme version of politicization' (Buzan et al. 1998: 23). The Copenhagen School notes that desecuritization refers to the reverse process. It involves the 'shifting of issues out of emergency mode and into the normal bargaining processes of the political sphere' (Buzan et al. 1998: 4). For example, the end of the Apartheid regime in South Africa represents an illustration of the desecuritization of the race question in South African society and of its reintroduction into the political domain.

An act of securitization refers to the accepted classification of certain and not other phenomena, persons, or entities as existential threats requiring emergency measures. The Copenhagen School relies on a two-stage process of securitization to explain how and when an issue is to be perceived and acted upon as an existential threat to security. The first stage concerns the portrayal of certain issues, persons, or entities as existential threats to referent objects. The initial move of securitization can be initiated by states but also by non-state actors such as trade unions or popular movements. Non-state actors are thus regarded as important players in the securitization model. Yet securitization tends to be a process dominated by powerful actors that benefit from privileged positions. Indeed, the move of securitization depends on, as well as reveals, the power and influence of the securitizing actor, which as a result often happens to be the state and its elites (Collins 2005).

The usage of a language of security does not mean, however, that the issue is automatically transformed into a security question. Instead, the consensual establishment of threat needs to be of sufficient salience to produce substantial political effects. The second and crucial stage of securitization is completed successfully only once the securitizing actor has succeeded in convincing a relevant audience (public opinion, politicians, military officers, or other elites) that a referent object is existentially threatened. Only then can extraordinary measures be imposed. Because of the urgency of the accepted existential threat to security, constituencies tolerate the use of counteractions outside the normal bounds of political procedures.

Central to the two-stage process of securitization is the importance of the 'speech act'. The latter is defined as the discursive representation of a certain issue as an existential threat to security. The Copenhagen School considers the speech act to be the starting point of the process of securitization. An issue can become a security question through the speech act alone, irrespective of whether the concern represents an existential threat in material terms. A securitizing actor uses language to articulate a problem in security terms and to persuade a relevant audience of its immediate danger. The articulation in security terms conditions the audience and provides securitizing actors with the right to mobilize state power and move beyond traditional rules. As discussed above, the security concern must be articulated as an existential threat (Buzan et al. 1998). This significant criterion enables the Copenhagen School to link a broadly defined security concept to the question of survival and thus to the reasoning found within a traditional approach to security studies. This avoids a broad and loose conceptualization of security that could too easily become meaningless.

Successful act of securitization

Governments and political elites have a certain advantage over other actors in seeking to influence audiences and calling for the implementation of extraordinary measures (Collins 2005). In a democratic system, a government benefits from the legitimacy of having been elected by the electorate. This gives it a significant advantage when seeking to convince an audience of the need for emergency actions in response to an existential threat. In democratic societies, the audience still has the right, however, to reject the speech act—namely, the representation of a certain issue as an existential threat.

An important question to examine is whether an act of securitization is more likely to succeed in authoritarian states where the military plays a central role in national politics (Anthony et al. 2006). The formulation of threat perceptions and the decision-making process are often dominated in undemocratic societies by the military as well as by bureaucratic and political elites. The influence of social pressure and aspirations on the securitization or desecuritization of political matters remains limited. Yet this is not to say that an audience is not part of the securitization move or that it is not expected to authorize the adoption of emergency measures, but, rather, that the audience excludes the wider population and consists solely of political elites and some state institutions such as the military. In such a context, political elites can abuse extreme forms of politicization to achieve specific political objectives and consolidate their grip on power. While the wider population may reject the speech act and consider the emergency measures adopted as a result to be illegitimate, the securitization act is nevertheless successful, having convinced a more restrictive audience on the existential nature of the threat (Collins 2005).

It should be clear by now that the Copenhagen School regards security as a socially constructed concept. In that sense, the School is primarily constructivist in its approach. What constitutes an existential threat is regarded as a subjective matter. It very much depends on a shared understanding of what constitutes a danger to security. A person in authority first needs to speak the language of security and demand the adoption of emergency measures. The discourse of the securitizing actor has to be articulated in a fashion that convinces an audience. In other words, a collective has to accept a specific issue as an existential threat to a referent object. Consequently, every act of securitization involves a political decision and results from a political and social act (Anthony et al. 2006). Only in a successful case will standard political procedures no longer be viewed as adequate to counter the threat.

In contrast to a realist approach to security studies that focuses on the material nature of the threat, the Copenhagen School predicts that an act of securitization can either succeed or fail depending on whether a separate audience accepts the discourse. As a result, it naturally asks why some acts tend to fail while others succeed. The Copenhagen School also examines why some questions are securitized in the first place while others are not. It argues that this will not just depend on material factors.

Extraordinary measures and motives for securitization

The Copenhagen School asserts that a successful act of securitization provides securitizing actors with the special right to use exceptional means. It indicates, however, that the success of the process does not depend on the adoption of such actions. It is natural to ask what is meant by 'extraordinary measures'. The latter go beyond rules ordinarily abided by and are therefore located outside the usual bounds of political procedures and practices. Extraordinary measures are expected to respond to a specific issue that is posing an existential threat to a referent object. The adoption and implementation of extraordinary measures involve the identification and classification of some issue as an enemy that needs to be tackled urgently. The types of measures to be adopted in response will obviously depend on the circumstances and the context of the threat. An existential threat to the environment, a sector of the economy, or a state ideology will demand different emergency responses (Collins 2005).

Some shortcomings of the Copenhagen School's interpretation of extraordinary measures should be mentioned. One can rather easily anticipate the types of emergency measures to be introduced by a state. Yet it is less clear what would form an extraordinary measure for a non-state actor after it has successfully convinced an audience of the existential nature of a threat. For instance, what would constitute an extraordinary measure that goes beyond standard political procedures for non-governmental organizations such as Greenpeace and Christian Aid? Moreover, one may question the significance of a securitization process when it does not go hand in hand with actions and policies to address the ostensible threat. According to the securitization model, transforming an issue into a security question requires only the audience's acknowledgement that it is indeed a threat. The adoption of extraordinary means is not a requirement. Buzan, Wæver, and de Wilde (1998: 25) specifically indicate that 'we do not push the demand so high as to say that an emergency measure has to be adopted'. This means that a securititizing actor can make successful speech acts while still deciding to address the existential threat through standard political procedures rather than extraordinary measures (Collins 2005). Yet it can be argued that a complete act of securitization really consists of and demands both discursive (speech act and shared understanding) and non-discursive (policy implementation) dimensions (Emmers 2004; Collins 2005). In this case, a security act would therefore depend on successful speech acts (discursive dimension) that persuade a relevant audience of the existential nature of the threat as well as the adoption by the securitizing actor of emergency powers (non-discursive dimension) to address the so-defined threat.

A series of motives and intentions can help us explain a securitizing act and the subsequent implementation of extraordinary measures (Anthony, Emmers, and Acharya 2006). Securitizing injects urgency into an issue and leads to a sustained mobilization of political support and deployment of resources. It also creates the kind of political momentum necessary for the adoption of additional and emergency measures. The securitization of an issue can thus provide some tangible benefits, including a more efficient handling of complex problems, a mobilizing of popular support for policies in specific areas by calling them security relevant, the allocation of more resources, and so forth. These achievements might not be obtained if the same problems were regarded only as political matters.

Yet it is crucial to highlight the danger of securitization. The process can be abused to legitimize and empower the role of the military or special security forces in civilian activities. This is particularly relevant in emerging democracies or countries where the division between the military and civilian authority is blurred. With the growing articulation of issues as threats in a post-9/11 context, an act of securitization can lead to the further legitimization of the armed forces in politics as well as to the curbing of civil liberties in the name of security in well-established democratic societies. Elites can use a securitizing act to curtail civil liberties, impose martial law, detain political opponents or suspected terrorists without trial, restrict the influence of certain domestic political institutions, or increase military budgets (Anthony et al. 2006). Few checks and balances are normally imposed on implemented emergency measures opening the door for possible abuse. In undemocratic societies, the greater public is not invited to speak out and is thus unable to prevent the dangers associated with an act of securitization. To highlight the potential danger linked to an act of securitization, Kyle Grayson (2003) uses a Frankenstein's Monster analogy. This metaphor for securitization helps us understand how powerful the securitizing actor can become as a result of the process as well as the loss of control that arises from a strategy that opens the door to extraordinary security actions.

Keeping Grayson's Monster metaphor in mind, it is not surprising that the Copenhagen School does not regard an act of securitization as a positive value or as a required development to tackle specific issues (Williams 2003). It argues instead that societies should, as much as possible, operate within the realm of normal politics where issues can be debated and addressed within the standard boundaries of politicization. Consequently, a process of desecuritization is described by Buzan and Wæver as particularly important to reintroduce a matter into a standard politicized level. Risks to society and abuse of authority can be prevented by desecuritizing an issue and reincluding it into the normal political domain.

> **KEY POINTS**
>
> - A successful act of securitization provides securitizing actors with the right to use exceptional means.
>
> - What constitutes an extraordinary measure is not always well defined.
>
> - A series of motives and intentions can explain an act of securitization.
>
> - An act of securitization can lead to excesses and abuse of power. It can easily be abused by authoritarian regimes and/or in the name of the defence of civil liberties.
>
> - Desecuritization can be beneficial, as it reintroduces an issue into a politicized sphere.

Limitations of the securitization model

The Copenhagen School provides a framework to determine how, as well as by whom, a specific matter becomes securitized or desecuritized. Yet, despite the School's prominence in the security-studies literature, the dynamics of securitization and desecuritization remain insufficiently understood empirically (Anthony et al. 2006). The Copenhagen School has so far primarily concentrated on framing a theoretical approach to security studies while paying insufficient attention to empirical research. Questions that need to be explored empirically include why some moves of securitization succeed in convincing an audience while others fail to do so. It is also necessary to analyse why some issues are articulated and treated as existential security threats while others are not. In other words, empirical studies on the path that leads to the securitization of public issues might lead to a better understanding of the transition from the politicized to the securitized end of the spectrum and vice versa. Finally, the Copenhagen School has not given much attention to assessing the policy effectiveness of extraordinary measures nor to the unintended consequences that they might provoke (Anthony et al. 2006). It is, however, important to determine empirically whether acts of securitization contribute to an effective handling of specific issues. Securitizing an issue may in fact not contribute to a solution, as desecuritization might instead be a more fruitful approach.

The Copenhagen School is also criticized for being Euro-centric (Anthony et al. 2006). This Euro-centricism is less obvious though in the case of *Security: A New Framework for Analysis*, which seeks to provide a broad theoretical approach to security studies. Still, the notion of societal security, for example, which is at the core of the Copenhagen School and emphasizes society rather than the state as the primary referent object (Tow 2001), very much derives from a European experience. It refers to borderless societies that are said to exist in Europe as a result of political and economic integration. Societal security, which is examined in Chapter 13, is linked to the construction of a collective European identity and should be dissociated from state security, which relates to the preservation of national sovereignty and territorial integrity. The existence of a similar sense of community in many other regions or parts of the world is disputable.

Furthermore, it is open to debate whether the securitization model contributes to the study of international security in parts of the world that can easily be analysed through a realist model. North East Asia is still very much defined, for example, by a strategic structure determined by realist characteristics. Concerns of a traditional mould continue to trouble the North East Asian region, including the protracted Korean peninsula problem and the risk of the proliferation of weapons of mass destruction, cross-straits tensions between China and Taiwan,

and ongoing diplomatic furores between Japan, on the one hand, and China and South Korea on the other, over the historical legacy of the Pacific War and disputed islets. The fragility of bilateral ties between China and Japan is a key concern for peace and stability in the entire region. From a US and Japanese perspective, China and its rising power also continues to present the most powerful long-term challenge to the East Asian regional order. In such a context, security is still regarded as being essentially about geopolitics, deterrence, power balancing, and military strategy. The state and its defence from external military attacks remain the primary focus of security policies. Hence, although the securitization model can indicate the various 'speech acts' as well as responses from specific audiences and the possible implementation of extraordinary measures, it may in such strategic environments not be able to reveal much more than rational theories, such as realism.

Another shortcoming touches on the blurred distinction between the political and security realms (Anthony et al. 2006). The Copenhagen School needs further to define and clarify the boundaries between politics and security. The School defines securitization as an extreme version of politicization, which contributes to the possible confusion and overlap along the spectrum of depoliticized, politicized, and securitized issues. As it stands, the model may not be able sufficiently to dissociate an act of securitization from a case of severe politicization. The distinction that may exist between these processes can be blurred depending on the political context and existing circumstances (Anthony et al. 2006). For instance, the separation between the political and security domains traditionally remains indistinct in undemocratic societies. Moreover, matters that are articulated in security terms even by democratically elected governments may continue to be located within the political domain and addressed through standard political procedures. Despite the use of speech acts, solutions for the resolution of non-military challenges are frequently found in the realm of politics. Furthermore, and as will be discussed in the next section, more needs to be said about the political motives to securitize an issue. Politicians can use the language of security towards public matters in order to boost their popularity and enhance their chances of re-election. Taking a tough stance on sensitive questions such as undocumented migration, for example, can help them win support among the electorate. Such examples of securitization could be regarded, therefore, as illustrations of politicization.

Finally, the securitization model raises some important questions about the role of academia. Are academics and analysts meant to be and act solely as observers or as advocates—securitizing or desecuritizing actors in their own right—when studying a securitizing move? The Copenhagen School expects analysts to distinguish themselves from a securitization act and the role of the securitizing actor. Yet the distinction may be obscured by a variety of factors. For example, ever since the terror attacks in the United States on 11 September 2001, terrorist experts have been widely present in the media and sometimes even in contact with intelligence agencies. It can be argued, therefore, that such repeated interventions blur the separation between academic analysis and politics and transform the analyst into a separate and influential securitizing actor that is part of the securitizing move.

KEY POINTS

- The securitization model is still relatively new. More empirical research is required to better understand the dynamics of securitization.

- The Copenhagen School is often viewed as Euro-centric, reflecting European security concerns and questions.

- The boundaries between securitization and politicization are sometimes blurred.

- The securitization model raises questions about the role of scholars and analysts.

Cases of securitization

Securitization of undocumented migration

The securitization of undocumented migration has become a recurrent event. Migration is a complex social phenomenon that is influenced by economic, political, socio-cultural, historical, and geographical factors. Economic determinants, especially poverty and economic disparities, are the prime motivation for migrants to leave their countries of origin. They are in pursuit of better opportunities to earn an income and improve their quality of life. Besides the phenomenon of economic migration, political circumstances also explain the movement of populations. Inter-state wars, domestic conflicts of ethno-nationalist origin, and authoritarian regimes with appalling human-rights records create waves of political refugees leaving their countries of origin in the hope of escaping persecution and violence. Migrants face restrictive immigration policies and reduced legal immigration opportunities. This leads to a growing reliance on illegal methods either to enter or to remain in a specific country, including overstaying the expiry of a valid tourist visa or work permit. Since the 1990s, the issue of undocumented migration has also been increasingly linked to organized criminal groups, which now largely control the smuggling and trafficking of people. It is estimated by the United States State Department that as many as 900,000 people might be trafficked annually across international borders.

Undocumented migration can be articulated by politicians and perceived by specific audiences as representing a threat to the political, societal, economic, as well as cultural security of a state and its society (Graham 2000). Undocumented migration is said to undermine the security of national borders and thus to be a threat to the national sovereignty of a state (political security). It can also have a negative

Migration

The Australian Immigration Minister Philip Ruddock said 'whole (Middle East) villages are packing up to come to Australia and the nation was facing "a national emergency".'

O'Connor (2002).

Discussing strip searches of children, then Australian Prime Minister John Howard told Melbourne radio station 3AW: 'It sounds stark and authoritarian, but if you are dealing with situations where people are using children in an exploitive way—which sometimes occurs—then I think that kind of thing is justified.'

Way and Polglaze (2001).

The then leader of the UK Conservative Party Michael Howard spoke on asylum and immigration on 22 September 2004: 'And we have lost control of our asylum and immigration system. At a time when Britain faces an unprecedented terrorist threat, we appear to have little idea who is coming into or leaving our country.'

BBC News (2004).

effect on the fabric of a society and its economic welfare by affecting social order and increasing unrest and crime rates (societal security). Moreover, migrants are often portrayed as a threat to the lifestyle and culture of the receiving country. In addition to being blamed for contributing to a rise in crime and other social problems, undocumented migrants are sometimes described as economic migrants who are claiming asylum to take advantage of national social benefits or take away jobs from the local population (economic security). Hiring undocumented workers tends to be much cheaper for local employers, as the latter do not have to cover their welfare or medical costs. Viewed as cheap labour, undocumented migrants are regarded as threatening employment opportunities. In reality, they mostly end up doing low-skilled jobs that nationals refuse to do. Finally, the arrival of immigrants from a common ethnic or religious group can be perceived

as causing a shift in the racial composition of a country and diluting its cultural identity.

The handling of the undocumented migration issue by the John Howard government in 2001 represents an interesting case of securitization (Emmers 2004). Undocumented migration had started to have a significant political impact in Australia since the late 1990s. Pauline Hanson and her political party, the One Nation Party, transformed the immigration issue into a popular political rallying point. Hanson had proclaimed her extreme views on immigration, the Aborigines, and asylum-seekers. She won a seat in the Australian federal parliament as an independent candidate in 1996 and created the One Nation Party in 1997. The John Howard government first adopted a hard line on undocumented migration in the summer of 2001 over the *Tampa* incident. The *Tampa*, a Norwegian freighter, had rescued 460 Afghans on their way to Australia to claim asylum. Approaching its territorial waters, the Australian government refused the right of entry to the *Tampa* and ordered the ship to turn away. After the ship had failed to obey, Howard ordered units of the Special Air Service (SAS) to take control of the ship and prevent it from reaching Christmas Island or mainland Australia. A military operation had thus been undertaken to avoid asylum-seekers from coming to Australia.

The Australian Prime Minister John Howard, used, together with the issue of terrorism in a post-9/11 environment, the migration theme in his re-election campaign in November 2001. The prime minister explained that he did not want undocumented migrants who had been smuggled into Australia to jump ahead of other people recognized as genuine asylum-seekers by the Australian authorities. The smuggling of undocumented migrants into Australia was also described as a threat to the national sovereignty and territorial integrity of the state. The government indicated that it could not give the impression that it was losing control over its borders, control that is so essential to national sovereignty. Finally, after the terrorist attacks of 9/11, the Australian authorities were concerned that terrorists might be among the migrants smuggled into Australia. The questions of terrorism and undocumented migration were therefore to some extent intertwined in public discussions.

The referent objects in this case of securitization were the national sovereignty and territorial integrity of Australia (military and political security), the fabric of society (societal security), and economic welfare (economic security). The securitizing actor was the John Howard government. The audience consisted of the Australian public opinion (Emmers 2004). Despite a lot of domestic debates and fierce criticism, the audience generally accepted the interpretation of events set forward by the securitizing actor and acknowledged the need to implement extraordinary measures to respond to the threat. Opinion polls suggested that a majority of Australians supported Howard's hard line on undocumented migration. While migration was certainly not the sole reason for success, his conservative coalition was re-elected for a third term in office in November 2001. In other words, the securitizing actor used a discourse of security that convinced an audience of the threat posed by the smuggling of undocumented migration into Australia.

Beyond the use of rhetoric, the Howard government adopted and implemented a series of extraordinary measures to reduce the number of asylum-seekers reaching Australia (Emmers 2004). Such measures included the automatic detention of asylum-seekers in camps while waiting for their applications to be processed and the interception of ships carrying asylum-seekers off the coast of Australia and their diversion to Pacific Islands for processing. The Australian government built immigration detention centres both on its territory and abroad. Asylum-seekers were interned on the Australian territory of Christmas Island, a remote island in the Indian Ocean located about 1,800 kilometres from Western Australia. Offshore refuge centres were also built on Mauru and on Manus Island, in Papua New Guinea, to detain asylum-seekers until their applications were processed. Finally, the Australian Federal Police (AFP) and the Australian Defence Force (ADF) increased their capabilities to ensure border and domestic security against people smuggling, terrorism, and other threats.

Securitization of drug trafficking

The securitization of the illicit trafficking and abuse of drugs has become a recurrent event. Drug trafficking is a transnational criminal activity and is probably the largest international crime problem in the world. The global trade of illicit drugs is believed to be worth as much as US$400 billion a year. Drug trafficking is connected to other categories of transnational crime. It is the prime generator of money laundering and is linked to arms smuggling (drug dealers often outgun police forces), organized crime, corruption, illegal migration, and, in some cases, terrorism. Drug trafficking is viewed as a threat to societal security by increasing drug consumption and addiction, raising the level of violent crime, affecting the health of the consumers, spreading HIV/AIDS through intravenous drug use, and undermining family structures. In addition to its social consequences, drug trafficking has significant economic and political effects. It creates shadow economies, distorts financial institutions, undermines national economies, and fuels the problem of money laundering. It also erodes the rule of law, promotes corruption, and undermines border security. This is examined in detail in Chapter 25.

The so-called war on drugs waged by Thailand in 2003 is an example of a securitizing act (Emmers 2004). The consumption of illicit drugs in the country is a dramatic problem that primarily involves young adults. The most serious trend in Thailand has been the rapid increase in the use of synthetic drugs. Besides the health and social consequences of illicit drug consumption, many in Thailand view the drug-trafficking activities coming from Burma as a significant national-security issue. In response, the then Thai Prime Minister, Thaksin Shinawatra, declared war on drugs in February 2003, vowing to the Thai population to eliminate the narcotics problem within three months. The prime minister stated at an anti-drugs event in late March 2003: 'The drugs problem is a threat to national security. Thus my government has declared war on drugs and

❝
❞ **KEY QUOTES 9.2**

Thaksin and the War on Drugs

'I am serious about taking action against drug traffickers. Government officials, police in particular, must take action too as these traffickers destroy youths' lives, ruin the economy and damage the country.'

Nation (2004).

'We must go after all traders and producers. They are not suitable to be part of our society. They deserve to be put in jail. Drug traders who fight back must be dealt with decisively.'

Tunyasiri (2003).

'Although we have destroyed most of the drug networks it does not mean that the drug problem is totally wiped out. They are like germs: they'll resurrect themselves when our body is weak.'

Agence France Presse (2003).

'But increasingly problems such as terrorism, in all kinds of form, the trafficking of narcotic drugs, or even the SARS epidemic have equally threatened our security, especially our national economic security. The latter represents the kind of non-traditional threats to security that could strike at the very heart of any nation. Because what these threats often aim at is to destroy the economic confidence of a nation. Confidence, being the most important component of a successful economy, once destroyed or even seriously impaired, could drive the whole economy to total collapse.'

Shinawatra (2003).

placed drugs eradication as the nation's most urgent agenda' (BBC News 2003).

In this case of securitization, the referent objects were the national sovereignty and territorial integrity of Thailand (military and political security), the integrity and stability of the political system (political security), the Thai population (societal security), and the economic development and prosperity of the country (economic security). The securitizing actor was the Thai Prime Minister Thaksin Shinawatra and his government. Finally, the audience consisted of the Thai public opinion (Emmers 2004).

Opinion polls indicated that the audience generally accepted the articulation of drug trafficking as a threat to Thailand's national security and its society as well as the need for it to be addressed through extraordinary measures. Repeated pollsters indicated strong public approval of the anti-drugs campaign. The audience therefore accepted the interpretation of events set forward by the securitizing actor and acknowledged the need for emergency action. According to the Copenhagen School, this indicates a successful act of securitization —the securitizing actor had used a discourse of security and an audience had been convinced by the existential threat posed by drug trafficking to the referent objects.

The war on drugs led to the implementation of extreme measures as well as to a series of abuses (Emmers 2004). The interior ministry, the police and local authorities published blacklists of suspected drug producers, traffickers, and dealers. The blacklists were widely criticized in the media and by non-governmental organizations because of their lack of accuracy. This led to concern that the police might accuse innocent people of being drug producers or traffickers. It was also reported that more than 2,500 people had been killed primarily between February and April 2003. The Thai government blamed inter-gang warfare for most of the killings. Thaksin announced: 'It is bandits killing bandits' (Cochrane 2003: 35). Most of the killings were not investigated, nor did they lead to arrests. Human-rights groups argued that a 'shoot-to-kill policy' had been put in place. They suspected the police of taking matters in their own hands and executing traffickers as part of the war-on-drugs campaign. Despite domestic and international criticism of the extra-judicial killings, repeated polls indicated that Thai public opinion generally supported the implementation of extraordinary measures.

The war in Iraq and the failure of securitization

We have so far noted two cases of a completed act of securitization. This is not to say, however, that all

- The illicit trafficking and abuse of drugs has recurrently been securitized.

- Narcotics are viewed as a threat to political, societal, economic, and health security.

- Thailand declared war on drugs in 2003. The Thai population (audience) generally accepted the articulation of drug trafficking as a threat to Thailand and its society.

- The implementation of extraordinary measures led to abuses.

moves of securitization succeed in convincing a specific audience on the existential nature of a threat. In fact, as mentioned above, the Copenhagen School anticipates that some speech acts will fail to do so. A relevant example is the failure by US President George W. Bush and British Prime Minister Tony Blair to convince the international community on the existential threat posed by Saddam Hussein and his regime in Iraq. In his State of the Union address on 29 January 2002, President Bush had already characterized Iraq together with North Korea and Iran as an 'axis of evil'. The US administration later sought to justify the removal of Saddam Hussein through military force by linking the issue of international terrorism to the threat of the proliferation of weapons of mass destruction (WMD). The language of security was therefore utilized to justify the need for the implementation of emergency and extraordinary measures (the immediate use of military force to dispose of a foreign regime). In the meantime, critics of the American position questioned Iraq's WMD capabilities and the accuracy of its immediate threat to international peace and stability. The WMD capabilities of Iraq were also said to be less than those of Libya, North Korea, or Iran.

Opponents to the use of military force called for a diplomatic resolution to the crisis through efforts at the United Nations (UN). The UN Security Council

KEY QUOTES 9.3

Bush and the Iraq War

'Iraq is the latest battlefield in this war. Many terrorists who kill innocent men, women and children on the streets of Baghdad are followers of the same murderous ideology that took the lives of our citizens in New York, in Washington, and Pennsylvania. There is only one course of action against them: to defeat them abroad before they attack us at home.'

President Addresses Nation, Discusses Iraq, War on Terror, Fort Bragg, North Carolina. 28 June 2005) http://www.whitehouse.gov/news/releases/ 2005/06/20050628-7.html

'The threat comes from Iraq. It arises directly from the Iraqi regime's own actions—its history of aggression, and its drive toward an arsenal of terror. Eleven years ago, as a condition for ending the Persian Gulf War, the Iraqi regime was required to destroy its weapons of mass destruction, to cease all development of such weapons, and to stop all support for terrorist groups. The Iraqi regime has violated all of those obligations. It possesses and produces chemical and biological weapons. It is seeking nuclear weapons. It has given shelter and support to terrorism, and practices terror against its own people. The entire world has witnessed

Iraq's eleven-year history of defiance, deception and bad faith.'

President Bush Outlines Iraqi Threat Remarks by the President on Iraq Cincinnati Museum Center–Cincinnati Union Terminal. Cincinnati, Ohio. 7 October 2002, http://www.whitehouse.gov/news/releases/2002/10/20021007-8.html

'While there are many dangers in the world, the threat from Iraq stands alone – because it gathers the most serious dangers of our age in one place. Iraq's weapons of mass destruction are controlled by a murderous tyrant who has already used chemical weapons to kill thousands of people. This same tyrant has tried to dominate the Middle East, has invaded and brutally occupied a small neighbour, has struck other nations without warning, and holds an unrelenting hostility toward the United States.'

President Bush Outlines Iraqi Threat Remarks by the President on Iraq Cincinnati Museum Center–Cincinnati Union Terminal. Cincinnati, Ohio. 7 October 2002, http://www.whitehouse.gov/news/releases/2002/10/20021007-8.html

adopted, in November 2002, a new resolution that allowed UN inspectors to go back to Iraq and search for WMD after a four-year absence. In early 2003, Mr Hans Blix, head of the UN weapons inspectors, pointed out that Iraq had failed to cooperate pro-actively. Yet he also announced that, in the two months of inspections in Iraq, his team had not found any WMDs, or, in the parlance of the time, a 'smoking gun'. In the meantime, the military build-up continued in the Gulf, with the US and British military sending more and more troops and equipment.

The opposition to the war was not limited to a diplomatic level but was characterized instead by a broad popular movement. Although the United Kingdom was a key member of the US coalition, the wider UK population did not accept the government's speech act describing Saddam Hussein's regime as an existential threat to international peace (Collins 2005). This was indicated by opinion polls as well as by massive and repeated demonstrations against the war. Aware that they would not be able to get a UN mandate to attack Iraq, the United States and the United Kingdom launched Operation Iraqi Freedom on 20 March 2003. The opposition to the war remained particularly strong in most parts of the world. Even after the start of the hostilities, the US administration and the British government failed to convince the wider international community of the necessity and legitimacy of the conflict. The continuing demonstrations against the war reflected these elites' lack of legitimacy and perceived abuse of power. The process of securitization therefore failed to move beyond its first stage.

KEY POINTS

- Moves of securitization can fail. This results from the audience rejecting the speech act articulated by the securitizing actor.

- US President George W. Bush and British Prime Minister Tony Blair generally failed to convince the international community of the existential threat posed by Iraqi President Saddam Hussein.

- Members of the coalition sought to justify the military removal of Saddam Hussein linking the issues of international terrorism and the proliferation of WMD.

- The linkage was not accepted by most other members of the UN Security Council nor by the wider international community.

Conclusion

The Copenhagen School, and its securitization model, is a framework for security studies that encapsulates both state security and non-traditional security concerns. It allows for non-military matters to be included in security studies while offering a coherent understanding of the concept of security. It provides a framework to determine how, why, and by whom a specific matter becomes securitized, and thus succeeds in distinguishing security and non-security threats. The securitization and desecuritization model makes it possible to adopt a broader conceptualization of security without losing the central coherence of the term. In that respect, the Copenhagen School greatly contributes to the security-studies literature.

The Copenhagen School structures its securitization model around a series of salient questions and steps. First, it asks who the securitizing actors might be—those who initiate a move of securitization through the speech act. These include not only policy-makers or bureaucracies, but also transnational actors (international institutions, non-state actors, civil society), and even individuals. Second, who or what is to be protected? States and governments are no longer the sole referent objects of security, as individuals, communities, economies, eco-systems, and others are all alternative referents for security. Third, from what kinds of threats are the referent objects to be protected? The security concern must be articulated as an existential threat, thus linking the concept of security to the question of survival. Fourth, who decides on what is a security issue? The act of securitization is completed only once a relevant audience (public opinion, politicians, military officers, or other elites) is convinced that the so-called security issue represents an existential threat to the referent object. Finally, what means are to be used to tackle the existential threat? Once the act of securitization is completed, extraordinary measures can be imposed that go beyond rules ordinarily abided by. The emergency measures are thus located outside the normal bounds of political procedures.

Nonetheless, the chapter has also stressed the dangers of securitization, particularly in an undemocratic political system where the wider population is unable to reject an illegitimate speech act and the emergency measures adopted as a result. Even in democratic societies, there is the risk of an act of securitization leading to the curbing of well-established civil liberties in the name of security. This is especially relevant in a post-9/11 context and the growing articulation of issues as existential threats. The pejorative and possibly negative connotations of securitizing an issue have been stressed through several illustrations as well as the preference for a desecuritizing approach. Finally, the chapter has highlighted some of the shortcomings of the Copenhagen School and its securitization model. These include the Euro-centric nature of the Copenhagen School, the sometimes blurred distinction between securitization and politicization, as well as the need for a deeper understanding of the dynamics of securitization through more empirical research.

QUESTIONS

1. Why are some issues considered as security questions while others are not?
2. How is a process of securitization completed?
3. Is an act of securitization generally dominated by powerful actors? Why?
4. Is securitization more likely to succeed in authoritarian states? Why?
5. What are the benefits of securitizing or desecuritizing an issue?
6. Assess the dangers of securitization.
7. What are some of the shortcomings of the securitization model?
8. How is drug trafficking a national-security problem?
9. Did the process of securitization fail in the case of Iraq? Why?

FURTHER READING

■ Doty, R. L. (1999), 'Immigration and the Politics of Security', *Security Studies*, 8/2 – 3: 71 – 93. The article offers 'lenses' for understanding security, arguing that a one-dimensional understanding of security is inadequate for both scholars and policy-makers.

■ Hansen, L. (2000), 'The Little Mermaid's Silent Security Dilemma and the Absence of Gender in the Copenhagen School', *Millennium: Journal of International Studies*, 29/2: 285 – 306. This paper presents a critique of the Copenhagen School by raising gender issues and other blind spots of securitization.

■ Kenney, M. (2003), 'From Pablo to Osama: Counter-Terrorism Lessons from the War on Drugs', *Survival*, 45/3: 187–206. The author looks at lessons from the war on drugs and suggests the need for policy-makers to address the 'demand side' of terrorism in the war on terror.

■ Matthews, J. T. (1989), 'Redefining Security', *Foreign Affairs*, 68/2: 162–77. This essay argues for a redefinition of national security that incorporates resource, environmental, and demographic issues.

■ Rudolph, C. (2003), 'Security and the Political Economy of International Migration', *American Political Science Review*, 97/4: 603–20. The article examines how migration affects the security of four advanced industrial states, namely the United States, Germany, France, and Great Britain.

■ Salehi, R., and Ali, S. H. (2006), 'The Social and Political Context of Disease Outbreaks: The Case of SARS in Toronto', *Canadian Public Policy*, 32/4: 373–85. This paper addresses the impact of government policies and politics on the diffusion as well as transmission of the Severe Acute Respiratory Syndrome Coronavirus (SARS-S-CoV) within a local Toronto context.

IMPORTANT WEBSITE

● http://www.idss-nts.org   This website contains information about the Institute of Defence and Strategic Studies (IDSS) Project on Non-Traditional Security in Asia, funded by the Ford Foundation. It is an information hub for policy-makers and academics working on non-traditional security and offers analytical tools by analysing the dynamics of securitization and desecuritization.

Visit the Online Resource Centre that accompanies this book for lots of interesting additional material: www.oxfordtextbooks.co.uk/orc/collins2e/

10

Historical Materialism

ERIC HERRING

Reader's Guide

This chapter begins with an outline of the social scientific, philosophical, and political dimensions of historical materialism (HM) and sketches how it connects to security and Security Studies as a field of academic enquiry. It goes on to explore the relationships between HM and approaches to security in wider context (realism, liberalism, social constructivism, and gender) and then to various perspectives on security (securitization and the sectoral approach, peace studies, critical security studies, and human security). This is followed by an elaboration of what HM involves, including its diversity, value, and potential pitfalls. Accompanying the text are Think Point 10.1 on using HM to understand arms production and the arms trade with the UK as a case study, and Think Point 10.2 on using HM to understand the connections between development and security. The conclusion provides an overall assessment of the contribution of HM to the scholarship and politics of security.

Introduction

Historical materialism (HM) is rightly seen as one of the key paradigms (systems of thought) of the social in its broadest sense alongside realism and liberalism. In this chapter I will treat HM as a particular version of Marxism (the system of thought based on the ideas of Karl Marx and Friedrich Engels in the mid- to late nineteenth century) that also tends to draw on other theories and that takes into account subsequent historical changes that required the modification of Marx's ideas. HM has three dimensions—the social scientific, the philosophical, and the political (Therborn 2008: ch. 3)—which will be considered in turn.

First, some scholars approach HM as social science, meaning that they assume that fact and value (judgements of worth such as right and wrong) can be separated sufficiently to generate theoretically grounded claims that can be tested against evidence. In other words, description (what is), explanation (why it is), and prescription (what should be) are treated as separable. As social science, HM offers analyses of how particular forms of the ownership and control of the production of goods and services shape the emergence of classes, how related forms of politics, the social, and the individual develop, and how conflicts between classes generate change. At its most useful, HM is not only about economics, does not assume that the economic drives everything else, and considers how this all operates at all levels from individuals to the global. The 'historical' part of HM refers to the indispensability of the empirical, both in terms of the facts of particular phenomena such as wage levels but just as importantly in terms of the character of entire phases of world history. A sensitivity to historical specifics and context provides the means to develop necessary qualifications to HM's theoretical generalizations. The 'material' part of HM refers to its focus on the class and productive basis of societies (which entails entire ways of living and being).

Second, as philosophy, HM involves a commitment to the systematic use of reason in order to grasp the nature of social reality. It is particularly interested in the ways that the material and the ideational are part of each other—for example, that, the development of capitalism (defined in some detail below) required the development of ideas of rightness and naturalness of private property. In this sense it contrasts with approaches that focus purely on discourse (the social construction of meaning between people through their words and actions). HM is interested in how changes in particular structures and the inequalities of power associated with them are vital to the rise and fall of discourses. HM is particularly well suited to being grounded in the philosophical approach known as critical realism (Cruickshank 2007). This is not the same as the realism depicted in Chapter 2 of this book, because that realism also involves a specific social scientific theory of world politics that HM rejects, even if there is at the philosophical level some common ground. Critical realism assumes, as does HM, that there are social structures independent of discourses about them that have the capacity to have particular effects and have more potential to change in some ways rather than others. This is a second sense of the term 'material' in HM. The critical realist notion that any existing social structure contains within it the potential for change has particular resonance with HM, as HM is interested in how existing class relations can be transformed.

This philosophical interest in the potential for change links to the third dimension of HM—namely, the political. For many, HM is irredeemably tainted by having been the official ideology of the Cold War Communist states and in particular the extremely repressive regimes of the Soviet Union under Joseph Stalin and China under Mao Zedong. Both regimes were directly responsible for the deaths of millions of their citizens. There have been plenty of apologists over the years for that kind of repression.

Third, HM is also associated with a different politics. This involves serious commitment to the human rights espoused by liberals but with much more emphasis on economic rights as part of what is variously known as the global justice, anti-capitalist, anti-globalization or alter-globalization (alternative-globalization) movement. Their most obvious practical expression is in the meetings since 2001 of the World Social Forum, which defines itself as a space 'of groups and movements of civil society opposed to neoliberalism and to domination of the world by capital and any form of imperialism' (World Social Forum 2002). The global justice movement is diverse and decentralized, which is both a strength and a weakness. Many in that movement see hope for the practical expression of their ideas in the rise since the early 1990s of Latin American left-wing social movements, political parties, and elected governments committed to redistributing wealth to the poor and resisting US domination and neoliberal economics (deregulated, privatized capitalism with countries' economies open to foreign corporations to invest and then remove the profits abroad without hindrance) (Rodríguez-Garavito et al. 2008). This movement has also taken heart from the spectacular problems faced from 2007 onwards by the neoliberalizing global financial system. Policies such as the nationalization of banks, shutting down tax havens, and introducing strict regulation by states went from being wild radicalism to mainstream common sense in 2008, though the reversal of neoliberalism is limited thus far. However, without a clear alternative to capitalism or route to getting there, if the global justice movement is to retain any credibility for its claims to care about welfare of most of humanity, it must in the short term also be concerned with how capitalism can be saved while some of capitalism's more extreme manifestations are reined in. Indeed, there is a long-standing strand within HM thinking that regards capitalism as having both desirable dimensions in terms of its unleashing of human productive capacities as well as undesirable ones in terms of the repression, poverty, and environmental degradation.

This brief outline already indicates many connections with security. If security is defined narrowly as actual or perceived freedom from violence and threats of violence for political purposes, HM has as much to say about why such threats arise, whose interests they serve, the legitimacy of the threats and violence used to try to secure them, and how change might come about to close down the space for threats and violence. In terms of scholarship, the field of security studies is seen in HM terms to have been created to service dominant interests in the Cold War and hence was on the opposite side of the class divide from HM scholars in the West. It meant that the concept of security was seen by HM scholars as politically suspect. HM scholars were divided over their attitude to the Cold War Communist states but were generally seen by realists and liberals to be on the side of those states. In this atmosphere, HM was unlikely to be central to security studies even as it managed to be one of the three key paradigms of international relations (IR) scholarship. Furthermore, HM scholars have considered the concept of security to be inferior as a focal point of research in comparison with HM's own already well-developed concepts, which they see as necessary for understanding the issues that are supposedly the preserve of security studies. However, in the post-Cold War period, as security studies has become more diverse with more left-wing security analysis being published, HM is increasingly featuring in those publications. The next section of this chapter elaborates on the relationship between HM, security, and security studies.

KEY POINTS

- Historical materialism (HM) has social scientific, philosophical, and political dimensions. HM argues that particular forms of the ownership and control of the production of goods and services result in related national and transnational class conflicts.

- HM sees material economic forces as playing a powerful role in the emergence of social ideas and in generating social change. It is usually but not necessarily associated with the political goal of transcending capitalism.

- The framework offered by HM provides a way of putting security issues in context and analysing them holistically.

- During the Cold War, security studies and HM scholars mostly viewed each other with suspicion politically. However, in the post-Cold War period, the diversification of security studies is resulting in an increased role for HM ideas.

Historical materialism, security, and security studies

This section examines how HM relates to perspectives that put security in a wider context (realism, liberalism, constructivism, and gender) and then relates it to key approaches to security (securitization and the sectoral approach, peace studies, critical security studies, and human security). All these subjects have their own chapters in this book, and reference will be made to them.

Security in wider context

Realism

HM has something in common with realism in relation to the notion that there are discernible regularities in human society. HM sees these regularities as changing in form within each historical epoch, whereas realists are more likely to represent them as essentially timeless, even if they change in specific content (for an enduring statement of realism see Morgenthau 1978). Realists are also concerned with the operation of these contextual regularities in relation to the power of nation states and with how to ensure its effective exercise by them. For example, realists such as John Mearsheimer (2005) argued that the US-led invasion of Iraq was against US interests and motivated by the ideological wishful thinking of neo-conservatives (those who wished to use US military and other power resources to overthrow dictatorships and to establish liberal democracies and open deregulated capitalist economies). HM accepts that states are important but argues that states represent not national interests—something that it treats as a ruling-class ideological myth—but class interests, with the nature of classes and their interests being peculiar to each epoch. As it happens, E. H. Carr, one of the founding figures of realism, accepted this critique, a point missed by realists generally. Carr (1981: 80) wrote of the notion of there being a harmony of interests between classes:

> It is the natural assumption of a prosperous and privileged class, whose members have a dominant voice in the community and are therefore naturally prone to identify its interest with their own ... The doctrine of the harmony of interests thus serves as an ingenious moral device invoked, in perfect sincerity, by privileged groups in order to justify and maintain their dominant position.

Carr was using the term 'class' in the more general sense of social class (the hierarchical stratification of society), in comparison with HM's more specific use of it in relation to the mode of production (way of producing, distributing, and exchanging goods and services, including the wider social relations associated with that, such as ideas about the meaning of freedom, individuality, and so on). Advocates of HM want to assist the effective exercise of a particular state's power only if they see that state as representing working class interests, a situation that does not usually exist in the capitalist world. HM scholars do understand that social class is important (including for feelings of dignity to which human beings attach a great deal of value), and that class is a great deal more complex than a simple capitalist ruling class—working class distinction (for example, when the pension fund investments of workers mean that they are to a limited extent capitalists themselves) (Wright 1997; Sayer 2005). What they reject is the idea that the only form of class that matters is social class, and they focus predominantly on class in relation to capital.

Liberalism

Liberalism involves a belief, shared with HM, in progress and reason. Liberalism is grounded in a commitment to the idea of individuals with freedoms (including the right to private property enforced by states), with restrictions on their liberties only to the extent necessary to protect other individuals. These freedoms are nowadays couched in universal terms (applying to everyone). Liberals relate this to security in terms of the creation, defence, and extension of an international society, defined as the existence of shared norms and practices around the survival of diversity within universal values and also complex interdependence (mutual dependence and a high level of connectedness) that encourages peace by making war less valuable as a means of achieving political goals (Nye Jr. 2008). The most prominent activist HM scholar since the 1960s, Noam Chomsky (1973: 156), argues that liberal ideals are actually anti-capitalist in origin:

> With the development of industrial capitalism, a new and unanticipated system of injustice, it is libertarian socialism that has preserved and extended the radical humanist message of the Enlightenment and the classical liberal ideals that were perverted into an ideology to sustain the emerging social order. In fact, on the very same assumptions that led classical liberalism to oppose the intervention of the state in social life, capitalist social relations are also intolerable.

HM points out that the international society that contemporary liberals value rests on a capitalist system in which people do not control or own the means of production. This means that they are usually free in terms of not being slaves (owned by their employers) but are forced to sell their labour if they are not to starve or live in poverty: this lack of freedom is not named as such in contemporary liberalism.

Social constructivism

Social constructivism is not actually a theory of security. It is more a general approach to understanding social meaning. Its central premise is that meaning is created intersubjectively—that is, as a collective human product of interpretation of the words and actions. Hence, instead of taking social reality for granted (such as a particular way of thinking about terrorism), it looks at how social reality is produced through human interaction, so that it appears commonsensical rather than a specific interpretation that could be replaced by others (Weldes et al. 1999). Social constructivists are particularly interested in challenging the idea that security is about actors with settled identities acting to secure their existence (such as Pakistan building nuclear weapons to deter attack by India). Instead, they are interested in how identity is produced by actions in the name of security (such as Pakistan's building of nuclear weapons and the claims to justify them as being a bid to establish a particular identity for Pakistan by acting out that identity and getting others to act as if that identity is natural). HM has a social constructivist dimension, but it also offers a particular substantive theory of social change in which the material dimensions of societies and related class conflicts shape social construction. HM does accept a two-way process between the material and the socially constructed, and overlap between the two, but tends to focus on how the former shapes the latter within the class relations of entire epochs.

Gender

Gender is also not a theory of security or indeed a theory of anything. It is an issue that may be approached from numerous different theoretical standpoints. Marxist feminism is described by Caroline Kennedy-Pipe in Chapter 7 as follows: 'Marxist feminists work on the issue of class and gender. Their work highlights not only the subordination of women in the workplace but the general over-representation of women in the lowest socio-economic groups across the globe. They draw our attention to the links between economic deprivation, security, and vulnerability.' As Kennedy-Pipe hints, HM goes beyond treating class and gender as two separate categories that interact to an exploration of how particular modes of production can result in constructions of gender identities and relations that are functional for those modes of production.

Perspectives on security studies

The sectoral approach and securitization

The sectoral and securitization approaches have been developed together. Barry Buzan, Ole Wæver, and Jaap de Wilde (1998) represented security as having military, economic, environmental, societal, and political sectors, and this is reflected in the organization of the middle section of this book. HM's claim to be a better way of thinking about security lies in its holistic approach. In other words, instead of treating them as if they are five separate sectors, HM treats the suppose sectors as making most sense when examined together. The sectoral approach of Buzan et al. also sees security studies as having global, non-regional subsystemic, regional, and local levels and they argue that the referent object (that which is being secured) of military security is usually the state. These claims mean that their work is much more compatible within the realist and to a lesser extent the liberal paradigms than the HM paradigm: the focus is on states, the political and economic are treated as distinct from each other ,and class (whether national or transnational) as a referent is not part of the picture. The same can be said of their proposal of the categories of non-political, political, and security issues. Buzan et al. have also developed the concepts of securitization and desecuritization: instead of taking at face value whatever is currently labelled a security issue, they examine how issues become labelled that way (securitized) and how they cease to be labelled that way (desecuritized). Furthermore, they recommend that, for something to be categorized as a security issue, it should threaten survival and requires urgent and exceptional political action, and so they see security as a label that is overused. These (de)securitization ideas could be adapted for use within HM.

Peace studies

As indicated by Paul Rogers in his contribution to this volume, the well-established field of peace studies is geared towards the promotion of positive peace (harmonious, fulfilling social relations) as well as negative peace (absence of violence). It seeks to expose what Johan Galtung (1969) called '**structural violence**' (deaths and suffering caused by the way society is organized so that huge numbers of people lack the means necessary to avoid starvation, preventable illness, and so on). Its methods are social scientific and lean towards the empirical more than the theoretical, and it has an impressive track record of involvement in developing and implementing practical solutions to security problems, often at local level. HM shares with peace studies this opposition to structural violence, and provides a theoretically grounded argument as to why capitalism and related class relations are inherently structurally violent. Furthermore, many left-wing political activists whose thinking is grounded in HM engage in the kind of practical peace-building that is central to peace studies. HM has some more theoretical and more revolutionary elements within it, while peace studies has more atheoretical, liberal, and reformist elements. But there is also extensive overlap between the two.

Critical security studies

HM is much less prominent in critical security studies (CSS) than would be expected from the fact that HM is central to the origins of the critical theory on which much of CSS draws. It is difficult to find a piece of CSS scholarship that does not refer to Robert Cox's classic essay 'Social Forces, States and World Orders: Beyond International Relations Theory' published in *Millennium* in 1981 and republished with a postscript in 1985 in Robert O. Keohane (ed.), *Neorealism and its Critics*. However, what is generally missed is that the critical theory Cox proposes in this essay is explicitly an HM one, an argument he sets out at length. A focus on ideas and the discursive to the exclusion of historically located assessment of class conflict is not what he sees as critical theory. He concludes his postscript as follows (Cox 1985: 248–9):

> There is a structuralist Marxism which ... has analogies to structural realism, not in the use to which theory is put but in its conception of the nature of knowledge. There is a determinist tradition ... which purports to reveal the laws of

motion of history. And there is a historicist Marxism that rejects the notion of objective laws of history and focuses upon class struggle as the heuristic model for the understanding of structural change. It is obviously in the last of these Marxist currents that this writer feels most comfortable . . . as things stand in the complex world of Marxism, he prefers to be identified simply as a historical materialist. 🙿

In his chapter on CSS for this book, David Mutimer makes passing reference to Ken Booth's argument in favour of including Marxism within CSS but clearly positions CSS as post-Marxist (which claims to draw on but also to have transcended Marxism by having Marxist ideas playing a secondary role within an approach mainly drawing on other theorizing). Most of CSS is so post-Marxist as to be non-Marxist: what lingers are commitments to change and emancipation (freeing people from the constraints that prevent them from living full lives). For example, Karin Fierke's survey study (2007) *Critical Approaches to International Security* has no entry in the index for class or capital or neoliberalism and few mentions of Marx. It is structured around the concepts of change, identity, production of danger, trauma, human insecurity, immanent critique, and emancipation. Having scholarship that approaches CSS from a social constructivist and discursive focus is valuable. What is counterproductive is for CSS to be positioned as a whole in a way that takes little account of the contribution that HM can make.

Human security

Interest in the notion of human security has grown rapidly in the post-Cold War period (see Chapter 8). Its focus on ensuring freedom from fear, want, and indignity for individuals, social groups, and humanity as a whole gives it some appeal to peace studies and CSS scholars, whereas securitization scholars tend to argue for the retention of a focus on states (Buzan 2004a). The human security agenda looks very much like peace studies in its focus on structural as well as physical violence (although some proponents of this sub-field focus only on the latter), on its empirical rather than theoretical methods, and on practical reforms. People are often insecure because of repression by their own state, neglect by a functioning state, or the state being willing but unable to provide security. These are all powerful reasons for not focusing on the security of states and for not assuming that, if the state is secure, so are the people who live within its borders.

From an HM point of view, the idea of human security can be used in a progressive way to challenge repression, structural violence, and the prioritization of states over people. But HM also alerts the observer to the possibility that the idea of human security can be an ideological weapon of the dominant capitalist actors (Bilgin and Morton 2002; Gruffydd Jones 2008). Specifically, human security can be used to frame poverty and violence in states of the South (the part of the world that consumes minimally and in which many of the people are marginalized, uninsured, policed, and repressed) as having purely internal causes with no blame attached to the North (the part of the world that has high consumption levels, is deeply integrated into capitalism, and securitizes the South). It can then be used to justify imperial intervention by the North in Southern 'weak' or 'failed' states (states that cannot or will not meet the basic needs of most of their population). In other words, this intervention is supposedly for the benefit of the people of the South but can turn out to be mainly for the benefit of the capitalist ruling class of the North and also for a large proportion of the population of the North.

KEY POINTS

- HM has some aspects in common with realism, liberalism, and social constructivism but offers something distinctive in having as its central focus class conflict within capitalism.

- The notion that there are separate sectors of security that shape each other is challenged by HM's holistic approach, which regards these 'sectors' as fundamentally part of each other.

- HM sees capitalism itself as involving structural violence and sees the idea of human security as potentially being employed by dominant capitalist actors to justify policies that reinforce that structural violence.

- While CSS tends to neglect its HM roots, some scholars within CSS are drawing on it to analyse major contemporary security issues such as state terrorism and energy security.

A (slightly) closer look at historical materialism

Up to this point this chapter has been using a very simplified version of HM, which only hints at its content, value, diversity, and potential pitfalls. This section of the chapter takes a closer look, so that the ground is prepared for Think Point 10.1 on HM, arms production, and the arms trade. Even this closer looks is a mere glimpse of what historical materialism has to offer: the guide to further reading and the suggested web links at the end of this chapter offer routes towards deepening your grasp.

HM as it is defined in this chapter seeks to understand the world not via static abstractions and timeless generalizations but in specific historical epochs (currently the capitalist epoch) with a focus on how change occurs. For HM, the contemporary context is one of imperialism (relations of domination and subordination across societies), which connects the global order to particular forms of state–society relations in class terms (Cox 1985; see also Cammack 2007b). An important concept in this analysis is the notion of dialectic, which means that conflict between opposed social forces in particular contexts generates potential for change. Within capitalism, the central dialectic for HM is class struggle. In the realist and liberal paradigms, capitalism is seen as involving private property, the profit motive, competition, and freedom of contract with this system guaranteed by the state and international organizations. HM agrees with this at one level but disputes the notion that this is a free, just, mutually beneficial, and timeless system in tune with human nature. The representation of aspects of economics by realists and liberals as somehow non-political and private is regarded by HM as serving the interests of capitalists by allowing them to retain unelected and for the most part unaccountable control. Similarly, exploitation in the sense HM uses it refers to the fact that workers are paid less than the value that results from their labour and do not retain control of the remainder of that value: this surplus value as it is called in HM goes to the capitalist, who accumulates it as capital to spend or reinvest. Hence the concept of exploitation is used here both to describe something and also to make a negative value judgement on it. As for the notion that workers are free to work: HM points out that workers do not own the means of production and so are forced to sell their labour to capitalists who have the 'right' to buy it at less than the full value that results from it or even not at all. This produces extremes of inequality, with vast numbers of people suffering and going to an early grave because they are unable to sell their labour for much. This is a profound kind of insecurity, and the concepts HM offers can deepen our understanding of this structural violence and human (in)security, as it does not depoliticize explanations of why these phenomena exist and it is linked to a politics of trying to find alternative social orders that would overcome them. This lack of control by most people of their labour, in a context in which this is represented as natural and inevitable, is defined as alienation, and people often feel this alienation emotionally, as they spend most of their lives doing work they do not believe in just to survive (Schmidt 2000). This connects with the human security notion of freedom from indignity.

Capitalism was for Marx in these respects a repulsive way of running a society, even though he was also impressed by its unleashing of human productive capabilities. He thought that a just alternative would be a communist system—that is, one in which workers collectively owned and controlled the economy. In 1875 he set out as a principle of communism: 'From each according to his ability, to each according to his needs' (Marx 1875: ch 1, n.p.). He thought that, in a communist society, people would want to work at whatever they could contribute to the collective good rather than doing what work they had to do in order to be paid, and that what one received would vary depending on what one needed. The latter idea has significant purchase even in the present world order, as indicated by the existence of some, if variable, welfare rights. The former idea goes against most of the 'common sense' of our current system of individualism, alienated labour, and private reward for 'competing' successfully (on the basis of what is in reality unequal ability and unequal opportunity). However, Marx (1859: preface, n.p.) argued that the common sense of any age is a product of its material circumstances:

> The mode of production in material life conditions the general character of the social, political, and spiritual processes of life. It is not the consciousness of men that determines their existence, but on the contrary, it is their social existence which determines their consciousness.

Note that Marx's position here (elsewhere in his work he took a less firm stance) is excessively rigid for most contemporary HM scholars in claiming that the material determines all else. This determinism, as it is known, has mostly given way to a perspective within HM that emphasizes the need to explore empirically and in historical context the relationships between the material and the rest of social life and that explores the ways in which they are mutually constitutive (not separate from each other and then shaping each other but fundamentally bound up with what they are). The point of continuing relevance is that willing socially valuable work, from this point of view, which in a capitalist era might seem absurdly unrealistic, would, Marx thought, seem natural in a communist one. Even in the capitalist era there are numerous examples of willing work without material reward in the voluntary sector that might suggest such possibilities on a wider scale and also of cooperatives (businesses owned and controlled by workers).

 THINK POINT 10.1

Historical materialism, arms production, and the arms trade

Realists see the arms trade as a rational instrument of the state to advance the national interest strategically and economically: it is about profit and jobs, strengthening friendly states, gaining influence over other states, or maintaining an independent military-industrial base. Some HM research argues that taxpayer subsidies to arms companies mean that the arms trade is not nearly as profitable as it is usually made out to be, that there are more effective ways to create jobs, that arms sales are a weak instrument of influence, and that the increasing tendency for the parts of weapons to be produced in different countries means that there is no independent military-industrial base anyway, especially for countries other than the United States (Mayhew 2005).

Liberals usually favour voluntary or legal codes of conduct as a way of discouraging sales of weapons that are likely to be used for external aggression or internal repression or that waste the money of poorer countries. It is often pointed out that these codes of conduct have been violated by liberal democratic states and are vague and weakly monitored (Saferworld 2007). HM scholars accept this but point out that there would be a deeper problem even if codes of conduct were operating effectively by the criteria of those who created them. Specifically, codes of conducts promote the idea that there is a legitimate arms trade that is beneficial in relation to security, the economy, and society. In contrast, HM scholars argue that the so-called legitimate arms trade has a range of pernicious effects (Rodríguez-Garavito et al. 2008). For example, they argue that it encourages militarism, which is the belief that militarization is a good thing in itself and preferable to alternative means of achieving goals even when those alternative means are more effective (Bacevich 2006). Militarism can also involve turning to military means without serious consideration of non-military alternatives.

The idea of a military-industrial complex was first coined by US President Dwight D. Eisenhower in 1961: by this he meant coalitions of military and industrial interests that promoted their own sectional interests in government policy making at the expense of national interests. Instead, HM treats the arms trade as a much bigger problem of militarized capitalism in which there is a revolving door between, and overlap of, elites within government, the military, arms industries, and academia who conduct the arms trade in their class interest (Melman 1974, 2003; CAAT 2005; Stavrianakis 2005a, b, 2006). Furthermore, this militarized capitalism operates at a global level with a hierarchical and imperial capitalist order, with the arms industries not separate from the state but deeply integrated into it as part of national and transnational capitalist elites who profit from arms sales despite their costs through subsidies, war, and diversion of resources from other purposes (Wendt and Barnett 1993).

In a capitalist system, corporations prioritize control and then profit. For HM, arms production and arms trading are basically a militarized manifestation of this (see Think Point 10.1). The logical function of humanity and the physical environment in such a system is to be mobilized to generate profit for capitalists in ways that do not challenge their control. This may involve pressuring people to work harder and for longer hours for the lowest wages possible and inducing them to use their non-working hours spending those wages. When people have the things they need, wants are created through advertising and wants cannot be satisfied through purchasing: more wants must be created all the time, and relations of all kinds must be monetized as far as possible. Capitalism has an inherent drive towards turning previously non-monetary social relations into monetary relations (commodification) and the actual functioning of items has, for capitalism, no inherent value: the purpose of goods is to generate profit. Capitalism involves many contradictions (social relations that pull in opposite directions at the same time). For example, on the one hand the state has a vital role in preserving freedom for capitalists, but the needs of the state may require it to reduce that freedom to protect its own interests. Another is that capitalism involves pressure to push down wages (thus increasing the surplus value from production) but also to increase wages (thus increasing demand for what is produced).

KEY POINTS

- Central concepts within HM include imperialism, dialectic, surplus value, exploitation, commodification, and contradictions, as well as class.

- These concepts help HM to develop its argument that lack of ownership and control of the means of production is a fundamental cause of life-threatening insecurity for huge numbers of people.

- The view that the material determines or even is the main force shaping our ideas about the world is mostly seen in contemporary HM as too rigid and as paying insufficient attention to how the material and the ideational mutually constitute each other.

- Seeing the arms trade as a form of militarized capitalism helps to explain the existence of seemingly pointless, dangerous, and/or subsidized arms production and arms trading.

Avoiding the potential pitfalls of historical materialism

Among HM scholars there is considerable disagreement about the likelihood or desirability of revolution (fundamental, possibly rapid, transformation of class relations) or how revolution relates to reform (incremental modification of class relations that leaves their fundamental elements intact). There is also disagreement about the extent to which conscious political efforts can bring about revolution or whether it would occur mainly through the working-out of class conflict. In its determinist form, HM proclaims to have discovered the objective laws of history that are unfolding towards the inevitable transition from capitalism to communism. In its more open form focused on class conflicts within capitalism, HM accepts that history has been unfolding in so many unanticipated ways thus far that we should continue to expect the unexpected. See Think Point 10.2 for an overview of how HM scholars have responded to the evolving connections between development and security.

It may even be that capitalism will for the indefinite future find a way to reform and indeed change

THINK POINT 10.2

Using historical materialism to understand the development-security nexus

In realist and liberal analysis, insecurity prevents development and lack of development generates insecurity. The questions that then arise from these perspectives is whether it is possible to promote development that leads to security, whether you need security first, or whether you can and must promote both at the same time. Realists look for ways rationally to promote the national interest in this situation, while, for liberals, states, international organizations and non-governmental organizations need to find ways to promote their common values in relation to these issues. HM's major contribution to thinking on the development–security nexus is to put this narrow analysis of the interaction of two policy sectors into a global and historical perspective.

The focal point of debate in HM analysis is whether the realist and liberal approaches to the development–security nexus legitimize an unequal world in which low levels of material welfare in the South is the norm for the long term and in which the North can use violence if necessary to enforce that inequality (e.g. Duffield 2001, 2007; Barkawi 2005; Davis 2006). In all the criticism of capitalism that HM involves, it is easy to forget that some HM scholars see capitalism as having progressive as well reactionary dimensions in relation to development. For example, capitalism, especially in its phase where territories across the world were subjected to direct imperial rule, involved enormous brutality in terms of physical violence and the shattering of indigenous societies. From Marx's perspective, this was negative in terms of its human cost but also positive in terms of being necessary to take those societies from their pre-capitalist feudal systems (with ordinary people bound through custom to be subservient to tribal and other leaders) through capitalism as a necessary stage to

socialism (state control of the means of production) and then communism (popular control of the means of production) (see Warren 1980). Even if one does not take this determinist line, one can still see respects in which capitalism has been progressive in terms of releasing human creative potential and producing goods and services that are life enhancing. HM also has overlapping strands—underdevelopment (e.g. Gunder Frank 1971), world-system (Wallerstein 2004), or post-development (Escobar 1995) analysis—which argue that in its current form capitalism has ceased to play this developmental role or never did play it in much of the world. These HM scholars argue that the areas of the world that have less advanced capitalism have been frozen into a position of supplying raw materials and a limited range of fairly unsophisticated goods to the advanced capitalist world. They also criticize as colonialist any approach, including that of Marx, that sees the capitalism of the North as the normal form of development.

In terms of ways forward with regard to development and security, HM debates put specific policy recommendations into the context of discussing whether the South needs to insulate itself from globalization and seek more national solutions to its problems or pursue an alternative form of globalization (Escobar 1995; Duffield 2007; Broad and Cavanagh 2009). Some HM scholars also argue for a fundamental change in the frame of reference from an imperial one serving the interests of the global North to a post-colonial one (Barkawi and Laffey 2006) in which security studies is not based on the question of what the global North should do to deal with the problems posed by the global South; in which the problem of development is not assumed to be the global South's lack of the global North's qualities; in which the role of the South in the development of the North is fully recognized; and in which opposition (including armed opposition) to the global North by actors in the global South is not assumed automatically to be illegitimate.

so dramatically that its positive dimensions overwhelmingly eclipse its negative ones. Capitalism may turn out to be manageable in a way that is environmentally sustainable and able to deliver high living standards and work perceived as fulfilling for virtually all. Or it may turn out catastrophically in environmental and human terms. Ruling out either of these outcomes and insisting on the inevitable

triumph of communism seem to be crude dogmatism (over-confidently sticking to a claim, interpreting facts to fit, and not taking alternatives seriously).

Other pitfalls to be avoided are reductionism (insisting that all phenomena are really about one thing, such as claiming that all aspects of security can be explained as forms of class conflict) or left functionalism (insisting that everything that the capitalist ruling class does is in its interests—such as economic sanctions on Iraq up to 2003, the invasion of Iraq in 2003, the way the occupation was conducted, and then the agreement made in 2008 that US forces should withdraw). These weaknesses are not inherently part of HM; careful scholarship can avoid them.

KEY POINTS

- Some versions of HM suffer from a variety of weakness such as claiming to have uncovered the objective laws of history with communist revolution as the inevitable outcome, explaining everything as being about class struggle, or interpreting everything that capitalists do as serving the interests of capitalism.

- These weaknesses are not necessarily part of HM.

- The contribution of HM to understanding the evolving connections between security and development illustrates the argument that HM is a crucial resource.

Conclusion

The key figure in the founding of CSS, Ken Booth (2007: 197), has stated with regard to class: 'in what is supposed to be a post-Marxist age this is a much-ignored referent, despite massive life-threatening and life-determining insecurity being the direct result of poverty' (see also Booth 2007: 49–56). As Booth (2005a: 261) has also commented: 'The Marxian tradition offers a deep mine of ideas that are especially useful for thinking about ideology, class, and structural power.'

There is increasing interest in HM as an open, flexible approach that involves synthesis with other theoretical approaches rather than a closed system of thought that excludes others. Some HM scholars are drawing on the work of Antonio Gramsci and Michel Foucault to develop a 'cultural political economy' approach so that the discursive and the material are taken equally seriously (Jessop 2004; Sum, n.d.). Others are engaging with the work of those such as Louis Althusser to show that the critical power of HM is maximized when it treats capitalism as an entire social order rather than just a kind of economy, when it engages with subjectivity (what people think and feel) as a force for action and change rather than seeing subjectivity as merely a product of material forces, and when it develops that analysis in relation to concrete historical circumstances rather than simply in the abstract (Laffey and Dean 2002).

HM scholars are producing substantial studies in the field of security, such as energy security (see Chapter 22) and particular cases of contemporary conflict such as Colombia (Stokes 2005). In their chapter on terrorism in this volume (Chapter 20), Brenda and James Lutz indicate correctly that Marxism-Leninism (the version of Marxism developed by and in the name of Russian revolutionary leader V. I. Lenin) has been the ideology of some terrorist groups. Doug Stokes (2005) and Ruth Blakeley (2009) have shown that HM is also a major resource for making sense of state terrorism in the service of capitalism. Their work brings up to date and revises the classic earlier analysis of this subject by Noam Chomsky and Edward Herman (1979). Indeed, the entire agenda of security studies could be tackled productively using the analytical tools of HM. In so doing, we would do well do bear in mind the following injunction by Cox (1985: 206–7): 'Above all, do not base theory on theory but rather on changing practice and empirical-historical study, which are a proving ground for concepts and hypotheses' (see also Cammack 2007b: 1).

QUESTIONS

1. What are the social scientific, philosophical, and political dimensions of historical materialism?

2. Historical materialism is a key paradigm of international relations thought and yet it is absent from most of security studies: why has this been the case and why might that be changing?

3. What does historical materialism share with realism and liberalism? What does it offer that is distinctive in comparison with realist and liberal thinking about security?

4. Why do historical materialists reject a sectoral approach to thinking about security in favour of a holistic one?

5. Historical materialists accept that states are important for security but see states as reflecting class rather than national interests: what are the implications of this approach?

6. What are the links between historical materialism and critical security studies?

7. How can historical materialism improve our understanding of structural violence and human security?

8. What do historical materialists mean when they argue that arms production and the arms trade are forms of militarized capitalism?

9. What are the potential pitfalls of a historical materialist approach to understanding security and how might they be avoided?

10. What can historical materialism tell us about the relationships between development and security?

 FURTHER READING

■ Blakeley, Ruth (2009), *State Terrorism and Neoliberalism: The North in the South,* London: Routledge. Wearing its HM perspective lightly and applying it effectively, this significant scholarly contribution shows that Northern liberal democracies have been involved in state and non-state terrorism in the South as part of their efforts to integrate it into a neoliberalized global political economy.

■ Chomsky, Noam, and Herman, Edward S. (1979), *The Washington Connection and Third World Fascism: The Political Economy of Human Rights,* i, Boston: South End Press. Still relevant today for the HM-rooted analytical framework it provides, Chomsky and Herman provide extensive evidence for their argument that a key priority for US foreign policy is making the world safe for US corporate interests and that the USA is willing to establish and back brutal dictatorships if necessary to achieve that goal.

■ Davis, Mike (2006), *Planet of Slums*, London: Verso. Davis provides a gripping analysis of the rise of the 'global informal working class', a section of humanity marginal to capitalism or used ruthlessly by it, mostly living in slums around the world and often treated as a security threat to be contained and coerced. While not explicitly HM in perspective, Davis's work is comfortably compatible with it.

■ Duffield, Mark (2007), *Development, Security and Unending War: Governing the World of Peoples*, Cambridge: Polity. Michel Foucault's notion of 'biopolitics' (regulation of the biological, social, and economic processes of human populations ostensibly for their benefit) is central to this powerful analysis. The book's central theme of a world divided into the privileged and secure trying to deny equality to the impoverished and insecure and contain them through aid and coercion has much in common with some aspects HM thinking.

■ Marx, Karl ([1890] 1976), *Capital: A Critique of Political Economy*, i, 4th edn., London: Penguin in association with *New Left Review*. This classic is a demanding but often still vivid and fresh read today. Go to http://davidharvey.org/ and be guided through it chapter by chapter in thirteen fascinating video lectures by David Harvey, one of the world's leading Marxist scholars, who, consistent with that perspective, operates across the stifling boundaries of a range of disciplines.

■ Rodríguez-Garavito, César, Barrett, Patrick, and Chavez, Daniel (2008), *The New Latin American Left: Utopia Reborn*, London: Pluto. Since the early 1990s, Latin America has seen the rise of numerous left-wing governments, parties, and social movements. This book assesses this phenomenon, significant for the fact that most of Latin America has managed to overturn domination by US-backed neoliberalizing military dictatorships.

■ Rupert, Mark, and Smith, Hazel (2002) (eds.), *Historical Materialism and Globalization*, London: Routledge. This outstandingly good collection of essays demonstrates that HM has great potential for understanding and indeed assisting the progressive potential of the new social movements, many of them transnational, that have sprung up in opposition to unrestrained capitalism.

■ Rupert, Mark, and Solomon, Scott (2006), *Globalization and International Political Economy*, Lanham, MD: Rowman & Littlefield. HM ideas are used by Rupert and Solomon to critique globalizing capitalism and show how it is being contested through violent and non-violent means. Those ideas enable them to integrate the themes of gender, class, imperialism, resistance, and terror into a coherent whole.

■ Stewart, Frances (2008) (ed.), *Horizontal Inequalities and Conflict: Understanding Group Violence in Multiethnic Societies*, London: Palgrave Macmillan. Stewart runs the Centre for Research on Inequality, Human Security and Ethnicity (CRISE) at the University of Oxford (go to www.crise.ox.ac.uk/), which studies the relationships between inequalities of various kinds and violence among ethnic groups in Latin America, South East Asia, and West Africa. This liberal scholarship is useful for its proposed policies to reduce inequalities and ameliorate their negative impacts, and an application of an HM perspective on inequality would enhance its value.

■ Stokes, Doug, and Raphael, Sam (forthcoming), *Imperial Logics: Global Energy Security and US Intervention*, Baltimore, MD: Johns Hopkins University Press. This valuable book looks beyond the usual Middle East focus regarding energy security: it explains the connections between US use of counter-insurgency warfare to stabilize oil-rich states in Africa, South America, and Central Asia and increased rivalry for diminishing energy supplies. It demonstrates the value of HM for explaining the vital links between phenomena that are too often treated as if they have little to do with each other.

 ## IMPORTANT WEBSITES

● http://www.zmag.org/.   Z Communications is a huge online nexus of analysis and discussion in many languages for left-wing activists, journalists, and scholars, including those who combine those roles.

● http://www.caat.org.uk/   The Campaign Against the Arms Trade (CAAT) is a non-governmental organization (NGO) that aims to reduce and eventually to end the arms trade and the militarization of arms-producing countries. From an HM perspective, CAAT is significant in that it challenges the arms trade as such rather than particular corrupt or counterproductive aspects of it and frames the arms trade as a militarized capitalism.

● http://www.globalwitness.org   Global Witness is an NGO that exposes the corrupt exploitation of natural resources and international trade and plays a significant role in promoting policies to end impunity, resource-related armed conflict, environmental degradation, and human rights abuses. Although it is liberal rather than HM in perspective, its campaigns and reports are valuable grist to the HM mill.

● http://www.marxists.org   The Marxists Internet Archive is a vast resource in dozens of languages containing the writings of numerous selected Marxists, a thematic archive, a historical archive, and a searchable encyclopaedia. You can go to this to put into context the classic Marxist quotations that will become familiar to you.

 Visit the Online Resource Centre that accompanies this book for lots of interesting additional material: www.oxfordtextbooks.co.uk/orc/collins2e/

PART 2

Deepening and Broadening Security

11

Military Security

MICHAEL SHEEHAN

Chapter Contents

- Introduction
- Approaches to military security
- Traditional military-security studies
- War
- Alliances and neutrality
- Deterrence
- Cooperative security and arms control
- The cost of military security
- Conclusion

Reader's Guide

This chapter examines the continuing importance of military security. It notes that international relations has historically seen security almost entirely in terms of the military dimension, before going on to review the impact of the broadening of the concept of security on approaches to the study of its military dimension. It then analyses the key aspects of the traditional approach to military security and some of the most common ways in which states have sought to acquire it historically, such as war, alliances, and, more recently, nuclear deterrence. The chapter then reflects on some of the difficulties in acquiring military security, and ways in which its pursuit can sometimes reduce, rather than increase, security, before concluding with a reminder of the continuing centrality of military security, even within a significantly broadened understanding of security as a multifaceted concept.

Introduction

The concept of security has been central to the study of international relations since its inception as a discipline, but has had a restricted definition for most of that period. Barry Buzan (1991a: 7) argued in 1991 that security was an 'essentially contested concept' and that the study of international relations was marked by 'unsolvable debates' about the meaning of security. Actually this is far from being the case; such debates are a comparatively recent phenomenon. For most of the twentieth century there was in fact a scholarly consensus regarding the understanding of security, and that consensus limited its meaning to *military* security, so that in practice security studies was synonymous with strategic studies, the study of the relationship between military power and the achievement of political objectives. States were seen as entities that provided 'collective goods' to their citizens, of which the most important was freedom from external attack (Kapstein, 1992: 14). As Baldwin (1997: 9) has noted, 'paradoxical as it may seem, security has not been an important analytical concept for most security studies scholars. During the Cold War, security studies was composed mostly of scholars interested in military statecraft.' In the post-Cold War period, the move to broaden the concept of security has been largely successful, with additional security 'sectors' taking their place alongside the military domain. But it is important to recognize that military security retains a central place in the expanded definition of security, and for governments remains an absolute priority. Military issues remain paramount, because 'a state and its society can be, in their own terms, secure in the political, economic, societal and environmental dimensions, and yet all of these accomplishments can be undone by military failure' (Buzan 1991b: 35). Military forces capable of defending the country and supporting its foreign policy remain central to state security. It therefore remains a priority in terms of the attention paid to it by International Relations as an academic discipline.

Approaches to military security

The traditional approach to studying military security was dominant during the Cold War, and remains intellectually hegemonic in the United States even in the post-Cold War era, though it has lost its predominance elsewhere. In the traditional approach, security is a military phenomenon, military capabilities take a priority in budgetary allocation by governments, and the projection and deterrence of military force is central to understanding the workings of international politics.

In an early realist contribution to the study of national security, Arnold Wolfers (1962: 150) noted that threats can result from a psychological construction as well as an empirical reality. Wolfers pointed out that 'security, in an objective sense, measures the absence of threats to acquired values, in a subjective sense, the absence of fear that such values will be attacked'. His insight was not followed up for several decades, which was unfortunate, since it opens the analyst to a more social-constructivist understanding of security in all its forms.

It is possible to study military security through non-realist analytical lenses, however. Rather than making the realist assumption that the structural realities of the international system are a given, which define the need for particular forms of military capability and policy, it is possible to adopt a social-constructivist approach, which sees all human reality as the product of human interaction and capable of being interpreted in different ways, and altered by human actions. In this approach, cultural factors and norms become central to the analysis (Adler and Barnett 1998). It is also important to be aware that the security of the state is an essential, but not always sufficient, condition for making its citizens secure.

Because of the prevalence of 'expeditionary wars' and humanitarian interventions in the post-Cold War period, alternative conceptions of security such as the 'human security' approach can also be related to military security. The traditional military objective of defeating or destroying enemy armed forces is inadequate when post-war 'peace building' or national reconstruction of the defeated state is a crucial policy objective. States also feel obliged to take account of the United Nations' call for the creation of a 'culture of protection' in situations of armed conflict. Wartime and post-war human security needs therefore need to be integrated into military security policies and in key procedures, from war plans to military training. In addition, national militaries must increasingly plan for missions in which they need to operate successfully alongside civilian government personnel and non-governmental organizations. Soldiers cannot be expected to be 'armed social workers', but the presence of such trained civilian staff may be crucial to the long-term success of the military operation (Lamb 2007). A European Union advisory panel has proposed the creation of a new type of mixed military–civilian formation, a division-sized (15,000 personnel) 'Human Security Response Force' of which two-thirds would be military and one-third police and civilian social and development specialists (Barcelona Report 2004). However, the idea that military and non-military security instruments should form part of such a 'networked-security' approach remains controversial for many civil society groups, who see this development as simply the 'militarization' of the other security sectors.

In 1977 Snyder introduced the concept of strategic culture in understanding the way that countries formulate and implement military-security policies. In contrast to the structuralist approach of neorealism, Snyder argued that societies' beliefs and historical behaviour patterns are crucial for understanding their policy decisions. Factors such as the continuing influence of national myths and social and political norms (Wendt 1996) help shape the boundaries of what a government considers vital or not, acceptable or not, achievable or not, urgent or not, and influences the manner in which governments seek to implement their policy choices.

A more 'critical' approach to military security would also note that, in the 'real' world, ontology is changing. In their wars on terror both the United States and Israel have deployed their armed forces abroad in large-scale military operations, the USA in Afghanistan (post 2001) and Israel in Lebanon (2006) and Palestine (2009), where the operations were directed not against the armed forces of those states, or to secure the territory, but in pursuit of sub-state insurgent or terrorist forces (al-Qaeda, Hisbollah, Hamas). In Columbia, US forces have been operating against insurgent forces linked with the international drugs trade. This is a very different use of military capability from the realist state-to-state logic, although the use of military forces in the counter-insurgency role has a long historical pedigree. Prior to the development of national police forces in the nineteenth century, the military were the only force the state had at its disposal for such purposes.

In addition, a critical approach to military security is valuable in recognizing that in many parts of the world the 'military security' threat facing a population, and sometimes facing the national government, is not the armed forces of neighbouring states, but those of the state itself. The 'threat' to states such as Argentina, Chile, Greece, South Korea, Nigeria, Pakistan, and many others in recent decades has been military coups against the national government, followed by long periods of brutal military dictatorship. The cosy assumption that a state needs to maximize its own military capabilities to face external threat safely takes no account of these realities. In 1948, Costa Rica abolished its armed forces in recognition of the fact that they, not those of other countries, were the real threat.

Focusing on population rather than the state is also typical of the social constructivist approach, which highlights the implications of notions of 'identity' for military security. Where realism sees identities as essentially fixed, the social constructivist approach sees them as being more fluid, and this has important implications for the use of force in international relations. Conflict can be the forge in which national identity is formed, rather than a struggle between pre-existing rival identities, as Campbell (1998b) argues was the case during the Bosnian War in the early 1990s. Campbell (1992) in fact insists that the state itself is constructed through the practice of pursuing militarized security against real or imagined external threats.

The social constructivist approach to security is useful because, in Onuf's words (1989), the international system is 'a world of our making'. The meaning that governments and individuals attach to events is crucial—for example, President George W. Bush seeing the 9/11 attacks as part of a war, rather than a terrorist attack requiring a policing response, or the way in which the understanding of 'child soldiers' has evolved in recent decades, or whether the conflict in Bosnia was a 'civil war' or an 'invasion'. The socially constructed meaning societies give to events shapes the way they respond to them, and interpretations of 'national interest' are crucial in underpinning national security policies.

Governments can choose to 'securitize' certain issues and not others. While the US government under President George W. Bush saw the struggle against terrorism as an aspect of military security, for example, its European allies tended to view it in terms of traditional policing and counter-subversion policies. The decision as to whether or not to place an issue within the military-security discourse will reflect the political objectives of those promoting the move. Militarization (in the conceptual sense), like theory, is 'always for someone and for some purpose'. It is not a politically neutral step; it will be taken because it advances the objectives of an influential group within the national polity.

KEY POINTS

- Military security has both an objective and a subjective dimension.

- While realist approaches have dominated the study of military security, other approaches, such as constructivism, can also be employed.

- A constructivist approach identifies alternative possibilities where a structuralist approach sees constraints as defining.

Traditional military-security studies

Prior to the expanding of the definition, security was understood in overwhelmingly military terms and was seen as meaning 'military protection against the threats posed by the armed forces of other states'. It was further assumed that the referent object of security, the thing that needed to be made secure, was the state. Thus, military security was about identifying actual and potential military threats from other states, and coping with them, either by acquiring sufficient levels of appropriate military capability oneself, or by allying with other states that possessed such a capability. The ultimate mechanism for maintaining security was the resort to war. Thus Lippmann (1943: 51) argued that 'a nation is secure to the extent to which it is not in danger of having to sacrifice core values, if it wishes to avoid war, and is able, if challenged, to maintain them by victory in such a war'. The study of military security is, therefore, the central concern of strategic studies, and one of the central concerns of security studies. In this regard, one can think of security studies as a subset of international relations, and strategic studies as a subset of security studies, the latter focusing solely on the military dimension of security in terms of the threat and use of force to achieve political objectives.

For traditionalists, the requirement for governments to focus their attention on military rather than other forms of security was seen as being a result of the structure of the international system. For traditional realists, the key element of the system is that it is an anarchy—that is, there is no world government. States are therefore obliged to produce their military security through their own efforts, and these efforts will seem threatening to other states in the system, causing them to respond in kind, and triggering an arms race spiral as a result of this 'security dilemma'. This produces what Snow (1991: 1) called the 'violent peace'. John Herz (1950: 158), who originated the term 'security dilemma', argued that it had crucial domestic as well as international implications because it resulted in 'power-political, oligarchic, authoritarian and similar trends and tendencies in society'. In this regard it has implications for the other security sectors as well, particularly political and societal security.

This was important, because the traditional security approach assumed that the domestic political order was stable and essentially peaceful, whereas there was an arena of 'necessity, contingency and violence beyond the state' (Dalby 1992b: 105). In reality, the boundaries of military security are themselves necessarily somewhat fluid. Since the perception of a 'threat' implies the recognition of vulnerabilities,

military security must encompass internal elements such as actual or potential insurgencies and terrorism, ideological division, nationalist pressures, in fact any 'national weaknesses that might be exploited by an enemy' (Freedman 1992: 754).

As well as this specific ontology (understanding of what it was that was being studied), traditional military security studies also operated with a very particular positivist epistemology (or understanding of what constituted legitimate knowledge). This was based upon empiricism, naturalism, and objectivism (Smith 1996: 18). A 'scientific objectivism' was held to be characteristic of the way that military security issues were studied (Wyn Jones 1996). Military security theorists assumed that the scientific method was applicable both to the natural and the social worlds (naturalism), and that it was possible for security analysts to remain objective by distinguishing between 'facts' and 'values' (objectivism). Finally, analysis, following the scientific method, would proceed through empirical validation or falsification. The 'real world' would be investigated, without bias or ideology influencing the results. As outlined by Walt (1991: 222), 'security studies seeks *cumulative* knowledge about the role of military force. To obtain it, the field must follow the standard canons of scientific research.' The study of military security is in this sense seen as a search for 'truth'.

Although security realism is often contrasted with idealism, there are idealistic elements within the realist world view in this regard. As Reus-Smit (1992: 17) notes, many traditional security specialists effectively see the state as an 'idealized political community', where the survival and well-being of the population as a whole is aggregated into a minimalist notion of state security. It is this assumption that allows Buzan (1991a: 328), for example, to claim that 'national security subsumes all other security considerations'. For critics such as Booth (1991: 320) this is illogical, since it gives priority to 'the security of the means as opposed to the security of the ends'.

Military power is relative to the situation in which a state tries to use it. It was a fatal error by Iraq under Saddam Hussein to think that, because its army performed well against Iran, it was capable of standing up

---

KEY QUOTES 11.1

The security dilemma

'When states seek the ability to defend themselves, they get too much and too little—too much because they gain the ability to carry out aggression; too little because others, being menaced, will increase their own arms and so reduce the first state's security. Unless the requirements for offence and defence differ in kind or amount, a status quo power will desire a military posture that resembles that of an aggressor. For this reason others cannot infer from its military forces and preparations whether the state is aggressive. States therefore assume the worst. The others intentions must be co-extensive with his capabilities.'

Jervis (1991: 92 – 3).

to the forces of the United States. How much military capability is deemed to be enough depends partly on what threats exist, and partly on what a state wishes to do with its military capabilities, both in terms of its overall defence strategy and on whether it sees the security of other states as also crucial to its own security, and thereby feels a need for power projection capabilities.

For most of the Cold War period, therefore, thinking about security in the heavily armed states of the developed world focused not on security in a broad sense, but rather on what were seen to be the requirements for maintaining the balance of power in the nuclear age, through policies of deterrence, alliance formation, and force projection. These ideas were reflected in the writings of key scholars such as Brodie, (1959), Kissinger (1956), and Schelling (1960b).

More recently, contributors to realist thinking have divided into somewhat different *neoclassical* realist approaches that have differing assumptions on the implications of the security dilemma for

military security. Offensive realism operates with a traditional interpretation of the security dilemma, in which rivalry and conflict is inevitable. Defensive realists, in contrast, do not assume that the international anarchy always leads to conflict. It can often produce relatively peaceful areas of the world, where states do not face any insurmountable military security threats, so that major external military dangers are seen as exceptional and unusual, rather than the norm (Rose 1998:149).

KEY POINTS

- Traditional security approaches focused on military threats posed to the state in an environment characterized by the security dilemma.

- Security specialists used a positivist methodology, emphasizing the scientific method.

- Post-Cold War realists have divided into groups with differing assumptions about the implications of the security dilemma.

War

States acquire and maintain military capabilities ultimately because they face the possibility of war. The problem of war has always been foundational to the study of international relations and central to security studies. Security studies has always operated with a Clausewitzian perspective on war: that war is not a social aberration or mass psychological disorder, but rather is simply a rational instrument of policy, in the same way as diplomacy or economic sanctions. It is a continuation of politics by other means. War, according to Clausewitz, is a political activity, 'intended to compel our opponent to fulfil our will'. It is simply a brutal form of bargaining.

In the 1970s and again in the 1990s it became fashionable in some academic circles to argue that war was on the decline and the use of military force as a foreign-policy instrument was

increasingly unattractive for states. Most of this writing originated in America and Western Europe, two areas of the international system that had certainly become less dangerous environments since the end of the Second World War.

Advocates of this logic argued that foreign-policy objectives had become more intangible, that there was less emphasis on territorial expansion and more emphasis on trade. States now sought to win friends and influence people, rather than to invade and occupy their territories. Nuclear weapons had proved to be effectively unusable, great powers had failed dismally to achieve their military objectives in wars in Vietnam (the USA) and Afghanistan (the USSR), and the international system seemed dominated by states with major constraints on their armed forces, such as Germany and Japan. Some went so far as to suggest that, at least between the major powers, war was becoming obsolete.

Certainly war is a risky option to resort to. Of all wars occurring between 1815 and 1910, 80 per cent were won by the governments that started them. But 60 per cent of the wars between 1910 and 1965 were lost by the initiating state. But, in the post-Cold War period, war does not seem to have lost its salience for military security. The debates about it have rather been concerned with the nature of the wars that have taken place and the implications of revolutionary developments in military technology.

One area of debate has concerned the question of whether or not a 'revolution in military affairs' (RMA) has been underway in the post-Cold War period. The term revolution suggests a sudden and radical break with the past, and it has been suggested that the technological superiority of American military forces revealed in the 1991 Gulf War showed that just such a revolution had occurred. This interpretation placed great emphasis on technological developments. However, sceptics such as Lambert have cautioned against overemphasizing the significance of technological change, while underestimating the importance of changes in doctrine and organization.

Kaldor and Münkler have engaged with the issue of whether the wars typical of the post-Cold War period differ in form sufficiently from previous eras that they can be termed 'new wars'. While Kaldor (1999), argues that such wars are indeed a new phenomenon, Münkler (2005) disagrees, arguing that such a view lacks historical depth, but that a 'new terrorism' is the central challenge facing contemporary states.

In the 'new-wars' thesis, identity politics are central to the explanation of political violence. Kaldor argues that the conflicts typical of the post-Cold War period have been struggles to control the state in order to assert a particular understanding of national identity. A feature of such conflicts is that they are internal to the state, taking the form of insurgencies and civil wars. They therefore lend themselves to a constructivist analysis, rather than a traditional analysis of military security.

KEY POINTS

- War remains a legitimate instrument of national policy for states.

- War between the major powers risks consequences that have dramatically reduced its attractiveness.

- Technological and doctrinal changes may be driving a revolution in military affairs.

- Since 1991 the dominant form of warfare has been intra-state rather than inter-state.

Alliances and neutrality

One method of acquiring military security is to become a member of a military alliance. Security analysis has thus historically also paid attention to the issues relating to the attractiveness or otherwise of alliance membership, usually linking it to structural realist explanations of international politics (Waltz 1979; Gilpin 1981). States will seek membership of such an alliance if they believe that their own resources are inadequate to maintain their sovereignty and security, and will make common cause with states that share their goals, or at least perceive similar threats. Alliance formation is particularly notable when a potential hegemonic power threatens the other states in the system. Alliance theories are often linked to balance of power theory. While some scholars argue that states automatically ally to 'balance' against a threatening state (Walt 1987), others argue that states are just as likely to 'bandwagon'—that is, to ally with the likely winning hegemon. In practice, the reasons for joining alliances vary widely.

More powerful states may also create alliances in order to extend their protective umbrella over weaker friendly states. Alliances are often seen by members not so much as essential tools for balancing against a potential hegemon, but rather as mechanisms for exercising influence over allies, whose own military security policies may increase the dangers to their allies—for example, by drawing them into confrontations or expeditionary commitments against third parties. They allow states to restrain or exert pressure on states within the alliance framework (Osgood 1968; Ikenberry 2001). While the idea that states prefer to join alliances with states that share common cultures or ideologies appears logical, such 'affinity theories' have not been confirmed by detailed studies of alliance formation (Russett 1971; Walt 1987).

The obligations assumed as members of an alliance vary significantly between organizations. Because of its size and longevity, NATO can sometimes be seen as a 'typical' alliance. In reality it is a very unusual alliance, completely unlike most others in history. Alliances vary in terms of issues that cause them to be created, the situations in which military commitments are triggered, the degree of military integration that takes place within the alliance, the numbers of allies, the geographical scope of the alliance, and many other factors.

CASE STUDY 11.1

NATO

The North Atlantic Treaty Organization (NATO) was created in 1949 with the signing of the Washington Treaty. NATO is a military alliance that has expanded in the post-Cold War period and by 2009 comprised twenty-eight countries from North America and Europe. It was originally created as an insurance against a revival of German militarism after the Second World War and as a collective defence initiative against the perceived threat from the Soviet Union.

The key clause of the Washington Treaty is Article 5, which declares that each ally will treat an attack against one Ally as an attack against all and respond with its own military forces as if it itself had been attacked. Article 4 of the treaty ensures consultations among Allies on security matters of common interest. The NATO members routinely consult each other on security matters, a habit that has become ingrained over six decades since 1949. In the post-Cold War period, NATO expanded its remit and geographical zone of operations, to allow it to become a collective security organization, operating in counter-insurgency warfare in Afghanistan, as well as peacekeeping in Kosovo.

Although its longevity and political influence encourage a perception of NATO as a 'typical' alliance, in reality NATO is historically unique. In terms of the length of time it has existed, the fact that it has done so in peacetime, rather than wartime, the degree of military integration among its members, and a number of other factors, NATO is an institution without precedent or parallel in recorded human history.

Most military alliances are assembled for the purpose of waging war, and end when the war is concluded. Their purpose is to coordinate the allies' common war effort to maximum effect. Integration of forces is unusual. NATO is unusual, both in that it is a peacetime alliance and in that it has remained in existence for sixty years, outlasting the disappearance of all its original reasons for being created. Alliances tend to have brief existences because they require the harmonization of many conflicting interests, which becomes more difficult over long periods particularly if there is not an overwhelming sense of commonly perceived external threat.

Critics of alliances argue that they contribute little to a state's military security, and are destabilizing for the international system. Wright (1965: 774) argued that they simply generate opposing alliances and are incompatible with collective security, since they promote a selective response to acts of aggression. However, Kegley and Raymond (1982) found that on balance alliances make a positive contribution to peace and security as long as the alliance structure is flexible and when alliance commitments are considered binding by the member states.

Nevertheless a state is likely to avoid alliance membership if it feels strong enough to maintain its security unaided, or if it feels that its sovereignty will be compromised by alliance membership, or that the obligations and risks involved outweigh the potential benefits. Many states have historically sought security, not by joining alliances, but, on the contrary, by declaring neutral or non-aligned status. Occasionally **neutrality** is forced upon a state. Austria's neutral status was not a national political choice, but rather the price imposed by the superpowers in return for ending their military occupation and restoring Austrian sovereignty in 1955. Finnish neutrality was a conscious choice by Finland's government, but one taken in the knowledge that any other option would be likely to trigger a renewed Soviet invasion after 1945. Other states, such as Sweden, have seen neutrality as providing more security, sovereignty, and freedom than entry into a military alliance dominated by one or more of the great powers (Joenniemi 1988: 53). Neutrality does not come cheap. Because they do not have access to the military capabilities of allied states, neutral countries typically have to maintain large armed forces and institute systems of national service.

Neutrality is a legal status. A neutral state must remain outside military alliances in peacetime, and refrain from activities that might seem to align it too closely with the members of any existing alliances. In return, its neutral status will (or at least should) be accepted by the belligerent states in wartime. In the post-Cold War period, collective security organizations have become more prominent than collective defence bodies, but, given that the systemic factors promoting alliance formation have changed little in the post-Cold War period, alliances are likely to remain important mechanisms by which states pursue military security (Snyder 1997: 78).

KEY POINTS

- Military security can be pursued unilaterally by relying on one's own capabilities, multilaterally via alliance membership, or unilaterally via a policy of neutrality.

- States join alliances to compensate for their own relative military weakness.

- Alliances vary significantly in terms of their membership, objectives, and obligations.

- Some states have historically preferred to remain neutral rather than join alliances.

Deterrence

For most of the Cold War period, not only did 'security' studies in the developed world focus almost exclusively on military security, but within that focus there was an enormous, if perhaps understandable, emphasis on the study of the issue of nuclear deterrence. The stress on deterrence occurred despite the fact that nuclear weapons were never actually employed in war during the Cold War.

Early writers on nuclear weapons believed that they would be a 'powerful inhibitor to aggression' and would lead military security policies to become designed to avert wars rather than to win them (Brodie 1946: 73). In practice, the impact of nuclear weapons was more complicated. They did act as an inhibitor of full-scale war between the nuclear-armed great powers during crises (Kennedy 1969), but had no impact on those states (the vast majority) that did not possess such weapons. The existence of nuclear weapons certainly encouraged superpower diplomatic caution during the Cold War, and also encouraged the superpowers to pursue arms control. But it also encouraged the development of a balance-of-power system that tried to limit the propensity for superpower military engagement worldwide, and stabilized a nuclear balance where the superpowers constantly strengthened themselves so as not to have to fight.

In terms of generating a sense of security, military power can serve a number of ends. Where feasible, defence is the goal that all states aim for first. If defence is not possible, deterrence is generally the next priority. The defensive use of military power revolves around two purposes. The first is to ward off an attack. Should this not succeed, the second purpose is to minimize the damage to oneself if attacked.

The deterrent use of military power works with a different logic. Deterrence is based upon the threat of retaliation. It seeks to prevent an adversary from doing something by threatening him with unacceptable punishment if he does it. The threat of retaliation or punishment is directed at the adversary's population or industrial infrastructure. It is effective only if the adversary is convinced you have both the will and the power to carry out the threat. Hence deterrence can be judged successful only if the retaliatory threat has not had to be carried out.

Nuclear weapons have paradoxically made those that possess them more militarily secure than any previous states in history, and more militarily insecure than any other states in history. Everything depends on the effectiveness of deterrence. Robert Art (1980: 22). argues that nuclear security buys conventional power projection capability: 'precisely because security can be bought so cheaply with nuclear weapons is each superpower able to use the bulk of its defence dollars on conventional forces, which can be readily employed and more finely tuned'.

Deterrence produces security not by physically obstructing a certain course of action, as defence does, but by threatening a response that makes the action seem disproportionately costly and therefore unattractive in the first place. In practice this

> **KEY QUOTES 11.2**
>
> ### Deterrence and defence
>
> 'Defence is possible without deterrence and deterrence is possible without defence. A state can have the military wherewithal to repel an invasion without also being able to threaten devastation to the invader's population or territory. Similarly, a state can have the wherewithal to credibly threaten an adversary with such devastation and yet be unable to repel his invading force. Defence, therefore, does not necessarily buy deterrence, nor deterrence defence. A state that can defend itself from attack, moreover, will have little need to develop the wherewithal to deter. If physical attacks can be repelled or if the damage from them drastically minimized, the incentive to develop a retaliatory capability is low. A state that cannot defend itself, however, will try to develop an effective deterrent if that be possible.'
>
> Art (1980: 7).

is not entirely straightforward. Deterrence will work only if the threatened state clearly possesses the capability to inflict overwhelming retaliation, successfully convinces the adversary that it would be certain to do so if attacked, and is able to communicate clearly what is and is not acceptable within its deterrence doctrine. All these requirements are problematical in various ways. There are additional issues related to commitments to allies. Against a fellow nuclear-armed state, the willingness to use nuclear weapons is tantamount to committing suicide. Such a 'passive' deterrent threat may be credible when one's own population is threatened, but an 'active' deterrent threat, to follow the same course in defence of an ally, is much more difficult to make credible.

There are also clear moral issues. Actually to carry out the threat of retaliation is for a state to commit genocide against its enemies. This would be in breach of all existing laws of war, and the moral codes of all the world's major religions. Given social norms against blackmail and violent intimidation of other people, and particularly those who threaten violence against children, the old, or the helpless, it is debateable whether even the *threat* to use nuclear weapons is morally acceptable. Such issues spawned a large and lively scholarly literature (see, e.g., Elshtain 1992).

Michael McGwire argues that the 'theology' of deterrence encouraged the development of an arcane language that disguised the brutal realities of nuclear weapons' 'countervalue' rather than, say, city-targeting strikes. It also assumed a particular kind of worse-case analysis, where an enemy course of action needed only to be conceivable for it to be included in the threat assessment. Finally, because 'retaliation' actually meant genocidal mass murder of civilian populations, deterrence encouraged continual efforts to paint the adversary as a people deserving of such a terrible fate (McGuire 1986: 24–9). This critique is another example both of the importance of cultural determinants of military security thinking, and of the potential disjuncture between 'state' and 'population' logics when pursuing military security.

A number of authors have argued that the characteristics of the nuclear balance of power since the end of the Cold War are so different from the 1945–91 period that the world has now entered the Second Nuclear Age. The number of nuclear-weapons states will continue to increase, but the stability of deterrent relationships will decrease, so that a failure of deterrence and an outbreak of nuclear war becomes more likely.

> **KEY POINTS**
>
> - Nuclear deterrence theory dominated Cold War security studies.
>
> - Nuclear deterrent relationships can increase and decrease security simultaneously.
>
> - Deterrence has very different moral implications from policies based upon defence.
>
> - The Cold War was the First Nuclear Age. The post-Cold War period may represent a Second Nuclear Age, with different implications for the pursuit of military security.

Cooperative security and arms control

Traditional approaches to military security assume that the existence of the international anarchy leads inevitably to the security dilemma. However, a number of scholars such as Wendt (1992: 407), have argued that while the anarchy may indeed exist, it is not inevitable that it should produce a security dilemma, and might indeed encourage cooperation among states. The operation of the security dilemma is a result of the practices of states, not of the structure of the system, and practices can change. Scholars such as Young (1968) and Jervis (1970), drew attention to the psychological aspects of the way in which policy-makers constructed their images of security.

One example of states seeking to circumvent the difficulties of the security dilemma is through practices of cooperative security such as the pursuit of arms control and disarmament. A feature of the search for military security in the Cold War period was the pursuit of arms control. It was recognised that a purely adversarial relationship between nuclear armed states was far too dangerous and that therefore efforts should be made to negotiate agreed constraints on military capability in certain areas, particularly with regard to weapons of mass destruction.

Classical disarmament theory assumed that weapons, rather than being a route to security, were a cause of insecurity. They were seen as both deepening tensions between states, and making them more likely to resort to the use of force in times of crisis (Claude 1964: 262–3). The solution was therefore to reduce armaments, thereby reducing tension. Booth

(1975: 89) described this approach by paraphrasing Clausewitz as 'a continuation of politics by a reduction of military means'. Arms control is a more conservative approach to building military security, though it can lead to disarmament in the longer term. Arms controllers did not see weapons as producing insecurity merely by their existence. On the contrary, they believed that weaponry was a normal and acceptable part of international relations (Bull 1961: 8). The arms control community therefore promoted the creation and maintenance of balances of power in which arms control would complement unilateral force improvements as the route to military security (Lefever 1962: 122).

Arms control as an approach to military security sought to distinguish between 'those kinds and quantities of forces and weapons that promote the stability of the balance of power and those which do not; to tolerate or even to promote the former and to restrict the latter' (Bull 1961: 61). Thus while disarmament always implies weapon reductions, arms control may simply freeze numbers, or even increase them through mutual consent. Schelling and Halperin (1961: 2) defined the objectives of arms control as being 'reducing the likelihood of war, its scope and violence if it occurs, and the political and economic costs of being prepared for it'. This was a clear attempt to address the 'costs of security' discussed earlier. In practice

however, subsequent decades of experience with arms control demonstrated that these objectives often conflicted with one another. Increasing the number of survivable nuclear weapons may make war less likely, but increases the cost of preparing for it, and the death and destruction if it occurs. Developing complex verification regimes, such as those for the 1993 Chemical Weapons Convention reduce the likelihood of war, and the death and destruction if it occurs, but still increase the cost of being prepared for it.

One problem that policymakers encountered in subsequently implementing arms control was that politicians and the general public expected agreements to produce numerical balances, what Krepon (1984: 130) called 'optical parity'. But, as Schelling (1985–6) pointed out, this reflected a shift from a concern with the *character* of weapons to an obsession with numbers. Bertram also argued that what is important was 'who could do what' rather than 'who had what'. But, from the point of view of economics and public perceptions, numbers are clearly important. Nevertheless, the arms control approach led to the conclusion of a large number of important agreements during the Cold War period, which can be held to have had a significant stabilizing function.

CASE STUDY 11.2

The INF Treaty

The Intermediate Nuclear Forces (INF) Treaty was signed in 1987 between the United States and the Soviet Union. It addressed a problem that had been souring relations between NATO and the Warsaw Pact over the previous decade, the deployment of large numbers of nuclear missiles in both halves of Europe, with ranges capable of striking most of the cities on the Continent. A new round of weapon modernization by both sides in the late 1970s and early 1980s raised tensions dramatically and led to the initiation of arms-control negotiations in an attempt to resolve the problem.

The INF Treaty when it came turned out to be of enormous historical significance. In order to ease the verification

difficulties involved, the two sides agreed to eliminate all weapons in this category, rather than simply reduce the numbers each side could possess. This removed 3 per cent of all nuclear weapons in the world and for the first time eliminated an entire category, making the agreement a disarmament as well as an arms control treaty. Moreover, in order to facilitate monitoring of compliance with its terms, the Soviet Union agreed to unprecedented intrusive verification techniques, which not only opened up the possibility of a range of other ambitious arms control agreements, but also signalled a change in Soviet attitudes so profound that it indicated that the Cold War was coming to an end.

In the post-Cold War period arms control lost momentum. A number of agreements were signed in the first half of the 1990s, but these represented the tidying-up of the Cold War agenda. Arms control became less central both to the practice of military security after 1991 and to scholarly debates about the best way to sustain such security. The very different international political environment called for what Daalder (1993) described as 'threat deconstruction'. However, while progress largely halted in some areas, arms control thinking was applied to some new areas, such as light weapons and to the issue of conventional weapons proliferation.

KEY POINTS

- Arms control has become an important cooperative dimension of efforts to acquire military security through mutual restraint.

- Arms control does not challenge the central role of weaponry and military power in the international system, but focuses on problems produced by specific weapon systems and relationships.

- In the post-Cold War period arms control lost much of its salience, but remains a useful tool for pursuing security.

The cost of military security

Analysts of international relations have reflected not only on the nature of security and alternative military strategies for maximizing it, but also on the fact that some of these strategies can be self-defeating, or generate security problems in other dimensions of the broader security agenda. Military security is of a different moral order to the other security sectors. The right of a people to defend their independence and way of life by maintaining and, if necessary, employing military capabilities is recognized under international law. However, as Klaus Knorr (1970: 50) said 'military power is ultimately the power to destroy and kill, or to occupy and control, and hence to coerce', and it therefore has rather different implications to the pursuit of environmental security for example.

There are also economic and political issues. Military power can be acquired only by enormous effort in terms of the commitment of manpower and economic resources. All states struggle to acquire and maintain what they consider to be adequate military forces, and democratically elected governments therefore face particular difficulties in deciding upon the appropriate level of military capability. There are two main reasons for this. In the first place, such capability is extremely expensive to acquire, and high levels of

defence spending may be unpopular, especially during long period of peace. Defence spending generates 'opportunity costs', the value of the social good a government could not invest in because it chose to spend the money on military capabilities. When President Eisenhower was asked the cost of the latest American bomber, he replied that the cost was 'a modern brick school in more than thirty cities, or two fully equipped hospitals'.

Acquiring military security is neither simple nor straightforward. One issue that overlaps with issues of economic security is the question, not so much of how much military capability does a state *need* to be secure, but how much can it *afford*? States often acquire less military capability than they would ideally like. The costs of acquiring such capability are real. The demand for security is a normative demand, it is the pursuit of a particular value. As Wolfers (1962: 150) noted, security is a value 'of which a nation can have more or less and which it can aspire to have in greater or lesser measure'.

The pursuit of military security requires states to make sacrifices in terms of spending on other social, or even security, goals that they might have. State resources are relatively scarce, and therefore the decision to spend resources on acquiring military security means such decisions are inevitably a subject for 'moral judgement' (Wolfers 1962: 162).

Secondly, the concentration of military power that a government feels is required to defend a democracy against its enemies in certain ways poses an inherent threat to the very values it is designed to protect. A state can become dangerously 'militarized' by such efforts. And the *use* of military force may damage democratic values, since it represents an undemocratic mechanism—the resort to force and violence to resolve disputes, rather than using dialogue and compromise, as would be expected in the domestic democratic context. In wartime civil rights are invariably weakened, and normally abhorrent practices such as the use of torture may be condoned.

Efforts to acquire military security may generate security problems of their own. Increasing the size of national armed forces may trigger an arms race with other states, for example, and require modified policies, such as the addition of arms-control initiatives. Acquiring substantial military capabilities may also encourage states to pursue military options when non-violent instruments still had the capacity to succeed. The use of force is seen both as legitimate for states, but also as a threat to the stability of the system, but the perception of the possibility of military threats from external actors ensures that states continue to maintain such capabilities.

The inhibitions in the use of violence between states are considerable, and they rest on the most basic kind of self-interest. Violence is seldom the most effective way of settling disputes. It is expensive in its methods and unpredictable in its outcome. However no state (with the exception of Costa Rica) has yet found it possible to dispense with armed forces. The capacity of states to defend themselves, and their evident willingness to do so, provides the basic framework within which the business of international negotiations is carried on. Every new state since 1945 has considered it necessary to create armed forces.

KEY POINTS

- Military security is expensive to acquire.

- The 'costs' of doing so are social as well as economic.

- Acquiring military capability can have consequences that threaten as well as secure a state's values.

Conclusion

The expansion of the concept of security has moved the focus of security studies away from a purely military understanding. Nevertheless, military security remains an absolutely crucial dimension of security as a whole. Governments continue to invest considerable resources in attempting to acquire it, and analysts of international relations seek to understand military security both in its own right and in relation to efforts to increase security in the non-military realms. Military security is extremely expensive to acquire, and the opportunity costs in terms of the human security agenda are profound. Efforts to increase military security can have unintended counterproductive consequences in the military or other fields. Questions about how much, and what kind of, military capability to seek in relation to perceived threats remain at the heart of the study of security.

QUESTIONS

1. Why is it important to study military security?

2. Are governments correct in prioritising military security?

3. To what extent is the requirement for military security produced by the international anarchy and the security dilemma?

4. Has the end of the Cold War invalidated the arguments for security policies based on nuclear deterrence?

5. In what ways can military security be said to have objective and subjective reality?

6. How useful is arms control as a means of achieving military security?

7. What are the strengths and weaknesses of the traditional realist approach to military security?

8. To what extent can the military-security environment be said to be 'socially constructed'?

9. Is war becoming obsolete as an instrument of national policy?

10. In what ways can the pursuit of military security leave a state perceiving itself as less secure?

 FURTHER READING

■ Anthony, I., and Rotfeld, A. (2001) (eds.), *A Future Arms Control Agenda,* Oxford: Oxford University Press. A useful collection of essays reflecting on the potential utility of arms control in the post-Cold War period.

■ Baylis, John, Wirtz, James J., Gray, Colin S. (2010) (eds.), *Strategy in the Contemporary World,* Oxford: Oxford University Press. Excellent collection of essays on the relationship of military power to international security.

■ Biddle, Stephen (2004), *Military Power: Explaining Victory and Defeat in Modern Battle,* Princeton: Princeton University Press. A good recent study of the issues involved in attempts to use force to increase military security in conventional terms.

■ Freedman, L. (2004), *Deterrence,* Cambridge: Polity Press. A brief and effective study that provides a clear and well-structured explanation of the nature and history of nuclear deterrence.

■ Kaldor, M. (1999), *New and Old Wars: Organised Violence in the Global Era,* Cambridge: Polity. Kaldor offers a controversial take on the nature of war in the post-Cold War era. Some of her arguments are disputable, but the book is provocative, thoughtful, and worthy of study.

■ Minear, L., and Weiss, T. G. (1995), *Mercy under Fire: War and the Global Humanitarian Community,* Boulder, CO: Westview Press. A very good study of the complexities of using traditional military capabilities in humanitarian interventions.

■ Sloan, E. (2002), *The Revolution in Military Affairs,* Montreal: McGill-Queens Press. A good survey of the issues involved in the RMA debate.

 IMPORTANT WEBSITES

● http://www.armscontrol.org   The Arms Control Association is a national non-partisan membership organization that seeks to build public understanding of and support for effective arms-control policies. It produces the journal Arms Control Today and its website provides information on a range of issues relating to military security.

- http://www.defenselink.mil   The web portal for the United States Department of Defense, a crucial resource for understanding contemporary US defence policy and thinking.

- http://www.fas.org   The website of the Federation of American Scientists. Provides excellent resources on the military capabilities and policies of key states.

- http://www.sipri.org   The website of the excellent Stockholm International Peace Research Institute.

 Visit the Online Resource Centre that accompanies this book for lots of interesting additional material: www.oxfordtextbooks.co.uk/orc/collins2e/

12

Regime Security

RICHARD JACKSON

 Chapter Contents

- Introduction
- The weak-state insecurity dilemma
- Security strategies in weak states
- Explaining insecurity in weak states
- Conclusion: prospects for the weak state

 Reader's Guide

This chapter examines the unique security dilemma facing developing countries. It begins with an explanation of the security threats facing states with weak institutional and coercive capacity and lack of national cohesion—what are called weak states—before going on to look at the kinds of security strategies that weak-state elites typically adopt to try and manage their predicament. Referred to as an 'insecurity dilemma', and in contrast to the security dilemma facing strong, developed states, the problem faced by weak states is a security environment in which the primary threats to security originate from internal rather than external sources. The chapter goes on to examine a number of competing theoretical explanations for how the weak state predicament arose and why it persists. It concludes with a brief discussion of international attempts to build security in weak states, and the long-term prospects of transforming weak states into strong states.

Introduction

By any measure of security, the disparity between the wealthy, developed countries of the global North and the rest of the world could not be greater. Citizens of the small group of highly developed nations face no real threat of major war and enjoy abundant food supplies, economic prosperity, comparatively low levels of crime, and enduring political and social stability. Even the threat of terrorism is extremely minor compared to the everyday risks of accident or disease. Contrary to the 'culture of fear' that exists in many Western societies, at no time in history have individuals in these countries enjoyed such high levels of safety, prosperity, and stability.

By contrast, the majority of people living in developing countries face profound security challenges, including perennial threats of intra-state war and communal violence, poverty and famine, weapons proliferation and crime, political instability, social breakdown, economic failure, and, at its most extreme, complete state collapse. At the most basic level of physical security, between twenty million and thirty million people have lost their lives in more than 100 intra-state wars in developing regions since 1945. Around 90 per cent of the victims were civilians, and tens of millions of people were displaced by the fighting, many of whom have remained refugees for decades after. Depending upon what measure is used, there are between twenty and forty intra-state wars ongoing in any given year, all of them in developing countries. In a great many more developing nations serious internal political violence, such as military coups or rebellions, ethnic or religious violence, campaigns of terrorism or riots and disorder, is a constant threat.

In addition, half a million people are killed every year by light weapons, frequently during criminal violence and almost all in developing countries. Added to these military threats, an estimated 40,000 people die every day from hunger and tens of millions of others die annually from diseases such as influenza, HIV-AIDS, diarrhoea, and tuberculosis. Tens of millions more suffer from chronic poverty, lack of employment opportunities, inadequate health, declining education standards, and environmental ruin. There is, in other words, a profound disjuncture between the kinds of security enjoyed by the small group of developed nations and the kind of security environment inhabited by the majority of the world's population. From a global perspective, insecurity is actually more the norm than security is.

This situation provides us with important reasons for trying to understand the nature and consequences of insecurity in the developing world. Empirically, we need to understand why virtually all war and major political violence since 1945 continues to take place in the developing world, and why most of it originates from internal rather than external sources. Conceptually, there is an urgent need to find appropriate theories and concepts that can accommodate the unique character of the security situation in these countries. Such approaches are a necessary starting point for devising more appropriate and more effective international security policies. From a normative perspective, there are clear humanitarian imperatives to try and deal with the immense suffering caused by the lack of basic security in the world's 'zones of instability'. Finally, enlightened self-interest dictates that we make a real effort to resolve the fundamental inequality in security between the developed and developing worlds. Globalization means that insecurity in any part of the world cannot be contained within increasingly porous national borders; security is, to a large extent, interdependent. In many ways, terrorism, gun crime, illegal migration, the drugs trade, and environmental damage are all spillover effects of persistent insecurity in the developing world.

In this chapter we shall try to make sense of the profound security challenges facing developing countries and the unique security dilemma they find themselves trapped in. We shall examine the nature of the main security threats facing developing nations, the key security strategies that they have adopted to deal with these threats, and the domestic and international causes of their security predicament. The argument we wish to advance in this chapter is that, unlike the developed nations of the global North, the primary security threats facing weak states are potentially catastrophic and originate primarily from internal, domestic sources. They include, among others, the threat of violent transfers of power, insurgency, secession, rebellion, genocide, warlordism, and, ultimately, state collapse and anarchy.

Moreover, these internal threats are rooted in the fundamental conditions of statehood and governance, thereby creating an enduring 'insecurity dilemma' (Job 1992) for ruling elites: the more elites try to establish effective state rule, the more they provoke challenges to their authority from powerful groups in society. In this context, regime security—the condition where governing elites are secure from violent challenges to their rule—becomes indistinguishable from state security—the condition where the institutions, processes, and structures of the state are able to continue functioning effectively, regardless of the make-up of the ruling elite. For weak states, the domestic sphere is actually far more dangerous and threatening than the international sphere.

Given this inversion of the accepted conception of the classical security dilemma (in which military threats originate primarily from other unitary states in an anarchic international system), it is not surprising that the weak state insecurity dilemma has received little attention in the orthodox security-studies literature. By focusing on a limited number of states (the great powers and developed countries), a limited set of military threats (Soviet expansionism, foreign invasion, nuclear proliferation, rogue states, international terrorism), a limited array of security strategies (national defence, deterrence, arms control, alliances), and employing a restricted conception of security (externally directed 'national security'), the security challenges facing the majority of the world's population have been largely sidelined in academic studies. Consequently, there are real limits as to what traditional or orthodox security-studies approaches can tell us about the nature and causes of insecurity in weak states today. Widening and deepening our understanding of security therefore necessitates a new set of diagnostic tools that allow us to get to grips more fully with the security challenges facing the vast majority of the world's people and the unique kind of states they inhabit.

KEY POINTS

- There is a profound disjuncture between the security challenges facing developed and developing countries.

- There are important empirical, conceptual, normative, and self-interested reasons to attend to the security of developing regions.

- Weak states face a unique set of security challenges that originate primarily from internal sources.

- Orthodox approaches to national security are severely limited in what they can tell us about the conditions of security in weak states.

The weak-state insecurity dilemma

The unique insecurity dilemma facing weak states is largely a function of the structural conditions of their existence. Weak states lack the most fundamental of state attributes—namely, effective institutions, a monopoly on the instruments of violence, and consensus on the idea of the state. Consequently, as incomplete or 'quasi-states' (Jackson 1990), they face numerous challenges to their authority from powerful domestic actors. In order to understand how this condition of insecurity arises in the first place, we need to examine the primary structural characteristics of weak states and the nature of the internal security threats they face.

Weak states

Assessing state strength can be a difficult and controversial exercise; scholars tend to apply different measures. Thomas (1987) associates state strength/ weakness with institutional capacity and distinguishes between two forms of state power: despotic power and infrastructural power. Despotic power refers to the state's coercive abilities and the exercise of force to impose its rule on civilians. By contrast, infrastructural power refers to the effectiveness and legitimacy of the state's institutions and its ability to rule through consensus. States may be 'weak' or deficient in one or both of these capacities, but, as a general rule, strong states have less need to exercise coercive power because their infrastructural power makes it unnecessary. Paradoxically, the more a weak state exercises coercive power, the more it reinforces its 'weakness' and corresponding lack of infrastructural power.

In contrast, Buzan (1991a) argues that states consist of three primary components: a physical base, institutional capacity, and the 'idea of the state'. For Buzan, state strength/weakness rests primarily in the less tangible realm of the 'idea of the state' and the extent to which society forms a consensus on, and identifies with, the state. Weak states, therefore, 'either do not have, or have failed to create, a domestic political and social consensus of sufficient strength to eliminate the large-scale use of force as a major and continuing element in the domestic political life of the nation' (Buzan 1983: 67).

Migdal (1988) provides a counterpoint to both these formulations. He defines state strength in terms of state capacity, or 'the ability of state leaders to use the agencies of the state to get people in the state to do what they want them to do' (Migdal 1988: p. xvii). But then he reverses attention to how soci-

ety and groups within it tolerate, permit, or resist the development of the state. He argues that most developing societies end up in a state/society stand-off where the state confronts powerful social forces with substantial coercive force, which in turn provokes violent resistance. In Migdal's view, weak states are less the issue than strong societies. This internal balance of power between state and society militates against the emergence of prototypical Western-style nation states.

In summary, three dimensions of state strength appear to be important: (1) infrastructural capacity in terms of the ability of state institutions to perform essential tasks and enact policy; (2) coercive capacity in terms of the state's ability and willingness to employ force against challenges to its authority; and (3) national identity and social cohesion in terms of the degree to which the population identifies with the nation state and accepts its legitimate role in their lives.

Empirically, it can be seen that most developing nations are weak or deficient in most if not all of these dimensions. Or, they have overdeveloped coercive capacities but lack infrastructural capacity and social consensus. As a consequence of these fundamental deficiencies, weak states typically display all or many of the following characteristics: institutional weakness and an inability to enact national policy or perform basic state functions such as tax collection and providing law and order; political instability, as evidenced by coups, plots, rebellions, and frequent violent changes of government; the centralization of political power in a single individual or small elite who command the machinery of government to run the state in their own interest; unconsolidated or non-existent democracies; ongoing economic crisis and structural weakness; external vulnerability to international actors and forces; intense societal divisions along class, religious, regional, urban–rural, and/or ethnic lines; lack of a cohesive or strong sense of national identity; and an ongoing crisis of legitimacy for both the government of the day and the institutions of state in general.

The most important characteristic of weak states is their frequent inability to establish and maintain a monopoly on the instruments of violence. Even in states with well-developed coercive power, civilian governments do not always retain the absolute loyalty of the armed forces and face a constant threat of military intervention. For most weak states, however, the armed forces are ill equipped, poorly managed, and prone to factional divisions. At the same time, a range of social actors—rival politicians with their own private armies, warlords, criminal gangs, locally organized militias, armed and organized ethnic or religious groups, and private security companies or mercenaries—are powerful enough to resist the state's attempt to enforce compliance. In such a situation, even the most minimal requirement of statehood—the monopoly on the instruments of violence—is largely out of reach.

At the other end of the scale, and in complete contrast, it is suggested that *strong states* have the willingness and ability to 'maintain social control, ensure societal compliance with official laws, act decisively, make effective policies, preserve stability and cohesion, encourage societal participation in state institutions, provide basic services, manage and control the national economy, and retain legitimacy' (Dauvergne 1998: 2). Strong states also possess high levels of socio-political cohesion that is directly correlated with consolidated participatory democracies, strong national identities, and productive and highly developed economies. Most importantly, strong states exist as a 'hegemonic idea', accepted and naturalized in the minds of ordinary citizens such that they 'consider the state as natural as the landscape around them; they cannot imagine their lives without it' (Migdal 1998: 12).

Crucially, the notion of weak and strong states is not a binary measure but rather a continuum along which states in the real world fall. Moreover, it is a dynamic condition. States can move back and forth along the continuum over time given sufficient changes to key factors: weak states can become strong by building a strong sense of national identity, for example; and strong states could potentially weaken through increased social conflict brought on by immigration, for example. Most states in developing regions fall towards the weak end of the state-strength continuum.

KEY POINTS

- The key dimensions of state strength/weakness are infrastructural capacity, coercive capacity, and national identity and social cohesion.

- Weak states are typically characterized by institutional weakness, political instability, centralization of power, unconsolidated democracy, economic crisis, external vulnerability, social divisions, lack of national identity, and an ongoing crisis of legitimacy.

- The most important characteristic of weak states is their lack of a monopoly on the instruments of violence.

- State strength or weakness is a dynamic continuum along which states can move; it is possible for weak states to become strong states and vice versa.

Threats to weak states

Because of their debilitating structural characteristics, weak states face a number of internal and external security challenges. *Internally*, weak states face the continual threat of violent intervention in politics by the armed forces. Such interventions can take the form of *coup d'état*, mutiny, rebellion, or revolt over pay and conditions. There have been literally hundreds of coup attempts in Latin America, Asia-Pacific, and the Middle East, and nearly two-thirds of Africa's states have experienced military rule since independence. Military rulers still govern numerous developing countries.

Weak states also face serious threats from **strongmen**, individuals or groups who exercise a degree of coercive and/or infrastructural power in their own right and who challenge the authority of the state. They may be semi-legitimate actors such as politicians or traditional and religious leaders who nonetheless command large followings and private access to weaponry. Alternately, they may be criminal gangs or **warlords**—charismatic individuals who command private armies and enforce a kind of absolutist rule in areas under their control, primarily for the purposes of pursuing illegal commerce. Examples of such strongmen include the drug cartels in Colombia,

Myanmar, and Afghanistan, and some of the rebel leaders in Africa during the 1990s, such as Charles Taylor, Foday Sankoh, and Jonas Savimbi. If the state fails to accommodate or placate such groups, they may launch a violent challenge to the regime.

In other cases, weak states face challenges from various social groups such as ethnic groups, religious movements, ideological factions, or local militias who organize for self-defence. Owing in large part to pre-existing divisions, the inability of the state to provide adequate welfare, and the tendency to employ excessive coercion, a great many ethnic groups in weak states have organized politically and militarily to protect their interests. Gurr's *Minorities at Risk* project (2000) found more than ninety ethnic minorities were either actively engaged in violent conflict with the state or at medium-to-serious risk of significant political violence. Similarly, in a number of Middle Eastern and Asian countries, such as Algeria, Egypt, Saudi Arabia, Indonesia, and, more recently, Thailand, religious groups have launched violent challenges to the state. Ideologically driven groups also continue to threaten weak states, from the Maoist insurgency in Nepal to the Zapatistas in Chiapas, Mexico. It is a sad fact that virtually all armed groups in weak states—state armies, warlord factions, and local, ethnic, and religious militias—employ large numbers of child soldiers (for more on child soldiers see Chapter 26).

A final internal threat can come from the steady erosion of state institutions and processes. Increasing lawlessness and the eventual collapse of governmental institutions can create a power vacuum in which the ruling elite simply becomes one of several factions struggling to fill the void and claim the formal mantle of statehood. At various times during the conflicts in Liberia and Somalia, for example, several different factions claimed to be the legitimate government at the same time, despite lacking the necessary control of territory or governing institutions required for formal recognition. In the final analysis, any of these threats— military intervention in politics, warlords and strongmen, ethnic demands for secession or state collapse—may lead to sustained bouts of all-out intra-state war.

Because of their internal fragility, weak states also face a variety of *external* threats. Lacking the infrastructural or coercive capacity to resist outside interference, weak states are vulnerable to penetration and intervention by other states and groups. Powerful states may directly invade or may sponsor a coup or rebellion in order to overthrow a regime, such as the American invasions of Grenada, Panama, Afghanistan, and Iraq, and French intervention in numerous African states. Alternately, the provision of significant quantities of arms and military assistance to rebel movements, such as American support to UNITA in Angola and Soviet support for the Vietcong in Vietnam, can pose a serious threat to the ruling elite. Often, support for rebel factions or coup plotters can come from sources closer to home, such as rival neighbouring states. A great many regional rivals—such as India–Pakistan, Uganda–Sudan, Somalia–Ethiopia, Iran–Iraq—have threatened each other in this manner. In addition, very small weak states can be threatened by the tiniest of external groups: mercenary coups and invasions have been launched against the Seychelles, the Maldives, the Comoros, and, more recently, Guinea-Bissau, sometimes by no more than a few dozen men. In most cases, the coups were thwarted only through assistance from powerful allies such as France or India.

A related external threat comes from the spillover or contagion of conflict and disorder from neighbouring regions. Lacking the necessary infrastructural capacity to control their borders effectively, weak states can often do little to prevent the massive influx of refugees, fleeing rebels, arms smuggling, or actual fighting. Major external shocks like this can seriously threaten the stability of the weak state. The Rwandan genocide in 1994 spilled over into Zaïre, a weak and failing state; the shock eventually led to the overthrow of the Mobutu regime, invasion by several neighbouring states and large-scale factional fighting (see Case Study 12.1).

Related to this, weak states are threatened by the uncontrollable spread of small arms and light weapons. In the hands of warlords, criminals, and private militias, these weapons pose a real challenge to the authority of the state and can intensify existing conflicts and seriously undermine peace efforts. Light, portable, durable, and easy-to-use (even by children) small and light weapons are easily obtained through legal and illegal channels, and, once in use, have a tendency to spread throughout the region. An estimated $5 billion worth of light weapons are traded illegally every year to the world's conflict zones, killing an estimated half a million people per year in criminal activity and civil violence.

> ### KEY POINTS
>
> - Internally, weak states are threatened by military factions, rival 'strongmen' such as warlords or criminals, rebellions from minorities, institutional collapse, and disorder and ultimately, intra-state war.
>
> - Externally, weak states are threatened by interference from powerful international actors, contagion and spillover from neighbouring states and the small-arms trade.

The weak-state 'insecurity dilemma'

The combination of state weakness and internal threats creates a security challenge unique to weak states. It is distinctive because it arises from meeting *internal* threats to the regime in power, rather than *external* threats to the existence of the nation state. The inability of the state to provide peace and order creates a contentious environment where each component of society—including the ruling elite or regime—competes to preserve and protect its own well-being. This creates a domestic situation similar to the neorealist conception of structural anarchy where groups create insecurity in the rest of the system when they try to improve their own security. To distinguish this internally oriented condition from the classical *security dilemma*, it is helpful to think of it as an insecurity dilemma. This condition of insecurity is self-perpetuating because every effort by the regime to secure its own security through force provokes greater resistance and further undermines the institutional basis of the state and the security of the society as a whole.

In a sense, the weak-state insecurity dilemma is caused by an initial and profound lack of 'stateness', in particular, the inability to establish a monopoly on the instruments of violence. This failure can be both normative—in the sense that the state has failed to convince the population that armed resistance is wrong or counterproductive—and practical—in that the state cannot physically disarm and control all its rivals. Either way, the lack of a political and institutional centre with a monopoly of force creates an insecurity spiral—a semi-permanent situation of 'emergent anarchy'—where armed groups are forced to engage in self-help strategies.

Thus, within the weak-state context, where ruling elites use the machinery of government primarily to secure the continuation of their rule, the concept of *national security*—the security of a whole socio-political entity, a nation state with its own way of life and independent self-government—is wholly inapplicable. In practice, the idea of state security—the integrity and functioning of the institutions and idea of the state—and regime security—the security of the ruling elite from violent challenge—become indistinguishable. Because of the fusion of state and government, when a particular regime is overthrown, as the Syad Barre regime was overthrown in Somalia in 1991, the entire apparatus of the state collapses too. In this sense, weak-state security *is* regime security.

> ### KEY POINTS
>
> - The weak-state insecurity dilemma is primarily an internal condition based on the contradiction between societal and state power.
>
> - It is engendered by a lack of 'stateness', most importantly, the failure to establish a monopoly on the instruments of violence.
>
> - The weak-state insecurity dilemma transforms national or state security into regime security.

Security strategies in weak states

The structural characteristics of weak states and the unique insecurity dilemma in which they are trapped severely constrain the range of policy options open to ruling elites. Essentially, the conditions of governance create a semi-permanent condition of 'crisis politics' or 'the politics of survival' (Migdal 1988) in which short-term strategies of regime security substitute for long-term state-building policies.

Elite security strategies

Weak state elites typically employ a mix of internal and external strategies aimed at regime survival. *Internally*, elites employ a mix of carrot-and-stick approaches to challengers. First, lacking both infrastructural capacity and wider social legitimacy, weak-state elites are often forced to rely on coercive power and state intimidation to secure continued rule. This entails creating or expanding the security forces, spending large sums of the national income on military supplies, and using violence and intimidation against real and perceived opponents of the regime. This is perhaps the most common survival strategy of weak-state elites, and it is reflected in the appalling human-rights record seen in a great many developing countries. Typically, regimes try to suppress opposition through the widespread use of torture and imprisonment, assassination and extra-judicial killings, disappearances, the violent suppression of political expression, forced removals, destruction of food supplies, and, in extreme cases, genocide, mass rape, and ethnic cleansing.

A key dilemma for elites is that the instruments of coercion—the armed forces—can themselves develop into a threat against the regime. For this reason, elites sometimes deliberately weaken the armed forces by creating divisions, establishing elite units such as presidential guards, and fomenting rivalry between different services. Such divide-and-rule strategies are also used against other potential sources of opposition, such as state bureaucracies, religious groups, traditional authorities, and opposition politicians. From this perspective, the deliberate undermining or hollowing-out of state institutions can be a rational and effective means of preventing the rise of potential centres of opposition to the regime.

On the other side of the ledger, elites sometimes find it easier to try and create positive inducements for supporting the regime. Typically, this entails the establishment of elaborate patronage systems, whereby state elites and various social groups are joined in complex networks of mutual exchange. In this way, corruption acts as a form of redistribution and a means of integrating the state in an informal power structure. Such systems may extend to strongmen in a form of elite accommodation (Reno 1998). Warlords or political leaders with private armies may be permitted control over a particular area, have state resources diverted their way, or be given exclusive control over a particular commercial activity, for example, in exchange for an agreement not to try and overthrow the regime or encroach on its other activities. In the settlement ending the war in Sierra Leone, the warlord leader of the rebel Revolutionary United Front (RUF), Foday Sankoh, became Minister for Mines in an attempt to buy his loyalty. Different kinds of accommodation have sometimes been found with the drug cartels in Colombia and Myanmar.

Ethnic manipulation or 'the politics of identity' is another typical strategy in weak states. In what is a form of divide and rule borrowed from colonialism, elites will sometimes deliberately foment inter-communal conflict as a means of preventing the emergence of united opposition to the regime. At other times, it is simply a method of rooting a regime's power base in what is seen to be a reliable source of support. Thus, elites will favour certain groups in the allocation of state resources, oppress minorities viewed as hostile, create minority scapegoat groups during times of unrest, and appoint members of the elite's own ethnic group to positions of power. Such strategies are frequently successful, as ethnic consciousness is usually well developed and readily exploitable in many developing societies.

A final internal strategy involves the careful manipulation of democratic political processes. Because of their external vulnerability, a great many weak states have been forced by international donors—developed states and international financial institutions (IFIs) such as the IMF and World Bank—to begin the process of democratic reform. A great many weak-state rulers have successfully managed the transition to multi-party democracy and retained control of the state, primarily through careful manipulation of internal opponents and external perceptions. Typically, this involved monopolising and controlling the media, the co-option of opponents, setting up fake parties to split the vote, gerrymandering, ballot rigging, candidate and elector disqualification, and manipulating the electoral rules. Constructing the outward appearance of democracy without any substantial concessions can actually function to bolster regime security by giving it a degree of international legitimacy.

In addition to these internal strategies, weak-state elites also look to form alliances with powerful *external* actors as a means of bolstering regime security. An increasingly prevalent strategy has been to employ foreign mercenaries or private military or security companies as force multipliers. There are nearly a hundred private military companies (PMCs) operating in 110 states around the world (see Key Quotes 12.1). Often working closely with oil and mineral companies, the industry is thought to be worth as much as $100 billion per year. Weak states employ private-security contractors, because they see them as being more effective and reliable than many national militaries. With superior weapons and training, these private armies have often proved to be decisive in securing weak-state survival against various internal threats. In Angola and Sierra Leone, the notorious PMC Executive Outcomes turned the tide against rebel forces, recapturing diamond mining areas in the process.

More formally, weak states seek out alliances with powerful states that can help to guarantee

---

KEY QUOTES 12.1

Private military companies

'Private military companies—or PMCs, as the new world order's mercenaries have come to be known—allow governments to pursue policies in tough corners of the world with the distance and comfort of plausible deniability. The ICIJ investigation uncovered the existence of at least 90 private military companies that have operated in 110 countries worldwide. These corporate armies, often providing services normally carried out by a national military force, offer specialized skills in high-tech warfare, including communications and signals intelligence and aerial surveillance, as well as pilots, logistical support, battlefield planning and training. They have been hired both by governments and multinational corporations to further their policies or protect their interests.

Some African governments are little more than criminal syndicates—warlords such as Charles Taylor, the president of Liberia, or more sophisticated elites, such as the rulers of Angola. But to sell diamonds and timber and oil onto the world market requires foreign partners.

The people doing the extracting, the bribing, the arms dealing, and the deal-making are South African, Belgian, American, Israeli, French, Ukrainian, Lebanese, Canadian, British, Russian, Malaysian, and Syrian. They are a class of entrepreneur that operates beyond borders, often unaccountable to shareholders and unfettered by the regulation they would encounter in their own countries. They have become influential political players in the countries in which they operate.'

van Niekerk (2002).

regime survival. During the Cold War, many weak states obtained military support from one or other of the superpowers in exchange for political and strategic assistance in the East–West confrontation. In Africa, at least twenty countries entered into defence agreements with France; subsequent military intervention by French troops was decisive in keeping several West African regimes in power, including Zaïre/DRC (see Case Study 12.1), Togo and Ivory Coast. At present, the war on terror is providing weak states with another opportunity to bolster their internal security: in exchange for cooperation in fighting terrorism, the United States provides countries like Pakistan, Saudi Arabia, Indonesia, and Uzbekistan (see Case Study 12.2) with vital military and economic assistance. External intervention of this kind can be crucial for keeping internal rivals at bay and ensuring regime security.

Finally, weak-state elites sometimes join together with other weak states in regional defence arrangements designed primarily to prop each other up. For example, under new multilateral security agreements, both the **Economic Community of West African States (ECOWAS)** and the **Southern African Development Community (SADC)** have since 1990 intervened a number of times in member states to overturn coups or secure governments from overthrow by rebel forces. Thus, the creation of regional security architecture, including regional peacekeeping forces, can function as a strategy of mutually reinforcing regime security.

Security outcomes

The perennial conundrum facing weak-state elites lies in the contradiction between ensuring the short-term security of the regime and the long-term goal of state making. Many of the security strategies described above are, in the long-run, self-defeating, as they further undermine the foundations of the state, provoke even more serious opposition from social groups, and delay genuine state consolidation. For most weak-state elites, however, there is no way out of this dilemma; if they neglect regime security in favour of more genuine state-building activities such as strengthening state institutions and forging a sense of national identity, they are just as likely to be overthrown in a coup or toppled by a rebellion. Thus, with few genuine alternatives, elites have to persist with policies that could eventually lead to complete state disintegration and collapse.

Ultimately, of course, a key outcome of these strategies is that the weak state, or rather the regime, becomes the greatest single threat to the security of its own people. In weak states, individual citizens often face a much more serious threat from their own governments than they do from the governments of other states. Instead of ensuring individual and social security, the continual use of coercion makes the state the primary threat to security. Moreover, the threat is affected on several levels: repression and identity politics threatens their physical survival through the spread of violent conflict; and deliberately undermining state institutions and patronage politics threatens their welfare and livelihood.

KEY POINTS

- Internal security strategies include repression and military expansion, employing mercenaries and private military companies, using divide-and-rule strategies, deliberately undermining state institutions, patronage politics and elite accommodation, identity politics, and democratic manipulation.

- External security strategies include employing private military companies and mercenaries, entering into external defence agreements with Great Powers, and joining in regional defence organizations.

CASE STUDY 12.1

Anatomy of a weak state: the Democratic Republic of Congo

The central African state of the Democratic Republic of Congo (DRC) has always been a weak state. It has suffered from tremendous insecurity since its founding, and ruling elites have employed all the classic regime security strategies to avoid being toppled.

At independence in 1960, Congo was poorly prepared for full statehood, with irrational national boundaries, underdeveloped state institutions, poor infrastructure, a fragile economic base, and only 100 university graduates to fill the civil service. In the first four years of independence, the country was plunged into civil war, with three main factions vying for power and the mineral-rich Shaba province attempting to secede. Order was established only with the help of a large-scale United Nations Operation. In 1965, Mobutu Sese Seko took power in a military coup.

Throughout his rule, Mobutu faced numerous threats to his regime: military rebellions, dissident movements, attempts at secession, mercenary revolts, invasions and violent disputes, and conflict spillover from neighbouring states. Cobalt and copper-rich Shaba province was invaded by mercenaries and exiled dissidents on four occasions.

Following the pattern of weak-state rules, Mobutu employed a number of classic regime-security strategies. He employed mercenaries to subdue the country in the first years of his rule, bribed opposition politicians to join the government, suppressed opposition movements, engaged in identity politics, hollowed out state institutions to prevent the rise of potential opponents, and split the armed forces into several factions to avoid coups and rebellions. Externally, he allied with the United States, providing a conduit for getting arms to Angola's UNITA rebels. In exchange, he received massive amounts of military and economic aid, which he then used to manage internal opposition. French paratroopers and American logistical support helped Mobutu to defeat an invasion of Shaba in 1978.

In 1996, a rebel alliance led by Laurent Kabila and backed by Rwanda emerged in the east of the country in the chaos engendered by the spillover of the 1994 Rwandan genocide. Within a few months, and despite employing a mercenary army, Mobutu's regime collapsed. The Kabila-led alliance soon fell apart, however, and full-scale civil war broke out in 1998. Rwanda and Uganda intervened on the side of different rebel factions, while Angola, Namibia, and Zimbabwe sent troops to support the Kabila government. Africa's 'first world war' raged until peace accords were signed in 2003, leading to elections and the withdrawal of most foreign occupying forces. However, the war continues in mid-2009 in eastern DRC, despite the presence of a UN peacekeeping force. The UN estimates that more than five million people have lost their lives in the conflict. Despite a recognized central government, the DRC continues to exist as a semi-collapsed state, with various warlords, ethnic militia, criminal enterprises, and foreign entrepreneurs engaged in large-scale looting, trade monopolization, and the exploitation of minerals.

KEY POINTS

- The long-term effect of elite security strategies is to reinforce insecurity for both the regime itself and the wider population.

- In extreme cases, elite security strategies can lead to complete state collapse.

 CASE STUDY 12.2

Anatomy of a weak state: Uzbekistan

The Central Asian country of Uzbekistan gained its independence from the Soviet Union in 1991. From 1924 to 1991 Uzbekistan had been governed as an outlying colony in the Soviet Empire. Consequently, at independence it shared many of the weaknesses of other post-colonial and post-Soviet states, such as an externally oriented, dependent economy, weak national institutions, overdeveloped coercive capabilities, a legitimacy crisis, and a history of authoritarianism.

President Islam Karimov, a former Communist Party boss, has ruled Uzbekistan since its independence from the Soviet Union in 1991. Throughout this period, the Karimov regime has been under constant threat from dissidents and anti-government campaigners, crime syndicates and drug traders, a small-scale terrorist campaign, opposition Islamic groups, and spillover from the conflicts in Afghanistan and Tadjikistan.

Karimov has clung to power using a variety of regime-security strategies, most commonly severe repression against real and potential opponents. Despite nominal constitutional protections, the government has banned public meetings and demonstrations, restricted the independent media, arrested thousands of opposition political and religious supporters, and used horrific torture and murder to suppress dissent. Uzbekistan presently has the worst human-rights record in the former Soviet Union. Other internal strategies used by Karimov to maintain power have included the clever manipulation of elections and referendums, rewriting the constitution to centralize

all power in the president and endemic corruption among government officials.

Externally, Karimov's primary strategy was to ally the regime with the United States in the War on Terror. In 2002, the two countries signed a Declaration of Strategic Partnership. In return for hundreds of millions of dollars of economic and military support, Uzbekistan provided the USA with military bases from which to conduct missions in Afghanistan, coercive interrogation facilities for terrorist suspects in the controversial rendition programme, and diplomatic support for US policies in the United Nations.

However, the US–Uzbek partnership came under severe strain following the military crackdown against anti-government demonstrators in the city of Andijan in May 2005, when hundreds of unarmed civilians were killed and injured. Following US criticism of the appalling human-rights situation in Uzbekistan, and the imposition of sanctions by the European Union, Karimov ordered the closure of US military bases in the country. In response to the deterioration in relations with the USA, Karimov turned instead towards building closer relations with Russia. Despite the easing of tensions with the West in 2008, in mid-2009 Uzbekistan remains firmly aligned with Russia.

Explaining insecurity in weak states

There are different theories about the causes of weak-state or regime insecurity. Taken together, they can tell us a great deal about how conditions of insecurity evolve and persist, despite international assistance. State-making theories explore the origins of the weak-state insecurity dilemma in the initial state-construction process. Warlord politics theories explore the impact of neoliberal globalization and the end of the Cold War on the choices facing weak-state elites. The combination of the inherited structural features of statehood and the nature and processes of the international context explain much about why weak states find it so difficult to escape from their insecurity dilemma.

State-making theories

Observing weak-state insecurity, scholars like Ayoob (1995) have suggested that these conditions represent a normal stage in the long-term state-building process from which strong states will, in time, emerge. Taking a historical view, they argue that the European experience proves that state building is a long and traumatic process, taking several centuries to complete and involving a great deal of bloodshed. Typically, it entailed sustained and bloody conflict between a centralizing state and powerful social forces before a monopoly on violence was achieved. It also took determined and sometimes violent efforts to weld disparate groups of people into a single national identity. Significantly, representative institutions emerged only gradually, after a powerful central state and a cohesive sense of national identity had been established.

The argument is that what has been observed in developing countries since the mid-twentieth century is a similar process of state consolidation to that experienced by European states in past centuries, but with additional obstacles that were absent during the European experience. For example, unlike European states, today's weak states have to cope with the ongoing effects of colonial rule, which includes: the imposition of alien doctrines and institutions of statehood; irrational territorial boundaries and the lack of national identity; societies divided along class, religious, and ethnic lines; stunted and dependent economies; and an entrenched culture of political violence. These factors make the state-building process even more difficult than it might have been.

The contemporary state-building process is also constrained by a shortened time frame. Unlike European states, weak states today are expected to become effective, fully functioning, democratic states within a few decades. Moreover, they are expected to do it without the violence, corruption, and human-rights abuses that accompanied the European state-building process. Established international norms and rules, such as the protection of minority and human rights and the right of self-determination (which often encourages ethnic rebellion), also complicates the state-building process. A particularly problematic norm is the inviolability of statehood. Once a state achieves independence and is admitted to the United Nations, its status cannot be revoked or its territory subsumed into another state, no matter how unviable it proves to be in practice. Thus, unlike European entities such as Burgundy and Aragon, which could not complete the state-building process and were absorbed into larger, more viable units, today's weak states must struggle on indefinitely.

In short, according to this approach, we can expect weak states to experience a great deal more bloodshed and violence over an extended period until stronger, more representative states emerge. Until then, they will remain 'quasi-states'—states possessing the nominal features of statehood, such as international recognition, but lacking the infrastructural capacities to create and secure a sense of genuine national identity (Jackson 1990).

KEY POINTS

- Scholars like Ayoob suggest that the conditions of insecurity in weak states are an expression of the historical state-building process.

- The European state-building process was similarly bloody and long.

- Weak states face the state-building process in an environment constrained by the experience of colonialism, a shortened time frame, and problematic international norms.

Warlord politics

During the Cold War, many weak states maintained a semblance of stability and integration through various forms of elite and social accommodation. The primary means of accommodation was the construction of a patrimonial or *redistributive state*—a system of patronage where state resources were distributed to supporters through complex social and political networks. The redistributive state was frequently maintained by direct superpower assistance, loans and development assistance from international financial institutions, and periods of high-commodity prices that supplied its primary national income. Temporary disruptions to the stability of the weak-state redistributive system came from sudden falls in commodity prices, wider economic shocks (such as the oil shocks), and the sudden loss of superpower support (which could be compensated for by switching to the other superpower, as Somalia did in the 1970s). In many cases, these shocks resulted in serious internal violence.

The end of the Cold War signalled a period of profound transformation in the international system.

A major consequence of the end of superpower conflict was the decline of military and economic support for many weak states. At the same time, international financial institutions began to demand changes in the economic and political policies of weak states—what are called 'conditionalities'—in exchange for continuing loans and assistance. In keeping with the global trend of privatization and deregulation, weak states were forced by lenders and investors to sell off and downsize government bureaucracies. These developments severely disrupted the redistributive state and forced rulers to find new ways of accommodating rival strongmen and restless social groups.

Somewhat paradoxically, elite strategies have since involved the deliberate creation of state collapse and social disorder. This entails hollowing out state institutions, fragmenting the armed forces, and creating parallel informal armed groups, thereby spreading the means of violence even further into society. The logic of 'disorder as a political instrument' is that, within the context of a collapsing state, elites can pursue forms of commercial activity that are not possible under normal circumstances, such as trading in illegal commodities, looting, protection rackets, coercive monopolies, and the like. Thus, exploiting the shadow markets engendered by neoliberal globalization, and in alliance with local strongmen and multinational companies, weak-state elites have created a new kind of political economy, what Reno (1998) has called 'warlord politics'. Crucial in this enterprise is the ability to employ private companies to perform state roles, especially the task of providing regime security.

As an alternative political-economic system, warlord politics provides elites with several advantages. It permits commercial activity and accumulation in the grey or shadow regions of the global economy, tapping into resources that would otherwise be unavailable to weak-state elites and that are desperately needed to buy protection from rivals. In this sense, warlord politics facilitates the process of elite accommodation needed to keep regimes safe from violent overthrow. It also prevents the emergence of mass social movements because civil society finds itself trapped between a rapacious state and well-armed networks of strongmen pursuing their own illiberal agendas.

In short, warlord politics represents an innovative response to rapid global change that permits the survival of the regime under harsh new conditions. From this perspective, state collapse and widespread disorder are not a temporary aberration in the normal functioning of the state, but a new form of regime security forced on weak-state elites by changes in the wider international system. Warlord political systems have been in existence for several decades now, and have become a part of the political landscape from West and Central Africa to Colombia, Haiti, Chechnya, Afghanistan, Myanmar, and the Balkans—among others.

> **KEY POINTS**
>
> - The end of the Cold War and the adoption of conditionalities by IFIs severely disrupted the redistributive state.
>
> - Weak-state elites responded by developing new and innovative forms of political economy based on shadow and predatory commercial activities called 'warlord politics'.
>
> - Warlord politics works to control internal threats from strongmen and mass movements.

Conclusion: prospects for the weak state

In this chapter we have examined the conditions of insecurity that affect the majority of the world's states. We have suggested that the insecurity dilemma facing developing countries is both profound and unique, and is rooted in the fundamental structures and processes of incomplete statehood.

The conditions of insecurity in weak states are the result of three interrelated factors: the historical state-making process; the structures and processes of the present international system; and the security strategies employed by weak-state elites. In the context of profound internal threats and constraining external conditions, national security becomes a matter of maintaining short-term regime security. The pursuit of regime security, however, is itself a profoundly contradictory process; short-term policies of regime security undermine the more important state-building project—and the security of the state and society.

From this perspective, weak-state insecurity appears to be an inescapable condition. There have been very few clear-cut cases where weak states have made a successful transition to state consolidation and genuine national security. The fundamental security challenge facing weak states lies in achieving greater levels of stateness and moving towards improved levels of genuine state strength. The challenge, therefore, lies in the willingness and ability of weak-state elites to substitute short-term regime security strategies for long-term state-building strategies.

Should regimes choose to take the state-building project seriously, the process will undoubtedly be long and difficult, not least because a number of entrenched internal and external obstacles to effective statehood remain. These include: the continued distorting effects of colonialism; the processes of neoliberal globalization and the imposition of external conditionalities; small-arms proliferation; continuing external intervention by powerful actors; the existence of constraining international norms; and debilitating internal conditions such as poverty, social division, weak institutions, and the like. The global war on terror launched in the wake of 9/11 has also had a negative effect on the state-building project, as the fight against terrorism has largely diverted international attention and resources from poverty eradication, democracy promotion, and peace-building activities. Weak-state elites have also been able to brand their internal enemies as terrorists, and, just as during the Cold War, receive military support in exchange for cooperation in the fight against terrorism (see Case Study 12.2). In other words, the new war on terror has allowed weak-state elites to reprioritize regime security over state building and receive vital international support for their efforts.

As during the Cold War, the problems of weak-state insecurity take a low priority on international agendas compared to the interests of the Great Powers. So far, solutions to the weak-state security dilemma have not moved far beyond the establishment of multi-party democracy and free markets. For neo-conservatives, it is sometimes argued that forceful 'regime change' and perhaps even a liberal or benign recolonization, such as occurred in Germany and Japan after the Second World War, is the only effective long-term solution. Others stress the need for humanitarian intervention to protect the security of civilians and promote human rights. They argue that 'cosmopolitan peace-keeping' (Kaldor 1999) and so-called peace-building missions are required to transform violent domestic politics in weak states into long-term peace and stability. In practice, both approaches are based on a similar liberal perspective, which envisages a minimal state devoted to protecting individual and market freedoms. The main problem is that, thus far, despite decades of effort, no case of enforced neoliberalization, through either conditionalities, regime change, or peace building, has succeeded in transforming a weak state into a strong state.

Given the enormous challenges facing weak states, and recognizing the fundamental inequities of the state project itself and the failure thus far to reform illiberal weak states, some radical commentators have suggested that state building should be abandoned in favour of alternative forms of political organization based on either smaller units—city states or ethnic groups, for example—or larger units—such as regional organizations like the European Union. The first option, sub-state political organizations, seems impractical in regions that are awash with weapons, criminal gangs, and poverty; the case of Somalia, which has been without a functioning central government since 1991, is informative in this regard. The second option, regional organization, is similarly not without its limitations. While it has had a modicum of success in the European Union, in regions characterized by weak states, underdevelopment, and instability, such as Africa or Latin America, regional processes are severely constrained in what they can achieve.

In the end, overcoming the internal and external obstacles to state building in the developing world will require tremendous political will and resources, and the elaboration of alternative and innovative approaches to state-building assistance. More importantly, it will require fundamental reform of international economic and political structures, including the international trade in weapons. Given the present preoccupation with international terrorism and the lack of enthusiasm by the world's developed states for debt relief, development, and curbs on the small-arms trade, the short-to-medium-term future of the weak state looks as bleak as it ever was (for more on the arms trade see Chapter 23).

? QUESTIONS

1. In what ways are orthodox approaches to security limited in their explanation of the weak-state insecurity dilemma?

2. What are the primary differences between weak and strong states?

3. Outline the main internal and external security threats facing weak states.

4. What makes the security dilemma in weak states unique?

5. What are the differences, if any, between national security, state security, and regime security in the weak-state context?

6. What domestic and international strategies do weak-state elites adopt to try to manage their security challenges?

7. What are the main internal and external obstacles to state building for weak states?

8. What impact has the end of the Cold War and the onset of globalization had on the weak-state security predicament?

9. Is abandoning the state-building project in favour of alternative forms of political organization a realistic solution to the weak-state security dilemma?

10. What role should the international community play in the state-consolidation process?

 FURTHER READING

■ Ayoob, Mohammed (1995), *The Third World Security Predicament: State Making, Regional Conflict, and the International System*, Boulder, CO: Lynne Rienner. Provides an informative analysis of the weak-state security predicament in its internal, regional, and international dimensions.

■ Buzan, Barry (1991), *People, States and Fear: An Agenda for International Security Studies in the Post-Cold War Era*, 2nd edn., Boulder, CO: Lynne Rienner. A seminal reformulation of security beyond its traditional focus to include the security predicament facing the majority of weak states in the world.

■ Holsti, Kalevi J. (1996), *The State, War, and the State of War,* Cambridge: Cambridge University Press. An empirical analysis of contemporary warfare, which demonstrates that internal war within weak states has been the primary form of international conflict since 1945.

■ Job, Brian (1992) (ed.), *The Insecurity Dilemma: National Security of Third World States*, Boulder, CO: Lynne Rienner. A very useful collection of essays from leading experts on some of the key dimensions of security in developing states.

■ Kaldor, Mary (1999), *New and Old Wars: Organised Violence in a Global Era*, Cambridge: Polity. A provocative and original statement on the changing nature of warfare and the need for new approaches to peacekeeping in weak states.

■ Musah, Abdel-Fatah, and Kayode Fayemi, J. (2000) (eds.), *Mercenaries: An African Security Dilemma*, London: Pluto. Provides a fascinating collection of essays on the security dilemma associated with the intervention of mercenaries in Africa's weak states.

■ Reno, William (1998), *Warlord Politics and African States*, Boulder, CO: Lynne Rienner. Provides a compelling analysis of how weak-state elites have adapted governance strategies to the opportunities and constraints of neoliberal globalization.

■ Rich, Paul B. (1999) (ed.), *Warlords in International Relations*, London: Macmillan. An insightful collection of essays by leading experts on the role of warlords, the small-arms trade, private military contractors, and other security challenges facing weak states.

■ Thomas, Caroline (1987), *In Search of Security: The Third World in International Relations*, Boulder, CO: Lynne Rienner. An original formulation of the weak-state security predicament.

■ Zartman, I. William (1995) (ed.), *Collapsed States: The Disintegration and Restoration of Legitimate Authority*, Boulder, CO: Lynne Rienner. An important collection of essays on the nature, causes, and consequences of weak-state decay and collapse.

IMPORTANT WEBSITES

● http://www.iansa.org   The International Action Network on Small Arms is a global network of civil-society organizations working to stop the proliferation and misuse of small arms and light weapons. The website contains resources on all aspects of small-arms proliferation and international efforts to regulate the trade.

● http://www.iss.co.za   The Institute for Security Studies is a leading research institution on all aspects of human security in Africa. The website contains news, analysis, and special reports on all aspects of security in Africa.

● http://www.systemicpeace.org/inscr/inscr.htm   The Integrated Network for Societal Conflict Research (INSCR) programme at the Center for International Development and Conflict Management, the University of Maryland, coordinates major empirical research projects on armed conflict, genocide, and politicide, minorities at risk, regime types, and state failure. The website has links to all the major projects and datasets.

 Visit the Online Resource Centre that accompanies this book for lots of interesting additional material: www.oxfordtextbooks.co.uk/orc/collins2e/

13

Societal Security

PAUL ROE

Chapter Contents

- Introduction
- A duality of state and societal security
- Society and societal identity
- Threats to societal identity
- Defending societal identity
- Societal security dilemmas
- Conclusion

Reader's Guide

This chapter explores the concept of societal security. It starts by looking at how society came to be conceived as a referent object of security in its own right. It then goes on to discuss the so-called Copenhagen School's understanding of both society and societal identity, showing how societal security is tied most of all to the maintenance of ethno-national identities. In looking at threats to societal security, through examples such as the former Yugoslavia and Northern Ireland, the chapter discusses a number of those means that can prevent or hinder the reproduction of collective identity, and, in turn, at how societies may react to such perceived threats. The concept of a societal security dilemma is then introduced to show how societal security dynamics can spiral to produce violent conflict. The chapter concludes by considering some of the main critiques of the concept as an analytical tool.

Introduction

Throughout the 1980s and early 1990s significant moves took place designed to take security studies beyond the confines of the dominant realist and neorealist paradigms. For the most part, such moves were made possible by the winding-down and eventual end to the Cold War. The decreasing threat of nuclear war opened the way for the emergence of other, non-military conceptions of security. For example, writing at the end of the 1980s Jessica Tuchman Mathews (1989: 162–77) suggested that international security be rethought to include resource, environmental, and demographic issues. Mathews, together with a number of like-minded others (see, e.g., Ullman 1983; Booth 1991), came to be known as the 'wideners': those wishing to broaden the concept of security out of its military-centric confines. One such widener was Barry Buzan.

The term 'societal security' was first introduced by Buzan in *People, States and Fear* (1991a). In the book, societal security was just one of the sectors in his five-dimensional approach, alongside military, political, economic, and environmental concerns. In this context, societal security referred to the sustainable development of traditional patterns of language, culture, religious, and national identities, and customs of states (1991a: 122–3). Each one of Buzan's five sectors was formulated within the confines of an essentially neorealist framework: all the dimensions remained as sectors of national—that is, state—security. 'Society' was just one section through which the state might be threatened. Furthermore, threats in the military

sector were seen as primary: as the priorities given to each dimension depended on their relative urgency, Buzan argued that military security was still the most expensive, politically potent, and visible aspect of state behaviour (1991b: 35). Hence: 'A state and society can be, in their own terms, secure in the political, economic, societal and environmental dimensions, and yet all of these accomplishments can be undone by military failure' (1991b: 37).

Although recognizing Buzan's vital contribution to the 'broadening' of international security, a major contention was that introducing more sectors of state security was simply not enough. While security studies was indeed beginning to move away from its preoccupation with military issues, it was still very much state-centric in its focus. What was required, therefore, were other referent objects of security: that international security should be 'deepened' as well as broadened brought with it a refocusing on what or indeed who should be secured, from the individual through to the global level. (For a fuller discussion of human versus state security, see Chapter 8.) Set against this, the concept of 'societal security' came to mark out a distinct third, and indeed middle, position; one that was reluctant to consider notions of either human or global security, but one that was also in agreement that the realist and neorealist approach to international security had become just too narrow. As a result, this middle position began to talk about the security of other collectivities, or 'societies'.

A duality of state and societal security

In the 1993 book *Identity, Migration and the New Security Agenda in Europe*, Ole Wæver, together with Buzan, Morten Kelstrup, and Pierre Lemaitre, suggested that 'societal securities' had become increasingly important vis-à-vis concerns over state

sovereignty in contemporary, post-Cold War Europe. Most crucially, the writers claimed that Buzan's previous five-dimensional approach to international security had now become untenable as a context for societal security. They suggested a reconceptualization: not five sectors relating to the state, but instead a duality of state and societal security. Although society was retained as a dimension of state security, it also became a referent object of security in its own right.

The key to this reconceptualization was the notion of *survival*. While state security is concerned with threats to its sovereignty—if a state loses its sovereignty, it will not survive as a state—societal security is concerned with threats to its identity—if a society loses its identity, it will not survive as a society. States can be made insecure through threats to their societies. But state security can also be brought into question by a high level of societal cohesion. This relates to those instances where a state's programme of homogenization comes into conflict with the strong identity of one or more of its minority groups. For example, during the 1990s the 'Romanianness' of the Romanian state was compromised as the large Hungarian minority in the Transylvania region of the country further asserted its 'Hungarianness'. In other words, the more secure in terms of identity these societies are, the less secure the states containing them may feel. For Wæver (1993: 25) and his collaborators, in this way traditional security analysis had created 'an excessive concern with state stability', and thus had largely removed any sense of 'the "security" of societies in their own right'.

As a concept, societal security was conceived very much as a reaction to events in Europe, in both the East and in the West. In the West, the process of European Union (EU) integration meant that political loyalties were increasingly being shifted, either upwards to the EU level itself, or downwards to the level of the regions, thus weakening the traditional link between state and society. Meanwhile, in the East, the collapse of some of the former socialist countries showed starkly the conflict between adherence to the state (Federal Yugoslavia) or adherence to its constituent groups (Serbs, Croats, Bosnian Muslims). As an analytical tool, the concept has therefore mainly been employed in a very much European context (see,

e.g., Huysmans 1995; Herd and Lofgren 2001; Roe 2002). However, its applicability arguably goes much further, in particular to those 'weak states' in parts of South East Asia and sub-Saharan Africa. And more will be said about this in the conclusion to this chapter.

KEY QUOTES 13.1

The importance of societal security

'In the West and the East, at the centre and the periphery, cultural identity and societal security have become the central theme of political attitudes and conflicts'.

Hassner (1993: 58).

'With the increasing intertwining of security and identity, a new agenda has emerged, both for policy-makers struggling with the dilemmas and uncertainties of post Cold-War Europe, and for academics trying to make sense analytically and conceptually of this changed continent ... exploring the interface between security and identity can shed considerable light on the structural dynamics and underlying trends of contemporary European politics.'

Aggestan and Hyde-Price (2000: 1).

KEY POINTS

- To begin with, societal security was just a sector of state security. This is where the state can be destabilized through threats to its language, culture, religion, and other customs.

- The societal-security concept was (re)conceived in the light of the processes of integration in Western Europe and disintegration in Eastern Europe.

- Societal security was reconceptualized as a referent object of security in its own right.

- Societal security concerns the maintenance of collective identity: if a society loses its identity it will not survive as such.

- Societal security represents a middle way between notions of individual and global security.

Society and societal identity

Put simply, society is about identity: it is about the self-conception of collectivities and individuals identifying themselves as members of that collectivity. Thus, societies are units constituted by a sense of collective identity. Wæver (1993: 17) defines collective identity as simply 'what enables the word *we* to be used'. In this sense, however, a 'we' identity can vary a great deal as to the kind of group to which it applies, the intensity to which it is felt, and the reasons that create a sense of it. Moreover, societies are composed of, and support a multitude of, different identities. That is to say, societies are multiple-identity units. How, then, is it possible to talk about a society's identity?

According to Anthony Giddens (in Wæver 1993: 19), there are two main ways to think about society. The first one is something fixed that has boundaries marking it off from other similar units. The second one is something that is constituted by social interaction; society is viewed rather as a fluid concept, referring more to a process than to an object. For Wæver (1993: 19), however, defining society as a process arguably reduced it to more or less any classification of 'we'—a view of society that cannot easily be employed in the analysis of international security. The interest for the so-called Copenhagen School, as in particular Buzan and Wæver came to be known, was in 'societies operating as units in the international system', where their reactions to threats against their identity have politically significant effects. Accordingly, Wæver distinguished between society and 'social group'. Here, societal security is concerned with the security *of* society as a whole, but not the security of groups *in* society (social group).

Wæver (1994: 8) notes that security action is 'always taken on behalf of, and with reference to a collectivity . . . that which you can point to and say: 'it has to survive, therefore it is necessary . . .'. From this there are two main points to keep in mind. The first one is that for the collectivity there are distinctive kinds of behaviour that cannot be reduced to the individual level. Like state security, societal security must be approached as the security of societies having more than, and thus being different from, the sum of their constituent individual and social groups. Thus, society is viewed as an entity possessing a reality of its own. The second one, and following on from the first, is that societies must also be seen as having the right to survive. For example, while farmers might be considered as a distinct social group, the argument is a difficult one to make that 'farmers' also constitute a significant entity operating alongside the state in political terms. Moreover, the argument that farmers automatically have some kind of right always to be farmers is a difficult one to sustain, as farms are routinely allowed to go out of business for a number of reasons. (However, when farming, as in the case of France in particular, is tied very closely to a particular notion of collective identity—in this instance 'Frenchness'—then farmers may become part of a societal security agenda: farms in France going out of business represent a loss of what it means to be French.)

Such difficulties over defining society can be tackled further by pinning the relationship between society and societal identity to a more easily definable unit. Wæver refers to Giddens' view that, as 'units', modern societies are most often nation states or based on the idea of the nation state. Indeed, Wæver (1993: 19) claims that the nation is a special case of society characterized by: attachment to territory, or at least a sense of homeland; a continuity of existence across time, from past generations to the present; and a sense of being one of the entities that make up the social world. In this way, though, the idea of nation and state are often blurred. Buzan, Wæver, and a further collaborator, Jaap de Wilde (1998: 121), recognize all too well that the problem with *societal* is that the related term *society* is often used to refer to state population. Taking the example of Sudan, they emphasize that 'Sudanese society is that population contained by the Sudanese state but which is composed of many societal units (e.g. Arab and black African). This is not our use of societal; we used societal for communities with which one identifies.' Thus, while, on the one hand, nation can be defined in relation to 'citizenship', on the other hand, it can also be defined in terms of 'ethnicity'. And this distinction is often characterized by the terms 'civic nation' and 'ethnic nation'.

Nations perform a number of roles—most prominently, the marking of borders, thereby staking claim to control a territory. For much of the time, though, the concept of nation is underpinned by common cultural (more often than not ethnic) bonds. Nations are, in this regard, very much a response to the need for identity. Belonging to a distinct culture tells us 'who we are', and it is this process of self-identification that is key to nations.

Although nationality and ethnicity are indeed often mingled, nation and ethnic group can be distinguished in the following terms: a nation strives for a state of its own, whereas an ethnic group acts within the state as it exists. Anthony D. Smith (1993: 48–62) suggests that an ethnic group constitutes a nation when it has become 'politicized': when the group is not only bound by a distinct culture, but also begins to act as a cohesive political unit. Smith's formulation is a useful one—although it must be kept in mind that politicized ethnic groups do not always strive for statehood. Nations, therefore, are often predicated on ethnicity. Shared ethnic origins provide nations with some sort of legitimacy over claims for territory and political autonomy. Thus, with regard to society, Wæver duly employs the label 'ethno-national' group.

Perhaps the only rival to ethno-national identity as a political mobilizer is religion. Religion possesses the ability to reproduce its 'we' identity more or less unconsciously across generations. It is also able to generate a feeling of self-identification, which can

be as intense as that of nationalism. Moreover, where religious and ethno-national identities reinforce each other (Catholic Croats, Orthodox Serbs), this can produce very defined and resilient identities.

Wæver (1993: 23) concludes that the main units of analysis for societal security are 'politically significant ethno-national and religious entities', and accordingly defines societal security as 'the ability of a society to persist under changing conditions and possible and actual threats. More specifically, it is about the sustainability, within acceptable conditions for evolution, of traditional patterns of language, culture, association, and religion and national identity and custom.'

But just what 'possible and actual threats' might Wæver be referring to? The next section tackles this question.

KEY POINTS

- Societies are units formed by a sense of collective identity, where collective identity is defined as what enables the word 'we' to be used.

- For security analysis, societies are different from social groups. Societies have a reality of their own, they can operate as units in the international system, and they are invariably seen as having the right to survive.

- Nations and states are sometimes difficult to distinguish. Societies may be nation states, but do not always refer to state population.

- Society most often equates to ethno-national group, although religious groups may also be relevant units for analysis.

- Societal security can be defined as the maintenance of distinct ethno-national and religious identities.

Threats to societal identity

Objective definitions of threats to societal security are as problematic as they are for states. Indeed, perhaps more so. Given the sometimes fluid nature of collective identities, not all changes to it will necessarily be regarded as threatening. Some

change will be seen as the natural process by which groups respond to meet changing historical conditions. Nevertheless, some processes invariably carry with them the potential to harm societal security.

Threats to societal security exist when a society perceives that its 'we' identity is being brought into question, whether this is objectively the case or not. Those means that can threaten societal identity range from the suppression of its expression to interference with its ability to reproduce itself across generations. This, according to Buzan (1993: 43), may include 'forbidding the use of language, names and dress, through closure of places of education and worship, to the deportation or killing of members of the community'. Threats to the reproduction of a society can occur through the sustained application of repressive measures against the expression of identity. If the institutions that reproduce language and culture, such as schools, newspapers, museums, and so forth, are shut down, then identity cannot easily be passed on from one generation to the next. Moreover, if the balance of the population changes in a given area, this can also disrupt societal reproduction.

As a referent object of security, society can be harmed through all of Buzan's five dimensions: societal, military, political, economic, and environmental. And, while some of the sectors are talked about at greater length in Chapters 11, 12, 14, and 15, it is worth describing here their specific relationship to societal identity.

The five sectors of security

Buzan et al. (1998: 121) have divided threats in the societal sector of security into three main categories: migration, horizontal competition, and vertical competition. In cases of migration, the host society is changed by the influx of those from outside; by a shift in the composition of the population. Think of examples in the early 2000s in the UK, where immigrants, particularly from countries such as Pakistan, India, and Bangladesh, have been accused of intensifying the formation of ghettos in major conurbations such as Greater London and the West Midlands, and where fears have likewise grown over competition for often scarce local resources such as education and health care. Horizontal competition refers to groups having to change their ways because of the overriding

linguistic and cultural influences of others. For example, in the Soviet Union many of the republics were 'Russified'; Russian language and culture came to dominate over Latvian, Estonian, Ukrainian, and Kazakh identities, to name but a few. Finally, vertical competition refers to those instances where, because of either integration or disintegration, groups are pushed towards either wider or narrower identities, as was the case in the former Yugoslavia.

In the military sector, it is invariably the case that an external military threat will threaten the society or societies within the state. Here, threats to societal security can arguably be seen mainly in terms of depopulation—where enough members of the society are killed (or sometimes deported) either to hinder or to prevent collective identity being transmitted from one generation to the next.

However, some societies within invaded states may not always view armed aggression as a threat. Some minorities may be liberated either from their own regimes or from occupation by a foreign power. Besides, while external military aggression will invariably threaten state sovereignty, it may not necessarily pose a concomitant danger to the society's identity. Take, for example, Nazi Germany's invasion of France in 1940. There was an obvious potential to threaten both the French state and French society. However, while French sovereignty was indeed violated, for the most part French society remained relatively secure: French identity was not, to any significant extent at least, intentionally suppressed. Contrast this with Hitler's prior invasion of Poland in 1939: hand in hand with the military threat to the Polish state was also a political–societal threat to Polish identity: the Poles' Slavic identity coupled with the Nazi's policy of *Lebensraum*. As such, except when invasion is specifically designed towards the harming of state populations, such threats are mainly directed against either the maintenance of political autonomy (puppet states) or the survival of the incumbent regime (regime change).

Military threats to societies may also come from internal aggression. Perhaps the clearest example of this is when a regime, representing one ethnic group, uses its armed forces to suppress other minorities (for more on this see Chapter 12).

In the political sector, threats to societies are most likely to come from their own government, usually in the form of the suppression of minorities. And in this way political and military threats to societal identity will be closely linked. Political threats can often be mitigated by the state itself: for example, certain legislation can be introduced in order to protect societal identity. However, when the state machinery is overwhelmingly controlled by a dominant society, then not only might the state be unwilling to provide societal security but it may itself be posing the threat.

The economic sector of security is for the most part characterized by how the capitalist system can undermine cultural distinctiveness by generating global products (televisions, computers, and computer games), attitudes (materialism and individualism), and style (English language), thereby replacing traditional identities with contemporary 'consumer' ones.

In the environmental sector, threats to societies can occur especially when identity is tied to a particular territory. This is certainly the case when culture is adapted to a way of life that is strongly conditioned by its natural surroundings. Threats to the environment may thus endanger the existence of that culture and sometimes the people themselves. For example, the loss of huge swathes of the Amazon rainforest has seriously affected many of its indigenous peoples in terms of their traditional existence as hunter-gatherer communities. In addition to deforestation, pollution, climate change, and desertification also pose similar threats to societal security.

Genocide, 'culturecide', and the Yugoslav wars

If carried out on a large enough scale, many such threats to societal security come to correspond with the definition of genocide as set out under the terms of the 1948 UN Genocide Convention. According to Article 2 of the Convention, genocide refers to acts that intend to destroy, physically or biologically, 'national, ethnical, racial or religious groups'. This was highlighted only too starkly during the conflict in Rwanda (see Case Study 13.1) and the wars in the former Yugoslavia. The now well-known horrors of ethnic cleansing saw the intentional killing, violence against (including sexual), and deportation of peoples on the part of all parties to the Yugoslav conflicts, although such acts were perpetrated most by the Bosnian Serb army and paramilitaries. We can think not only of the 1995 massacre of an estimated 8,000 Bosnian Muslim men and boys at Srebrenica, but also of the existence of many camps in towns, such as Foca, where women were imprisoned and subjected to rape and other forms of sexual violence.

In addition to ethnic cleansing, however, what some have termed cultural cleansing was also a prevalent practice. By contrast, cultural cleansing is perpetrated not against members of the group as such, but against manifestations of group culture. This involved the deliberate destruction of churches, mosques, libraries, and monuments across much of Bosnia-Hercegovina and parts of Croatia, and was

---

KEY QUOTES 13.2

The effects of cultural cleansing

'You have to understand that the cultural identity of a population represents its survival in the future. When Serbs blow up the mosque of a village and destroy its graveyards and the foundations of the graveyards and mosques and then level them off . . . no one can ever tell this was a Muslim village. This is the murder of a people's cultural identity.'

Boeles (1990).

'In extreme circumstances, systematic discrimination threatens communal groups' most fundamental right, the right to survival. Many groups also face cultural discrimination and the risk of de-culturation or so-called cultural genocide in the form of pressures or incentives to adopt a dominant culture, or denial of cultural self-expression.'

Gurr (1993: 6).

intended to wipe out hundreds of years of history from the former Yugoslavia. It is what some writers have described as 'culturecide', and it strikes right against the very core of societal identity (see Key Quotes 13.2).

Culturecide, or 'cultural genocide', is not a part of the Genocide Convention, although Raphael Lemkin (1944), who is seen as being the originator of the term 'genocide', did propose a cultural component to it. Lemkin argued that the destruction of cultures was every bit as disastrous as the physical destruction of nations. Although not clearly defined, the UN's 1994 Draft Declaration on the Rights of Indigenous Peoples does use the term 'cultural genocide'; amongst other provisions, Article 7 calls for prevention against the deprivation of 'cultural values' and against any imposed forms of 'assimilation or integration by other cultures'. Indeed, the term 'cultural genocide' (culturecide) is used regularly by politicians, scholars, and human- and minority rights activists to describe threats to societal security. For example, in 2008 the Dalai Lama accused China of cultural genocide, referring to ethnic Chinese immigration into Tibet and the restrictions placed on Buddhist worship.

CASE STUDY 13.1

The Rwandan genocide

The 1994 genocide in Rwanda was provoked by the assassination of the country's president, Juvenal Habyarimana, in April of that year. Over the course of the following three months, up to as many as three-quarters of a million Tutsis are estimated to have been killed by Hutu militias, the most notorious of these being the *Interahamwe*.

Historically, Tutsis, who at the time of the genocide made up around 15 per cent of Rwanda's population, had been privileged over Hutus by the country's aristocracy and, in this way, the difference between the two groups was as much economic and social as it was ethnic. However, under Belgian administration a strict system of racial classification served both to exaggerate and to reinforce ethnic difference: Tutsis were considered superior by virtue of being seen as more 'white' looking by their colonial rulers. Following an uprising in 1959 and the establishment of an independent republic in 1961, the new, Hutu-dominated government retained racial classification as a means of subordinating the Tutsi minority. Government suppression resulted in the flight of tens of thousands of Tutsis from Rwanda, and culminated in an invasion by Tutsi rebels from neighbouring Uganda in 1990.

From a societal security perspective, perceived ethnic differences were used by the majority Hutus to reinforce grievances over the privileges historically enjoyed by the minority Tutsis: Tutsis were murdered and expelled because of their ethnic identity, and not just because of their prior economic and social standing. The ideology of 'Hutu Power' articulated a culturally defined disdain for, and superiority over, Tutsis: Tutsis were portrayed as foreigners, and Hutu propaganda frequently depicted them as cockroaches and rats. Moreover, as in the former Yugoslavia, the majority of rapes perpetrated by Hutu militias against Tutsi women were carried out with the express intention of trying to destroy Tutsi culture.

Skjelsbaek (2001: 219).

Against perceived threats through all five dimensions of security, societies can react in two ways. First, by trying to move the threat onto the state's security agenda—and actions taken by states to defend their societies are quite common. However, second, societies can also choose, or may be forced, to defend themselves through non-state means. As Buzan (1993: 56–7) enquires: 'What happens when societies cannot look to the state for protection . . . ?' Unable to turn to the regime to guarantee their survival, societies will have to provide for their own security; they will be in a self-help situation. And just how societies help themselves is the matter of the next section.

KEY POINTS

- Objectively defining threats to societal security is difficult, especially so as some changes to group identity will be seen as a natural response to shifting historical circumstance.

- Societal identity can be threatened from the suppression of its expression through to interference with its ability to reproduce itself across generations.

- Ethnic cleansing; the deliberate killing, violence against, and deportation of members of one society by another, and cultural cleansing, the systematic destruction of institutions and symbols designed to promote and maintain group identity, are two prominent manifestations of threats to societal security, and were widely employed, for example, during the wars in the former Yugoslavia.

- Societies can be threatened through all five of Buzan's sectors of security, although the societal and military dimensions are perhaps the most important.

- States often take measures to defend their own societies. But, in multi-ethnic states in particular, societies may find themselves in self-help situations, where they are compelled to provide for their own security.

Defending societal identity

Perhaps most evidently, societal identity can be defended using military means. This is particularly the case if identity is linked to territory: the defence of the historic homeland. If the threat posed by one group to another is military (armed attack from a neighbouring society), then some kind of armed response is invariably required. However, in such a scenario, societal security dynamics are likely closely to resemble those of armed aggression between states: defending societal identity becomes much the same as defending state sovereignty. Therefore, in order to show how societal security can be used as a distinct (from state security) analytical tool, the remainder of this section turns its attention to the intra-state level of analysis, and to multi-ethnic states where societal insecurities are most often apparent.

While some societies (as states or quasi-states) may very well have an army or at least some kind of militia that can be utilized for defence, the vast majority of intra-state groups possess no such exclusive means of protection. For them, members of the group will either make up part of the state's armed forces as a whole, or have military forces composed of the same ethnic group in a neighbouring state.

Facing a threat in identity terms, such groups are therefore left with two main options: first, they can try to form their own militia/defence force as a means or protection, although this can prove to be extremely difficult; or, second, they can try to defend their identity using non-military means.

Non-military means of defence

At the intra-state level, the vulnerabilities felt by many groups may often derive not so much from armed aggression as from demographic processes and political–legal means designed to deprive societies of beliefs and practices vital to the maintenance of their culture. Returning to the example of ethnic cleansing, Robert Hayden (1996: 784) highlights how, for example, such threats to societal identity can be shaped very much by demographic considerations: 'Within areas in which the sovereign group is already an overwhelming majority, homogenization can be brought about by legal and bureaucratic means, such as denying citizenship to those not of the right group.' In more mixed areas, however, Hayden goes on, homogenization requires more drastic measures such as killing and physical expulsion. And, although it is only the attempted extermination of the minority group in this regard that has been widely recognized as ethnic cleansing, 'it is important to recognize that legal and bureaucratic discrimination is aimed at bringing about the same result: the elimination of the minority'.

When the nature of the threat is non-military (legal, bureaucratic), countervailing measures are also likely to be so. In the *Identity, Migration* book, Wæver et al. (1993: 191) suggest that for threatened societies 'one obvious line of defensive response is to strengthen societal identity'. This can be done, Wæver (1995: 68) notes succinctly, by defending culture 'with culture'; and consequently 'culture becomes security policy'. The idea of defending culture with culture is a slightly tricky one to unpack, but John Hutchinson provides a useful starting point. Hutchinson (1944) describes the project of what he calls **cultural nationalism**. Cultural nationalism is designed to generate a strong feeling of self-identification. It emphasizes various commonalities such as language, religion, and history, and downplays other ties that might detract from its unity. In this sense, cultural nationalism celebrates what is special about our *identity* (see Key Quotes 13.3). Self-identification, as such, often takes place because societal identity has been threatened: 'Our present identity has become too weak. We therefore need to change it and make ourselves strong again'.

Defending societal identity through cultural nationalism can be seen in the case of relations between the Protestant and Catholic communities in Northern Ireland.

In Portadown, the Protestant Orange Order has struggled to maintain what it sees as its historic right to march down the predominantly Catholic Garvaghy Road. Likewise, many of the town's Catholic inhabitants have protested, claiming that the march is highly provocative. For the Orange Order, not to march is tantamount to surrender: 'We have been walking down this road for generations. Why should we stop now?' In this way, the right of the Orange Order to march is inextricably bound up with the maintenance of its Protestant identity: it is the right to express who *we* are, where *we* come from (and indeed, where *we* are going). It is a societal security requirement. However, for the Catholic community the march is a celebration of the Protestant victory at the 1690 Battle of the Boyne, and thus represents a serious attack on their own identity. As Michael Ignatieff (1993: 169) points out, the victory of William of Orange over the Catholic King James 'became a founding myth of ethnic superiority ... The Ulstermen's reward, as they saw it, was permanent ascendancy over the Catholic Irish.'

In the face of what many Protestants have come to see as the erosion of their ascendant status in the province, Orange Order marches are a cultural-nationalist strategy aimed at strengthening their identity: the celebration of the self.

In perhaps more concrete terms, collective identity can be strengthened when cultural nationalist strategies are manifest as **cultural autonomy**. Cultural autonomy entails the granting of certain rights in relation to the means of cultural reproduction: the control of one's own schools, newspapers, religious institutions, and so forth.

Similarly, societal groups may also employ 'ethnic' or '**political nationalism**' as a means of defence. Unlike cultural nationalism, political-nationalist projects have an explicit territorial element to them.

🎧 KEY QUOTES 13.3

The project of cultural nationalism

'[C]ultural nationalists establish ... clusters of cultural societies and journals, designed to inspire spontaneous love of the community in its different members by educating them to their common heritage of splendour and suffering. They engage in naming rituals, celebrate national cultural uniqueness and reject foreign practices, in order to identify the community to itself, embed this into everyday life and differentiate this against other communities.'

Hutchinson (1994: 124).

Political nationalism, as manifest in **political autonomy**, often involves self-government along a wider range of issues, such as the ability to control some of its own legal and financial affairs (for example, as with the Basques in Spain). In this way, political autonomy usually equates to some kind of autonomous region within the state. In its most extreme expression, though, and if threats to societal identity are seen as particularly severe, political-nationalist projects may seek outright independence outside of the existing state structure.

In this way, the concept of societal security and questions of human and minority rights become closely linked. Both Will Kymlicka (2001) and Gwendolyn Sasse (2005) have discussed the implications of framing minority rights as a security issue: Kymlicka argues that using the language of (societal) security effectively prevents thinking about the provision of minority rights in terms of justice, while Sasse shows how actors, such as the OSCE's High Commissioner for National Minorities (HCNM), are increasingly cognizant of the balance between security and rights (or justice) based concerns. Similarly, Paul Roe (2001; 2004) has talked about the role of the HCNM in mitigating societal security dilemmas (see the following section), and has also made the argument that societal security concerns are an inherent quality of minority-rights provisions (see Key Quotes 13.4).

KEY QUOTES 13.4

Societal security and minority rights

' "First of all, a minority is a group with linguistic, ethnic or cultural characteristics which distinguish it from the majority. Secondly, a minority is a group which usually not only seeks to maintain its identity but also tries to give a stronger expression to that identity" . . . Or, in the language of the Copenhagen School, being a minority, and thus pursuing minority rights, is a matter of societal security.'

Roe (2004: 288).

KEY POINTS

- Military means may often be used to defend societal identity. This is particularly the case when identity is linked to territory.

- At the intra-state level, however, many societal groups may have no such means of armed protection. Forced to provide for their own security, such groups are compelled to employ non-military countermeasures.

- Cultural-nationalist strategies can be used to defend societal security. When manifest as cultural autonomy,

this involves the control over those institutions that are responsible for cultural reproduction, such as schools and churches.

- Political-nationalist strategies are also a means of defending collective identity. Political autonomy, however, is more territorially based and thus involves a much greater measure of self-government within the state.

- Secession is the most extreme form of defence for societal security.

Societal security dilemmas

Thus far, the chapter has noted the importance of societal security, in particular with relation to Europe's security agenda. It has talked about how societal identity can be threatened, and how threatened societies can respond to those dangers. In this section, the notion of a societal-security dilemma is discussed.

The purpose is to highlight how societal security dynamics can escalate to the point of violence and war, and, importantly, to show how conflict in this way can be generated by non-military concerns.

In the *Identity, Migration* book, Buzan (1993: 46) suggests that, by analogy with relations between states, it may be possible to talk of **societal security dilemmas**, and that societal security dilemmas might explain why some ethnic conflicts 'come to acquire a dynamic of their own'. But what does a societal security dilemma look like? How does it operate? How is it different, if at all, from the traditional (state) security dilemma? And what effects might it produce? Chapter 2 touches on the concept of the security dilemma. But for our purposes here it is useful briefly to revisit the concept.

The (state)security dilemma

For the most part, the security dilemma describes a situation where the actions of one state, in trying to increase its security, causes a reaction in a second, which, in the end, decreases the security of the first. Consequently, a process of action and reaction is manifest whereby each side's policies are seen to threaten the other. Thus, at the core of the concept lies an escalatory dynamic. The key to this escalatory dynamic is *ambiguity* and *uncertainty*.

States usually try to increase their security by building up their arms. But most arms that can be used for defence can also be deployed for offensive purposes. A tank, for example, can just as easily be employed to attack a neighbour's territory as it can to defend one's own. Arms, therefore, are invariably ambiguous in nature; on the one hand, they are a means to protect oneself, while, on the other, they are a way of harming others. And it is this crucial role that arms play in being able to generate both security and insecurity that has led the vast majority of writers to conceive of the security dilemma in almost exclusively military terms.

In turn, the ambiguity of military postures creates uncertainty about the intentions of one's adversary. Faced with the indistinguishability between offence and defence, decision-makers must come to distinguish between 'status quo' states and 'revisionist' states.

Accordingly, decision-makers are forced to assume the worst. In an anarchical, self-help system, it is prudent to equate capabilities with intentions:

what the other can do, it will, given the opportunity. Countervailing measures are therefore taken, generating a spiral of insecurities, which, in the context of states, is often manifest as arms racing.

The societal security dilemma

But how can this equate to societies, rather than states? While collective identity can certainly be threatened by military means, as has been pointed out, societal insecurities and responses to those insecurities may often be non-military in nature. In other words, thinking about a societal security dilemma also prompts the shift to a non-military security dilemma. In this way, a first question is what can create ambiguity if not arms?

For societal security dilemmas, ambiguity can stem from the two sides of nationalism; cultural (positive) and ethnic (negative). Many writers describe ethnic (political) nationalism in rather malign terms, often characterized in this regard with the annexation of territories and the disintegration of states. By contrast, cultural nationalism is often seen as more benign, as it tends to work within existing state structures. The goal of cultural nationalists is to amend the current order and not overturn it: it is more 'status quo' than 'revisionist' (see Key Quotes 13.5).

> ## KEY QUOTES 13.5
>
> ### The two sides of ethnicity
>
> 'On the one hand, ethnicity … is often perceived as backward and dangerous. On the other hand, [some] authors tend to view ethnicity as … the self-expression of the threatened and the marginalised. Ethnicity can be both positive and negative. Of course, the divisive nature of contemporary ethno-nationalism, its violent boundary makings, its exclusiveness, etc., must also be viewed as considerable challenges to the modern international system, as well as potentials for violence and wars. One must not forget, however, that ethnicity has also a potential for internal group solidarity and loyalty.'
>
> Lindholm (1993: 24).

In practice, however, clear distinctions between cultural nationalism and political nationalism are often difficult to make. Indeed, Hutchinson (1994: 125) himself notes that cultural nationalist projects may sometimes employ ethnic nationalist strategies in order to secure their goals. That is, cultural nationalism sometimes may be compelled to change itself from a solely cultural movement into a political one in order to get its concerns onto the state agenda, or to be able to expand into a genuinely mass movement in order to realize its desires. In certain circumstances, then, cultural nationalism might be conflated with political nationalism. And ambiguity might thus be apparent in the sense that cultural nationalist movements come to resemble a political nationalist project; the desire for cultural autonomy becomes confused with that for political autonomy. But how might this happen?

Within the state, the desires of the group will either be communicated verbally and/or be presented in written form through official memoranda and manifestos. In such a context, such desires may not be clearly articulated to others—a problem that can be compounded if insufficient communicative channels exist within the state. Moreover, certain verbal and/or written pronouncements may contradict previous ones. Others may thus be thrown into confusion, causing them to misperceive the group's intentions. Dominant actors may employ exaggerated threat perceptions. This is often with the intention of mobilizing political support in order to sustain and create national or local power bases. For each scenario, countervailing measures might then be taken, which, in turn, can result in an action–reaction process and the subsequent outbreak of ethnic violence and war. In this way, Roe (2002, 2005) uses the societal security dilemma to explain the outbreak of ethnic violence between Hungarians and Romanians in the Transylvania region of Romania in 1990. He argues that misperception over questions of greater cultural and political autonomy for the region's ethnic Hungarians caused many Romanians to view this as a threat to their own status as a majority identity.

KEY POINTS

- A societal security dilemma occurs when the actions taken by one society to strengthen its identity causes a reaction in a second, which, in the end, weakens the identity of the first.

- In societal security dilemmas, actors may be uncertain as to whether the other is employing either a cultural-nationalist (cultural autonomy) or political-nationalist (political autonomy/secession) strategy. Assuming the worst can lead to a spiral of nationalisms and, finally, violent conflict.

- As an explanation for ethnic conflict, societal security dilemmas can highlight those important non-military dynamics that traditional (state) security dilemmas miss.

Conclusion

Thus far, the chapter has shown the importance of societal security concerns and how the concept can be used profitably as an analytical tool. However, the Copenhagen School has not been without its critics. And in this concluding section some of the major contentions are considered.

The charge of reification

A first, and perhaps most fundamental, criticism concerns the Copenhagen School's view of the construction of collective identity. In a comprehensive critique of the societal security concept, Bill McSweeney (1996: 82) charges Wæver, Buzan, and their fellow collaborators with reification. He claims that both 'society' and 'identity' are treated as 'objective realities, out there to be discovered': seen in objectivist terms, societies and societal identities are 'things' that somehow naturally exist. McSweeney (1996: 85) takes a more constructivist view in which society is rather a fluid entity: 'Identity is not a fact of society; it is a process of negotiation . . .'. Thus, society is constantly being constructed and reconstructed, and to talk about *a* (single) societal identity as such is difficult if not near impossible. In short, what is at stake here is whether societies, like states, can be seen as objects around which security dynamics can be observed.

However, as Tobias Theiler (2003: 54), in a review of the societal security concept, makes clear, the Copenhagen School 'manage[s] to mount a persuasive defence'. In a direct response to McSweeney's contentions, Buzan and Wæver (1997) refute the charge of objectivism, arguing that theirs is also a constructivist approach. Unlike McSweeney, though, they claim that, while societal identities are indeed socially constructed, once constructed they can also be regarded as, at least temporarily, fixed. Theiler (2003: 254) agrees, noting that, when 'beliefs and institutions become deeply sedimented', they 'change only very slowly'.

As an analytical tool, therefore, societal security is useful in accounting for specific events in specific places at specific times. An example of this is Graeme P. Herd and Joan Lofgren's study (2001) of societal-security concerns between the Baltic States and their Russian minorities during much of the 1990s.

Who speaks for society?

A second major criticism concerns the separation between state and society. In particular, the question arises as to who speaks for society if not the state. Certainly, where state and society coincide, in the case of relatively homogenous nation states, societal security concerns are invariably articulated by the government or by major political parties, the very same voices that speak on behalf of the state. In such an instance, to the observer state security and societal security may very well appear as pretty much one and the same. However, while the voice may indeed often be the same, the 'grammar' may nonetheless be different: state security concerns come hand in hand with the language of sovereignty, while societal security concerns come hand in hand with

the language of identity. The point here is essentially tied to the Copenhagen School's notion of securitization, which is discussed at length in Chapter 9. For purposes here, though, what is important to keep in mind is that, although state and society may be coterminous, *how* the referent object is threatened gives rise to different responses.

Sometimes, though, as has already been discussed, states and societies do not coincide. And in these instances the voices of state security and societal security may be different. For minority groups, societal-security concerns are not always voiced from within the government, unless minority political parties are part of the ruling coalition. Minority groups may at least have some kind of representation within the legislature. If not, though, such societies will be forced to articulate their concerns outside the state apparatus. In this regard, cultural elites (writers, poets, academics) can try to mobilize their societies against the government (majority group).

The dangers of speaking societal security

From this second criticism comes a third, and it concerns the political implications of voicing societal security. As Michael Williams (1998) points out, although, on the one hand, McSweeney charges the Copenhagen School with objectivism, but, on the other hand, he also notes how the societal-security concept is dangerously subjectivist too. Politicians can use perceived threats to societal security to legitimize racists and xenophobic political agendas. For example, defending 'our' identity against 'theirs' can serve to characterize immigrant communities as dangerous Others who must either be assimilated or expelled (see Key Quotes 13.6). There is certainly a risk here, but a risk that Wæver (1999: 337) believes is worth taking: 'This danger [of giving rise to fascist and anti-foreigner voices] has to be offset against the necessity to use the concept of societal security to try to understand what is actually happening.' This is what Jeff Huysmans (2002) has called the 'normative dilemma' of writing security.

Applying the concept elsewhere

While not really a substantive criticism of societal security, a final point worth considering is whether the concept has a potentially wider application outside Europe. As was mentioned, the Copenhagen School's thinking about societal security was very much a response to the European Security agenda of the 1990s—to the processes of Western integration and Eastern disintegration. So what about elsewhere?

As an analytical tool, societal security is particularly effective for understanding the security concerns of multi-ethnic states: relations between the regime (majority group) and the country's minority groups. And this is the focus of the so-called Third World Security School (see, e.g., Job 1992; Ayoob 1995). For many countries in the Third World, the greatest threats are often internal. During the process of nation building, where minority identities are assimilated into the majority, state regimes may often require minority groups to give up all, or part, of their cultural distinctiveness. These ethnic differences, together with the state's inability to provide for certain sections of its people, cause the population to express its loyalty elsewhere. And it is this lack of cohesion between the state and its societies that defines the state as 'weak'. Weak states provide propitious conditions for the study of societal insecurities, and the security-studies literature is utilizing it (Collins 2003; Caballero-Anthony et al. 2006).

? QUESTIONS

1. In what ways does societal security mark a departure from more traditional thinking about security? Cannot realist and neorealist approaches adequately capture the dynamics of nationalism and ethnic conflict?

2. What is the difference between society as a sector of security and society as a referent object?

3. How far can 'societies' be seen as rational, instrumental actors?

4. Is there a clear distinction to be drawn between societies and 'social groups'?

5. In what way might societies be said to have a right to survive?

6. Are societies, as the Copenhagen School claim, all about identity?

7. How can multi-ethnic states threaten the societal security of their minority groups? How can minorities try to counter these threats?

8. How differently does, for example, a map of Europe look seen through a societal-security rather than a state-security perspective?

9. Is the Copenhagen School right in saying the European security agenda has become increasingly concerned with questions of group identity?

FURTHER READING

■ **Aggestam, L. and Hyde-Price, A. (2000) (eds.),** *Security and Identity in Europe*, **London: Macmillan.** Excellent coverage of key issues facing European security; including NATO enlargement, EU integration, and the wars in the Balkans.

■ **Buzan, B., Kelstrup, M., Lemaitre, P., Tromer, E., and Wæver, O. (1990),** *The European Security Order Recast: Scenarios for the Post-Cold War Era*, **London: Pinter.** Precursor to the Identity, Migration book, this is the Copenhagen School's exploration of the new, emerging European security agenda through Buzan's five dimensions.

■ **Katzenstein, P. J. (1996) (ed.),** *The Culture of National Security: Norms and Identity in World Politics*, **New York: Columbia University Press.** Perhaps the most important edited collection concerning the impact of norms and identity on security and foreign policy and behaviour.

■ **Lapid, J., and Kratochwil, F. (1999) (eds.),** *The Return of Culture and Identity in IR Theory*, **Boulder, CO: Lynne Rienner.** Edited volume that covers the 'constructivist turn' in international relations from the Copenhagen School to postmodern and poststructural approaches.

■ **McSweeney, B. (1999),** *Security, Identity, and Interests: A Sociology of International Relations*, **Cambridge: Cambridge University Press.** Provides excellent critiques of existing constructivist approaches to security and identity.

■ **Roe. P. (2005),** *Ethnic Violence and the Societal Security Dilemma*, **London: Routledge.** One of the few books that successfully combines questions of identity with traditional security-studies scholarship.

■ **Weldes, J., Laffey, M., Gusterson, H., and Duvall, R. (1999),** *Cultures of Insecurity: States, Communities, and the Production of Dangers*, **Minneapolis, University of Minnesota Press.** Introduces sociological and anthropological approaches in examining the cultural production of insecurity in local, national, and international contexts; from the Korean War, to the Cuban Missile Crisis, to the conflicts in the Middle East.

 IMPORTANT WEBSITES

● http://www.ciaonet.org Provides access to a wide range of working papers, journals, and policy briefs, including previous COPRI works.

● http://www.systemic peace.org Official website of the 'Center for Systemic Peace'. Contains datasets, project reports, including Ted Robert Gurr's 'Minorities at Risk' and an extensive library of bibliographical references for works that examine violent conflicts from both a human and societal security perspective.

● http://www.hrw.org Excellent resource for news releases, publications, reports, and event lists concerning human and minority rights in Europe and elsewhere.

 Visit the Online Resource Centre that accompanies this book for lots of interesting additional material: www.oxfordtextbooks.co.uk/orc/collins2e/

14 Environmental Security

JON BARNETT

✔ **Reader's Guide**

This chapter discusses the concept of environmental security. It explains the way environmental security has both broadened and deepened the issue of security. It describes the evolution of the concept as a merger of international environmental agreements, efforts by the peace movement to contest the meaning and practice of security, the proliferation of new security issues in the post-Cold War era, and the growing recognition that environmental changes pose grave risks to human well-being. The chapter examines the different meanings of environmental security, and then it explains four major categories of environmental security problems—namely, the way environmental change can be a factor in violent conflict, the way environmental change can be a risk to national security, the way war and preparation for war can damage the environment, and the way environmental change can be a risk to human security. It explains how environmental security can mean different things to different people and can apply to vastly different referent objects in ways that sometimes have very little to do with the environment.

Introduction

In its most basic sense insecurity is the risk of something bad happening to a thing that is valued. For example, people who value their jobs are concerned about the risk of unemployment, families who value having enough to eat are concerned about the regular supply of food, governments that value power are concerned about losing office, and countries that value peace are concerned about the possibility of war. So, security can apply to many different things that are valued (referent objects such as jobs, health, organizations, countries) and refer to many different kinds of risks (unemployment, lack of food, change of government, war). Given this, it is not surprising that the environment has been seen as a referent object of security, and that environmental change has been seen as a security risk. These and other connections between the environment and security fall under the heading of environmental security, and this chapter provides a critical overview of this concept.

Like the broader field of security studies, approaches to environmental security are diverse and reflect many theoretical perspectives. Environmental security is one of a number of 'new', non-traditional security issues that have served to deepen and broaden the concept of security. It helps to deepen security, as it entails considering not just the security of states, but also the security of the 'global' environment as well as its many nested subsystems, and various social systems. It broadens security by considering risks other than war—principally the risks posed by environmental change—to the things that people value. Further, like the concepts of gender security and human security discussed in this book (see Chapters 7 and 8), environmental security is sometimes a *critical* security project in that it is used by some people to ask questions about who and what is being secured—and from what risks—by orthodox security policies (see also Chapter 6 of this book).

Like security studies more generally, environmental security has entailed much research of a more practical kind. There have been numerous attempts to assess the extent to which environmental change causes violent conflict within and between countries (this is examined in the fourth section of this chapter). There are explanations of the ways in which environmental change may undermine national security (explained in the fifth section of this chapter). There have been investigations of the ways in which war and preparations for war affect the environment (discussed in the sixth section of this chapter). Finally, there has been a growing body of research that investigates the linkages between environmental change and development issues such as poverty and human security (as explained in the seventh section of this chapter). These research endeavours have influenced policy development in some countries, in intergovernmental organizations such as the United Nations and NATO, and in non-governmental organizations such as the World Conservation Union and Greenpeace; for example, the Institute for Environmental Security has detailed the use of environmental security policies and practices in thirteen countries and eight intergovernmental organizations (Kingham 2006).

For all this research and policy development, there remains a debate about the usefulness of the environmental security concept. From an environmental perspective, there are concerns that the concept has lead to a militarization of environmental issues. From the perspective of the dominant security paradigm, there are concerns that the concept has undermined the 'hard' business of national-security analysis and planning. Associated with this debate are questions about the uniqueness of environmental security, given the difficulties of distinguishing between environmental problems and environmental *security* problems, and between security problems and *environmental* security problems. For most proponents of environmental security, however, its utility is the way it bridges the gap between security researchers and policy-makers and those working in the environmental field, creating new fusions of theory, and new opportunities for dialogue. These issues are discussed in the last section of this chapter.

KEY POINTS

- The environment can be both an object to be secured and a source of risk.

- Environmental security means different things to different people.

- Environmental security has contributed to both a broadening and a deepening of security.

- Environmental security has both critical and applied dimensions.

- There are debates about the usefulness of environmental security.

The origins of environmental security

Environmental security emerged as an important concept in security studies because of four interrelated developments beginning in the1960s. The first of these was the growth of environmental consciousness in developed countries. A number of events stimulated and sustained the growth of the environmental movement at this time. Notable among these was the publication in 1962 of Rachel Carson's widely read book *Silent Spring* (also serialized in the *New Yorker*), which explained the impacts of pesticide DDT on animals and the food chain. Carson was among the first of many people whose use of print and electronic media have created and sustained awareness of environmental issues; others include notable personalities such as David Attenborough, Jacques Cousteau, and David Suzuki.

The number of environmental non-governmental organizations—of which there may now be more than 100,000 worldwide—also seriously began to grow in the 1960s. From an international relations perspective, a notable development was the creation of large international environmental non-governmental organizations such as the World Wildlife Fund (1961), Friends of the Earth (1969), and Greenpeace (1971). Their functions have grown to include networking across countries, research, awareness raising, policy development and

monitoring, capacity building, fund raising, and lobbying at local, national, and international forums. Their issue agenda is similarly broad, extending beyond conservation to include environmental justice, gender inequities, genetic engineering, indigenous rights, nuclear non-proliferation, poverty alleviation, sustainable energy technologies, and waste management.A growing number of non-governmental organizations of various scales and in various locations are incorporating environmental security issues into their work, including the African Centre for Technology Studies, the Global Environmental Change and Human Security project, the International Institute for Sustainable Development, the Stockholm Environment Institute, and the Worldwatch Institute.

The 1970s also saw the beginning of international summits on environmental issues, and a proliferation of international agreements on environmental issues. According to the United Nations Environment Programme (itself established in 1972), there are 144 regional and 97 global environmental agreements relating to the environment, more than three-quarters of which were signed after 1972 (see Background 14.1). The first major global environmental summit was arguably the United Nations Conference on the Human Environment (UNCHE) held in Stockholm in 1972. It initiated a number of intergovernmental investigations, meetings, and agreements on global environmental problems. These merged at times with parallel investigations into development and common security, and culminated in the 1987 report of the World Commission on Environment and Development (WCED) entitled *Our Common Future*. The WCED report popularized the term 'sustainable development', and it introduced the term 'environmental security' (see Key Quotes 14.1). It set the scene for the watershed United Nations Conference on Environment and Development (UNCED) held in Rio de Janeiro in 1992, which has had follow-up conferences in 1997 and 2002.

BACKGROUND 14.1

Major multilateral environmental agreements

1946	International Convention for the Regulation of Whaling
1963	Treaty Banning Nuclear Weapon Tests in the Atmosphere, in Outer Space and under Water
1971	Convention on Wetlands of International Importance especially as Waterfowl Habitat (Ramsar)
1972	Convention on the Prevention of Marine Pollution by Dumping of Wastes and Other Matter (London Convention)
1972	Convention for the Protection of the World Cultural and Natural Heritage
1973	International Convention for the Prevention of Pollution for Ships, 1973, and Protocols (MARPOL)
1973	Convention on International Trade in Endangered Species of Wild Fauna and Flora (CITES)
1979	Convention on Long-Range Transboundary Air Pollution
1982	United Nations Convention on the Law of the Sea
1983	International Tropical Timber Agreement
1987	Montreal Protocol on Substances that Deplete the Ozone Layer
1989	Basel Convention on the Control of Transboundary Movements of Hazardous Wastes and their Disposal
1992	Convention on Biological Diversity
1992	United Nations Framework Convention on Climate Change
1996	Comprehensive Nuclear Test Ban Treaty
1997	Kyoto Protocol to the United Nations Framework Convention on Climate Change
2000	Cartegena Protocol on Biosafety to the Convention on Biological Diversity
2001	Stockholm Convention on Persistent Organic Pollutants

KEY QUOTES 14.1

Environmental security

'A comprehensive approach to international and national security must transcend the traditional emphasis on military power and armed competition. The real sources of insecurity also encompass unsustainable development . . .'

'Environmental stress can thus be an important part of the web of causality associated with any conflict and can in some cases be catalytic.'

'Poverty, injustice, environmental degradation and conflict interact in complex and potent ways.'

'As unsustainable forms of development push individual countries up against environmental limits, major differences in environmental endowment among countries, or various stocks of usable land and raw materials, could precipitate and exacerbate international tension and conflict.'

'Threats to environmental security can only be dealt with by joint management and multilateral procedures and mechanisms.'

WCED (1987: ch. 11).

The second major development leading to the emergence of environmental security was attempts from the 1970s onwards by a number of scholars to critique orthodox security discourse and practices by highlighting their inability to manage environmental risks to national and international security. This is the origin of the critical component of environmental security. Among the first attempts to do this were Richard Falk's *This Endangered Planet* (1971), and Harold and Margaret Sprout's *Toward a Politics of Planet Earth* (1971) (see Key Quotes 14.2). Both books argued that the international political system needs to comprehend and collectively to respond to common environmental problems, as they pose threats to international stability and national well-being. These ideas about environmental interdependence and common security have remained key themes of environmental security studies.

It was not until 1983, when Richard Ullman published an article titled 'Redefining Security',

that the idea that environmental change might cause war was seriously proposed. Ullman defined a national security threat as anything that can quickly degrade the quality of life of the inhabitants of a state, or that narrows the choices available to people and organizations within the state. He suggested that environmental degradation is 'likely to make *Third World* governments more militarily confrontational in their relations with the advanced, industrialized nations' (Ullman 1983: 142). Ullman's paper was published in a highly influential US-based security journal (*International Security*), suggesting that, when environmental security is narrowly interpreted as being about national security and armed conflict, it has more purchase with the orthodox security-policy community. A number of environmental scientists have also argued that environmental degradation will induce violent conflict (see Key Quotes 14.2).

These early arguments for the connections between the environment and security were very

---

KEY QUOTES 14.2

Environment and security

'We need to revamp our entire concept of "national security" and "economic growth" if we are to solve the problems of environmental decay.'

Falk (1971: 185).

'The thrust of the evidence is simply that the goal of national security as traditionally conceived—and as still very much alive—presents problems that are becoming increasingly resistant to military solutions.'

Sprout and Sprout (1971: 406).

'Neither bloated military budgets nor highly sophisticated weapons systems can halt deforestation or solve the firewood crisis.'

Brown (1977: 37).

'The pressure engendered by population growth in the Third World is bound to degrade the quality of life, and diminish the range of options available, to governments and persons in the rich countries.'

Ullman (1983: 143).

'Conflict over resources is likely to grow more intense.'

Ullman (1983: 139).

'If a nation's environmental foundations are depleted, its economy will steadily decline, its social fabric deteriorate, and its political structure become destabilized. The outcome is all too likely to be conflict, whether conflict in the form of disorder and insurrection within the nation, or tensions and hostilities with other nations.'

Myers (1986: 251).

'It is thus inescapable that any concept of international security must in the last analysis be based on this obligate relationship of humankind with its environment.'

Westing (1986: 195).

'Climate change acts as a threat multiplier for instability in some of the most volatile regions of the world.'

CNA Corporation (2007: 6).

much of peripheral concern to Western security institutions occupied with the 'hard' business of winning the Cold War. For the United States and its allies, security meant national security from the military and ideological threat of the Soviet Union and its allies, and the principal strategy to achieve this was to build and to maintain military superiority. However, one notable event troubled this pure vision of security. In 1973 the Organization of Petroleum Exporting Countries (OPEC) restricted oil exports, leading to a quad-rupling of the price of oil on world markets. This showed that the industrial capacity that under-pinned the military superiority of the West was vulnerable to the dictates of the suppliers of energy. This event firmly established the idea of energy security into mainstream security planning.

The end of the bipolar world order created by the Cold War created something of a 'vertigo' for security policy and security studies, and for a few years the old ways of thinking about security became less obviously relevant (O'Tuathail 1996). This 'vertigo', combined with the growing environ-mental consciousness of people in developed coun-tries, the call for common security approaches in *Our Common Future*, and preparations for the UNCED Rio conference, created the intellectual and policy space for environmental security to enter the mainstream as one of a suite of 'new' security issues (Dalby 1992a). So, from 1989 onwards there were many more publications and studies on environmental security, including in prominent security journals. These were to have some influence on policy, particularly in the United States (Barnett 2001). This shift in the stra-tegic landscape is the third reason why environ-mental security is now an important concept in security studies.

The fourth reason why environmental security has become an important concept in security studies is because of the growing recognition that environmental changes do not merely pose risks to ecosystems; they also pose risks to human well-being. For the most part, research into environmental change has focused on understanding large-scale environmental proc-esses, and not its outcomes on peoples' needs, rights, and values, meaning that important issues of development, distribution, power relations, and conflict have been somewhat over-looked (O'Brien 2006). Yet it is now well under-stood that environmental change poses real risks to human security by undermining access to basic environmental assets such as productive soils, clean water, and food; by contributing to violations of civil and political rights such as to the means of subsistence and health; and by restricting people's access to the economic and social opportunities they need to develop mean-ingful lives. As this recognition has grown, envi-ronmental security has become an important concern of development studies, and this has resulted in increased dialogue between security, development, and environmental researchers and policy-makers.

KEY POINTS

- Environmental security emerged as an important con-cept in security studies because of:

  ○ the development of environmentalism in developed countries after the 1960s;

  ○ attempts to contest the meaning and practice of secu-rity from an environmental standpoint;

  ○ changes in strategic circumstances, in particular the end of the Cold War;

  ○ growing recognition of the risks environmental changes pose to human security.

- There are now a large number of multilateral environ-mental agreements.

- Both political scientists and environmental scientists have contributed to the development of the concept of environmental security.

Major interpretations of environmental security

Since the early 1990s environmental security has been an important concept in security studies and increasingly also in environmental studies. Yet the meaning of environmental security is ambiguous, perhaps because of the vagueness of the words *environment* and *security*. The basic meaning of environment is the external conditions that surround an entity, but it can be more accurately defined as the living organisms and the physical and chemical components of the total Earth system (Boyden et al. 1990: 314). Security is also an all-encompassing yet vague concept, which has perhaps been best defined by Soroos (1997: 236) as 'the assurance people have that they will continue to enjoy those things that are most important to their survival and well-being'. The ambiguity of these words has given rise to many different meanings of environmental security.

Six principal approaches to environmental security can be discerned from the literature (see Table 14.1). First, environmental security can be seen as being about the impacts of human activities on the environment. This interpretation of environmental security—sometimes also called 'ecological security'—emphasizes at least implic-

itly that it is ecosystems and ecological processes that should be secured, and the principal threat to ecological integrity is human activity (see Think Point 14.1). In this view humans are secured only in so far as they are part of the environment (Rogers 1997). This view draws on both Green philosophy and ecological theory to challenge security thinking by demanding a shift in the reason for action from individual and national interest to a concern for the overall welfare of the entire social-ecological system of the planet. Perhaps because it is so radical this explains why this ecological security view is on the periphery of environmental security thinking.

The second key approach to environmental security focuses on common security. The causes and impacts of some environmental problems are not confined to the borders of nation states. Some problems such as ozone depletion and climate change are very 'global' in nature in that they are caused by cumulative emissions of gases from many countries, which in turn affect many countries. However, to say that these problems are 'global' is not to say that all countries are equally responsible for them, or that all countries

Table 14.1 Six key interpretations of environmental security

Name	Entity to be secured	Major source of risk	Scale of concern
Ecological security	Natural environment	Human activity	Ecosystems
Common security	Nation state	Environmental change	Global/regional
Environmental violence	Nation state	War	National
National security	Nation state	Environmental change	National
Greening defence	Armed forces	Green/peace groups	Organizational
Human security	Individuals	Environmental change	Local

THINK POINT 14.1

Human impacts on . . .

Land

- In the past 40 years nearly one-third of existing cropland has been abandoned because of erosion.

- 25 per cent of all land is affected by some form of land degradation.

Forests

- During the 1990s 16.1 million hectares of natural forests were cleared each year.

- Between 1990 and 2000, 3 million hectares of forests were cleared in Africa, Latin America, and the Caribbean.

Biodiversity

- 184 species of mammals, 182 species of birds, 162 species of fish, and 1,276 species of plants are critically endangered (extremely high risk of extinction).

- Approximately 27,000 species are lost every year.

Freshwater

- Eighty countries containing 40 per cent of the world's population experienced severe water shortages in the mid-1990s.

- Approximately half of the world's wetlands were lost during the twentieth century.

Coastal and Marine Areas

- Approximately half of all mangrove forests were cleared in the twentieth century.

- 58 per cent of the world's coral reefs are threatened.

The Atmosphere

- Concentrations of CO_2 have increased by 30 per cent since 1750.

UNEP (2002, 2005).

and communities are equally at risk from them (see Case Study 14.2 and Think Point 14.2). Other environmental problems, such as acid rain, smoke haze, and water scarcity and pollution, are often caused by, and impact on, more than one country. This means that groups of countries with similar environmental problems cannot easily unilaterally achieve environmental security, and so their common national security interests require collective action. This is the rationale behind the many meetings and treaties discussed in the previous section. However, while many environmental problems are to some degree 'common', no two countries have exactly the same interests, and all have sovereign rights. For these reasons multilateral environmental agreements have not significantly halted environmental degradation. The four other major approaches to environmental security are each discussed in the following sections.

KEY POINTS

- Both 'environment' and 'security' are ambiguous concepts.

- Interpretations of environmental security differ according to the entity to be secured, the source of risk to that entity, and the solutions proposed.

- Most interpretations of environmental security do not require much change in security thought and practice because they are concerned with the nation state and/or the risk of armed conflict.

- The ecological security and human security approaches to environmental security challenge the security-policy community to consider alternative objects of security, and alternative security risks.

Environmental change and violent conflict

The connections between environmental change and violent conflict have been a central and long-standing concern of environmental security studies. The critical questions, which have yet to be conclusively answered, are whether environmental change contributes to violent conflict, and, if so, to what degree and in what ways?

Early writing on the connections between environmental change and violence borrowed heavily from realist international relations theory and focused largely on resource scarcity and conflict between states. Gleick (1991), for example, argued that there were clear connections between environmental degradation and violence, suggesting that resources could be strategic goals and strategic tools, and that resource inequalities could be a source of conflict. The early contributions from Ullman and Myers (see Key Quotes 14.2) also canvassed the possibility of inter-state war caused by resource and environmental problems. The possibility of war between counties with shared water resources was often highlighted (see Case Study 14.1). A variant of this 'water-wars' thesis is the proposition that climate change may cause war. However, the idea that environmental change may cause wars between countries has been discredited by researchers such as Deudney (1990) and Barnett (2001), as well as by liberal theories about the ways complex interdependence and trade mitigate against resource wars, and by subsequent waves of research on environmental conflicts (see Peluso and Watts 2001).

Population growth and its links to environmental degradation and subsequently violent conflict were also a theme of early writing on environmental violence (see, e.g., Myers 1987). Yet the linkages between both population growth and environmental change, and environmental change and violent conflict, are not overly straightforward. Poverty and technology are critical additional variables. In low-income and

---

CASE STUDY 14.1

Water wars?

The idea that countries might fight over water has been widely discussed by academics, politicians, and in the media. For example, for Thomas Naff (1992: 25), 'the strategic reality of water is that under circumstances of scarcity, it becomes a highly symbolic, contagious, aggregated, intense, salient, complicated, zero-sum, power- and prestige-packed issue, highly prone to conflict and extremely difficult to resolve.'

Most commentators suggest that a future water war is most likely to occur in the Middle East, a region already rife with religious, ethnic, and political tensions. Attention was first drawn to the problems of shared waterways and water scarcity in the region by the Egyptian Foreign Minister Boutrous Boutrous-Ghali, who later became Secretary General of the United Nations, who reportedly observed that 'the next war in our region will be over the waters of the Nile, not politics' (cited in Gleick 1991: 20).

There are 261 major river systems that are shared by two or more countries. Yet this geographical misfit between water and national boundaries does not necessarily imply that states will fight over water. Indeed, Aaron Wolf (1999) has demonstrated that, despite rapid population growth and increased demand for water for agriculture, industry, and cities in the twentieth century, there were only seven minor skirmishes over international water, in contrast to the signing of 149 new water-related treaties. Countries, it seems, are more likely to cooperate than fight over water. With respect to the Middle East too, detailed analyses by a number of scholars such as Allan (2002), Libiszewski (1997), and Lonergan (1997) find that there is indeed no reason to expect conflict over water in the near future.

technology-poor societies more people means more consumption of natural resources for food, fuel, and shelter, but it can also mean more labour, and this can lead to more environmentally sustainable forms of production and consumption. In high-income and high-technology societies people consume up to a hundred times more resources and energy than people in developing countries. For example, while India had 17 per cent of the world's population in 2007, it produced only 4.7 per cent of the world's carbon-dioxide emissions in 2004, whereas the United States, with 4.6 per cent of the world's population in 2007, produced 22 per cent of all greenhouse-gas emissions in 2004 (World Bank 2009c). These differences imply that the aggregate number of people is not as important as the amount of resources they consume and the volumes of waste they produce.

The relationship between population, environmental change, and violent conflict was most systematically explored by the Project on Environment, Population, and Security at the University of Toronto. The project began in 1994, and was heavily informed by an earlier paper by its Director, Thomas Homer-Dixon (1991). The Toronto Project carried out numerous case studies to investigate the links among population growth, renewable resource scarcities, migration, and conflict. These studies examined cases where there had been violent conflict, and then they sought to determine the influence of environmental factors in the generation of those conflicts. At around the same time another project—the Zurich-based Environment and Conflict (ENCOP) Project directed by Guenther Baechler (1999)—also conducted case studies on the linkages between environmental degradation and violence. Both projects ended in the late 1990s.

Common findings of both projects are that: unequal consumption of scarce resources contributes to violent conflicts; violent conflicts where environmental scarcity is a factor are more likely in low-income resource-dependent societies; population pressure can indirectly be a contributing factor to violent conflict; and, when mechanisms that enable adaptation to environmental scarcity fail, violent

conflict is a more likely outcome. Both Homer-Dixon (1999) and Baechler (1999) find that environmental change is not an immediate cause of conflict, but it can at times be an exacerbating factor. Both also find that environmental change is unlikely to be a cause of war between countries.

Since the Toronto and ENCOP Projects there have been three further developments in environmental violence research. The first of these has been a series of quantitative analyses of aggregated data to test the relationships between various environmental and social variables such as resource scarcity/abundance, population growth, and income inequality. These studies have tentatively shown that 'strong states' tend to be less prone to internal conflicts, whereas states undergoing significant economic and political transitions are relatively more prone to internal violent conflict (Esty et al. 1999). A number of them suggest that it is the abundance of natural resources as much as their scarcity that drives armed conflict (Collier 2000; de Soysa 2000). They have also shown that poverty is an important causal variable in internal wars. Because these studies are constrained by the quality of data they use, and lack detailed field-based observations, their findings are inevitably somewhat uncertain (Conca 2002).

The second new development in environmental violence research seeks to learn from peaceful responses to environmental change rather than from instances of violence. This is an important approach if the goal of research is to help prevent conflicts, because understanding what works to promote peace is as important as understanding what causes violent outcomes. Thus far the focus of this research has been on cooperation between states over shared resources such as rivers and seas (Conca and Dabelko 2002). This research endeavour serves as a useful reminder that cooperation among people and groups is also an outcome of common environmental problems.

The final new approach to environment and violence research involves detailed field-based studies of places that have experienced environmental problems and violence. These studies have stressed the importance of unequal outcomes of social and environmental changes. For example, inadequate distribution of the returns from resource extraction activities has been a factor in violence in West Kalimantan (Peluso and Harwell 2001), the Niger Delta (Watts 2001), and Bougainville island (Böge 1999). They show that a range of intervening economic, political, and cultural processes that produce and sustain power are seen as more important in causing (and preventing and resolving) violent conflict than the actual material environmental changes that take place.

KEY POINTS

- There are no strong causal relationships among population growth, environmental change, and violent conflict.

- Environmental change is not an immediate cause of conflict, but it can at times be an exacerbating factor.

- Environmental change is unlikely to be a cause of war between countries.

- Groups experiencing common environmental problems can also cooperate to address those problems.

Environmental change and national security

Most interpretations of environmental security take existing theories of national security, and then factor in environmental issues. Regardless of whether or not environmental change may cause violent conflict within or between states, in many less subtle ways it can undermine national security.

Environmental change can weaken the economic base that determines military capacity. In some developed countries, and in most developing countries, natural resources and environmental services are important to economic growth and employment. Income from and employment in primary sectors such as agriculture, forestry, fishing, and mining, and from environmentally dependent services like tourism, may all be adversely affected by environmental change. It has been widely reported, for example, that China's rapid economic growth—which has funded its military modernization programme—is ecologically unsustainable because of water shortages, water pollution, and land degradation. So, in some cases, if the natural capital base of an economy erodes, then so does the long-term capacity of its armed forces. Because it exposes people to health risks, environmental change can also undermine the human development that Sen (1999) considers important for economic growth. It can also weaken the legitimacy and stability of ruling regimes by decreasing the income they gain from resource-based rents or taxes, thereby undermining their ability to provide welfare, employment, and key services (Kahl 2006). In other words, if economic development can be ecologically unsustainable, then national security can be similarly unsustainable.

While many environmental problems countries face are principally caused by internal developments within those countries, some problems are largely beyond their control. Examples of this include the impacts of global emissions of ozone-depleting substances on rates of skin cancer in southern latitudes, the legacies of nuclear-weapons tests conducted during colonial times in French Polynesia and the Marshall Islands, the impacts of the Chernobyl nuclear-reactor accident in 1986 on East European countries, the impacts of forest fires in Indonesia on air pollution in Malaysia and Singapore, and the impacts of global emissions of greenhouse gases on low-lying countries and countries with high climatic variability (for example a 45 cm rise in sea level will potentially result in a loss of 11 per cent of Bangladesh's territory, forcing some 5.5 million people to relocate) (see Case Study 14.2). Transboundary flows differ from traditional external security threats in that

CASE STUDY 14.2

Climate change and atoll countries

Atolls are rings of coral reefs that enclose a lagoon that contain small islets with a mean height above sea level of approximately 2 meters. There are five countries comprised entirely of low-lying atolls: Kiribati (population 85,000), the Maldives (population 309,000), the Marshall Islands (population 58,000), Tokelau (population 2,000), and Tuvalu (population 10,000).

Climate change is likely to cause sea levels to rise by between 9 and 88 cm by the year 2100. Atoll countries are highly vulnerable to sea-level rise because of their high ratio of coastline to land area, lack of elevated land, soft coastlines, relatively high population densities, and low incomes to fund response measures. Also, climate change is likely to result in more intense rainfall events and possibly more intense droughts. The combined effect of these changes on atoll societies is likely to include coastal erosion, increases in flooding events, freshwater aquifers becoming increasingly contaminated with saline water,

and decreasing food security because of reduced harvests from agriculture and fishing. The World Bank estimates that by 2050 Tarawa atoll in Kiribati could face an annual damages bill equivalent to 13–27 per cent of current Kiribati GDP.

This combination of changes in mean conditions and extreme events driven by climate change may mean that atoll countries are unable to sustain their populations, a possibility with even a moderate amount of climate change. This danger to the sovereignty of the atoll countries is arguably greater than anything any single country could impose; indeed, nuclear testing in the Marshall Islands and severe fighting in Kiribati during the Second World War had relatively minor impacts compared to the risks posed by climate change. This risk that climate change poses to national sovereignty is a very clear case of national (and human) environmental insecurity.

Barnett and Adger (2003).

they are uncontrolled and most often unintended; in this respect they are 'threats without enemies' (Prins 1993).

However, understanding environmental problems as national security issues is not unproblematic. Daniel Deudney (1990) offers three reasons why linking environmental issues to national security is analytically misleading. First, he argues that military threats are different from environmental threats in that military threats are deliberately imposed and the cause of the threat is easily identifiable, whereas environmental threats are accidental and their causes are often uncertain. Second, Deudney argues that linking environmental issues to national security may not have the effect of mobilizing more attention and action on environmental problems, but, rather, it may serve to

strengthen existing security logic and institutions. There are reasonable grounds to consider that this has been the case—for example, a 2007 study by the CNA Corporation argued that climate change 'poses a serious threat to America's national security' and concluded that part of the solution was that the US 'Department of Defense should enhance its operational capability' (CNA Corporation 2007: 6, 8; see also Background 14.2). Deudney's third argument against environmental security is that environmental change is not likely to cause wars between countries (as discussed in the previous section). So, while there is some basis for considering environmental problems as national security problems, the problem remains one of interpretation—of what constitutes national security, of whom it is for, and of how it is to be achieved.

Armed forces and the environment

Linking environmental change with security inevitably means addressing the linkages between the

most important of security institutions—the military—and the environment. It is when

BACKGROUND 14.2

The 1998 National Security Strategy

The 1998 *National Security Strategy* was the first major national security policy statement to include environmental issues in a significant way. Here are some excerpts:

- 'The same forces that bring us closer increase our interdependence, and make us more vulnerable to forces like extreme nationalism, terrorism, crime, environmental damage and the complex flows of trade and investment that know no borders' (White House 1998: p. iii).

- 'We seek a cleaner global environment to protect the health and well-being of our citizens. A deteriorating environment not only threatens public health, it impedes economic growth and can generate tensions that threaten international stability. To the extent that other nations believe they must engage in non-sustainable exploitation of natural resources, our long term prosperity and security are at risk' (White House 1998: 5).

- 'Crises are averted—and US preventative diplomacy actively reinforced—through US sustainable development programs that promote voluntary family planning, basic education, environmental protection, democratic governance and the rule of law, and the economic empowerment of private citizens' (White House 1998: 8).

- 'The current international security environment presents a diverse set of threats to our enduring goals and hence to our security . . . [including] terrorism, international crime, drug trafficking, illicit arms trafficking, uncontrolled refugee migrations and environmental damage [which] threaten US interests, citizens and the US homeland itself' (White House 1998: 10).

KEY POINTS

- Environmental change can put at risk the quality and quantity of resources available to a country.

- Environmental change can put at risk the economic strength of many countries.

- Environmental change poses risks to population health in many countries.

- Some environmental risks come from beyond a country's borders, and are unintentional.

- Linking environmental issues to security issues may not help solve environmental problems.

---

considering the role of militaries that some of the most profound contradictions with the concept of environmental security are raised. The goal of most militaries is to win wars, and so they train for and sometimes fight wars with devastating consequences for people and the environment. This contrasts considerably with the goals of the environmental movement to achieve sustainable development and peace.

Warfare almost always results in environmental degradation. The use of nuclear weapons in Japan, defoliants in Vietnam, depleted uranium ammunition in Kuwait and Kosovo, the burning of oil wells in Kuwait, the destruction of crops in Eritrea, and the draining of marshes in south-eastern Iraq are all examples of the direct impacts of war on the natural environment. In most cases the consequences of these impacts last well beyond the end of fighting.

Warfare also has indirect—but in many ways more extensive—impacts on the environment. In many cases, spending on fighting is sustained by resource extraction, and in some cases it is resources that are the principal source of conflict. For example, timber in Cambodia and Burma, gems in Afghanistan, and diamonds in Sierra Leone have all been sources of income for armed groups. In these kinds of conflicts, control over and extraction of resources is of paramount concern and the environmental and social impacts of extraction are not considered. Violent conflict almost always involves denial of territory to

THINK POINT 14.2

The environmental impacts of armed forces

- In the 1980s the US military was the largest holder of agricultural land in the Philippines.

- The US nuclear weapons programme was conducted in thirty-four states and covered 2.4 million acres of land; clean-up costs are expected to be in the order of US$200–300 billion.

- Nuclear tests have been carried out at seven sites in the South Pacific, making four islands completely uninhabitable and causing above-average cancer levels in residents of the Marshall Islands.

- The former Soviet Union dumped up to 17,000 containers of nuclear waste and up to 21 nuclear reactors into the Barents and Kara seas.

- The US military generates more toxins than the top five US chemical companies combined.

- In the United States in the 1980s there were 26 US military bases with significant toxic hazards; clean-up costs were estimated to be over US$400 billion.

- Worldwide use of aluminum, copper, nickel, and platinum for military purposes exceeded the combined demand for these materials in all the developing countries.

- One quarter of all the world's jet fuel is consumed by military aircraft.

- The US military – industrial complex may be responsible for at least 10 per cent of the US total CO_2 emissions, making it responsible for some 2 – 3 per cent of total global emissions or more than those of all Australia, Finland, Sweden, and New Zealand combined.

Renner (1991); Seager (1993); Heininen (1994); Dycus (1996).

opponents, sometimes with associated environmental impacts. Landmines are often used, and there are now over 100 million landmines lying in 90 countries denying access to land for productive purposes. Countries particularly affected include Angola, Afghanistan, Cambodia, and Iraq.

War also affects economic development in ways that impact indirectly on the environment. Money spent on weapons, for example, is money that could have been spent on social and environmental activities. War deters foreign investment and aid, disrupts domestic markets, and often results in a decline in exports. It depletes and damages the labour force, creates a massive health burden, and destroys productive assets such as factories and communications and energy infrastructure. War often results in increased foreign debt, increased income inequality, reduced food production, and a reduction in GDP per capita. It also creates refugees and internally displaced people. There were 19.2 million people of concern to the UNHCR at the start of 2005, including 9.2 million official refugees. There are a further 5.4 million people

who have been displaced but remain within their countries of origin.

These environmental, economic, and social effects of war all negatively impact on people's access to the kinds of resources they need to develop themselves in ecologically sustainable ways. They also reduce the amount of economic resources available to governments and communities to implement environmental policies and programmes, restrict access to the kinds of technologies needed for sustainable economic growth, suppress educational attainment and restrict the policy learning necessary for understanding and responding to environmental problems, damage the infrastructure needed to distribute resources such as water, electricity and food efficiently and equitably, and weaken the institutions and social cohesion necessary for a society to manage its environmental problems. So, armed forces wage war, and war is extremely bad for environmental security.

As well as causing major environmental impacts in times of war, in times of peace militaries also cause environmental damage. They may indeed be the single largest institutional source of environmental degradation in the world. This raises serious questions about the possibility of militaries having a positive role in environmental protection and recovery. Despite this, in the 1990s the United States Department of Defense (DOD) claimed it made a positive contribution to environmental security, through, for example, supporting 'the military readiness of the US armed forces by ensuring continued access to the air, land and water needed for training and testing' and contributing to 'weapons systems that have improved performance, lower cost, and better environmental characteristics' (Barnett 2001: 79). This, and other responses by the United States, suggests that what the DOD is securing through these 'environmental security' measures is its own capacity to wage wars.

The idea that environmental change may be a cause of armed conflict also has implications for armed forces. If environmental change is likely to make for a more unstable international environment through environmentally induced wars, for example, then this suggests that armed forces are still required to help manage these negative effects. In this way arguments about the threats environmental change poses to security help to justify existing security institutions like the armed forces, even though they may have significant environmental impacts.

KEY POINTS

- Armed forces have very different goals from the environmental movement.

- War causes environmental damage.

- War is harmful to sustainable development.

- Armed forces are major consumers of resources and major polluters.

Environmental change and human security

The concept of environmental security refers to a sector of security (the environment) rather than a referent object to be secured. Thus, it is possible to talk of the environmental security of the international system, of nation states, and, as explained in this section, of people (human security) (see also Chapter 8). The environment is one the seven sectors identified in the United Nations Development Program's (UNDP 1994) early definition of human security (the others being economic, food, health, personal, community, and political security), and so for some time now environmental change has been identified as a human security issue.

Whereas the ways in which environmental change threaten the welfare of the international system and states are somewhat ambiguous and hypothetical, the ways in which it affects the welfare of individuals and communities is obvious (see Case Study 14.3). People are environmentally insecure in all sorts of ways, and for all sorts of reasons. Broadly speaking the determinants of environmental insecurity are: where people live and the nature of environmental changes in those places; how susceptible people are to damage caused by environmental changes; and people's capacity to adapt to environmental changes. For example, subsistence farmers in the mountains of East Timor rely almost exclusively on their own farm produce for food, they earn very little if any money (on average less than US$0.55 cents per day), their farms do not have irrigation, the soils they farm in are not very fertile and are eroding, infrastructure for storing and transporting food is not well developed, agricultural productivity is low, and rainfall is variable. So, in seasons where the rain fails, food production falls and farmers have no ability to supplement their diet with other food sources because they cannot afford to purchase food. As a result, hunger and malnutrition are widespread in East Timor in drought years. In this case, the environmental insecurity of Timorese farmers is a function of the physical properties of their environments—they live in steep mountainous areas with thin soils and variable rainfall, and they also depend on farming as their only source of livelihood; if they had alternative sources of income, they could afford to buy food. The capacity of East Timor's farmers to adapt to land degradation and water shortages is constrained by poverty: if they had more money, they could afford to invest in irrigation systems, soil-erosion control programmes, food-storage systems, tractors, and fertilizers to increase production so that food would not be scarce during drought years. The causes of this environmental insecurity of Timorese farmers lie not so much in the environmental characteristics of where they live, but rather in the deep rural poverty caused by twenty-five years of violent occupation of East Timor by the Indonesian armed forces.

A comparison between Timorese farmers and Australian farmers underlies the ways in which human environmental insecurity is more socially created than naturally determined. Australian farmers live in similar environmental conditions (thin soils and variable climate), but they eat little if any of their own production, which is instead sold on markets, irrigation is widely available, food transport and storage systems are modern and efficient, fertilizers and pesticides are easily afforded, high levels of government support are available, and there is a wide array of options for off-farm income. Therefore, when drought strikes Australia, farmers do not go hungry; at worst they lose some livestock and some income. For both Timorese and Australian farmers climate variability is likely to increase because of climate change, and, while it will be difficult for Australian farmers to adapt to sustain their existing income levels, for Timorese farmers it may well be even more difficult for them to maintain enough food to keep their children healthy.

CASE STUDY 14.3

Climate change and the right to health

Article 12.1 of the International Covenant on Economic Social and Cultural Rights states that everyone has the right to 'the highest attainable standard of physical and mental health'. Climate change is and will increasingly violate this right. The WHO (2002) estimates that, in addition to causing excess deaths, climate change is already causing the additional loss of some 5.5 million disability-adjusted life years (the sum of years of healthy life lost due to illness). Climate change will exacerbate the incidence of infectious diseases such as malaria, waterborne diseases such as diarrhoea and cholera, and cardio-respiratory diseases. In Africa, for example, one estimate suggests that malaria exposure will increase by 16–28 per cent under a range of climate-change scenarios, which is significant, given that 445 million people are already exposed to malaria each year in Africa, leading to over 1 million deaths a year. The WHO (2002) also estimates that climate change already causes the loss of some 2.8 million disability-adjusted life years due to malnutrition (slightly over half of all the disease already caused by climate change). This constitutes a violation of the right to be free from hunger (Article 11.2).

WHO (2002).

Environmental change therefore does not undermine human security in isolation from a broad range of social factors, including poverty, the degree of support (or discrimination) communities receive from the state, the effectiveness of decision-making processes, and the extent of social cohesion within and surrounding vulnerable groups. These factors determine people and communities' capacity to adapt to environmental change so that the things that they value are not adversely affected. In terms of environmental change, for example, upstream users of water, distant atmospheric polluters, multinational logging and mining companies, regional-scale climatic processes, and a host of other distant actors and larger-scale processes influence the security of individuals' use of natural resources and services. Similarly, in terms of the social determinants of insecurity, larger-scale processes such as warfare, corruption, trade dependency, and economic liberalization affect people's sensitivity to environmental changes and their capacity to adapt to them. Finally, past processes such as colonization and war shape present insecurities, and ongoing processes such as climate change and trade liberalization shape future insecurities.

Understanding human environmental insecurity therefore requires understanding the larger-scale past and present processes that create wealth in some places and poverty in others, and environmental change in some places and not in others. Think Point 14.3 describes some of the existing levels of inequality that generate environmental security for some people, and environmental insecurity for others. Therefore, even though the focus of human security is the individual, the processes that undermine or strengthen human security are often extra-local. Similarly, then, the solution to human environmental insecurity rests not just with local people, but also with larger-scale institutions such as states, the international system, the private sector, civil society, and consumers in developed countries. In this respect, even an approach to environmental security that focuses on human security cannot avoid taking into account nation states and their security policies.

THINK POINT 14.3

Inequality and environmental insecurity

Inequalities in consumption

- The wealthiest 10 per cent of people in the world account for 59 per cent of all consumption.

- The poorest 50 per cent of people in the world account for 7.2 per cent of all consumption.

- The wealthiest 20 per cent of people in the world:

  consume 58 per cent of all energy resources;

  consume 84 per cent of all paper;

  own 87 per cent of the world's vehicles.

- The poorest 20 per cent of people in the world:

  consume 4 per cent of all energy resources;

  consume 1.1 per cent of all paper;

  own less than 1 per cent of the world's vehicles.

Inequalities in pollution

- The average person in a developed country causes as much pollution as 30 people in developing countries.

- The wealthiest 20 per cent of people in the world produce 53 per cent of all carbon-dioxide emissions; the poorest 20 per cent produce 3 per cent.

Unequal insecurity

- Of the people living in developing countries:

  60 per cent do not have basic sanitation,

  37 per cent do not have access to electricity,

  30 per cent do not have access to clean water.

- Every year poor-quality water in developing countries results in 5 million deaths due to diarrhea, 3 million of which are children.

- Air pollution causes 175,000 premature deaths a year in China.

UNDP (1998); World Bank (2008b).

Environment or security?

Security is a power word. When a problem is identified as a security issue it can lead to state monopolization of solutions (see Chapter 9) (Wæver 1995). Environmentalists have used environmental security to 'securitize' environmental problems—to make them matters of 'high' politics that warrant extraordinary responses from governments equal in magnitude and urgency to their response to more orthodox security threats. They have also used environmental security to highlight the opportunity costs of defence spending, and the environmental impacts of military activities, including war. This is the 'political rationale' of environmental security (Soroos 1994).

This securitizing move has to some degree raised the profile of environmental issues among foreign and security policy-makers and agencies, so that there is a general recognition that environmental changes can in some sense be considered as security issues. These changes relate mostly to a broadening of the issue of security, but there has arguably been little real change in policy and action in terms of the referent object of environmental security. The focus of much of the research and writing on environmental security on environmental violence, on environmental threats to national security, and on greening the armed forces suggests that it is the environmental security of the state that still matters most for the security-policy community. Indeed, the concept of environmental security and its messages of impending danger may have helped security institutions to appropriate environmental issues in ways that help to maintain national security business as usual.

For the environmental and peace movement, therefore, environmental security has not lead to a trading-off of military security for environmental security, or increased resources committed to solving environmental problems. Instead, environmental problems have been militarized; the emphasis has been placed on environmental change as a cause of violent conflict rather than human insecurity; and on addressing environmental threats from other places as opposed to attending to domestic causes of environmental change. In this respect, much that is called 'environmental security' has had little to do with the environment, and much to do with security.

Despite all these arguments, there are some good reasons for continuing to use the concept of environmental security. It has gained some purchase with development agencies, as it helps to capture the environmental dimensions of social vulnerability. It communicates the critical nature of environmental problems such as climate-change impacts on atoll countries, or the health impacts of water pollution, better than standard concepts like sustainability or vulnerability. Environmental security can also serve as an integrative concept to link local (human security), national (national security), and global (international security) levels of environmental change and response. Further, in that it involves merging international relations with development studies and environmental studies, environmental security helps produce new fusions of knowledge and awareness. It offers a common language that facilitates the exchange of knowledge among people from diverse arms of government, civil society, and academia across both the developed and developing worlds. Finally, environmental security still helps to contest the legitimacy of the dominant security paradigm by pointing to the contradiction between simple state-based and military approaches to national security, and the complex, multi-scale and transboundary nature of environmental flows.

Conclusions

Environmental security has been one of the key new security issues that has helped to broaden the meaning of security in the post Cold War period.

It is the product of: efforts by the environmental movement to raise the profile of environmental issues and contest the practices of national security; the increasing recognition that environmental problems demand common security approaches and the growth in multilateral environmental agreements; and the strategic vacuum created by the end of the Cold War. Therefore, despite some twenty years of prior thinking about the connections between the environment and security, it was not until the 1990s that the concept of environmental security came to prominence and featured regularly in academic journals, in the speeches by politicians and security bureaucrats, and in the work of environmental organizations.

There are many different interpretations of environmental security because there are many different approaches to security and an even broader range of approaches to environmental change. At two ends of the spectrum of views are those people who follow the orthodox national security paradigm, who understand environmental security as being about the ways in which environmental change might be a cause of armed conflict between countries; and environmentalists, who tend to see environmental security as being about the impacts of human activities—including military activities—on the environment. Somewhere in the middle ground are those who are concerned about the ways in which environmental change undermines human security.

The most influential interpretations of environmental security are those that fit well the orthodox security paradigm. In particular, arguments that environmental change may be a cause of violent conflict between and within countries, and suggest that environmental problems in other countries are threats to national security, have all largely been accepted by the security-policy community and the armed forces—especially in the United States. So, environmental security is still largely understood to be about threats to the nation state rather than to the environment *per se*, to other states, or to individuals. This suggests that, while environmental security may have broadened the meaning of security, it has been less successful in deepening it. This is not to say, though, that for some countries environmental change is not a major security problem, as the example of climate change and atoll countries shows.

The growing attention paid to environmental change as a human security issue does not fit so well with the Western security-policy community. It does, however, have some appeal to the development-policy community and to environmental groups and organizations. In the future it is likely that the concept of environmental security as human security will become more central in the fields of environmental studies and development studies, and figure more prominently in their respective policy domains. Research and policy will extend to include the impacts of environmental change on women and children, on livelihoods, and on human development. There may also be more research and policy development on institutions for cooperation on common environmental problems at a range of scales.

In the same way that environmental security did not gain much purchase with the security-policy community during the Cold War, it has received far less attention since the 9/11 attacks in the United States. This suggests that environmental security is a second-order security problem, which is considered only in times when more conventional dangers from armed aggression do not dominate national-security concerns. The immediate future of the environment as a security issue may therefore be determined by the relevance of other security problems. However, in the longer term environmental issues may well become paramount security concerns, as the impacts of certain environmental problems seem set to increase—for example, concentrations of greenhouse gases in the atmosphere are ever increasing and so therefore will sea levels and the intensity of climatic hazards such as cyclones, floods, and droughts; problems of nuclear waste have not been dealt with and the stockpile is still growing; and water demand is increasing but supply is relatively fixed. So, the relevance of environmental security will most probably increase until such time as truly common and cooperative approaches implement serious reforms to achieve forms of social organization that are ecologically sustainable. In this sense, current practices of national security are a significant barrier to achieving environmental security for all people.

? QUESTIONS

1. Is environmental security about the impact of humans on the environment, or about the impact of environmental processes on things that people value?

2. What reasons explain why there has been so much effort devoted to finding connections between environmental change and violence?

3. What are the implications of calling environmental problems security issues?

4. Can armed forces enhance environmental security?

5. What kinds of environmental problems are national security issues? For what reasons?

6. What kinds of environmental problems are human security issues? For what reasons?

7. What causes someone to be environmentally insecure?

8. How is it that the securitization of environmental issues may have helped to secure security?

9. How could the human security and national security approaches to environmental security be reconciled?

10. What are the most appropriate policies to provide environmental security? Who should implement them?

≋ FURTHER READING

 Barnett, J. (2001), *The Meaning of Environmental Security: Ecological Politics and Policy in the New Security Era,* London: Zed Books. A critical examination of different approaches to environmental security which promotes a human security approach.

■ Conka, K., and Dabelko, G. (2002) (eds.), *Environmental Peacemaking,* Baltimore: John Hopkins University Press. The first major book that focuses on cooperation over environmental problems.

■ Dalby, S. (2002), *Environmental Security*, Minneapolis: University of Minnesota Press. A critical geopolitical perspective on environmental security that incorporates insights from environmental history and ecological theory.

■ Diehl, P., and Gleditsch, N. (2001) (eds.), *Environmental Conflict*, Boulder, CO: Westview Press. An extensive collection of largely quantitative studies of the causal relationships between population, environment, and conflict.

■ Homer-Dixon, T. (1999), *Environment, Scarcity, and Violence*, Princeton: Princeton University Press. Summarizes the author's highly influential work on environmental scarcity and violence.

■ Kingham, R. (2006) (ed.), *Inventory of Environmental Security Policies and Practices: An Overview of Strategies and Initiatives of Selected Governments, International Organisations and Inter-Governmental Organisations*, The Hague: Institute for Environmental Security. An inventory of the policies and programmes of governments and international organizations on environmental security.

■ Peluso, N., and Watts, M. (2001) (eds.), *Violent Environments*, Ithaca, NY: Cornell University Press. A collection of detailed field-based qualitative case studies of environmental disputes.

■ WCED (1987), *World Commission on Environment and Development, Our Common Future*, Oxford: Oxford University Press. A foundational report on the environment and common security.

 IMPORTANT WEBSITES

● http://www.wilsoncenter.org/ecsp The Environmental Change and Security Program at the Woodrow Wilson International Center for Scholars is the pre-eminent centre for environmental security studies in the United States. The site contains a wealth of information including the influential Environmental Change and Security Project Report.

● http://www.gechs.org The Global Environmental Change and Human Security (GECHS) Project conducts policy-relevant research on environmental change and human security. This site contains some useful publications, including policy briefings, and an extensive set of links to related sites.

● http://www.unep.org The United Nations Environment Program provides leadership on environmental issues within the UN system. Among other things, this site contains information about global environmental issues, summits, and treaties.

 Visit the Online Resource Centre that accompanies this book for lots of interesting additional material: www.oxfordtextbooks.co.uk/orc/collins2e/

15

Economic Security

CHRISTOPHER M. DENT

Chapter Contents

- Introduction
- Contemporary thinking on economic security
- A new conceptual approach to economic security
- Conclusion

Reader's Guide

'Economic security' is an increasingly used phrase but also a relatively undertheorized concept in the political economy literature. This chapter examines how recent thinking on economic security has developed and presents a new conceptual approach to it. There are generally two largely separate discourses on economic security: micro-level analyses concentrate on 'localized' agents such as individuals, households, and local communities, whereas macro-level economic security tends to focus on nation states (or other entities capable of conducting a foreign economic policy) and their engagements in the international economic system. It is the latter discourse with which this chapter is concerned, and in this context the definition of economic security advanced here is *safeguarding the structural integrity and prosperity-generating capabilities and interests of a politico-economic entity in the context of various externalized risks and threats that confront it in the international economic system*. More specifically, it is contended that the pursuit of economic security essentially orientates foreign economic policy (FEP) objectives. The new conceptual framework presented here is centred on eight different 'objective typologies' of economic security, the exposition of which forms the main discursive function of this chapter.

Introduction

The increasing attention afforded to **economic security** can be primarily attributed to the broadening of security conceptualization after the end of Cold War (Ullman 1983). Hence it joins other 'new' sectors that have more substantively extended the usual scope of security concerns beyond the traditional politico-military domain. Economic security remains a highly contested concept, not least because scholars have approached it from various disciplinary perspectives. Sociologists and anthropologists tend to adopt a micro-level approach. As I later argue, political scientists still working in the framework of traditional security studies have been more concerned with what I refer to as the **economics–security nexus** rather than economic security *per se*. The new conceptual framework offered here is international political economic in perspective, and thus does not claim disciplinary universalism. However, the very multidisciplinary nature of international political economy (IPE) makes it a useful approach to take by its ability to connect and synthesize different disciplinary insights into a holistic framework of analysis.

In general terms, economic security analysis may be divided into two narratives, or what can be called a dyadic narrative. On the one hand, *micro-level* economic security concentrates on 'localized' agents such as individuals, households, and local communities, and is primarily concerned with safeguarding their livelihoods (Liew 2000; Zalewski 2005). In developing country studies this often concentrates on food security issues. On the other hand, *macro-level* economic security generally deals with FEP powers (for example, nation states) and their engagement in the international economic system. Notwithstanding the broadening of the domestic–international interface in an era of globalization, these two discourses have remained largely separate in the academic literature. Yet there are, of course, overlaps between them—as when FEP powers persist in agricultural protectionism in order to safeguard the livelihood of their rural communities (for example, Japan, the European Union (EU)). Thus, state authorities have economic security duties to fulfil at both the micro and macro levels. Furthermore, multi-level analysis that considers the economic security predicaments of both micro-level and macro-level agents are sometimes, but not frequently, presented (Draguhn and Ash 1999; Liew 2000). However, most economic security analyses can be distinguished as either predominantly domestic (that is, micro-level) or international (that is, macro-level) in their point of departure, and it is the latter level of analysis that is the focus of this chapter.

Contemporary thinking on economic security

Post-Cold War ascendancy

The recent growth in interest in macro-level economic security is very much a product of the post-Cold War period. Hence, it derives from the respective shifts from geopolitics to geoeconomics, from military superpowers to economic superpowers, and hence from politico-ideological competition to economic competition. As Stremlau (1994: 18) observed in the early 1990s, 'we are entering an era when foreign policy and national security will increasingly revolve around our commercial interests, and when economic diplomacy will be essential to resolving the great issues of our age'. Early post-Cold War analyses on the subject considered the emerging (geo)economic foundations of future security systems. During this time, the focus was very much on how the old bipolar geopolitics had given way to a new tripolar world structure of economic superpowers (the USA, the EU, and Japan), and intense debate surrounded which of these 'triadic' powers or regions would emerge pre-eminent in the twenty-first century (Thurow 1992; Albert 1993). Thus, economic security analysis was then largely fixated on geoeconomic competition, and endeavours to consolidate regional integration (for example, the Single European Market, the North American Free Trade Agreement (NAFTA)) were broadly aligned to this. A more cooperative approach between the triadic powers emerged, however, by the mid-1990s, with the USA and East Asian states drawing closer together within the Asia-Pacific Economic Cooperation (APEC) forum, the EU and the USA signing the New Transatlantic Agenda in 1995, and the EU and East Asia initiating the Asia–Europe Meeting (ASEM) dialogue framework in 1996 (Dent 2001).

The policy shift towards a more cogent economic security approach was particularly conspicuous in the USA. Economic security became a key issue in discussions within both the National Security Council (NSC) and the Council on Foreign Relations (CFR) from the early 1990s. In January 1993, US President Bill Clinton expanded the NSC's membership to include, among others, the Treasury Secretary and the newly created office of Assistant to the President for Economic Policy, thus acknowledging the greater role of economic issues in the formulation of national security policy. Moreover, shared staffing between the NSC and the newly created National Economic Council was intended to bring greater security-policy coherence on these issues. Later on, in May 1997, a second-term report from the Clinton administration entitled 'A National Security Strategy for a New Century' listed 'to bolster America's economic prosperity' as one of three core objectives, the others being 'to enhance our security with effective diplomacy and with military forces' and 'to promote democracy abroad'. In these new policy developments, Clinton went beyond previous efforts operationally to integrate US economic policy with national security. Similar shifts to economic-security thinking were visible in the perceptions and actions of many other foreign-policy elites. The 9/11 terrorist attacks on the USA further enhanced comprehensive security thinking amongst security-policy circles, incorporating economic security considerations more closely into the strategic calculus. The targets chosen by the terrorists were in themselves very significant, as they intended to cause chaos in the USA simultaneously in the security domain by attacking the Pentagon, and in the economic domain by attacking the World Trade Center, the very totem of American corporate and financial power. The choice of a high-profile 'economic' target was important in so far as the al-Qaeda terrorists sought to extend the target spectrum beyond politico-military sites—for example, embassies or naval vessels.

The economics–security nexus

Social science studies on the connections between economics and politico-military security have been made for some time. According to Mastanduno (1998), these date back to the 1930s and 1940s, when Jacob Viner, E. H. Carr, Albert Hirschman, and Edward Mead Earle were the first prominent academics to take an interest in the economics–security nexus. However, the subject was surprisingly neglected in the early post-war period, despite being a particularly strong feature of US foreign policy (Leitzel 1993; Mastanduno 1998). It took the global shocks of the 1970s and the emergence of IPE as an academic discipline essentially to change this. Yet, the economics–security nexus can be and should be differentiated from that of economic security itself. Technical aspects of the former generally include:

- *the economics of military security (or military security economics)*, which concern allocative, productive, techno-industrial, infrastructural, and cost-price aspects of resourcing military security capabilities;

- *the subordination of economic policies to security policy interests*, involving the use of FEP measures to support wider foreign-policy objectives, or 'low politics' directly serving the needs of 'high politics';
- *the subordination of security policies to economic interests*, which, at a general level, could relate to making the world safe for the expansion of capitalist activities, with this typically attributed to a hegemonic state's duties.

It is admittedly often difficult to establish whether a certain policy action was specifically driven by economic and politico-military security objectives when the intention was to realize both, as witnessed in both the USA's and the EU's generally positive approach to China's accession to the World Trade Organization (WTO). Furthermore, the view that both economic policy and traditional security policy measures can be used to affect similar intended outcomes is linked to the fungibility of power argument, which contends that threats on the economic front (for example, sanctions) can achieve security aims, and vice versa. Such actions establish credible links between action in one domain and a goal in the other. However, the continued preoccupation with this linkage in the mainstream literature may have been at the expense of developing more cogent ideas about what specifically constitutes the pursuit of economic security in the international system.

This problematical and somewhat unrefined (and even sometimes confused) relationship between the economics–security nexus and economic security dates back some time. Knorr's contribution (1977) to the early economic security debate was indicative of the rather negative terms in which many scholars of the Cold War period thought about economic security. According to him, the manifestation of economic security policies becomes most apparent when a country 'consciously chooses to accept economic inefficiency to avoid becoming more vulnerable to economic impulses from abroad or when a country stresses national approaches at the expense of international integration' (Knorr 1977: 14). This

suggested that high opportunity costs were incurred in making economic security choices: in other words, there were clear trade-offs between pursuing economic security objectives and more 'welfare-rational' economic policy objectives. For example, US government embargoes on a wide range of US exports to the Soviet Union denied American firms access to this foreign market, thus leading to an under-exploitation of their competitive advantage in a number of industries (for example, information technology) and the subsequent under-optimization of production and resource efficiencies, leading to net welfare losses. This is because American firms like IBM could have gained greater scale economy cost reductions through expanded export production targeted at the Soviet Union market that generated these efficiencies. The legacy of this Cold War thinking persists strongly in that many scholars still equate economic security with aspects of the economics–security nexus, or remain strongly preoccupied with the economics–security nexus rather than advancing theories on economic security itself (Harris and Mack 1997; Soeya 1997; Sperling et al. 1998).

Defining the empirical domain and concepts of economic security

Distinguishing the empirical domain of economic security from the economics–security nexus can be problematic, as recognized by a number of scholars. Buzan, Wæver, and de Wilde (1998) ask whether the pursuit of economic security merely represents the securitization of economic issues, and furthermore are scholars simply wishing to define it by their attempts to distinguish between politicized economics and security spillovers from the economic sector into others. They conclude that the question of economic security concerns the relationship between the political structure of anarchy and the economic structure of the market, and avoid merging security and economy into a single analytical construct.

At the fundamental level, security relates to guarding or guaranteeing the safety of some entity from extant dangers. Determining the economic security of *what* and of *whom* connects with our prior discussion over micro-level and macro-level economic security. In this context, we must consider the relationship between an FEP power's physical economic functions and capacities (for example, infrastructural, techno-industrial), on the one hand, and the interests of its associated economic agents (which may be extra-territorial, or transnationalized, such as multinational enterprises or migrant workforces), on the other. Hence, this raises the old problem of differentiating agent from structure, given their mutually constitutive links. For instance, the corporate interests of an agent (for example, a firm) may form a critical part of the economy's export capacity (a structural aspect), and this agent may represent a substantial proportion of the FEP power's broader economic structure—as, for example, in the case of Samsung in South Korea. Our discussion on micro-level and macro-level economic security has already acknowledged the connections between localized agents and FEP powers pursuing economic security in the international system with the former's interests in mind. It was also previously implied that FEP protagonists (see Key Ideas 15.1 for terms of reference) are charged with identifying and realizing the economic security interests of the economic agents deemed to constitute the FEP power, on both

an individual (for example, a firm lobbying the government on a specific market-access issue) and a collective basis. In this sense, the economic security of both agent and structure in the international system is combined, as will be illustrated further in the exposition of the new conceptual framework below. This framework is also founded on the notion that establishing more definitive economic security objectives helps better identify economic security motivations behind foreign (economic) policy actions, thus further defining the empirical domain of economic security.

KEY POINTS

- The growing interest in economic security analysis should be understood in a post-Cold War context, centring on the respective shifts from geopolitics to geoeconomics, from military superpowers to economic superpowers, and hence from politico-ideological competition to economic competition.

- Linkages between economic policy and traditional or politico-military security policy—the economics–security nexus—have always existed but have become increasingly entwined.

- Despite this closer interlinkage, the study of the economics–security nexus and economic security are not the same, and one often gets confused with the other in the academic literature. Furthermore, many studies of 'economic security' do not explain what is meant by the term.

A new conceptual approach to economic security

Introduction

The pursuit of economic security broadly defines FEP objectives. The conduct of FEP itself can be said to fall into two domains (Dent 2002). The first of these can be referred to as *technical policy realms*, which themselves can be subcategorized into a *core* element (trade, FDI, international finance, and foreign-aid policies) and an *associative* element (for

example, industry policy), whereby the former possesses a more overt and cognitive international focus while the latter is subordinately allied to the former in some functionally supportive, often competitiveness-enhancing, manner. The second domain is *economic diplomacy*, which broadly concerns the means and parameters within which trade, investment, and other international economic relations are conducted between representative agents of different FEP powers. Economic diplomacy can generally be viewed from different levels of engagement, modalities, exercises of power, and bargaining processes.

Furthermore, our model of FEP analysis incorporates three 'orienting' interactive dimensions: (1) *cognitive-ideological approaches* relate to key ideological 'nodes' of thought (for example, liberalism, neo-mercantilism), value-system traditions, the accommodation of economic culture, and other ideational or value-based factors that shape the thinking behind FEP formation; (2) *contesting 'actor-based' influences* examine how different domestic (for example, trade unions, industrial associations), international (for example, foreign governments, international economic organizations) and transnational actors (for example, TNCs, transnational civil society) seek to affect FEP

KEY IDEAS 15.1

Key terms of reference

Key terms of reference used throughout this analysis are as follows. *FEP formation* is a general term for the structure, conduct, and process of foreign economic policy. *FEP protagonists* relate to actors that are responsible for the directing (political or quasi-political leadership) or managing (bureaucratic leadership) of foreign economic policy. These normally relate to central government representatives but can also include those from sub-state units (for example, local government), supranational or inter-governmental units (such as the EU), and even, in some cases, representatives drawn from business or civil society. *FEP powers* refer to the polities that these protagonists represent. These are typically nation states or some other state form and can include sub-state units (for example, states within a federated union such as the USA), supranational, or inter-governmental units (for example, the EU), city states (for example, Singapore) or quasi-states (for example, Taiwan). Lastly, *stakeholding FEP constituencies* relate to any groups with a direct interest in, or even leverage over, FEP formation. These can include FEP protagonists themselves, as well as representations from business, civil society, and institutional communities.

---

formation; (3) the third concerns the conceptual framework of *'generic' economic security objectives* itself, which is outlined in the latter half of this article. Thus the pursuit of economic security forms just one (but nevertheless central) aspect of FEP formation. Key terms of reference used in our analysis can be found in Key Ideas 15.1.

Establishing a definition of economic security

The new conceptual approach to economic security advanced here is founded on a definition that emphasizes a threat-minimizing and opportunity-maximizing take on economic security, the pursuit of which involves *safeguarding the structural integrity and prosperity-generating capabilities and interests of a politico-economic entity in the context of various externalized risks and threats that confront it in the international economic system*. Here, *politico-economic entity* broadly equates with an FEP power with respect its own territorial economy and extraterritorial (for example, transborder or transnational) economic interests. Hence, FEP protagonists may work to safeguard the transnational commercial interests of its home-based or hosted foreign multinational enterprises (MNEs). Thus, FEP powers are focused on different forms of transnational economic space. This may be relatively localized and comparatively distant—for example, where the global connections of 'home-based' firms are extensive. Moreover, FEP powers may work with others to safeguard the security of their transnational economic space through regional and multilateral modes of cooperation—for example, the EU and the WTO.

The *structural integrity* aspect of the definition relates essentially to maintaining the internal construction of the economy during its interactions in the global economy, and its ability to meet the basic demands of economic agents located therein. Where meaningfully applied, this can be linked to proximate notions of the economy's survival in the international system and thus the prevention of its structural collapse—a rare event in absolute total terms, although this depends on your interpretation of 'structural collapse'. Some appear in a new politico-geographically defined form (for example, East Germany), whereas in other cases apparent structural collapses may apply to certain aspects of the economy (for example, Iceland's financial system in the 2008/9 global financial crisis—see Case Study 15.3). Structural integrity is, therefore, an essential economic security objective. The *prosperity-generating capabilities and interests* aspect broadens the conventional boundaries of the economic security concept beyond its usual attention to minimizing direct and immediate economic vulnerabilities. Safeguarding prosperity-generating capabilities and interests works towards this objective anyway through reducing the future scope for economic security risks, vulnerabilities, and threats, constituting a sort of 'insurance policy' or 'preventative medicinal' approach. The development and safeguarding of the prosperity-generating capabilities and interests may concern 'technical' (for example, trade–industry policies) or 'relational' (for example, economic diplomacy) aspects. Moreover, these too can be linked to welfare maximization—both localized and global—and the externalization of FEP interests, such as championing the interests of home MNEs in their operations abroad.

In comparing these last two aspects of the base definition, safeguarding the 'structural integrity' of the FEP power is more defensive in connotative action, whereas safeguarding 'prosperity-generating capabilities and interests' relates more to promotive or enhancing actions. As such, 'safeguarding' in this latter context involves proactive measures for advancing the FEP power's economic security interests. Instances include foreign economic policies that cultivate certain prosperity-generating functions within the economy, such as the development of strategic export production capabilities—for example, semiconductors in the IT sector. Strengthening economic diplomacy ties with other FEP powers may also foster trade, foreign investment, or finance-related linkages that serve similar economic security objectives.

The objective typologies of economic security

The objective typologies of economic security presented here further develop the concept and definable pursuits of economic security, as well as the contention that it provides a suitable focal lens for FEP analysis. These typologies may be considered facets of the same analytical lens, which refracts in different ways in accordance to various factors such as issue linkage, interdependence variables, fungibility of power, and so on. The objectives of FEP are naturally difficult to compartmentalize, made more so by their differential modalities—for example, tactical, strategic. However, attempts at classification are viable if a *generic* rather than a *specific* approach to classifying different types of FEP objectives is considered. This new framework of economic security analysis is based on eight different typologies.

Supply security

In basic terms, supply security concerns the securing of key supply chains involving foreign sources. It therefore relates particularly to the various structures of supply through which an FEP power acquires foreign materials, components, and technologies, and exercises of economic diplomacy may be necessary to maintain the integrity of these structures. These structures in turn ultimately serve the supply base of the economy, which itself may be thought of in infrastructural terms from the perspective of economic agents (that is, individuals, firms) who stand to gain external economies of scale and scope from an enhanced supply base. Thus, supply security can affect the ability of producers to remain or improve their competitiveness, to access key materials and technologies, and to help retain the economy's general prosperity-generating capabilities and interests. As Case Study 15.2 discusses, China's emerging economic relationship with Africa is substantially founded on supply-security imperatives.

In a globalizing world economy, supply diversification (rather than self-dependence) plays an important element of a vulnerability management strategy of economic security, especially in specific circumstances or a general environment marked by closed, costly, or unpredictable access. This tends to be the case when FEP powers or firms impose certain supply restrictions, or where oligopolistic-monopolistic concentration exists in the international markets. Both situations can create quantitative and cost uncertainties for 'supplied' FEP powers and producers therein, compromising their ability to respond effectively to changes in international competitive conditions. Foreign economic policy measures—both 'policy-technical' (for example, trade policy) and economic diplomacy actions—are utilized to address such economic security predicaments. For example, US aid is currently used to develop the oil-exporting capacities of ex-Soviet Union republics as a means to diversify America's dependence on Middle East sources.

Market-access security

This broadly concerns the FEP power's securing of the best access possible to key foreign markets. This is particularly crucial for export-oriented economies with small domestic markets, although this has become a prime economic diplomacy objective of all FEP powers. Exploiting foreign-market potential has long been perceived as a means to generate prosperity for the exporting country, essentially through the foreign 'earnings' procured by export sales. It is also increasingly linked to the 'structural-integrity' dimension of economic security by foreign-market access helping facilitate domestic techno-industrial restructuring by providing outlets for extra-nationally produced goods from relevant industrial sectors. For example, the development of ascendant sectors, such as biotechnology, often depends on attaining minimum efficiency scale levels of production, and domestic demand alone may be insufficient to help reach this position. Likewise, alleviating the economic and social hardships associated with the structural decline of 'sensitive' industries in Western economies, such as steel, may be achieved by improved foreign-market demand for these products.

Large economies, such as the USA and Japan, tend to enjoy the benefit of domestic-market self-sufficiency, and therefore one could argue they are not so concerned with market-access security. Of course, it is more complicated than that. The USA, for instance, is compelled to seek improved market access because of its persistent trade-deficit predicament: exports must help pay for its burgeoning import bill. Japan's aggressive export policies and practices, and its huge trade surpluses, can be primarily attributed to the state's lingering neo-mercantilist ideology and the global market strategies of Japanese MNEs. Furthermore, foreign-market competition has intensified for all firms and has thus become a prominent FEP issue. This is largely because globalizing processes have made markets more porous from both the domestic and the foreign perspective. Domestic-market-oriented firms now face greater competition from foreign rivals, and thus must look to foreign markets themselves to compensate. Similarly, firms now compete with others outside their respective domestic markets more than before. Thus, European and Asian firms compete more vigorously for US market share and across a wider range of product sectors.

Finance-credit security

Finance-credit security entails ensuring in so far as possible the financial solvency of the FEP power in the international system, as well as its maintenance of access to, or influence or control over sources of, international credit. Since the 1990s, this has become an acute economic security concern of developing countries in the context of Third World debt and of other countries that have required significant IMF assistance—for example, South Korea and Argentina. The pursuit of finance-credit security is perhaps the most problematic of all economic security typologies. Developments in financial globalization have made at least national-level attempts to maintain finance-credit security in the international system an extremely complex and difficult task (Kahler 2004). The risk of exchange-rate volatility has increased for many FEP powers since the 1990s, owing primarily to the ever-larger and unpredictable international currency transactions that occur daily in global money markets.

The role of increasingly powerful currency speculators has been at the centre of most financial crises over the last decade or so, most notably during the EU exchange-rate mechanism crisis of 1992/3 and the East Asian financial crisis of 1997/8 (see Case Study 15.1). Indeed, cooperative acts between FEP powers have come increasingly to characterize their pursuit of finance-credit security objectives. Connections here may be made to the complex interdependence of financial globalization, and how therefore deepening connectivity between different national and regional financial systems presents the imperative for greater cooperation on matters of international finance. Thus, finance-credit security interests are closely aligned to those of systemic security and alliance security. Those FEP powers with very large foreign-exchange reserves (for example, China, Japan, Russia, India) have tended, though, to rely on these resources as the basis for pursuing an independent finance-credit security policy. However, there are very few that are conceivably able to attain this position, given the financial reserves available to foreign-currency speculators, as Hong Kong (in 2009 the world's ninth largest forex retainer) found out during its efforts to maintain exchange-rate stability through market interventions at the time of the East Asian financial crisis (see Case Study 15.1).

Techno-industrial capability security

Preserving and developing the ability of the economy to generate prosperity, productivity, and other welfare-creating factors through techno-industrial means involves maintaining the economy's position as close as possible to the technological frontier. This may derive from indigenous or foreign sources, and relate to issues of access and acquisition of foreign technology. These capabilities may be

---

CASE STUDY 15.1

The 1997/8 East Asian financial crisis

The 1997/8 financial crisis made a profound impact on East Asia, bringing about significant political and economic change to many countries in the region. The crisis also clearly demonstrated the power and influence of financial speculators in the international economic system, and the general risks associated with 'ungoverned' financial globalization. The 1997/8 crisis caused much soul-searching within the IMF, not least because only in 1996 it had praised Thailand for recent reforms it had made in its financial policies. Attempts at future crisis aversion at the regional level have centred on ASEAN Plus Three (APT) frameworks of cooperation between the Association of South East Asian Nations (ASEAN) and the North East Asian states of Japan, China, and South Korea. Both the Chiang Mai Initiative of bilateral currency swap agreements between APT member states (sixteen agreements concluded by 2008 totalling US$85 billion) and the Asian Bond Market Initiative (devised to foster longer-term regional financial governance development) may be understood as regional economic security endeavours that seek better to manage the growing financial and economic interdependence between East Asian states. In addition, the crisis further revealed how finance-credit security depends not just on financial resources or inter-state cooperation but also on smart approaches to international financial policy. Leading up to the crisis, most if not all of the region's governments had embarked on programmes of financial liberalization from the late 1980s and early 1990s onwards. However, in many instances this was implemented within a weak institutional framework. In other words, financial markets were liberalized but without a proper institutionalization of market order. For example, firms were now free to borrow large sums from foreign banks and other financial institutions, but these were not closely monitored or supervised by the government authorities. Consequently, the huge foreign debts run up by firms significantly compromised the finance-credit security interests of these East Asian states. It was no surprise, therefore, that those that had developed smart regulatory and institutional capacities in their international finance policies, such as Taiwan and Singapore, came through the regional crisis contagion relatively unscathed. While the financial liberalization may serve the finance-credit security interests of FEP powers by improving access to sources of foreign credit, smart regulatory approaches to international financial policy *per se* are equally, if not more, important.

deployed to meet specific foreign economic policy objectives (for example, export competitiveness, attracting high-tech foreign investment, improving the FEP power's relative techno-industrial position in the international economic system, and so on); conversely, certain FEP actions (for example, trade–industry policy, economic diplomacy) may be used to assist the development of techno-industrial capabilities. Moreover, there is a strong 'strategic' association with the improvement of an FEP power's techno-industrial capabilities. Green (1996: 31) defines a strategic industry as one that 'is essential to the economic and national security interests of the state and one that engages in an activity that affects the national economy with critical forward and backward linkages through the existence of positive externalities'. As such, certain forms of strategic industrial activity perform key 'structural-integrity' functions through the roles they play via upstream and downstream linkages. This can be seen by the importance of steel production in manufactured products, and information technology as a critical process in service provision. In addition, the underlying technology of strategic industries often provides the foundation for productivity growth, and thus the potential for advancing the FEP power's prosperity-generating capacities and interests. This is particularly found in higher-tech industrial activity by its ability to add value and positively transform both the structural and the prosperity-linked prospects of the FEP power.

'Higher-tech' industry itself is, of course, a relative term, depending on whereabouts on the techno-industrial ladder FEP powers are generally positioned, but all have an interest in promoting strategic industry development. High-tech industry competition and cooperation between developed FEP powers has been well documented. For developing FEP powers, strategic industry or trade policies may be vindicated in economic welfare terms, in that developing countries are promoting the development of infant industries that eventually intensifies international competition in a positive, global welfare-enhancing manner in the future. Furthermore, WTO rules still permit developing countries to subsidize new industries where necessary and to ensure that subsidies are result-oriented through the imposition of performance standards (Amsden and Hikino 2000).

Socio-economic paradigm security

This concerns the 'defence' of a society's preferred socio-economic paradigm (for example, the East Asian developmental statist, European social market, Anglo-Saxon market liberal, and Middle Eastern socio-religious forms of 'economic model') and its welfare goals where defined. It often entails the resistance of foreign pressure to adapt to new international norms that are associated with a counter-paradigm. For those FEP powers with a strong statist tradition, as found in East Asia, this may relate to various levels of resistance (for example, societal, state bureaucratic) to neoliberalism. In addition, certain states may deem it a critical objective of their foreign economic policy to defend their socio-economic paradigm against others perceived to threaten it directly. Taiwan's FEP in relation to China may be seen thus, although socio-economic paradigm security should not be equated with the defence of sovereignty rights. This economic security typology also involves maintaining the integrity of the socio-economic paradigm and the prosperity-generating capabilities and interests that may be associated with it. The latter entails issues of prosperity distribution (for example, growth with equity) and prosperity-generating method (for example, free markets or guided markets). In addition, socio-economic paradigms evolve over time in their adaptation to changing domestic and international conditions. However, certain paradigmatic fundamentals (for example, underlying ideologies and cultural values; embedded institutional and relational frameworks) may remain largely unchanged. For instance, the ideals of liberty and individualism are intrinsic to neoliberalism, just as institutionalized state–society relations are important to developmental statism.

We may see the concept of 'socio-economic paradigm' as interchangeable with parallel concepts of 'economic system', 'capitalist culture', or 'socio-business order'. The international system is characterized by balances of convergence and competition between the different socio-economic paradigms of FEP powers, or groups of FEP powers. In a generalized example, many currently subscribe to the view that Anglo-Saxon 'market-liberal' capitalism has proved itself superior not just to communism but also to other capitalist paradigms. They point to evidence from the 1990s, where resurgent US, UK, and Australian economies clearly outperformed their continental European and East Asian capitalist counterparts. Their reasoning was premised on the argument that, in an era of globalization, those economies that had liberalized and deregulated were best positioned to exploit opportunities arising in an increasingly barrierless world economy and its emergent transnational economic spaces. The extent to which such neoliberal convergence between different capitalist systems has occurred is highly debatable, and the USA's economic troubles during the 2000s—in particular the 2008/9 global financial crisis (see Case Study 15.3)—offer scope for revisionist analysis on the above argument.

Transborder community security

Transborder community security involves the addressing of local regionalized concerns that may either precipitate transborder economic crises or affect localized interdependence issues—for example, sub-regional economic integration projects. These often centre on transborder spillovers or externalities that require market-failure correction policies, and hence the management of a shared transborder economic space. They may thus also focus on issues from other security sectors such as pollution, drug trafficking, and economic migration. The development of transborder communities may therefore emerge out of the need to tackle common economic security challenges. The geographic scale of these communities tends to range from sub-national locales (for example, provinces) contiguous to those from neighbouring countries to wider regional collectives involving a group of nation states. Moreover, it is generally the case that relatively small FEP powers that are surrounded by a large number of others are more susceptible to transborder community security issues. It will often be the case that the structural integrity and development of participating FEP powers' economies are in some way closely connected, or that potential future changes in one can have a profound impact on another. This may be particularly applicable to those states with larger neighbours (such as Canada and the USA, Ireland and the UK, Taiwan and China) and may therefore entail dependency relationships.

To draw upon an example from East Asia, Singapore's 'growth-triangle' relationship with the Malaysian province of Johor to the north and Indonesia's province of Riau to the south and west is essentially driven by the imperatives of the city state's own techno-industrial restructuring. Other kinds of subregional projects that seek to develop or manage transborder economic spaces are evident around the world, and in contrast may be founded on pre-existing transnational business networks or common natural resource management—for example, international river zones. Addressing both the interdependence opportunities and threats associated with transborder community security issues are hence linked to safeguarding an FEP power's prosperity-generating capabilities and interests in a number of ways. Issues arising from other new security sectors, such as transborder immigration and pollution, are expected to have a potentially profound impact upon these capabilities and interests. In the early 1990s, Sweden provided funds to Poland that were designed to minimize the latter's 'export' of acid rain, which was decimating parts of Sweden's agriculture industry as well as incurring substantial clean-up costs. This provides an example of how the pursuit of transborder community security objectives often connects foreign economic policy with 'new-sector' foreign-policy domains, in this specific case with foreign environmental policy. Mitigating adverse transborder spillover effects may involve different economic diplomacy responses, ranging from defensive unilateral measures (for example, strict immigration regulations) to acts of cooperative bilateralism, to the development of plurilateral or multilateral frameworks in which comparatively broad transborder community security challenges may be mutually confronted. With respect to the 'interdependence-opportunities' dimension, different FEP powers can exploit these through cultivating effective transborder divisions of labour or by rational and equitable approaches to sharing common transborder resources. Over all, the more localized nature of transborder community security issues differentiate them from those related to the maintenance of systemic security, which tend to be more global in nature.

Systemic security

Systemic security concerns the common interests of FEP powers in upholding the integrity of the international economic system, entailing cooperative and concessionary acts to uphold multilateral regimes of systemic governance, facilitate inter-state bargains, and maintain overall systemic stability. Hence, there is a strong international public-goods dimension to this economic security typology,

regarding in particular issues of the provision, distribution, and consumption of these 'goods'. Furthermore, systemic security would be emphasized by neoliberals as being a most important pursuit of economic security generally, although neoliberals tend to question the viability of pursuing economic security objectives anyway. This argument is based on their view that capitalism (the dominant economic paradigm) by its very nature propagates a state of constant insecurity in the international economic system that derives from the competitive dynamics it creates. As Buzan (1991a: 235) comments, 'capitalism is by definition a competitive system, the whole dynamic of which depends on the interplay of threats, vulnerabilities and opportunities in the market'. Thus, neoliberals generally contend that economic security is a mirage and at best can be achieved only in relative terms, although this is surely a universal predicament that applies to any pursuit of security. Neoliberals further

---

✒ CASE STUDY 15.2

The emerging China – Africa development relationship

During the 2000s, China has strengthened its economic relationship with a number of African countries through a combination of trade, investment, and development-aid deals. For example, in 2007 China signed an agreement whereby its state-owned firms would invest up to US$12 billion on economic and social development projects in exchange for rights to mine copper and cobalt ore in Congo of an equivalent value. A year earlier, China and Angola agreed to a similar US$10 billion arrangement on access to Angola's oil reserves and infrastructure development. Since the mid-1990s, China has invested US15$ billion in developing Sudan's oil-production capacity, in return securing around two-thirds of Sudan's oil-export contracts. Beijing has signed similar deals with South Africa (manganese mining), Niger (uranium), Zambia (copper), and various other African countries. In 2007, China pledged US$20 billion to finance trade and infrastructure projects across the continent over the next three years. This emerging development relationship between Africa and China may be understood from various economic-security perspectives. Taking first *supply security*, China has sought access to vital energy and natural resources

to help maintain the pace of its rapid industrial development. For example, copper is an essential commodity required in the production of electronics and information and communication-technology products. Whilst still the world's sixth largest oil producer, China became a net importer of oil in 1993. Africa was identified as a strategic oil-supply partner in the mid-1990s to help diversify China's still heavy dependence on Middle East-sourced oil. From Africa's supply security perspective, China has now become an important source of new capital and technology. This also connects with *techno-industrial capacity security* motives, as China's investments have made substantive contributions to Africa's infant industry development in sectors such as textiles and other labour-intensive manufactured products. In terms of *market-access security*, China too has become a market of growing significance for its key African partners. China – Africa trade has been growing at around 40 per cent a year since the early 2000s. Notwithstanding criticism of how Chinese investments have helped prop up dubious political regimes on the continent, China has offered *finance-credit security benefits* to many African countries through the closer development aid and finance partnerships cultivated since the 1990s.

propose that economic insecurity is not to be feared but embraced in so far as positive responses to foreign competitive threats lead to disciplined improvements in efficiency and productivity. In addition, attempts by losers of this competitive game to 'securitize their plight' merely represent desperation to change the game's rules (Buzan 1991a: 109). More generally, neoliberals tend to subordinate vulnerability issues in the pursuance of 'plenty', which can be optimized only in a free and open global economy.

However, the issue is not whether or not economic security is a mirage, but rather whether FEP powers *respond positively* to the conditions of economic insecurity that confront them: addressing economic insecurity poses a set of opportunities as well as threats, neither of which should be avoided. Moreover, the maximization of global welfare is contingent upon the security (that is, the stability) of the international economic system: a 'free and open global economy' ultimately depends on the provision of international public goods to ensure both its stability and its positive development. It could, therefore, be argued that maintaining *systemic security* is the *de facto* core economic-security concern of neoliberalism, with systemic support being the neoliberal FEP power's implicit path to pursuing economic security. Furthermore, even ardent neoliberal FEP powers follow broader economic-security aims and strategies (US Council on Competitiveness 1994; Mastanduno 1998). We too should consider the neoliberal institutionalist view regarding complex interdependence and the need for cooperative exercises in international economic security (Keohane and Nye 1977; Oye 1986). The governance architecture of systemic security lies primarily in multilateral economic institutions such as the WTO and IMF, which in turn are key depositories and custodians for the aforementioned international public goods. Regional institutions such as the EU and APEC may also contribute positively towards systemic security where multilateral utility functions have been developed.

From another perspective, Marxists and structuralists stress that economic security concerns arise from significant asymmetries in both global

---

CASE STUDY 15.3

The 2008/9 global financial crisis

Just as the 1997/8 East Asian financial crisis was triggered by a specific event (Thailand's de-pegging of its currency from the US dollar), so was the case with the 2008/9 global financial crisis, the trigger here being the mass defaulting of sub-prime mortgages in the United States. Yet, as with the 1997/8 crisis, there were broader underlying reasons behind the unfolding of the 2008/9 crisis, primarily concerning deep structural fault lines that had emerged in the banking systems of many key countries. This has posed challenges to the *finance-credit security* of these countries and, owing to the nature of financial globalization, *systemic security* risks to the world economy as a whole. Those nations whose banks had bought substantially into the sub-prime mortgage market and other high-risk lending arrangements were particularly susceptible. Iceland was perhaps the most high-profile case, where a third of the population saw its savings evaporate, all three of its major banks collapsed, and the country was essentially bankrupt, being the first Western country to seek IMF assistance in over thirty years. Iceland's economy has 'survived' the crisis, but its finance-credit capabilities and structures are likely to remain weak for some time yet. International financial institutions and national governments undertook measures to assist individual countries as well as the global financial system as a whole. Even market-liberal nations such as the United States implemented various extreme forms of state intervention (including nationalization of private firms) and a raft of new regulatory measures in attempts to safeguard finance-credit security. North American and European banks and other financial organizations had become especially entangled in the crisis. Most of their East Asian counterparts were relatively much less exposed to risk, having exercised more caution in their lending policies after learning the lessons from the 1997/8 financial crisis. However, East Asian economies were significantly affected in terms of *market-access security* from the crisis, causing a drastic decline in consumer spending on mass-produced goods made in the region.

economic development and balances of power within the world capitalist system, from which lead an accordingly uneven distribution of economic vulnerability amongst FEP powers. Those in the periphery and semi-periphery naturally possess higher vulnerability coefficients, their relative weakness making them more susceptible to economic security risks and exogenous threats. This predicament can be linked to Lee's argument (1999) that the economic security interests of weaker FEP powers are focused on maintaining their structural integrity.

Alliance security

This economic security typology is essentially subservient in character, in that it broadly entails maintaining and developing international economic partnerships with state and non-state actors in pursuance of those economic security objectives already discussed. These partnerships may take various forms, ranging from donor–client alliance relationships to looser cooperative or coordinative arrangements between relatively equal partners. As one would expect, the pursuit of economic alliance security objectives is essentially predicated on cooperative ventures. Indeed, we have previously highlighted how the complex interdependence associated with advancing globalizing processes presents an *a priori* case for FEP powers to adopt a more cooperative approach to economic security generally. This is certainly what neoliberal institutionalists would stress; moreover, non-state actors may play a critical part in this cooperative process. Milner (1992) argues in her examination of cooperative behaviour in international relations that cooperation concerns goal-directed behaviour that produces mutually shared benefits over and above those yielded by noncooperative behaviour. Different types of this behaviour include: *tacit cooperation*, which occurs without communication or explicit agreement; *negotiated cooperation*, which derives from an explicit bargaining process; *imposed cooperation*, where the stronger party in a relationship forces the other(s) to enter into cooperative arrangement, its coercive features making this

somewhat anomalous, although there are clear links here to **hegemonic stability theory**.

The problematics associated with this latter category is linked to a broader dilemma emphasized by Lee (1999: 21), who contends that, for an FEP power, it must, on the one hand, seek to 'preserve its internal autonomy and economic sovereignty from being exploited by external interference', while, on the other, 'it needs to invite external forces in order to ensure the enhancement of domestic welfare'). Neo-realists would certainly concur that economic alliance security interests are subject to the vicissitudes of anarchic inter-state competition, whereby alliances quickly form and then quickly dissolve or are soon renegotiated in accordance to changing nation state interests over time. Thus, cooperative frameworks of economic alliance security are essentially transient in nature, and are ultimately dependent upon coincidental alignments of national interests forming in the international economic system.

Inter-relationships between different typologies

When examining what inter-relationships exist between different economic security typologies, we should initially make the point that the first four typologies discussed (supply, market access, finance credit, techno-industrial capability) can be viewed as more 'technical'-policy focused, whereas the second four (socio-economic paradigm, transborder community, systemic, alliance) are generally more relational in nature or economic-diplomacy focused. Furthermore, certain relationships between typologies may be co-reinforcing or even conflictual, thus creating in the latter case dialectical tensions between different foreign economic policy goals. To begin with, there are natural overlaps between these different typologies. For example, securing better access to sources of international credit may be deemed either a supply-security or finance-credit-security objective. Techno-industrial capability security may also be served by supply security, where, for example, an infusion of foreign technology through inward FDI or other means enhances the latter. Furthermore, the pursuit of socio-economic paradigm security and market-access security interests may be mutually aligned, as we mentioned in connection with the USA's exposition of neoliberal advocacy and free trade and free markets generally. An instance of conflicting economic-security interest can arise when FEP powers are fostering certain foreign economic alliances and market-access deals (for example, bilateral free-trade agreements) that may run to the pursuit of systemic security interests (for example, upholding WTO multilateralism). In addition, the hierarchy of typologies in any set of generic FEP objectives will be primarily determined by the interaction of contesting influences from different stakeholding FEP constituencies and cognitive-ideological approaches adopted by FEP protagonists. Moreover, the aforementioned tendency of these typologies to overlap sometimes can make constructing such a hierarchical ordering difficult to establish.

KEY POINTS

- The pursuit of economic security broadly determines how a nation state or other state-like entity defines their foreign economic policy (FEP) objectives.

- We can define the pursuit of economic security itself as safeguarding the structural integrity and prosperity-generating capabilities and interests of a politico-economic entity (for example, a nation state) in the context of various externalized risks and threats that confront it in the international economic system.

- Eight different 'objective typologies' of economic security may be developed from this definition that help us further conceptualize and theorize on economic security

analysis, especially with respect to identifying different types of economic security interests.

- These objective typologies are: supply security, market-access security, finance-credit security, techno-industrial capability security, socio-economic paradigm security, transborder community security, systemic security, alliance security.

- Understanding the interlinkages between these different objective typologies is also important—for example, how the pursuit of one may be in conflict with another, or work in concert with another.

Conclusion

Economic security is an increasingly discussed but still much undertheorized concept. This chapter has presented a new conceptual framework of economic security analysis as an attempt to advance its theoretical development. In setting its context, we have examined the key theoretical and methodological issues pertaining to economic security analysis. Important distinctions have been made between the dyadic pursuits of micro-level and macro-level economic security, as well between economic security generally and the economics–security nexus. Regarding the latter, it has been argued that it is particularly important to distinguish between their respective empirical domains while acknowledging inter-sectoral connections between the politico-military security and economic security. This was examined at various fundamental levels, which in turn provided the discursive platform for the base definition of the new conceptual framework presented here, which posited that the pursuit of economic security entailed *safeguarding the structural integrity and prosperity-generating capabilities and interests of a politico-economic entity in the context of various externalized risks and threats that confront it in the international economic system.* Moreover, it was this pursuit in its multifarious forms that broadly oriented the foreign economic policy (FEP) objectives of states and state-like powers (for example, the EU, local provincial governments). From this definition, a series of eight different 'objective typologies' of economic security were developed. These form the substantive structure of the new conceptual framework, and hence provide the analytical lens through which we can understand the definable generic nature of FEP objectives. It is therefore hoped that this chapter has also made a valuable contribution to the linked discourses of economic security and foreign economic policy analysis.

? QUESTIONS

1. Why is it important to distinguish between micro-level and macro-level studies of economic security?

2. How did the end of the Cold War impact upon economic security analysis?

3. Why is it important to distinguish between economic security analysis and the economics – security nexus?

4. Why is it that, in the international economic system, it is not just nation states for which we need to consider the economic security interests?

5. Under what objective typology or typologies of economic security would you assign managing a freshwater resource shared by two neighbouring countries? Explain your reasoning.

6. Under what objective typology or typologies of economic security would you assign averting the collapse of multilateral trade negotiations at the WTO? Explain your reasoning.

7. Under what objective typology or typologies of economic security would you assign region-level endeavours to address international worker migration issues? Explain your reasoning.

8. Under what objective typology or typologies of economic security would you assign international coordinated actions to address the 2008/9 global financial crisis? Explain your reasoning.

9. Under what objective typology or typologies of economic security would you assign Singapore's signing of a free-trade agreement with the United States? Explain your reasoning.

10. Under what objective typology or typologies of economic security would you assign Japan conferring a new multi-billion-dollar foreign-aid programme to South East Asia? Explain your reasoning.

FURTHER READING

■ Buzan, B., Wæver, O., and de Wilde, J. (1998), *Security: A New Framework of Analysis,* Boulder, CO: Lynne Rienner. The chapter on economic security views the concept from the author's ground-breaking work on 'securitization'. The whole book is very thought provoking.

■ Dent, C. M. (2002), *The Foreign Economic Policies of Singapore, South Korea and Taiwan,* Cheltenham: Edward Elgar. The theorization on economic security presented in this chapter primarily derives from this work. Here, I place the pursuit of economic security as the main determining factor of foreign economic policy objectives generally.

■ Kahler, M. (2004), 'Economic Security in an Era of Globalisation: Definition and Provision, *Pacific Review,* 17/4: 485 – 502. This article critically examines economic security in today's globalizing world economy. Amongst other things, it questions whether economic security issues can be identified as being specifically national in an era of globalization, and moreover cautions against thinking that globalization just brings greater economic insecurity for nation states and regions.

■ Lee, C. (1999) 'On Economic Security', in G. Wilson-Roberts (ed.), *An Asia-Pacific Security Crisis? New Challenges to Regional Stability,* Wellington, New Zealand: Centre for Strategic Studies. This paper makes a very good review of other key works and also offers some useful ideas on the economic security conceptualization.

 ## IMPORTANT WEBSITES

● http://www.whitehouse.gov/nsc US National Security Council.

● http://www.whitehouse.gov/issues/economy US White House.

● http://www.centerforsecuritypolicy.org/200/c220.xml Center for Security Policy's site on Economic Warfare.

● http://www.globalpolicy.org/social-and-economic-policy.html Global Policy Forum site on Social and Economic Policy.

 Visit the Online Resource Centre that accompanies this book for lots of interesting additional material: www.oxfordtextbooks.co.uk/orc/collins2e/

16

Globalization, Development, and Security

NANA K. POKU

 Chapter Contents

- Introduction
- Definitions and key concepts
- Human security and level of analysis
- Globalization of insecurity: human-security framework
- Transformative agenda for development
- Conclusion

 Reader's Guide

Globalization is affecting security not only at the state level, but at the level of individuals' day-to-day lived experience. While this is true across the globe, in specific ways it may be particularly significant for the people of the South, where the twin challenges of freedom from want and freedom from fear are the most pervasive. This chapter reveals the different ways in which globalization impacts on the relative vulnerability of real human beings and communities, rather than abstract states. It does so by requiring disaggregation of data. Thereby, it unmasks official, state-level statistics, national positions, explanations, and power structures, which obscure as much if not more than they reveal, be they the product of international organizations or governments. The overall premise of the chapter is that people matter and are an appropriate focus of concern for the international-relations community.

Introduction

Globalization has set in motion a process of far-reaching change that is affecting everyone. New technology, supported by more open policies, has created a world more interconnected than ever before. This spans not only growing interdependence in economic relations—such as trade, investment, finance, and the organization of production globally—but also social and political interaction among organizations and individuals across the world. At the same time, there is also a shrinking of the world brought about by the third technological revolution that has enabled us to travel both vicariously and instantaneously to almost all regions of the world. The potential for good is immense—the growing interconnectivity among people across the world is nurturing the realization that we are all part of a global community. The nascent sense of interdependence, commitment to shared universal values, and solidarity among people across the world can be channelled to build enlightened and democratic global governance in the interest of all.

Palpably, the benefits of globalization are enormous, as a result of the increased sharing of ideas, cultures, life-saving technologies, and efficient production processes. For the leading international financial institutions (IFIs)—the World Bank and the International Monetary Fund (IMF)—the global market has demonstrated great productive capacity, which, if unhindered by state regulations, can deliver unprecedented material progress while contributing significantly to reducing poverty. Yet, we are far from realizing this potential; the current phase of the globalization process is generating unbalanced outcomes, both between and within countries.

Indeed, the euphoria the process has generated, and continues to generate, serves to disguise the very real social and economic inequalities that are not merely leftovers from the past, but the results of the globalizing process itself. Most obviously, global welfare inequalities have mushroomed alongside the noted advancements in technological developments and the rapid expansion of trade and investment.

Wealth is being created, but too many countries and people are not sharing in its benefits; nor do they have any voice in shaping the process. For the three-quarters of the world's population caught on this side of the globalization fence, the process has not met any of their basic needs; many live in the limbo of the informal economy without formal rights, livelihoods, or the legitimate prospect of better futures for their children. In what follows, I will use a **human security** lens to explore and evaluate some of the impacts of globalization on the notion of development and security across communities and societies in the developing world. Following definitions of key concepts and ideas, the chapter is divided into three parts: the first part explores in some detail *what* is meant by human security and why it is a useful concept for furthering our understanding of the outcomes of globalization; the second part suggests that the *disaggregation of data* required by a human security approach, in terms of both *level* and *scope of analysis*, offers the opportunity for a deep understanding of the complex results of globalization; and the third part considers how the human-security concept can be used in policy response for development, to overcome multiple human insecurities.

Definitions and key concepts

The problem of socio-economic development and concomitant improvement of level of living, or quality of life, is certainly one of the outstanding issues confronting humankind. Development appears to be a question not of national endowment, as are natural resources or population size, but of capabilities, such as the utilization of resources, technology, and socio-economic institutions. A definition of *development* would include the process of more effective use of resources and increased efficiency in production and distribution, which results in a greater volume and diversity of goods and services for less human physical labour. To this, one would have to add the distributional aspect within society as being, perhaps, the most important facet. In other words, the distribution of wealth or the more equitable distribution of income constitutes the highest forms of development. In this sense, the issue of 'human rights' transcends political and civil rights, to include socio-economic rights, such as rights to health, shelter, education, housing, employment, and rights for minorities, and becomes central to development. For the core dimensions of poverty, see Background 16.1.

Most analysts, following the United Nations Development Programme (UNDP) report of 1994, have embraced the notion of 'human security' as a concept for both understanding and assessing the notion of development in the modern world. The UNDP defines *human security* as encompassing two foundational freedoms at the heart of the UN charter: freedom from *want* and freedom from *fear*. Freedom from want describes a condition of existence in which basic material needs are met, and crucially in which there is a reasonable expectation that protection will be afforded during any crisis or downturn—natural or man-made—so that survival is not threatened. Human security as freedom from fear describes a condition of existence in which human dignity is realized, not only embracing physical safety, but going beyond that to include meaningful participation in the life of the community, control over one's life, and so forth. This suggests a radical account of politics as freedom from domination/exploitation, not simply the freedom to choose, as advocated by the liberal tradition in international relations. Thus, while material sufficiency lies at the core of human security, in addition the concept encompasses non-material dimensions to form a qualitative whole. In other words, human security embraces the whole gamut of rights—civil, political, economic, social, and cultural.

By contrast, *human insecurity* refers to a condition of vulnerability, in which human beings' physical or material wellbeing is threatened. Such threats may be due to natural disasters, such as cyclones or volcanic eruptions, or man-made disasters, such as rising sea levels, mud slides, oil spillages, nuclear and chemical explosions, and so on. They may be due to political conflict within or between states. Also, they may arise from the fundamental structure of the global economy in which decision-making power is concentrated in the core capitalist states, commodity producers are continually disadvantaged, and billions of people live precariously on the edge, where life is structured by lack of reliable access to material resources. Particular events arising within the global economy or broadly within the process of globalization (for example, financial crises that are due to poor management, at levels from the global to the national) can cause instant havoc to the livelihoods of millions.

Globalization is clearly the buzzword of the new millennium, but its use is often imprecise. Since as early as the seventeenth century, the world has appeared to shrink, as individuals (usually men of European origin) have travelled around it with ever-greater ease, incorporating societies they encounter into their web of wealth creation. Over the same period, very diverse countries have been drawn together (whether willingly or unwillingly) by a multitude of economic, social, and political forces. This has led to the world becoming more globally interconnected at many different levels. Since about the 1980s, these trends have accelerated dramatically, leading some to argue that we now inhabit a globalized world that is qualitatively different from that of the past—that we are living through a unique phase in human history.

Commentators offer many interpretations of these developments, but there is broad consensus on the key trends under review. The first is what Anthony Giddens (1990) has described as the intensification of worldwide social relations and increasing global interdependence. The second is expressed in David Harvey's description (1989) of 'the compression of space and time through the development of new technologies'. What these trends mean in practice is that economic, financial, technical, and cultural interchanges between different countries are now happening more quickly and more often in ways that are transforming the everyday lives of many individuals and communities around the globe. The question to be addressed here is how these trends have affected countries across the developing world, and their peoples.

KEY POINTS

- Development. The process of more effective use of resources and increased efficiency in production and distribution, which results in a greater volume and diversity of goods and services for less human physical labour, and, importantly, the distribution of wealth or the more equitable distribution of income within society.

- Human security. Freedom from want—where basic material needs are met, so as not to threaten survival; and freedom from fear—going beyond physical safety to include meaningful participation in the life of the community, control over one's life, and freedom from political domination/exploitation.

- Human insecurity. A condition of vulnerability, in which human beings' physical or material well-being is threatened.

- Globalization. Trends that in practice mean that economic, financial, technical and cultural interchanges between different countries are now happening more quickly and more often in ways that are breaking down national borders and transforming the everyday lives of many individuals and communities around the globe.

BACKGROUND 16.1

The core dimensions of poverty

Economic capabilities are the ability to earn an income, to consume, and to have assets, which are all key to food security, material well-being, and social status. These aspects are often raised as important by poor people, along with secure access to productive financial and physical resources: land, implements and animals, forests and fishing waters, credit and decent employment.

Human capabilities are based on health, education, nutrition, clean water, and shelter. These are core elements of well-being, as well as crucial means to improving livelihoods. Diseases and illiteracy are barriers to productive work, and thus to economic and other capabilities for poverty reduction. Reading and writing facilitate communication with others, which is crucial to social and political participation. Education, especially for girls, is considered the single most effective means for defeating poverty and some of its major causal factors—for example, illness (in particular HIV/AIDS) and excessive fertility.

Political capabilities include human rights, a voice, and some influence over public policies and political priorities. Deprivation of basic political freedoms or human rights is a major aspect of poverty. This includes arbitrary, unjust, and even violent action by the police or other public authorities, which is a serious concern of poor people. The politically weak have neither the voice in policy reforms nor secure access to resources required to rise out of poverty.

Socio-cultural capabilities concern the ability to participate as a valued member of a community. They refer to social status, dignity, and other cultural conditions for belonging to a society, which are highly valued by the poor themselves. Participatory poverty assessments indicate that geographic and social isolation is the *main* meaning of poverty for people in many local societies; other dimensions are seen as contributing factors.

Protective capabilities enable people to withstand economic and external shocks. Thus they are important for preventing poverty. Insecurity and vulnerability are crucial dimensions of poverty with strong links to all other dimensions. Poor people indicate that hunger and food insecurity are concerns along with other risks like illness, crime, war, and destitution.

OECD (2009).

Human security and level of analysis

The challenge of poverty and inequality is long-standing. In the mid-1970s the developing countries, through the UN system, had called for a New International Economic Order. This call had fallen on deaf ears, and from the late 1970s onwards the discursive UN system gave way to the less democratic international financial institutions, the IMF and the World Bank, under the direction of the G7, since 1999 the G20. While some limited progress was made over the next twenty-five years to address specific social concerns, such as increasing the number of people with access to clean water, in general inequality grew within and between states as the IFIs sought to promote debt repayment by governments and peoples of the developing world or the South, and global economic integration, via economic and political restructuring.

By the early 1980s, symptoms of rising poverty along with deepening inequalities were evident almost everywhere across the developing world. In pursuit of appropriate mitigation strategies, the IFIs identified domestic policy weakness of the countries in the developing world as the main culprit in accounting for the region's economic position. Based on this assumption, governments were 'encouraged' to adopt Structural Adjustment Programmes (SAPs) as a crucial prerequisite to receiving vitally needed loans. The word 'encouraged' is used very loosely here, because, in almost all cases, there was little choice on the part of the recipient states but to follow the recommendations from the IMF and the World Bank.

Table 16.1 represents sectoral figures for the impact of SAPs on agricultural growth over a twenty-year period. It is clear from the table that SAPs had very little impact on the sector. The more worrying observation is that the trend can be replicated across all the major indicators of economic growth. In almost all its evaluation reports, the World Bank (1989, 1990, 1994, 1996, 1998) observed this trend, but attributed its cause not to the poor designs of SAPs, but to their implementation. For the nature of SAPs see Table 16.2. In the World Bank's words (1984: 14), 'no country has achieved a sound macro-economic policy stance, and there is considerable concern that the reforms undertaken to date are fragile and that they are merely returning the continent to the slow growth path of the 1960s and early 1970s'.

In truth, it is not clear whether the lack of effective implementation results from the recipient governments' unwillingness to undertake reforms (as the World Bank claims) or from the objective conditions of the economies not permitting the kind of adjustment being recommended. Despite two and half decades of adjustment policies, this debate remains large unresolved. The only certainty, however, is that SAPs often had an immediate and at times detrimental impact on the welfare of the

Table 16.1 Agricultural growth rate (median) under SAPs in all developing regions, 1981–2000 (%)

	1981–1986	1987–1993	1994–2000
Large improvements	4.2	2.4	2.0
Small improvements	3.1	2.8	2.2
Deterioration	2.3	3.3	3.0
All countries	3.1	2.8	2.3

Source: Author, using base data from World Bank and IMF.

poorest members of society, especially as they affect food prices, costs of education, and payment of medical services (see Table 16.2). In the case of Africa, for example, the promotion of exports for debt repayment and the cutting of public expenditure on welfare in a region where 100 million people are undernourished; where there is 1 doctor for 36,000 people, compared with 1 for 400 people in industrial countries; and where nine out of ten of the HIV-infected people worldwide reside, is tantamount to a scandal. One author has even referred to SAPs as a form of economic genocide. 'When compared to genocide in various periods of colonial history, its impact is devastating. SAPs directly affect the livelihood of more than 4 billion people' (Chossudovsky 1996).

The mid- to late 1990s witnessed growing dissatisfaction with the performance of neoliberal economic development policies throughout the South and former Eastern bloc, within specific constituencies in the G7 countries such as church groups and social justice NGOs, and even among some individuals within the World Bank. The failure of structural adjustment, coupled with the social reversals brought about by specific currency crises in the late 1990s, further eroded confidence in the model and added fuel to this protest movement. The Jubilee 2000 campaign to write off Third World debt was highly effective in mobilizing a transnational alliance of global citizens who could not easily be dismissed by G7 governments as anarchists and troublemakers. Demonstrations at Seattle, Genoa, and so on led some within G7 governments and the IMF and World Bank to question the political expediency of continued application of neoliberal development without modification. Indeed, there was concern amongst such groups that the global economic integration project might be derailed if the benefits of the project were not more evenly

Table 16.2 Impact of common structural adjustment measures

Intended result	Policy	Common impact on the poor sub-Saharan
Reduced budget deficit, freeing up money for debt servicing	Reducing government expenditure	Reduced health, education, and social-welfare spending and the introduction of cost recovery and user fees put health care and education beyond the reach of many ordinary people. Public-sector redundancies and salary freezes lead to fewer teachers and doctors.
Increased efficiency	Privatization of state-run industries	Massive lay-offs and increased unemployment with no social-security provision push families deeper into poverty.
Increased exports, boosting foreign-exchange reserves needed for debt repayment	Currency devaluation and export promotion	Cost of imports soar, including vital resources such as imported medicines. Moreover, export prices fall because many countries are promoting the same exports under SAPs, so countries are still no better off.
Reduced inflation	Raising interest rates	Farmers and small companies can no longer afford to borrow money and are forced to reduce production or go out of business.
Increased efficiency in food production	Removal of price controls	Basic food prices rise, putting even further pressure on already stretched household budgets.

distributed, and if civil society groups could not be made to understand the benefits of globalization.

Human security emerged from this general dissatisfaction with globalization. The concept has resonance for those scholars, global citizens, and policy-makers who are trying to make sense of the political world at the beginning of the twenty-first century and to devise appropriate policies for dealing with global challenges. It follows that human security represents a conscious attempt to relocate the security discourse, to move it from the impersonal terrain of inter-state relations and to embed it in a global social structure composed of humanity. In the process, the concept enables the analyst to challenge the notion of two separate worlds in which domestic security is set against the contrasting insecurity in the global political arena.

The UNDP *Human Development Report* (1994) puts the position this way: 'The concept of security has for too long been interpreted narrowly: as security of territory from external aggression, or as protection of national interest in foreign policy or as global security from threat of nuclear holocaust ... forgotten were the legitimate concerns of ordinary people who sought security in their daily lives.' The UNDP critique is clear and powerful. By placing the poor, the disadvantaged, the voiceless, the underrepresented, and the powerless at the core of the security agenda, the Human Security discourse recognizes that, for the majority of the people in the world, apparent 'marginal' or 'esoteric' concerns—such as environmental security, food security, and economic security—are far more real and immediate threats to their daily survival than inter-state wars. (See Chapter 8 for more on human security.) A human security approach requires us to explore issues relating to (i) level and (ii) scope of analysis.

Level of analysis

Human security requires a disaggregated (data separated into its component parts) and therefore richer, more sophisticated, exploration of the very complex and sometimes contradictory impacts of globalization on actual human experience across the globe. Mechanistic state-level analyses of security, which place the state at the centre of analysis, are based on zero-sum games, assumptions of governmental legitimacy, and impermeable borders. Human-security analysis places the individual at the centre of analysis and, in disaggregating the idea of the 'national', which in the South is not strong in many places, focuses on the perceptions and lived experience of real people and their communities rather than abstract nations or states.

Similarly, regarding development, in contrast to orthodox state-based analyses based on national income and expenditure data, the human security approach invites far greater disaggregation of data, and a consideration of additional criteria, thus potentially offering a fuller, richer, more meaningful picture. We are all well aware of the shortcomings of national averages; and, yet, measurements of development, poverty, water and food availability, and a host of other indicators have for too long relied on national per-capita averages. These often paint a very partial picture, and can be very misleading. Development economist Ravi Kanbur (2002) has highlighted the importance of disaggregation, using the example of Ghana to show that, while national data indicate a decrease in the poverty index over the period 1987–91, disaggregation of the data by region reveals that the poverty index for entire regions of the country worsened. He suggests further that disaggregation undertaken along lines of gender, ethnicity, race, etc., would reveal a complex picture.

A human security approach forces us to think about how global, national, and local structures/forces interrelate, and their cumulative impacts on individuals and communities. It requires us to ask: to what extent does the current form of globalization impact on the experience of human vulnerability across the globe, and how do governments at various levels mediate outcomes? What is the lived experience of globalization, and who is responsible for it? What does it look like to most of humanity? What does it feel like? Consider not politicians in Washington or Brussels, nor members of the core workforce of highly skilled people integrated into the global economy; but rather the majority of citizens, precarious workers, or the rest, the expanding pool of people in First and Third World states excluded from international production. What of those hopelessly marginalized by the globalization process, such as the over one billion people who are unemployed? How do the 1.4 billion people (more than one-quarter of the population of developing countries) living on $1.25 or less a day (for purchasing power parity, see Think Point 16.1) (World Bank 2008a: 1) feel about the current order? How do the HIV/AIDS sufferers in Africa feel, knowing that medication exists, but they cannot afford it, and that their governments either cannot or will not provide treatment? In contrast, how do the super rich 1 per cent of the global population—earning annually as much as the poorest 57 per cent of humanity combined (World Bank 2008a), and growing worldwide in relative wealth—experience the current form of globalization, living behind high walls and electronic fences, and with private security forces?

THINK POINT 16.1

What is purchasing power parity?

Purchasing power parity (PPP) is used to enable comparison of price levels between countries. PPP allows us, for example, to compare the price of a basket of products in one country, to the price of a similar basket of products in another country, allowing for variation in basket composition according to economic and socio-cultural differences between countries, but with each basket providing equivalent satisfaction or utility. PPP converts local currencies to a common currency, such as the US dollar, and involves the systematic collection of price data on hundreds of representative and carefully defined products and services consumed in each country. The international poverty line is calculated at purchasing power parity.

As an example: a person in India living on the international poverty line, set by the World Bank at $1.25 PPP per capita (or person) per day, would not actually have $1.25 a day (or the equivalent in Indian rupees) to spend in India, but would have only the equivalent purchasing power of spending $1.25 in the United States—perhaps, for example, the ability or power to purchase a loaf of bread.

OECD (2006: 261); World Bank (2008b: 1).

Scope of analysis

Human security provides a useful starting point for thinking about the inter-related nature of many current and future global political challenges. It requires us to investigate and reflect holistically on matters that affect the security of real people and their communities, and, where appropriate, to make connections in a way that traditional state-based analysis—whether in terms of the security debate or the development debate—has failed to do. Thus, it invites a consideration of whatever factors affect the security of human beings, ranging from state-sponsored repression, to international hostilities, to the climate, to environmental degradation or resource depletion, to the unregulated activities of multinationals, to fluctuating commodity prices, or to capital market volatility. Human security requires an analysis of the interconnections between these factors, as a necessary step to addressing the security concerns of human beings. For example, if mining companies fail to respect the local environment and render insecure the lives of local people, then an understanding of the vulnerability of those communities requires an analysis not only of the company, but of the national government that has failed to regulate the company in the public interest, and of the complicity of the global institutions that are promoting trade and investment liberalization via conditional loans without due regard to local impact.

Globalization of insecurity: human security framework

Manifestly, the benefits of globalization are enormous, as a result of the increased sharing of ideas, cultures, life-saving technologies, and efficient production processes. Yet, the euphoria these developments generate can often serve to disguise the very real social and economic inequalities that are not merely leftovers from the past, but the results of the globalizing process. Most obviously, global welfare inequalities have mushroomed alongside the noted advancements in technological developments and the rapid expansion of trade and investment. Take, for example, the gap in income and investment patterns since about 2000. In 2007, the richest 20 per cent of the world's population spent more than 75 per cent of the world total, while the poorest 20 per cent spent less than 2 per cent (World Bank 2008b: 4), or, in another way, the gap between the richest and the poorest 20 per cent of the world had increased to 86:1 and widens every day (UNDP 2008).

Similarly, at the beginning of this decade, the Organization for Economic Cooperation and Development (OECD) countries held over three-quarters of the accumulated stock of **foreign direct investment (FDI)** and attracted over 60 per cent of new FDI flows (see Table 16.3). In so far as FDI went to the developing countries (South), it was concentrated in ten countries, with China alone accounting for more than one-third (see Think

Point 16.2 for what constitutes FDI). Thus, foreign-investment resources are being concentrated on those countries—such as Thailand, Indonesia, Colombia, Malaysia, Taiwan—that are performing most strongly in global trade (OECD 2009). Eight countries that accounted for 30 per cent of developing country GDP absorbed

---

 THINK POINT 16.2

What is foreign direct investment?

Foreign direct investment (FDI) occurs where an entity—for example, an individual, a public or private enterprise, a government, or a group of entities—owns at least 10 per cent of a foreign (that is, non-resident) enterprise, with the aim of developing a long-term relationship between investor and enterprise. The Organization for Economic Cooperation and Development (OECD) proposes that FDI forms an essential part of the rapidly evolving process of international economic integration, creating direct, stable, and long-lasting links between economies. Furthermore, the OECD argues that FDI encourages the transfer of technology and knowledge capacity across borders, and enables the host economy to market its products more widely, internationally. Lastly, under the right policy environment, FDI, as an additional source of funding for capital investment, can be used to support enterprise development.

OECD (2009).

Table 16.3 Foreign direct investment (as percentage of global FDI flows), 1997–2008

Indicators	1997	1998	1999	2000	2006	2008
Developed countries	56.8	69.8	77.2	79.1	80.1	
Developing countries and economies	39.2	27.2	20.7	18.9	18.0	
Asia	22.4	13.8	9.3	11.3	11.2	
Latin America	14.9	12.0	10.3	6.8	6.8	
Africa	2.3	1.2	1.0	0.7	0.7	
Africa (as a percentage of developing countries)	5.88	4.63	4.72	3.78	3.87*	3.11**

* UNCTAD data 2009.

** UNDP 2009.

Source: ADB Statistics Division and IMF.

around two-thirds of total FDI (World Bank 2009: 14). At the other extreme, the forty-eight less-developed countries (LDCs) received around $800 million in FDI in 2008—roughly the same size as flows into Brazil, and less than 1 per cent of the total transfer to developing countries.

This uneven distribution of global investment patterns, with its associated selectivity and polarization of societies, has given rise to: a growing gap between the rich and poor within and between nations—in particular between North (the developed world) and South (developing world); the destruction of quality jobs and their replacement by casualization and temporary jobs brought by a process of subcontracting of so-called non-core business activities; growing unemployment, in particular in the developing countries, which goes hand in hand with poverty, which itself leads to more social problems; and mass migration in pursuit of adequate standards of living. As a result, a true process of immiseration is now observable in many parts of the world, particularly within developing countries. The facts of global inequalities are truly staggering: the richest twenty-five million Americans have an income equal to that of almost two billion people combined, while the assets of the world's three richest men, even after the recent fall in the value of stock markets, is greater than the com-

bined income of the world's LDCs with a population of more than 600 million (UNDP 2009).

The statistics show a bleak picture for global inequalities, particularly for the worst affected region: Africa. With a fifth of the world's population, Africa is home to one in three poor persons in the world, and four of every ten inhabitants live in what the World Bank (2006) classifies as a 'condition of absolute poverty'. Close to half the population of the continent live on less than a dollar a day. More worrying still, Africa is the only region in the world where both the absolute number and the proportion of poor people have *increased* in the last decade. If current trends continue, by 2015 half of the world's poor will live in Africa. It is also the case that income and wealth distributions are extremely unequal in many countries. Currently, a number of countries experience improved economic growth, but lack the policies and the will to redistribute the increased wealth, and inequality is therefore likely to increase rather than diminish. As regards links with the global economy, dependence on external resources, even for budgetary support, continues to increase, but the actual flows have fallen short of requirements. Commodity prices continue to fluctuate whilst the overall terms of trade are unfavourable (see Figure 16.1a).

In order to investigate different facets of human security, it is practical to break it down into measurable components. One way to do this is to see the Millennium Development Goals (MDGs) as expressions of threats to human security. Although they do not quite capture the non-material participatory aspect of human security, the MDGs provide tangible expressions of core aspects of human well-being—the first of which is to 'halve the proportion of people living in absolute poverty by 2015' (UNDP 2009). As shown above, sub-Saharan Africa is far from achieving this crucial objective, and is the only region in the world, not even making progress towards reaching it. This would require GDP growth of close to 7 per cent in every country. This is not happening, and, while some countries are recording impressive growth rates, this is not the case overall, and, where growth is taking place, it is only to a limited extent invested in such a way as to benefit the poor.

The second target of the first MDG is to halve the proportion of people who suffer from hunger (see Table 16.4). However, sub-Saharan Africa has made very little progress in eradicating hunger and malnutrition (see Figure 16.1b).

Indeed, the numbers of people suffering malnutrition has increased to well over 200 million in recent decades and the problem is especially severe in Central, East, and Southern Africa, where it is estimated that almost half of the population of 360 million is undernourished (see Figure 16.2).

Women and children are especially vulnerable to food insecurity and malnutrition, with the latter being especially important as a cause of under-5 mortality (UNDP 2009). Trends were actually reversed during the 1990s in those countries most affected by adverse growth in Gross Domestic Product and by the effects of HIV/AIDS. UNDP/UNICEF recently concluded that, 'during the 1990s, the spread of HIV/AIDS had a devastating effect on families and communities. The loss of productive capacity among families affected by HIV/AIDS had a major impact on food production and on nutritional well-being' (UNDP 2008).

Education is an important gateway to employment, as well as increased awareness of health and other issues that have the potential to increase individual and household well-being and reduce insecurity. Being out of school constitutes vulnerability in itself, in that, across Africa, the children not in school are the poorest and the most isolated. Although there has been overall progress in terms of total primary enrolment rates, which increased by 38 per cent between 1990 and 2000 (UNESCO 2008), these figures mask country and regional variations, and the problems surrounding the relevance of education, completion rates, and progression. Only 46 per cent of girls in sub-Saharan African complete primary

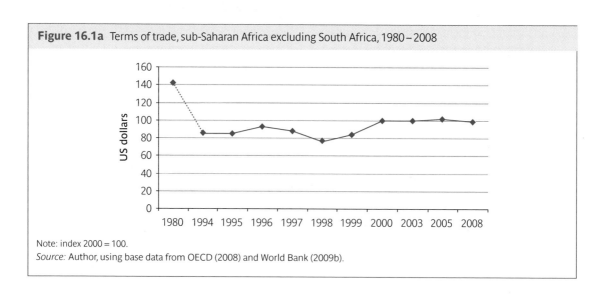

Figure 16.1a Terms of trade, sub-Saharan Africa excluding South Africa, 1980–2008

Note: index 2000 = 100.

Source: Author, using base data from OECD (2008) and World Bank (2009b).

Table 16.4 The Millennium Development Goals (MDGs) and targets

Goals	Targets
Goal 1 Eradicate extreme poverty and hunger	Target 1 Halve, between 1990 and 2015, the proportion of people whose income is less than $1 a day Target 2 Halve, between 1990 and 2015, the proportion of people who suffer from hunger
Goal 2 Achieve universal primary education	Target 3 Ensure that by 2015 children everywhere, boys and girls alike, will be able to complete a full course of primary schooling
Goal 3 Promote gender equality and empower women	Target 4 Eliminate gender disparity in primary and secondary education, preferably by 2005 and in all levels of education not later than 2015
Goal 4 Reduce child mortality	Target 5 Reduce by two-thirds, between 1990 and 2015, the under-5 mortality rate
Goal 5 Improve maternal health	Target 6 Reduce by three-quarters, between 1990 and 2015, the maternal mortality ratio
Goal 6 Combat HIV/AIDS, malaria, and other diseases	Target 7 Have halted by 2015 and begun to reverse the spread of HIV/AIDS

Figure 16.1b Increase in the proportion of the population who are hungry

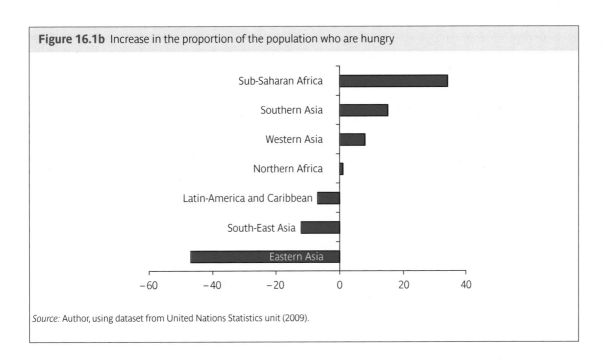

Source: Author, using dataset from United Nations Statistics unit (2009).

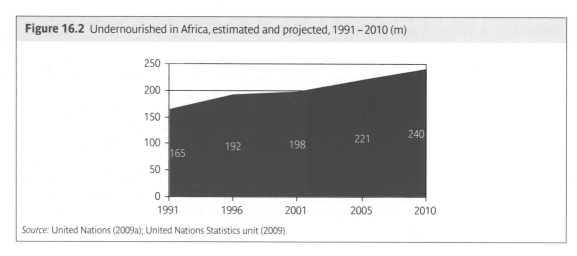

Figure 16.2 Undernourished in Africa, estimated and projected, 1991–2010 (m)

Source: United Nations (2009a); United Nations Statistics unit (2009).

school, and in seven countries have a 20 per cent less chance of starting primary school than boys (Benin, Niger, Burkina Faso, Chad, Ethiopia, Guinea Bissau, and Mali) (UNESCO 2008). The situation is likely to be extremely bad in those countries for which there are no reliable data available—the Democratic Republic of Congo (DRC), Somalia, and Liberia.

The target is that, by 2015, children everywhere, girls as well as boys, will be able to complete a full course of primary schooling. However, achieving universal primary education, as promoted through Education For All (EFA) goals of universal access and completion, is unlikely to be achieved by 2015 by most of the African countries, especially the poorest with large rural populations. This is especially true if the sole strategy for achieving EFA is based on the linear expansion of existing public school programmes. Clemens (2004) notes that data from ninety countries indicate that increasing enrolment from 50 per cent to 90 per cent takes an average of fifty-eight years, and, they assert, reaching 95 per cent enrolment by 2015 will require historically unprecedented growth rates; as we have noted earlier, this is not happening. Sub-Saharan Africa has made only marginal progress on closing the gender gap in primary and secondary enrolment since 1990, and the pace of change required is the most dramatic of any region. At the current rate of progress, gender parity in primary education in sub-Saharan Africa will not be reached until 2038— and this does not mean that every African girl will have claimed her right to primary and secondary

education by that date; it means only that there will be as many girls enrolled in school as boys by 2038 (World Bank 2008c).

While African countries saw some progress in educating children during the 1990s, this was not nearly enough to meet the goal set for 2015. In over a third of countries, every other child is not in school; while some countries have increased their enrolment rates (such as Uganda and Malawi), other countries actually experienced declines (such as Central African Republic, Lesotho, and South Africa) (see Figure 16.3).

There continue to be significant urban–rural gaps in enrolment, and in some countries the enrolment ratio in urban areas is some 2–3 times higher than for rural populations. Unless the educational targets are substantially achieved by 2020, then not only will millions of children be deprived of their right to basic education, but many of the other MDG targets will also be unachievable. A better-educated population is essential for the achievement of democratic states in Africa and for improvement in systems of governance. It is wholly improbable that economic growth and poverty reduction targets can be met without a better-educated and skilled population, and a more educated population is essential for improving labour productivity. Improved access to education for girls is also crucial for achieving progress on maternal and under-5 mortality, and for progress generally in the area of reproductive health.

Death is the ultimate threat, and MDG 3 encompasses two aims: to reduce by two-thirds the under-5

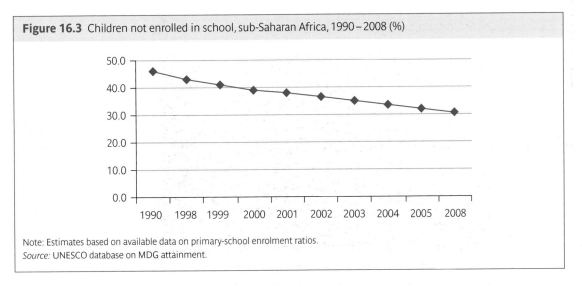

Figure 16.3 Children not enrolled in school, sub-Saharan Africa, 1990–2008 (%)

Note: Estimates based on available data on primary-school enrolment ratios.
Source: UNESCO database on MDG attainment.

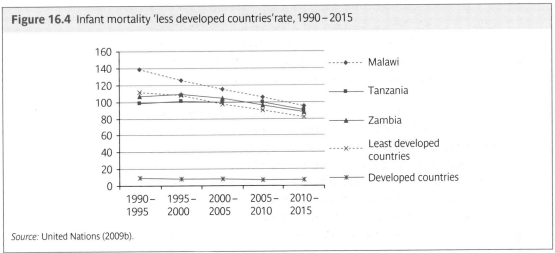

Figure 16.4 Infant mortality 'less developed countries' rate, 1990–2015

Source: United Nations (2009b).

mortality rate by 2015, and to reduce by three-quarters the maternal mortality ratio by the same date. At the present time, 15 per cent of all children in Africa will not live to see their fifth birthday. Progress in decreasing the infant mortality rate seems to have been reversed during since the late 1980s, and some countries, such as Zambia, Malawi, and Tanzania, have actually seen increases in infant mortality because of HIV/AIDS (see Figure 16.4). There also remain significant gaps between urban and rural rates in many countries, and it is clear that the probability of a child dying is much greater in poorer families than in richer ones (the probability is twice

as high for children in the bottom 20 per cent of the income distribution as it is in the top 20 per cent).

African countries currently account for about one-third of all maternal deaths worldwide, with about 250,000 women dying during pregnancy and childbirth every year. These trends seem, if anything, to have worsened since 2000, in part associated with deteriorating health-care systems (see Figure 16.5). But the primary problem, apart from poor access to health care, continues to be the continued high levels of fertility, and thus persistently high risks of maternal mortality. The comparative rates of maternal mortality between developing country regions strikingly emphasizes the gap between

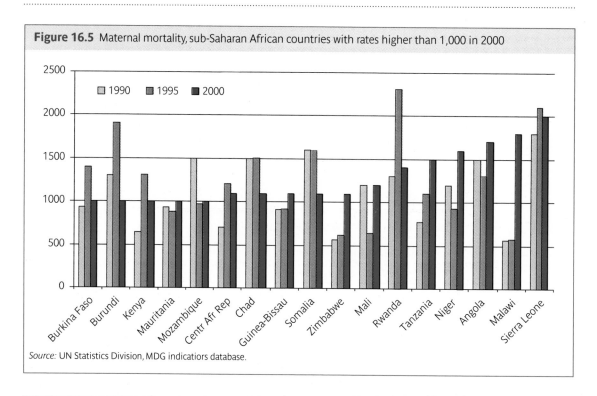

Figure 16.5 Maternal mortality, sub-Saharan African countries with rates higher than 1,000 in 2000

Source: UN Statistics Division, MDG indicatiors database.

KEY POINTS

- In the context of globalization, the threats posed to many people are of a wide variety, of lower intensity, and less well defined. Human security provides a framework for understanding these threats as they affect ordinary people and communities, by placing people at the centre of analysis, instead of states.

- The uneven distribution of global investment patterns with its associated selectivity and polarization of societies has given rise to: a growing gap between the rich and poor within and between nations; the destruction of quality jobs and growing unemployment; and mass migration in pursuit of adequate standards of living.

- Under World Bank and IMF SAPs in developing countries, government actions and control are seen as the cause of inflation, debt, and economic retrogression, while the private sector is promoted as the creator of efficiency and growth. Cuts in government expenditure have forced up the costs of primary education and health care beyond the reach of many ordinary people, while rushed privatization has resulted in mass unemployment, and the removal of price controls and the devaluation of the national currency have led to the cost of living spiralling upwards.

- Of the 1.4 billion people defined by the World Bank as the poorest—that is, those surviving on less than $1.25 per day—70 per cent are female. Poor women are often caught in a damaging cycle of cultural bias and gender discrimination that further exposes them to poverty, exploitation, and disease, most notably HIV/AIDS.

Africa and other regions—in Africa a woman faces a 1 in 13 chance of dying in childbirth compared with 1 in 160 in Latin America and 1 in 280 in East Asia.

The gendered links between health, poverty, and global restructuring can be illustrated with parti-cular clarity through the HIV/AIDS epidemic (Poku 2006). This began as a disease primarily affecting men who have sex with men in developed countries, but has become a major killer of poor women. Last year more that 1.3 million women died from AIDS, and there are now more than 16.4 million women living with HIV/AIDS. Since the mid-2000s, the proportion of women among people who are HIV positive has risen from 41 per cent to 47 per cent. The reasons behind this shift in the epidemiology of the disease are complex, but very often poverty is the context within which infection occurs.

Transformative agenda for development

For some commentators the securitization of issues related to livelihoods is quite problematic, not least because it risks mixing up the quite different agendas of international security, on the one hand, and social security and civil liberties, on the other. Barry Buzan, for example, readily accepts the case for studying the interplay between the international and domestic security agendas, but cautions against a reductionist approach that prioritizes the individual security above the collective good. He puts the position this way: 'while a moral case for making individuals the ultimate referent can be constructed, the cost to be paid is loss of analytical purchase on collective actors, both as the main agents of security provision, and as possessors of a claim to survival in their own right' (Buzan 2004a). Roland Paris (2001) pursues the theme further, noting that 'existing definitions of human security tend to be extraordinarily expansive and vague, encompassing everything from physical security to psychological well-being'. This, he argues, provides policy-makers with little guidance in prioritizing competing policy demands, and academics with little sense of what is to be studied.

Individuals are not free standing, but take their meaning only from the societies in which they operate: they are not some kind of bottom line to which all else can or should be reduced or subordinated. So if, as Buzan has stated, human security sought simply to collapse all the possible referent objects for security into a single one, then he would be right to caution against such a process, as it would exclude the claims of both collective and non-human (for example, environmental) referent objects in a way that defies both other moral claims and the actual practices of securitization. Indeed, reductionism of this type would not only eliminate the distinctiveness of international security—being about interaction among social collectivities; it would also challenge the viability of security studies as a discipline. It is perhaps this potential realization that worries Roland Paris so much! This, of course, is not to say that Paris and others may not have a fundamental point: namely, the need for greater prioritization of the issues covered under the umbrella of human security and relatedly the development of improved analytical tools better to understand these issues.

In reality, however, the critics of human security have missed a fundamental point about the utility value of the concept. The very breadth and inclusiveness of the concept serves a political function that perhaps explains the enthusiasm with which it has been embraced by practitioners of development. Far from being a reductionist concept, human security should be conceived as emancipatory; encompassing and empowering the hopes and aspirations of a group of people—development practitioners, NGOs, donor organizations—for a better world: a world in which children are not allowed to die from preventable diseases; where epidemics like HIV/AIDS are not allowed to decimate an entire continent; where ethnic prejudice is not allowed to result in gratuitous violence or, worse, genocide; where women are not illegally trafficked or sexually abused; and where corruption is not allowed to continue to reduce millions of people to a bleak and vulnerable future. These are issues with an emotional charge of a kind that only a subjectifying narrative can fully convey, and around which a coalition of forces are needed to bring radical political change.

A consideration of the values underpinning human security suggests that policies devised in support of its achievement must be geared towards social transformation, not in the sense proposed by the neoliberal agenda, but rather in the sense of the radical politics of equality, solidarity, sustainability, and so forth. The human security approach offers a conceptual shift, which is necessary to meet the changed conditions of mutual vulnerability that increasingly characterize the globalized world. An analysis based on simple 'one-size-fits-all' national security or national-development indicators is limited. A human-

KEY POINTS

- For some commentators the securitization of issues related to livelihoods is quite problematic, not least because it risks mixing up the quite different agendas of international security, on the one hand, and social security and civil liberties, on the other. However, they have missed the fundamental point about the utility value of the concept. The very breadth and inclusiveness of the concept serve a political function that perhaps explains the enthusiasm with which it has been embraced by practitioners of development—encompassing and empowering the hopes and aspirations for a better world.

- A consideration of the values underpinning human security suggests that policies devised in support of its achievement must be geared towards social transformation, not in the sense proposed by the neoliberal agenda, but rather the radical politics of equality, solidarity, sustainability, and so forth.

- An analysis based on simple 'one-size-fits-all' national security or national-development indicators is limited. A human security analysis, by contrast, is more in tune with lived experience on the ground, where 'multiple factors affect the existence of concrete people', charging us to identify causes of insecurity wherever we find them and to work to overcome them at multiple levels.

security analysis, by contrast, is more in tune with lived experience on the ground, where ' multiple factors affect the existence of concrete people' (Nef 1999: 23). It charges us to identify causes of insecurity wherever we find them—including within the structure and functioning of the global whole—and to work to overcome them at multiple levels.

This contrasts sharply with the largely 'business-as-usual' approaches that hang on to the state as the primary referent, whether emanating from the security community—for example, the securitization of issues such as disease, environmental change, and so on (Buzan, Wæver, and de Wilde 1998) or the development community—for example, voices calling for a reassessment of rational choice, and standard national development and poverty indicators (e.g. Sachs 2009). For Jorge Nef (1999: 23), adherence to such modified orthodoxies is limiting, because it fails to engage with the most important question: 'whose security and whose interests are at stake, or more specifically, of what the connection is between the abstract public, or "national" interest and the specific and concrete interests of diverse national and international constituencies'.

Conclusion

The global social problems arising today and the trends predicted for future decades are not amenable to grand solutions, nor can they be tackled by discrete, bounded sovereign states. The latter do not exist in practice, and, even if they did, they could not use the old security frame of referents to tackle the increasing range of transboundary problems that confront humanity. In a globalized world, environmental problems and disease recognize neither social nor political boundaries. Consequently, if the rich world helps address the problem in the poor world, it is helping secure not just 'them', but 'us' too. The human-security framework offers a conceptual vehicle through which to direct this assistance in a way that responds to the multiple factors affecting the existence of people as individuals, families, and communities, and to identify causes of insecurity wherever they can be found, and to work to overcome them at multiple levels.

QUESTIONS

1. Outline the key features of globalization and insecurity?

2. Can security ever be conceived of in the human interest?

3. Is human security simply the expansion and securitization of human rights?

4. The pursuits of state security and human security are fundamentally at odds. Discuss.

5. Are the pursuits of state security and human security fundamentally at odds?

6. Does the human-security approach necessarily undermine the concept of state sovereignty?

7. 'While a moral case for making individuals the ultimate referent can be constructed, the cost to be paid is loss of analytical purchase on collective actors, both as the main agents of security provision, and as possessors of a claim to survival in their own right.' (Barry Buzan.) Discuss.

8. Assess the role of international financial institutions in the growing inequalities between the rich (North) and poor (South) countries in global politics.

FURTHER READING

■ Glenn, John (2008), *Globalization: North – South Perspectives,* Oxford: Routledge. This book provides a very good introduction to globalization and its impacts across the developed and developing world.

■ McGrew, Anthony, and Poku, Nana K. (2007), *Globalization, Development and Human Security,* Cambridge: Polity. This book contains a series of essays by leading scholars on the challenges that globalization is posing for development.

■ Scholte, Jan Aart (2005), *Globalization: A Critical Introduction*, 2nd edn., Basingstoke: Palgrave Macmillan. This is an excellent and highly accessible book, exploring the dimensions of globalization, and the rise of superterritoriality.

■ Thomas, Caroline (2000), *Global Governance, Development and Human Security,* London: Pluto Press. This is one of the finest books on human security and the challenges posed to it by globalization.

■ United Nations Development Programme (1994), *Human Development Report*, Oxford: Oxford University Press. This seminal work by the UNDP introduced the notion of human security to the world as a conceptual framework for understanding the globalization and its differential impacts across the globe.

IMPORTANT WEBSITES

● http://www.un.org/millenniumgoals United Nations Millennium Development Goals (MDGs). This website provide access to the MDGs and documents related to it.

● http://www.humansecurity-chs.org/activities/meetings/first/overview.pdf   Commission on Human Security 'Overview for the Commission on Human Security'. This link is to the Human Security Commission's report.

● www.undp.org/publications/annualreport2008/downloads.shtml   The UNDP *Human Development Report* (Oxford: Oxford University Press). All the formal documentation of globalization and inequality can be found in the various UNDP reports stored on this site.

● http://www.unctad.org/en/docs/ldc2002_en.pdf UNCTAD, *The Least Developed Countries' Report: Escaping the Poverty Trap*, Geneva. UNCTAD is the best source on issues of global trade and poverty.

 Visit the Online Resource Centre that accompanies this book for lots of interesting additional material: www.oxfordtextbooks.co.uk/orc/collins2e/

PART 3

Traditional and Non-Traditional Security

17

Coercive Diplomacy

PETER VIGGO JAKOBSEN

Reader's Guide

Coercive diplomacy involves the use of threats and/or limited force in order to convince an actor to stop or undo actions already undertaken. The use of threats/limited force may, but need not, be accompanied by offers of inducements in order to enhance the adversary's incentive to comply with the coercer's demand. Coercive diplomacy has become part and parcel of Western conflict management since the end of the Cold War, but the Western states have been bad at translating their overwhelming military superiority into coercive diplomacy successes. In addition to explaining this failure, this chapter will relate coercive diplomacy to other threat-based strategies such as deterrence and compellence. It will explain the increasing resort to coercive diplomacy since the Cold War, indicate when the strategy is likely to be employed by Western-led coalitions, explain why coercive diplomacy succeeds and fails, identify the limitations of the strategy, and assess the prospects for its successful use in the future.

Introduction

The principal strategic challenge facing the Western states and the international community as a whole during the Cold War was the avoidance of great-power war. The risk that a local armed conflict could escalate into nuclear war between the two superpower blocs naturally put a premium on policies and instruments that sought to prevent this worst-case scenario. The principal mission performed by Western military forces during this period was thus to deter the Soviet Union from attacking their homelands. This mission disappeared with the collapse of the Soviet Union and was replaced by the more challenging one of managing the disorder emanating from internal wars in weak or failing states, mass violations of human rights committed within the borders of sovereign states, and efforts by a small number of states and non-state actors to acquire or develop weapons of mass destruction (WMD). Instead of preventing Western adversaries from acting, the principal post-Cold War challenge has been to persuade, coerce, and, on occasion, force them to change their behaviour.

The favourable geopolitical environment characterized by an overwhelming Western military superiority and a low risk of hostile great-power intervention generated pressures on, as well as incentives for, Western policy-makers to use threats and force in order to promote their interests. It is, therefore, not surprising that they began to use coercive diplomacy and force more often than had been the case during the Cold War. Coercive diplomacy was employed against Iraq in the run-up to the 1991 Gulf War and subsequently in the various crises created by the Iraqi unwillingness to cooperate with the United Nations (UN) inspectors seeking to determine whether Iraq had terminated its WMD programmes; it was employed by the Western powers in the Balkans in their attempts to manage the armed conflicts in Bosnia and in Kosovo; and the United States employed it against the military

leadership in Haiti to reverse the overthrow of the first democratically elected president.

The 9/11 attacks on the World Trade Center and the Pentagon in 2001 reinforced this trend by increasing the American willingness to threaten and use force to counter the threats emanating from mass casualty terrorism, WMD proliferation, and failing states (White House 2002). Since 9/11 coercive diplomacy has been employed in attempts to coerce Iran, Iraq, Libya, and North Korea to stop their development of nuclear weapons; and in attempts to coerce the Taliban in Afghanistan to stop supporting al-Qaeda. Finally, it has also been employed in the so-called war against terror to coerce states, terrorist groups, and non-state actors from cooperating with al-Qaeda and affiliated groups.

Success does not explain the increased resort to coercive diplomacy. Coercive diplomacy failed to coerce Iraq to comply fully with UN and US demands between 1990 and 2003; it failed to coerce the Taliban to stop supporting al-Qaeda; success came at a high cost in Bosnia and Kosovo, where thousands were killed before the North Atlantic Treaty Organization (NATO) in the end had to bomb the Serbs to the negotiating table; and its effectiveness with respect to coercing non-state actors and terrorist groups to stop their support and cooperation with al-Qaeda and its associates is unclear. To date, the strategy's potential for peaceful conflict resolution has been realized only three times: in 1994, when Haiti's generals were coerced to step down; in 2001, when Pakistan was coerced to stop supporting the Taliban; and in 2003, when Libya was coerced to terminate its support for terrorism and its nuclear programme. But even though the strategy has not been particularly successful and its potential for peaceful conflict resolution is realized only rarely, it is likely to remain central to Western conflict management because of the continuing need to stop or undo hostile and destabilizing actions.

The difficulty of translating Western military superiority into coercive diplomacy success came as a surprise to Western governments in both Bosnia and Kosovo. This difficulty is less surprising from a theoretical perspective, as the existing theories regard coercive diplomacy as a high-risk, hard-to-use strategy. But the theoretical understanding of coercive diplomacy remains wanting in several respects. A better understanding of the strategy and its requirements for success is, therefore, required to enhance the strategy's potential for resolving conflicts short of war.

KEY POINTS

- The end of the Cold War rivalry made it easier for Western states to threaten and use force because the risk of uncontrollable escalation vanished.

- Coercive diplomacy has become an integral part of Western crisis and conflict management.

- Western military superiority should make coercive diplomacy easier to conduct successfully.

- It has proved difficult to use coercive diplomacy to stop or reverse acts of aggression, end (support for) terrorism, and end WMD programmes.

- Coercive diplomacy will continue to play a central role in Western conflict management in the foreseeable future, because the need to stop or undo undesirable actions remains a key challenge.

- Understanding the conditions under which coercive diplomacy succeeds or fails represents a major challenge for theory and practice.

What is coercive diplomacy?

Coercive diplomacy seeks to resolve crises and armed conflicts without resorting to full-scale war. It relies on threats and the limited use of force to influence an adversary to stop or undo the consequences of actions already undertaken. The use of threats and limited force (sticks) may be coupled with the use of inducements (carrots) to enhance the adversary's incentive to comply with the coercer's demand, but the stick has to instil fear in the mind of the adversary for the strategy to qualify as coercive diplomacy. If compliance is not caused, partly at least, by fear of the coercer's threat, then coercion has not taken place. A strategy that stops aggression or a WMD programme by buying off the opponent constitutes appeasement, not coercive diplomacy.

Compellence is another term for coercive diplomacy, but it covers a broader set of phenomena. Whereas coercive diplomacy only covers reactive threats employed in response to actions taken by an adversary, compellence also involves threats aimed at initiating adversary action. A threat to coerce a state to give up part of its territory would thus count as compellence but not as coercive diplomacy, because the latter covers only situations where the adversary has made the first move.

It is also the reactive nature that distinguishes coercive diplomacy from its sister strategy of deterrence, which involves the use of threats to influence adversaries not to undertake undesired actions in the first place. Deterrence is used before the adversary has acted, whereas coercive diplomacy is employed once the adversary has taken the first step. Deterrence was the cornerstone of the Western strategy employed against the Soviet Union during the Cold War. The Western states threatened to respond to a Soviet attack by using nuclear weapons in the hope that it would convince the Soviet leadership that an attack on the Western states would be too costly. If a deterrent threat fails to prevent an attack, the coercer then has to consider whether to respond by threatening to use force to influence the enemy to stop the attack and withdraw, to use limited force to influence the enemy to do so, or to use full-scale or brute force to force it to stop and withdraw.

Whereas the use of threats and limited force count as coercive diplomacy, the use of brute force to defeat the attacker does not. Coercive diplomacy is employed in order to avoid or limit the use of force. It is an influence strategy that is intended to obtain compliance from the adversary without defeating it first. It leaves an element of choice with the target; it has to make a decision whether to comply or to fight on. Full-scale or brute force, on the other hand, aims at defeating the adversary. It seeks not to influence but to control by imposing compliance upon the adversary by depriving it of any say in the issue at hand. The 2001–2 Afghanistan War illustrates this difference. The United States initially threatened to attack the Taliban regime unless Osama bin Laden and other key al-Qaeda leaders were handed over and their training camps closed. Non-compliance then led to American air strikes on key military installations, coupled with threats of escalation. In the first phase of the war, the United States refrained from attacking the Taliban frontlines and from providing direct military support to the Northern Alliance, the Afghan groups that were fighting the Taliban. It also, somewhat unconvincingly, offered to leave the Taliban regime in place if it complied with US demands. When the United States became convinced that compliance was not forthcoming, it escalated its use of force to defeat the Taliban. At that stage the American strategy changed from influence to control.

The distinction between limited force and full-scale/brute force is crucial, because resort to brute force means that coercive diplomacy has failed. It is important to understand that this distinction is not based on the number of bombs dropped on the adversary. The distinction rests on the purpose that the use of force seeks to accomplish and the element of choice left to the adversary. Coercive diplomacy uses limited force as a bargaining tool. It is used to increase the costs of non-compliance and to threaten with more of the same unless compliance is forthcoming. It always leaves room for the adversary to decide whether to comply or not. Brute force does not leave such a choice; its purpose is to defeat the adversary. The resort to brute force means that diplomacy has been abandoned and that the coercer has lost faith in negotiation and decided to impose its will by force.

The distinction can be difficult to make in practice, but a useful rule of thumb is that use of air and sea power will usually be limited in nature, as it leaves the decision whether to comply or to suffer more attacks to the adversary. The air campaigns in the 1991 Gulf War and the 1999 Kosovo War provide examples of the use of limited force as part of coercive diplomacy strategies. The ground war that followed the air campaign in the Gulf War signified a shift from coercive diplomacy to brute force. Once the land campaign had begun, force was no longer used to 'persuade' Iraq to withdraw its forces from Kuwait, but rather physically to throw them out. As a consequence, the initiation of the land war also meant that coercive diplomacy had failed.

Note that this definition of 'limited' force allows for major use of force. The strategic air campaigns waged against Germany and Japan during the Second World War thus constitute limited force according to this definition, even though the number of bombs dropped and the damage inflicted were enormous. For this reason, limited force is typically defined as 'demonstrative' or 'symbolic' use, meaning 'just enough force of an appropriate kind to demonstrate resolution and to give credibility to the threat that greater force will be used if necessary' (George and Simons 1994: 10; Art 2003: 9). This definition is vague and hard to employ in practice, which is why this chapter defines 'limited' in terms of how force is used rather than in terms of how much. The practical implication is that the scope for coercive diplomacy success is broadened. NATO's air campaign in the Kosovo conflict is thus counted as a coercive diplomacy success in this chapter, whereas the more conventional definition employed by Art, George, and others will result in the coding of this case as a failure.

The distinction between coercive diplomacy and full-scale use of force cannot be made solely on the basis of how force is used, however. When coercive diplomacy is used as part of an escalation sequence, which culminates in brute force, as was the case in the 1991 Gulf War, the 2001–2 Afghanistan War, and the 2003 Iraq War, it has to be determined whether the coercer was pursuing a peaceful solution or merely using threats and limited force in order to legitimize the resort to brute force that

followed. One way to do this is to consider whether the coercer deliberately made demands that it knew that the adversary could not meet, and whether the adversary was denied sufficient time to comply. If that is the case, the conclusion must be that the coercer preferred war to adversary compliance. It has been debated in the wake of the 2003 Iraq War whether the Bush administration preferred regime change to compliance in order to get rid of Saddam Hussein once and for all. If that were the case, the American use of threats in the run-up to the war would not qualify as coercive diplomacy.

KEY POINTS

- Coercive diplomacy seeks to resolve crises and armed conflicts short of full-scale war.

- It is a reactive strategy relying on threats, limited force, and inducements to influence an adversary to stop or undo the consequences of actions already undertaken.

- Coercive diplomacy is an influence strategy that leaves the choice between compliance and defiance to the adversary.

- Full-scale or brute force is a control strategy that deprives the adversary of any choice by forcing compliance upon it.

- Escalation from limited to brute force means that coercive diplomacy has failed.

- Use of threats and limited force constitute coercive diplomacy only if the coercer prefers compliance to full-scale war.

Theories and requirements for success

Whereas the study of deterrence, which enjoyed a dominant position in the field of strategic studies during the Cold War, has produced books and articles enough to fill an entire library, the works on coercive diplomacy and compellence do not fill more than a bookshelf. Whereas an Internet search for deterrence produces 7.81 million hits, coercive diplomacy and compellence produce only 94,700 and 17,500 hits respectively.

Although the practice of coercive diplomacy, as it has been defined here, has always been an integral part of crisis and conflict management, theorizing about it has not been a popular pastime. Only two major theoretical works exist: Thomas C. Schelling's *Arms and Influence* (1966), which coined the term compellence, and Alexander L. George et al.'s *Limits*

to Coercive Diplomacy (1971), which pioneered the study of coercive diplomacy. These classic works continue to shape the study of coercive diplomacy today. Schelling deductively identified five conditions necessary for success, but he did not try to formulate specific policy prescriptions or confront his conditions with empirical evidence (see Key Ideas 17.1).

In contrast, George and his associates employed an inductive research strategy with the objective of developing a policy-relevant theory. They relied on case-study analysis to identify fourteen factors influencing the outcome of coercive-diplomacy attempts (see Key Ideas 17.2). George and his associates distinguish between contextual variables and conditions favouring success, and the idea is that they should be used by decision-makers at different

KEY IDEAS 17.1

Schelling's necessary conditions for compellence success

1. The threat conveyed must be sufficiently potent to convince the adversary that the costs of non-compliance will be unbearable.

2. The threat must be credible in the mind of the adversary; he must be convinced that the coercer has the will and the capability to execute it in case of non-compliance.

3. The adversary must be given time to comply with the demand.

4. The coercer must assure the adversary that compliance will not lead to more demands in the future.

5. The conflict must not be perceived as zero-sum. A degree of common interest in avoiding full-scale war must exist. Each side must be persuaded that it can gain more by bargaining than by trying unilaterally to take what it wants by force.

Adapted from Schelling (1966: 1, 3–4, 69–76, 89).

KEY IDEAS 17.2

George and Simons' checklist of factors influencing the use of coercive diplomacy

Contextual variables

1. Global strategic environment
2. Type of provocation
3. Image of war
4. Unilateral or coalitional coercive diplomacy
5. The isolation of the adversary

Conditions favouring success

1. Clarity of objective
2. Strength of motivation
3. *Asymmetry of motivation*
4. *Sense of urgency*
5. Strong leadership
6. Domestic support
7. International support
8. *Opponent's fear of unacceptable escalation*
9. *Clarity concerning the precise terms of settlement of the crisis*

Note: *Italicized* factors are deemed 'particularly significant' for success.

George and Simons (1994: 271–4, 287–8, 292).

stages of the policy-making process. The contextual variables should be used initially to decide whether coercive diplomacy is a viable strategy in a given crisis. The success variables enter the decision-making process in the second stage only if analysis of the contextual variables suggests that a coercive diplomacy strategy may work. The success variables are then supposed to help policy-makers in the task of conceiving an effective strategy.

The main strength of Schelling's theory is its coherent and parsimonious nature. But parsimony is also its greatest weakness, as its highly abstract nature makes it difficult to use in practice. Schelling offers no help to policy-makers wanting to know how to devise a potent threat, to make a threat credible in the mind of the opponent, or to assure the adversary that compliance will not lead to new demands. Schelling himself gave up when asked by the Johnson administration to use his theory to devise an air campaign against North Vietnam in 1964. The administration then had a go itself, but the result—Operation Rolling Thunder—failed to coerce the North Vietnamese to comply with US demands (Kaplan 1983: 330–6).

The problem is exactly the opposite with the George and Simons' checklist, as the high number of factors makes it hard to use and coercive-diplomacy outcomes difficult to explain. It is hard to know which of the many factors actually cause success or failure in a given case. According to George and Simons, success is unlikely unless all their nine success conditions are present, but logically the presence of their four 'particularly-significant' conditions should suffice. One would expect the opponent to comply if it fears unacceptable escalation, perceives the balance of interest as unfavourable, feels the need to comply as urgent, and regards the terms of settlement as clear. Even more problematic is the failure to operationalize several of the factors in a way that makes it possible to measure whether they apply or not in a given crisis. The three of the four conditions deemed 'particularly significant', asymmetry of motivation, opponent's fear of unacceptable escalation, and urgency for compliance, can be measured only after the fact. This significantly reduces the analytic value of their checklist.

Jakobsen's *ideal policy* attempts to overcome the weaknesses in Schelling's and George's work (see Key Ideas 17.3). The *ideal policy* was developed with two objectives in mind. The first was to reduce the number of success conditions to a more manageable number. For this reason it is narrower in scope and developed to apply to attempts to counter aggression only, but its logic should hold for attempts to counter terrorism and WMD acquisition as well. The second was to operationalize the success conditions to make it possible to determine whether they apply or not in specific crises. To minimize the risk of excluding important factors, the *ideal policy* incorporates Schelling's necessary conditions for success and the conditions that George and Simons deem particularly significant.

The first success condition in the *ideal policy* is designed to make the threat so potent that non-compliance will be too costly for actors that have resorted to force. Opponents who have resorted to force have signalled a willingness to accept high costs to achieve their goals, making it reasonable to assume that threats of force will be required to make non-compliance too costly in most cases. The poor record that economic sanctions have with respect to

stopping or reversing military aggression supports this assumption (Jakobsen 1998: 27). That sanctions usually take a long time to work is another reason why they are ill suited for stopping military aggression, which in most cases will require swift action.

It is not enough merely to issue a threat of force, however. The nature of the military action threatened is very important. To make non-compliance too costly, the coercer must threaten to defeat the adversary or deny him his objectives quickly with little cost in terms of blood and treasure. The threat has to be designed in this way to accomplish two things. The first is to create the fear of unacceptable escalation in the mind of the opponent, which George and Simons emphasize as particularly significant for success. A threat to deny the opponent what it so desperately wants is the most direct way to do this. The second is to make the threat credible in the eyes of the opponent; threats of quick, low-cost defeats are essential to this end. In the light of the difficulties that Western democracies have with respect to sustaining domestic support and suffering casualties in conflicts not threatening their vital interests, opponents will regard Western threats involving a commitment to fight a protracted war in such conflicts as bluff. A threat to fight a prolonged war will be credible in the eyes of the opponent only if the coercer's vital interests are directly threatened. Threats to defeat the opponent quickly with few costs are hence essential for credibility in most cases. In practice this means that the coercer not only needs to enjoy a significant military superiority; it must also be capable of denying the opponent the ability to retaliate and impose costs on the opponent. The coercer must, in the words of Byman et al. (1999), enjoy 'escalation-dominance'. The lack of escalation dominance and the perception that vital interests were not at stake explain the failure of the Western powers to coerce the Bosnian Serbs between 1992 and 1995. Western coercion was invariably countered by a variety of Bosnian Serb responses aimed at undermining Western resolve. Typical were empty promises to comply with Western demands, threats aimed at deterring the Western

KEY IDEAS 17.3

Jakobsen's ideal policy (1998) identifying the minimum conditions for success

1. A threat of force to defeat the opponent or deny him his objectives quickly with little cost.
2. A deadline for compliance.
3. An assurance to the adversary against future demands.
4. An offer of inducements for compliance.

powers from executing their threats and acts of escalation such as hostage taking. The Bosnian Serbs used hostage taking of UN personnel to neutralize NATO air strikes with great success between April 1994 and July 1995, when the Western powers took effective measures to reduce the vulnerability of their troops in Yugoslavia to retaliation (Jakobsen 1998: 107).

To maximize credibility, a threat of quick defeat backed by the required capability is not sufficient, however. A deadline for compliance must accompany it. The literature on misperception and deterrence failure shows that decision-makers finding themselves in no-win situations are likely to interpret the actions and signals made by their opponent in a manner consistent with their own expectations and desires (Jervis 1976). An actor being asked to stop or undo an act of aggression or terminate a costly WMD programme can hence be expected to be prone to wishful thinking. It follows that failure to set a deadline for compliance is likely to be interpreted as evidence that the coercer lacks the will to implement the threat. Opponents will simply not perceive a threat of force as credible unless it is accompanied by a deadline for compliance. A deadline for compliance hence constitutes the second condition in the *ideal policy*. Apart from reducing the risk of misperception and miscalculation, a deadline also serves to reduce the scope for delaying tactics and counter-coercion.

Assurance against new demands must also be included in the *ideal policy* to enhance the prospects of success. As pointed out by Schelling, the opponent's incentive to comply will be significantly reduced if he fears that compliance will merely result in new demands. George and Simons make the same point when they stress clear terms of settlement as a 'particularly-significant' condition for success. The Finnish refusal to hand over a few small islands to the Soviet Union in 1939 illustrates the importance of providing assurances. Fear that compliance would result in more demands played an important role in their refusal, which triggered the Winter War (Jakobsen 1961: 139).

Use of inducements is the fourth and last ingredient in the *ideal policy*. Inducements should be used as sweeteners or face-savers to help an opponent fearing the coercer's threat to comply with a minimum of humiliation. By increasing the opponent's incentive to comply, inducements help to prevent zero-sum situations (Schelling's fifth condition), and they also serve to give more credibility to assurances against future demands. (The cases summarized below clearly demonstrate that the use of inducements enhance the prospects of success.) Inducements are involved in most of the successes and absent in most of the failures. The findings are not so strong as to suggest that inducements are necessary for success, but strong enough to suggest that inducements are important facilitators that may make the difference between success and failure.

The *ideal policy* improves upon Schelling's and George's lists of success conditions in at least three ways. First, it can explain the outcome of attempts to use coercive diplomacy to stop/undo military aggression just as accurately with fewer conditions. Second, all the conditions in the *ideal policy* framework are operationalized so that it becomes easier to determine whether they are present or not in a given case. Third, it is an analytical tool that requires little knowledge about the opponent. It rests on the claim that one can explain and predict outcomes of coercive diplomacy attempts against aggressors by focusing on the policy pursued by the coercer and black-boxing the opponent. If the coercer lacks the capability and the will to meet the requirements of the *ideal policy*, coercive diplomacy can be expected to fail. While it goes without saying that a coercer needs a good understanding of the adversary and actionable intelligence to devise the most effective mix of threats and inducements in a real-world crisis, the *ideal policy* remains useful because it highlights what the coercer at a minimum must do to succeed, and because actionable intelligence is scarce on most Western adversaries.

This said, implementation of the *ideal policy* does not guarantee success. Whereas non-implementation of the *ideal policy* is a recipe for failure, its implementation only maximizes the probability of success.

A coercive diplomacy attempt meeting the requirements of the *ideal policy* may fail because of factors outside the coercer's control, such as misperception or miscalculation by the opponent, or because the opponent prefers to fight and lose to preserve honour rather than complying with the coercer's demand.

It cannot, and is not intended to, explain why a government decided (not) to implement the *ideal policy*. A complete theory should also specify the conditions under which Western governments will be willing to meet the requirements for success. These conditions are discussed further in the conclusion.

KEY POINTS

- Coercive diplomacy is an understudied strategy.

- Schelling and George laid the foundations for the study of coercive diplomacy.

- Jakobsen's *ideal-policy* framework focuses on the use of coercive diplomacy to counter aggression.

- The *ideal-policy* framework explains and predicts coercive diplomacy outcomes with a minimum of success conditions on the basis of the coercer's actions only.

- A complete theory should also specify when the success conditions are likely to be met.

The challenge of defining success

Defining coercive diplomacy success is easy in theory. Coercive diplomacy succeeds when the communication of a threat or the use of limited force produces adversary compliance with the coercer's demands. Non-compliance equals failure. In practice, four factors complicate the task of defining success. First, most studies of coercive diplomacy define success in binary terms: coercive diplomacy either fails or succeeds. The problem with this approach is that success in most cases is a question of degree. Coercers may settle for partial compliance or reduce their demands in the negotiation process that coercive diplomacy by definition involves. To give an example, Serbia complied with NATO's demands regarding Kosovo in 1999 only after NATO had lowered its demands. This has led some to claim that Serbia was not coerced by NATO, and that Serbian compliance resulted from NATO's concessions and the loss of Russian support.

This example also illustrates a related second problem: that it will often be difficult to isolate the effect that the threat of force or the use of limited force has had in a specific case. As discussed earlier, compliance must partly be caused by fear for

coercion to have taken place. This was undoubtedly the case in Kosovo, as Serbian compliance (and Serbia's loss of Russian support) would not have been forthcoming in the absence of NATO's air campaign. The stick does not have to be sufficient for success, however, since it would certainly be wrong to regard a case where both inducements and sticks proved necessary for compliance as a coercive diplomacy failure. The question to ask is consequently not whether the stick employed as part of coercive diplomacy strategy was sufficient for success, but whether it was a necessary contributing factor.

Third, the price of success must be weighed against the degree of coercion employed. Ideally, coercion should not be required at all to solve disputes. But, if the threshold from persuasion to coercion is crossed, the degree of successfulness is negatively correlated with the amount of coercion (and inducement) required for compliance. When the threshold between limited and brute force is crossed, coercive diplomacy fails. The challenge, in short, is to obtain compliance without having to use force.

Table 17.1 Measuring success

Strategies	Diplomacy	Coercive diplomacy (CD)		War
Instruments	Persuasion and inducements	Threats, sanctions (and inducements)	Limited force (and inducements)	Full scale/ brute force
Degree of success	CD unnecessary	Cheap CD success	Costly CD success	CD failure

Finally, it is important to distinguish between tactical/temporary and strategic/lasting success. Western use of coercion has generally been protracted affairs involving a series of inconclusive coercive diplomacy exchanges that resulted in tactical/temporary successes followed by new acts of non-compliance. Western use of coercion in Bosnia from 1992–5 is a case in point. It involved seven major coercive diplomacy exchanges each involving (1) acts of aggression committed by the Bosnian Serbs, (2) a response from the Western powers in the form of a demand coupled with a threat of force, and (3) the response to this threat from the Bosnian Serbs. Three of these exchanges can be considered tactical/temporary successes because Western threats coerced the Serbs to back down and comply with Western demands. From a strategic perspective, they cannot be considered successes, however, because compliance did not last for long.

These considerations lead to the operationalization of success depicted in Table 17.1. Coercive diplomacy successes resulting from the use of threats and sanctions (inducements may, but need not, be employed) are classified as cheap successes, whereas successes resulting from the use of limited force count as costly ones. Escalation to brute force means that coercive diplomacy has failed.

KEY POINTS

- Coercive diplomacy succeeds when a threat or limited use of force is necessary for compliance.

- Escalation from limited to brute force represents failure.

- Coercive diplomacy success is a question of degree.

- Success is negatively correlated with the amount of coercion (and inducements) required to obtain compliance.

- It is important to distinguish between temporary and lasting successes.

- To be genuine, coercive diplomacy success has to be lasting.

Western use of coercive diplomacy, 1990–2008

Western use of coercive diplomacy involving threats and use of limited force has sought to end and undo acts of aggression, acts of terrorism, and attempts to acquire WMD in the post-Cold War era. To qualify as a case of coercive diplomacy, explicit threats, sanctions, or limited force have to be employed by a Western coercer. Cases involving implicit threats and show of force such as the crises between the United States and China over Taiwan have consequently been excluded from the list below. The cases have been identified in the studies listed in the Further Reading at the end of the chapter and the coding is based on the information provided in these studies.

The literature shows that coercive diplomacy primarily has been employed to stop and undo acts of aggression. A total of twenty-one coercive-diplomacy exchanges have taken place between Western states and various aggressors in eight different conflicts. Twelve exchanges ended in failure, five resulted in temporary successes followed by new acts of non-compliance, three resulted in costly lasting successes requiring limited use of force, and only one resulted in cheap success in which compliance was obtained without a shot. The *ideal policy* identifying the minimum requirements for success was implemented to the letter in only six exchanges, all of which resulted in temporary or lasting successes.

Table 17.2 Western use of coercive diplomacy to stop/undo acts of aggression, 1990–2008

Location	Demand	Adversary	Coercive strategy*	Outcome
Iraq Round 1 1990–1991	Withdraw from Kuwait	Iraq	• sanctions • threats of force • deadline	Failure; escalation to limited force
Round 2 January–February 1991	Withdraw from Kuwait; leave heavy weapons behind	Iraq	• sanctions • limited use of force • deadline	Failure; escalation to brute force
Slovenia 1991	End aggression	Serbia (Yugoslavia)	• sanctions • deadlines • inducements • assurances	Failure; compliance not caused by coercion
Croatia 1991–1992	End aggression	Serbia	• sanctions • deadlines • inducements • assurances	Failure; compliance not caused by coercion
Bosnia Round 1 June 1992	End shelling of Sarajevo airport and interference with relief operation	Serbia and the BSA	• weak military threat • sanctions • deadline • inducements • assurances	Temporary success
Round 2 August–November 1992	End aggression and interference with relief efforts	Serbia and the BSA	• weak military threats • no-fly zone • tighter sanctions • inducements • assurances	Failure
Round 3 April 1993	End aggression; sign peace plan	Serbia and the BSA	• weak military threats • threat to arm Bosnian forces • tighter sanctions	Failure

Table 17.2 (Continued)

Location	Demand	Adversary	Coercive strategy*	Outcome
Round 4 August 1993	Withdraw forces from positions overlooking Sarajevo	Serbia and the BSA	• weak military threats • deadline • inducements • assurances	Failure; appeasement not coercion
Round 5 February 1994	Withdraw heavy weapons from Sarajevo	Serbia and the BSA	• *credible military threats* • *deadline* • *inducements* • *assurances*	Temporary success
Round 6 April 1994	Stop offensive; withdraw from Gorazde	Serbia and the BSA	• limited use of force • threats of escalation • deadline • assurances	Temporary success
Round 7 August–September 1995	Stop attacks; cease military activities; withdraw heavy weapons	Serbia and the BSA	• *limited use of force* • *deadline* • *inducements* • *assurances*	Costly success
Haiti Round I 1991–1992	Step down; restore president to power	Haitian military	• ineffective sanctions	Failure
Round 2 1993–April 1994	Step down; restore president to power	Haitian military	• more sanctions • deadline	Failure
Round 3 May–September 1994	Step down; restore president to power	Haitian military	• *credible military threat* • *deadline* • *inducements* • *assurances*	Cheap success
Somalia Round 1 1992–May 1993	End fighting and interference with relief operation; hide weapons	Several Somali clans	• *threats and limited use of force* • *deadlines* • *inducements* • *assurances*	Temporary success
Round 2 June–October 1993	End fighting; disarm and hand over power to representative councils	Several Somali clans	• threats and limited use of force	Failure; escalation to brute force
Iraq 1996	Withdraw from Iraqi Kurdistan	Iraq	• attack with 44 cruise missiles** • expansion of no-fly zone	Costly success
Kosovo Round 1 June 1998	End violence; start negotiations; withdraw forces	Serbia	• sanctions • weak military threats • deadline • inducements • assurances	Failure

Table 17.2 (Continued)

Location	Demand	Adversary	Coercive strategy*	Outcome
Round 2 September– October 1998	End violence; withdraw some forces; accept deployment of observer force	Serbia	• *sanctions* • *credible military threats* • *deadline* • *inducements* • *assurances*	Temporary success
Round 3 February–March 1999	Give NATO access throughout Serbia; withdraw from Kosovo; accept referendum on independence	Serbia	• sanctions • credible military threats • deadline	Failure
Round 4 March–June 1999	End violence; withdraw from Kosovo; accept peace plan	Serbia	• *sanctions* • *limited use of force* • *deadline* • *inducements* • *assurances*	Costly success

*Italic indicates implementation of the *ideal policy.*
**Unilateral US attack. All other cases are coalitional.

Notes: BSA = Bosnian Serb Army

Western governments have sought to stop four WMD programmes during the period. Nine coercive diplomacy exchanges ended in four temporary successes followed by subsequent non-compliance, two failures, and one cheap success; two exchanges were ongoing at the time of writing. In none of the cases was the *ideal policy* implemented, as it proved impossible to use force to deny the adversary's objectives quickly with little cost. Threats of force were not employed explicitly during the negotiations, which led to Libya's decisions to terminate its WMD programmes and its support for terrorist activities in 2003. On the contrary, assurance against regime change was crucial for success.

Table 17.3 Western use of coercive diplomacy to suspend or end WMD programmes, 1990–2008

Location	Demand	Adversary	Coercive strategy	Outcome
Iraq Round 1 1992–1993	Stop violating the no-fly zones and obstructing UN inspections	Iraq	• sanctions • limited use of force	Temporary success
Round 2 December 1997– February 1998	Stop obstructing UN inspections	Iraq	• sanctions • credible military threats • deadline	Temporary success
Round 3 November 1998	Stop obstructing UN inspections	Iraq	• sanctions • credible military threats • inducements	Temporary success

Table 17.3 (Continued)

Location	Demand	Adversary	Coercive strategy	Outcome
Round 4 2002–2003	Declare all WMD programmes, plants, and materials; cooperate with UN inspectors	Iraq	• economic sanctions • air strikes • credible military threats • threats of regime change • deadlines	Failure; partial Iraqi compliance triggers US-led escalation to brute force
Libya Round 1 1992–1997	End WMD programmes; cease terrorist activities; hand over terrorist suspects; provide compensation	Libya	• sanctions • weak threats of force • threats of regime change	Failure
Round 2 1997–2003	End WMD programmes; cease terrorist activities; hand over terrorist suspects; provide compensation	Libya	• sanctions • implicit threats of force • carrots • assurances	Cheap success
North Korea Round 1 1993–1994	Freeze nuclear programme	North Korea	• US sanctions • threats of UN sanctions and force • inducements • assurances	Temporary success
Round 2 2002–	End nuclear programme	North Korea	• US sanctions • indirect threats of force • inducements • assurances	?; ongoing negotiations
Iran 2002–	End nuclear programme	Iran	• weak threats of sanctions • and force • deadlines • inducements	?; ongoing negotiations

Finally, Western states used coercive diplomacy against state sponsors of terrorism and al-Qaeda on eight occasions. It is difficult to tell whether it had any effect against Iraq and Sudan, it failed against Libya, al-Qaeda, and the Taliban on three occasions, and two cheap successes were obtained against Libya and Pakistan. The *ideal policy* was employed to the letter only against Pakistan.

Table 17.4 Western use of coercive diplomacy to stop support for or use of terrorism, 1990–2008

Location	Demand	Adversary	Coercive strategy*	Outcome
Libya Round 1 1992–1997	End WMD programmes; cease terrorist activities; hand over terrorist suspects; provide compensation	Libya	• sanctions • weak threats of force • threats of regime change	Failure

Table 17.4 (Continued)

Location	Demand	Adversary	Coercive strategy*	Outcome
Round 2 1997–2003	End WMD programmes; cease terrorist activities; hand over terrorist suspects; provide compensation	Libya	• sanctions • implicit threats of force • carrots • assurances	Cheap success
Iraq 1993	Stop targeting the USA	Iraq	• attack with 23 cruise missiles**	?
Sudan 1998	Stop support and use of terrorism	Sudan and al-Qaeda	• UN and US sanctions • attack with 6–7 cruise missiles**	Sudan?; al-Qaeda failure
Afghanistan Round 1 1998–2001	Stop support and use of terrorism; hand over Osama bin Laden	Taliban and al-Qaeda	• attack with 60–70 cruise missiles** • sanctions	Failure
Round 2 September–October 2001	Stop support and use of terrorism; hand over al-Qaeda leadership	Taliban and al-Qaeda	• sanctions • credible threats of force • deadline • inducements	Failure; escalation to limited force
Round 3 October 2001	Stop support and use of terrorism; hand over al-Queda leadership; accept power-sharing arrangement	Taliban and al-Qaeda	• sanctions • use of limited force and threats of escala- tion • deadline • inducements	Failure; escalation to brute force
Pakistan Round 1 2001	End support for Taliban; support US war against Afghanistan	Pakistan	• *threats of sanctions and* *force** • *deadline* • *inducements* • *assurances*	Cheap success

* Italic indicates implementation of the *ideal policy.*

* * Unilateral US use of coercive diplomacy. All other cases are coalitional.

KEY POINTS

- The Western states obtained only six lasting successes in thirty-six coercive-diplomacy exchanges, and five of them were preceded by failures in earlier exchanges.

- Coercive diplomacy scored only three cheap successes in thirty-six attempts.

- Use of the *ideal policy* resulted in success, but it was implemented in only seven exchanges.

- The Western states are most likely to use coercive diplomacy to counter acts of aggression.

- Threats and limited use of force are very difficult to employ successfully to stop terrorism and WMD.

Why coercive diplomacy is hard

Several factors complicate the use of coercive diplomacy, and some of them are inherent in the nature of the strategy and in attempts to use it to counter aggression, terrorism, and WMD acquisition. The difficulties are further compounded by practical challenges related to the design of effective strategies meeting the requirements for success.

Inherent difficulties

Coercive diplomacy is tough, because the requirements for success are contradictory. To succeed the coercer must frighten and reassure the adversary at the same time. It must create fear of uncontrollable escalation and a sense of urgency in the mind of the adversary and convince it that compliance will not lead to further demands in the future. It is no easy task to use threats or limited force without hardening the adversary's motivation to resist, and equally hard to offer inducements and assurances to prevent this without appearing weak.

That success ultimately rests on perceptual, psychological, and emotional factors adds to the difficulty. Since success hinges on cooperation from the adversary, there is always a risk that misperception or miscalculation will defeat even a well-executed strategy meeting all the requirements for success. Adversaries finding themselves in what they may perceive as no-win situations will be prone to wishful thinking. That this was the principal reason why coercive diplomacy failed to persuade Saddam Hussein to withdraw his forces from Kuwait prior to the start of the fighting in 1991 cannot be ruled out.

The likelihood that this might happen is enhanced by the fact that compliance requires a visible change in behaviour—for instance, withdrawal of military forces or termination of a nuclear programme. As a consequence, compliance is not only likely to be perceived as humiliating; it may also be positively dangerous for the adversary's leaders, since their surrender may be perceived as a betrayal and trigger attempts to overthrow them by democratic or military means. Standing up to the coercer may also make the leadership more popular, since the use of coercion may produce a rally-around-the-flag effect. History shows that populations and groups tend to unite behind their leaders in times of crisis or war; even unpopular leaders may benefit from this effect.

In addition to these complications that apply to the use of coercive diplomacy in general, its use to counter aggression, terrorism, and WMD poses special problems of their own. Such cases are especially hard, because actors engaging in such behaviour are fully aware that force might be used to stop them. Most actors fearing hostile military responses will be deterred from resorting to force or terrorism or embarking on a high-cost, high-risk gamble to acquire WMD. Actors engaging in such behaviour are likely to perceive their vital interests as threatened and regard the issues at stake in zero-sum terms. As a consequence, the room for compromise that coercive diplomacy requires for success may simply not exist. This will almost certainly be the case if the coercer is demanding regime or leadership change, as was the case in Haiti, in Afghanistan (see Case Study 17.1), and in the crisis preceding the 2003 Iraq War. Leaders fearing for their hold on power or their lives have little incentive to comply, unless they are faced with certain defeat and offered very juicy inducements such as golden exiles. The American ability to do this paved the way for coercive success in Haiti in 1994, but it is unlikely to be possible very often. Similarly, threats and limited use of force will not impress terrorists willing to die for their cause.

Finally, the political scope for offering inducements to such adversaries may be very limited. This problem was underlined by the argument made by the British and American governments during the 1990–1 Gulf conflict that Saddam Hussein did not deserve any inducements, because he should never have attacked Kuwait in the first place. A similar logic applies to state sponsors of terrorism, terrorists, and actors pursuing WMD. Offers of inducements to convince North Korea and Iran to stop their nuclear programmes have thus been criticized along the same lines.

CASE STUDY 17.1

Failure in Afghanistan

Pre-9/11 context

At the time of the 9/11 attacks, the United States was already engaged in a coercive diplomacy campaign against the Taliban regime. Cruise missiles had been employed in an attack on al-Qaeda targets in 1998 and the following year sanctions were imposed in an attempt to coerce the Taliban to extradite Osama bin Laden. The Taliban flatly refused to force him out or hand him over to an 'infidel nation', however (Crenshaw 2003: 328).

US response to the 9/11 attacks

On 20 September 2001 the United States issued a public ultimatum to the Taliban demanding that the Taliban immediately hand over the al-Qaeda leadership and close the terrorist camps in Afghanistan. These demands were accompanied by threats of force and an offer to leave the Taliban regime in place. While the credibility of the threats were enhanced by military preparations, strong international support, and successful coercion that cut the Taliban off from Pakistani support, the Taliban had more reason to question the American offer to leave the regime in place. The Taliban response was defiant. It engaged in counter-coercion and refused to hand over Osama bin Laden and associates. The United States then began to bomb military air fields and the few high-value targets that Afghanistan presented to US air power: command centres, air defence systems, and leadership residences. The

United States also began to provide military materiel and financial support to the Northern Alliance, the Afghan groups that were fighting the Taliban.

Escalation to brute force and failure

On 11 October 2001 the United States offered to end its use of force in return for compliance with the American demands. Now regime change had been added to the list of demands. The Taliban regime now had to go, but prospects of participation in a future Afghan government were held open for moderate members of the existing regime. The Taliban responded with defiance, and the United States then began to bomb Taliban front-line positions and offer direct military support to the Northern Alliance. The Taliban had no response, and their regime quickly collapsed.

Was the Taliban impossible to coerce?

The Taliban had no reason to doubt American resolve, and threat credibility could not have been higher. Their failure to comply may consequently have stemmed from the belief that the USA would seek their overthrow whether they complied or not, religious/ideological beliefs ruling out compliance, an inability to comply, or a combination of the three. If the Taliban effectively depended upon financial and military support from al-Qaeda for regime survival, as the Central Intelligence Agency (CIA) concluded (Woodward 2001), then it may simply not have been able to comply with US demands.

Practical problems

In addition to the inherent difficulties, practitioners trying to put a strategy together face a set of practical problems, of which five stand out as particularly hard to overcome. To devise an effective mix of threats and inducements the coercer needs a good understanding of the adversary's mindset, motivations, interests, behavioural style, and decision-making process. In addition, actionable intelligence is required to target the adversary's forces, bases, and WMD installations. A poor understanding of the adversary and lack of intelligence has been a major obstacle limiting the effectiveness of Western coercion in the post-Cold War era. The widespread tendency in the West to label adversaries as rogue, irrational, fanatical, funda-

mentalist, crazy, and uncivilized is indicative of this problem, and it has been compounded by the inability to penetrate their societies and organizations to obtain the intelligence required to threaten with effective military action. The problem has been particularly acute with respect to terrorist groups and the Iranian, Iraqi, and North Korean nuclear programmes.

It is not only the different nature of the adversaries that complicates the use of Western coercion. Their tendency to rely on irregular or asymmetric military strategies such as guerrilla warfare or terrorism also complicates the use of coercive diplomacy by making it hard to threaten and, if need be, defeat the opponent's military strategy quickly with little cost. Actors, be they states or non-state actors, adopting such strategies offer few high-value targets to destroy or hold at risk and deny Western forces the ability to rely on air power to win quickly with little cost. As a consequence, threats and use of force either have little utility or require high-risk operations involving ground troops over an extended period of time. The Serbian success with respect to neutralizing the effectiveness of NATO air power forced NATO to contemplate a high-risk invasion with ground forces, and the effectiveness of guerrilla strategy with respect to neutralizing Western military superiority is also illustrated by insurgencies in Iraq and Afghanistan. The cases summarized above demonstrate that the ability to deny Western forces quick low-cost victories have a strong deterrent effect upon Western decision-makers in crises and conflicts that do not threaten their vital interests directly.

A related problem is the difficulty of verifying compliance with respect to terrorism and WMD. While it is easy to verify whether an aggressor withdraws or not, it is very hard to verify whether a state stops covert support for terrorist activities, whether terrorist groups cease from engaging in terrorist activities, or whether states or non-state actors stop clandestine efforts to acquire WMD. This has been a problem in all the WMD and terrorist cases summarized in Table 17.4.

A fourth practical problem is the need to coerce several opponents with conflicting interests at the same time. This will often be the case when coercive diplomacy is being used to manage internal conflicts where several parties are fighting each other. Western decision-makers faced this problem in Bosnia and Kosovo, where the parties fighting the Serbs on several occasions resisted Western attempts to find a diplomatic solution and sought to persuade Western states to help them defeat the Serbs instead. The Kosovo Liberation Army (KLA) was highly successful in this respect, as its policy of attacking Serbian civilians to provoke Serbian forces to retaliate against Kosovo Albanian civilians in the end convinced NATO leaders of the need to use force against the Serbs and deploy a large peacekeeping force in Kosovo. Thus the KLA effectively got NATO to evict Serbian forces from Kosovo, something it could never have done by itself (see Case Study 17.2).

CASE STUDY 17.2

Costly success in Kosovo

The context

Kosovo had long been regarded as a powder keg when violence finally broke out in the spring 1998. The Serbian security forces responded to the armed bid for independence launched by the Kosovo Liberation Army (KLA) with excessive use of force, which immediately drew international condemnation and mediation aimed at ending the violence.

Half-hearted coercion

NATO governments threatened to undertake air strikes in June 1998 unless the fighting ended and the Serbian forces were withdrawn from Kosovo. Threat credibility was, however, undermined by Russian opposition and visible opposition to the use of force within NATO. The situation was further complicated by KLA insistence on independence and their unwillingness to meet American negotiators.

Western governments consequently settled for a symbolic deployment of fifty observers and turned a blind eye as the Serbs launched a major offensive to defeat the KLA.

Temporary success

In October implementation of a coercive strategy meeting the requirements of the *ideal policy* paved the way for a deployment of 2,000 unarmed observers in Kosovo. To obtain Serbian compliance, NATO postponed its deadline twice and allowed more than 20,000 Serbian personnel to remain in Kosovo. The underlying sources of conflict were not addressed, and, since the KLA was not party to the agreement and vowed to fight on, few believed that the agreement would serve to end the violence.

Escalation to limited use of force

Continued fighting resulted in peace negotiations, the failure of which resulted in a NATO ultimatum demanding that Serbs sign the proposed peace agreement or face air strikes. The proposed agreement gave NATO unimpeded access to all of Serbia, involved a deployment of a large NATO force in Kosovo and a referendum on the future status of Kosovo that could only lead to independence. The Serbs were not offered any inducements or assurances to facilitate their compliance, and the context was not conducive to coercive diplomacy success: China and Russia opposed the use of force, forcing NATO to attack without a UN mandate, several NATO members had questioned the wisdom of resorting to force and the United States had publicly ruled out the use of ground forces. Against this background it is hardly surprising that Milosevic decided to fight and hold out for a better agreement rather than comply. By ruling out the use of ground forces, NATO guaranteed President Milosevic that Kosovo would not be taken from him unless he agreed to hand it over, and this left him with considerable leverage.

Explaining Serbian compliance after 78 days of bombing

Milosevic exploited this leverage to obtain a better agreement than the one he had been offered before the bombing. The final agreement made no mention of a referendum on Kosovo's future, it affirmed Serbia's sovereignty and territorial integrity, NATO was not granted access to Serbia proper, and the NATO force deployed in Kosovo had a UN mandate and Russian participation. In addition to these inducements and assurances, three other factors account for Milosevic's decision to comply. The first was NATO's ability to maintain its unity and escalate its bombing campaign, the second was a credible threat of a ground invasion if the bombing failed, and the third was the loss of Russian support. Taken together these new factors meant that the requirements of the *ideal policy* had been met.

A fifth problem stems from the need to engage in coalitional coercion. Western coercion is usually coalitional and conducted with a mandate from an international organization such as the UN or NATO. While coalitional coercive diplomacy holds a number of advantages in terms of burden sharing, enhanced legitimacy, and increased isolation of the adversary, these advantages may be offset by the difficulty of creating consensus on the need to threaten and use force. Since coercive diplomacy is a high-risk and potentially high-cost strategy, states tend to free ride and be unwilling to put their troops in harm's way in conflicts that pose no direct threat to their own security. As a consequence, coalitional consensus on the need to threaten and use force usually requires the presence of one or more great powers that are willing to take the lead and bear most of the costs in blood and treasure that the use of force involves (Jakobsen 1998: 138–9).

Even with effective great-power leadership, coalitional coercive diplomacy may still lack the necessary credibility in the eyes of the adversary, however. Disagreements within the coalition may convince the adversary that the coalition will either fall apart once the battle has been joined or fail to escalate the use of force sufficiently to make non-compliance too costly. Belief that they would be able to undermine coalition unity by engaging in counter-coercion and propaganda campaigns probably provides an important part of the explanation why Saddam Hussein refused to withdraw from Kuwait without a fight in 1991 and why it took a seventy-eight-day bombing campaign to persuade Milosevic to leave Kosovo in 1999.

KEY POINTS

- It is difficult to frighten and reassure the adversary at the same time.

- Compliance hinges on psychological, perceptual, and emotional factors outside the coercer's control.

- Coercive diplomacy against aggressors, terrorists, and actors seeking WMD is especially hard, because such opponents are likely to perceive the issues at stake in zero-sum terms.

- It has proved difficult to obtain the knowledge and intelligence required to devise effective coercive strategies.

- Actors relying on terrorism or guerrilla strategies are hard to target and coerce militarily.

- It is extremely difficult to verify whether opponents have stopped terrorist activities or WMD programmes.

- Coalitional coercive diplomacy requires great-power leadership to be effective.

Conclusion

Coercive diplomacy is an attractive strategy, because it can be used to stop and/or reverse acts of military aggression, terrorism, and attempts to acquire WMD with limited or, at the best of times, no use of force. While coercive diplomacy is a low-cost strategy when it succeeds, failure may be very costly, as the coercer then faces the grim choice of backing down or executing his threat. This is a choice that Western policy-makers have been facing often since the end of the Cold War. The strategy's potential for peaceful conflict resolution has been realized in only three of the thirty-six Western coercive diplomacy exchanges since 1990, and the number of lasting successes for the period 1990–2008 is six. This is hardly an encouraging success rate and a stark reminder that coercive diplomacy is a high-risk, hard-to-use strategy.

The conditions for success are clear in the abstract and coercive diplomacy generally succeeds when the Western states meet the requirements of the *ideal-policy* framework: (1) make credible threats of force and/or use limited force to defeat the adversary's gains quickly with little cost; (2) issue deadlines for compliance; (3) offer inducements; and (4) reassure opponents that compliance will not trigger new demands. The problem is that Western governments rarely devise coercive strategies that meet these requirements. As a consequence, the main problem is not misperception, miscalculation, or irrationality on the part of Western adversaries, as it is often claimed (see, e.g., Tarzi 2005). The main problem is that the Western states either lack the will to threaten and use force in the manner prescribed by the *ideal policy* framework, or, conversely, when the willingness to do so exist, they fail to couple the stick with adequate inducements and credible assurances.

It is a paradoxical feature of coercive diplomacy that the prospects of cheap success are highest when the coercer is willing to go all the way and escalate to brute force if need be. Unfortunately for Western decision-makers, it was all too apparent that they lacked the willingness to do so in most of coercive diplomacy exchanges they were involved in during the 1990s. Western policy-makers were very reluctant to put their troops in harm's way in Somalia, the Balkans, and Haiti. After the traumatic withdrawal from Somalia, the Western and especially the American preoccupation with force protection undermined the initial attempts to coerce the military leadership in Haiti and the Serbs in Bosnia and Kosovo, and it also played a major role in deterring Western governments from launching a timely intervention to stop the genocide in Rwanda in 1994.

This problem did not go away after 9/11; it continues to apply to most contemporary conflicts that are unrelated to the war on terrorism. Western governments remain extremely reluctant to threaten and use force credibly to end armed conflicts on the African continent, for example, preferring to leave the management of these conflicts to the UN and Africa's regional organizations. As was the case in the 1990s, coercive diplomacy will be employed effectively to counter aggression only in conflicts that pose no direct threat to Western security, provided that the prospects of military success are high and the risk of casualties low. Very few contemporary conflicts fit this description.

The problem is the opposite when Western states use coercive diplomacy to counter terrorism and WMD acquisition. In these conflicts 9/11 has made a huge difference. After the fall of the Taliban and Saddam Hussein, few actors engaged in terrorist and WMD activities are likely to doubt Western resolve with respect to threatening, and using, force. In these conflicts the principal problem from a coercive diplomacy perspective is that Western decision-makers tend to see these confrontations in zero-sum terms and make demands that give the adversaries little incentive to comply. American demands for regime change are likely to crowd out the prospects of coercive diplomacy success in most cases, as it gives the opponents no incentive to cooperate. American demands for regime change made coercive diplomacy success next to impossible to obtain in the confrontations with the Taliban and Saddam Hussein, and credible assurances that regime change would not be pursued were key in the successful negotiations that coerced Libya to terminate its support for terrorism and its nuclear programme. Similarly, it is hard to see the regimes in North Korea and Iran giving up their nuclear programmes as long as they have good reason to believe that the United States is seeking their overthrow.

While the Libyan case suggests that coercion coupled with skilful use of assurances and inducements can coerce states to end WMD programmes, the prospects of success look considerably less bright with apocalyptical terrorist groups, like al-Qaeda.

The principal problem here is not unwillingness to use inducements and assurances, but lack of feasibility. Such groups are hard to locate and target militarily, engaged as they are in a zero-sum struggle and willing to die for their cause. Against these actors it is possible to use coercive diplomacy only indirectly to coerce state sponsors and less radical terrorist groups to stop their cooperation with al-Qaeda and affiliated groups.

It is, in short, unlikely that coercive diplomacy will have a higher rate of success in the near future than it has enjoyed since the end of the Cold War. Western governments will simply not be able to meet the requirements for success very often. Western policy-makers would therefore be well advised to strive harder to prevent the need for coercive diplomacy from arising in the first place.

? QUESTIONS

1. Why has the Western use of coercive diplomacy increased since the end of the Cold War?

2. What distinguishes coercive diplomacy from brute force?

3. Consider the pros and cons of the definition of limited force employed in this chapter.

4. How do you determine whether the coercer wants to avoid the use of force or is using coercive diplomacy to legitimize it?

5. List the advantages and limitations of the *ideal policy* framework.

6. Why is it difficult to define coercive diplomacy success?

7. Does the implementation of the *ideal policy* yield the predicted results?

8. List the factors complicating the use of coercive diplomacy.

9. Why is coercive diplomacy unlikely to become more successful in the foreseeable future?

10. How could Western governments reduce their need for coercive diplomacy and force to counter aggression, terrorism, and WMD?

FURTHER READING

■ Art, R. J., and Cronin, P. M. (2003) (eds.), *The United States and Coercive Diplomacy*, Washington: United States Institute of Peace. Applies refined version of George's theory to eight new cases. Useful case studies, but analytic value reduced by inconsistent coding of cases and outcomes as well as vague definitions of key concepts.

■ Art, R. J., and Cronin, P. M. (2007), 'Coercive Diplomacy', in C. A. Crocker, F. O. Hampson, and P. Aall (eds.), *Leashing the Dogs of War: Conflict Management in a Divided World*, Washington: United States Institute of Peace, 2007,

299–318. Overview article summarizing the findings of the work above; contains short discussions of thirteen cases.

■ Bratton, P. C. (2005), 'When Is Coercion Successful? And Why Can't We Agree on It?', *Naval War College Review*, 58/3: 99–120. Good review of the various definitions of success employed in the coercion literature.

■ Byman, D., and Waxman, M. (2000), *Confronting Iraq: US Policy and the Use of Force since the Gulf War*, Santa Monica, CA: RAND, MR-1146-OSD. Analyses use of coercive diplomacy against Iraq 1991–8.

■ Freedman, L. (1998) (ed.), *Strategic Coercion: Concepts and Cases*, Oxford: Oxford University Press. Discusses strategic coercion, coercive diplomacy, and compellence and contains eight case studies.

■ George, A. L., Hall, D., and Simons, W. E. (1971), *The Limits of Coercive Diplomacy: Laos, Cuba, Vietnam*, Boston: Little, Brown. The initial formulation of George's theory applied to three cases.

■ George, A. L., and Simons, W. E. (1994) (eds.), *The Limits of Coercive Diplomacy*, 2nd rev. edn., Boulder, CO: Westview. Refined version of theory presented in 1971 volume applied to seven cases.

■ Jakobsen, P. V. (1998), *Western Use of Coercive Diplomacy after the Cold War: A Challenge for Theory and Practice*, London: Macmillan Press. Develops and tests the *ideal policy* concept in three cases and identifies the conditions under which Western governments are most likely to threaten and use force.

■ Jentleson, B. W., and Whytock, C. A. (2005–6), 'Who "Won" Libya? The Force–Diplomacy Debate and its Implications for Theory and Policy', *International Security*, 30/3 (Winter): 47–86. Refinement of George's theory applied to Libya.

■ Pape, R. A. (1996), *Bombing to Win: Air Power and Coercion in War*, Ithaca, NY: Cornell University Press. Very influential work introducing the distinction between punishment and denial to the study of coercion. Contains five case studies.

■ Schelling, T. C. (1966), *Arms and Influence*, New Haven: Yale University Press. The theory of compellence is presented and the concept is distinguished from deterrence and brute force.

🌐 IMPORTANT WEBSITES

● http://www.crisisgroup.org   The International Crisis Group's website contains high-quality analysis of ongoing and potential armed conflicts.

● http://www.globalsecurity.org   GlobalSecurity.org contains useful background information on armed conflicts past and present as well as developing news stories in the fields of defence and security.

● http://www.rand.org   The Rand Corporation's website contains excellent studies of coercion and air power available in full text.

 Visit the Online Resource Centre that accompanies this book for lots of interesting additional material: www.oxfordtextbooks.co.uk/orc/collins2e/

18 The Role of Intelligence in National Security

STAN A. TAYLOR

 Chapter Contents

✔ **Reader's Guide**

This chapter explores the tenuous and complex yet critical relationship between security and intelligence. Following some basic introductory remarks, including definitions and a theoretical framework, it presents an overview of some of the more significant intelligence services in major Western nations, describes the variety of intelligence disciplines (the ways intelligence is collected) followed by a discussion of what is called the intelligence process—the way information needs are defined by decision-makers and what happens between then and the time they receive that information. After giving examples of intelligence successes and failures in modern history, the chapter concludes with a discussion of some of the ethical issues involved in intelligence and a brief discussion of the security/intelligence environment in the twenty-first century.

Introduction

Security is a fundamental goal of all states. To support that search for security, all states use intelligence, to one degree or another, to enhance decision making. The significance of intelligence has been recognized for centuries. In one of the earliest recorded uses of spies, Moses sent spies into Canaan to 'spy out the land' to see whether or not the Israelites could occupy it. The Chinese general Sun Tzu (*c.*500 BC) devoted the last chapter of his still widely read book, *The Art of War*, to the role of spies. Sun Tzu, like most early users of intelligence, sought information about the military capabilities and plans of potential enemies. Roman armies under Caesar scouted the movements and capabilities of enemy troops, and the fortunes of medieval statecraft often depended on the quality of the intelligence collected (see Key Quotes 18.1).

Although the desire and need for intelligence has been constant for centuries, the information available, the technology of communications, the means of collection, and the speed and accuracy of turning raw information into finished intelligence for decision-makers have all changed dramatically. These changes have become the critical and defining characteristics of what is now called the information age. Both the information sought and the means by which it was sought were one thing in, for example, the industrial age. But they are completely different in a post-industrial, post-service economy information age, where governments, businesses, and common social intercourse are all driven by the need for and availability of information, as well as by the need, at times, to keep information secret from others.

KEY QUOTES 18.1

Sun Tzu on intelligence

'Thus, what enables the wise sovereign and the good general to strike and conquer, and achieve things beyond the reach of ordinary men, is foreknowledge. Now this foreknowledge cannot be elicited from spirits; it cannot be obtained inductively from experience, nor by any deductive calculation. Knowledge of the enemy's dispositions can only be obtained from other men. Therefore, enlightened rulers and good generals who are able to obtain intelligent agents as spies are certain for great achievements.

If you know the enemy and know yourself, you need not fear a hundred battles. If you know yourself and not the enemy, for every victory you will suffer a defeat. If you know neither yourself nor the enemy, you are a fool and will meet defeat in every battle.'

Sun Tzu, *The Art of War*, trans. Lionel Giles, ch. 13, 'On Spies'; 13:006 in the Shonsi system.

KEY POINTS

- The collection, analysis, and use of intelligence are ubiquitous—all states do this to one degree or another.

- Intelligence has been used by rulers and generals from earliest times to the present.

- The information available, as well as the means to collect and analyse it, have changed dramatically in the information age.

Definitions and theory of intelligence

The term 'intelligence', as used in this chapter, refers to the collection, analysis, production, and utilization of information about potentially hostile states, groups, individuals, or activities. It differs from other sources of information in that it is often, though not always, collected clandestinely and states attempt to keep other states from obtaining it. It may also include special activities meant to influence the foreign or domestic policies of other states without revealing the source of the influence. Intelligence also refers to the government entities that collect and analyse information as well as to the process by which this function is performed.

A general theory of intelligence can be drawn from cybernetics, a discipline developed in 1947 by mathematician Norbert Weiner and others. The word 'cybernetics' comes from a Greek word meaning helmsman or governor—one who steers a ship. A helmsman must use skill, intuition, and constant feedback from the environment to permit accurate steerage of the vessel. Thus, a cybernetic system is one in which the constant feedback of information modifies the behaviour of the system in order to achieve a desired end. It can be as mundane as a thermostat that persistently monitors the temperature of a room in order consistently to maintain a desired temperature or as complex as a robot that relentlessly reads the nature of its environment in order to accomplish programmed tasks.

Cybernetics is a perfect metaphor for the role of intelligence as applied to statecraft. Decision-makers are the helmsmen, the governors, who must use skill, intuition, and iterative feedback to maintain security for a state. Intelligence, whether defined as process, product, or people, involves collecting and analysing almost limitless data about international events and providing that information to the state's decision-makers. Heads of state and their foreign-policy and national security bureaucracies, at all times, must be aware of threats to the state's national security and must receive information (intelligence) that will allow them to steer their state safely through the hazardous waters of international affairs.

KEY POINTS

- Intelligence refers to the process of defining needs, collecting and analysing information, and providing information needed by decision-makers to make sound decisions about a state's policies.

- Intelligence also refers to the process by which this is done, to the people and institutions that do it, and to the occasional use of secret activities to influence a foreign state's policies.

- The theory of cybernetics assumes that the intelligence process is but part of the flow of information that then acts as feedback to maximize a state's efficiency in achieving its foreign-policy goals.

Intelligence services of different nations

Every nation collects, analyses, and uses intelligence—some merely spend more than others to do so. This section outlines a general organizational sketch for most nations and examines in greater detail the intelligence services adopted by certain countries. While 'spies have been around for centuries ... intelligence services are new' (Knightley 1986: 5). They began in most countries as military intelligence units supplying information to commanders and were usually cut back or eliminated when hostilities ended. The early national intelligence services that appeared in the last three decades of the nineteenth century were generally small, poorly funded, and somewhat obscure. It was not until around the turn of that century that truly national intelligence services appeared in Western states. Sometime between 1900 and 1920 nearly every major European power had a permanent national intelligence organization with worldwide interests. But America lagged behind. In spite of fairly active and effective military intelligence units, the USA did not create a permanent civilian intelligence organization with global interests until 1947.

In general, most large and globally active nations have some or all of the following types of intelligence agencies, although the nature of each agency will vary according to the different political cultures, legal systems, and bureaucratic styles of the country:

1. an overall supervisory office or group of offices charged with coordinating the several different agencies that make up a country's intelligence community (IC);

2. an agency responsible for collecting, analysing, and producing intelligence drawn from foreign countries and other external sources;

3. an agency responsible for collecting, analysing, and producing intelligence about domestic threats to security;

4. an agency responsible for the collection and distribution of signals intelligence (sigint);

5. an agency that works under the direction of the military department or departments of a government to provide intelligence required by military forces;

6. depending on the size and global involvement of the nation, agencies specifically charged with anti-terrorism; the development, operation, and exploitation of satellite and overhead imagery; counterintelligence; border protection; and other special functions.

See Background 18.1 for a summary of these organizations for six countries.

While all nations have intelligence communities carrying out most of the above functions, many differences exist between them. The greatest differences appear in the size, scope, nature of the supervisory structures, and the extensiveness of public accountability through legislative oversight.

Historically, intelligence organizations and operations were shrouded in secrecy. Quite often the organizations were created and controlled by a very small number of government officials. In some nations it was not uncommon for intelligence operations to be directed against citizens or other branches of their own governments. The intelligence services of totalitarian governments typically have been unrestrained in their domestic operations. Their efforts have been directed more against their own citizens than against foreign intelligence targets.

In the early twenty-first century, only the US, UK, Chinese, and Russian services can claim to have truly global intelligence coverage and activities, with Germany and France close behind them. The US intelligence community is by far the largest and best funded, but the British services are taken very seriously, partially because of their successful history and relationship with the USA. Russian intelligence is still very extensive and continues to be directed against Russian citizens and groups, though less so than during the Soviet period. Germany and France are the only other Western nations with extensive intelligence services, but both are hampered by fragmentation and by chequered pasts. Chinese intelligence is also global and focuses more on economic intelligence than do other national services. The global overseas Chinese community greatly facilitates Chinese collection efforts, just as the Jewish Diaspora benefits Israeli intelligence collection.

In 1976, the USA became the first nation to place its IC under permanent legislative oversight. Since that time, most democratic nations have followed suit to one degree or another. Australia and Canada moved in this direction in 1979 and 1984, respectively, with most other European nations following suit through the 1980s and 1990s (Born et al. 2005: 4). European nations did this partially in response to changing interpretations of certain provisions of the European Declaration of Human Rights. The degree of oversight varies from nation to nation, with the USA being the most extensive and Russia and China being the least. Although there is growing sentiment for legislative oversight of intelligence services and operations, particularly in democratic nations, certain branches of some intelligence services still operate under executive supervision only.

Intelligence communities of six major nations

	United Kingdom	United States	Russia	France	Germany	China
Supervisory structure	1. Prime Minister 2. Foreign Minister (for SIS and GCHQ) 3. Home Secretary (for MI5) 4. Special Cabinet Committees 5. Joint Intelligence Committee (JIC)	1. President 2. National Security Council (NSC) 3. Director of National Intelligence (DNI) 4. Secretary of Defense for DIA, NSA, GIA, and Uniformed Services Intelligence	1. President 2. Russian National Security Council 3. Permanent Interbranch Commissions of the Russian National Security Council 4. Ministry of Defence (for the GRU)	1. Prime Minister 2. General Secretary for National Defence 3. Inter-departmental Intelligence Committee 4. Domestic Security Council 5. Minister of Defence	1. Chancellor 2. Parliamentary Control Commission (PKK) 3. German Federal Armed Forces (for MAD) 4. Federal Ministry of the Interior (for BfV)	1. President 2. Communist Party Central Committee 3. General Staff Department for the Central Military Commission 4. People's Liberation Army (PLA; for the Second and Third Departments)
Foreign intelligence	Secret Intelligence Service (MI6)	Central Intelligence Agency (CIA)	Foreign Intelligence Service (SVR)	General Directorate for External Security (DGSE)	Federal Intelligence Service (BND)	Ministry of State Security (MSS)
Domestic intelligence	Security Service (MI5)	Federal Bureau of Investigation (FBI)	Federal Security Service (FSB)	General Intelligence (RG)	Federal Office for the Protection of the Constitution (BfV)	Ministry of Public Security (MPS)
Signals intelligence	Government Communications Headquarters (GCHQ)	National Security Agency (NSA)	Federal Agency for Government Communications and Information (FAPSI)	Intelligence and Electronic Warfare Brigade (BRGE)	Office for Radio Monitoring of the Federal Armed Forces (AFMBw)	Third Department (a.k.a. Technical Department)
Military intelligence	1. Defence Intelligence Staff (DIS) 2. Various Military Service Intelligence Groups	1. Defense Intelligence Agency 2. Various Military Service Intelligence Groups	Main Intelligence Administration (GRU)	1. Directorate of Military Intelligence (DRM) 2. Directorate for Defence Protection and Security (DPSD)	1. Office of Intelligence of the Federal Armed Forces (ANBw) 2. Military Security Service (MAD)	1. Second Department 2. PLA Navy 3. PLA Airforce
Other	1. Defence Geographic and Imagery Intelligence Agency (DGIA) 2. National Criminal Intelligence Service (NCIS) 3. Metropolitan Police (Scotland Yard)	1. Department of Homeland Security (DHS) 2. National Reconnaissance Office (NRO) 3. National Geospatial-Intelligence Agency (NGA)	1. Federal Protective Service (FSO) 2. Ministry of Internal Affairs (MVD) 3. Federal Border Service (FPS)	1. Central Information Systems Security Division (DCSSI) 2. Directorate of Territorial Security (DST)	1. State Offices for the Protection of the Constitution (LfV) 2. Federal Office for Information Technology Security (BSI)	1. New China News Agency 2. 8341 Unit – Central Security Regiment

Intelligence collection disciplines

Each different method of collecting intelligence is referred to as an intelligence discipline. These disciplines are usually divided into two general types—human intelligence collection (or humint in intelligence jargon) and technical intelligence collection (techint) (see Background 18.2).

Humint

The use of spies or human intelligence (humint) is the oldest such discipline. It may not be, as it is often called, the second oldest profession, but, for as long as tribes, clans, nations, or empires have been

---

BACKGROUND 18.2

Intelligence collection disciplines

Acronym	Definition
HUMINT	*Human intelligence*. Information collected by intelligence officers usually stationed in foreign nations.
TECHINT	*Technical intelligence.* Originally referred to information about weapons systems but now used to refer to intelligence collected from the interception of a variety of electronic signals by the use of sophisticated technical means.
SIGINT	*Signals intelligence*. All kinds of information collected through various electronic devices, including the following sub-disciplines.
IMINT	*Imagery intelligence*. Any photographic or digital images collected by orbiting (satellite) or ground-based (aeroplanes or Unmanned Ariel Vehicles) systems.
PHOTINT	*Photographic intelligence*. An earlier term for IMINT. Used widely to describe both film and digital photographs taken from satellites.
COMINT	*Communications intelligence*: The interception of communications between two or more parties.
TELINT	*Telemetry intelligence*. The interception of data transmitted during the testing of various kinds of weapons systems.

ELINT	*Electronic intelligence.* The interception of electronic emissions emanating from weapons and tracking systems.
MASINT	*Measures and Signatures Intelligence.* A more recent form of SIGINT using more sophisticated devices that can sense material used in various types of modern weapons.
RADINT	Information derived from the use of radar signals emanating from overhead satellites, aircraft, or from ground-based sources.
OSINT	*Open Source Intelligence.* The collection of intelligence information from a wide variety of publicly available sources (media, government information, scholarly publications, etc.).

Adapted from Lowenthal (2003: ch. 5).

competing with one another, there have been spies. The methods used by these spies have changed over the centuries, but the goal has always been the same—to gain some advantage over an opponent by accessing his secrets, usually through stealthy observation or by intercepting written messages carried by couriers.

This kind of work has always required men and women who know the language and culture of the country to which they are assigned and who are comfortable living a double life.

Today's intelligence officers operate quite differently from the way they are portrayed in literature or cinema, however. They are seldom armed and are usually putative employees of a nation's diplomatic service working in a foreign country. While there, they attempt to recruit locals who have access to classified information and who, for whatever reason, may wish to reveal that information to them. An intelligence officer's primary responsibility is to develop secure ways to exchange information in a manner that will not compromise the person providing it.

Techint

Since the Cold War, technical intelligence (techint) has referred to all intelligence collected through technical means. Techint developed in response to three particular scientific and engineering advances: first, the development of wire-based electronic communications; second, the development of wireless electronic communications; and, third, the development of the aeroplane.

In the late 1830s, states began to communicate with their diplomatic and military personnel abroad over fixed, land-based telegraph wires. This also meant, however, that other states could tap into these wires and intercept communications. When wireless communications came along, these electronic signals could literally be plucked from the air. To prevent this incursion into a state's secrets, these transmissions were soon encrypted or encoded so they could not be read by others. This, of course, led to dramatic developments in intercepting, decryption, and decoding, which, obviously, led to equally dramatic developments in protecting communications.

A third widely used techint collection discipline became possible with the development of the aeroplane in 1903. The Wright brothers correctly believed their invention would be of critical use to military services. But long before aeroplanes were used as fighting weapons, they were used for aerial reconnaissance. In France, developments in photography made it possible to take pictures of troop locations from aircraft. Photographic intelligence (photint) was born when the first aerial photographs in a battle zone were taken by Italian aviators in the Italian–Turkish War in October 1911. By the latter half of the twentieth century, major powers were conducting surveillance by the use of aircraft, satellites, and (in the twenty-first century) unmanned aerial vehicles (UAVs).

The intelligence process

The intelligence process begins when national-security officials need to know something about other states or other global actors involved in world affairs whose actions might impinge on the security of their state. That specific need-to-know, along with literally hundreds of others, will be prioritized and eventually assigned to one or more entities that make up a state's intelligence community. The requested information may be about empirical and observable developments (WMD, types of weapons, foreign commitments, terrorism, and so on), or it may about intentions (what a state or group plans to do with its weapons). But, above all, the information is usually something that the target state or group does not want other states to obtain.

Next is the collection stage. Various intelligence agencies and sub-agencies will begin to collect information through a combination of all disciplines, particularly if the topic is prioritized at a high level. In the build-up to the 2003 Iraqi War, for example, nearly every intelligence entity in several major states was focused on Iraq. Satellite photography, airborne listening devices, and other highly sophisticated instruments were focused on intercepting public and private Iraqi communications. At the same time, some intelligence officers were interviewing defectors, émigrés, as well as official and non-official visitors to Iraq, while other officers were trying to develop sources of information within Iraq itself.

Following the collection stage, and often contemporaneous with it, some processing occurs. Material in foreign languages needs to be translated, photographs must be interpreted, and communications need to be decrypted or decoded. Because of sheer volume, translating intercepted communications may take many months and deciphering coded communications may take several years.

Analysis is the next stage in the intelligence process. All collected and processed information is eventually fed to analysts, who must place it into historical contexts and try to separate the valid information from the disinformation put out by the intelligence target to confuse any collecting state. Many consider analysis the most important and the most difficult stage in the intelligence process. Information sent to analysts is called raw or unfinished intelligence; it is often conflicting, ambiguous, or contradictory, but analysts try to turn it into what is called finished or actionable intelligence.

Production follows analysis. Obviously, critical and time-sensitive information will be delivered immediately to decision-makers. But most analysis is put into some finished form before being sent to decision-makers as an intelligence product. The product can take a variety of forms. It may be daily or occasional briefs to decision-makers or it may be what are called intelligence estimates—periodic printed assessments of important developments.

The final stage in the intelligence process involves the delivery of the information to those who requested it in the first place. Obviously, throughout the cycle additional related information gets added to the specific information gathered in response to the original questions, but it is at this stage that intelligence theoretically adds value to the decision-making process. Senior government officials, armed with the intelligence product, are able to pursue policies and practise statecraft in a more informed manner and, theoretically, are better able to enhance either state or alliance security.

The word *theoretically* must be emphasized. The intelligence cycle is logical and sound as described. It is also misleading. Unfortunately, many problems that can lead to intelligence failures enter into the process at virtually every stage (see Think Point 18.1).

Decision-makers often do not know which questions to ask. Few decision-makers before the mid-1990s, for example, were asking about Osama bin Laden and al-Qaeda. Other problems occur at the prioritization stage. A question, or set of questions, may not be given a high priority. For example, prior to 9/11, al-Qaeda was absent or low on the priority lists of several nations. The Bush administration came into office in 2001, in fact, with WMD in rogue states as its highest priority. Only after 9/11 did terrorism rise to the top of every list (Taylor and Goldman 2004: 425).

 THINK POINT 18.1

Intelligence failure or policy failure?

The phrase 'intelligence failure' is widely used but minimally understood. One of the frustrating facts of life faced by intelligence agencies in any country is that they are, in one sense, always in a 'lose – lose' situation. The phrase 'policy failure' is seldom heard, while the phrase 'intelligence failure' is heard with increasing frequency. If a government

initiative works, it will always be touted as a 'policy success' but seldom as an 'intelligence success'. If a government policy is not successful, accusations of 'intelligence failure' fill the media but 'policy failure' is seldom seen or heard. To add to the problem, in order to protect sources and methods, agencies must most often respond to questions with the ubiquitous words 'no comment'.

Processing and collecting failures also occur. Communications may not be translated, spy planes may be shot down, intelligence officers or their agents may be caught, or codes may not be broken. For example, although American cryptographers were intercepting vast amounts of Soviet coded messages in the 1940s, they could not decipher them. It was not until 1948 that the USA and Britain began to break Soviet communication codes. Starting in late 1942 and then with gradually increasing success into the late 1950s, what was called the VENONA Project revealed vast Soviet penetrations into the American, British, West German, French, and Australian governments. But often the decrypted messages were being worked on for between two and five years after they were intercepted. VENONA confirmed the treason of Kim Philby and the other Cambridge spies, Julius and Ethyl Rosenberg (the American atomic spies), Klaus Fuchs (the British atomic spy), Alger Hiss (an adviser to President Franklin D. Roosevelt), as well as Soviet spies in highly placed positions in virtually all Western governments, including the USA and Britain. But the decryptions either came

too late to prevent damage or could not be used in legal trials out of fear that their use would reveal to the Soviets that the West had broken their codes. Being able to read Soviet codes was deemed of higher value than the prosecution of traitors.

Most intelligence failures occur during the analysis stage. Analysts may be overwhelmed by too much intelligence or kept in the dark because of insufficient intelligence; they may have prejudices that cause them to emphasize unimportant clues or to ignore important ones. They may fall victim to groupthink or they may want to cook their analysis to fit a decision-maker's recipe. Or they may be overly cautious, so that they do not become embarrassed for being wrong and thus lose bureaucratic influence. A proliferation of analytical agencies within a nation's intelligence community contributes to this problem.

Finally, at any stage in the cycle, 'stovepiping' may occur. Either collectors or analysts may take what they deem to be pleasing information directly to the decision-maker and thus circumvent the critical analytical process. For example, at one point in the prelude to the 2003 Iraq invasion, two

American Defense Department officials took information directly to their superiors rather than submit it to intelligence community analysts. The information proved misleading and would have been seen in a better perspective had it gone through the normal analytical process.

KEY POINTS

- With only slight variations, every national government has an intelligence process that identifies critical intelligence questions, assigns tasks to various collecting agencies, processes and analyses information, and delivers it to decision-makers. In theory this process improves and informs the decision-making process and enhances national security.

- Breakdowns, often resulting from a failure to correlate and coordinate between agencies and sub-agencies, occur at virtually every stage of the process.

- Without detracting from the importance and difficulty of developing contacts inside hostile governments or terrorist groups, analysis is probably the most difficult and important stage in the process. Most intelligence failures arise in this stage.

Intelligence and security since the Second World War

A full understanding of the contributions of intelligence to security in modern times includes many developments during the first fifty years of the twentieth century. The role of British intelligence in getting America into the First World War (the Zimmerman Telegraph affair), the intelligence failure that got America into the Second World War (Pearl Harbor), the dramatic impact of cryptography during the Second World War (the Enigma development), and the amazing success of British counterintelligence in using Hitler's spies for their own purposes (the Doublecross operation) are all interesting and important.

Three Second World War intelligence developments set the stage for intelligence during the Cold War. First, the extensive sigint cooperation established between the UK and the United States led to the world's first intelligence treaty between nations. The BRUSA agreement of May 1943 followed a series of both formal and informal exchanges of personnel and information between Britain and the USA. Five years, and scores of negotiations later, this turned into the UK–USA Agreement (UKUSA). The treaty bound the UK, USA, Canada, Australia, and New Zealand to cooperate fully in the collection and sharing of sigint information. It even divided geographical collection responsibilities between those nations. UKUSA has weathered some difficult times—concern about Soviet penetration of British intelligence, the Suez crisis, and a small episode when New Zealand banned nuclear armed and powered vessels from its harbours in 1985—but it still exists into the twenty-first century.

Second, aerial overhead imagery, first begun during the First World War, became much more sophisticated during the Second World War. As that war ended and the Cold War began, Western nations believed it even more important to be able to obtain information about Soviet weapons developments through overhead imagery. Both American and British aircraft gathered sigint and imint intelligence by flying over international waters but as close to the Soviet territorial borders as possible. Then, in 1956, after the Soviets had rejected US President Eisenhower's Open Skies Proposal, the Americans put into service the U-2 spy plane—an aircraft that could fly directly over Soviet territory 70,000 feet in the sky and, it was believed, 20,000 feet beyond the range of Soviet planes and missiles, yet take photographs and other images that revealed a great deal about Soviet weapons systems. Within two years, virtually all Western hard intelligence about Soviet weapons developments came from U-2 overflights. That source ended on 1 May 1960, when the Soviets shot down a U-2 plane and captured its pilot, Gary Powers, alive.

Spy planes played a critical role in the discovery and documentation of Soviet missiles in Cuba in 1962 as well as in the discovery of Iraqi missile sites in 1991. But they were no longer used in flights over Soviet territory after the 1 May 1960 incident. Instead, the USA developed satellites that could take a variety of images from hundreds of miles in space either while orbiting the planet or when in geosynchronous orbit above Soviet territory. The first American satellite to cross Soviet territory was Discoverer 13 in August 1960. Discoverer 14, the next in the series, was responsible for more photographs of the Soviet Union than came from all U-2 overflights. The Soviets soon developed their own photographic satellites and the era of 'eyes in the sky' began. This gave both sides in the Cold War the ability to monitor weapons developments and to verify compliance with the arms control agreements that began in the 1970s. Contrary to what some believed at the time, intelligence gained from satellite reconnaissance actually added to international stability and even played a role in the eventual ending of the Cold War. In fact, it may be said that, in the absence of this intelligence source, arms-control agreements would have been unlikely.

The third Second World War development that both set the stage for, and carried into, the Cold War, was the intense human espionage conducted on both sides of the Iron Curtain. Before the war ended, the Soviet Union had more spies working against its allies than against its enemies. In the early post-war years, a remarkably large number of British, American, and West German citizens were working for Soviet intelligence. Senior British intelligence and Foreign Office personnel became traitors, and several well-placed US and West German bureaucrats and government officials betrayed their countries.

The so-called **Cambridge Five** compromised many British and American military and political secrets. At least three of them had access to strategic plans during the UN-approved, but US-led, Korean War. Early efforts to keep several Eastern European countries from falling into the Communist Bloc were frustrated by other compromises, and, as a result, scores of Western intelligence officers and local resistance fighters were betrayed and killed. Soviet intelligence officers in Britain and the USA recruited scientists and others working on the secret efforts to develop atomic weapons. When Klaus Fuchs, a German émigré scientist working on the British atomic project and later assigned to be part of the British team working on the US atomic project, fell under suspicion and was interrogated, the ring of 'Atomic Spies' began to unravel. Several critical scientific and engineering secrets were nevertheless betrayed to Soviet intelligence. As a result, the Soviet atomic bomb came five to seven years earlier than it otherwise would have come.

Soviet defectors who stayed in their positions yet reported to Western intelligence (Oleg Penkovsky, Adolf Tolkachev, and Oleg Gordievsky, for example) added to the intrigue of the latter half of the twentieth century, and large-scale and expensive intelligence agencies became a fact of life in most globally active states.

KEY POINTS

- The sigint capabilities of major powers came to play an increasingly significant role in international security matters.

- The Cold War saw the development of the first US peacetime civilian intelligence agency (the CIA), the formalization of intelligence cooperation through the UKUSA Agreement, the growth of spy–counterspy efforts on both sides of the Iron Curtain, and the heavy reliance on high-tech 'eyes-in-the-sky' surveillance.

- Overhead satellite reconnaissance, first instituted to assist in preventing future surprise wars, later came to be a valuable aid in stabilizing and reducing the tension of the Cold War.

Legal and ethical issues involving intelligence

The twenty-first century has seen an increase in the need for and use of intelligence and an increase in the ways it can be collected. But these developments have also raised even more questions about the legality and ethics of intelligence operations. Much has been written on this topic, but it is not as complicated as some think. First, the domestic laws of the collecting nation always permit (either expressly in statutes that create intelligence agencies or tacitly through the existence of such agencies) the sending of their own personnel abroad for such purposes. The nation recruits these people, trains them, pays them, and provides for their retirement.

Second, positive international law (bilateral and multilateral treaty obligations between states) is generally silent or permissive on the subject of espionage. Some interpret the presence of verification clauses in a variety of arms-control, disarmament, non-proliferation, and other international treaties as legitimizing that aspect of intelligence collection. Most of these treaties contain a clause to the effect that no state that is a party to the agreement will interfere with national technical means (NTM) of verification. NTM normally refers to overhead surveillance or other electronic collection techniques. Customary international law (traditional and accepted patterns of international interaction) is

ambiguous on the subject—most authors view the ubiquity of spying as evidence of some legitimacy, while a few view spying as illegal under virtually any circumstances.

Third, the laws of all nations prohibit their own citizens from revealing state secrets to other nations. In short, it is legal under the laws of one's own nation to be sent abroad to persuade citizens of other nations to do what their own laws prohibit and international law largely ignores.

Discussions of the ethics of intelligence collection usually treat two aspects. The first aspect is the relationship of means to ends. As long as the purpose of the espionage is to protect and enhance a nation's security, and as long as the means chosen are the least intrusive available, many deem intelligence collection as ethical, particularly if the state is democratic and affords its citizens human rights.

The second aspect refers to the overall international environment in which the collection occurs. In an anarchic international environment with minimal or no international sources of security beyond the individual nation, the 'others-do-it' theory is often used as an ethical justification of collection. That is, as long as other nations are spying on us and, in effect, are compromising our security, it is ethical for us to spy on them if it enhances our security.

KEY POINTS

- The growing importance of intelligence to national security has raised many questions about legal and ethical issues in both the collection and use of intelligence.

- The ubiquity of intelligence activities throughout the world suggests that nations do not consider it to be in violation of their own domestic law to support such activities.

- International law is largely silent on the legality of intelligence, although intelligence activities that violate the

sovereignty of other nations require careful thought and more sophisticated justification.

- Many treaties and agreements between nations tacitly acknowledge the use of NTM for treaty verification. In fact, many arms-control, disarmament, non-proliferation, and drug-control agreements are based on the assumption of intelligence collection techniques for verification purposes and would not exist were such intelligence activities not possible.

Covert action

Covert action (CA), sometimes called special activities, refers to activities carried out by one state to alter political or economic developments in another state while disguising the source of that influence. Thus, the 1986 surprise American bombing of Libya was a secret military action but was not a covert action, since no attempt was made to disguise the source of the attack. However, CIA attempts to assassinate Cuban leader Fidel Castro in the mid-1960s, although they failed, were meant to remain secret for ever.

Some of these activities are relatively benign and minimally intrusive; others clearly violate the UN requirement not to interfere with the political independence or territorial integrity of other states. At the least intrusive end of the continuum are such activities as financial or political support to friendly political parties, labour groups, popular movements, media, and so on in foreign nations, where the democratic process is generally intact but under siege from anti-democratic forces. Some scholars feel that no sovereignty is abridged in such cases, while others believe that any secret attempt to influence developments in another state is wrong.

At the other end of the continuum are CA operations to support favourable groups or factions involved in civil conflicts, secretly provide weapons or military personnel in such conflicts, engineer coups to remove unfriendly political leaders or even attempt assassinations (see Case Study 18.1).

While CA gets huge press attention, it actually involves a relatively small percentage of the time and money of most intelligence agencies. The CIA, the agency widely thought to conduct CA all over the globe, probably has less than 5 per cent of its personnel involved in CA and spends well over 90 percent of its budget on normal collection and analysis efforts (Gates 1987–8: 216). Getting accurate information about CA is very difficult. More is known about operations that fail than those that succeed. Failed operations become public and are frequently written about by

---

CASE STUDY 18.1

Assassinations

Few intelligence topics attract more interest than that of assassinations. Most are surprised to find that spy novels and cinema romanticize a topic that does not deserve to be romanticized. Political officials and military officers are killed during war and civil unrest. But those deaths are usually associated with military activities—they are normally not killed by intelligence officers. Most covert action assassinations in the twentieth century have been carried out only by Soviet and Israeli intelligence agencies. British, French, and American agencies have talked about assassinations, but, even in these cases, only one was actually attempted, and it failed.

The CIA has been accused of ordering the assassinations of several foreign political leaders. However, thorough examinations by a committee of the US Senate found that, while the CIA may have talked about getting rid of five foreign political officials, they actually attempted to do so in only one case. In the case of Fidel Castro, long time ruler of Cuba, the CIA ran several unsuccessful assassination attempts and, in one of the most bizarre developments in American history, actually subcontracted the job to the criminal Mafia on one occasion. All attempts failed.

Soviet intelligence agencies were quite successful in eliminating political émigrés. From the pick axe used to kill Leon Trotsky in Mexico to the poisoned pellets delivered on the end of an umbrella in the London Underground, Soviet agents, in many cases by their own admission, carried out many assassination plots during the Cold War.

Israeli intelligence agents methodically tracked and killed most of the PLO group that attacked Israeli athletes in the 1972 Olympics in Munich. Unfortunately, they also killed an innocent person in Norway in 1974.

journalists and scholars. Successful operations, however, remain covert or secret for many years.

The use of covert activities to alter developments in other nations is a singularly dangerous foreign-policy tool that must be used very sparingly. In fact, in the absence of similar activities by other nations, it would be easy to argue that, at least in peacetime, nations should refrain completely from any covert actions. Given the anarchic nature of the international environment, however, and as long as some nations engage in CA, other nations use that fact to justify their own CA.

Can covert action be justified?

Those who attempt to justify CA argue that it fills a gap between diplomacy and war. This is called 'the gap theory of covert action'. That is, after a state has pursued policies, beginning with the least intrusive and continuing up to the most serious diplomatic action, and war still appears to be inevitable, some argue that some variations of CA might be better than war and may actually prevent war.

One effort to make CA more ethically acceptable is to apply some of the principles drawn from the famous Just War Theory to CA. For example, one could argue a nation must consider six criteria before initiating CA.

1. *Essentiality*. The desired goal of the CA must be essential to national security. CA short of this should not be undertaken. CA should never be considered routine. It should be deemed essential by both executive and parliamentary institutions.

2. *Feasibility*. The proposed CA must be feasible. That is, it must involve resources that are available and that will not be jeopardized by routine domestic political changes.

3. *Last resort*. Covert action must be the best, if not the only, means to accomplish the desired goal. All too often policy-makers have turned to covert action, not because it was the best way to accomplish a task, but because it was seen as secret, and therefore, the easiest option. It should never be initiated merely because it is secret, because it will not remain secret for long.

4. *Legitimacy*. Approval procedures for CA must be spelled out clearly and must require the written approval of senior officials. Covert action is the most intrusive and potentially dangerous of all government foreign-policy tools and should not be authorized by word of mouth, by low-level officials, or, even worse, by operators in the field.

5. *Commensurability*. The degree of force, intrusiveness, and deception must be commensurate with the nature of the threat. In democratic nations, the public will usually support CA if such is the case. They will not support it if massive clandestine efforts appear to be in response to minor irritants or embarrassments and pursued merely because they are covert.

KEY POINTS

- Covert actions are secret activities by one state to influence political and economic developments in another state without the source of the influence being known.

- The overwhelming majority of covert actions are fairly benign, but some clearly violate the sovereignty of the target state.

- Assassination attempts by intelligence agencies are quite rare except in the case of the former Soviet Union and Israeli intelligence. The USA actually tried, unsuccessfully, to assassinate Fidel Castro, while other states have considered contingency plans for assassinations.

- Covert actions are a very small part of the operations of most intelligence agencies.

- Some believe that 'the Gap Theory' does justify CA; others believe that the Just War Theory can be adapted to evaluate the ethicality of Covert Actions.

6. *Popular support*. All CA, even those few carried out in complete secrecy, must be able to stand the light of public awareness eventually. When knowledge of CA eventually seeps out, governments must not be embarrassed by that knowledge.

Terrorism, Iraq, and the post 9/11 security environment

Few events have heightened the relationship between security and intelligence more than the al-Qaeda sponsored terrorist attacks that began in Somalia in 1993 and have continued up to the present day. Chapter 20 will discuss terrorism in more detail, but this chapter will highlight some of the ways these attacks have altered the security and intelligence environment.

First, the amount of public funds devoted to intelligence services and operations has increased markedly. While the budgets of intelligence agencies are usually secret, in a variety of very public ways it is clear that money is flowing into them at ever-increasing rates. In some cases, it is more money than the agencies themselves have requested; but, for obvious political reasons, legislative bodies have not wanted to seem cheap on this issue (Taylor and Goldman 2004: 421).

Second, an increasing percentage of intelligence spending is being targeted against terrorism. This is not surprising, but it is leaving other traditional intelligence targets (non-proliferation, transnational drugs and crime, and even WMD, for example) underfunded and ripe for surprise.

Third, the most immediate result of 9/11 was the 2001 invasion of Afghanistan, an Islamist government providing safe haven for Osama bin Laden and his al-Qaeda base. But, as that war progressed, some nations, particularly the USA and the UK, believed that Iraq was also supporting Islamist terrorism and was developing WMD that, in the hands of future terrorists, could be more damaging than hijacked aeroplanes.

Western intelligence organizations had been monitoring Iraqi developments for many years, at least since the first war against Iraq brought on by an Iraqi invasion of Kuwait in 1990. But the desire to attack terrorists any place they might be and to change regimes that might be harbouring terrorists triggered increased intelligence efforts against radical Islam. Virtually every Western intelligence organization significantly increased collection efforts against Iraq, especially after UN inspectors were forced out of Iraq in 1998. And, by 9/11, every Western intelligence organization (UK, US, German, French, and Israeli) believed that Iraq was continuing WMD development in violation of UN sanctions, that it had missiles with ranges beyond that proscribed by the UN, and that, within five to seven years, it could arm these missiles with nuclear weapons.

Failing to get UN approval for an invasion, the UK and the USA (with help from Australia, Poland, and, to a lesser extent, other states) launched an attack against Iraq in 2003. The war was over quickly, but the challenges of occupation and pacification proved to be much more than anticipated. Even more importantly, virtually no evidence was found to support the conclusions of the various intelligence reports on which the decision to go to war had been based. Some have called this one of the worst intelligence failures of all time (see Key Ideas 18.1).

Fourth, allegations of intelligence failure have brought about reform efforts in several Western nations. Since 9/11 the intelligence services of several major countries have been studied and investigated more than at any previous time in history. Two parliamentary inquiries and two additional commissions studied aspects of British intelligence. The Butler Commission made several recommendations

KEY IDEAS 18.1

What Went Wrong about Iraq? Four Theories

The following are summaries of theories that explain why both UK and US intelligence agencies were wrong about WMD prior to the 2003 invasion of Iraq. In fact, virtually all Western intelligence agencies, including Russia and Israel, were—to one degree or another—wrong about this. Each theory is followed by a brief evaluation.

1. *Intelligence Conspiracy Theory*. UK and US intelligence agencies were so anxious to get into a war with Iraq that they fed government decision-makers patently false information about the extent of WMD in Iraq.

Fact. No investigation of intelligence agencies in the UK or USA has turned up any evidence to support this theory. In fact, some agencies in both countries argued that no evidence of an advanced nuclear programme existed.

2. *Defence Intelligence Conspiracy Theory*. Defence-related intelligence agencies in both countries falsified evidence so they could get their military forces into Iraq.

Fact. Again, no investigation has provided any evidence to support this theory. However, at least within the American defence-related intelligence agencies, evidence supports the notion that some intelligence officials, anxious to please their superiors and to meet their strenuous and repeated requests for intelligence to support the invasion, relied on Iraqi defectors and other questionable sources for information that was not put through the normal intelligence cycle. This is referred to as 'cherry picking', providing unanalysed information to decision-makers.

3. *Groupthink Theory*. This theory asserts that, as intelligence analysts working on the issue of WMD in Iraq

evaluated and discussed available evidence, they gradually came to accept prevailing interpretations of ambiguous evidence because of a desire to conform to group beliefs.

Fact. No investigations have revealed the slightest hint that would justify this interpretation. Senior analysts in both the UK and USA have ridiculed this interpretation in confidential interviews with the author.

4. *Bureaucratic Pressure Theory*. This theory, often called 'cooking the intelligence to fit the decision-maker's recipe', argues that recurring appeals from senior decision-makers to find intelligence support for an Iraqi invasion caused analysts to interpret ambiguous evidence in a way that was most friendly to their supervisors, who had to deal frequently with the senior decision-makers.

Fact. This theory, with some modifications, is probably the best explanation of what happened. It is true that very senior decision-makers, close to the head of state in each country, met frequently with senior IC managers and asked for intelligence about WMD in Iraq prior to the invasion. No evidence exists that these decision-makers ordered intelligence to be fabricated. But they did repeatedly encourage the analysts to 're-evaluate' and 'keep looking', and this created within the analytical branches a sense of pressure to phrase the evidence in certain ways. It also led to the 'cherry picking' discussed above. This phenomenon was enhanced in a climate of multiple analytical centres across a nation's IC, each trying to gain bureaucratic advantages and favour. It is possible in some analytical centres that 'groupthink' became a factor at a certain point in the process.

---

about intelligence procedures that the Blair government accepted. In the USA, three congressional reports and scores of think-tank and other independent commissions made recommendations for reform. The most significant intelligence reform since the creation of the CIA in 1947 came about in 2005 with the creation of a National Intelligence Director (NID) along with a large support office. The bulk of these institutional and/or procedural reforms are meant to increase intelligence coordination within each nation and greater intelligence cooperation between nations.

Two ironies ought to be noted, however. First, throughout the modern history of intelligence, nearly every intelligence failure has been abetted, if not caused, by national intelligence communities grown so large and cumbersome that internal cooperation and external collaboration became scarce and difficult. At the same time, the political response to accusations of intelligence failure has usually been the creation of more agencies and sub-agencies, more money, and more personnel—thus feeding the very condition that contributed to the intelligence failure in the first place (Taylor and Goldman 2004: 421). Second, one effect of the global response to modern terrorism has been to diminish, in various ways and degrees in diverse countries, the very democratic conditions that people in democracies deem worthy of defence.

KEY POINTS

- Two approaches to combating contemporary jihadist terrorism have been to create new intelligence agencies and sub-agencies and to devote ever larger sums to counterterrorism. These very responses increase the cumbersome nature of intelligence agencies and diminish coordination and correlation—the very source of intelligence failures.

- The tendency to assume that the next terrorist attack will be like the last one takes intelligence assets away from the developments that may lead to the next, and different, attack.

- The 2003 Iraqi War (in ways merely part of the war on terrorism) was initiated on the basis of faulty intelligence brought about by decision-makers so hungry for supporting evidence that they could shop around for analytical products that supported their predilections and could use raw unprocessed intelligence if it supported their views.

- The question of whether the decision to invade Iraq was an intelligence failure or a policy failure is still open to debate, although sufficient blame exists to taint both decision-makers as well as the practices of some intelligence agencies.

Conclusion

From time immemorial, tribes, clans, empires, and nations have collected information about other groups in order to make more informed decisions when dealing with them. This information is called intelligence and its collection may well be the 'second oldest profession' in the world. As from the beginning, modern nations believe that the collection, analysis, and use of good intelligence will enhance their security in an anarchic world.

Nineteenth-century intelligence was generally minimal and focused on potential enemies. But by the beginning of the twentieth century, most global powers, with the exception of the USA, had both military and civilian intelligence agencies operating in times of peace as well as war. The first two wars of the twentieth century saw the growth and institutionalization of these agencies, which, at times, made significant contributions to the war effort. The Japanese surprise attack on Pearl Harbor in December 1941 convinced the Americans that they needed to have a civilian intelligence agency. More than any other war before it, the Second World War was an intelligence war. The famous British military historian John

Keegan (2003: 28) argues that intelligence does not win wars—that it takes the courage and skills of fighting men and women to do that. But, through the Second World War, intelligence made significant contributions to the war effort in many different ways—the war in the Pacific was turned around by intelligence, the war in the Atlantic profited from intelligence, counterintelligence efforts in Britain and the USA virtually eliminated German spies, and the intelligence-devised deception associated with the D-Day Invasion was critical.

Intelligence during the Cold War had two major characteristics. First, techint became extremely sophisticated. Spy planes, satellite surveillance, computer-assisted cryptography, and remote controlled listening and imaging devices changed the way much intelligence was collected. Second, humint became pervasive. State secrets of every major power were betrayed to other states. In the early days of the Cold War, most traitors were ideologically motivated. Westerners sympathetic to communism penetrated their own military, intelligence, and government structures. And Russians sympathetic to democratic ideals betrayed Soviet secrets to Western intelligence. But, as idealism faded, most traitors went into the business for money.

Keegan's pessimism about the role of intelligence might be more correct for the Cold War than for the shooting wars. One wonders, for example, about the net effect of all of the spy—counterspy interactions. To what degree were largely defensive intelligence activities on one side seen as provocative by the other (see Case Study 18.2)? Perhaps the best that could be said for Cold War intelligence is that the sophisticated verification and monitoring

---

📌 **CASE STUDY 18.2**

Operations Ryan and Able/Archer: The 'security dilemma' at work

The 'security dilemma' describes a condition in which insignificant, or even benign, actions on the part of one state can be interpreted as threatening to another state, particularly during times of crises such as the Cold War. The second state then takes what it deems are defensive actions, which are, in turn, interpreted by the first state as a confirmation of intended hostilities. This action and reaction may continue until actual hostilities break out. A set of Soviet and Western intelligence and political actions in the early 1980s illustrate this model.

In May 1981, Soviet Premier Leonid Brezhnev told a KGB conference that US President Reagan was preparing for a nuclear attack on the USSR. KGB head Yuri Andropov then announced Operation RYAN (Raketno Yadernoye Napdenie—Russian for nuclear missile attack), a combined KGB/GRU intelligence initiative that by 1983 involved nearly all Soviet Bloc intelligence services. Even though KGB American experts were sceptical of this interpretation of American intentions, Operation RYAN launched an enormous increase, both sigint and humint, in the monitoring of Western military planning.

Of course, Western intelligence collectors picked up this increased Soviet monitoring, and tensions increased even more. By 1983, conservative US President Ronald Reagan was in his third year in the White House and conservative British Prime Minister Margaret Thatcher was in her second term at 10 Downing Street. Western rhetoric (Reagan labelled the Soviet Union an 'evil empire' in March 1983 and announced his Strategic Defense Initiative in the same month) as well as Cold War policies (the December 1979 Soviet invasion of Afghanistan, Western and Islamic states' boycott of the Moscow 1980 Olympics, the American refusal to ratify the SALT II agreement, and Reagan's unilateral invasion of Grenada in October 1983, among others) had increased Cold War tensions to even greater heights.

In August 1983 the Soviets tested their first missile with multiple warheads—the SS-X-24. On the night of that test, Western intelligence put their entire missile test-monitoring collectors in place. Next, Soviet radar that was monitoring the flight paths of American sensor aircraft began tracking the flight of a civilian Korean passenger airliner (KAL 007), and early in the morning of 1 September shot it down with a loss of 269 lives. Because of pilot error, the jet had strayed off course and was over Soviet-controlled Sakhalin Island.

Western leaders denounced what they called 'uncivilized' behaviour, and the Soviet's Operation RYAN was seen as an even-more-threatening portend of Soviet intentions. President Reagan called for greater vigilance and called for a major diplomatic effort to keep attention focused on Soviet behaviour. On the other hand, Operation RYAN now seemed more important to Soviet leaders, who denounced NATO's placement of Pershing missiles into Western Germany on 23 November.

In the meantime, NATO, in reaction to Operation RYAN and the KAL 007 episode, launched a command exercise called Operation ABLE ARCHER in order to test communications and decision-making equipment and procedures in case it was necessary to invade the Soviet Union. This was essentially a command and control exercise and did not involve the movement of any military forces. But, as Richelson (1995: 386) states: 'While the Soviets and their allies monitored ABLE ARCHER, the United States and its allies used their SIGINT to monitor the monitors.' A senior KGB defector, Oleg Gordievsky, pointed out the dangers of such intelligence collection and military exercises when he said: 'The world did not quite reach the edge of the nuclear abyss during [these operations] . . . But . . . it had come close—certainly closer than at any time since the Cuban missile crisis of 1962' (Andrew and Gordievsky 1991: 605).

In mid-1984 tensions eventually resumed normal levels as it became clear that neither side was actually planning a nuclear attack. But Operations RYAN and ABLE ARCHER are still reminders of one of the potential hazards of intelligence-collecting activities.

abilities of the protagonists eventually reduced tensions, provided some stability, and may have prevented benign activities from being perceived as threatening and thus triggering violent responses. Moreover, a major source for political reform in the Soviet Union came from intelligence officers who had travelled and lived in Western nations more freely than other Soviet citizens were allowed. They could see the disadvantages of a command economy combined with a dictatorial political system and began to lead efforts for reform.

In the 1990s, just when people in many nations were thinking intelligence agencies could be eliminated or, at least, reduced, international terrorism provoked cries for increased intelligence. Terrorism was not new. It had been around literally for centuries. But the dramatic rise of terrorism sponsored by extremist Islamist groups raised the stakes to unprecedented heights. The al-Qaeda attacks beginning in the early 1990s challenged the security of many states as well as global stability. They, along with issues of weapons proliferation and international drug and criminal activities, have brought about the greatest expansion of intelligence agencies and the greatest infusion of money in history.

At the same time, the failures of intelligence agencies to predict al-Qaeda attacks and the faulty intelligence about WMD in Iraq have brought about unprecedented scrutiny and transparency of intelligence agencies. Heads of intelligence agencies are now public figures. Their operations have become so public that some believe the phrase 'secret intelligence' has become an oxymoron. Moreover, to prevent terrorists from organizing cells in a country, intelligence agencies, with parliamentary and legislative authority, have become more pervasive, and their very actions seem to some to threaten the civil liberties that characterize Western civilization. The modern security environment (terrorism, nuclear proliferation, transnational criminal activities—all occurring during unprecedented globalization) has brought about calls for stronger intelligence activities, while at the same time it has created concerns about the unintended consequences of intelligence activities.

When the intelligence process works well—when decision-makers ask penetrating questions, when collectors are creative and successful, when analysts paint accurate pictures, and when political pressures on intelligence agencies are at a minimum—when these conditions exist, intelligence can and has made valuable contributions to national security in every state. When the process does not work well, national security may be diminished and the foreign reactions intelligence activities generate may complicate diplomacy and increase international tensions.

? QUESTIONS

1. The word 'intelligence' has many meanings. What is the meaning used in this chapter?

2. If the gathering of intelligence is ancient, what has changed about it in the post-service economy information age?

3. How does the theory of cybernetics explain the function of intelligence?

4. While the intelligence community of every nation is somewhat unique, what functions are quite common between them?

5. In what ways has intelligence contributed to various arms control treaties and agreements?

6. What developments have changed technical-intelligence (techint) collection techniques?

7. How does the actual intelligence cycle or process differ from the theoretical one?

8. Do you think that intelligence collection violates international law? Why?

9. What significant techint development began in 1956 after the Soviets had rejected the American Open Skies proposal?

10. Do you agree or disagree with the author's attempt to apply the Just War Theory to covert actions? Why or why not?

11. Which do you think occurs more frequently, 'policy failures' or 'intelligence failures'?

12. What effect has contemporary jihadism had on intelligence activities in most Western nations?

13. Discuss how aggressive intelligence collection might actually increase international tension.

FURTHER READING

- Andrew, Christopher (1987), *Her Majesty's Secret Service: The Making of the British Intelligence Community*, London: Penguin. A thorough history of the origins of British intelligence. Andrew has also written the best histories of both American and Soviet intelligence in *For the President's Eyes Only: Secret Intelligence and the American Presidency from Washington to Bush* (New York: Harper Collins, 1995), and, with Oleg Gordievsky, *KGB: The Inside Story* (New York: Harper Collins, 1990).

- Born, Hans, Johnson, Loch K., and Leigh, Ian (2005) (eds.), *Who's Watching the Spies: Establishing Intelligence Service Accountability*, Dulles, VA: Potomac Books. The best introduction to the issues of democratic accountability and government oversight of intelligence from a global perspective.

- Herman, Michael (1996), *Intelligence Power in Peace and War,* Cambridge: Cambridge University Press. One of the only general works on intelligence that takes a somewhat theoretical and global perspective.

- Haufler, Hervie (2003), *Codebreakers' Victory: How the Allied Cryptographers Won World War II,* New York: New American Library, and Keegan, John (2003), *Intelligence in War: Knowledge of the Enemy from Napoleon to al-Qaeda*, London: Hutchinson. These take somewhat contradictory sides on the relationship between intelligence and military victory. Both are very readable.

- Johnson, Loch K. , and Wirtz, James J. (2004) (eds.), *Strategic Intelligence: Windows into a Secret World*, Los Angeles: Roxbury Press. The best, and nearly the only, intelligence anthology. Its contributors represent the best scholarship in the rapidly growing field of intelligence scholarship.

- Kahn, David (1996), *The Code-Breakers: The Comprehensive History of Secret Communication from Ancient Times to the Internet*, rev. edn., New York: Scribner. This book is pretty much what it claims to be—an excellent, definitive, and lengthy history of cryptography.

- Lowenthal, Mark M. (2006), *Intelligence: From Secrets to Policy*, 3rd edn., Washington: CQ Press. Takes a US-centric approach but may be the best short introduction to the intelligence process. It includes one chapter on the intelligence services of other major nations.

- Richelson, Jeffrey T. (1995), *A Century of Spies: Intelligence in the Twentieth Century*, Oxford: Oxford University Press. One of the better books with a multinational approach to modern intelligence history.

- *Intelligence and National Security* and the *International Journal of Intelligence and CounterIntelligence* are the two best academic journals on this topic. They address a wide range of intelligence topics and both are published by Routledge of the Taylor and Francis Group.

IMPORTANT WEBSITES

Official websites of national intelligence agencies or communities:

- http://www.csis-scrs.gc.ca   Canadian Security Intelligence Service.

- http://www.intelligence.gov   Official access point for all US intelligence agencies.

- http://www.mi5.gov.uk   UK domestic intelligence service – MI 5.

- http://www.gchq.gov.uk   UK signals intelligence agency.

Think tanks or research centres working on intelligence:

- http://fas.org   Homepage of the Federation of American Scientists, whose intelligence links and data are one of the best available about intelligence in all major nations.

- http://intellit.muskingum.edu   Best web-based bibliography.

- http://www.gwu.edu/~nsarchiv/   Quite critical, but still best documentary source about US intelligence.

- http://www.loyola.edu/dept/politics/intel.html   Best university intelligence web page with links to every available national intelligence service home page.

 Visit the Online Resource Centre that accompanies this book for lots of interesting additional material: www.oxfordtextbooks.co.uk/orc/collins2e/

19

Weapons of Mass Destruction

JAMES J. WIRTZ

 Chapter Contents

- Introduction
- Nuclear weapons
- Chemical weapons
- Biological weapons
- Conclusion

 Reader's Guide

Since the late 1990s, policy-makers everywhere have been deeply concerned about the possibility that weapons of mass destruction—chemical, biological, nuclear, and radiological weapons—are not only becoming fixtures in the arsenals of states, but might fall into the hands of terrorists. This chapter explains how these weapons work and the effects they might have if used on the battlefield or against civilian targets. It describes how they have been used in war and how they have shaped the practice of international politics.

Introduction

Although many observers hoped that the danger posed by weapons of mass destruction (WMD)—chemical, biological, nuclear, and radiological weapons—would fade with the end of the Cold War, these armaments continue to pose a worldwide threat. Some progress has been made in terms of rolling back WMD proliferation. Iraq no longer menaces its neighbours with its chemical arsenal, and its efforts to acquire nuclear and biological weapons have been thwarted. Libya has also abandoned its nuclear weapons programme. The international community has bolstered the non-proliferation regime by undertaking a series of diplomatic efforts, for example the Chemical Weapons Convention, the Biological Weapons Convention, the Proliferation Security Initiative, and the 2002 Moscow Treaty. The Barack Obama administration also seems determined to re-energize arms negotiations between the United States and Russia. Despite these concerted efforts, however, several state and non-state actors find WMD to be an attractive part of their arsenals. Black-market trade in nuclear materials, technology, and know-how is increasing. In 2004, revelations that the Pakistani scientist A. Q. Khan might have provided information about gas centrifuges (used to produce weapons-grade uranium) and nuclear-bomb designs to North Korea, Iraq, Iran, Libya, and Syria sent a shock wave through the non-proliferation community (Clary 2004; Albright and Hinderstein 2005). Indigenous nuclear programmes are also making existing proliferation safeguards obsolete (Braun and Chyba 2004). For some states, WMD provide a way to offset their inferiority in conventional armaments compared to stronger regional rivals or the United States and its allies. Leaders of these regimes probably hope that the threat of chemical, biological, or nuclear warfare might deter stronger opponents contemplating attack, defeat those opponents once battle has been joined, or even threaten domestic opponents (Lavoy et al. 2000). Weapons of mass destruction also serve as status symbols that highlight the 'success' of otherwise dubious regimes.

If the threat posed by WMD proliferation to state actors is of increasing concern, then the possibility that these weapons could fall into the hands of terrorists or even individuals is alarming. A chemical weapons attack against a major sporting venue could kill thousands of people, while a successful anthrax attack might place hundreds of thousands at risk. A 'dirty bomb', a device that uses high explosives to spread radioactive contamination, could poison scores of city blocks. It would be extraordinarily difficult for even a well-funded terrorist organization to construct a primitive gun-type nuclear weapon, but international terrorist networks, domestic terrorist organizations, or even individuals have the resources and materials to construct and use chemical, biological, and radiological weapons. Weapons of mass destruction have been used in terrorist attacks, albeit with relatively limited effects. In 1995, for instance, Chechen rebels planted radiological source (caesium-137) in Moscow's Izmailovsky Park, probably to show Russian authorities that they had the capability to make a 'dirty bomb'. The Aum Shinrikyo (Aum Supreme Truth) cult experimented with several toxic substances before launching their Sarin attack against the Tokyo subway in 1995 that injured thousands of people. In the wake of the 9/11 terrorist attacks against the World Trade Center and Pentagon, some person or group in 2001 used the US postal system to mail letters contaminated with anthrax, which was probably derived from materials supplied to US weapons laboratories.

Weapons of mass destruction vary greatly in terms of their availability, lethality, and destructive potential, and the ease with which they can be manufactured and employed. High-yield, lightweight nuclear weapons are some of the most sophisticated machines ever manufactured by humans, while some chemical and biological weapons have been available for centuries. What separates WMD from conventional weapons, created from chemical-based explosives, however, is their potential to generate truly catastrophic levels of death and destruction. A small nuclear weapon can devastate a city: the fission device that destroyed Hiroshima produced an explosive blast (yield) that was equivalent to about 20 kilotons (kt) of trinitrotoluene (TNT). A smallpox attack against an unprotected (unvaccinated) population could kill 30 per cent of its victims and leave survivors horribly scarred for life. Because of their ability to strike terror worldwide, these weapons are attractive as political instruments.

The remainder of this chapter will first describe the technology that underlies nuclear, chemical, and biological weapons, and explain how they are constructed. What is reassuring about this overview is the fact that, while these weapons can be extra ordinarily destructive, state and non-state actors would have to overcome significant technical hurdles before they could maximize their destructive power. The chapter will also describe their destructive effects, the systems used to deliver them, and the history of their use in war. It will then outline the impact these weapons have on national defence policy and international security.

Nuclear weapons

The design and development of nuclear weapons were based on advances in theoretical and experimental physics that began at the start of the twentieth century. By the late 1930s, Leo Szilard, a physicist who escaped Nazi persecution by fleeing to the United States, realized that it might be possible to construct an 'atomic bomb'. Unlike conventional (chemical) explosions, which are produced by a rapid rearrangement of the hydrogen, oxygen, carbon, and nitrogen atoms that are components of TNT, for example, Szilard suggested that a nuclear explosion could be created by a change in atomic nuclei themselves. If an atom of uranium-235, for instance, is fragmented into two relatively equal parts, the remaining mass of the two new atoms would have less mass than the original atom. The lost mass would be instantaneously converted into energy. Nuclear weapons are so powerful because, as Albert Einstein predicted, under certain conditions mass and energy are interchangeable ($E = MC^2$). The difficult aspect of setting off this interchange would be to create a device that would sustain a nuclear reaction for a fraction of a second before it is destroyed in the resulting nuclear explosion.

Szilard's opinion was not widely shared among American scientists or government officials, so he enlisted the aid of his friend, Albert Einstein, to bring the issue to the attention of President Franklin D. Roosevelt. In a letter dated 2 August 1939, Einstein informed Roosevelt that it was theoretically possible to construct an atomic bomb and that the Nazis might be hard at work constructing such a device. It took the USA entry into the Second World War to launch a full-scale project to construct a nuclear weapon, the UK–US Manhattan Project, which began in September 1942. The first nuclear (fission) device was ready for testing at Alamagordo New Mexico on 6 July 1945. It was quickly followed by the detonation of 'Little Boy' over Hiroshima on 6 August 1945 and 'Fat Man' over Nagasaki on 9 August 1945.

Fission weapons all share similar components: fissile material (for example, U-235 or Plutonium); chemical explosives; non-fissile materials to reflect neutrons and tamp the explosion; and some sort of neutron generator to help initiate the nuclear reaction. Weapons also need triggers, a mechanical safety, arming, and firing mechanisms. There are two basic types of fission weapons. 'Little Boy' was a gun-type fission device. This is the simplest and least-efficient nuclear weapon design (the design requires a relatively large amount of fissile material to produce a relatively small blast). In a gun design, two sub-critical masses of U-235 are fired down a barrel, striking each other at extremely high velocities producing a fission reaction. Gun-type devices, however, are rugged and have a relatively high probability of 'going critical'—that is, producing a nuclear detonation. The second design, an implosion-type device, uses high-explosive lenses to compress the fissile material—'Fat Man' utilized plutonium—until it reaches criticality. Implosion devices are relatively difficult to manufacture and assemble because the shaped charges that compress the fissile material need to be manufactured to critical tolerances and detonated with more than split-second timing. The physics and engineering behind the design and manufacture of nuclear weapons are widely available. What is far more difficult to acquire are highly enriched uranium (U-235) and plutonium. These materials are under safeguards, and their production and storage are monitored by the International Atomic Energy Agency (IAEA) and the declared and undeclared nuclear-weapons states themselves.

A fusion weapon is a three-stage bomb that uses an implosion device to trigger a fission reaction, which in turn detonates a fusion reaction (a process whereby one heavier nucleus is produced from two lighter nuclei). When the nuclei of light elements are combined, the resulting heaver element has less mass than the two original nuclei, and the difference in mass is instantaneously translated into energy. Often referred to as a thermo-nuclear weapon, or a hydrogen bomb, fusion weapons can be relatively small and lightweight, and pack virtually unlimited destructive force. During the Cold War, large nuclear weapons had yields in the millions of tons—megatons (mgt)—of TNT. On 31 October 1952, for example, the United States tested its first fusion device (Test Mike) at Eniwetok atoll in the Pacific Ocean. It produced a yield of about 10 mgt, which is equivalent to 10,000 kt. The most powerful nuclear weapon ever detonated was the Tsar Bomba (King of Bombs), which was a reduced-yield test of a 100-mgt bomb design. A product of Soviet science, the device was detonated with a 50-mgt yield on 30 October 1961 at the Mityushikha Bay Test range, Novayua Zemlya Island, producing a flash so bright that it was visible 1,000 km away. Bombs in the multi-megaton range generally have limited military utility since their destructive radius often exceeds the size of potential urban or military targets.

Nuclear-weapons effects

Compared to the devices we encounter in our everyday lives, nuclear weapons operate at the extremes of time, pressure, and temperature. The entire explosive process of a hydrogen bomb, for example,

Table 19.1 Nuclear-weapons states

Country	Fission Device	Fusion Device
United States	1945	1952
Soviet Union	1949	1953
United Kingdom	1952	1957
France	1960	1966
PRC	1964	1967
Israel	1967?	1973?
India	1974	1998?
Pakistan	1998	1998?
North Korea	2006	

occurs over the period of a few thousand nanoseconds (a nanosecond is 1/100,000,000 of a second). Pressure within a fusion bomb core can reach up to 8,000,000,000 tons per square inch and temperatures exceeding those found on the surface of the sun (6,000 °C). Nuclear weapons introduce galactic scale forces into a terrestrial environment, producing devastating consequences.

Nuclear-weapons effects are shaped by a variety of factors, including the weapon's explosive yield, its height of detonation, weather conditions, and terrain features. For example, an airburst occurs when the nuclear fireball does not touch the ground. Airbursts distribute the explosive blast and the radiation burst produced at detonation over a relatively wide area. Raising the height of burst lowers the pressure generated immediately below the detonation, but covers a larger area with somewhat lower overpressure. A ground burst maximizes the overpressure against a specific target—a missile silo or a command and control complex. A ground burst produces a great deal of fallout, because the fireball irradiates and lofts dirt and debris high into the atmosphere. Nuclear weapons can also be driven deep beneath the earth's surface in an effort to couple their explosive power more efficiently to the ground to destroy deeply buried and hardened targets.

All nuclear weapons produce similar effects, although the balance between these effects can be altered somewhat by design. An average nuclear weapon (about 100 kt) detonated in the atmosphere will deliver 50 per cent of its energy as blast, 35 per cent as thermal radiation, and about 15 per cent into gamma and residual radiation. A so-called neutron bomb, for instance, shifts some of the energy involved in a nuclear detonation from blast into radiation effects. Not all nuclear effects, however, are known or well understood. In the aftermath of a US high-altitude test of a 1.4 mgt weapon in 1962, for example, scientists were surprised to learn that the resulting electro-magnetic pulse (EMP) burned out street lights and fuses and opened circuit breakers 800 miles away in Oahu (Hansen 1988: 87). In the 1980s, scientists and analysts also debated

whether a full-scale nuclear exchange would plunge the world into nuclear winter (Turco et al. 1990). By contrast, nuclear blast and thermal effects can be predicted with great precision; the US military generally relies on blast effects to estimate the damage that will be produced by a nuclear detonation.

The best-known and most important nuclear-weapons effects are EMP, a thermal-light pulse, blast, and fallout. EMP and the thermal-light pulse are produced at the instant of detonation. Electromagnetic pulse occurs when gamma radiation interacts with matter (for example, the atmosphere)—a process known as the Compton effect. EMP produces a high-voltage electrical charge, which is harmless to humans, but can destroy electronic systems that are not specifically shielded against its effects. EMP effects are maximized by detonating weapons at relatively high altitudes (100,000 feet). In theory, a single high-altitude nuclear detonation could temporarily knock out most electronic systems in a medium-sized country. Thermal-light pulse, which lasts about two seconds, can cause flash blindness and fire. A 1-mgt airburst could produce flash blindness in individuals 53 miles away on a clear night and 13 miles away on a clear day. This airburst would cause first-degree burns on unprotected skin 7 miles away, second-degree burns at about 6 miles away, and third-degree burns at about 5 miles away.

A shockwave (a sudden rise in atmosphere pressure) and dynamic overpressure (wind) follow a few seconds behind the thermal light pulse. At about one mile away, a 1-mgt airburst will produce 20 lb per square inch (psi) overpressure and 470 mph winds, pressure sufficient to level steel-reinforced concrete structures. At 3 miles away, overpressure reaches 10 psi, producing winds of about 290 mph, sufficient to destroy most commercial structures and private residences. At 5 miles away, winds reach about 160 mph and overpressure reaches 5 psi, enough to damage most structures and subject people caught in the open to lethal collisions with flying debris. Blast effects were generally used by military planners to calculate casualty rates in a nuclear attack: it was estimated that about 50 per cent of the people living within 5 miles of a 1-mgt airburst would be either killed or wounded by blast effects.

Individuals can be exposed to the fourth nuclear effect, radiation, either in the initial nuclear detonation or from fallout, which is irradiated debris picked up by the nuclear fireball and lofted into the atmosphere. A REM (roentgen-equivalent-man) is a measure of radiation energy absorbed by living creatures. 600 REM is likely to produce lethal radiation sickness in an exposed population, while a dose of 300 REM would produce lethal radiation sickness in about 10 per cent of an exposed population (United States Congress 1979).

A dirty bomb uses chemical high explosive to disperse radioactive material. It relies primarily on radiation to produce a lethal effect. A dirty bomb's lethality thus would be governed by how far radioactive materials might be lofted by the conventional chemical explosive and the radioactivity of the material used in the bomb. Many observers believe that the explosive blast produced by a dirty bomb, not the radioactive material it disperses, would cause the greatest amount of actual damage. Panic set off by even a limited dispersion of radioactive material, however, might be more costly in terms of the disruption it causes than the actual casualties or damage to property produced by the detonation of a dirty bomb.

Methods of delivery

Nuclear weapons have taken a variety of forms over the years. Early weapons were relatively large and heavy; only four-engine bombers were capable of lifting them. With the advent of thermonuclear (fusion) weapons, the size and weight of weapons began to decrease as their yields increased. Nuclear 'warheads' were soon mounted on cruise missiles, medium-range ballistic missiles, and eventually intercontinental ballistic missiles (ICBMs) and submarine-launched ballistic missiles that were launched beneath the surface of the ocean from nuclear-powered submarines. By the 1970s, multiple independently targetable re-entry vehicles were being installed aboard US and Soviet ICBMs, giving both superpowers the ability to

strike up to a dozen targets with one missile. Nuclear warheads were soon available for air-to-air missiles that were to be fired by aircraft to knock down incoming bombers, artillery shells, and even man-portable demolition charges. Neutron warheads were created to arm interceptor missiles that were part of the Safeguard Anti-Ballistic Missile System, which was developed by the United States in the 1970s. Both superpowers also investigated the possibility of deploying Fractional Orbital Bombardment Systems (FOBS)—that is, parking nuclear weapons in orbit so that they could be armed and targeted following an alert from ground-control stations. Mercifully, officials on both sides of the Cold War divide thought better of living literally with a sword of Damocles over their heads, and in the 1967 Outer Space Treaty they banned placement of nuclear weapons in space.

Today, officials are worried about the possibility that terrorists might somehow manufacture or acquire a nuclear weapon or a radiological device. Although a missile or airborne attack is possible, there is much concern that a weapon might be smuggled into a country in one of the thousands of marine shipping containers that travel the world's oceans everyday. There is also a possibility that a weapon's components could be shipped separately and assembled on site. Local police forces and national intelligence agencies also closely monitor efforts to sell radioactive materials on the black market. In 1998, for instance, Mamdough Mamud Salim, an al-Qaeda operative, was arrested after attempting to buy 'enriched uranium' in Western Europe (Boureston 2002). Nuclear or radiological weapons manufactured by terrorists would probably be relatively crude, suggesting that they would be relatively large and difficult to transport. Small, man-portable nuclear devices (for example, atomic demolitions) were manufactured by the superpowers during the Cold War, which has raised concerns that these weapons might find their way onto the black market. In September 1997, for instance, the CBS news program *Sixty Minutes* reported that former Russian National Security Adviser Aleksander Lebed claimed that the Russian military had lost track of 100 'suit-case bombs', each with a yield of about 10 kt. Russian officials confirmed that such devices had been constructed, but it remains unclear if they have been secured or destroyed.

Impact on international politics

Despite the fact that it is over sixty years since nuclear weapons emerged on the world scene in 1945 and that they played a dominant role in the Cold War standoff between the North Atlantic Treaty Organization (NATO) and the Warsaw Pact, debate continues about their impact on world politics (Paul et al. 1998). Disarmament advocates bemoan the failure of the existing nuclear powers to reduce their reliance on nuclear weapons, the failure of the US Senate to ratify the **Comprehensive Test Ban Treaty**, and the decision of the George W. Bush administration to withdraw from the **1972 Anti-Ballistic Missile Treaty**, which in their mind threatens a new round in the arms race. They are also concerned that the non-proliferation regime is slowly losing ground, as several states continue to press ahead with covert and overt programmes to develop nuclear weapons. Others see the cup as half full. The United States and Russia have greatly decreased the size of their deployed nuclear forces—the 2002 Moscow Treaty cuts Russian and American nuclear forces to about 20 per cent of the level they reached during the Cold War. The international community has also taken a series of steps to address the issue of non-compliance with non-proliferation norms and to imbed international non-proliferation norms into domestic laws. United Nations Resolution 1540, for instance, obliged all nations to criminalize trafficking in WMD and to establish domestic controls over the export and use of materials that could be used in WMD programmes. Resolution 1540 extends the reach of existing international efforts to combat nuclear proliferation. The Global Initiative to Combat Nuclear Terrorism, announced jointly by President Bush and President Vladimir Putin in July 2006, refocuses international efforts in the battle against nuclear terrorism. It is a multinational effort to coordinate policy and transmit best practices.

Scholars are divided about the impact of nuclear weapons on world politics (Sagan and Waltz 2003). Some believe that a nuclear arsenal helps to deter attack by other states armed with conventional and nuclear weapons. The ability to retaliate with nuclear weapons after suffering an attack—known as a secure second-strike capability—is especially desirable, because it can effectively eliminate an opponent's potential gain produced by using nuclear weapons first, a situation known as crisis stability. Because even a few nuclear weapons can cause catastrophic destruction, and it is virtually impossible to defend against the effects of nuclear weapons, these scholars believe that they are truly revolutionary weapons that force militaries to concentrate on preventing, not fighting, wars (Brodie 1946). Some, focusing on Soviet–American relations during the Cold War, suggest that peace is the logical outcome, especially if potential enemies obtain secure second-strike capabilities: it is not logical for officials to engage in conflicts if they know in advance that a nuclear exchange will devastate, if not completely destroy, their country (Jervis 1989).

By contrast, proliferation pessimists worry that the superpower Cold War experience was at best an anomaly, and at worse a situation that often teetered on the brink of disaster. They worry that human frailty, communication failures and misperception, bureaucratic snafus, or psychological or technological breakdowns in a crisis can cause failures of deterrence, leading to inadvertent or accidental nuclear war. Others point to normal accidents—the inability to anticipate all human–machine interaction in complex systems—as a potential path to accidental nuclear war, especially because nuclear warning and command and control systems interact intensively during a crisis. Proliferation pessimists also point out that there is no guarantee that all militaries and governments will be good stewards of their nuclear arsenals. Those who possess nuclear weapons might take risks that expose their arsenals to sabotage, loss through theft, or accidental or inadvertent use. Some governments might use their newly found weapons not for deterrence purposes, but instead for purposes of intimidation or aggression. They might gravitate towards nuclear war-fighting strategies that seek to introduce nuclear weapons quickly and massively on the battlefield in an attempt either to pre-empt an adversary's use of nuclear weapons or to end a conflict with a quick knock-out blow.

Although the debate between optimists and pessimists continues, all agree that the spread of nuclear or radiological weapons to non-state actors or even individuals would be a global disaster. Existing deterrent strategies and capabilities do not address terrorist use of nuclear weapons. The threat that these nuclear weapons could fall into the hands of non-state actors will force states to heighten domestic surveillance and security efforts.

KEY POINTS

- A gun-type fission device is a relatively simple, reliable, and rugged nuclear weapon design that would be attractive to terrorist organizations or states developing a nuclear programme.

- Fusion weapons are highly complex devices that can produce enormous destructive energy from relatively small, light-weight packages.

- Primary nuclear effects are electromagnetic pulse, thermal-light energy, blast, and radiation.

- Although the risk of nuclear Armageddon has receded since the end of the Cold War, concerns are increasing that terrorists might acquire and detonate a dirty bomb or a gun-type device.

- Scholars continue to debate if nuclear weapons are a source of peace in world politics or an unjustified risk to international security.

Chemical weapons

Although poisons and chemicals have been used in war since ancient times, chemical weapons emerged in the late 1800s as part of the modern chemical industry. Scholars debate whether chemical weapons should be considered a weapon of mass destruction, because large quantities of chemical weapons often have to be used on the battlefield to have a significant effect against a prepared opponent, and these weapons have to be expertly employed to produce massive casualties. On 20 March 1995, for instance, the Aum Shinrikyo cult launched a sarin attack against the Tokyo subway system that resulted in twelve deaths. By contrast, the al-Qaeda attack against the Madrid train system on 11 March 2004 used conventional explosives and killed nearly 200 innocent civilians. What worries analysts, however, is that any state with a chemical industry could quickly convert production processes from civilian use to weapons manufacturing and that even readily available household products can be mixed to create relatively dangerous concoctions. Weapons can be created from commonly available chemicals using well-understood

technologies. Household insecticides, for example, are simply 'watered-down' nerve agents.

The first significant employment of chemical weapons occurred in the First World War, as both sides sought a way to break through the stalemate of trench warfare. On 22 April 1915, German units unleashed a cloud of chlorine gas (an asphyxiating agent) against allied lines at Ypres, Belgium, but failed to exploit the gap created in the French lines. Petrified by the sight of corpses that exhibited no obvious causes of death, attacking German soldiers refused to advance. The Germans introduced mustard gas (a blistering agent) on the battlefield on 12 July 1917. The Allies also developed their own blister agent, Lewisite, but it was just reaching the battlefield as the First World War came to an end. Although chemical weapons caused only about 4 per cent of the casualties suffered by all sides during the First World War, the use of gas on the battlefield affected societies everywhere as veterans related stories of helpless soldiers struggling to put on gas masks as they chocked to death or were

Figure 19.1 John Singer Sargent, *Gassed* (1918).

Source: Reproduced with permission from the Art Archive/Imperial War Museum.

blinded by blister agents. This imagery, best exemplified by the painting of a field dressing station in Arras, France, made by the American artist John Singer Sargent, highlighted the horror and cruelty of gas warfare (see Figure 19.1).

Although the Italians employed mustard agent against Ethiopia in 1935 and the Japanese attacked Chinese troops with chemical weapons in the 1930s, chemical weapons were not used extensively on Second World War battlefields. Many speculate that Adolf Hitler, a mustard-gas casualty in the First World War, was personally reluctant to be the first to introduce these weapons in Europe (although this apparent aversion did not stop the Nazis from using Zyclon-B, a prussic-acid-based substance used as a pesticide and disinfectant, to kill thousands of victims in gas chambers). In fact, only one major chemical-weapons incident occurred during the war. On 2 December 1943, a Nazi air raid on the harbour in Bari, Italy, damaged a merchant ship carrying 2,000 100 lb M 47A1 bombs filled with mustard agent. The accidental release of agent affected thousands of allied soldiers and civilians. It was not until the Iran–Iraq War, however, that chemical weapons were again employed on the battlefield. In 1982, Iraqi units, hard pressed by far more numerous Iranian forces, dispensed mass concentrations of the riot control agent CS to break up opposing formations. By 1983, Iraq was using mustard agents on

the battlefield and continued experimenting with more lethal agents and concoctions. In a February 1986 strike against al-Faw, the Iraqis employed a mixture of mustard and tabun (a nerve agent) against the Iranians, which resulted in thousands of casualties. Saddam Hussein's murderous regime also attacked its own citizens with chemical weapons. On 16 March 1988 Iraq forces sprayed a mixture of mustard and nerve agents over the Kurdish village of Halabja, killing more than 10,000 civilians.

Chemical-weapons effects

Chemical weapons vary in terms of their lethality, their complexity, and the way they cause injury and death. They also vary in terms of their persistence: some disperse quickly, allowing attacking troops to move through an area, while 'area denial agents', which might be used to attack an airfield to reduce the tempo of flight operations, might persist for a long time. Traditionally, chemical weapons have been characterized as blood agents, choking agents, blister agents, nerve agents, and incapacitants.

Blood agents, which are generally based on hydrocyanic acid (HCN), interfere with the body's ability to transport oxygen in the blood. Because cyanide has been used as a poison throughout history, several countries experimented with using this agent as a weapon. Owing to its high volatility—it evaporates quickly, making it hard to create a lethal concentration over a battlefield—most states long ago abandoned it as a toxic agent for military use.

Choking agents—phosgene and chlorine—get their name from the fact that their victims literally drown in the fluids produced when the tissues lining the lungs interact with the agent. Choking agents produce hydrochloric acid when they are inhaled, causing blood and fluid to infiltrate the lungs. Phosgene, which reacts with water in the body to produce hydrochloric acid, is a common industrial chemical that is more toxic than chlorine. Most of the deaths caused in the First World War by chemical weapons were caused by phosgene.

Blister agents are primarily intended to generate serious causalities in an opposing force, thereby placing enormous demands on supporting medical services. Before the development of more lethal nerve agents, sulphur mustard was considered to be the chemical weapon of choice. It exists as a thick liquid at room temperature, but can be suspended in air (that is, turned into an aerosol that can be inhaled) by using a conventional explosive. It can also be used to contaminate people, terrain, or equipment. Although the exact reason why mustard agent is an extreme irritant is not well understood, it causes severe blistering on exposed skin and mucous membranes. It can also cause temporary blindness. Long-term effects from a single moderate exposure to mustard agent are not usually lethal. The effects of mustard can sometimes take several hours to develop; Lewisite, another blister agent, works more rapidly than mustard.

Nerve agents are by far the most lethal chemical weapons. Invented during the 1930s as insecticides, they entered Nazi and Allied military inventories in the Second World War but were not used in combat. The name 'nerve agent' reflects the fact that these chemicals interfere with the body's neurological system by irreversibly inactivating acetyl cholinesterase (AChE), which 'deactivates' the neurotransmitter acetylcholine. Nerve agents bind to the active site of AchE, making it incapable of deactivating acetylcholine. Without an ability to deactivate acetylcholine, muscles fire continuously and glandular hypersecretion occurs (for example, excess saliva), leading to paralysis and suffocation. Second-generation nerve agents, G (German) series agents (GA) Tabun, (GB) Sarin, (GD) Soman, (GF) Cyclosarin, are considered to be non-persistent agents. G series agents are all water and fat soluble, and can enter the skin and cause lethal effects. Third-generation V Series—VX, VE, VG, VM—nerve agents, a product of British science, are persistent agents that are about ten times more lethal than Sarin. Less is publicly known about fourth-generation A-series agents (also known as 'Novichok' agents), a product of Soviet science. Exposure to high aerosol concentrations of nerve agents causes prompt collapse and death.

Incapacitants are used for riot control (CS or tear gas) or for personal protection (CN or mace). They are less toxic than other chemical weapons and usually do not produce lethal effects when used in the open at a proper concentration. Vomiting agents (adamsite) have been developed for use in combat. Both Soviet and US scientists also experimented with psychochemicals (that is, lysergic acid diethylamide [LSD] and BZ) in an effort to cause altered states of situational awareness. BZ was weaponized by the United States, but it was dropped from its arsenal because its effects were unpredictable. In October 2002, Russian security forces used an opiod form of fentanyl in an attempt to incapacitate Chechin separatists who were holding 800 hostages in a Moscow theatre. Owing to either a lack of prompt medical attention or an overdose of fentanyl, 126 people died from this 'incapacitant'.

Methods of delivery

Chemical weapons are delivered from either a line or a point source. Bombs, artillery shells, missile warheads, or parcels, for instance, are all point sources, because they deliver chemical weapons to a specific location. A line source, which is generated by a series of dispensing devices, a crop duster, or even a moving crop sprayer, creates a cloud or 'line' of gas that drifts towards the target. Wind, temperature, and terrain can affect the lethality and persistence of an agent. For example, a gallon of VX is sufficient to kill thousands of people, but only if individuals are brought into contact with the correct amount of agent to cause casualties. Agents can be blown off target, diluted by rain, or even solidify, if the temperature drops too low.

Because proper dispersal is the key to employing chemical weapons, analysts are most concerned about their use in closed venues such as sporting arenas or large buildings with ventilation systems that could be subject to tampering. Aum Shinrikyo targeted the Tokyo subway because of the large numbers of people who travel daily through its contained spaces and choke points. The cult experimented with a suitcase mechanism to deliver sarin aerosol in the subway: two small electric fans were used to disperse chemical agent after it was released from vials stored inside the suitcase. To conduct the actual attack, however, the cult relied on a far simpler method: they punched holes in plastic bags containing sarin and simply allowed the agent to evaporate in the subway cars.

Impact on international politics

By the 1970s, NATO militaries began to view chemical weapons as a deterrent, not as a weapon they preferred to use on the battlefield. Chemical weapons pose obvious difficulties in terms of transportation and handling, and most military observers agree there are safer and more efficient ways to hold targets at risk. Thus the preferences of military professionals helped to foster a taboo against the use of chemical weapons in war, restraint codified in the 1925 Geneva Protocol for the Prohibition of the Use in War of Asphyxiating, Poisonous, or Other Gases, and of Bacteriological Methods of Warfare. Although the Geneva Protocol banned first use of chemical weapons, it did not prevent states from stockpiling chemical munitions. The Chemical Weapons Convention (CWC), which entered into force on 29 April 1997, makes it illegal for signatories to possess or employ chemical weapons, with the exception of small samples used to test protective equipment. States party to the CWC are required to declare their existing stocks of chemical weapons, to identify facilities that were once involved in chemical-weapons production, and to announce when their existing stocks will be completely destroyed. The Organization for the Prohibition of Chemical Weapons (OPCW) is authorized to verify compliance with the CWC and can undertake challenge inspections when demanded by states parties (Larsen 2002).

While 148 nations have ratified the CWC, about twenty countries, some of which maintain a large chemical arsenal (for example, North Korea and Syria), have not signed the treaty. Most military analysts believe that these large arsenals would only have a modest effect on well-equipped and trained troops on the battlefield. In their view, a chemical arsenal is the 'poor man's' weapon of mass destruction, because it is based on old, relatively simple, and inexpensive technologies that have limited military utility. Nevertheless, if employed deliberately against relatively defenceless civilian populations, these weapons could wreak havoc. Analysts are most concerned that terrorist organizations or even individuals might gain access to poisonous chemicals that are part of industrial processes and attack urban targets. Iraqi use of chemical weapons in war is considered an anomaly. The fear is that Aum Shinrikyo's sarin attack might be a harbinger of things to come.

KEY POINTS

- There are five types of chemical weapons: blood agents, choking agents, blister agents, nerve agents, and incapacitants.

- Chemical agents can be persistent or non-persistent and can be delivered from a point or a line source.

- State and non-state actors with access to even a rudimentary chemical industry can acquire chemical weapons.

- The nearly universal Chemical Weapons Convention bans the manufacture or use of chemical weapons and allows signatories to possess only small amounts of agents for research into defensive equipment and prophylaxis.

Biological weapons

Biological weapons (BW) make use of living organisms or toxins to sicken or kill humans, animals, and plants. These organisms and toxins all occur in nature, which makes it difficult to differentiate natural disease outbreaks from a BW attack. BW is probably the most potentially destructive weapon known to humans in the sense that a single organism or infected individual can affect millions of human beings, although scientists debate the degree of difficulty any state or non-state actor might encounter in infecting large numbers of people quickly. Although extremely contagious diseases are generally not lethal, some, smallpox, for example, are easily transmitted and produce high **morbidity**. Sometimes, diseases that are considered relatively mundane can be extremely lethal: the 1918–19 Spanish Flu killed upwards of forty million people, striking hardest among healthy adults between the ages of 20 and 40.

Disease has been a part of war throughout history. Until recently, most people died in war from illness, not from wounds suffered in combat. Deliberate use of disease as a weapon of war, however, has been sporadic, producing mixed results. In 1346, Mongol invaders hurled the corpses of soldiers who had died from bubonic plague into the besieged city of Kaffa in a deliberate effort to spread disease. The Mongols did not know, however, that the causative bacteria of plague *Yersinia pestis* is spread by fleas that feed only on live hosts. At the end of the Seven Years War (1756–63), British forces apparently provided American Indians with smallpox-infected blankets, although it is difficult to determine whether or not they succeeded in infecting anyone, because smallpox was already endemic in the Americas and had decimated Indian populations about two hundred years earlier. During the First World War, German saboteurs apparently succeeded in infecting horses used by the allies with glanders. During the Second World War, the Japanese filled glass bombs with plague-infected fleas to spread disease, and Japanese scientists working in the infamous Unit 731 conducted biological warfare experiments on prisoners of war.

Although the United States, Britain, and Canada conducted research into the weaponization of Anthrax, Tularemia, Q-fever, Venezuelan equine encephalitis, and anti-agricultural agents, biological weapons were generally viewed in the West as lacking military utility. By contrast, Soviet researchers concentrated on perfecting a variety of biological agents during the Cold War and exploited the emerging science of genetic engineering better to weaponize naturally occurring diseases. According to Ken Alibek (2000), who was a leading figure in Biopreperat, the Soviet Union's complex of biological weapons facilities, Soviet science worked with a variety of bacteria (for example, an antibiotic-resistant strain of anthrax), viruses (for example, smallpox) and even haemorrhagic fevers (for example, Ebola). Although the 'Soviet' biological weapons programme apparently ended in Russia in the early 1990s, experts still debate what motivated the Soviets to undertake such an extensive BW programme. The Soviets probably saw their BW programme as a counter to the precision, global-strike complex that was emerging in NATO in the 1970s or as a way to retard Western recovery following an all-out nuclear exchange. The Soviets apparently loaded several SS-18 intercontinental ballistic missiles with plague in an attempt to provide Western survivors of a nuclear war with an additional reason to envy the dead.

Biological weapons effects

Although naturally occurring diseases have been a scourge of humankind, not every disease provides the basis for an effective biological weapon. An agent's storage, delivery, mode of transmission, and its very resilience (that is, how long can it survive in the environment) can shape its effects on a target population. Military professionals believe that most biological weapons are

Table 19.2 Possible biological warfare agents: bacterial and rickettsial agents

Agent/Disease	Organism	Lethality	Onset	Symptoms	Target
Anthrax	*Bacillus anthracis*	80% lethality, non-contagious	1–5 days	Pulmonary form: chest cold symptoms, respiratory distress, fever, shock death	Area attack
Brucellosis	Brucella	3–20% lethality, non-contagious	5–60 days	Fever, headaches, pain in joints and muscle fatigue	Area attack
Plague	*Yersinia pesstis*	80% lethality, contagious	2–3 days	High fever, headache, extreme weakness, haemorrhages in skin and mucous membranes	Area attack
Tularemia	*Francisella tularensis*	50% lethality contagious	2–10 days	Chills, fever, headache, loss of body fluids	Area attack
Q Fever	Coxiella burnettii	2% lethality non-contagious	10–40 days	Fever, headache, cough, muscle and joint pain	

Table 19.3 Possible biological warfare agents: viral agents

Agent/Disease	Organism	Lethality	Onset	Symptoms	Target
Smallpox	Variola virus	2–49% lethality, contagious	7–17 days	Severe fever, small blisters on skin, bleeding on skin and mucous	Area attack
Viral encephalitis	Eastern Equine Encephalitis (EEE) virus	80% lethality, non-contagious	1–14 days	Headache, general aches and pains, photophobia	Area attack
Viral haemorrhagic fevers	Ebola	80% lethality, contagious	4–21 days	Subcutaneous haemorrhage, bleeding from body orifices, headache, fever, stupor, convulsion	Area attack

simply too unpredictable in their effects to be a reliable weapon. Because they are easy to manufacture and can be potentially highly lethal in small quantities—any basic medical laboratory has the capability to cultivate a biological agent—biological agents might be attractive and available to terrorists. Relatively large industrial facilities are needed to produce militarily significant quantities of chemical weapons, but relatively small fermenters used to make legitimate vaccines, for instance, could be quickly converted to produce biological agents.

There are three varieties of biological agents: bacteria, viruses, and toxins. As an area attack agent, anthrax is probably the best-known bacterial agent. Its spores are extremely hardy (they can live for literally hundreds of years) and it can be spread quickly across large areas. Anthrax is not contagious, so its effects can be relatively contained and focused on specific targets. It also can be genetically engineered to be resistant to most antibiotics and it can be formulated with inert matter better to form an aerosol. These qualities make anthrax the agent of choice for many biological-weapons programmes. The cutaneous form of anthrax occurs in the animal industry and can be treated relatively easily; by contrast, the inhalation form of the disease is extremely dangerous. By the time the victim begins to show symptoms of inhalation anthrax, a near-lethal dose of toxins produced by the anthrax bacteria has already built up in the body. The Aum Shinrikyo cult attempted to disperse anthrax in Tokyo in 1996; they failed because they used a non-toxic vaccine strain of the virus. The terrorist who sent anthrax through the US mail in autumn 2001, however, used a deadly 'Ames' strain. which US weapons laboratories employ to test defensive equipment and prophylaxis (Stern 2000).

Although haemorrhagic fevers—Marburg, Lassa fever, or Ebola—are viral agents that could serve as potent weapons, policy-makers are most worried about the threat posed by smallpox. As smallpox was eradicated as a naturally occurring disease, global vaccination programmes were terminated, leaving entire generations unprotected against the disease for the first time in hundreds of years. Smallpox is an airborne virus that is about as contagious as the flu, but it has a lethality of about 30 per cent in its ordinary form (rarer malignant and haemorrhagic forms of smallpox are 100 per cent lethal). Smallpox vaccination can stop the disease, even if administered a few days after exposure, but, to prevent a pandemic, potentially millions of doses of vaccine need to be made quickly available. Reintroduction of general inoculation programmes, however, have not been advocated by public-health authorities, because the smallpox vaccine itself leads to about fifty instances of side effects per one million people vaccinated. The impact of a smallpox outbreak, however, cannot be underestimated. The 'Dark Winter' exercise run by the US Federal Emergency Management Agency in June 2001 was based on a smallpox outbreak in the American Midwest. Within 30 days, over 300,000 people in 25 states and 10 foreign countries had already contracted the disease. Smallpox truly has the capability of creating a global catastrophe.

Although toxins are not living organisms and are in fact a by-product of metabolic activity, they are generally discussed as a biological weapon. Toxins are probably best thought of as a poison, which is often used to attack specific individuals. Like chemical weapons, individuals have to be brought into direct contact with the toxin to suffer from its effects. Toxins, however, can be extremely lethal. Ricin, which is made from castor bean, kills by inhibiting protein synthesis within cells. Used as an assassination weapon—the Bulgarian dissident Georgy Markov was killed by a ricin injection in 1978—it can kill within three days. Because it can be made easily from readily available materials, many analysts believe that terrorists will seek to use ricin. In 2003, for instance, British officials arrested a terrorist who was plotting to smear ricin on the door handles of cars and buildings in London. In 2008, a man was sickened by the Ricin he had stockpiled in a Las Vegas hotel room. In 2004, Victor Yushchenko was badly disfigured from a toxin attack (see Think Point 19.1).

Methods of delivery

Biological agents are generally delivered in the form of an infectious aerosol. Precise preparation of the aerosol is crucial because the agent has to be the proper size to infect a host by lodging in the small alveoli of the lungs. Vectors—lice, fleas, mosquitoes—transmit disease in nature, but it would be difficult to use this mode of transmission as a military weapon because it is inherently difficult to control. Terrorists might attempt to infect individuals surreptitiously with a disease such as smallpox, but the disease is difficult to grow in vitro and the terrorists themselves

---

THINK POINT 19.1

Who poisoned Yushchenko?

Although toxins could be employed against troops in the field or against large groups of individuals in sporting arenas or transportation systems, history suggests that they often serve as an exotic weapon for assassination. In the latest example of attempted 'toxin assassination', Austrian doctors reported in December 2004 that Ukrainian presidential candidate Victor Yushchenko was suffering from dioxin poisoning. Yushchenko apparently developed symptoms—fatigue, pain, and disfiguring chloracne—quickly after he had apparently ingested TCDD dioxin in his food. The concentration of dioxin in Yushchenko's body, the second highest ever recorded, was at least 1,000 times more than is found in most people. Some observers speculate that dioxin was used because it would disfigure and sicken Yushchenko, literally making him an unattractive candidate to the Ukrainian electorate. Campaigning in extreme pain, and badly disfigured by dioxin, Yushchenko went on to ride the 'Orange Revolution' in Ukraine that followed the electoral fraud in the November 2004 presidential elections. He took office as the Ukraine's President on 23 January 2005.

---

would have to be vaccinated to work with the virus. Because smallpox vaccine is not readily available, seeking vaccine might allow public-health officials to detect some nefarious scheme. The difficulty of controlling infectious diseases should also give terrorists pause. Unleashing highly contagious diseases can backfire, because a pandemic does not respect religious, political, or cultural boundaries, although public-health services in rich countries are far more likely to cope with an outbreak of infectious disease than poorer countries whose health-care system is already stretched to the breaking point.

Impact on international politics

Following revelations in the early 1990s about the Soviet biological weapons programme and renewed concerns about biological warfare following the 1991 Gulf War, policy-makers devoted renewed attention to strengthening the 1972 Biological and Toxin Weapons Convention (BWC) by devising an inspection protocol similar to the verification mechanism embedded in the CWC. By late 2001, however, negotiations over an inspection protocol for the BWC reached an impasse. Officials concluded that it was too difficult to devise an inspection regime that could provide any significant insight into what was being manufactured in the tens of thousands of medical laboratories around the planet and that, regardless of the efforts of inspection teams, it was simply too easy to conceal work on biological agents. Efforts instead shifted from the diplomatic realm to strengthening domestic criminal laws against the manufacture or possession of biological weapons or agents and improving international health monitoring to spot the outbreak of infectious diseases.

Table 19.4 Possible biological warfare agents: toxins

Agent/Disease	Organism	Lethality	Onset	Symptoms	Target
Botulinum Toxin	*Clostridium botulinum*	80% lethality, non-contagious	1–5 days	Blurred vision, photophobia, paralysis	Proximity attack
SEB Toxin	*Staphylococcus aureus*	2% lethality	1–6 hours	Headache, sudden fever, nausea, vomiting	Proximity attack

Figure 19.2 Who poisoned Yushchenko? This combination image shows the changing face of Ukraine's opposition leader Viktor Yushchenko in file photos taken on 4 July 2004 (left) and 1 November 2004 (right).

Source: Reproduced with permission from Reuters/Gleb Garanich and Vasily Fedosenko.

KEY POINTS

- Biological weapons are derived from naturally occurring diseases and can be manufactured in medical laboratories.

- Biological weapons vary in terms of their lethality and whether or not they are contagious.

- Anthrax is a biological agent of great concern because it is a hardy, non-contagious agent that can be used to contaminate large areas. It can potentially directly infect many people quickly.

- The revolution in genetic engineering has been used to weaponize naturally occurring diseases.

Conclusion

In some respects, the WMD threat has greatly receded since the end of the Cold War. The number of deployed Soviet (Russian) and American strategic nuclear warheads has been reduced by 80 per cent since the 1990s, and US tactical nuclear weapons have largely been withdrawn from service. The threat of Armageddon produced by a massive nuclear exchange is now only a remote possibility. The International Non-Proliferation Regime has survived the 1998 Indian and Pakistani nuclear tests and a *de facto* nuclear test ban remains in place, despite the fact that the US Senate failed to ratify the Comprehensive Test Ban Treaty. The CWC and

BWC not only provide a basis in international law to stop the spread of these deadly chemical and biological agents, but they also serve as a useful diplomatic framework for devising new ways to stop the spread and use of these weapons. The Proliferation Security Initiative (PSI), for instance, is a new international undertaking to stop illicit trade in materials related to chemical, biological, and nuclear weapons. The PSI also reflects a shift towards counter-proliferation in the international effort to stop the spread of chemical, biological, and nuclear weapons. In the wake of revelations about A. Q. Khan's clandestine nuclear supply network and the interception of a shipment of North Korean SCUD missiles that were bound for Yemen, officials are taking more active steps to stop trade in illicit materials, weapons, and delivery systems.

Although Iranian efforts to develop a nuclear weapon or the fact that North Korea has a nascent nuclear arsenal dominates headlines, officials today are most concerned by the prospect that WMD is escaping the control of state actors. The biological and medical sciences are undergoing a period of revolutionary development based on advances in genetics and genetic engineering. These capabilities are now widely available to researchers and manufacturers. This raises the possibility that new biological weapons will inevitably find their way into the hands of individuals or non-state actors. The so-called renaissance in nuclear energy, the turn towards nuclear power as an answer to global warming and peak oil, also creates opportunities for more state and non-state actors to gain access to radiological materials and know-how. The emerging challenge is to devise ways to safeguard these nuclear, biological, and chemical technologies and materials in both a domestic and an international setting so that they cannot be diverted to nefarious purposes. Since the First World War, the use of WMD in war has been episodic. Nation states have mostly abandoned their chemical and biological arsenals. Terrorists' efforts to use chemical, biological, or radiological weapons have been largely ineffective. Nuclear weapons, the centrepiece of the Soviet–American Cold War competition, have been used on the battlefield twice. Lingering questions remain. Is there a taboo against the use of weapons of mass destruction? Have we all just been incredibly lucky?

? QUESTIONS

1. Why might nuclear weapons be a source of stability in international relations?

2. Why do you think that the use of weapons of mass destruction in war is relatively rare?

3. Why would terrorists be attracted to chemical, biological, radiological, or nuclear weapons?

4. What effect would another use of nuclear weapons have on world politics?

5. Toxins are often used against what type of target?

6. Which variety of WMD is most destructive? Which is most easily manufactured?

7. What steps should governments take to prevent WMD terrorism?

8. Is direct action or international negotiation the best way to counter the spread of WMD?

9. Do you think Aum Shinrikyo's experience with sarin will be emulated by other groups or individuals?

10. Do you think that weapons of mass destruction serve as status symbols in world politics?

FURTHER READING

■ Bernstein, Jeremy (2008), *Nuclear Weapons: What You Need To Know,* New York: Cambridge University Press. This volume offers a fascinating account of how scientific puzzles and technical hurdles were overcome in the quest to build nuclear weapons.

■ Croddy, Eric A., and Wirtz, James J. (2005) (eds.), *Weapons of Mass Destruction: An Encyclopedia of Worldwide Policy, Technology, and History,* 2 vols., Santa Barbara, CA: ABC-Clio. A handy reference on WMD.

■ Freedman, Lawrence (2003), *The Evolution of Nuclear Strategy*, 3rd edn, New York: Palgrave Macmillan. This is the best single volume on the history of nuclear arsenals and the strategic thinking that guided nuclear strategy.

■ Sagan, Scott D., and Waltz, Kenneth (2003), *The Spread of Nuclear Weapons: A Debate Renewed,* 2nd edn, New York: Norton. Provides an engaging debate between proliferation optimists and pessimists.

■ Schell, Jonathan (1982), *The Fate of the Earth*, New York: Knopf. This is probably the best description of the existential threat posed by the widespread use of nuclear weapons.

IMPORTANT WEBSITES

● http://www.cdc.gov   Center for Disease Control and Prevention. The Center provides information on diseases.

● http://www.ucsusa.org   Union of Concerned Scientists. Established in 1969, this is an independent non-profit alliance of more than 100,000 citizens and scientists concerned by the misuse of science and technology in society.

● http://www.ccc.nps.navy.mil   Center for Contemporary Conflict. Launched in 2001, the CCC conducts research on current and emerging security issues and conveys its findings to US and Allied policy-makers and military forces.

● http://nuclearweaponarchive.org   Nuclear Weapons Archive. The purpose of this archive is to illuminate the reader regarding the effects of these destructive devices, and to warn against their use.

● http://cns.miis.edu   Center for Nonproliferation Studies, Monterey Institute of International Studies. The Center strives to combat the spread of weapons of mass destruction (WMD) by training the next generation of non-proliferation specialists and disseminating timely information and analysis.

● http://www.fas.org/index.html   Federation of American Scientists. Formed in 1945 by atomic scientists from the Manhattan Project, the FAS conducts research and provides education on nuclear arms control and global security; conventional arms transfers; proliferation of weapons of mass destruction; information technology for human health; and government information policy.

Visit the Online Resource Centre that accompanies this book for lots of interesting additional material: www.oxfordtextbooks.co.uk/orc/collins2e/

20

Terrorism

BRENDA LUTZ AND JAMES LUTZ

Reader's Guide

This chapter analyses the threat that terrorism poses for countries and the world. Efforts to deal with terrorism can be considered within the framework of terrorism as warfare, terrorism as crime, and terrorism as disease. Which of these views is adopted determines what kinds of countermeasures countries will use in their effort to deal with terrorism. Terrorism is a technique of action available to many different groups; security measures that work with one group may not be effective with others. Dealing with terrorism in today's world can be a very complex process indeed.

Introduction

Terrorism has become an important phenomenon, as well as a major security issue for many countries. The attacks of 9/11 on the World Trade Center in New York City and the Pentagon near Washington DC highlighted the great damage that such attacks could cause. Since that time, large-scale attacks on tourist facilities on Bali in 2002 and again in 2005, on the commuter trains in Madrid in 2004, on a Russian middle school in Breslan in 2004, the suicide bombings in London in 2005, and the attack at Glasgow airport in 2007 all demonstrate the continuing threat that terrorism can pose. Further, the continuing terrorist campaigns that persist over time, such as the attacks in Iraq since the US invasion, have claimed many victims. It is not only the spectacular attacks that constitute a threat. The cumulative effects of such campaigns are important. Multiple attacks by a variety of dissident groups in Turkey between 1975 and 1980 left more than 5,000 dead and 15,000 injured (Bal and Laciner 2001: 106). This casualty toll is heavier than that sustained on 9/11. Casualty lists have demonstrated the continuing vulnerability of people everywhere to terrorism, and more recently concern has grown

that terrorists might use weapons of mass destruction (biological, chemical, radiological, or nuclear).

While terrorism is a technique that has been around for millennia and used by different groups, the more pressing concern for governments today is the groups that are currently threats. Groups have adapted to changing circumstances. During the Cold War, terrorist groups often gained the support of the Soviet Union or the United States or their respective allies. Today, there are no competing superpowers, and overt support for terrorist groups can generate a massive military response, as the Taliban regime in Afghanistan discovered. In response, terrorist organizations have developed networks that provide mutual assistance. Groups like al-Qaeda in some respects have network structures (see Case Study 20.1). Other terrorist groups have also developed linkages with criminal organizations, especially those involved in drug trafficking. Both the terrorists and the drug cartels benefit from weak governments that find it difficult to interfere with their activities. These loosely connected international networks can be more difficult to attack and defeat.

CASE STUDY 20.1

Al-Qaeda and decentralized structures

Al-Qaeda (the Base) provides the most prominent contemporary example of a terrorist group organized as a network. Before 9/11 al-Qaeda had a core of planners and close associates of Osama bin Laden and groups in individual countries that cooperated with this central group. Al-Qaeda, in turn, often provided financial and technical assistance to national groups in Muslim countries, especially those opposed to more secular and pro-Western governments or those groups opposed to Western influences that come with globalization and modernization. Al-Qaeda was even willing to fund terrorist projects presented to it by local groups if they held the promise of success (Nedoroscik 2002). Cooperation such as this permitted the group to extend its reach. It provided technical and financial support for the first attack on the

World Trade Center in 1993. It was much more centrally involved in the attacks on the US embassies in East Africa in 1998 and the 9/11 attacks on the World Trade Center and the Pentagon. Once Afghanistan was invaded, al-Qaeda maintained some of these network characteristics, but it also became a form of global leaderless resistance. Since 2002 the global jihadist movement has involved both network and leaderless resistance characteristics. The Madrid commuter train bombings of 2004, for example, involved participation by al-Qaeda agents. The London transit attacks in 2005 and probably the 2007 bombing attempt at Glasgow airport, on the other hand, were inspired by al-Qaeda, but they were undertaken independently by a local group of extremists who saw their attacks as part of the broader global jihad against the West (see also Table 20.8).

While terrorism and terrorists have been analysed from a variety of theoretical perspectives, one of the most useful has been proposed by Peter Sederberg (2003), who suggests that terrorism can be viewed from three perspectives. The first perspective is to think of terrorism in the context of an enemy to be defeated in war. The war analogy presumes that the use of military methods can be successful and that it is possible to achieve victory. A second perspective for dealing with terrorists is to rely on normal police techniques. The criminal analogy has two quite important implications. First, it suggests that terrorism, like crime, will not disappear; it can only be contained. Second, this approach is a reactive one—criminals are normally caught after they commit their crimes. The third perspective is to consider terrorism as a disease, emphasizing both symptoms and underlying causes. It assumes that there is a need for long-term strategies, even if there can be successes along the way in treating symptoms. The three perspectives, of course, are not mutually exclusive, but they represent dominant ways in which terrorism is viewed. They are important for analysing the phenomenon and for government officials who make choices in terms of how to deal with terrorist activity. Which perspective is adopted will suggest mechanisms for dealing with terrorism. Before 9/11, authorities in the United States largely dealt with acts of terrorism from the criminal perspective. Terrorists were caught (although it took time in some cases) and brought to trial (although not always convicted). Normal police techniques, including the use of informers and the infiltration of agents into potentially dangerous groups (like the Ku Klux Klan in the United States in the 1960s), drew upon conventional practices. After 9/11, however, the war analogy became dominant for the administration of President Bush, and references to the global war on terrorism appeared regularly. Others have suggested reforms and policy changes to deal with the causes of terrorism, but that has never been the main strategy adopted by the United States.

KEY POINTS

- Terrorism was a problem long before the 9/11 attacks.

- Terrorism can be viewed as a problem to be resolved by military means (war on terrorism), by normal police techniques (terrorism as crime), or as a medical problem with underlying causes and symptoms (terrorism as disease).

- How terrorism is viewed will help to determine which policies governments will adopt to deal with terrorism.

Concepts and definitions

There are a number of key concepts that are essential to any discussion of terrorism. The first is selecting a workable definition. A second concern involves targets and techniques, including the increasing concern about the danger that weapons of mass destruction present. A third key issue involves the prevalence of terrorism and the distinction between domestic and international terrorism, a distinction becoming more blurred with the passage of time. Finally, it is useful to distinguish among some basic types of terrorist groups, including ethnic, religious, and ideological.

Definition of terrorism

There has been a multitude of definitions used for terrorism, partially because of disagreements among commentators or analysts and partially because some definers seek to exclude groups that they support or to include groups that they wish to denounce. Courts and police agencies require definitions that permit prosecution and incarceration; political leaders may have different needs and agendas. A working definition that is relatively neutral recognizes the basic fact that terrorism is a tactic used by many different kinds of groups. It includes six major elements. Terrorism involves (1) the use of violence or threat of violence (2) by an organized group (3) to achieve political objectives. The violence (4) is directed against a target audience that extends beyond the immediate victims, who are often innocent civilians. Further (5), while a government can be either the perpetrator of violence or the target, it is considered an act of terrorism only if one or both actors is not a government. Finally, (6) terrorism is a weapon of the weak (Lutz and Lutz 2005: 7).

This definition excludes kidnappings for financial gains and excludes acts by individuals, even those with political objectives. Organization is essential for a successful campaign to bring about the political goals that are being sought. While the exact political objectives vary, they can include changes in government policies or practices, changes in government leaders or structures, demands for regional autonomy or independence, or a mix of such political issues. While organization is necessary for any chance of a successful campaign, individuals may operate in loose affiliation with a group. The individual dissidents may receive suggestions from leaders who maintain their distance from the operatives in the field in an organizational form that has come to be known as leaderless resistance. In such circumstances, individuals or small groups operate as part of a broader movement, even though they may not have direct links with a leadership. Groups as different as animal-rights organizations, the American militia movement, and global jihadists have relied on leaderless resistance tactics (Joosse 2007).

Terrorism has a target audience that goes well beyond the immediate victims. Ultimately terrorist violence is a form of psychological warfare that undermines opposition to their goals (Chalk

1996: 13). They generate fear in a target audience by attacking individuals who are representative of the larger group. This group can consist of members of the elite, supporters of the government, members of a particular ethnic or religious community, or the general public. Civilians are often chosen as targets, because they are more vulnerable than members of the security forces; furthermore, their deaths or injuries heighten the level of insecurity in the larger audience. It is often suggested that terrorist targets are chosen at random, but in fact terrorists usually pick their targets very carefully in order to influence an audience. The media often becomes important for this aspect of terrorism, since media coverage is very important for spreading fear, or at least in reaching the target audience more quickly, although target populations will usually become aware of attacks even when media attention is limited. Finally, terrorism is also a weapon utilized by the weak. Groups that can win elections or seize control of the government will do so; groups that cannot hope to win their objectives in other ways, however, may resort to terrorism.

While terrorism can involve governments as targets or perpetrators, it does not include cases during cold and hot wars, even when governments use actions designed to instil terror. These government-to-government attacks are a different security issue and are not included in definitions of terrorism, even if they involve massacres, atrocities, or war crimes, or even genocide. Governments, however, are often the targets of dissident terrorists. While governments usually oppose terrorists attacking their citizens, at times political leaders may tolerate terrorist attacks by private groups against enemies, potential dissidents, or unpopular minorities (ethnic, religious, cultural, or ideological). The government may fail to investigate or prosecute the perpetrators of the violence. In other cases governments may provide active support and in extreme cases even form death squads to attack their enemies while maintaining at least an illusion of deniability. While this governmental involvement in terrorism is quite important, it will not be the focus of this chapter, since the violence does not begin as a security concern (although violent groups that are tolerated may later challenge the government, as occurred with the Fascists in Italy). The use of private groups or death squads does correspond with the idea that terrorism is a weapon of the weak. Governments that are strong enough to deal with dissidents or to protect dissidents from private violence do not need to tolerate or use such forms of control.

Techniques and targets

The range of techniques available to terrorists is varied, but most activities are variations of standard practices—bombings, kidnappings, assaults including assassinations, and takeovers of buildings or planes or ships, invariably with hostages. Bombs can be used to damage property or in efforts to inflict casualties, sometimes in large numbers. Car bombs have increasingly become a favourite device for terrorist groups because of the damage that they can do. Kidnapping frequently provides a publicity bonanza for terrorist groups. In some cases ransoms from kidnappings have provided an important source of funding for terrorist organizations, and in other cases terrorists have been able to gain some concessions from governments in return for the release of the victims. Assaults are usually directed at individuals who represent a particular group (politicians, police, military personnel, journalists, and so on). Sometimes the intent is to wound, while in other cases the goal is the assassination of the individual or individuals. No one assassination is likely to bring about the changes the terrorists desire, but a campaign of such assassinations generates greater fear. Hostage situations in airline hijackings or the capture of buildings (the Japanese embassy in Peru in December 1996) demonstrate the vulnerability of society and generate publicity for the terrorist cause. Even when governments refuse to make major concessions, they will often publicize a list of demands by the terrorists or publish other kinds of communiqués.

Weapons of mass destruction (WMD) have become a special security concern for governments. There is a great fear that some terrorist groups will use biological, chemical, nuclear, or radiological (dirty) weapons to cause more casualties. To some extent, terrorist groups have already gained a psychological edge simply because of the fear of their use. There have been only a few such attacks to date. Aum Shinriyko, the Japanese cult, attempted to use nerve gas in the Tokyo subway system to cause mass casualties but failed. The anthrax attacks in the United States after 9/11 generated great fear, but there were only a few deaths. A single bomb might have killed more people, but the use of anthrax made the attacks more terrifying. Most terrorists, however, still prefer to stick to the tried-and-true techniques, at least until the utility of a new technique, such as car bombs, has been demonstrated.

One deadly technique that has been used by terrorists involves suicide attacks. Such attacks with bombs can be more deadly, since the detonation can occur at the last minute or when casualties will be maximized. Suicide attacks are not an especially new technique. The Assassins active from the eleventh through the thirteenth centuries expected to die, as did the anarchists who undertook assassinations in the late nineteenth century. Recent attacks have been more devastating, as with the airliners on 9/11 and bombers in Israel. Suicide attacks were first used on a large scale by the Liberation Tigers of Tamil Eelam (LTTE) in Sri Lanka, more commonly known as the Tamil Tigers. They were responsible for more suicide attacks than all other groups put together between 1980 and 2000 (Radu 2002). Such attacks have increased in various parts of the Middle East, Chechnya, and elsewhere in the twenty-first century. Many of these attacks have inflicted large numbers of casualties, while others have been directed against important political figures. Perhaps the greatest danger in the future is that a suicide attack might be combined with the use of biological, chemical, or radiological weapons. If the persons involved in the use of these weapons are willing to die in the effort, many of the problems involved in using WMD will have been reduced.

Terrorists have great flexibility in choosing their targets, and, if one target is too carefully protected, they can simply shift to another. Some other individual, building, or large gathering of people will serve to send the message that everyone in the target audience is vulnerable. The ability to find vulnerable targets may be greater in democratic states, since government security is likely to be weaker than in equivalent authoritarian societies. There are limitations on how much a democratic state can monitor its citizens and visitors. Democracies also provide greater publicity for the cause, since the media face few, if any, restraints. Further, even if the terrorists are caught, they will be tried in some type of impartial judicial setting where proof of guilt must be established. Of course, it is not only democratic countries that are vulnerable. Security forces may be weak in a variety of non-democratic political systems providing terrorist groups with opportunities to operate relatively freely.

Prevalence of terrorism

Terrorism has been present in the world for centuries. In recent years, better statistics have been available for such violence, especially incidents of international terrorism. Tables 20.1, 20.2, and 20.3 indicate the extent of international terrorist incidents by region, the injuries caused, and the deaths that resulted for 1991–2006. International terrorist incidents are considered to be actions where indigenous terrorists attack a foreign target (such as kidnapping foreign tourists), where terrorists launch an attack against a target in another country (the 9/11 attacks), or when a foreign country is used because it is convenient (IRA attacks against British soldiers in Germany). International attacks have been widespread. North America has been the scene of very few attacks, but the 9/11 attacks resulted in high casualties. Other attacks, such as the East Africa embassy bombings in 1998 and the attacks against tourists in Bali in 2002, resulted in higher casualties as well.

The distinction between domestic and international attacks has become increasingly blurred,

---

Table 20.1 International terrorist incidents, by region, 1991–2006

| Year | Region | | | | | | | |
	Africa	Asia	Eastern Europe *	Latin America	Europe	Middle East	North America	Total
1991	13	43	10	122	126	102	4	420
1992	33	20	7	81	70	59	2	272
1993	57	26	19	47	55	65	3	272
1994	85	22	21	55	51	73	3	310
1995	48	21	18	22	118	39	0	266
1996	39	42	13	40	58	44	2	238
1997	16	33	20	40	22	27	13	171
1998	22	22	31	15	37	34	0	161
1999	21	10	8	7	59	20	2	125

Table 20.1 (Continued)

Year	Region							
	Africa	Asia	Eastern Europe *	Latin America	Europe	Middle East	North America	Total
2000	9	14	1	15	38	29	0	106
2001	8	31	5	16	24	118	3	205
2002	8	59	13	20	24	173	1	298
2003	15	52	5	24	39	142	0	277
2004	7	50	12	12	26	288	0	395
2005	10	54	8	15	20	203	1	311
2006	19	55	1	4	15	147	0	241

*Former Communist countries of Eastern Europe and European successor states of the Soviet Union.

Source: Lutz and Lutz (2008: 42).

Table 20.2 Injuries caused by international terrorist incidents, by region, 1991–2006

Year	Region							
	Africa	Asia	Eastern Europe	Latin America	West Europe	Middle East	North America	Total
1991	3	86	12	41	36	58	0	256
1992	136	8	13	284	58	56	1	556
1993	146	1,237	101	29	116	2,677	1,045	2,677
1994	108	20	62	250	49	590	3	1,082
1995	52	5,207	30	5	229	485	0	6,082
1996	125	1,581	18	19	280	934	111	3,068
1997	60	339	3	7	3	455	4	871
1998	5,185	47	11	6	1	100	0	5,350
1999	113	0	0	0	2	6	0	121
2000	2	31	10	0	10	52	0	95
2001	6	78	0	1	2	949	2,337	3,373
2002	100	569	661	36	6	1,582	3	2957
2003	5	284	0	80	1	1,396	0	1766
2004	227	482	34	1	614	614	0	2023
2005	234	73	3	4	2	548	0	864
2006	114	95	0	19	0	245	0	473

*Former Communist countries of Eastern Europe and European successor states of the Soviet Union.

Source: Lutz and Lutz (2008: 43).

Table 20.3 Deaths resulting from international terrorist incidents, by region, 1991–2006

| Year | Region | | | | | | | |
	Africa	Asia	Eastern Europe	Latin America	West Europe	Middle East	North America	Total
1991	6	46	2	49	18	69	2	192
1992	35	20	2	43	12	33	0	145
1993	56	342	5	10	13	35	10	471
1994	126	15	17	122	7	146	2	435
1995	83	92	2	8	21	87	0	293
1996	197	171	11	26	23	142	1	571
1997	89	82	12	10	6	45	2	246
1998	305	36	4	2	0	30	0	377
1999	51	4	0	3	1	6	0	65
2000	15	7	0	3	2	20	0	47
2001	10	50	10	2	1	129	2982	3184
2002	89	321	163	19	0	375	3	970
2003	42	92	0	8	1	327	0	470
2004	39	89	6	3	192	403	0	732
2005	79	54	1	1	0	416	0	551
2006	39	81	0	6	0	168	0	294

* Former Communist countries of Eastern Europe and successor states of the Soviet Union.

Source: Lutz and Lutz (2008: 44).

especially when international terrorist networks are operating. British citizens undertook the attacks on the London transit system in 2005, but their nationality did not make this action a domestic one, since the attackers considered themselves to be part of the global jihadist movement. The assassination of a domestic leader on foreign soil would qualify as international terrorism, but the choice of a foreign country for the attack could simply be one of convenience. Domestic terrorism does not usually generate the media attention that international incidents can, but it is by far the most prevalent form of terrorism. Individual attacks that have caused mass casualties, such as the 9/11 attacks and

the bombings of the Madrid commuter trains or the bombings of the US embassies in East Africa, can inflate figures for individual years, but the greatest number of terrorist incidents, both domestic and international, has generally occurred in the Middle East, various parts of Asia, and Western Europe. For details see Tables 20.4, 20.5, 20.6, and 20.7. Terrorist violence also appears to be on the increase in the twenty-first century and is becoming more dangerous (Tan 2006: 241–4; Lutz and Lutz 2008: 42–5). Whether terrorism is addressed within the context of war, crime, or disease, it is not likely to be eliminated as a security concern in the immediate future.

Table 20.4 Incidents of domestic and international terrorism, by region, 1998–2004

Region	Year 1998	1999	2000	2001	2002	2003	2004
North America	6	8	9	39	16	18	6
Western Europe	284	433	372	550	342	372	271
Eastern Europe	313	86	27	104	215	125	167
East and Central Asia	20	—	—	23	12	13	15
South Asia	126	88	96	197	836	613	626
South East Asia and Oceania	27	28	72	122	96	30	49
Middle East	205	350	309	508	627	496	1291
Africa	107	53	28	27	29	29	36
Latin America	186	113	225	163	477	199	167
Totals	1,274	1,159	1,138	1,833	2,650	1,895	2,461

Note: No information reported for East and Central Asia in 1999 and 2000. Information is either lacking or the numbers are included in other regions.

Source: Start (2007).

Table 20.5 Injuries from domestic and international terrorism, by region, 1998–2004

Region	Year 1998	1999	2000	2001	2002	2003	2004
North America	2	14	0	11	3	0	0
Western Europe	145	34	153	213	1,914	114	653
Eastern Europe	260	775	234	259	1,236	689	1,232
East and Central Asia	20	—	—	23	3	1	43
South Asia	1,193	675	1,043	1,171	2,158	1,326	2,929
South East Asia and Oceania	94	104	601	494	975	394	406
Middle East	413	334	190	1,267	1,914	3,205	4,921
Africa	5,858	372	139	239	183	51	402
Latin America	120	25	176	306	757	473	1232
Totals	8,166	2,333	2,397	3,983	7,333	6,253	10,586

Note: No information reported for East and Central Asia in 1999 and 2000. Either the information is lacking or the numbers are included in other regions. Figures for North America for 2001 obviously do not include the uncertain number of injuries on 9/11.

Source: Start (2007).

Table 20.6 Fatalities from domestic and international terrorism, by region, 1998–2004

Region	Year 1998	1999	2000	2001	2002	2003	2004
North America	1	3	0	2,987	3	0	0
Western Europe	52	6	33	31	15	6	194
Eastern Europe	133	350	65	70	375	266	543
East and Central Asia	71	—	—	13	3	21	26
South Asia	585	201	297	440	1,017	803	883
South East Asia and Oceania	9	16	87	61	351	72	202
Middle East	168	113	60	257	564	907	2,598
Africa	1,078	93	37	289	129	109	388
Latin America	142	67	198	307	297	185	543
Totals	2,239	849	777	4,555	2,754	2,369	4,834

Note: No information reported for East and Central Asia in 1999 and 2000. Either the information is lacking or the numbers are included in other regions.

Source: Start (2007).

Table 20.7 Terrorism in the world (domestic and international) and Middle East

	Year 1998	1999	2000	2001	2002	2003	2004
Incidents total	1,274	1,159	1,138	1,833	2,650	1,895	2,461
Middle East	205	350	309	508	627	496	1291
Injuries total	8,166	2,333	2,397	3,983	7,333	6,253	10,586
Middle East	413	334	190	1,267	1,914	3,205	4,921
Deaths total	2,239	849	777	4,555	2,754	2,369	4,834
Middle East	168	113	60	257	564	907	2,598

Source: Start (2007).

KEY POINTS

- Statistics indicate that terrorism is actually increasing.

- Domestic terrorism is often not as newsworthy as international actions, but it accounts for a large majority of terrorist attacks.

- Terrorist groups can be very flexible in their choice of targets.

- Terrorist groups often find that democratic states or weaker authoritarian political systems are more inviting targets.

- Some groups may be willing to use weapons of mass destruction, but most terrorist organizations continue to rely on conventional weapons for their attacks.

Types and causes of terrorism

Terrorism has been widespread, and there is no single cause that explains outbreaks of this kind of violence. It is a complex phenomenon with many facets. Linked with the causes of terrorism are the motivations of the various organizations involved in the violence, motivations that provide some clues as to the underlying causes. These motivations can be used to categorize groups in terms of their objectives. The basic types are religious, ethnic or nationalist, and ideological. Additionally, there are groups that are more difficult to place into any particular category given the complexity of their motivations.

Categories

Religious groups obviously come to mind in the twenty-first century, given their prevalence in recent years. Al-Qaeda is the most prominent example since 2000, with the global nature of its attacks (see Table 20.8), but it is not the only such group in operation. There are other Islamic groups, some with linkages to al-Qaeda and the broader global jihadist

movement, that have been active in Indonesia, India, Egypt, Israel and the Occupied Territories, Algeria, the Philippines, and other countries. Religious terrorism, however, has not been limited to Islamic organizations; extremists' groups in other religious traditions have also used the technique. The violent anti-abortion activities in the United States are based in Christian viewpoints. Christian beliefs were used to justify ethnic-cleansing activities against Muslims in Bosnia. There was a guerrilla struggle in the Indian **Punjab** in the 1980s and 1990s that pitted **Sikhs** against Hindus. The Sikh uprising was in part a reaction to extremist Hindu groups in India that sought to reclaim the subcontinent for their religion and to drive out foreign religions, especially Islam and also Christianity. Jewish extremists justifying their actions by religious beliefs have used terrorist tactics against Palestinians. Aum Shinrikyo was willing to attack Japanese society and to cleanse it of the impure. Many religious groups are too weak to impose their views in other fashions, and terrorism then become the weapon that they use.

Table 20.8 Significant al-Qaeda attacks, 1993–2007

Date	Place	Target	Method	Fatalities
26 February 1993	New York City	World Trade Center	Car bomb	6
25 June 1996	Dhahran, Saudi Arabia	Khobar Towers housing US military	Truck bomb	19
7 August 1998	Nairobi, Kenya	US Embassy	Truck bomb	247
7 August 1998	Dar-es-Salaam, Tanzania	US Embassy	Truck bomb	10
12 October 2000	Aden, Yemen	*USS Cole*, USA	Explosives on boat	17
11 September 2001	New York and Washington, DC	World Trade Center and Pentagon	Airliners flown into buildings	2,973
22 December 2001	Paris–Miami flight	Airliner	Attempted attack with shoe bomb	0
11 April 2002	Djerba, Tunisia	Synagogue and tourist	Truck bomb	19
14 June 2002	Karachi, Pakistan	US consulate	Suicide car bomb	19

Table 20.8 (Continued)

Date	Place	Target	Method	Fatalities
6 October 2002	Mina al-Dabah, Yemen	French tanker	Boat bomb	1
12 October 2002	Bali, Indonesia	Western tourists	Car bomb	202
28 November 2002	Mombassa, Kenya	Israeli-owned hotel for tourists	Car bomb	16
12 May 2003	Riyadh, Saudi	Three compounds	Car bombs	25
16 May 2003	Casablanca, Morocco	Five sites	Suicide bombs	42
5 August 2003	Jakarta, Indonesia	Marriott Hotel	Car bomb	10
11 March 2004	Madrid, Spain	Commuter trains	Bombs	191
7 July 2005	London, England	Underground trains and buses	Suicide bombs	56
2 October 2005	Bali, Indonesia	Tourist hotel	Suicide bombs	26
30 June 2007	Glasgow, Scotland	Airport	Attempted suicide bomb	0

Sources: Poland (2005); Tan (2006).

Groups defined by their ethnic or linguistic identifications are another broad category (see Case Study 20.2). The Basque Euzkadi ta Askatasuna (ETA—Basque for Homeland and Freedom) has been seeking independence for the Basque region of Spain since 1959, and began using violence to achieve that goal in 1968. The Tamil Tigers continue to seek independence (or at least autonomy) for those areas of Sri Lanka where Tamils are a majority. Turkey has faced significant terrorist attacks from Kurdish separatist groups. A large number of anti-colonial groups in the past were ethnically based and used terrorism as one tactic in their efforts to gain independence. Algerian nationalists mounted a major urban terrorism campaign against the French in the late 1950s to supplement guerrilla activities. Greek Cypriots also used urban terrorism and guerrilla attacks against the British in the same period. In Palestine, Jewish settlers (who qualify as nationalist in this context, since most of the settlers were quite secular) relied only on terrorism in their successful efforts to force the British to leave the territory.

CASE STUDY 20.2

Palestinian Liberation Organization (PLO)

The struggle between the Israelis and the Palestinians is often seen as a religious conflict, but it was for many years primarily a clash of nationalisms. Most of the initial Jewish settlers were largely secular, and the original Palestinian resistance movements were overwhelming secular as well. Only in the 1990s did the Palestinian opposition take on overtly religious objectives, such as the creation of an Islamic Palestinian state in all of the Occupied Territories and Israel. The PLO always focused on Palestinian nationalism and stressed secular themes, so that it could appeal to both Muslim and Christian Palestinians. It was an umbrella organization that included many different Palestinian nationalist groups, but it never included avowedly Islamic groups. Fatah, the organization led by Yasser Arafat, was one of the most important organizations, but others like the Popular Front for the Liberation of Palestine (PFLP) combined leftist ideology with Palestinian nationalism. For them the Palestinians were an oppressed Third World people battling against the evils of global capitalism and its Israeli representatives in the Middle East. The PLO initially used guerrilla raids against Israel, but, after the defeat of the Arab armies in the 1967 war, it shifted to terrorism as

---

📌 **CASE STUDY 20.2** (Continued)

the remaining hope for creating a Palestinian homeland. At various times groups, such as the PFLP and others, left the PLO because of disputes with Arafat over the course of action to be followed—for example, when terrorist attacks

were limited, when they were discontinued, and when the agreement to create the Palestinian Authority was made in Oslo. Some of these organizations were eventually willing to rejoin the PLO.

Other terrorist groups have drawn their ideas from ideologies. There was a wave of terrorist violence in Europe in the 1970s and 1980s rooted in various leftist and Marxist ideologies. The Red Brigades in Italy, the Red Army Faction in Germany, and other groups in Europe were joined by Japanese groups, the Weathermen in the United States, and organizations in Latin America. The leftist wave was on the wane by the last part of the 1980s, when the collapse of communism in East Europe and the Soviet Union weakened the surviving groups even further. Some leftist groups have survived and have continued to be active in Nepal, Mexico, and Ecuador. Terrorist groups based in right-wing ideologies have also been present. Such groups were relatively weak in the years after the Second World War, but a great number of them appeared in the 1990s in Western Europe. These groups have often

been opposed to foreign influences, a large state, or leftist ideas. They have often targeted migrants and foreign workers, especially those from the Middle East, South Asia, or sub-Saharan Africa where cultural, ethnic, and religious differences often reinforced each other. These groups have their counterparts in the United States with xenophobic and anti-black groups. The Ku Klux Klan was once one of the largest of such groups (see Case Study 20.3). It was severely weakened in the 1960s and 1970s, but its place has been taken by a large number of smaller groups espousing some of the same racist and anti-foreign ideas. When groups from the left and right have battled each other, more conservative governments tolerated the violent right-wing groups that targeted members of the left. At times governments have used death squads against the leftist dissidents.

📌 **CASE STUDY 20.3**

The Ku Klux Klan (KKK)

The KKK is a classic American terrorist group that propounded racist and right-wing views in the 1950s and 1960s. It tried to terrorize Black Americans and their white supporters during the civil-rights struggle of those years. Lynchings, murders, and bombs were used in the failed attempt to dissuade people from agitating for equal rights. This period, violent though it was, resulted in hundreds of deaths. The most active period for the KKK was in the 1920s. In this period the KKK combined its racist orientation with opposition to the presence of Catholics, Jews, and Orientals. It was also opposed to the arrival of new immigrants (many of whom were Catholic or Jewish). In

these years the KKK had noticeable strength outside the Southern states; in fact, Indiana at one time had the largest membership of any state branch. The overall level of violence by racist and anti-foreign groups, including the KKK, was greater in this period with lynchings and murders totalling the thousands (Hofstader 1970: 65). Many of the dead were Black Americans, but members of other groups were also victims. Whites were at times the main targets, as they were considered more dangerous by the KKK because they had been contaminated by foreign ideas (Tucker 1991: 5). The KKK eventually declined, partially as a consequence of scandals that involved the leaders, including the leader of the Indiana chapter (Chalmers 1965: 167–70).

Some groups are more difficult to categorize. A number of right-wing groups in the United States incorporate Christianity into their ideologies

(sometimes in unusual ways). The IRA in Northern Ireland has mobilized support on the basis of Irish versus British nationalities, but the role of religion in the struggles in the province cannot be denied. Ideology has also appeared in this struggle since the Irish National Liberation Army (INLA) shared the ethnic Irish basis of the IRA but also included a Marxist-Leninist ideological component. In Colombia there were some straightforwardly Marxist-Leninist terrorist groups that operated in the country, but others such as the Revolutionary Armed Forces of Colombia (FARC) joined forces with drug cartels. In Peru in the 1980s and 1990s dissident organizations using terror combined leftist ideology with an ethnic appeal to the Indian communities that have been ignored by the Europeanized elite of the country. These Peruvian groups also developed links with the weaker drug cartels in that country. Drug cartels have cooperated with terrorist groups in many other countries as well, and there are increasing connections between criminal organizations and terrorist groups (Dishman 2005).

Causes

The causes of terrorism are in many ways similar to the causes of most other forms of political violence (such as riots, rebellions, coups, and civil wars). Individuals in a society become so discontented or frustrated with their inability to bring about what they see as necessary changes that they resort to violence. The dissidents have a perception that society and the political system discriminate or are unfair. What is ultimately important are the perceptions of the dissidents, although greater levels of exploitation may drive larger numbers to attempt violent change.

There are some specific factors, however, that can contribute to outbreaks of terrorism. Democracies with their limitations on the security forces provide opportunities for terrorists. Limited political participation and repression by government forces can also breed the necessary popular discontent for violence, but states with strong security forces and firm control of their societies can usually prevent terrorists from operating. Dissidents and potential dissidents can be jailed, suspects can be tortured, families can be held hostage, and convictions can be

guaranteed in the courts (if trials occur). When the Soviet Union was a strong centralized system, terrorism was virtually unknown. The successor states are weaker, and some like Russia have faced significant terrorist problems. It is the inability of the government of Colombia to function effectively in many parts of the country that has provided significant opportunities for guerrillas and terrorists, as well as the drug cartels, to survive and prosper. Similarly, the weak state structure in Lebanon for the last part of the twentieth century permitted terrorist groups to form and operate. Lebanon not only saw terrorism used in the struggles to control the country, but it became a base for terrorist groups operating elsewhere.

The processes involved with globalization have also contributed to outbreaks of terrorism. With faster communications and transportation, outside forces—usually Western—intrude into local societies. Economies are disrupted, and, even if winners outnumber losers, there are still losers. Further, local cultures, including religious components, are threatened by globalization, especially when it has been accompanied by secularization. Terrorism in many cases can be seen as a reaction to globalization. Leftist groups around the world have opposed the spread of capitalism and all its evils. Secular globalization also leads to religious and ethnic fragmentation (Ramakrishna and Tan 2003: 3–4). Many religious groups (Christian, Jewish, Muslim, Hindu) are opposed to the secularism that comes with modernity (Pillar 2001: 65). Right-wing, ethnocentric groups have opposed the dilution of their cultures by the outside ideas that accompany migrants, guest workers, and refugees. It is perhaps ironic that Muslims in the Middle East feel threatened by the intrusion of European or Western values at the same time that groups in Europe feel threatened by individuals from Middle Eastern cultures with Islamic ideas. Terrorism rooted in ethnic differences can also reflect the intrusion of outside forces, and groups like the Irish and the Basques fear the submergence of their language and culture into a larger ethnic identity (Dingley and Kirk-Smith 2002). There is another potential connection between democracy and nationalism that has come with globalization or that has been a response to it. Walter Laqueur (2001: 11) has suggested the overlap between democracy and nationalism provides more opportunities for terrorism. Nationalism provides a spark that can exacerbate ethnic differences, and democracy allows for the expression of opposing nationalist views. If Laqueur's analysis is correct, the wave of democratization that occurred at the end of the twentieth century may have increased the chances of new outbreaks of terrorism, although increasing democratization in stable countries may eventually remove many of the conditions that contribute to terrorism.

KEY POINTS

- There is no one cause of terrorism.

- Terrorism is a technique that is available to different kinds of groups pursuing different types of objectives.

- Terrorism is not unique to Islam or the Middle East.

- Globalization and responses to it can be linked to fresh outbreaks of terrorism.

Security measures

Leaders and governments facing terrorist attacks have to defend against these attacks. Since there is no one overwhelming cause or source of terrorism, partially because it is a technique that can be used by different groups for different causes, countermeasures become more difficult. Sederberg's threefold typology is relevant as a point of reference, because some security or counterterrorism measures are more in keeping with viewing terrorism as war, others fit terrorism as crime, and yet others are more relevant for the disease analogy. Counterterrorism measures can also be considered within the scope of prevention, response to attacks, international collaboration, and the effects of security measures on civil liberties.

Prevention

Prevention is normally associated with the concept of terrorism as war or crime. All governments will practice prevention—repression from the terrorist perspective—by seeking to arrest or eliminate those actively involved in the violence. Security forces attack the terrorists before they strike (war) or they are arrested after the attack (crime). Clearly, whichever concept of battling terrorism is chosen helps to determine security policies. The war conceptualization, for example, permits a stronger pre-emptive response. In actual fact, however, the military and police functions do not have a precise dividing line. Police forces dealing with dangerous criminals (terrorist or otherwise) may shoot first and ask questions later. In both the warfare and criminal models, there may be a desire to capture terrorists to elicit further intelligence, sometimes by offering shorter sentences to captured terrorist in exchange for information. Informers inside the terrorist groups can be key assets for the security forces for gathering intelligence. Using informers is hard in the case of small groups; they are usually too cohesive for effective infiltration. Larger organizations are easier to penetrate and gain information, but it is unlikely that all the operations of larger groups can be stopped except with the passage of time. Similarly, loose network groups such as al-Qaeda and right-wing extremist groups in the United States and Europe are unlikely to be dismantled because of any single intelligence coup, although actions based on successful intelligence gathering can weaken them.

Greater physical security measures are another preventive option that has merit, whether one views terrorism as war, crime, or disease. Not every possible target can be protected, but key installations, including potential sources of materials for weapons of mass destruction, however, need to be secured. In other cases security can be enhanced for many potential targets, even if all attacks cannot be prevented. Some terrorist activities might be foiled, and in other cases some members of the dissident groups may be captured or killed as a consequence of improved security. These preventative measures will not stop determined terrorists, who will seek other, more vulnerable targets (see Think Point 20.1). Increased security, of course, will mean increased costs, and the money spend on physical security and target hardening is not available elsewhere in the economy, which could result in important lost economic opportunities.

 THINK POINT 20.1

Security and the law of unintended consequences

Sometimes improved security can have unintended, and negative, consequences. In the 1960s and 1970s the United States and other countries suffered through a wave of airline hijackings. Individuals from a variety of groups (and loners with no cause but a desire for publicity) skyjacked airliners, issuing communiqués justifying their actions. Many of the aircraft were flown to Cuba or Algeria, where the hijackers received asylum in return for releasing the planes and passengers. In response to the hijackings, airport security was improved so that hijackings virtually ceased. Groups could no longer use this tactic to publicize their cause; therefore, some organizations shifted to planting bombs on the airliners to raise public awareness of their objectives. The terrorists even developed sophisticated bombs that would begin a countdown to detonation only when a certain altitude was reached. Eventually baggage security at airports improved so that only an occasional bomb could be successful placed on planes, but not before a number of airliners had been destroyed in mid-flight. In some ways the use of airliners on 9/11 was a response to the difficulties of placing bombs on aircraft. It is clear that defensive security precautions can be important, but committed terrorists can find new techniques (Enders and Sandler 2006: 5). These new techniques may be more deadly than the methods that were replaced.

Responses

Responses to terrorist attacks vary, either explicitly or implicitly, if terrorism is seen as warfare, crime, or disease. If the war analogy holds, retaliation and punishment become the norms. Pre-emptive strikes against training facilities or at headquarters, or even the assassinations of key individuals in the terrorist organizations are potential responses. The United States and its allies have attempted to follow this strategy against al-Qaeda, albeit with less than complete success. In their confrontations before the Oslo Accords, Israel and the PLO basically viewed their struggle in terms of covert warfare. Even though Israel considered the PLO and other Palestinian groups to be terrorists and definitely not soldiers, the context of the struggle was one of warfare. Israel has continued the same approach in dealing with attacks by Hamas and Islamic Jihad.

Arrest, capture, trial (fair or otherwise), and incarceration reflect the crime perspective. The ultimate goal of police forces is to deter action by demonstrating that criminals will be caught and punished. The same goal is present with terrorists; capture and punishment are inevitable. While the warfare analogy also presumes deterrence at times, deterrence is more central to a justice system. Pre-emptive strikes and assassinations are not normally part of the arsenal of crime fighting unless a government unleashes death squads as a form of state violence or permits groups allied with the government to attack in this fashion. In these circumstances governments have shifted from the crime perspective to one closer to the warfare analogy. The extent of pre-emption available in a normal criminal context is detention of suspects—sometimes for lengthy periods (but not indefinite ones), and perhaps judicial harassment of suspects. Hostage situations are one area where terrorism as crime is most frequently the response. It is frequently police forces that are better equipped and trained to deal with these kinds of situations. Even rescue attempts are not foreign to typical police practice. The war response might be more difficult for the hostages, since a military response might see them as potential casualties of a conflict with terrorists rather than considering their safety as the prime objective.

If terrorism is viewed as a disease, the range of responses will change. Since diseases have both symptoms and causes, this perspective requires that some of the responses related to the war and crime views be applied. Terrorist violence, as a symptom, will need to be dealt with by arrest or prevention. The disease perspective, moreover, leads to efforts to deal with the underlying causes. Reform packages may become part of the government response in an effort to reduce the appeal of the terrorist groups within the population. If ethnic or religious discrimination is present, laws forbidding discrimination may be passed. If poverty is perceived to be fuelling support for the terrorists, then governmental programmes to reduce poverty in a region or group may be instituted (at least if the funds are available). If the terrorists are operating in a colonial situation, then the ultimate reform that is possible is for the colonial power to grant independence. Of course, it has been argued that reforms will simply encourage the terrorist to continue the violence because they are being rewarded. As one leader of a terrorist groups argued, more was won by a few months of violence than by years of peaceful politics (Ash 2003: 63). Under these circumstances reforms may become concessions that fuel the violence rather than a mechanism for ending it; yet, there has been no compelling or consistent evidence that concessions encourage terrorists to continue to use violence to gain even more (Crenshaw 1998: 255). Like other counterterrorist approaches, sometimes concessions may work and sometimes they may make the circumstances worse.

There are other reasons why reforms will not always eliminate the presence of terrorism. Demands by the terrorist dissidents for the establishment of a religious state, a leftist government, the repression of a minority, or removal of all foreigners or foreign elements may not be acceptable to the majority. The leftists in the 1970s and 1980s in Europe wanted to do away with the international capitalist system, yet most Europeans wanted to continue to receive the benefits of capitalism. Most of the inhabitants of Puerto Rico do not want independence, but groups with this objective have used terror attacks against the United States. The spread of globalization or the intrusion of outside values and new cultures cannot be prevented. In other cases, extremist groups in the same country may have mutually incompatible goals. Extreme Jewish settler groups in Israel want complete control of the West Bank and all Palestinians to leave; Hamas wants to create an Islamic state in the whole of Israel, the West Bank, and the Gaza Strip. No Israeli government can meet the demands of both groups. In Turkey in the 1970s dissident terrorists from the left and the right attacked the Turkish government. There was no programme available that could meet the demands of both sides. In circumstances such as these, even a government or political leaders otherwise amenable to reforms will have to rely on other options.

International measures

International cooperation among countries is another important counterterrorist technique. Intelligence agencies operate best on their own soil or in their own region; national intelligence agencies are not equally effective everywhere. Collaboration among intelligence agencies, as has occurred in the European Union, therefore, will contribute to the prevention of terrorism. International cooperation can also provide the necessary support for reforms that reduce the severity of terrorism. Sanctions against countries aiding terrorists have worked in the past, but in 2009 there are few state sponsors that can be targeted. Military action was effective in toppling the Taliban regime in Afghanistan and ending its support for al-Qaeda, and this military action had widespread international support (unlike the later military action against Iraq). While cooperative international sanctions do not always work, it is important to note that they have not always failed.

A great deal of international diplomacy has involved attempts to define terrorism so that all countries could then take steps to eliminate terrorist groups. These efforts have faltered because countries often support or sympathize with dissidents who use violence against repressive governments. Governments in the developing world have wanted to avoid situations where anti-colonial struggles are labelled as terrorism. Most countries have not favoured too strict a definition, since they want the flexibility to avoid extradition or punishment of some political dissidents. It is hard to envision the United States accepting a terrorist label in 2003 for anti-Saddam Hussein dissidents had they attacked members of his regime. There have been some successes in the international sphere. Certain types of actions, such as air piracy, have been outlawed, and most members of the United Nations have signed these treaties and conventions (Pillar 2001: 77–9). These partial agreements are a positive step in the process of containing terrorism by defining certain actions as crimes. When global agreements are not possible, diplomacy can achieve agreements among smaller groups of countries, providing for greater cooperation and bilateral arrangements automatically to prevent asylum for individuals associated with certain groups. The United States and the United Kingdom, for example, eventually signed a bilateral agreement making the extradition of suspected IRA members from the United States easier.

Civil liberties in peril

A final concern that has appeared with counterterrorism efforts in many countries is the potential threat that such measures can have for civil liberties. While authoritarian states do not worry about this issue, there are limits on intelligence gathering and pre-emptive actions in democracies. Increased security measures can lead to infringements on the rights of citizens or foreign residents. In the United States,

the Patriot Act has permitted more intrusive searches and wiretaps, while persons captured overseas have been placed in indefinite detention at the Guantanamo Naval Base in Cuba. There have also been efforts to establish special tribunals to try suspected terrorists that would be expected to operate in ways to make conviction of suspects more likely than would be the case in normal courts. In Northern Ireland IRA intimidation of jurors led to the use of courts without juries, and preventative detention was also introduced. Special terrorism laws were passed in the United Kingdom in the wake of IRA attacks. The danger of wrongful convictions is possible even without special legislation; judges and juries may be quick to assume the guilt of suspected terrorists. Germany, France, and Australia—like the United Kingdom and the United States—passed new legislation after the events of 9/11, giving government security forces greater powers to detain and interrogate those suspected of terrorism (Haubrick 2003; Hocking 2003). In such circumstances there is always the danger of convicting innocent people (see Case Study 20.4). Civil liberties are in the least danger if terrorism is viewed as a disease where the root causes need to be treated. The crime model provide for some threat to civil liberties, but defenders of civil liberties frequently deal with the police and criminal justice system. The greatest danger comes when governments regard the battle against terrorism as warfare because most democratic countries permit greater restrictions on the rights of individuals during wartime. As a consequence, viewing the struggle with terrorism as war tends to bring with it the idea that temporary personal sacrifices of liberties may be necessary in the interest of victory.

CASE STUDY 20.4

Miscarriages of justice with Irish defendants

In 1974 IRA attack teams set off bombs in Woolwich in London and Guildford in Surrey that killed off-duty service personnel (and others). A month later two pubs in Birmingham were bombed. These bombings led to the passage of the Prevention of Terrorism Acts (Temporary Provisions)—since periodically renewed—which provided for longer detention of IRA suspects for questioning and other changes that facilitated intelligence gathering.

CASE STUDY 20.4   (Continued)

Four suspects (the Guildford Four) were arrested, convicted, and imprisoned on shaky evidence and coerced confessions. Their arrests also led to the arrest and conviction on weak forensic evidence of seven more suspects (the Maguire Seven). The bombings in Birmingham resulted in the conviction of six individuals (the Birmingham Six) with weak evidence and coerced confessions. Sixteen of the seventeen individuals were Irish, and the seventeenth was the English girlfriend of one of the suspects. The special interrogation procedures available to the authorities under the act permitted over-zealous police to coerce confessions and manipulate evidence to convict the individuals whom the police thought were guilty. Juries were clearly inclined to believe the police and doubtful of the Irish suspects. While there is no evidence that the police, the courts, or the government had a concerted policy to manufacture convictions, the climate of fear and the desire to convict someone for the bombings contributed to these miscarriages of justice (Lutz et al. 2002).

KEY POINTS

- Detection and prevention of terrorist attacks will not always be possible.

- Dealing with terrorism within the context of warfare is more likely to result in pre-emptive actions.

- Considering terrorism within the disease perspective places greater emphasis on reforms than either the crime or the war perspective.

- International cooperation for dealing with terrorism would appear to have natural limits, and any global agreements on a meaningful definition of terrorism are unlikely.

- The greatest threat to civil liberties in democracies comes in those contexts where the battle against terrorism is seen as being equivalent to war.

Conclusion

It is clear that terrorism will remain a major security threat for years to come. The ethnic, religious, and ideological disputes that have fuelled terrorism in the past have not disappeared. While ideological terrorism has declined somewhat since the end of communism, it has not disappeared as right-wing groups and fewer leftist groups continue to operate. Ethnically and religiously inspired terrorism remains very important. Groups that cannot attain their goals through the electoral process or government takeovers will often adopt terrorism as a technique. Globalization will continue to disrupt economic, political, social, religious, and cultural systems. Weak states will be inviting targets for attacks or provide terrorists with convenient bases. Government repression will generate opposition. Connections between terrorists and criminal groups could increase.

Providing security against terrorism will not be easy. There are too many targets. Terrorists have the advantage of being able to choose targets that are not defended. As one type of target is eliminated by protection, terrorists will substitute another (Enders and Sandler 2006). No one countermeasure will defeat terrorism—it has multifaceted causes and is a technique that can be used by many different groups. Success against one group will not guarantee success against another. Groups come from different backgrounds, have different kinds of support, and seek different objectives. Under these circumstances it would be amazing if there was one countermeasure that always worked. In some cases, normal police methods will be successful. Treating terrorism as crime, for example, could be quite appropriate when terrorists have links with drug cartels. Considering terrorism as war is relevant in cases where the dissident groups combine terrorism with guerrilla activities, as has been the case with the Tamil Tigers in Sri Lanka and the resurgent Taliban in Afghanistan. In other cases there may be some value in governments considering reforms as one means of weakening support for the dissidents or as a compromise to end violence. Looking at terrorism from the perspective of war, crime, or disease is useful for analysis and for pinpointing problems that can occur when one or the other of these particular approaches is taken, but many terrorist groups and situations do not fit neatly into any one situation. The necessary response will often be a mixture of elements involving all three, and determining the appropriate mix of security programmes and responses to terrorism will never be easy. Security measures for dealing with terrorist threats are likely to require flexibility, and government security forces will have to change techniques as circumstances change.

QUESTIONS

1. Which type of terrorism has been the most present in the Middle East, Asia, Europe, and the United States since the mid-1980s and why?

2. Which areas of the world are most vulnerable to terrorism and why?

3. What other categories of terrorism might be added to the religious, ideological, and ethnic varieties?

4. What role do the media play in international terrorism and domestic terrorism?

5. What techniques might be most effective in dealing with different kinds of terrorism? Why?

6. Does the appearance of leaderless resistance styles of terrorism or network systems create special problems for countermeasures?

7. Is terrorism best dealt with as war, crime, or disease in your country?

8. What counterterrorism measures would be most effective in dealing with terrorism in your country?

9. What changes (if any) will occur in the next decade in how terrorist groups operate? How will ways of providing security against terrorism change?

10. Are efforts to defeat or contain terrorism a great threat to civil liberties?

FURTHER READING

■ Bjorgo, Tore (2005) (ed.), *Root Causes of Terrorism: Myths, Reality, and Ways Forward*, London: Routledge. This volume provides a comprehensive survey of the types of terrorism (ethnic, religious, ideological, criminal) and techniques with reference to recent events.

■ Enders, Walter, and Sandler, Todd (2006), *The Political Economy of Terrorism*, Cambridge: Cambridge University Press. This book is a compilation of the authors' earlier work. It involves some empirical assessment of terrorism, but it also contains excellent overviews on key topics as well.

■ Hoffman, Bruce (2006), *Inside Terrorism*, rev. and expanded edn., New York: Columbia University Press. The new edition of this book, like its predecessor, is one of the best introductions to the topic of terrorist groups and terrorism.

■ Kegley, Charles W., Jr. (2003), (eds.) *The New Global Terrorism: Characteristics, Causes, Controls*, Upper Saddle River, NJ: Prentice Hall. This collection of short articles is still one of the best compilations of works in the field; it covers virtually all the basic issues from a variety of perspectives.

■ Laqueur, Walter (2001), *A History of Terrorism*, Brunswick, NJ: Transaction Publishers. This book is in part an update of Laqueur's many earlier works. It contains a broad overview of terrorism through time and details the difficulties of viewing terrorism from one or a limited number of perspectives.

■ Lutz, James, and Lutz, Brenda (2008), *Global Terrorism,* 2nd edn., London: Routledge. This textbook uses case studies to provide historical and geographical depth to the discussion of terrorism. While terrorism in the Middle East and by extremist Islamic groups is covered, the book clearly avoids concentrating on these topics to the exclusion of others.

■ Tan, Andrew H. T. (2006), *The Politics of Terrorism: A Survey*, London: Routledge. This volume is an excellent source of information. It contains chapters by individual authors on the various types of terrorism or techniques that are used as well as a very useful compilation of the types of groups that have been operating on some of the key terrorist incidents.

■ Tucker, Jonathan B. (ed.) (2000), *Toxic Terror: Assessing Terrorist Use of Chemical and Biological Weapons*, Cambridge, MA: MIT Press. This volume documents various attempts to use chemical and biological weapons by terrorist groups. Most ended in failures, although the attacks by Aum Shinrikyo in Japan have been an obvious exception. The conclusions drawn from the book about the relative danger of such attacks remain valid today.

■ Wilkinson, Paul (2006), *Terrorism versus Democracy: The Liberal State Response*, 2nd edn, London: Routledge. Wilkinson provides an overview of terrorism and terrorist groups and then discusses the effects that terrorism has had on Western democracies.

 IMPORTANT WEBSITES

● http://www.comw.org/rma Project on Defense Alternatives, Revolution on Military Affairs (RMA)—maintained by Commonwealth Institute, Cambridge, MA. This website provides access to papers and other works dealing with terrorism, including some papers (from conferences or as working papers) that are not readily available elsewhere.

● http://www.state.gov/s/ct/rls/crt United States Department of State site that has 'Patterns of Terrorism' for years 1991–2003 and 'Country Reports on Terrorism' for subsequent years. 'The Patterns of Terrorism' series was a compilation of international incidents around the world. The 'Country Reports on Terrorism' series lacks the statistics, but it does have information on terrorism on a country-by-country basis. In both sets of materials the data are not restricted to attacks involving the United States and against US interests or citizens abroad. Also see the NCTC website.

● http://wits.nctc.gov This website is associated with the National Counterterrorism Center (NCTC). This centre took over incident reports from the State Department (see above). It has a tracking system for incidents by country (Worldwide Incidents Tracking System) that is directly accessible from this site. The NCTC also published Reports on Incidents of Terrorism for more recent years. The volumes for individual years are more readily accessed with a search engine with the search term 'Reports on Incidents of Terrorism."

 Visit the Online Resource Centre that accompanies this book for lots of interesting additional material: www.oxfordtextbooks.co.uk/orc/collins2e/

21

Humanitarian Intervention

ALEX J. BELLAMY

Chapter Contents

- Introduction
- The case for humanitarian intervention
- The case against humanitarian intervention
- Towards responsibility to protect
- Conclusion

Reader's Guide

This chapter provides an overview of the debate between those who believe that the protection of civilians from genocide and mass atrocities ought to trump the principle of non-intervention in certain circumstances and those who oppose this proposition. This has become a particular problem in the post-Cold War world where the commission of atrocities in places like Rwanda, Bosnia, and Darfur prompted calls, in the West especially, for international society to step in to protect the victims with military force if necessary. Although it might seem morally appealing to intervene to protect populations from death and destruction, humanitarian intervention causes problems for international security by potentially weakening the rules governing the use of force in world politics. Since the end of the Cold War, a broad international consensus has emerged around a principle called the 'responsibility to protect' (R2P). This principle was based on an understanding of sovereignty as responsibility developed in the 1990s by Francis Deng and UN Secretary-General Kofi Annan, among others. The principle itself was developed by the International Commission on Intervention and State Sovereignty in 2001. The R2P holds that states have a responsibility to protect their citizens from genocide and mass atrocities and that the international community has a duty to help states fulfil their responsibilities and use various measures to protect populations when their own states are manifestly failing to do so.

Introduction

'Humanitarian intervention' refers to the use of military force by external actors for humanitarian purposes, usually against the wishes of the host government. There have been several humanitarian interventions since the end of the Cold War (see Table 21.1). In the 1990s, **genocide** in Rwanda (1994) killed at least 800,000, war in the former Yugoslavia (1992–5) left at least 250,000 dead and forced thousands more to flee. Protracted conflicts in Sierra Leone, Sudan, Haiti, Somalia, Liberia, East Timor, the Democratic Republic of Congo (DRC), and elsewhere killed millions more. Conflict in the Darfur region of Sudan has cost the lives of around 250,000 people and forced more than three million people from their homes (Coebergh 2005).

Approximately 90 per cent of the victims in these conflicts were civilians. In what Mary Kaldor (1999) famously described as 'new wars', civilian deaths are a direct war aim not an unfortunate by-product (see Slim 2008). Although most of these wars involved non-state militia groups, sometimes the worst perpetrators of crimes against civilians are states and their allies. According to one study, in the twentieth century around forty million civilians were killed in wars between states, whilst nearly six times that number were killed by their own governments (Rummel 1994: 21).

Historically, **genocides** have ended in one of two ways: either the perpetrators succeed in destroying their target group or they are defeated in battle.

Table 21.1 Interventions for ostensibly humanitarian reasons, post-Cold War era

Place	Date	Intervener	UN Authority?	Consent?	Type of Intervention	Outcome
Liberia	1990–7	ECOWAS–Nigeria	No—but later welcomed by UN	Initially, but ECOWAS then forcibly engaged with the Charles Taylor faction controlling most of the territory	Active combat against anti-government rebels	ECOMOG defeated Taylor in 1992, but Taylor elected president in 1997 elections
Iraqi Kurdistan	1991	USA, UK, France	Ambiguous	No—but little resistance	Establishment of safe area and no-fly zone	Kurds protected from Iraqi army
Somalia	1992–3	USA/UN	Yes	No government to seek consent from	Secure delivery of humanitarian relief, disarmament of warlords	Humanitarian relief delivered, but warlords resisted disarmament, prompting withdrawal after USA sustained casualties
Bosnia-Hercegovina	1993–5	NATO	Yes	Bosnian government consented, Yugoslav government/Bosnian Serbs did not	Limited airstrikes followed by deployment of rapid reaction force; large-scale air operations in 1995	Bosnian Serbs and Yugoslav government accepted Dayton peace accord

Table 21.1 (Continued)

Place	Date	Intervener	UN Authority?	Consent?	Type of Intervention	Outcome
Haiti	1994	USA	Yes	Yes; Haitian military leaders backed down prior to deployment of US forces	Deployment to restore elected government	Peacekeepers deployed to maintain order and disarm rebels
Rwanda	1994	France	Yes	Pre-genocide government had collapsed	Creation of safe areas at the end of genocide	Safe areas saved some lives, but the perpetrators of the genocide allowed to flee to safety in the DRC, destabilizing that country
Kosovo	1999	NATO	No	No— intervention opposed	Aerial bombardment to coerce compliance with the Rambouillet accords	After 78 days, Yugoslavia conceded and permitted deployment of KFOR
East Timor	1999	Australian-led coalition	Yes	Yes—Indonesia granted consent after economic pressure used	Deployment of peacekeepers to deter and end militia violence	Militia withdrew or laid down arms; INTERFET handed over to UN transitional administration
Liberia	2002	ECOWAS– Nigeria	No	No—intervention in support of rebels after they had made significant advances	Deployment of peacekeepers in support of new government	Handed over to UN Mission to Liberia (UNMIL)
Democratic Republic of Congo	2003	EU–France	Yes	The government consented but not the armed groups that controlled the town and its environs	Deployment of forces to prevent genocide in the town of Bunia after Ugandan withdrawal	Atrocities in Bunia deterred but pushed into countryside in Ituri province; handed over to UN Mission (MONUC)
Georgia	2008	Russia	No	No	Deployment of forces and airstrikes in response to Georgian assault on disputed territory of South Ossetia	Georgians forced to withdraw; Russia created buffer zone; strongly criticized by the West

Notes

1.   The table is illustrative not definitive.

2.   For the purposes of this table, 'humanitarian intervention' is taken to mean the use of military force for ostensibly humanitarian purposes; 'ostensibly humanitarian' means that the principal justification offered was humanitarian.

3.   Although humanitarian intervention properly understood includes only those cases where force is used without the consent of the host state, for illustrative purposes cases have been included where consent was in doubt (e.g. Liberia), where military and economic coercion was required to secure consent (Haiti and East Timor respectively), and where the government gave consent but did not control the territory under question (e.g. Congo).

This cold fact is borne out by recent cases. The 1994 Rwandan **genocide** ended with the defeat of the Rwandan government and *interehamwe* militia at the hands of a rebel group known as the Rwandan Patriotic Front (RPF). The war in Bosnia came to an end when the military balance turned in favour of a Croat–Muslim coalition backed by NATO airpower; NATO airpower brought ethnic cleansing in Kosovo to an end. The rate of killing in Darfur has declined since its peak in 2003–4 primarily because the *Janjaweed* militia and their government backers have largely succeeded in forcing their enemies into exile.

Facts like this pose a major challenge to international security. For both liberals and realists alike, security has traditionally been understood as the purview of states, and two of the main guarantors of national security are the principles of sovereignty and non-interference. According to this perspective, security is best pursued through a society of sovereign states that enjoy exclusive jurisdiction over a particular piece of territory and rights to non-interference and non-intervention that are enshrined in the Charter of the United Nations. This is often labelled 'Westphalian sovereignty', referring to the 1648 Peace of Westphalia, which is commonly reckoned to have instituted a world order based on the rights of sovereigns. This idea sits at the heart of contemporary international society's rules governing relations between states. Article 2(4) of the UN Charter forbids the threat or use of force by states in their dealings with one another and Article 2(7) prohibits the UN from interfering in the domestic affairs of its member states. There are only two exceptions to the ban on the use of force contained in Article 2(4): Article 39 gives the UN Security Council the right to authorize military action in cases where it identifies a 'threat to international peace and security' and Article 51 recognizes that all states have an inherent right to use force in self-defence.

The value of this Westphalian system of security rests on the assumption that states are the best guardians of their citizens' security. In other words, the security of the state is considered important, and worth protecting, because states provide security to individuals. It should be clear from the proceeding paragraphs, however, that this assumption is problematic. In the past, threats to human security have tended to come more from an individual's own state than from other states. This raises the question of whether there are circumstances in which the security of individuals should be privileged over the security of states. Should a state's right to be secure and free from external interference be conditional on its fulfilment of certain responsibilities to its citizens, not least a responsibility to protect them from mass killing?

If we think that there are circumstances in which the use of force for humanitarian purposes is legitimate, we are then confronted by a range of practical questions about the utility of force in promoting humanitarian objectives. It is widely accepted that, although it sometimes provides the only means of protecting civilians from grave harm, military force is a relatively blunt humanitarian instrument. It is much better, and cheaper, to prevent humanitarian catastrophes in the first place than to intervene and rebuild afterwards (Carnegie Commission 1997). Sometimes, as in Somalia in 1993 and Kosovo in 1999, armed intervention seems to make the situation worse. There are also claims that the potential for foreign intervention might encourage rebels to take up arms and provoke their government to attack the civilian population (Kuperman 2008).

In recent years, important progress has been made towards building an international consensus on some of these questions. Most notably, the R2P principle adopted by over 150 world leaders in 2005 and reaffirmed by the UN Security Council the following year in Resolution 1674 attempts to reconcile the twin concerns of state sovereignty and human security by setting out the responsibilities that states have towards their own citizens, and international society's responsibility in cases where states struggle or fail to meet their responsibilities. By situating the potential for humanitarian intervention within a broader continuum of measures such as early warning and capacity building designed to prevent crises erupting in the first place, the R2P also addresses some of the practical problems associated with humanitarian intervention.

The case for humanitarian intervention

Usually associated with liberalism and cosmopolitanism, the case for intervention is typically premised on the idea that external actors have a *duty* as well as a *right* to intervene to halt **genocide and mass atrocities**. For advocates of this position, the rights that sovereigns enjoy are conditional on the fulfilment of the state's responsibility to protect its citizens. When states fail in their duties towards their citizens, they lose their sovereign right to **non-interference** (Caney 1997: 32; Tesón 1998; 2003: 93). There are a variety of ways of arriving at this conclusion. Some liberal cosmopolitanists draw on the work of the German philosopher Immanuel Kant to insist that all individuals have certain fundamental rights that deserve protection (Caney 1997: 34). Some advocates of the Just War tradition arrive at a broadly similar position but ground their arguments in Christian theology. Paul Ramsey (2002: 20), for instance, based his argument on St Augustine's injunction that military force be used to defend or uphold justice and maintained that intervention to end injustice was 'among the rights and duties of states until and unless supplanted by superior government'.

Political leaders who adopt this position often argue that today's globalized world is so integrated that massive human rights violations in one part of the world have an effect on every other part. This social interconnectedness, they argue, creates moral

obligations. The leading proponent of this view was former British Prime Minister Tony Blair. Shortly after NATO began its 1999 intervention in Kosovo, Blair (1999) gave a landmark speech setting out his 'doctrine of the international community'. Blair maintained that globalization was changing the world in ways that rendered traditional views of sovereignty anachronistic. He argued that enlightened self-interest created international responsibilities for dealing with egregious human suffering, because, in an interdependent world, 'freedom is indivisible and when one man is enslaved who is free?' He also maintained that sovereigns had international responsibilities, because problems caused by massive human rights abuse in one place tended to spread across borders.

A further line of argument is to point to the fact that states have already agreed to certain minimum standards of behaviour and that humanitarian intervention is not about imposing the will of a few Western states upon the many, but about protecting and enforcing the collective will of international society. Advocates of this position argue that there is a customary right (but not duty) of intervention in supreme humanitarian emergencies (Wheeler 2000: 14). They argue that there is agreement in international society that cases of **genocide**, mass killing, and ethnic cleansing constitute grave humanitarian crises warranting intervention (see Arend and Beck 1993; Tesón 1997;

Donnelly 1998). They point to state practice since the end of the Cold War to suggest that there is a customary right of humanitarian intervention (Lepard 2002; Finnemore 2003). In particular, they point to the justifications offered to defend the American-, French-, and British-led intervention in Northern Iraq in 1991 to support their case. In that case, the British argued that they were upholding customary international law, France invoked a customary 'right' of intervention, and the USA noted a 're-balancing of the claims of sovereignty and those of extreme humanitarian need' (see Roberts 1993: 436–7).

This movement towards acceptance of a customary right of humanitarian intervention was reinforced by state practice after Northern Iraq. For instance, throughout the UN Security Council's deliberations about how to respond to the Rwandan **genocide** in 1994, no state argued that either the ban on force (Article 2(4)) or the **non-interference** rule (Article 2(7)) prohibited armed intervention to halt the bloodshed (see Barnett 2002), suggesting that armed intervention would have been legitimate in that case. What stood in the way of intervention in Rwanda was the fact that no government wanted to risk the lives of its own soldiers to save Africans. Throughout the 1990s, the Security Council expanded its interpretation of 'international peace and security' and authorized interventions to protect civilians in safe areas (Bosnia), maintain law and order and protect aid supplies (Somalia), and restore an elected government toppled by a coup (Haiti) (see Roberts 1993; Morris 1995; Findlay 2002). These cases prompted Richard Falk (2003) to describe the 1990s as 'undoubtedly the golden age of humanitarian diplomacy', whilst Thomas Weiss (2004) argued that 'the notion that human beings matter more than sovereignty radiated brightly, albeit briefly, across the international political horizon of the 1990s'. Progress did not stop, however, at the turn of the century. Since 2000 the Security Council has on several occasions mandated peacekeepers to protect civilians under threat in the Democratic Republic of Congo, Burundi, Côte d'Ivoire, Liberia, and Darfur (see Holt and Berkman 2006), though it has usually insisted on receiving the consent of the host government.

Although appealing, several aspects of this defence of humanitarian intervention are problematic. First, it is not self-evident that individuals *do* have universal and fundamental human rights. Parekh (1997: 54–5), for example, argues that liberal rights cannot provide the basis for a theory of humanitarian intervention because liberalism itself is rejected in many parts of the world. Realists argue that rights are meaningful only if they are backed up with the power to enforce them. For example, America's Bill of Rights is supported by the full coercive power of the US state. Given that there is no world government or police force with the capacity to enforce human rights globally, there are no meaningful international human rights. Second, critics argue that any norm endorsing the use of force to protect individual rights would be abused by powerful states, making armed conflict more frequent by relaxing the rules prohibiting it but without making humanitarian intervention any more likely (Chesterman 2001; Thakur 2004b).

Above all, however, is the charge that advocates of humanitarian intervention exaggerate the extent of global consensus about the use of force to protect human rights. There is a gap between what advocates would like to be the norm and what the norm actually is. The putative 'golden era' of humanitarian intervention in the 1990s included the world's failure to halt the Rwandan **genocide**, the UN's failure to protect civilians sheltering in its 'safe areas' in Bosnia, and the failure to prevent the widely predicted mass murder that followed East Timor's referendum on independence in 1999. The world stood aside as Congo destroyed itself, taking four million lives, and—more recently—failed to halt the mass killing in Darfur. Moreover, closer inspection of the relevant cases from the 1990s suggests that world leaders were much more hesitant than implied by advocates of humanitarian intervention. Most notably, the Security Council has still yet to authorize intervention against the wishes of a fully functioning sovereign state. The only instance of humanitarian intervention against a fully-functioning sovereign state was NATO's intervention in Kosovo, and this was conducted without the consent of the Security

Council. The 1991 intervention occurred in the wake of the first Gulf War, the 1992–3 intervention in Somalia occurred only after the state had effectively ceased to exist, military intervention in Bosnia was endorsed by the Bosnian government, the 1994 intervention in Haiti was finally conducted with the (albeit heavily coerced) consent of the country's military leaders, the French intervention in Rwanda in the same year occurred after the Rwandan Patriotic Front had defeated government forces and the *Interehamwe* militia, and peacekeepers were deployed in Darfur with the consent of the Sudanese government. We should, therefore, avoid the temptation of thinking that there was a 'rash' of humanitarian interventions in the post-Cold War era (Finnemore 2008: 197).

Finally, with the partial exception of British Foreign Secretary Douglas Hurd's claim in 1991 that the UK was upholding customary international law in Northern Iraq and Belgium's International Court of Justice defence of NATO's intervention in Kosovo, humanitarian interveners themselves have typically chosen not to justify their actions by reference to a new norm of humanitarian intervention

(see Wheeler 2000). This is principally because they are wary of making it easier for other states to justify the use of force—just as Russia did, for example, when it claimed to be acting as a 'peacekeeper' when it invaded Georgia in 2008.

KEY POINTS

- Liberals argue that all humans enjoy fundamental human rights and that this creates a right and duty to intervene in cases where fundamental human rights are abused on a massive scale. This moral duty is reinforced by globalization, which connects individuals.

- The post-Cold War era saw the development of a customary norm of humanitarian intervention, as international society responded to humanitarian emergencies in Iraq, the Balkans, Somalia, Rwanda, Haiti, East Timor, and elsewhere.

- Critics argue that the idea of fundamental human rights has little empirical purchase, that humanitarian intervention destabilizes international security, and that advocates overstate the progress made towards a new norm of humanitarian intervention in the post-Cold War era.

The case against humanitarian intervention

Nowadays, only a handful of marginal states—often with atrocious human rights records themselves (such as Cuba, Iran, Venezuela, Zimbabwe)—are prepared to argue that humanitarian intervention is *never* warranted. Even China, the state most closely associated with defence of the principle of non-interference, publicly acknowledges that massive humanitarian crises are a 'legitimate concern' for international society and that the UN Security Council is entitled to take action in such cases. By and large, therefore, contemporary opposition to humanitarian intervention focuses on the questions about who can *legitimately authorize* intervention, *in what circumstances*, and the effectiveness of using military force for humanitarian purposes.

Opponents of humanitarian intervention maintain that international peace and security requires something approximating an absolute ban on the use of force outside the two exceptions set out by the UN Charter—Security Council authorization (Chapter VII) and self-defence (Article 51). The starting point for this position is the assumption that international society comprises a large number of diverse communities each with different ideas about the best way to live. The world is made up of democratic states of different types (for example, social democracies in Scandinavia, authoritarian democracy in Russia, and market democracy in the USA), states organized according to religious principles (for example, Iran), monarchies (for example, Tonga and Saudi Arabia), dictatorships, and communist states (for example, China, Cuba) and each state houses communities with very different cultural values. According to this view, international security is based on rules—the UN Charter's rules on the use of force first among them—that permit the peaceful coexistence of these very different types of states and societies (see Jackson 2002). In a world characterized by radical disagreements about how societies should govern themselves, proponents of this view hold that unfettered humanitarian intervention would create global disorder as states waged wars to protect and violently export their own cultural preferences.

What is more, a right of humanitarian intervention would open the door to potential abuse. Historically, states have shown a distinct predilection towards 'abusing' humanitarian justifications to legitimize wars that were anything but humanitarian in nature. Most notoriously, Hitler insisted that the 1939 invasion of Czechoslovakia intended to protect Czechoslovak citizens whose 'life and liberty' were threatened by their own government (in Brownlie 1974: 217–21). Some commentators have argued that the US and UK abused humanitarian justifications in an ill-fated attempt to legitimize the 2003 invasion of Iraq, emphasizing the humanitarian case for war as it became clear that the legal reasons given (the existence of Iraqi weapons of mass destruction (WMD)) were ill-founded (see Bellamy 2004; cf. Morris and Wheeler 2006). Similar claims could also be made about Russia's use of humanitarian arguments to justify its 2008 invasion of Georgia (see Case Study 21.1). It was precisely because of the fear that states would exploit any loophole in the ban on the use of force that the delegates who wrote the UN Charter in 1944–5 issued a comprehensive ban with only two limited exceptions. According to Simon Chesterman, without this general ban there would be *more war* in world politics but not necessarily more humanitarian interventions. Chesterman (2001: 231) argues that states refrain from intervening in humanitarian emergencies, not because they are constrained by law, but 'because states do not want them to take

place. Creating a humanitarian exception to the ban on force would not enable more humanitarian interventions, but it would make it easier for states to justify self-interested invasions. 'On balance', Thomas Franck and Nigel Rodley (1973: 278) warned in 1973, 'very little good has been wrought' in the name of humanitarian intervention.

Finally, it is important to note that a majority of states continue to oppose humanitarian intervention—seeing it as a dangerous affront to another core principle, the right to self-determination. The General Assembly's 1970 Declaration on Principles of International Law Concerning Friendly Relations stated categorically:

> No state or group of states has the right to intervene, directly or indirectly, for any reason whatever, in the internal or external affairs of any other state. Consequently, armed intervention and all other forms of interference or attempted threats against the personality of the state or against its political, economic and cultural elements, are in violation of international law.

This position was clearly in the ascendancy during the Cold War. In 1977, when Vietnam invaded Cambodia and ousted the murderous Pol Pot regime, responsible for the death of some two million Cambodians, it was condemned for violating Cambodian sovereignty. China's representative at the UN described Vietnam's act as a 'great mockery of and insult to the United Nations and its member states' and sponsored a resolution condemning Vietnam's 'aggression'. The United States agreed. Its ambassador argued that the world could not allow Vietnam's violation of Cambodian sovereignty 'pass in silence' as this 'will only encourage Governments in other parts of the world to conclude that there are no norms, no standards, no restraints' (in Wheeler 2000: 90–1). France argued that 'the notion that because a regime is detestable foreign intervention is justified and forcible overthrow is legitimate is extremely dangerous. That could ultimately jeopardize the very maintenance of law and order' (in Chesterman 2001: 80). These sentiments persist. Nearly thirty years after

The misuse of humanitarian justifications: Russia's 2008 intervention in Georgia

In August 2008, Russia responded to Georgian incursions into the disputed territory of South Ossetia, which was formally part of Georgia, with a large military intervention. Backed up by the aerial bombardment of key Georgian cities, including Georgia's capital Tblisi, Russian forces pushed the Georgian army out of South Ossetia and another disputed territory, Abkhazia, and established a buffer zone over 20 miles inside Georgia proper. Russia's foreign minister, Sergei Lavrov, accused Georgia of committing 'genocide' in South Ossetia and argued that its intervention was a legitimate exercise of its 'responsibility to protect', a principle being widely used by the UN.

These justifications, however, were rejected by analysts and won little support from international society, with even China refusing to support Russia's position despite calls for it to do so. First, although the Organization for Security and Cooperation in Europe (OSCE) has suggested that Georgian forces probably did fire the first shots, there is no empirical evidence to support Russia's claims that Georgia was committing 'genocide'. Whilst it is likely that individual war crimes were committed during the short war, it seems that

Georgian, Russian, and South Ossetian forces all committed crimes to some extent. As such, the claim that Georgian crimes justified the intervention is as dubious as America's claim that the invasion of Iraq was justified by that country's possession of weapons of mass destruction. Second, the Global Centre for the Responsibility to Protect argued that the scale of Russia's assault on Georgia far exceeded that which was necessary to protect South Ossetians. In particular, Russian forces entered Georgia proper, attacked ports and cities that were unrelated to South Ossetia, and used force in the other disputed territory of Abkhazia. This suggests that the protection of South Ossetia was not Russia's principal objective. Third, the Global Centre argues that R2P does not give legal cover for armed intervention absent a Security Council resolution (GCR2P 2008).

For these reasons, Russia's intervention in Georgia seems to be a clear case of 'abuse'. The Russian government specifically invoked R2P and used humanitarian justifications to justify armed intervention, but its claims were not supported by the evidence. The situation in South Ossetia was not as Russia described it, and, even if it were, Russia's use of force went well beyond that necessary for human protection purposes.

the Vietnamese experience, Pakistan argued against intervention to halt the Sudanese government-sponsored atrocities in Darfur on the grounds that 'the Sudan has all the rights and privileges incumbent under the United Nations Charter, including to sovereignty, political independence, unity and territorial integrity' (United Nations Security Council 2004).

Finally, realists especially claim that humanitarian intervention should be avoided because it does not work and is an inappropriate use of armed force. It does not work, they argue, because foreign intervention tends to prolong wars and create unstable peace. For realists, war is the ultimate test of strength, and stable post-war peace is produced by the victory of one side over the other, which then forces actors to realign their behaviour in accordance with the new distribution of power. Because foreign intervention reduces the proportion of wars that end in outright victory, it leaves behind an unstable peace

that is likely to reignite (Luttwak 1999). Realists also argue that armed force should only ever be used in the national interest and that humanitarian intervention is therefore imprudent.

There are a number of problems with these positions as well, however. First, the overriding assumption that states protect their citizens' rights and cultural differences does not hold in every case, as the examples offered at the beginning of this chapter attest. Second, critics argue that this perspective underestimates the wealth of customary practice suggesting that sovereignty carries responsibilities as well as rights (see Tesón 1997). Third, although there are a few notorious historical cases, the fear of abuse is exaggerated (Weiss 2004: 135). It is fanciful to argue that denying a state recourse to humanitarian justifications for war would make them less war prone. It is highly unlikely that either Hitler in 1939 or Bush and Blair in 2003 would have been deterred from waging war by the absence of a plausible humanitarian justification. Fourth, the critics of humanitarian intervention overlook the wide body of international law relating to basic human rights and the consensus on grave crimes such as genocide (see Scheffer 1992; Mertus 2000). Finally, the realist claim that intervention produces unstable peace is not supported by empirical studies, which show that well-equipped peace operations can significantly reduce the likelihood of war reigniting (Fortna 2008).

In summary, almost all governments recognize that crimes such as **genocide** and mass killing are a legitimate concern for international society. Some governments, international officials, activists, and analysts argue that sovereigns have a responsibility to protect their citizens from mass killing and other abuses, and, when they fail to do so, others acquire a right to intervene. A majority of the world's governments, however, argue that this responsibility does not translate into a right of humanitarian intervention without the authority of the UN Security Council because that would contradict other cherished principles, including the rule of non-aggression and the right to self-determination. Since the end of the Cold War, the UN Security Council has authorized collective intervention to protect populations from mass killing. In this sense, there is a norm of UN-sanctioned humanitarian intervention (Wheeler 2000), but it is heavily circumscribed in practice to cases where the host state has collapsed or where the recognized government is not the target of intervention and lends its support. This presents a dilemma about what to do in cases where some governments believe that intervention is warranted to save people from genocide and **mass atrocities** but where there is no consensus in the Security Council. This dilemma was exposed by NATO's decision to intervene in Kosovo in 1999. The debate sparked by this case provided a catalyst for a fundamental rethink of the way that international society conceptualizes the relationship between sovereignty and human rights.

KEY POINTS

- There is broad consensus that there are circumstances in which the use of force for military purposes might be justified, but critics argue that humanitarian intervention is legitimate only as a last resort, in the very worst of cases, and only when authorized by the UN Security Council.

- The rule of non-intervention is important because it protects weak states from strong states and preserves cultural diversity.

- A general right of humanitarian intervention is likely to be abused by states that would use humanitarian arguments to justify self-interested acts of war. This would damage international security without a corresponding improvement in human security.

Towards responsibility to protect

Three events in the 1990s prompted academics, politicians, and international organizations to consider a fundamental rethink of the relationship between sovereignty and human rights. In 1994, the world stood aside as Hutu militia massacred over 800,000 Tutsi and Hutu civilians in the Rwandan **genocide**. A year later, Bosnian Serb forces overran the UN protected 'safe area' of Srebrenica. They separated the men and boys from the women and slaughter 7,600 of them in the days that followed. In 1999, NATO bombed the Federal Republic of Yugoslavia to coerce its leader, Slobodan Milosevic, into ceasing the ethnic cleansing of Kosovar Albanians. NATO was forced to act without a UN mandate because

Russia and China believed that the situation in Kosovo was not serious enough to warrant humanitarian intervention and therefore threatened to veto any proposed resolution authorizing intervention.

Events like these prompted new thinking about the nature of sovereignty, which developed some old ideas about the sovereign's responsibility to protect its citizens. The first person to begin thinking along these lines was Francis Deng, a former Sudanese diplomat who was appointed the UN Secretary-General's special representative on internally displaced people in 1992. In a book published in 1996, Deng and his co-authors argued that 'sovereignty carries with it certain responsibilities for which governments must be held accountable. And they are accountable not only to their own national constituencies but ultimately to the international community. In other words, by effectively discharging its responsibilities for good governance, a state can legitimately claim protection for its national sovereignty' (Deng et al. 1996: 1). According to Deng, legitimate sovereignty required a demonstration of responsibility. Troubled states faced a choice: they could work with international society to improve their citizens' living conditions or they could obstruct international efforts and forfeit their sovereignty (Deng et al 1996: 28). Conceptualizing sovereignty as responsibility removed the validity of objections to international assistance and mediation based on the principle of non-interference.

The questions surrounding NATO's intervention in Kosovo prompted UN Secretary-General Kofi Annan to enter the debate and make a vital contribution. In his annual address to the General Assembly in 1999, he insisted that 'state sovereignty, in its most basic sense, is being redefined by the forces of globalization and international cooperation'. He continued, 'the state is now widely understood to be the servant of its people, and not vice versa. At the same time, individual sovereignty—and by this I mean the human rights and fundamental freedoms of each and every individual as enshrined in our Charter—has been enhanced by a renewed consciousness of the right of every individual to control his or her own destiny' (Annan

1999: 2). Annan also pointed to three critical concerns. First, intervention should be understood broadly to cover measures short of armed force that could be used to prevent and halt humanitarian emergencies. Second, sovereignty alone was not the principal barrier to effective action to protect human rights. Just as significant, Annan argued, was the way in which member states defined their national interests. Third, international society should make a long-term commitment to rebuild states and societies once a conflict is over.

Together, Deng and Annan pointed towards a new way of thinking about sovereignty as responsibility. The Canadian government then created the International Commission on Intervention and State Sovereignty (ICISS), chaired by Gareth Evans and Mohammed Sahnoun, to develop a way of reconciling sovereignty and human rights (see Evans 2008). The Commission's report, released in late 2001, was premised on the notion that, when states are unwilling or unable to protect their citizens from grave harm, the principle of non-interference 'yields to the responsibility to protect' (ICISS 2001: p. xi). The concept of R2P that it put forward was intended as a way of escaping the logic of 'intervention versus sovereignty' by focusing not on what interveners were entitled to do ('a right of intervention') but on what was necessary to protect civilians threatened by genocide and mass atrocities. Influenced by Annan and Deng, the ICISS argued that the R2P was about much more than just military intervention. Appropriate responses to humanitarian emergencies included non-violent measures such as diplomacy, sanctions, and embargoes, and legal measures such as referring crimes to the International Criminal Court. Furthermore, in addition to the 'responsibility to react' to massive human suffering, the ICISS insisted that international society also had responsibilities to prevent rebuild polities and societies afterwards. Of the three responsibilities, the Commission identified the 'responsibility to prevent' was the single most important (ICISS 2001: p. xi). In relation to decisions about the use of force for humanitarian purposes, the Commission proposed the adoption of criteria that included just-cause

The responsibility to protect: principles for military intervention

(1) The Just Cause Threshold

Military intervention for human protection purposes is an exceptional and extraordinary measure. To be warranted, there must be serious and irreparable harm occurring to human beings, or imminently likely to occur, of the following kind:

A. large scale loss of life, actual or apprehended, with genocidal intent or not, which is the product either of deliberate state action, or state neglect or inability to act, or a failed state situation; or

B. large scale 'ethnic cleansing', actual or apprehended, whether carried out by killing, forced expulsion, acts of terror or rape.

(2) The Precautionary Principles

B. Right intention: The primary purpose of the intervention, whatever other motives intervening states may have, must be to halt or avert human suffering. Right intention is better assured with multilateral operations, clearly supported by regional opinion and the victims concerned.

C. Last resort: Military intervention can only be justified when every non-military option for the prevention or peaceful resolution of the crisis has been explored, with reasonable grounds for believing lesser measures would not have succeeded.

D. Proportional means: The scale, duration and intensity of the planned military intervention should be the minimum necessary to secure the defined human protection objective.

E. Reasonable prospects: There must be a reasonable chance of success in halting or averting the suffering which has justified the intervention, with the consequences of action not likely to be worse than the consequences of inaction.

(3) Right Authority

A. There is no better or more appropriate body than the United Nations Security Council to authorize military intervention for human protection purposes. The task is not to find alternatives to the Security Council as a source of authority, but to make the Security Council work better than it has.

B. Security Council authorization should in all cases be sought prior to any military intervention action being carried out. Those calling for an intervention should formally request such authorization, or have the Council raise the matter on its own initiative, or have the Secretary-General raise it under Article 99 of the UN Charter.

C. The Security Council should deal promptly with any request for authority to intervene where there are allegations of large scale loss of human life or ethnic cleansing. It should in this context seek adequate verification of facts or conditions on the ground that might support a military intervention.

D. The Permanent Five members of the Security Council should agree not to apply their veto power, in matters where their vital state interests are not involved, to obstruct the passage of resolutions authorizing military intervention for human protection purposes for which there is otherwise majority support.

E. If the Security Council rejects a proposal or fails to deal with it in a reasonable time, alternative options are:

I. consideration of the matter by the General Assembly in Emergency Special Session under the 'Uniting for Peace' procedure; and

II. action within area of jurisdiction by regional or sub-regional organizations under Chapter VIII of the Charter, subject to their seeking subsequent authorization from the Security Council.

F. The Security Council should take into account in all its deliberations that, if it fails to discharge its responsibility to protect in conscience-shocking situations crying out for action, concerned states may not rule out other means to meet the gravity and urgency of that situation – and that the stature and credibility of the United Nations may suffer thereby.

(4) Operational Principles

A. Clear objectives; clear and unambiguous mandate at all times; and resources to match.

B. Common military approach among involved partners; unity of command; clear and unequivocal communications and chain of command.

C. Acceptance of limitations, incrementalism and gradualism in the application of force, the objective being protection of a population, not defeat of a state.

D. Rules of engagement which fit the operational concept; are precise; reflect the principle of proportionality; and involve total adherence to international humanitarian law.

E. Acceptance that force protection cannot become the principal objective.

F. Maximum possible coordination with humanitarian organizations.

ICISS 2001: (pp. xii–xiii).

thresholds and precautionary principles (see Key Quotes 21.1).

The ICISS report was received most favourably by 'like-minded' states including Canada, the UK, and Germany, which had, since the intervention in Kosovo, been exploring the potential for developing criteria to guide global decision making about humanitarian intervention. The USA rejected the idea of criteria on the grounds that it would not commit itself to intervening in places where it had no national interests, and that it would not be bound to criteria that would constrain its right to decide when and where to use force (Welsh 2004: 180). China and Russia argued that the UN was already equipped to deal with humanitarian crises

through the Security Council and suggested that, by countenancing unilateral intervention, the ICISS report risked undermining the UN Charter. Opinion outside the Security Council was also sceptical. The Non-Aligned Movement (NAM) rejected the R2P, though the 'Group of 77' developing states in the UN General Assembly suggested that the R2P be revised to emphasize the principles of territorial integrity and sovereignty (Bellamy 2006: 151–3).

These concerns were taken on board, and, at the 2005 World Summit, over 150 world leaders adopted a declaration affirming the R2P, which was itself subsequently reaffirmed by the UN Security Council in 2006 (see Key Quotes 21.2).

KEY QUOTES 21.2

Responsibility to protect and the 2005 World Summit

138. Each individual state has the responsibility to protect its populations from genocide, war crimes, ethnic cleansing and crimes against humanity. This responsibility entails the prevention of such crimes, including their incitement, through appropriate and necessary means. We accept that responsibility and will act in accordance with it. The international community should, as appropriate, encourage and help States to exercise this responsibility and support the United Nations in establishing an early warning capability.

139. The international community, through the United Nations, also has the responsibility to use appropriate diplomatic, humanitarian and other peaceful means, in accordance with Chapters VI and VIII of the Charter of the United Nations, to help protect populations from war crimes, ethnic cleansing and crimes against humanity. In this context, we are prepared to take collective action, in a timely and decisive manner, through the Security Council, in accordance with the Charter, including Chapter VII, on

a case-by-case basis and in cooperation with relevant regional organizations as appropriate, should peaceful means be inadequate and national authorities are manifestly failing to protect their populations from genocide, war crimes, ethnic cleansing and crimes against humanity. We stress the need for the General Assembly to continue consideration of the responsibility to protect populations from genocide, war crimes, ethnic cleansing and crimes against humanity and its implications, bearing in mind the principles of the Charter and international law. We also intend to commit ourselves, as necessary and appropriate, to helping States build capacity to protect their populations from genocide, war crimes, ethnic cleansing and crimes against humanity and to assisting those which are under stress before crises and conflicts break out.

140. We fully support the mission of the Special Adviser of the Secretary-General on the Prevention of Genocide.

United Nations (2005d).

According to the UN Secretary-General, Ban Ki-moon, who succeeded Kofi Annan in 2007, the R2P rests on three pillars:

> 1. the responsibility of the state to protect its own populations from genocide, war crimes, ethnic cleansing and crimes against humanity;
>
> 2. the international community's commitment to assist states in meeting these obligations;
>
> 3. the international community's responsibility to respond in a timely and decisive manner when a state is manifestly failing to protect its population, using Chapters VI (peaceful means), VII (coercive means authorized by the UN Security Council) and VIII (regional arrangements).

Ban Ki-moon (2008); Luck (2008)

The approach adopted by the UN Secretary-General has been described as 'narrow but deep' (Luck 2008: 1). The R2P applies only to a narrow category of cases (**genocide**, war crimes, ethnic cleansing, and crimes against humanity) but requires a deep commitment from states. International society is expected to shoulder the responsibility of preventing **genocide** and **mass atrocities** by helping states to build the necessary capacities, developing early warning systems and being prepared to act 'upstream' of an outbreak of violence with a range of diplomatic, humanitarian, legal, and other peaceful measures. Heeding the concerns of states such as Russia and China, the R2P insists that military intervention be authorized by the UN Security Council and rules out unilateral force.

The World Summit's declaration on the R2P received a mixed reception. Todd Lindberg (2005) described it as nothing less than a 'revolution in consciousness in international affairs'. Prominent international lawyer Simon Chesterman agreed, arguing that 'what we're seeing is a progressive redefinition of sovereignty in a way that would have been outrageous sixty years ago' (in Turner 2005). Others were more equivocal. John Bolton, the American Ambassador to the UN and a well-known realist and UN-sceptic, described the R2P as 'a moveable feast of an idea that was the High Minded *cause du jour*' and said of the World Summit Outcome Document: 'I plan never to read it again. I doubt many others will either' (Bolton 2007: 213–14).

To what extent has the R2P advanced and replaced debates about humanitarian intervention? One group of critics complain that the principle amounts to little more than an assault on state sovereignty. They argue that it is little different from the interventionist doctrines put forward by liberals in the 1990s and has all the negative connotations associated with humanitarian intervention (e.g. Chandler 2005). A second group of critics make the opposite point. Michael Byers (2005), for example, argued that the 2005 World Summit Outcome Document watered down the original R2P concept to such an extent that the new principle would not advance the humanitarian intervention debate or protect threatened populations. Some commentators have taken to labelling the post-2005 principle 'R2P lite' because of the limitations it placed on humanitarian intervention (for the scope of R2P, see Case Study 21.2).

Whilst the first group of critics ignore the fact that the R2P has been adopted by world leaders of all stripes and carefully limits the scope for armed intervention, the second group focus too heavily on the question of armed intervention and underestimate the potential impact of the commitment to the R2P. Thus, whilst we need to be mindful of the principle's limitations, as the UN Secretary-General's special adviser, Edward Luck, has pointed out, there are several good reasons for thinking that the R2P is likely to make a lasting impact on international peace and security (see Key Ideas 21.3). Ultimately, however, the R2P will be judged not according to its ability to help finesse difficult judgements about humanitarian intervention but by the extent to which it reduces the frequency with which the world is confronted with an apparent choice between 'sending in the Marines' or standing aside (Feinstein 2007) in the face of unconscionable inhumanity. See Case Study 21.3 for an analysis of the first, and so far only, resort to R2P.

CASE STUDY 21.2

The scope of R2P: Myanmar and Cyclone Nargis

On 2 May 2008, Cyclone Nargis struck Myanmar, devastating the Irrawaddy delta region and leaving much of the region under water. Over 130,000 people were killed and around 2.5 million affected. Despite the massive scale of the humanitarian catastrophe and the government's obvious inability to respond in an effective and timely fashion, Myanmar's military regime refused to grant the UN and humanitarian agencies access to the affected areas. The disaster happened shortly before a constitutional referendum planned for 10 May, and the regime decided to go ahead with that referendum, despite the humanitarian crisis in the country's south. Frustrated by the lack of progress, the French Foreign Minister, Bernard Kouchner, proposed that the UN Security Council invoke the R2P to authorize the delivery of aid without the consent of the government of Myanmar. Kouchner argued that there was no moral difference between deaths caused by direct killing and those caused by deliberate neglect and that, if the government failed in its responsibility to provide life-saving assistance to its populations, the international community had a duty to act, even without the consent of the host government.

Kouchner's proposal was flatly rejected out of hand by the Chinese government, which argued that the responsibility to protect did not apply to natural disasters. John Holmes, the UN's Under-Secretary-General for Humanitarian Affairs and Emergency Relief Coordinator, described Kouchner's call as unnecessarily confrontational. The British Minister for International Development, Douglas Alexander, rejected

it as 'incendiary' and Britain's UN Ambassador, John Sawers, agreed with the Chinese view that R2P did not apply to natural disasters. In the end, concerted diplomacy by ASEAN and the UN Secretary-General, reputedly helped by the threat that the Security Council would invoke R2P if Myanmar did not cooperate, persuaded the government to grant access.

There are four main reasons for thinking that it was right to reject calls for R2P to be applied in this case. First, the principle applies only to genocide, war crimes, ethnic cleansing, and crimes against humanity. However immoral Myanmar's position was, there was no prima facie case for arguing that its denial of access constituted a breach of one of those crimes. Second, the idea that aid could have been effectively delivered without government consent was fanciful. With much of the region under water, much of the aid dropped from planes would have ended up in water, and, with the Myanmar army in control of the land, there would have been no way of ensuring that the aid reached those who most needed it. A land intervention would have taken too long to organize and would, in all probability, have massively increased the loss of civilian life. Third, the invocation of R2P would have been opposed by Asian members of the Security Council, making it impossible to create a common position on the crisis. Finally, invoking R2P in a controversial case such as this would have damaged the principle itself, making it more difficult to use it to stimulate international action in more clear-cut cases (see Asia-Pacific Centre for the Responsibility to Protect 2008).

 CASE STUDY 21.3

Operationalizing R2P in Darfur

At the time of writing, the situation in Darfur remains the only case in which UN Security Council has invoked the R2P Security Council Resolution 1706 (2006), which called for the creation of a large peacekeeping force to protect civilians in Darfur, specifically referred to the R2P principle. However, the UN and African Union have encountered serious obstacles in their effort to translate R2P from words to deeds in this case, leaving some analysts to argue that R2P has 'failed' its first test (e.g. de Waal 2007).

The conflict began in earnest in 2003, after a few years of sporadic fighting over land and access to water between some of the different groups. In April 2003, rebel groups

captured the border town of Tine and attacked al-Fashir airport. The government responded by 'outsourcing' the counter-insurgency to local militia leaders. In return for their military support, the government basically gave the militia a free hand to attack civilians, steal livestock, and destroy homes. The war they waged was primarily a war of genocide on the civilian population designed to curb support for the rebel groups, occupy land, secure access to water, and steal booty. The consequences are well known. Over 250,000—and by some estimates as many as 400,000—civilians have been killed. Another 2.5 million have been forcibly displaced and live either rough or in one of the 230 refugee camps for displaced people that dot the countryside in Darfur and Chad. The violence has

CASE STUDY 21.3   (Continued)

decreased since 2003–4, but in many regions this is only because the government's *janjaweed* militia succeeded in seizing the land and driving out or butchering their civilian targets.

The international response to the crisis in Darfur is best described as tepid. With the West unwilling to commit troops to a peacekeeping operation and the Security Council unable to agree on measures such as targeted sanctions and a no-fly zone, the African Union (AU) dispatched a small force (AMIS) to monitor a ceasefire in 2004. The ceasefire collapsed almost as soon as it had been signed and the small AMIS force, which numbered 7,000 at its peak (covering an area the size of France), proved utterly incapable of protecting civilians or preventing other breaches (Williams 2006). The West now focused its efforts on getting a UN peacekeeping force deployed. This required a peace agreement, and the USA led an effort to deliver such an agreement. However, the process did not receive high-level support in the West and resulted in an agreement being forced through against the will of several rebel leaders. As a result, the rebel groups began to fracture and the violence persisted. Although the UN got its peace agreement, with violence persisting member states remained unwilling to commit troops and the Sudanese government refused to grant its consent. In the end, a compromise was reached whereby the UN entered into an agreement with the AU to deploy a 'hybrid' operation managed by both organizations. In the absence of additional resources, however, the new UNAMID mission mainly comprised rebadged AMIS peacekeepers. Progress was

made, however, on other aspects of the international community's engagement with Darfur – the Security Council imposed limited sanctions on the Sudanese government and referred the matter to the International Criminal Court.

There are three main reasons why the international response to the atrocities in Darfur has been so tepid. First, the situation in Darfur is highly complex and there is little agreement about the most appropriate type of response. Even among activists there is no agreement on the best course of action. Some focus on the need to get sufficient numbers of peacekeepers into Darfur, whilst others argue that this is a distraction from the main game of securing a political settlement and delivering humanitarian aid (see Flint and de Waal 2008). Second, the crisis in Darfur is not a political priority for the West. Western priorities are focused elsewhere, in Afghanistan, Iraq, and the Balkans. As such, they are reluctant to commit the resources and political capital needed to lead on Darfur. Third, many states—particularly China and several Arab states—have actively blocked coercive measures on the grounds that they impinge on Sudanese sovereignty (see Williams and Bellamy 2005).

The Darfur case suggests that a lot more work is needed to figure out the best way of translating R2P from words to deeds in real-world cases, both in terms of the measures that are necessary to protect populations from harm and in terms of the politics of consensus building.

KEY IDEAS 21.1

The impact of the responsibility to protect

1. R2P is a politically potent concept based on a consensus produced by one of the largest gatherings of heads of state ever seen.

2. The Outcome Document specifically points to the prevention of genocide, war crimes, ethnic cleansing, and crimes against humanity.

3. The Outcome Document points to the kinds of tools, actors, and procedures that could form the basis for operationalizing the R2P.

4. The process of negotiating the Document and forging consensus required compromise by both sides of the intervention debate and produced a shared conception of sovereignty as responsibilvity that bridges the divide.

Based on Luck (2008: 3).

KEY POINTS

- The R2P principle attempts to replace the debate about humanitarian intervention with a new consensus based on the principle of sovereignty as responsibility and duties to prevent genocide and mass atrocities, react appropriately to them, and rebuild states and societies afterwards.

- The R2P rests on three pillars: (1) each state's responsibility to protect its own populations; (2) the international community's commitment to help states fulfil their responsibility; (3) the international community's responsibility to take timely and effective measures, using

Chapters VI, VII, and/or VIII of the UN Charter, when a state is manifestly failing in its R2P.

- Critics argue that the R2P is either simply a reincarnation of liberal arguments in favour of humanitarian intervention or a piece of meaningless rhetoric that will make little difference in practice.

- The promise of R2P is not that it will make it easier to decide when to launch humanitarian interventions but that it will reduce the need for interventions in the first place.

Conclusion

The R2P is an attempt to reconfigure the relationship between sovereignty and human rights and replace the debates about humanitarian intervention covered in the first part of the chapter with a new consensus that focuses on protecting populations from genocide and mass atrocities. Traditionally, it was assumed that international security required strict adherence to the principles of sovereignty and non-interference and that, in cases where the security of states and individuals collided, the former should be privileged. After the Cold War, many governments and scholars argued that in grave situations sovereignty should be suspended and humanitarian intervention permitted. This produced an irresolvable debate about who had the right to authorize such interventions and in what circumstances, in a context where even governments that advocated human rights were deeply reluctant to risk their troops to save imperilled people overseas. This debate pitted sovereignty against human rights.

But, if sovereignty is understood as a responsibility to protect, as Kofi Annan and Francis Deng argued in the 1990s, then the role of international society becomes one of enabling and supporting sovereigns in discharging their responsibilities to their citizens. The R2P holds

that this is not just a matter of charity but a matter of responsibility, because the very foundations of sovereignty and international society are individual human rights. As a result, international society has a responsibility to ensure that sovereigns fulfil their duties by preventing and reacting to cases of genocide, mass killing, and ethnic cleansing and helping to rebuild societies afterwards. This responsibility was acknowledged at the 2005 World Summit and reaffirmed by the UN Security Council in Resolution 1674, but there remains much work to be done by states, international organizations, and non-governmental organizations to ensure that all this makes a difference to those in need and succeeds in replacing the debate about humanitarian intervention.

The challenge now is to translate the R2P from words to deeds and to change the practice of how the world responds to genocide and mass atrocities. If the principle continues to develop and gain momentum, chapters about humanitarian intervention might become obsolete as global institutions, regional organizations, and individual states develop the capacities better to prevent and respond to genocide and mass atrocities. It is not yet clear, however, whether changing the terms of debate has altered its fundamental logic. The test will come partly in how the world responds to new and emerging crises—and the slow, inadequate, and half-hearted response to Darfur does not bode well in this regard—and partly in how successful reform of the UN and regional organizations proves to be in building the necessary capacities, decision-making capabilities, and political will.

QUESTIONS

1. To what extent is the consent of the host government an important consideration in relation to humanitarian emergencies?

2. Why do liberals think there is a moral duty to help endangered populations in far-away countries? Is their argument plausible?

3. To what extent does international security depend on the UN Charter's rules on the non-use of force (Article 2(4)) and non-interference in the domestic affairs of sovereigns?

4. Did a new norm of humanitarian intervention develop in the 1990s? What sort of norm was it?

5. What is the likelihood that a right of humanitarian intervention would be abused by powerful states to justify aggressive war? Does the R2P increase or reduce that likelihood?

6. Should armed intervention always be authorized by the UN Security Council? Why?

7. To what extent do you think that the R2P principle replaces humanitarian intervention?

8. Is the principle just 'hot air' or a rehashed version of the liberal defence of humanitarian intervention?

9. What is the scope and meaning of the R2P?

10. What needs to be done in order to translate the R2P from words to deeds?

11. What are the potential merits and weaknesses of humanitarian intervention in the following cases: Darfur, Myanmar, Zimbabwe, Congo, Georgia.

FURTHER READING

■ Bellamy, A. J. (2009), *Responsibility to Protect: The Global Effort to End Genocide and Mass Atrocities,* Cambridge: Polity Press. Presents an account of the emergence of the R2P and the challenges of translating it from words to deeds.

■ Bellamy, A. J., and Williams, P. D. (2009), *Understanding Peacekeeping,* 2nd edn., Cambridge: Polity Press. A comprehensive introduction to peacekeeping covering history, over twenty-five case studies and contemporary challenges.

■ Chesterman, S. (2001), *Just War or Just Peace? Humanitarian Intervention and International Law,* Oxford: Oxford University Press. An excellent account of the legal issues relating to humanitarian intervention.

■ Evans, G. (2008), *The Responsibility to Protect: Ending Mass Atrocity Crimes Once and for All,* Washington: Brookings Institution. A powerful defence of the R2P and insider's account of the ICISS experience.

■ ICISS (2001), International Commission on Intervention and State Sovereignty, *The Responsibility to Protect,* Ottawa: IDRC. Report making a landmark contribution to the field.

■ Weiss, T. G. (2007), *Humanitarian Intervention: Ideas into Action,* Cambridge: Polity Press. A compelling introduction to the theory and practice of humanitarian intervention.

■ Welsh, J. (ed.) (2004), *Humanitarian Intervention and International Relations*, Oxford: Oxford University Press. A superb collection that covers the ethical, legal, and political dilemmas provoked by humanitarian intervention.

■ Wheeler, N. J. (2000), *Saving Strangers: Humanitarian Intervention in International Society*, Oxford: Oxford University Press. Remains the best account of humanitarian intervention in the 1990s and earlier.

 IMPORTANT WEBSITES

● http://www.un.org   The website of the UN; contains information about Security Council and General Assembly debates on humanitarian intervention and the responsibility to protect, as well as the organization's work on conflict prevention, peacekeeping, peace building, and human rights.

● http://www.responsibilitytoprotect.org   The website of the World Federalist Movement's project on R2P; contains an excellent archive of reports and other documents.

● http://www.globalr2p.org   The website of the Global Centre for the Responsibility to Protect, which aims to advance the principle through research and outreach.

● http://www.r2pasiapacific.org   The website of the Asia-Pacific Centre for the Responsibility to Protect.

● http://www.reliefweb.int   A UN-run website that provides information to humanitarian agencies in the field.

 Visit the Online Resource Centre that accompanies this book for lots of interesting additional material: www.oxfordtextbooks.co.uk/orc/collins2e/

22 Energy Security

SAM RAPHAEL AND DOUG STOKES

Chapter Contents

- Introduction
- The problem of energy security
- Energy security and IR theory
- Energy security and human insecurity
- Energy security and the United States
- Conclusion

Reader's Guide

This chapter examines growing concerns over global energy security, as accelerating demand for fossil fuels by industrialized economies is matched by increasing uncertainties over future energy reserves. With a particular focus on the politics of oil (as the key global energy source), it will assess the ways in which increasing energy *insecurity* amongst the world's major powers will impact upon international security more broadly, and will discuss different understandings of the likelihood of future 'resource wars' and a new era of geopolitical rivalry. The chapter will also examine the impact that the search for energy security by states in the global North has upon the human security of communities in the oil-rich global South. Finally, the chapter will examine the central role played by the United States in underpinning global energy security in the post-war era, and the impact that this has had for oil-rich regions.

Introduction

'Energy security' is a term in vogue. The intersection of a number of trends—rising global demand for energy, fears of dwindling supplies, increased instability in many of the energy-rich regions, and concerns about the potential future devastation wrought by climate change—ensures that the sources, locations, and stability of world energy supplies have become a common subject for debate. For the purposes of this chapter, we will define 'energy security' as follows:

Energy security exists when there are energy sources large enough to meet the needs of the political community (the energy demands), which include all military, economic and societal activity. Those sources must be able to deliver such quantities of energy in a reliable and stable manner, and for the foreseeable future. As soon as these conditions are not met, there exists a problem of energy (in)security.

This is our definition of 'energy security', but captures—we think—what is meant by the term when used by academics and politicians alike.

Many communities live in conditions of energy *insecurity*. Across the global South in particular, regular shortages of energy supply are a fact of life, even where abundant local sources of energy exist (as daily power cuts in post-invasion Baghdad demonstrated). Such insecurity has a significant effect on the quality of life for many, with health, education, and transport services often severely affected. In contrast, for most of those living in the industrialized and rapidly industrializing states of the North, the existence of robust infrastructure ensures that the problem of energy security manifests differently. For these societies, the existence of stable energy supply at a *state* level is usually sufficient to ensure enough energy for the entire population. For example, as long as the United Kingdom receives a supply of energy to meet the overall demand of its citizens, the existence of a high-quality national grid within the UK ensures that any one community can almost always be guaranteed reliable and sufficient supply.

Over recent decades, government officials, analysts, and academics alike have identified energy security as a growing problem, affecting states in the North as much as, if not more than, those in the South. Indeed, given the rapid industrialization of large regions of the globe, and the transformation of lead economies into those dependent upon copious amounts of fossil fuels, energy security has become elevated to a key political and economic problem of modern times. Moreover, this problem intersects with a range of wider security concerns covered elsewhere in this book. The existence of reliable supplies of energy clearly underpins economic activity, and can be seen as a prerequisite for any significant degree of *economic security*. In attempting to ensure the stability of supplies, core powers are increasingly militarizing their approach to energy security. This, as we shall see, may have significant consequences for *international security*, as inter-state cooperation threatens to break down into a struggle over the control of key energy reserves. Likewise, this militarization often has a profound impact upon the *human security* of those living in oil-rich regions in the South, as the use of armed force is used to 'stabilize' energy-rich areas. Oil wealth has other impacts upon states in the South, with *regime security* often becoming intimately bound up with the collection of oil 'rents' (a method of income generation that allows governments to become politically insulated from their citizens). This process often leads to negative consequences for *development and security*, as oil wealth fails to filter down to the wider population. And lastly, of course, the huge reliance of the world on fossil fuels as a source of energy, and the likely continuation of this fact, will ultimately impact widely upon us all, as understood through the lens of *environmental security*.

Overall, then, the problem of energy security intersects with a host of other security issues, and is rising up the agenda of international politics as governments are increasingly concerned over the quantity and reliability of their state's energy sources. And, given the causes of this problem, discussed in the next section, it is likely to be a central security issue well into the twenty-first century.

KEY POINTS

● The degree of energy security experienced by each political community is measured by the reliable and stable supply of enough energy to meet the energy demands of the present, and into the near future.

● Many communities live in a state of energy insecurity, although the problem tends to manifest differently in the global North, as compared to the South. Robust energy infrastructure in industrialized economies means that energy security here is best considered at the state level.

● For energy-intensive economies of the North, the search for energy security is intimately wrapped up with notions of economic security, and may affect wider dynamics of international security, with the potential for inter-state conflict over key resources in the future.

● For oil-rich regions in the South, the drive to achieve energy security by the core powers has an impact upon the human security of local communities, whilst oil wealth often insulates leaders from the wider population, with consequences for notions of regime security and development.

The problem of energy security

At one level, the growing problem of energy (in)security is simple to explain. Demand for energy use is growing—and in all likelihood will continue to grow for the foreseeable future—whilst it is not at all clear that reliable and stable sources of supply will continue to match this. This leads to a growing 'energy gap' between demand and supply, which in turn exacerbates concerns amongst leaders over the sources of future supply. Overall global consumption of marketed energy stood at just over 460 quadrillion British thermal units (qBtu) in 2005.[1] This level is forecast to rise *by over 50 per cent* during the medium term, to nearly 700 qBtu by 2030. This is a truly staggering rate of increase, which will significantly dictate the nature of the energy problem over the coming decades. Those states that are currently responsible for the majority of the world's energy consumption—the industrialized states of North America, Europe, East Asia, and Australasia that make up the Organization for Economic Cooperation and Development (OECD)—are set to increase their consumption by almost 20 per cent by 2030, as economic growth leads to sustained increases in energy demand. However, it is the future rise in demand by the newly emergent major economies of the non-OECD (projected to increase by 85 per cent by 2030) that will primarily account for increased global consumption. In particular, the rapid growth of the Chinese and Indian economies is drastically changing the energy map of the world: together, they accounted for less than 8 per cent of overall consumption in 1980; by 2005 this share had grown to 18 per cent; by 2030 it is projected to be no less than 25 per cent. Indeed, by 2030 Chinese energy use is projected considerably to outstrip that of the United States, which in 2008 accounted for over 20 per cent of global consumption. It is unsurprising, therefore, that some have referred to an emerging 'Chindia Challenge', destined to exacerbate the coming

---

[1] Unless otherwise stated, all data in this section are drawn from the authoritative *International Energy Outlook 2008*, a publication from the US Department of Energy (see EIA 2008).

problem of energy insecurity (Klare 2008). The vast majority (87 per cent in 2005) of global energy consumption is sourced from fossil fuels, whether oil, coal, or natural gas, with the remainder made up from nuclear and renewable sources. And, in particular, oil is crucial to the workings of industrialized and industrializing economies, providing the basis for much of the world's transportation, industrial production, and commercial activity. The 2008 consumption of 84 million barrels per day (mbpd) is forecast to rise by 35 per cent by 2030, ensuring that the production of an additional 29 mbpd will be required to meet growing demand; equivalent to *three times* Saudi's production in 2008.

Given uncertainties over the size and stability of global supply, this projected rise in demand is likely to be problematic. Although most governmental and industry analyses have tended to forecast rises in oil, gas, and coal production sufficient to meet growing demand, these have usually been based on a scarcity of hard data, and a tendency of oil-rich countries and oil companies to overstate the size of reserves in their possession. Indeed, as the International Energy Agency have argued, the moment of 'peak oil' may come far sooner than previously thought. This moment—whereby the discovery and exploitation of new oil reserves will no longer match or exceed the decline in production levels from existing reserves, thus leading to an overall decline of production—may be just several years away (Monbiot 2008).

Equally important is the fact that, by and large, those states that consume the most energy do not have sufficient domestic supplies to meet their demand. In other words, the globe's key powers are, with few exceptions, driven to import their energy supplies from other states. As will be explored next, this mismatch between the geographical distribution of world energy stocks and the location of the largest energy consumers creates what we will call an 'energy-security nexus', whereby energy security becomes irretrievably entwined with the wider foreign and security policies of key states.

The energy-security 'nexus'

Almost every powerful state in world politics (with the exception of Russia, Canada, and the UK) requires large volumes of imported oil to sustain the demand from its domestic economies. The USA, China, and India need to import over half of their oil requirements, whereas members of the G8 such as Japan, France, Germany, and Italy are almost wholly reliant on foreign oil. Moreover, this reliance is set to grow, as increased demand from powerful states is not matched by rises in domestic production. In fact, the shortfall between consumption and production for the core powers—the extent to which they are reliant upon imports—is set almost to double by 2030. For China, this rise is even more dramatic: as annual oil consumption more than doubles by 2030, relatively static levels of domestic production ensure that the resulting 'energy gap' is set to grow massively. Chinese leaders will need to source an *additional* 8.6 mbpd from foreign sources by 2030, almost *quadrupling* the amount of oil needing to be imported into the country.

This fact ensures that controlling the conditions under which this resource is produced, exported, and delivered to consumers has become a key strategic concern for powerful states. In the post-colonial era, where formal notions of imperial control no longer frame North–South relations, political, economic, and even military intervention in oil-rich regions by the world's core powers has continued to play itself out on the ground. In particular, the *stability and friendly orientation* of key oil-producing states and regions is a central concern for strategists, and foreign and security policies have often reflected this fact. In regions where instability is often endemic, and where there exists a range of forces seeking to challenge existing social orders (and thus potentially jeopardize the flow of oil under conditions favourable to the major consumers), these powers have often acted to bolster those governmental and non-governmental forces considered 'friendly'. Billions of dollars of economic and military assistance have been granted to oil-rich regimes by the core powers, often in direct competition with one another for influence. Ensuring that enough oil keeps on flowing—and that local governments are sufficiently responsive to the needs of the larger economies—is a priority for consuming states.

Attempts to exert control over energy reserves in the South have consequences for the extent to which cooperation between core powers can be sustained. Indeed, the potential for an emerging set of geopolitical rivalries over this form of control has implications for international security more broadly. What

these implications might be depends largely upon the theoretical framework employed. In the next section we will briefly explore competing understandings of the role played by energy in international politics, and the consequences of growing energy insecurity for international security.

KEY POINTS

- Growing concerns over energy security derive from rapidly increasing global demand for energy (set to rise by 50 per cent by 2030), allied to rising fears over the size of key energy stocks and the likelihood of being able to exploit them in the future. The emerging 'Chindia Challenge' is especially significant in this regard, given the huge rises in energy consumption forecast for the Chinese and Indian economies.

- The fact that most of the world's largest energy consumers do not hold sufficient domestic reserves of key sources (especially oil) ensures that energy security becomes irretrievably entwined with wider foreign and security policies.

- An energy-security 'nexus' exists, whereby a central priority for core powers becomes ensuring that friendly and stable governments exist in the oil-rich South. This objective is a key determinant of foreign policy, and influences the nature of diplomacy and assistance.

- This strategy has potential consequences for international security, as larger states compete over the politics of control with regards to producing states. It also has consequences for those living in the oil-rich South, particularly given that the core powers often support non-democratic regimes in the name of 'stability'.

Energy security and IR theory

Liberalism and energy security

According to received liberal wisdom, the irrepressible spread of liberal democratic rule in the post-Cold War era, tied to free-market capitalism, has ensured that many more regions now benefit from an order that has brought peace and stability to the West since 1945. Processes of 'globalization' are accelerating, and a vastly increased set of interlinkages between states ensures that national interests are increasingly subsumed by the logic of transnational economic cooperation. The potential for inter-state competition has consequently reduced, and many liberals now see war between the major powers as an obsolete phenomenon.

In this reading, the increasing reliance by the core powers upon the oil reserves in the global South is unlikely to lead to major conflict. International energy markets—which dictate production levels, major transit routes, and prices—mediate relations between

producers and consumers, as well as between major consumers. The interests of all core powers are highly enmeshed, as the energy security of each state cannot be divorced from that of others. All major players want to maximize the stability of the flow of oil onto the market, and to minimize fluctuations over the prices that everyone pays. Moreover, this common interest is not dependent on where each state physically receives its oil from; it is the stability of the overall market that is of concern. The US government has acknowledged this fact:

> We should not ... look at energy security in isolation from the rest of the world. In a global energy marketplace, US energy and economic security are directly linked not only to our domestic and international energy supplies, but to those of our trading partners as well ... because the price of our domestic and imported oil is determined by a world market, our energy security interests *transcend the source of our physical supplies.*

National Energy Policy Development Group (2001: 8–3; emphasis added).

For liberals, then, the interconnected nature of today's global economy ensures that energy security for one is dependent upon energy security for all, and that all core powers have the same interests in maintaining and extending the conditions under which this market operates. As long as this economic order exists, conflict between major powers over energy reserves is highly unlikely.

Realism and energy security

In contrast to liberals, realist thinkers are increasingly sceptical about the durability of the current liberal order, and point to several disturbing trends that may signal a return to an era of greater geopolitical confrontation. 'Resource wars', in particular over energy sources, present a clear possibility for a breakdown in international cooperation, as states begin to compete (and eventually conflict) over the control of major reserves. For Michael Klare (2008: 30), the key thinker in this regard, we are witnessing

> the energy equivalent of an arms race to secure control over whatever remaining deposits of oil and natural gas are up for sale on the planet, along with reserves of other vital minerals. This resource race is already one of the most conspicuous features of the contemporary landscape and, in our lifetimes, may become *the* most conspicuous one—a voracious, zero-sum contest that, if allowed to continue along present paths, can only lead to conflict among the major powers.

In this light, energy scarcity is likely to lead to future disruptions in the global system and the emergence of a 'new international energy order', characterized less by liberal free-market trading than by statism and neo-mercantilism. This realist understanding does well to explain recent moves by powers outside the liberal core—most noticeably China—to circumvent the international market in energy. For Beijing, such moves are driven by a sense of deep concern about the sheer degree of American dominance over Persian Gulf oil, which will allow Washington to control the flow of oil during any period of heightened Sino-US tension (Downs 2000: 45). As a result, Chinese planners are pursuing direct, bilateral deals with oil-rich regimes across the world, which results in the trade of oil outside the global marketplace.

In particular, realists point to the strategic rivalries at play in the Caspian Basin. Since the scale of the reserves became clear in the mid-1990s, Russia, China, and the USA have been vying for influence over the oil-rich regimes of Central Asia and the Caucasus. Military and economic aid has flowed from each power, and the issue of pipeline route has become key. In this context, a strategic priority for Washington has been to loosen Moscow's traditional dominance of the region through pushing for the construction of westward-pointing pipelines, bypassing Russian territory to reach international markets. In return, Moscow and Beijing have been working to minimize American influence in the region. Clearly, such rivalry presents a challenge to the current liberal order, and may signal the beginning of intensified inter-state competition and conflict (Klare 2008: 115–45). In this light, the 2008 Russian invasion of Georgia (a key oil-transit state), and the NATO response to this, may be a harbinger of the forthcoming era.

Historical materialism and energy security

From a historical-materialist (HM) perspective, liberal and realist accounts miss a central aspect of the picture. Indeed, one cannot understand the importance of energy and its influence on international politics without placing it within the context of the development of global capitalism, and without exploring the role of key states in defending and expanding this economic system. Oil remains the lifeblood of the current order—an order that is based upon an unequal (and deeply unjust) distribution of wealth and power in favour of capitalist economic elites. In this regard, those who benefit most from the prevailing order are driven to ensure that the flow of energy under favourable conditions continues to underpin their position in the global system.

There are disputes from within the HM tradition over exactly how and why control of oil supplies is sought by leading capitalist states. In what we will call the 'blood-for-oil' thesis, intervention by core capitalist powers in oil-rich regions is designed to serve specific corporate interests, especially those of 'Big Oil'. In this reading, the capitalist state is little more than an instrument for ruling economic elites, with foreign policy subsumed under a logic of profit maximization. Ian Rutledge (2006: 65) provides a clear example of this form of analysis when he describes figures such as US Vice President Dick Cheney as a 'single-minded representative of oil capitalism', and someone who 'would not hesitate to mould US foreign policy into a form conducive to the business opportunities and profit maximisation so earnestly sought after by the huge energy multinationals of which his own company was a leading representative'.

In contrast to such 'instrumentalist' accounts, others working within the HM tradition have stressed the 'relative autonomy' of capitalist states, whereby they act primarily for the interests of the capitalist world order *as a whole*, rather than for the interests of specific capitalists (such as the oil sector). Such accounts stress the managerial role assumed by core powers (and by Washington in particular), whereby they work to ensure the smooth operations of a global economy beneficial to all. In this reading, overt competition over the world's oil stocks will continue to be overwhelmingly pacified, as rival centres of power opt to work within the framework of the liberal international economic order. Within this, international oil companies (IOCs) are granted the freedom to make independent commercial decisions over where to invest, with the role of capitalist states one of maintaining an international environment required for private capital to operate with security and profits.

In this reading we are not, in the face of increased tension between major powers, seeing a return to widespread geopolitical rivalry, especially given that the global hegemon (the USA) and many other key states remain dedicated to an order based on a largely positive-sum, open-door trading regime. For the capitalist core, by far the most preferred future scenario is a China (and Russia and India) that remains pacified and subordinated within liberal economic order.

KEY POINTS

- The likelihood of increased international competition and conflict over energy reserves depends upon the theoretical framework employed, with realists generally pessimistic about the future sustainability of the liberal economic order.

- A key question in this regard is how core powers will begin to relate to each other as energy stocks dwindle: will they continue to cooperate through current open-door trading regimes, or will they retreat behind nationalist barriers? And what will this mean for the likelihood of inter-state conflict?

- Historical materialists stress the importance of control of the world's energy reserves to the development of global capitalism, and examine how and why core capitalist states have worked to ensure this control is maintained.

Energy security and human insecurity

Of all the regions in the global South, oil-rich zones are often some of the most unstable. **Dutch disease**—whereby substantial oil income drives up exchange rates, slowing overall growth and 'hollowing out' non-oil sectors—affects many oil-rich economies. In parallel, these regions tend to have a set of *political* problems that have the potential to exacerbate existing instabilities and generate new ones. In particular, as the economist Joseph Stiglitz (2003) has made clear: 'Control over natural resource wealth provides leaders with little incentive to share power, and gives leaders the means with which to buy legitimacy rather than earn it through elections.' Authoritarian state forms can be more easily sustained in oil-rich regions, given that the centralization of wealth works to insulate the ruling strata from popular pressure for reform. The prevalence of non-democratic governance can be seen across the oil-rich Middle East, Caspian Region, and West Africa, where the power of corrupt dictatorships is largely based upon the huge wealth generated through the energy sector.

In turn, the reduction of legitimate political space for most of the population, combined with often-vast inequalities in wealth distribution (as the oil 'rents' are retained within a small circle of economic and political elites), can easily breed domestic unrest. Across the oil-rich South, a wide variety of social and political forces have arisen to challenge the current distribution of power, and the conditions under which energy stocks are released onto international markets. Most of these adopt peaceful means of protest, although increasingly these have been matched by armed campaigns against the prevailing order, as groups turn to violence in order to achieve their goals. Attacks on energy infrastructure and foreign oil

---

CASE STUDY 22.1

Oil and resistance in the Niger delta

The extraction and exportation of oil in the Niger delta has generated significant internal instability within Nigeria, as extreme poverty combines with widespread environmental degradation as a direct result of oil operations. A wide range of groups in the delta have been active in the region. Particularly high profile has been the peaceful campaign by the Ogoni community, which coalesced in the early 1990s around the Movement for the Survival of the Ogoni People (MOSOP). Consisting of a collection of trade unions, church bodies, women's associations, and student unions, MOSOP (1990) declared that 'over 30 years of oil mining have led to the complete degradation of the Ogoni environment', and that 'we as a people must through all lawful and non-violent means fight for social justice and fair play for ourselves and our progeny'. The group has been key in organizing mass protests against oil operations on Ogoni land—acts of popular expression that led ultimately to the execution of nine Ogoni activists by the Nigerian state (including, infamously, MOSOP's President, Kenule Saro-Wiwa).

In addition to lawful means of protest, groups in the delta have taken to direct action. Oil facilities and platforms have been occupied. In May 1998, for example, over 100 unarmed Ijaw Youth Council members occupied Chevron's Parabe oil platform in order to demand more local employment and greater efforts to clear up pollution. This was followed by the release of the *Kaiama Declaration* in December 1998, which stated the group's intent to 'cease to recognise all undemocratic decrees that rob our peoples/communities of the right to ownership and control of our lives and resources', and demanded 'the immediate withdrawal from Ijawland of all military forces of occupation and repression by the Nigerian state' (Ijaw Youth Council 1998). This tactic was repeated by 600 Itsekiri women in 2002, who peacefully occupied ChevronTexaco's Escravos export terminal for ten days, shutting down around 25 per cent of the country's production (International Crisis Group 2006a: 15).

Increasingly, however, such peaceful protests have been matched by armed campaigns in the delta. Two groups in particular—the Movement for the Emancipation of the Niger Delta (MEND) and the Niger Delta People's Volunteer Force (NDPVF)—have emerged in recent years, and use armed force explicitly as part of a campaign to seize 'total control' of the Niger delta's oil wealth. MEND, for example, is explicitly fighting for 25–30 per cent of oil revenues to be returned to local communities in the delta (International Crisis Group 2006b: 3–5). It aims to achieve this by halting the current activities of the oil sector. By attacking oil workers and facilities, MEND has declared that: 'It must be clear that the Nigerian government cannot protect your workers or assets. Leave our land while you can, or die in it. Our aim is to totally destroy the capacity of the Nigerian government to export oil' (BBC News 2006b).

workers have increased, and these have often tied in with wider insurgent campaigns for greater autonomy and control over resources. The ideological base supporting these movements is highly dependent on each situation, ranging from leftist groups in Colombia to ethno-nationalist groups in the Niger Delta (see Case Study 22.1), to al-Qaeda-affiliated groups in Saudi Arabia.

Regardless of the specificities of each case, these forms of resistance all—to varying degrees—present a major challenge to the security of oil operations in the region, and therefore to the energy security of consuming states. As with other forms of foreign investment, the confidence and smooth operation of oil capital is deeply affected by political instability. In this sense, conditions in much of the oil-rich South give grave concern for those powers reliant upon a steady flow of energy from these regions, not least because it may adversely affect the commercial decisions of IOCs about where to invest. This has translated into a focus by these states on 'critical infrastructure protection', in order to ensure the smooth operation of the oil sector in the face of 'terrorist' threats. Organizations such as NATO have emphasized that 'protecting energy infrastructure at home only provides a partial response to the challenge posed by energy security', and that European and North American dependence on foreign energy supplies ensures that they have 'an interest in enhancing protection of energy infrastructure in producing and transit countries, and of energy routes worldwide' (NATO 2007).

This interest has seen a rise in military assistance provided to oil-rich states. However, and of key importance in relation to the impact on human security, this aid is not simply designed to provide static defence for oil infrastructure. It is also provided in order to ensure a wider stability of prevailing social orders, where these are considered favourable for energy-consuming states. In other words, given the presence of forces in the oil-rich South who would overturn existing forms of governance, and who may alter the terms under which

oil is supplied to the major powers, it often becomes important for those powers to support incumbent regimes in their fight against sources of 'instability'. The rationale for militarized intervention in this regard has been clearly spelt out by policy analysts in the field:

> It is … reasonable to ask who, among present-day occupants of the international stage, would like to see a great deal changed? To which the immediate answer would obviously be the ramshackle assemblage of rogue states and revolutionary movements whose machinations consume such a disproportionate share of time and attention from the defense establishments around the world … military planners and civilian strategists are [inclined] to point to the potential threat that terrorists and other disenfranchised groups pose to global energy markets; and indeed they have good reason to.

Moran and Russell (2008).

This focus on the threat posed to international energy markets by 'disenfranchised groups' in the South has led to the provision of a particular form of military assistance by the core powers. Alongside pipeline protection and anti-kidnapping training, local security forces are being equipped to *actively* deploy against a wide range of armed and unarmed groups. Often refracted through the lens of 'counter-insurgency' or 'counterterrorism', this aid has often had grave consequences for those sections of civil society pushing for change (however moderate). Groups that in some way challenge the rule of incumbent elites in oil-rich regions are often recast as 'terrorist' or 'subversive' threats, thereby legitimating the use of armed force in response. Indeed, a cursory examination of the human rights records of security forces in the oil-rich South leaves no doubt of the effects on human security of their campaigns to ensure regime security (and, indirectly, global energy security).

In parallel, IOCs have often resorted to the employment of force in order to guarantee the security of their investments. On the ground, this has been carried out through close cooperation with both host-nation security forces and private military companies (PMCs). PMCs are employed by oil corporations throughout the global South to protect specific installations, create localized zones of stability to allow operations to continue unimpeded, and even to influence wider dynamics of conflict in the region. In this way, they 'act as "investment enablers", providing clients with robust security that make otherwise extremely risky investment options safe enough to be financially viable. In the midst of conflict, they create localized stability that reduces costs and increases investment values' (Singer 2003: 80–1). Throughout the oil-rich South, such operations have led to extensive human rights abuses. Indeed, according to John Ruggie (2006) in his work for the UN, the extractive sector 'utterly dominates' the record of documented abuses by transnational corporations in the South, accounting for most of the 'allegations of the worst abuses, up to and including complicity in crimes against humanity, typically for acts committed by public and private security forces protecting company assets and property; large-scale corruption; violations of labour rights; and a broad array of abuses in relation to local communities, especially indigenous people'. In many cases, the outsourcing of security requirements to private companies is used to ensure 'plausible deniability' in the face of any abuses that result.

KEY POINTS

- The drive to maximize and stabilize the flow of oil onto international markets has profound implications for populations in producing states, as oil wealth insulates ruling elites from the need to ensure political accountability and a fair distribution of economic resources.

- Ongoing social injustice has spurred many groups to challenge the prevailing order, through both peaceful protest and armed insurgency. Although motivated by a wide range of ideological commitments, such movements present a common threat to the interests of oil corporations, local economic and political elites, and the energy-consuming states of the global North.

- Often supported by one or more of the major powers, and working alongside oil corporations, non-democratic governments in oil-rich regions routinely deploy their security forces to ensure 'stability' is maintained.

- 'Stability' in this context refers to the absence of challenge to the status quo, and the pursuit of this objective has severe ramifications for human security in the regions. Operating through the lens of 'counter-insurgency' or 'counterterrorism', local security forces often engage in repeated human-rights violations in order to remove threats.

Energy security and the United States

As the global hegemon, granted a primary role by other powers for the maintenance of the liberal order—and as the lead capitalist state with by far the largest economy—the United States has long been concerned with ensuring the security of the world's energy supplies. This has translated into a post-war strategy of political, economic, and military intervention in oil-rich regions, precisely in order to stabilize and maximize global energy production. In this section, we will begin to unpack the logic behind this strategy, before briefly examining the record of intervention by Washington.

In addition to the substantial domestic reliance on foreign sources of oil—where the USA uses 24 per cent of all the oil consumed in any one day, and needs to import most of this (Energy Information Administration 2008)— American grand strategy vis-à-vis the rest of the world is firmly premised upon establishing and retaining control of major oil reserves. In other words, there is a geostrategic, as well as a purely economic, logic driving concerns over 'energy security'. In particular, the sustained projection of American military power is fully predicated upon receiving an uninterrupted supply of vast quantities of oil. The Pentagon is by far the largest single consumer of oil in the world, with fuel now representing more than half of all cargo transported by the US military (Department of Defense 2007). Likewise, playing a key role in stabilizing global oil production provides the USA with immense structural power in relation to other core powers. Given that any serious challenger to US primacy would require unfettered access to vast quantities of oil, and that preventing the emergence of any such challenge is a core theme of US strategy, control of this commodity has long been a key objective for the American state. Zbigniew Brzezinski (2003–4: 8), President Carter's former National Security Adviser, captured this wider, structural logic when he argued:

> America has major strategic and economic interests in the Middle East that are dictated by the region's vast energy supplies. Not only does America benefit economically from the relatively low costs of Middle Eastern oil, but America's security role in the region gives it indirect but politically critical leverage on the European and Asian economies that are also dependent on energy exports from the region.

It is in this context that US control over the Persian Gulf has long been considered so important. By 2008, the region sat on top of no less than 61 per cent of all proven reserves in the world, and will provide 33 per cent of global oil production by 2030. In particular, Saudi Arabia remains central for US strategic planners, given that it holds more than 20 per cent of the entire global stock of oil and—along with other regional producers—over 80 per cent of the world's 'excess production capacity' (Energy

Information Administration 2007). Controlling this region, and Saudi Arabia in particular, is therefore a key priority for any state wishing either unparalleled energy security or wider geopolitical hegemony. This is the logic driving US strategy towards the Persian Gulf.

US hegemony, oil, and intervention in the Middle East

The centrality of oil from the Middle East has long been understood by US planners. As early as 1944, for example, a report by the Office of Strategic Services (the forerunner of the CIA) concluded that, in relation to the Middle East, Washington's key national interests were 'oil, airbases and future markets', whilst the US State Department urged a 'substantial and orderly expansion of production in Eastern Hemisphere sources of supply, principally the Middle East' (Klare 2004: 30; Layne 2006: 47–8). In particular, the USA has long worked to forge close relations with Saudi Arabia. President Roosevelt committed the USA in 1945 to secure the Saudi monarchical dictatorship from external and internal threat, in return for an agreement to export oil cheaply onto international markets. This strategic posture was concretized with the 1951 deployment of the United States Military Training Mission (USMTM): a large-scale, Pentagon-led advisory mission still in position in the 2000s. Militarizing the relationship between the Saudi state and people has been a long-term goal of the USA, which has worked continuously (and alongside a wide range of PMCs) to 'stabilize' the regime from internal 'subversion' (see Case Study 22.2).

This long-standing strategy towards Saudi Arabia was matched, before 1979, by a strategy to ensure the 'stability' of Iran, as the second significant oil state of the region. This played itself out through a CIA-sponsored coup against the democratically

CASE STUDY 22.2

US counter-insurgency assistance and PMCs: stabilizing the Saudi regime

The United States has long worked to ensure the stability of the Saudi dictatorship, given that this regime has provided the best means through which to access the country's oil reserves. Security assistance to Saudi Arabia has been designed explicitly to insulate the Saudi monarchy from internal unrest, given that—in President Reagan's words—'there is no way we could stand by and see [the country] taken over by anyone that would shut off that oil' (Maynes 1995: 105). This has been achieved primarily through the training and arming of the Saudi Arabian National Guard (SANG), a paramilitary force designed to consolidate the rule of the Saudi dictatorship and highly trained in internal warfare and counter-insurgency (CI) techniques. And central to the provision of US expertise in this regard has been the activities of private military companies (PMCs), which have been deployed *en masse* by Washington. Contracts between the Saudi regime and US-based PMCs run into billions of dollars, and have resulted in 35,000–40,000 private security personnel deploying to the country at any one time in order to buttress the military and internal security forces (Wells, Meyers, and Mulvihill 2001). Central to this assistance effort has been the Vinnell Corporation, which has been paid hundreds of millions of dollars to train the SANG, including the provision of CI doctrine, operational training in small-unit tactics and advanced infantry manœuvres, and equipment. As one Vinnell official told *Time* (1975): 'We are not mercenaries because we are not pulling triggers. We train people to pull triggers. Maybe that makes us executive mercenaries.' This relationship continues to be central to US planning,

with huge sums dedicated by the Pentagon to bolstering Saudi internal security. In just one example, the Pentagon notified Congress in October 2005 of the possible provision of $918 million of equipment to support the modernization of the SANG. The package included 144 armoured personnel carriers, water cannon vehicles, command, control, and communications equipment, and tens of thousands of assault rifles with grenade launchers, as well as scopes and sights for sniper weapons systems. According to US officials, the SANG 'needs these defense articles so that it can effectively conduct security and counterterrorism operations' (Defense Security Cooperation Agency 2005).

Although increasingly wrapped up in the language of 'counterterrorism', assistance to the SANG has been designed to provide the means for the Saudi regime to suppress *any* domestic challenge to its rule, with overt activity by unionized workers or political activists targeted through widespread imprisonment and torture. Stabilizing the pro-US regime and keeping the oil flowing has required the continual policing of the Saudi population and the severe suppression of any significant protests. This has included the crushing of dissent over oil revenues by workers in 1978, the slaughter of over 400 people in protests against the Saudi authorities in 1987, right through to the 2007 imprisonment of 700 people who, according to the Saudi Ministry of the Interior, 'were not involved in terrorist acts' but were simply suspected of 'harbouring extremist thoughts' (Human Rights Watch 2007). Overall, the attempt to ensure energy security by Washington has had profound effects on the human security of Saudis who may be working for a more just future.

---

elected president, Mossadegh, after he moved to nationalize Iranian oil reserves and pull away from American and British influence. With a pro-US regime installed, Iran became the largest single purchaser of American arms in the world, and between 1972 and 1977 US military sales to Iran reached a staggering $16.2 billion (Bill 1988: 202).

However, this 'twin-pillar' strategy suffered a calamitous setback in 1979, with the Iranian Revolution and the Soviet invasion of Afghanistan both ensuring that powerful counter-hegemonic forces were present in the region. In response, the outgoing Carter administration

swiftly announced a clear commitment to retain Washington's primacy in the Persian Gulf, through a policy of *direct intervention* in the face of any major threat to the flow of oil. To give teeth to his new doctrine, Carter ordered the formation of a Rapid Deployment Force (RDF) that could speedily assemble for forward power projection in the region. This force was later upgraded by Ronald Reagan to a full-scale regional command, US Central Command (CENTCOM). This has since been the central vehicle through which US power is exercised across the Persian Gulf. CENTCOM provides the key instrument for applying overwhelming military force throughout the region at any point that supplies appear threatened—a function acknowledged by its Commander-in-Chief, Anthony Zinni (1998): the command's military strategy towards the region was, he said, 'basically energy driven', with the significant oil deposits in the region 'one of the prime considerations in determining our interests'.

These interests have underpinned US strategy towards the region throughout the post-Cold War era, and explain Washington's response to the Iraqi invasion of Kuwait in August 1990, as well as the continued presence of significant numbers of US troops in the region throughout the 1990s. As the leaked draft of the 1992 Defense Planning Guidance made clear, in the Persian Gulf 'our overall objective is to remain the predominant outside power in the region and preserve US and Western access to the region's oil' (Tyler 1992). Ultimately, after the election of Bush and the attacks of 9/11 had provided a window of opportunity for US strategists, this objective translated into the campaign against Saddam Hussein, in order to remove a key threat to US power in the region. Although US officials strenuously denied that oil factored into the strategic planning surrounding regime change in Iraq, this logic was clearly at play. Indeed, the continuing centrality of this interest has been acknowledged by the former Chairman of the US Federal Reserve, Alan Greenspan:

> If Saddam Hussein had been head of Iraq and there was no oil under those sands, our response to him would not have been as strong as it was in the first Gulf War. And the second gulf war is an extension of the first. My view is that Saddam, looking over his 30-year history, very clearly was giving evidence of moving towards controlling the Straits of Hormuz, where there are 17, 18, 19 million barrels a day [passing through. Given that,] I'm saying taking Saddam out was essential.

Woodward (2007).

US strategy of diversification

Continuing instability in the Persian Gulf, not ameliorated by the invasion and occupation of Iraq, has led to rising levels of concern amongst US planners as to the sheer vulnerability of an American economy, and a wider global position, which are both ultimately reliant on the steady flow of oil from this region. This is especially the case given the physical concentration of oil production and transportation from the Persian Gulf, which ensures that high-profile targets exist for those forces wishing to reduce exports levels. This was brought home in dramatic style after the failed suicide bombing of the Abqaiq oil-processing plant in Saudi Arabia in February 2006. Had this been successful, output from a site through which two-thirds of the country's oil passes would have been drastically affected, with overall exports from Saudi Arabia potentially halved for up to a year (BBC News 2006a). Likewise, almost all this oil travels through the 21-mile-wide Strait of Hormuz, which is clearly vulnerable to closure or severe disruption. In this way, the beating heart of US power rests upon an exceptionally fragile set of conditions. This has been acknowledged by key US officials, with former US President George W. Bush (2007) clear that this dependence 'leaves us more vulnerable to hostile regimes, and to terrorists—who could cause huge disruptions of oil shipments, and raise the price of oil, and do great harm to our economy'.

As a result of this vulnerability, US planners have pursued a dual approach to ensure the highest possible degree of global (and, by extension, American) energy security. On the one hand, as we have seen, the USA has sought to entrench its dominance over the Persian Gulf. On the other hand, however, Washington has increasingly pursued a policy of energy diversification away from the Persian Gulf. Through this, US planners aim to supplant Middle Eastern oil supplies with those from other oil-rich regions within the South, with increasing efforts to cultivate new sets of relationships with alternative oil suppliers. Focusing on states in the Caspian Basin, West Africa, and Latin America—regions that together are thought to hold around 220 billion barrels of oil (not significantly less than Saudi Arabia)—Washington has increased the amount of military and economic assistance provided to oil-rich regimes. Employing this strategy, the USA has worked to establish its hegemony over these zones, so as to stabilize and maximize production levels, and to integrate local political economies within the wider US-led order.

As in the Persian Gulf, this strategy has relied upon an explicit militarization of state–society relations through extensive levels of security assistance, and a reorientation of local security forces away from concerns over external security and towards the provision of internal defence. As one key report from the Center for Strategic and International Studies declared: 'Stability in petroleum exporting regions is tenuous at best', and is threatened by a wide range of domestic forces, including 'pipeline sabotage in Nigeria, labour strikes in Venezuela … and civil unrest in Uzbekistan and other [former Soviet Union] states' (Cordesman and Al-Rodhan 2005: 8). Ensuring domestic stability, often through the use of counter-insurgency training and equipment, has become a central means by which the USA attempts to maintain energy production in these regions. Needless to say, this has continued to have profound implications for local populations, as vocal elements from civil society are recast as subversive threats to 'peace and stability'.

KEY POINTS

- The USA has adopted a lead role in the post-war era in ensuring an adequate degree of global energy security. This has translated into extensive military deployment in oil-rich regions, and a wide array of interventions in order to stabilize friendly political and economic orders.

- The strategy has been pursued to secure enough oil for the American economy, but also to secure American primacy vis-à-vis friendly and rival powers. In this way, there is a geostrategic logic to US energy interventions, running alongside a purely economic logic.

- This logic has fed into a long-standing strategy of ensuring US dominance in the Persian Gulf, through the provision of military and economic aid to allied states, and through the presence and use of huge numbers of US troops. The invasion of Iraq in 2003 can be best understood as an implementation of this overall post-war strategy (albeit under the guise of a uniquely unilateralist and militarist American administration).

- Increasingly, the USA is attempting to supplant its dominance over the Persian Gulf with the integration of other oil-rich zones within the US-led order. Again, this is being largely achieved through the militarization of state–society relations in those regions, in order to stabilize energy production. And again, this has consequences for the human security of those in the wider oil-rich South.

Conclusion

As we have seen, energy security involves a complex nexus of geopolitical, economic, and strategic concerns, which link together distant regions of the globe, and disparate security concerns. Rising demand for energy, and the likelihood that this will continue to be met by fossil fuels, are matched by increasing uncertainties over the size and stability of remaining stocks. This will, almost inevitably, lead to a rising prominence of concerns over energy security, and an increasing possibility of intensified inter-state competition (and even conflict) over energy reserves. As we have examined, there exist a number of different theoretical approaches to understanding the nature of the current energy order, and these emphasize different aspects of the coming challenge. Liberal theorists stress the positive-sum nature of US oil hegemony, the openness of the market mechanism, and the ways in which the liberal order serves to pacify resource rivalry. In contrast, realist theorists tend to stress the inherent likelihood of a return to geopolitical tensions as a result of increased oil demands, and the strong potential for major powers to direct their strategic primacy towards a more 'mercantilist' direction. Lastly, historical-materialist theorists stress the close interrelationship between energy security and the maintenance of a capitalist economic order, and consider the likelihood of future conflict through this lens.

Unsurprisingly, each of these approaches reveals important dimensions of contemporary and future global energy security. The global oil regime *is* a liberal one, in the sense that major powers can and do participate within it to the benefit of all. In 2008, there are certainly no moves by the USA, as the hegemonic 'stabilizer' of this regime, towards a more economically nationalist stance in relation to oil acquisition and control. This was perhaps underscored when the Chinese National Petroleum Company—an arm of the key strategic rival to US hegemony—acted within the US-led liberal order to sign a $3 billion oil deal with Iraq, the first of its kind after the invasion (CNN 2008). As such, talk of a new 'Great Game', and the inherent likelihood of conflict and rivalry, is perhaps overblown. However, it is also true that increased economic turbulence as

a result of the global financial crisis of 2008–9 could see the gradual erosion of the liberal logic and the re-emergence of strategic rivalries. This is where the historical-materialist position has a great deal of purchase, in so far as the history of energy security cannot be disaggregated from the development of capitalism, and by extension the processes of imperialism and neo-imperialism within contemporary global politics. The invasion of Iraq, Obama's continued insistence that US troops will remain there (albeit in an smaller number and an advisory role), and the expansion of oil interests to regions outside the Persian Gulf, all point to an older form of Western meddling in the resource-rich global South.

This is perhaps the central point of this chapter: when we speak of security, we must always ask 'whose security' and 'whose insecurity'. The current global oil regime has meant that core powers have often become intimately involved with the politics of oil-producing regions, and have often pursued foreign policies for a form of 'stability' that has not always worked in the interests of the majority of people in those regions. Energy security for some has often meant human insecurity for others, and this is likely to continue to be so as long as contemporary society is heavily dependent upon the uninterrupted and cheap supply of energy from fossil fuels.

? QUESTIONS

1. What is meant by 'energy security'?

2. Why do medium-term projections paint a picture of increased future energy insecurity?

3. How might the problem of energy security impact upon wider aspects of international security?

4. How does the quest for energy security by states in the North generate human insecurity for people in the South?

5. In what ways have movements in the South attempted to resist what they see as the exploitative nature of current energy ownership and production structures?

6. What is meant by the 'peak oil moment', and how might this lead to increased energy insecurity?

7. How likely is a return to an era of geopolitical rivalry, driven by so-called resource wars?

8. Why does the USA have such a long record of military intervention in oil-rich regions of the global South?

9. What is military assistance to oil-rich states in the South primarily designed to achieve?

10. What role did oil play in the 2003 invasion of Iraq?

FURTHER READING

■ Klare, M. (2004), *Blood and Oil: How America's Thirst for Petrol is Killing Us*, London: Penguin. A penetrating critique of America's drive to control energy reserves, both in the Middle East and more widely. Argues that this strategy is, in fact, generating insecurity for the United States.

■ Klare, M. (2008), *Rising Powers Shrinking Planet: The New Geopolitics of Energy*, New York: Metropolitan Books. In this book, Klare outlines his vision for an emerging new international energy order, based on a rejection of the free-market order and a return to statism and neo-mercantilism. Up to date and highly readable.

■ Layne, C. (2006), *The Peace of Illusions: American Grand Strategy from 1940 to the Present*, Ithaca, NY: Cornell University Press. Using detailed empirical analysis, this book lays out a convincing argument as to the continuity of American strategy in the post-war era. Although ranging far wider than oil, his analysis has direct relevance for thinking about the US role in underpinning global energy security.

■ Leech, G. (2006), *Crude Interventions: The United States, Oil and the New World (Dis)Order*, London: Zed Books. Focusing on the effects of US intervention in the oil-rich South, this volume charts the degree to which abusive regimes are supported by the West (and the USA in particular), and the complicity of these powers in the human-rights violations that result.

■ Stokes, D., and Raphael, S. (forthcoming), Imperial Logics: US Hegemony and Global Energy Security, Baltimore, MD: Johns Hopkins University Press. In this book, we chart the long-standing American strategy to control oil-rich zones in the South, and the ways in which this control translates into the wider US objective of maintaining its primacy within the current liberal order. We pay particular attention to the attempt by US planners to 'stabilize' oil-rich zones, through the provision of military assistance to counter 'subversive' threats to its interests. Detailed case studies of Latin America, the Caspian Basin, and West Africa examine Washington's current strategy of energy diversification, and the consequences this has for the peoples living in these regions.

IMPORTANT WEBSITES

● http://www.eia.doe.gov The Energy Information Administration. An agency of the US Government, housed within the Department of Energy, the EIA provides official energy statistics (including production, export, and consumption data for all forms of marketed energy), in-depth country briefs, and authoritative forecasts up to 2030.

● http://www.energybulletin.net Energy Bulletin. A clearing house for information regarding energy security and the upcoming peak in global energy supply. Organized by energy source, region, and issue, this site gathers many useful and respectable analyses of the issue.

● http://www.gwu.edu/~nsarchiv National Security Archive, an independent, non-governmental research institute located at the George Washington University. Collects, analyses, and publishes declassified documents on US foreign policy, obtained through the US Freedom of Information Act. Much of these are published online, and provide a fascinating insight into US interventions in the Middle East and other oil-rich regions.

● http://www.business-humanrights.org/ Home Business and Human Rights Resource Centre, a UK- and US-based charity dedicated to providing information on the human-rights impacts—positive and negative—of corporate activities. A very detailed section on the energy sector, with over 4,800 entries searchable by company, countries, or issue. Publishes media articles, first-hand accounts, UN reports, and sought responses from corporations.

Visit the Online Resource Centre that accompanies this book for lots of interesting additional material: www.oxfordtextbooks.co.uk/orc/collins2e/

23

The Defence Trade

JOANNA SPEAR AND NEIL COOPER

 Chapter Contents

- Introduction
- Explaining the arms dynamic
- Trends in defence expenditure
- The content of the contemporary defence trade
- Conclusion

Reader's Guide

This chapter discusses key aspects of the contemporary defence trade. It begins by examining the main theoretical approaches that have been developed to explain why states acquire defence equipment. This section includes an analysis of the action–reaction, domestic factor, and technological imperative models as well as a brief discussion of the military–industrial complex thesis. It concludes by considering the various ways in which the symbolic meaning attached to military technology may influence decisions on both the acquisition and the sale of defence equipment.

The chapter then examines trends in both defence expenditure and defence exports. With respect to the former, it highlights, in particular, the way in which the US war on terror has legitimized a return to Cold War levels of defence expenditure and how the vast amounts expended on defence by the USA is creating a growing technology gap between it and other producers. With respect to the latter, the chapter draws on the notion of 'tiers' in the defence market to analyse trends in the defence export trade, focusing on the policies of specific states that can be viewed as exemplars of each tier. This section also includes a brief discussion of the role played by non-state actors in the supply of defence material as well as an examination of demand factors in the market. The final section of the chapter outlines the changes in the content of the contemporary defence trade, in particular the shift away from the supply of complete major weapons systems to the provision of upgrades, dual-use technologies, communications equipment, spare parts, and training.

Introduction

This chapter aims to outline both the dynamics underpinning the acquisition of defence technology and the various features of the contemporary export market in defence goods. The first section briefly outlines the main schools of thought that have been developed to explain why states acquire arms. We then go on to outline the key trends in defence expenditure both globally and for key states, as well as examining post-Cold War trends in the defence export market and the way the market itself is changing. We use the term 'defence trade' throughout this chapter when discussing the export market to indicate that the post-Cold War market involves much more than the supply of arms.

Explaining the arms dynamic

This section will examine the various attempts to conceptualize the factors that drive actors to acquire weapons and defence technology.

Perhaps the first point to note is that academic analyses of the motivations underpinning the acquisition of defence equipment more commonly refer to the arms dynamic, which can be understood as 'the entire set of pressures that make actors (usually states) both acquire armed forces and change the quantity and quality of the armed forces they already possess' (Buzan and Herring 1998: 790). The arms dynamic can be distinguished in two important ways. First, one can make a distinction between arms dynamics that have different levels of intensity—for example, build-down, maintenance, competition/build-up, and arms racing (Buzan and Herring 1998: 75–81). Second, one can also distinguish between the notion of a primary arms dynamic, which describes the set of pressures to acquire armed forces that are experienced by major arms producers, and a secondary arms dynamic, which describes the set of pressures experienced by part-producers or non-producers, who are far more reliant on defence imports and who may therefore be open to a different mix of pressures.

There have been various attempts to theorize the processes that drive the arms dynamic, but they are commonly differentiated according to whether they emphasize either action–reaction factors, domestic factors, or what is termed the technological imperative. We also discuss the symbolic meaning attached to weapons as a factor influencing the acquisition of defence equipment. These are not necessarily mutually exclusive models, however. Indeed, most commentators on the arms dynamic would probably take the view that, for most, if not all, societies with significant military forces, some combination of these models is likely to be in operation. Rather, the key question concerns the extent to which one or the other factor predominates.

Action – reaction

The action–reaction model assumes that actors increase either the quantity or quality of their military forces in response to increases on the part of potential adversaries. The pressure for states to act in this way is rooted in the conditions of the security dilemma, under which any attempt by states to provide for their own defence are, regardless of intent, viewed by others as potentially threatening (Herz 1950; Snyder 1984; Wheeler and Booth 1992)—not least, because a self-help international system creates pressures for states to make worst-case analyses of the actions of others.

The action–reaction model is at the heart of the notion that particularly intense rivalries can give rise to arms races. However, there remain significant debates about exactly what characteristics distinguish arms races from the regular operation of the arms dynamic (Hammond 1993), whether arms races make conflict more likely or less, and, indeed, whether the concept has any explanatory value at all (Gray 1986). Similarly, critics point to a number of key problems in the action–reaction model. These include questions over the timing of reaction and whether the concept needs to (and can) incorporate anticipatory reactions based on assumptions about what potential enemies might do in the future. These issues are particularly salient given the long lead times involved in the development of major weapons systems, which means that by the time a weapon actually rolls off the production line the threat it was originally designed to respond to may well have changed or disappeared altogether—the example of the Typhoon noted in Case Study 23.1 being a case in point. Other issues concern the scale of the activity required before one can identify a reaction, the form in which a reaction occurs (quantitative, qualitative, like for like, like for unlike), and the extent to which broader factors such as strategic culture and economic constraints limiting the ability of governments to react need to be taken into account, or whether doing so essentially undermines the model itself.

Moreover, specific studies of the weapons-acquisition process tend to highlight the fact that strategic necessity may often be of marginal significance in the decision to procure specific weapons. For instance, Farrell has contrasted the concern over micro-wastage in US weapons procurement (for example, political controversies over the excessive cost of basic equipment such as hammers or toilet seats) with the macro-wastage that arises from spending on billion dollar weapons systems that are not actually needed (Farrell 1997).

Domestic factor explanations

In these explanations emphasis is placed on the idea of a domestic arms dynamic that, to varying degrees, is self-generating and not strongly linked to the external actions of other states. Domestic factor explanations can be broadly subdivided into four types: bureaucratic/organizational explanations, political explanations, economic explanations, and military–industrial complex perspectives. Bureaucratic or organizational explanations emphasize the idea that defence-procurement decisions can be understood either as the outcome of bureaucratic politics—bargaining between different sets of policy actors—or as a reflection of particular organizational cultures, such as the traditions and military doctrines of the armed services (Allison 1971; Farrell 1996, 1997).

Political explanations focus on the role that domestic political considerations may play in both defence budgeting and weapons acquisition. These can include a concern with the way public opinion influences defence spending (Hartley and Russet 1992) or, alternatively, with the way in which politicians may use increases in defence spending to garner political support (Nincic 1982: 32–3; Mayer 1991: 203–7). A common feature of political explanations focused on the USA emphasizes the way in which electoral funding from defence contractors has the potential to shape the attitudes of legislators towards budgeting and procurement decisions and/or the way electoral considerations lead members of Congress to promote weapons and defence contracts that will benefit their constituents irrespective of their merit (Stiles 1995: 74–6). This latter phenomenon is known as 'pork-barrel' politics, although there is evidence to suggest the phenomenon may be more apparent than real (Lindsay 1991; Mayer 1991).

Economic explanations can take a number of forms. First, some analyses emphasize the way in which increases in defence spending are sometimes used by governments to provide a boost to the economy in times of economic downturn or to protect jobs in particular regions or industrial sectors (Cooper 1997: 9–12). Second, it is argued that the need to maintain a viable defence industrial base can create a 'follow-on imperative' under which governments place orders simply to keep companies and skilled workers in being rather than as a function of any immediate military necessity. At its worst, according to Kaldor (1982), the follow-on imperative can combine with the innate conservatism of the military to produce successive incremental changes to existing major defence systems that result in 'baroque weapons'. Such weapons are hugely expensive, overly sophisticated to the point that their effectiveness in combat is debatable, frequently break down, and are ill suited to the real military needs of the armed forces. Third, Marxist analyses have argued that military expenditure and war production are intimately linked to the needs and nature of capitalism, either because spending on defence is necessary for the maintenance of capitalism as an economic system, or because it produces specifically capitalist forms of weaponry, or because it is linked to capitalist imperialism (Baran and Sweezy 1966; Shaw 1984; Stavrianakis 2005b).

Elements of the various domestic factor explanations—bureaucratic, political, economic—have often been combined in approaches that explain defence-equipment acquisition as a function of the military–industrial complex. Although the term was coined by President Eisenhower in his 1961 farewell speech, some of the key ideas underpinning the term had already been elaborated by C. Wright Mills in his book *The Power Elite*. For Mills (1956: 198) there was a coincidence of interest that existed between economic, political, and military actors, which had led to the creation of a permanent war economy in the USA and 'a nation whose elite and whose underlying population have accepted what can only be called a military definition of reality'. The notion of a military industrial complex or iron triangle (Adams 1982) was particularly popular in accounts of US defence procurement policy in the 1960s, 1970s, and early 1980s. However, whilst there is a significant body of work that utilizes the term with respect to both the USA (Lens 1970; Melman 1970; Stiles 1995) and other states (Ikegami-Andersson 1992; Conca 1997), there is little consensus on what groups form part of the complex, how powerful it is in relation to other groups in society, and how much cohesion it really has.

Nevertheless the concept has experienced something of a resurgence of late. For example, James Der Derian (2001) has produced a variant of it in his concept of a military–industrial–media–entertainment network, whilst others have attempted to rework it to take account of new mechanisms by which defence industrial interests are promoted. In the UK, for instance, Mayhew (2005) has highlighted the disproportionate influence of the defence industry on the numerous, and often unaccountable, task forces, policy review, and advisory groups established by the Blair government to advise on aspects of defence policy. Similarly, the influence of the defence industry in policy task forces established by the European Commission has been taken as evidence of an emerging EU military–industrial complex (Slijper 2005). It is also worth noting that a series of transnational mergers and other linkages amongst defence companies has led to debates about the globalization of the defence industry (Bitzinger 2003). For some, this may presage an era of global private arsenals: relatively few defence-industrial giants possessing near monopoly control over 'world weapons' sourced from a variety of countries (Markusen 1999).

Technological-imperative explanations

Technological imperative (TI) explanations can take a number of forms. One approach places particular emphasis on the way the predominance of military research and development activity—both at the domestic and the global level—creates an autonomous push for the continued development of weapons technology that is distinct from broader action–reaction and domestic–factor processes (Thee 1986). This also raises questions about the extent to which military research distorts the direction of the civilian economy (Buzan and Sen 1990). Other studies, however, are more sceptical about the extent to which technology or the influence of technologists is an independent force in the arms dynamic highlighting the way social forces, military culture, the direction of resources, and strategic goals have a significant influence in determining what technologies are taken up and in what ways (Mackenzie 1990).

A second and more contemporary way of understanding the idea of a technological imperative is to view military modernization as a process that is both fuelled and shaped by an underlying process of permanent technological change in the civil sector. This has become a particularly popular conception, given the way in which civil advances in electronics, computing, and IT are feeding into contemporary military technology, producing what some see as a revolution in military affairs (RMA) (see below). Whereas during the Cold War it was common to talk of 'spin-offs' from military technology to the civil sector, since the mid-1990s it has been more usual to see 'spin-ons' from civil technologies to the military sector.

It is also argued that the spread of specific Western military technologies (for example, the weapons system), underpinned by military aid, commercial sales, and military training programmes provided to allies, has produced a global military culture that has established the possession of capital-intensive high-tech weapons supported by professional armies as the norm. Not only does this underpin broader relations of dependency between developed-world suppliers and developing-world recipients, but it results in the acquisition of weapons that are inordinately expensive and that may actually be unsuitable for recipients (Wendt and Barnett 1993).

To the extent that states then attempt to establish the domestic production of defence goods in this context, it is also possible to describe a global military order or hierarchy of states (Krause 1992; Held et al. 1999: 87–148) of the sort that we outline below, where different states have attained different levels of production capability but where all are geared around essentially the same models (if not sophistication) of technology.

A related aspect of this debate is the idea that the traditional model of defence technology (dominant since the end of the Second World War), based around high-tech weapons systems and perpetual advances in capability, produces inexorable real-term rises in weapons costs. For some this is producing a form of **military Malthusianism**—in which there is a growing mismatch between the cost of weapons and the ability of national defence budgets to afford them. In this view, states are thus likely to be faced with either purchasing fewer weapons or cheaper versions of existing models, or opting out of the current global military culture (Scheetz 2004).

The symbolic meaning of weapons

The notion of a global military culture also highlights the way in which motivations for the acquisition of defence technology may have less to do with objective threats and the military application of technology and more to do with the meanings attached to such technology. Indeed, given the limits on most national defence budgets and the high cost of modern weaponry, it can be argued that, for most states in the international system, the conventional idea that arms, and even armed forces, are acquired to enable actors to fight independent wars is far from the reality. Thus, weapons and armed forces may more often be acquired for reasons of national prestige, as symbols of statehood, as both agents and symbols of modernization, as vehicles to cement alliances, or simply to act as trip-wires that signal a state of emergency to which others may be expected to respond.

Postmodernists take such ideas even further, arguing that the practice of foreign policy is not about responding to objective threats but about manufacturing an 'Other' against which an imagined political identity can be forged. In this context, the acquisition of armies and arms are both an outcome of this manufacturing of the other and part of a series of performative acts by which borders, identities, and difference are inscribed (Campbell 1998a).

Similarly, the decision to provide or prohibit the supply of weapons may be a function of the specific meaning attached to them. Thus, from this perspective what is interesting about the ban on the production and trade in landmines is not so much the arguments about how odious they may or may not be as weapons but how, within a few short years, a particular meaning came to be attached to them as odious weapons where no such meaning had previously existed. Similarly, Mutimer (2000) has highlighted how the language used to describe the transfer of conventional weapons ('defence trade', 'arms trade', and so on) invokes a commercial metaphor that is implicitly legitimizing even when it is deployed by critics decrying the activities of the 'merchants of death'.

KEY POINTS

- The notion of an 'arms dynamic' refers to the set of pressures that make actors acquire armed forces and adjust their quantity and quality.

- Action–reaction explanations of the arms dynamic explain defence-equipment acquisition as a response to the external actions of potential adversaries.

- Domestic-factor explanations emphasize the idea that the arms dynamic is primarily self-generating and is a function of bureaucratic, economic, or domestic political factors.

- Technological imperative explanations understand the arms dynamic either as a function of the disproportionate influence of military research and development (R&D) or as fuelled by perpetual modernization in the civil sector.

- Symbolic explanations suggest that both the acquisition and the prohibition of defence technology may be a function more of the meanings invested in weapons than of strategic necessity or any inherent qualities they may have.

Trends in defence expenditure

In this section of the chapter we first highlight key differences between the high-technology defence trade and the trade in low-technology equipment. We then outline the trends in defence expenditure, highlighting some of the major players and other states who illustrate key trends.

Within the defence market there is a clear distinction between the high-technology defence trade and the low-technology defence trade. The distinction is in terms of the suppliers, the recipients, the money involved, the attention paid to the deals, and the degree to which the trade is seen as political.

Somewhat counter-intuitively, the high-tech defence trade is increasingly depoliticized and seen primarily in terms of economics, whereas the supply of second-hand and low-tech weapons is often highly politicized, as these are the weapons that are being used in conflicts. This disparity is highlighted by the two examples of defence sales outlined in Case Studies 23.1 and 23.2.

One thing that both of the deals show is that there is over-supply in the defence trade, and this means that at the low-tech end weapons are cheap and plentiful, and at the high-tech end competition to make sales is intense. This leads analysts to characterize the market as a buyer's market.

Defence expenditure includes not only weapons and equipment but wages, training, pensions, and so on. Defence expenditure on equipment can be through either domestic procurement (that is, buying from a firm in your state) or international purchase.

The high point in global defence expenditures came in the mid-1980s during the Cold War, when significant percentages of gross domestic product (GDP) were channelled into defence spending. However, global defence expenditure is now on the

---

CASE STUDY 23.1

A high-technology sale

Key aspects of the high-tech defence trade can be illustrated by examining one big defence sale: the December 2005 announcement by BAE Systems and the British government of a deal to supply Saudi Arabia with the Eurofighter *Typhoon*. From this we can see the following.

● Defence sales are now discussed primarily in terms of economic and employment issues. There was no discussion of the impact of the sale on the military balance in the region, nor of the threat that these aircraft will guard against. This may be because the *Typhoon* is seen by some critics as unsuited to Saudi Arabia's defence needs. Indeed, the sale became politically controversial only once it was mixed with allegations of corruption linked to a previous sale to the Saudi regime (see below).

● So keen were the British to secure the deal that they have pledged that the first twenty-four aircraft will be drawn from the British Royal Air Force's production run of eighty-nine fighters. Thus, the Royal Saudi Air Force will get some of the fighters before the British do (Hoyle 2005).

● The deal has been valued at anything between £8 billion and £20 billion, depending on how many aircraft and what equipment the Saudis acquire (Hope 2005). It has been touted as securing 14,000 British jobs for a decade and will secure defence industry jobs throughout Europe.

● Upon news of the deal, BAE Systems shares increased 6 per cent in value (R. Smith 2005).

● Following past precedents, the Saudi government is expected to pay in a mix of cash and oil.

● In order to secure the deal both Prime Minister Blair and Defence Minister Reid visited Saudi Arabia and agreed a crucial memorandum of understanding, promising to 'establish a greater partnership in modernising the Saudi Arabian Armed Forces and developing close service-to-service contacts especially through joint training and exercises' (cited in *Guardian* 2005). Thus the British government's commitment was vital to making the deal.

● The Saudi government reportedly threatened to renege on the deal as part of a broader campaign to get the British to abandon an investigation by the Serious Fraud Office (SFO) of corrupt payments to Saudi officials on an earlier arms deal dating back to the 1980s. The investigation was eventually cancelled in December 2006 after sustained pressure on the SFO by a range of government officials. Various reasons were cited for abandoning the investigation, including limited prospects of a successful prosecution and the need to maintain intelligence cooperation with the Saudis. However, many reports also emphasized the need to protect British defence jobs as a key factor determining government pressure on the SFO.

● Although this has been spun as a British deal, the *Typhoon* is made by a consortium of BAE Systems, the European aerospace group EADS, and Italian Alenia Aerospazio.

● BAE Systems will be involved in a number of offset deals, whereby the cost of the purchase is offset by investment in the Saudi economy. Saudi Arabia routinely asks for 30 per cent offsets into commercially viable businesses on all defence sales. This deal includes defence-technology transfers and establishing defence facilities in the country (Hoyle 2005). Past offset deals between BAE Systems' predecessor British Aerospace and the Saudi Arabian government included education and training, joint ventures such as that to establish the pharmaceutical firm Glaxo Saudi Arabia (*Gulf Industry* 2004), and one to produce polymers for the paint and adhesives market (British Offset). These offsets were designed to diversify the Saudi economy, but the track record is of significant underperformance.

---

rise again and is estimated to have been $1,339 billion in 2007, representing a 45 per cent increase in real terms since 1998 and amounting to 2.5 per cent of world GDP and $202 per capita (SIPRI 2008a: 175). The main trends in defence expenditure that can be discerned here are as follows (see also Figure 23.1).

United States military expenditure is higher, in real terms, in the late 2000s than at any time since the end of the Second World War, although the growth of the US economy means that expenditure as a share of both GDP and total US government outlays is still relatively low. The sheer size of the US defence budget means that in 2008 it accounted for 48 per cent of global defence expenditure (Hellman and Sharp 2008).

In the case of the *USSR/Russia*, the end of the Cold War and the collapse of the economy meant defence expenditures were dramatically decreased, at great cost

---

> ### CASE STUDY 23.2
>
> #### A low-technology sale
>
> In 1994 war was raging in the former Yugoslavia and the position of the Muslim-led government of Bosnia-Hercegovina looked particularly dire. The United Nations had imposed an arms embargo on the region intended to stop the fighting, but it had the counter-productive effect of giving an advantage to Serb forces that had access to the defence industries of the former Yugoslavia.
>
> There was some pressure from the US Congress to lift the embargo, but British Foreign Secretary Douglas Hurd said he did not want to 'level the killing field' (Sims 2001), and the US government was concerned about the precedent that unilaterally breaching the embargo would have on their attempts to keep United Nations' sanctions on Iraq. President Clinton therefore declined to act.
>
> However, the Croatian government (which had recently made peace with Bosnia) secretly approached the Clinton administration and asked if the USA would object if it created an arms pipeline to Bosnia (*Newshour* 1996). The administration replied that it neither approved nor objected to that, tacitly giving Croatia the go-ahead.
>
> The weapons came from Iran—via Turkey and Croatia—to Bosnia and involved cooperation from sub-state Islamist groups such as the Afghan Mojahedin and pro-Iran Hezbullah to get the arms into the country and to the Bosnians (Wiebes 2003).
>
> - The weapons were small arms, anti-tank weapons, surface-to-surface missiles, and mortars. Many tons of the weapons were transferred at relatively low cost.
>
> - Part of the reason for the large shipments was that Croatia imposed a high 'transit tax' on all the weapons, creaming off between 20 and 50 per cent of every shipment (Aldrich 2002).
>
> - The deal was financed by Saudi Arabia.
>
> - The weapons deals were seen as providing a political entrée into Bosnia for Iran. Subsequently the Clinton administration was heavily criticized by its Republican opponents for tacitly approving the deal, as it allowed Islamists to establish a foothold in Bosnia, where they trained and fought beside the Bosnian Muslims (Cox 1996).
>
> - Whilst the USA was involved in arming the Bosnians, Ukraine, Greece, and Israel were arming the Bosnian Serbs.
>
> This then was a highly political arms transfer, with minimal economic significance, but that was justified on the grounds that it helped ensure the survival of the Bosnian government and led the way to the Dayton Peace Accord of 1995.

to the traditionally cosseted defence industrial complex. Since 1998 growth in oil revenue has permitted a 160 per cent increase in military expenditure.

In the period from 1998 to 2007 *China's* military expenditure experienced a real terms increase of 202 per cent (SIPRI 2008a: 195). Nevertheless, the data in Table 23.1 might be understated for a number of reasons. The first is the current undervaluation of the Chinese currency, the renminbi. Second is that the cost of living is cheap in China (though rising), so pensions, wages, and so on are relatively low. Third is that the People's Liberation Army is a major entrepreneur within the economy and earns money that goes into defence spending as well as being engaged in arms production that is not covered in national defence expenditure statistics.

Britain and France still invest major resources in their militaries. Despite significant pressure to shift spending into social programmes, both regard themselves as significant military players and have sought efficiency savings and economies of scale through joint purchases rather than contemplating large cuts in defence spending. British defence spending has been rising because of operations such as Sierra Leone, Afghanistan (where it assumed control of the ISAF (International Security Assistance Force) in 2006), and Iraq. Nevertheless, there is increasing discussion of British military 'overstretch', primarily in terms of personnel.

A panel reported to the French Defence Minister in 2005 that all EU spending on military hardware is equal to a third of the USA's equipment budget,

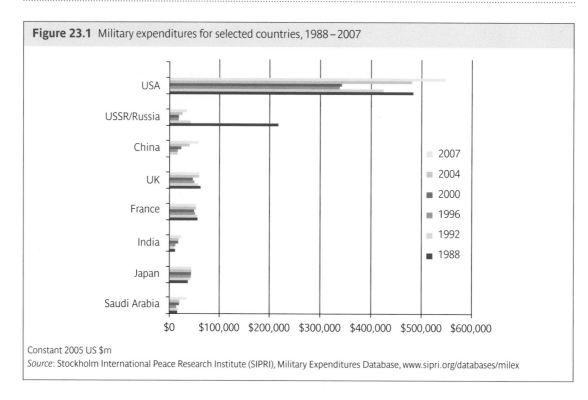

Figure 23.1 Military expenditures for selected countries, 1988–2007

Legend: 2007, 2004, 2000, 1996, 1992, 1988

X-axis: $0, $100,000, $200,000, $300,000, $400,000, $500,000, $600,000

Countries: USA, USSR/Russia, China, UK, France, India, Japan, Saudi Arabia

Constant 2005 US $m

Source: Stockholm International Peace Research Institute (SIPRI), Military Expenditures Database, www.sipri.org/databases/milex

while R&D spending across the whole EU is around one-fifth of US expenditure, suggesting an ever-widening technology gap between the USA and Europe with implications for alliance operations and the future of European defence sales (Anderson 2005).

Japan has surprisingly significant and steady levels of defence spending, despite a constitution that limits its military forces to a self-defence role. Japan's military spending did not diminish with the end of the Cold War, in large part because its major concern is China, whose spending has been rising.

India's military expenditure has risen since the end of the Cold War, when it lost the support of its traditional ally USSR/Russia (including subsidized defence sales) and had to prepare to protect itself alone. India perceives major (conventional and nuclear) threats from China and Pakistan and is fighting an insurgency against Pakistani-supported militants in Kashmir.

Saudi Arabia is a puzzle, as it has relatively high levels of military expenditure but does not have a well-regarded defence capability. The answer is that Saudi Arabia uses its military expenditure to buy allies and mutual defence agreements; it needs a less able force of its own if it knows that the USA, France, and Britain (its major defence suppliers) will come to its aid if it is threatened. Nevertheless, expenditure has risen by 60 per cent in real terms since 2004 (see Table 23.1), contributing to a 62 per cent real-terms increase in Middle East defence expenditure between 1998 and 2007 (SIPRI 2008a: 202).

A number of the countries we have considered here are also significant defence-equipment producers and exporters. Every unit that they sell abroad gives them a lower unit price on military equipment that they buy from their defence industries. This makes competition for all sales significant and for big defence contracts very intense. Indeed, the variety of subsidies, offset, and financing deals now offered by exporters to secure deals has led critics to suggest that, despite the huge sums involved, the economic benefits of defence sales to the economies of major exporters may actually be negligible or even non-existent (Hartung 1996; Ingram and Davis 2001).

Table 23.1 Selected suppliers and their three largest recipients, 1985–9

Supplier	Rank	Value US $m (at constant 1990 prices)	Global market share (%)	No. of recipients	Top three recipients
USSR	1	69,289	37	42	India (20%)
					Iraq (14%)
					Syria (9%)
USA	2	56,465	30	87	Japan (16%)
					South Korea (9%)
					Spain (7%)
France	3	12,332	7	75	Saudi Arabia (20%)
					India (11%)
					Iraq (11%)
China	4	10,131	5	21	Iraq (29%)
					Saudi Arabia (17%)
					Iran (16%)
UK	5	9,512	5	60	Saudi Arabia (21%)
					India (20%)
					USA (6%)
Germany	6	6,684	4	46	Turkey (22%)
					Argentina (11%)
					Netherlands (10%)
Others		22,087	12		
Total		186,501	100		

Note: Figures may not add up owing to the conventions of rounding.
Source: Stockholm International Peace Research Institute (SIPRI), Arms Transfers Database, www.sipri.org/databases/armstransfers

Suppliers and recipients in the defence market

With the end of the Cold War, defence sales went down significantly and began to climb again consistently only in 2003 (see Figure 23.2).

In order to categorize suppliers we use the notion of 'tiers' in the defence trade developed by Keith Krause (1992). The first-tier suppliers are at the highest levels of technological sophistication across the entire range of defence production. Second-tier suppliers have some R&D capabilities and some areas of innovation, but the majority of their defence products are below the cutting edge. Third-tier suppliers show little technological sophistication and often do not progress much beyond slightly modifying products made under licence. All the figures listed in Think Point 23.1 are from the Stockholm International Peace Research Institute (SIPRI) website and are expressed in constant 1990 dollars (which means that the figures are comparable). Although more than 100 countries are involved in the defence trade, the sales of the USA, Russia, France, Germany, and the UK combined accounted

Table 23.2 Selected suppliers and their three largest recipients, 2003–7

Supplier	Rank	Value US $m (at constant 1990 prices)	Global market share (%)	Total No. of recipients	Top three recipients
USA	1	34,499	31	71	South Korea (12%) Israel (12%) UAE (9%)
Russia	2	28,382	26	45	China (45%) India (22%) Venezuela (5%)
Germany	3	10,889	10	49	Turkey (15%) Greece (14%) South Africa (12%)
France	4	9,544	9	43	UAE (41%) Greece (12%) Saudi Arabia (9%)
UK	5	4,766	4	38	USA (17%) Romania (9%) Chile (9%)
China	9	2,057	2	25	Pakistan (30%) Iran (23%) Bangladesh (11%)
Others		21,391	19		
Total		111,528	100		

Note: Figures may not add up owing to the conventions of rounding.
Source: Stockholm International Peace Research Institute (SIPRI), Arms Transfers Database, www.sipri.org/databases/armstransfers

---

THINK POINT 23.1

Suppliers of weapons

FIRST-TIER SUPPLIERS

USA

The USA accounted for almost a third of global defence sales in the five years to 2007, with exports amounting to $34,499 million, making it the top supplier in the world—a status it has held consistently since the end of the Cold War.

US companies dominate the top 100 defence firms, and account for 63 per cent of the combined sales of the top 100 firms in 2006 (SIPRI 2008a: ch. 6).

Russia

Russia accounted for 26 per cent of global defence sales between 2003 and 2007.

Although Russia has retained its position as the world's second largest exporter, its future sales are not assured, as it did not invest sufficiently in new weapons systems during the 1990s and it is losing market share to the USA (in the high-technology realm) and to plucky challengers such as Ukraine (in the low-technology realm).

SECOND-TIER SUPPLIERS

Germany, France, and the UK

Germany was ranked third in the 2003–7 period, France fourth, and the UK fifth. Their combined sales accounted for 23 per cent of world exports.

These suppliers are fighting hard to maintain their shares of the defence trade. This means competing against, teaming with, and trying to sell to the US—which is actually the most lucrative defence market in terms of buying power.

THIRD-TIER SUPPLIERS

Israel

Israel was ranked twelfth in the list of major defence equipment exporters for 2003–7 with sales of $1,635 million, some 1.5 per cent of the global market.

Sales are considered vital for Israel, which has pursued a 'niche' strategy, leading the development of Unmanned Aerial Vehicles (UAVs) and keeping a healthy portion of that market.

South Korea

South Korea was ranked twentieth in 2005 and sixteenth in 2006.

Despite the state of the market, South Korea wants to become a major supplier in order to reduce its dependence on defence purchases from abroad. Since the 1990s, South Korea has encountered both technological and political barriers to progress but continues to expand its defence industrial base, most recently moving into space research.

China

From being ranked as the fourth largest exporter in the late 1980s, China was ranked ninth in the 2003–7 period, with just 2 per cent of market share.

Technologically China is in the third tier, but sells significant amounts of defence goods abroad and is the only state in this tier manufacturing land, sea, and air systems.

Chile

Chile was no longer in the top fifty-five suppliers in 2006.

Chile is facing market exit, because of fierce competition in the third tier.

Brazil

Brazil came thirty-first in the supplier rankings for the 2003–7 period, with sales of $110 million. .

Brazil is struggling to maintain its share of the market, aided by the firm Embraer, which has a presence in both the civil and defence sectors.

MARKET ENTRANTS

Ukraine

Ukraine's defence sales amounted to $1,731 million for the 2003–7 period, making it the eleventh largest supplier of defence equipment.

This is an impressive performance for a new supplier, but is based on it selling old Soviet weapons and newly produced Soviet-era designs. Ukraine is competing directly with Russia and winning sales by selling more cheaply.

Non-State Actors

Particularly at the low-tech end of the trade, states are no longer the only sources of supply. Arms traders, brokers, firms acting independently (sometimes legally, sometimes not), private security companies, and even individuals selling things on E-Bay are some of the alternative sources of supply. These suppliers have grown in response to the imposition of arms embargoes by the United Nations, and are meeting the demand for illicit weapons.

---

for 80 per cent of major conventional weapons exports during the period 2003–7.

To consider recipients briefly, there have been important structural changes that are affecting the demand for major weapons, with old Cold War protagonists for the most part scaling back high-technology procurement (exceptions being areas of lingering tension such as the Korean Peninsula). The reality is that there are fewer major recipients in the market than there are suppliers. In this buyer's market recipients are able to play suppliers off against each other to extract the best possible deals. The top five recipients of defence equipment are detailed in Table 23.3.

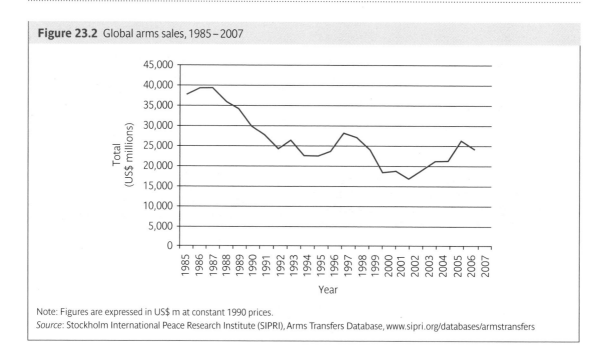

Figure 23.2 Global arms sales, 1985–2007

Note: Figures are expressed in US$ m at constant 1990 prices.

Source: Stockholm International Peace Research Institute (SIPRI), Arms Transfers Database, www.sipri.org/databases/armstransfers

The most important regional defence markets are East Asia and the Middle East. The rise in importance of non-state recipients should also be considered. Sales opportunities previously thought too risky because of the legal and ethical difficulties involved are now being considered and even actively pursued by some suppliers. Moreover, the use of middlemen and brokers has allowed some states to benefit from making transfers to non-state actors such as terrorist groups, without having to pay any direct political price.

Table 23.3 Top five recipients of defence equipment, 2003–7

Recipient	Value of defence imports (US$ million)	Percentage of global defence imports
China	13,463	12
India	9,105	8
UAE	7,467	7
Greece	7,170	6
South Korea	5,536	5
Others	51,919	62
Total	111,528	100

Source: SIPRI (2008b).

The content of the contemporary defence trade

The twenty-first century is witnessing changes in the substance of the defence trade, with moves away from the supply of complete major weapons platforms (aircraft, ships, and so on). For example, in 1998 the premier defence supplier, the USA, transferred 180 aircraft around the world. By 2004 the number was down to 51. The trade is moving towards the purchase of upgrades, dual-use technologies, communications equipment, and spare parts. Indeed, a lot of what counts as the high-tech defence trade does not look anything like a weapon—hence our abandonment of the term 'arms trade'. Amongst the key trends in the trade are the following.

Modernization of platforms and upgrades. In an era of constrained procurement budgets, the emphasis is on various forms of **force multipliers** to be incorporated into existing platforms (for example, new engines, weapons pods), as opposed to new purchases. Indigenous modernization is also occurring, as recipient states apply their ingenuity to improving weapons they bought. Upgrades offer the opportunity to hybridize weapons systems: marrying Western technologies to eastern platforms—or vice versa. For

example, Israeli and Russian cooperation to upgrade MiG fighters offers the opportunity to install advanced Western avionics (some of which were developed for the Lavi fighter) into the solid platforms of the Soviet era (Sher 1995: 40).

Retro-fitting. The increasing trade in upgrades involves the retro-fitting of sophisticated new technologies to existing systems. The move to modular weapons systems means that retro-fitting and upgrading are increasingly practised and can extend the life of a basic platform significantly.

Re-transfers. There is an increasing trade in re-transfers (second-hand sales). Weapons and weapons platforms that are surplus to requirements are sold on rather than stored or scrapped (*Flight International* 1994; Tusa 1994). They are a challenge to new sales, as they tend to be cut price and are often fairly sophisticated technologies.

Dual-use technologies. A major trend in the international market is towards the supply of technologies, whose spread is more difficult to control. Part of this greater trade is accounted for in **dual-use technologies**—those with both legitimate civil and military applications. For example, computers and software that can coordinate air-traffic control can also coordinate battlefield operations or missile attacks. There is increased pressure within states to loosen the controls over dual-use exports—on the grounds that, in the aftermath of the Cold War, the security risks attached to such sales are much lower.

The trade in dual-use goods brings into the market a whole stratum of new firms and (possibly) states. In addition to the deliberate marketing of goods as militarily useful, there is an increasing range of goods not marketed with military intent, but having latent military applicability. One of the more extreme examples of latent military applicability was the Sony PlayStation2. According to Japanese trade officials, these video game consoles contain a graphics processing facility fast enough to help guide some types of missile towards their target (McCurry 2000).

Systems Integration. With the hybridization of weapons systems comes the birth of a new type of defence sale: systems integration to make the different systems work together. The work requires highly skilled personnel. Israel has made good inroads into this area of the market.

Training. Countries like India and Israel are marketing their ability to train fighter pilots—in India's case, in response to the perceived inadequacy of Russian support services. Israel trained fifteen Ugandan pilots to fly the three MiG-21 fighters the state acquired in 1998. Israel Aircraft Industries upgraded the fighters, and the pilots spent a year in Tel Aviv undergoing training (*Xinuha* 2000). Corporate giants such as SAIC, BDM, and its subsidiary Vinnell Corporation are primarily high-technology suppliers but have diversified into military training. They are contracted by the Saudi Arabian government to upgrade and train its armed forces in the use of mainly US weaponry (Shearer 1999: 84).

People. The transfers of personnel are taken to higher levels in the Middle East, where several countries employ foreign military specialists not just to maintain and repair equipment, but actually to use it. For example, Saudi Arabia has for many years

employed foreign nationals such as Pakistanis (on leave from their national armed forces) to fly their fighter planes. This enables the Pakistanis to maintain a large, well-trained reserve force without incurring massive costs (Lock 1998). For Saudi Arabia, this helps to fill a skills and employment gap.

Software and Software Source Codes. Modern weapons increasingly rely on sophisticated software. Of fundamental importance are the software source codes. Simply put: 'These codes provide a blueprint of how a specific system's software works and are at the heart of nearly all modern weaponry. The codes are the keys to understanding everything about a weapon, including its avionics, communications and guidance system' (*Defense News* 1999: 56).

In some instances these valuable commodities are 'black boxed' by a supplier to ensure that, although the systems work, the technology is protected and cannot be reverse engineered. However, in a buyer's defence market, the would-be recipients often demand access to software source codes as the price for securing the deal.

Leasing. States do not always purchase weapons nowadays; there are also attractive leasing deals on offer. For example, in 2001 Hungary struck a deal to lease 14 *Gripen* fighters from the Swedish Air Force and in 2004 the Czech Republic struck a similar leasing deal (*Air Force Technology* 2006).

Revolution in Military Affairs (RMA). This is the term given to a basket of military technologies and approaches to warfare that has the potential to 'transform' the nature of military operations. The introduction of precision-guided munitions and 'smart' weapons has resulted in conventional weapons achieving previously unimaginable levels of lethality and accuracy. There have also been improvements in materials, aircraft design, and military avionics, which led to the emergence of a new generation of 'stealthy' aircraft and ships. The advantage—and the problem—of stealth is that it reintroduces the possibility of surprise attack. Equally important have been technological improvements in **stand-off missiles**— that is, missiles launched from weapons platforms miles outside the theatre of operation, which are then guided to a distant target.

Developments on the non-weapons side of the equation include electronic warfare technologies, sensors, radars, and night-vision equipment. These technologies act as **force multipliers** through permitting the real-time relay of vital information to the battlefield and by allowing all-weather and night use of military hardware.

One interesting aspect of the RMA is the increased use of unmanned aircraft. These unmanned aerial vehicles (UAVs) were initially thought of in terms of reconnaissance missions, but since 2001 they have been deployed in a variety of lethal missions, including remote attacks in Yemen, Afghanistan, Pakistan, and elsewhere.

Taken together, these technological trends have the potential to revolutionize the battlefield. To date the only country able to reap the technological advantage has been the United States. The US technological edge—amply demonstrated by the Gulf Wars of 1991 and 2003—has, however, not proved so useful in the counter-insurgency campaigns in Iraq and Afghanistan, though there is increasing adaptation of some of these technologies for urban guerrilla warfare.

Small Arms and Light Weapons (SALW). A more instantly recognized form of defence trade is in SALW, where business has been facilitated by an abundance of supplies from excess post-Cold War stocks, lower transport costs as a consequence of globalization, sustained demand from a number of internal conflicts that have occurred since the end of the Cold War and the reality of porous borders. With respect to the latter, for instance, one study identified 21 known arms-trafficking routes into Colombia from Venezuela, 26 from Ecuador, 37 from Panama, and 14 from Brazil (Cragin and Hoffman 2003).

KEY POINTS

- The post-Cold War defence export market has been characterized by a move away from the supply of complete weapons systems to the provision of upgrades, dual-use technologies, communications equipment, and spare parts.

- The term 'revolution in military affairs' is often used to describe the way in which simultaneous advances in a number of technologies are deemed to be radically transforming, or have the potential to transform, the way military operations are conducted.

Conclusion

Like all issues in international relations, the main focus of academic engagement with the defence trade has shifted in response to changes in the nature of global politics. Thus, in the Cold War, the concern was to investigate the ways in which defence expenditure, weapons acquisition, and defence sales were determined by superpower rivalry via the logic of action–reaction or, alternatively, to investigate how superpower rivalry was actually driven by the institutionalization of the military–industrial complex and the mechanisms of military aid. The end of the Cold War, however, saw a relative decline in the study of such factors and a turn to research on those aspects of the defence trade that seemed more germane to the political concerns of the day—at the higher end of the defence trade this has been reflected in a concern with the mechanisms of nuclear proliferation, whilst, at the lower end of the trade, research and policy activity has focused on the role played by the trade in small arms in sustaining the 'new wars' of the post-Cold War. As we have already noted, this both reflected and reinforced the fact that the conventional trade in major weapons has become profoundly depoliticized.

Interestingly, however, the war on terror and its various corollaries—for example, the huge increase in US defence expenditure and (at least in some cases) a renewed emphasis on the politics as well as the economics of defence sales and military aid—appears to be producing something of a renewed concern with issues such as the relationship between an apparent threat (now understood as global terrorism) and defence spending, or with the existence, role, and nature of a putative military–industrial (media-entertainment) complex. Nevertheless, this has yet to translate into solid academic work on these issues.

In addition some areas of study that were only beginning to emerge towards the end of the Cold War have become far more consolidated—in particular the challenge of fighting a stateless and globally networked enemy, combined with the opportunities presented by an apparent RMA, has spurred academic and policy engagement with the idea of network-centric warfare and the implications this is having, and will have, for our way of doing war. These are interesting and important issues for a new generation of security analysts to explore.

? QUESTIONS

1. Which model of the arms dynamic is more convincing and why?

2. Does the notion of a military–industrial complex still have relevance, given the globalization of the defence industry and the growing emphasis on dual-use technologies?

3. To what extent does the symbolic meaning attached to defence technology determine both supply and demand in the defence trade?

4. 'Arms embargoes simply create new market opportunities for illicit weapons dealers.' Discuss.

5. To what extent has the content of the defence trade changed and what does this imply for attempts at regulation?

6. Is it accurate for commentators to refer to a revolution in military affairs, and if so, what are its likely consequences?

7. To what extent has the transfer of major conventional weapons been depoliticized in the post-Cold War era?

8. What are the differences between the licit and illicit trade in small arms?

9. Defence exports are often justified on the basis of the economic benefits they provide to the economies of suppliers. What is the evidence to support this contention?

10. Evaluate the arguments for and against the UK's sale of the Eurofighter *Typhoon* to Saudi Arabia.

FURTHER READING

▪ Bitzinger, Richard A. (2003), *Towards a Brave New Arms Industry?* Adelphi Paper 356, London: International Institute for Strategic Studies. An excellent survey of what Bitzinger describes as the 'hub and spoke model' of arms industry globalization.

▪ Buzan, Barry, and Herring, Eric (1998), *The Arms Dynamic in World Politics,* London: Lynne Rienner. A revised (and improved) follow-up to Buzan's *Introduction to Strategic Studies*, this is essential reading for students wishing to understand the various debates on the arms trade and the methods for controlling it.

■ Der Derian, James (2001), *Virtuous War: Mapping the Military–Industrial–Media–Entertainment Network,* Boulder, Co: Westview. At its worst, this book lapses into self-indulgent travelogue, but it nevertheless manages to reinvent the notion of the military industrial complex for the post-Cold War era and contains important insights into the relationship between modern military technology, the media, and the nature of modern warfare.

■ Farrell, Theo (1997), *Weapons Without a Cause: The Politics of Weapons Acquisition in the United States,* London: Macmillan. Although somewhat dated now, this nevertheless remains an excellent account of the factors that influence procurement decisions, particularly in the USA.

■ Hammond, Grant T. (1993), *Plowshares into Swords: Arms Races in International Politics, 1840–1991,* Colombia, SC: University of South Carolina Press. An impressive attempt to refine the concept of arms racing based on a number of case studies dating back to the nineteenth century.

■ Krause, Keith (1992), *Arms and the State: Patterns of Military Production and Trade,* Cambridge: Cambridge University Press. This book provides a thorough analysis of the history and structure of the arms trade.

■ Markusen, Ann (1999), 'The Rise of World Weapons', *Foreign Policy, 114* (Spring): 40–51. This is a provocative analysis of the challenges implied by the globalization of the defence industry.

■ Mutimer, David (2000), *The Weapons State: Proliferation and the Framing of Security,* Boulder, CO: Lynne Rienner. This is the definitive postmodern take on both nuclear proliferation and the defence trade more generally.

■ Smith, Ron (2009), *Military Economics: The Interaction of Power and Money,* Palgrave Macmillan. An accessible introduction to the field of defence economics geared towards undergraduates and non-specialists alike.

There are two very good yearbooks on aspects of the defence trade:

■ The Stockholm International Peace Research Institute (SIPRI) publishes *The SIPRI Yearbook: Armaments, Disarmament and International Security* (Oxford: Oxford University Press). This contains extensive quantitative data on military expenditure and the defence trade. It also has excellent analytical essays on features of the trade such as the activities of key defence firms.

■ The Small Arms Survey publishes an annual *Small Arms Survey* (Oxford: Oxford University Press) and is a major attempt to get over the problem of lack of information about the trade in SALW.

There are a number of defence magazines that provide good coverage of the trade.

■ Defense News is published in the USA and comes out weekly. *Jane's Defence Weekly* is published in the UK. Both have excellent coverage of the market. Their websites are also provide vital insights into the defence trade.

IMPORTANT WEBSITES

● http://www.sipri.org   The SIPRI website, an excellent source of information on global military expenditures.

● http://www.smallarmssurvey.org   The Small Arms Survey, the key source on SALW issues.

● http://www.fas.org/   The Federation of American Scientists provides good coverage of all aspects of the defence trade as well as web links to relevant reports. It also publishes an annual newsletter, *Arms Sales Monitor*.

● http://www.basicint.org   The British American Security Information Council engages with a wide range of defence-related issues from nuclear weapons to the small arms trade.

- http://www.cdi.org/index.cfm   The Centre for Defense Information covers a wide range of defence-related topics, including the arms trade and small arms.

- http://www.worldpolicy.org/projects/arms/index.html The Arms Trade Resource Centre of the World Policy Institute is a particularly useful resource for information on the US defence trade.

 Visit the Online Resource Centre that accompanies this book for lots of interesting additional material: www.oxfordtextbooks.co.uk/orc/collins2e/

24

Health and Security

STEFAN ELBE

Contents

- Introduction
- Health and human security
- Health and national security
- Health and bio-security
- Conclusion

Reader's Guide

Three different links between health issues and security concerns are increasingly drawn by policy-makers and scholars. First, health and security have become more closely associated within the framework of *human* security. That framework draws attention to a range of diseases, such as HIV/AIDS, malaria, and tuberculosis, that are endemic in the low-income countries and that continue to cause millions of deaths annually. Second, some newly emerging infectious diseases, such as SARS and avian flu, are also being considered as threats to the national security of several states. Given the contemporary speed and rate of international travel, even states with wide-ranging public health infrastructures feel vulnerable to new infectious diseases that may initially emerge outside their borders. Finally, linkages have also been established between health and security within the context of international efforts to combat terrorism, especially in terms of preparing for the spectre of a terrorist attack using a disease-causing biological agent such as anthrax, smallpox, or plague. The chapter concludes by contrasting two different ways in which this emerging health – security nexus can be conceptualized.

Introduction

Health issues are back on the international agenda—and not just as a matter of low politics. They are 'back' in the sense that they had already become the subject of international diplomacy as early as 1851, when delegates of the first International Sanitary Conference gathered in Paris to consider joint responses to the cholera epidemics that had overrun the European continent in the first half of the nineteenth century. Yet during the twentieth century the pertinence of controlling potentially pandemic microbes was gradually overshadowed by the more pressing concerns of avoiding the spectre of renewed wars, and the ever-present potential for a nuclear confrontation. The twentieth century's deep addiction to war, coupled with its important advances in medicine, reinforced the view in the West that the world was moving in a direction in which infectious diseases would eventually be controlled—exemplified so quintessentially by the confident declaration made in 1948 by US Secretary of State George Marshall that the conquest of all infectious diseases was imminent. This confidence has been profoundly shaken.

At the outset of the twenty-first century there is once again considerable international anxiety about a host of potentially lethal 'rogue' viruses circulating the planet—including relatively new ones such as H1N1 swine flu, the highly pathogenic strand of avian influenza and the corona virus responsible for Severe Acute Respiratory Syndrome (SARS). Other infectious diseases such as HIV/AIDS, tuberculosis, and malaria remain endemic in many developing countries and have made devastating comebacks—often in drug-resistant forms. At the same time, states in the West and elsewhere remain apprehensive about the consequences of a potential terrorist attack using biological weapons. Collectively, these concerns have begun to displace the optimism of the twentieth century, giving way to a renewed sense of unease. Nothing reflects this more poignantly than the fact that the responses to these health issues are increasingly articulated in the language of security.

Health and human security

The framework of human security was pioneered by the United Nations Development Program in its 1994 *Human Development Report* and seeks to redress the perceived imbalance in security thinking that predominated during past decades. By developing a 'people-centric' account of security revolving around the needs and welfare of ordinary individuals, rather than predominantly around the protection of sovereign states, human-security activists wish to challenge the narrow twentieth-century equation of security with the absence of armed conflict between states. Specifically, the *Human Development Report* outlined seven areas or components of human security that policy-makers should henceforth devote greater political attention and capital to: economic security (poverty, homelessness), food security (famine and hunger), health security (disease, inadequate health care), environmental security (ecological degradation, pollution, natural disasters), personal security (physical violence, crime, traffic accidents), community security (oppression, discrimination), and political security (repression, torture, disappearance, human rights violations) (UNDP 1994: 24–5). As part of this broader approach to security, the report also did not fail to highlight the considerable burden that infectious diseases continue to pose in the developing world—including HIV/AIDS, tuberculosis, and malaria. It is estimated that these three diseases alone cause between four and five million people to die every year.

Whilst the initial *Human Development Report* did not define the notion of 'health security' in greater detail, the subsequent 2003 report of the Commission on Human Security—*Human Security Now*—filled this gap by devoting an entire chapter to 'health security'. 'Good health', the report (Commission on Human Security 2003: 96) argued, 'is both essential and instrumental to achieving human security'. It is essential in the sense that human security is ultimately about protecting lives, and this is not possible to achieve without also reducing the scale of a range of lethal diseases. The report argued further that health is also 'instrumental' for human security because it allows sick adults to resume work, helps secure the material well-being of families, allows children to stay in school, and so on. Endemic diseases are thus both *direct* threats to human security because they can cause death, and also broader, *indirect* threats to human security because, where the burden of disease is substantial, this has knock-on ramifications for several other dimensions of human security. These relationships can be illustrated very well in relation to challenges that the global AIDS pandemic poses for many developing countries.

'As a global issue', Peter Piot (2001) argued in his former capacity as director of the Joint United Nations Program on HIV/AIDS (UNAIDS), 'we must pay attention to AIDS as a threat to human security, and redouble our efforts against the epidemic and its impact'. UNAIDS is the specialized United Nations agency tasked with addressing the international spread of HIV/AIDS. Established in 1995, UNAIDS is located at the centre of a complex network of various United Nations programmes and affiliated organizations, including the World Health Organization and the World Bank. Its political objectives are to mobilize leadership for effective action against the spread of HIV/AIDS, to monitor and evaluate its spread, and to support an effective response. As such, UNAIDS also collates international statistics about the extent of the AIDS pandemic. It is actually very difficult to determine exactly how many

people are living with HIV/AIDS in the world and how many are dying from AIDS-related illnesses. Generating such data would not only be impossible in the light of immense financial and logistical constraints, but would also necessitate testing virtually every member of the human population for HIV—raising difficult ethical questions around compulsory testing. Nevertheless it is estimated by UNAIDS (2007) that around two million people die annually of AIDS-related illnesses, while a further 2.5 million people continue to become newly infected with the virus every year (see Table 24.1). Contrary to widespread belief, HIV/AIDS is not at all confined to sub-Saharan Africa. Every region of the world currently has a significant number of people living with HIV/AIDS.

Health security

Beyond this direct mortality, HIV/AIDS also has ramifications for a range of other elements of human security. In countries where **prevalence rates** are high, HIV/AIDS affects health security more generally by placing additional stresses on health-care facilities, which are frequently already stretched in the first place. A study of the impact of HIV/AIDS on the health sector in South Africa conducted in 2003 found that the AIDS epidemic is having several negative impacts. It is causing the loss of health-care workers and generating increased levels of absenteeism, with just under 16 per cent of the health-care workforce in the Free State, Mpumalanga, KwaZulu-Natal, and North West provinces being HIV-positive. It also found that the rise in the number of HIV/AIDS patients seeking clinical care had led to an increased workload for health-care staff, as well as lowering staff morale. With some 46.2 per cent of patients in public hospitals being HIV-positive, the study concluded that at times non-AIDS patients have even been 'crowded out' of the system in order to accommodate patients living with HIV/AIDS (Shisana et al. 2003). A study from Kenya based on

Table 24.1 Regional HIV and AIDS statistics, 2007

Region	Adults and children living with HIV/AIDS	Adults and children newly infected with HIV	Adult and child deaths due to AIDS
Sub-Saharan Africa	22.5 million	1.7 million	1.6 million
Middle East and North Africa	380,000	35,000	25,000
South and South-East Asia	4 million	340,000	270,000
East Asia	800,000	92,000	32,000
Oceania	75,000	14,000	1,200
Latin America	1.6 million	100,000	58,000
Caribbean	230,000	17,000	11,000
Eastern Europe and Central Asia	1.6 million	150,000	55,000
Western and Central Europe	760,000	31,000	12,000
North America	1.3 million	46,000	21,000
Total	33.2 million [30.6 million–36.1 million]	2.5 million [1.8 million–4.1 million]	2.1 million [1.9 million–2.4 million]

Source: UNAIDS (2007: 7).

a sample of hospitals detected similar trends, with an increase in AIDS-related admissions and 50 per cent of patients on medical wards living with HIV/AIDS. Focus-group discussions conducted in the context of the study also revealed that one of the reasons why the Kenyan health-care systems had such high levels of attrition, with scores of personnel leaving the sector, was a fear of becoming infected with HIV (in addition to high workloads, poor remuneration, and poor working conditions) (Cheluget et al. 2003). A study of the impact of Swaziland in turn estimates that up to 80 per cent of bed occupancy in the medical and paediatric wards is related to HIV/AIDS (Kober and van Damme 2006). The human-security ramifications of HIV/AIDS are therefore not confined to the direct mortality caused by the illness, but also result from the ripple effects of the disease through much wider social structures—including health-care systems.

Economic security

Defined as 'an assured basic income—usually from productive and remunerative work, or in the last resort from some publicly financed safety net' (UNDP 1994: 25)—economic security is another important component of human security affected by HIV/AIDS. Although only few have been conducted, those household studies carried out to date suggest the impact to be twofold. Households affected by HIV/AIDS are likely to experience a reduced earning capacity, as persons are unable to work, or are tied down to caring for the affected family member. A 2002 comparative study of rural and urban households in South Africa conducted by Booysen and Bachman (2002) showed that those households affected by HIV/AIDS have on average only 50–60 per cent of per-capita income of non-affected households. HIV/AIDS additionally generates new costs for treatment and, in the case of death, additional funeral expenditures, legal costs, medical bills, and so forth (Drimie 2003). Other studies carried out by the World Bank similarly suggest increased expenditure by these households on medical care and funerals, as well as a reduction in spending on non-food items (see Barnett and Whiteside 2006: 203–5). HIV/AIDS can thus have an additional impact on human security in that it can undermine the ability of individuals and households to ensure their economic security.

Food security

HIV/AIDS can also affect food security, defined as requiring 'that all people at all times have both physical and economic access to basic food. This requires not just enough food to go round. It requires that people have ready access to food' (UNDP 1994: 27). The crucial point here is that the physical availability of food is only part of the equation when it comes to food insecurity. Even when such food is physically available, people may still hunger and starve if they do not have access or entitlement to this food. During many famines, the problem is the lack of purchasing power and the poor distribution of food, rather than the absence of food itself. This distinction is crucial, because HIV/AIDS can generate food insecurities by skewing the access of certain individuals and groups to food. The negative impact of HIV/AIDS on food security has prompted the famine researcher Alex de Waal to advance a 'new-variant famine' thesis, which argues that 'AIDS attacks exactly those capacities that enable people to resist famine. AIDS kills young adults, especially women—the people whose labor is most needed' (de Waal 2002). A study carried out by the Food and Agriculture Organization of 1,889 rural households in northern Namibia, southern Zambia, and around Lake Victoria in Uganda found that households affected by HIV/AIDS, particularly if they are headed by women, are finding it increasingly difficult to ensure their food security (FAO 2003). A study of fifteen villages in three districts of Malawi

carried out by Shah et al. (2002) found that many households affected by HIV/AIDS experienced loss of labour (70 per cent), reported delays of agricultural work (45 per cent), leaving fields unattended (23 per cent), changing crop composition (26 per cent), but much of the impact depends on when the disease arrived (that is, pre- or post harvest), the existence of other stress factors, and the relative economic status of households. Although HIV/AIDS is, therefore, unlikely to create a 'supply-shock' in terms of food production in and of itself, HIV/AIDS can nevertheless have negative implications for households by interacting in complex ways with their ability to secure access to food (de Waal 2006: 89–92; Gillespie 2006).

In these ways the AIDS pandemic illustrates very clearly how widespread, lethal diseases not only represent direct threats to human security, but can also shape other components of human security—including health security, economic security, and food security. Taken in conjunction with the large number of lives the disease claims annually, many in fact consider HIV/AIDS to represent one of the world's most pressing contemporary human-security threats. It is precisely one of those crucial contemporary issues that the human security framework wishes to highlight and where its advocates would like to see increased international coordination in terms of scaling up the prevention, treatment, and care for people living with HIV/AIDS, as well as for people affected by other endemic diseases such as malaria and tuberculosis. This emphasis on health issues within the framework of human security renders the latter one of the principal sites in contemporary world politics where health issues are increasingly being discussed, deliberated, and responded to in the language of security—albeit in a context in which the meaning of security is itself significantly expanded and redefined. Considering health issues as threats to human security is, in the end, much more a case of definitional fiat, and of redefining security, than it is of making substantially novel empirical claims about the impact of these diseases in developing countries.

Health and national security

Links have also been drawn between health and national security. Here, too, the case of HIV/AIDS is instructive in that it shows how infectious diseases can simultaneously bear upon human security and national security concerns. Within the state-centric perspective of national security, HIV/AIDS has received further attention by policy-makers since the late 1990s, because it was feared that the disease could have a detrimental impact on the armed forces of the worst affected countries. Evidence about the impact of HIV/AIDS in the armed forces is very patchy and subject to considerable controversy. Yet there is some evidence that HIV/AIDS is posing considerable challenges to the operational efficiency of several armed forces (see Case Study 24.1).

The impact of HIV/AIDS on the armed forces can also have wider international ramifications, because armies with significant levels of HIV prevalence occasionally contribute to peacekeeping operations. Since the late 1990s HIV/AIDS has thus begun to pose additional logistical and political problems for such peacekeeping operations, as it becomes increasingly well known that some peacekeepers are at a special risk both of contracting and of spreading HIV when and where they are deployed (see Case Study 24.2). These impacts on the armed forces and on international peacekeeping operations give the AIDS pandemic an important national security dimension as well.

HIV/AIDS is not the only infectious disease that has been framed as such a national security concern.

Wealthy states in particular have begun to express much wider anxieties about how a range of new infectious diseases threaten their populations and economies in the twenty-first century. An influential report issued in 1992 by the Institute of Medicine in the United States entitled *Emerging Infections: Microbial Threats to Health in the United States* already warned that the emergence of the AIDS pandemic illustrated how 'some infectious diseases that now affect people in other parts of the world represent potential threats to the United States because of global interdependence, modern transportation, trade, and changing social and cultural patterns' (Lederberg et al. 1992: p. v). By the end of the decade, these anxieties had reached a sufficient level for parts of the US government to officially designate such infectious diseases as threats to national security. The United States National Intelligence Council, for example, produced an influential and widely cited National Intelligence Estimate entitled *The Global Infectious Disease Threat and its Implications for the United States*. The findings of the report, declassified in January 2000, confirmed many of these fears by pointing out that, since 1973, at least thirty previously unknown disease agents have been identified (including some for which there is no cure such as HIV, Ebola, Hepatitis C, and the Nipah virus). It also found that in this same period at least twenty older infectious diseases have re-emerged, frequently in drug resistant form—most notably amongst them tuberculosis, malaria, and cholera. The report

The South African National Defence Force (SANDF)

Information about the impact of HIV/AIDS on Africa's armed forces is extremely difficult to obtain because of its sensitive nature. Even in those militaries that test soldiers for HIV/AIDS, officials are extremely reluctant to make such information public, as it may well point to potential weaknesses in the armed forces. Over the past years some information has nevertheless begun to emerge about the ways in which HIV/AIDS has begun to affect the South African National Defence Force (SANDF).

South Africa is already home to the largest number of persons living with HIV/AIDS in Africa. The adult (aged 15–49) HIV prevalence rate among the civilian population is estimated by UNAIDS to be 21.5 per cent, and, according to the South African Department of Health, more than six million people have now been infected with HIV in the country. The South African National Defence Force (SANDF) claims that HIV prevalence in the armed forces is around 23 per cent, which is slightly higher than the civilian population and which amounts to roughly 16,000 soldiers. Many analysts believe that in reality this figure may be much higher, perhaps as high as 40 per cent, which would put the number closer to 28,000. Even the official figure is high enough, however, to prompt the United States and SANDF to set up a programme aimed at establishing the rate of HIV infection in the armed forces more conclusively and evaluating the effects of anti-retroviral treatments on SANDF. Because of human rights considerations, SANDF cannot force its soldiers to be tested, but SANDF has now set up a programme where soldiers can come forward voluntarily to be tested. Initially 1,089 soldiers came forward to be tested, of whom 947 (89 per cent) tested positive. The average age of those who tested positive was 34 years, and 60 per cent of them were married. Although this figure is not representative of SANDF as a whole (most of those who came forward to be tested probably suspected that they were HIV-positive already), it leaves no doubt that the issue of HIV/AIDS is rapidly becoming very serious for many armed forces in Africa.

In the light of these figures, senior officials in SANDF have expressed serious concern about the impact of HIV/AIDS on the military's combat readiness because of the high levels of absenteeism the illness induces. They estimate that a soldier in the early stages of illness will be absent on average 20 days a year, which rises to 45 days for soldiers displaying symptoms. Soldiers who have developed full-blown AIDS are estimated to be absent on average for a minimum of 120 days per year. SANDF believes that it will lose between 338,000 and 560,000 working days annually because of the illness. SANDF is also concerned with the fact that many of those most affected by HIV/AIDS in SANDF are in the age group of 23–32, which is the age group from which most of the operationally deployable soldiers, officers, non-commissioned officers, and highly skilled members of the armed forces are drawn. HIV/AIDS may thus hollow out this middle rank, creating gaps and shortfalls within the armed forces. This impact is all the more difficult because of South Africa's leadership role on the African continent and because the country wishes to play an expanding role in African peacekeeping operations, which it can only do with a healthy military.

---

concluded: 'New and re-emerging infectious diseases will pose a rising global health threat and will complicate US and global security over the next 20 years. These diseases will endanger US citizens at home and abroad, threaten US armed forces deployed overseas, and exacerbate social and political instability in key countries and regions in which the United States has significant interests' (National Intelligence Council 2000).

By their very nature infectious diseases lend themselves particularly well to such securitizations. They are usually caused by microbes that are imperceptible to the human eye. Consisting, in the case of viruses, merely of a piece of nucleic acid (DNA or RNA) wrapped in a thin coat of protein, they exist at the very margins of our conceptions of life. Human beings could be exposed to them at any time without knowing it, and yet suffer a quick and violent death not long thereafter. They are, in this respect, 'silent' and 'invisible' killers. Perhaps nothing is more frightful to many people than a lethal danger they have no way of detecting. Even the famous microbiologist Louis Pasteur, who explored the germ theory of disease, eventually developed an obsessive fear of microbes, refusing to shake hands with people, carefully wiping his plates before eating, and on more than one occasion even examining food served as dinner parties with his portable microscope. As in

---

CASE STUDY 24.2

United Nations peacekeeping in Sierra Leone

On 17 July 2000 the United Nations Security Council passed Resolution 1308 in order to address the issue of HIV/AIDS in peacekeeping operations. The resolution expressed concern at the potentially damaging impact of HIV/AIDS on the health of international peacekeeping personnel, and demanded that the United Nations make HIV/AIDS training a central component of pre-deployment and ongoing training for peacekeepers. The United Nations Department of Peacekeeping Operations together with the Joint United Nations Program on HIV/AIDS (UNAIDS) subsequently began to look at the links between HIV/AIDS and peacekeeping operations in greater detail. The detailed analysis (Bazergan 2002) of the role that HIV/AIDS played during the United Nations Mission in Sierra Leone (UNAMSIL) was an important step forward in this regard and revealed some of the problems and complexities associated with the issue of HIV/AIDS in peacekeeping operations.

The United Nations Security Council authorized this mission in the West African state of Sierra Leone on 22 October 1999 under the powers granted to it by Chapter VII of the United Nations Charter. The aim of the mission was to cooperate with the government and the other parties in implementing the Lomé Peace Agreement and to assist in the implementation of the disarmament, demobilization, and reintegration plan. To this end the Council approved a deployment of up to 17,500 troops to the country, including 260 military observers and up to 170 civilian police personnel. In total, some thirty-eight countries contributed peacekeepers, military observers, or civilian police to the mission. There was consequently concern that, as with other recent peacekeeping operations in Africa, such a deployment might facilitate the spread of HIV/AIDS in Sierra Leone.

Under current policy, the United Nations Department of Peacekeeping Operations (UNDPKO) cannot ensure that only HIV-negative peacekeepers are deployed. Indeed,

UNDPKO does not preclude HIV-positive soldiers who do not show clinical manifestations of AIDS from peacekeeping operations on human rights grounds. Nevertheless, it *recommends* that persons living with HIV not be selected by troop-contributing countries, (1) because medical treatment in peacekeeping missions may not be adequate to meet the medical needs of these persons; (2) because exposure to endemic infections and exhaustive immunization requirements may be detrimental to their health; and (3) because of the risk of transmitting HIV to medical personnel, fellow peacekeepers, and sex workers in the mission. This is only a recommendation, however, and UNDPKO has no strict enforcement mechanism. Indeed, the UN does not test these troops and does not request such information from troop-contributing countries.

The case of UNAMSIL showed that ultimately relying on the troop-contributing countries to fulfil these recommendations is problematic. Although most countries that contributed to the mission in Sierra Leone officially claimed to be engaged in pre-deployment testing, at least four UNAMSIL peacekeepers died between November 1999 and March 2002, while another ten soldiers were sent back to their country of origin because they were symptomatic of AIDS, pointing to considerable weaknesses in many countries' pre-deployment testing. As long as this remains the case, the United Nations cannot effectively preclude the possibility that in some instances UN peacekeepers may spread the virus where and when they are deployed. In order to address this problem further, the United Nations now also deploys AIDS advisers with peacekeeping missions and has developed a plastic AIDS awareness card that was piloted in Sierra Leone. The card includes basic facts about the transmission and nature of the disease, a 'pocket' to hold a condom, and it reiterates the peacekeeper's code of conduct. The card is now produced in several languages and is routinely deployed to peacekeepers around the world. Its effectiveness has yet to be properly evaluated, however.

---

other areas of life, uncertainty tends to breed anxiety. It is this innate and all too human fear of microbes that makes them particularly amenable to being portrayed not just as important health issues, but as national security threats as well. Since 2003 two infectious diseases in particular have been portrayed as such national security threats.

SARS

Widely regarded as the first infectious disease epidemic of the twenty-first century, SARS is thought to have emerged in the Guangdong Province of China in November 2002—a region known for its lively markets where human and livestock mingle in close proximity. Symptoms of the new disease included a high fever, a dry cough, and shortness of breath or breathing difficulties. However, it was not until 11 February 2003 that the Chinese Ministry of Health forwarded reports of 305 cases of acute respiratory syndrome to the World Health Organization, by which time at least five deaths had been reported in Guangdong Province. The new disease appeared to confirm all the earlier fears about how a newly emerging infectious disease could rapidly spread across the globe through modern transport infrastructure. Perhaps nothing exemplified this more clearly than the fate of Dr Liu Jianlun, a local Chinese doctor who initially treated patients infected with the new disease. He subsequently travelled from Guangdong Province to Hong Kong in order to attend a wedding. He stayed on the ninth floor of the four-star Metropole hotel (in Room 911), where the disease quickly began to spread to other guests staying on that floor of the hotel. In epidemiological terms he is now referred to a 'super-spreader'; the World Health Organization ultimately attributes more than 4,000 worldwide cases of SARS to this doctor alone (National Intelligence Council 2003: 10). Those who became infected by him subsequently travelled as far as Singapore, Hong Kong, Vietnam, Ireland, Canada, and the United States, where they, in turn, infected more than 350 people directly or indirectly. Another doctor who had treated the first cases of SARS in Singapore too reported symptoms before boarding a flight from New York back to Singapore on 14 March, and had to disembark prematurely in Frankfurt, Germany, for immediate hospitalization and isolation.

Wide-ranging international cooperation amongst scientists and laboratories revealed that SARS is caused by a new coronavirus, which is believed to have crossed over from the animal to the human population. This is because evidence of infection with the coronavirus could also be found in several animal groups, including Himalayan masked palm civets, Chinese ferret badgers, raccoon dogs, and domestic cats.

By the time the last human chain of transmission was broken in July 2003, there had been 8,098 reported SARS cases, causing 774 deaths in 26 different countries. SARS killed about 10 per cent of those infected, although the chances of survival in the event of an infection were heavily depended upon the age of the victim. Less than 1 per cent of persons aged 24 years or younger died from the disease, up to 6 per cent of those aged 25–44 years old died, and up to 15 per cent of persons aged 44–64 years old died. The great risk was for persons aged 65 or older, of which 55 per cent succumbed (National Intelligence Council 2003: 16). Geographically, SARS left its deepest mark in Asia, with China, Taiwan, and Singapore accounting for more than 90 per cent of cases, although notable outbreaks also occurred in Toronto. Moreover, the effects of the SARS outbreak were not confined to these deaths alone.

The disease also caused widespread fear amongst populations around the world, especially as there was no cure readily available, and its transmission patterns remained unclear for a considerable period of time. People thus began to wear masks covering their noses and mouths, began to avoid public places such as restaurants and cinemas, and ceased to travel. In conjunction with the decision of many investors to put investment plans in the region on hold, the SARS outbreak also had considerable economic consequences for the region. The travel and tourism sectors were particularly badly hit, with room bookings and airline seat bookings in several cases being down more than 50 per cent on previous years. In countries such as China, Singapore, and Canada public-health agencies also implemented quarantine and isolation procedures, restricting the movements of those perceived to be at risk of being infected with the virus. Some countries even introduced thermal scanners at airports in order to detect people with symptoms of fever. Although it ultimately proved possible to contain SARS through quarantine and other public-health measures, many policy-makers felt that the writing was now clearly on the wall and that things could have been much worse, especially if the coronavirus had achieved more efficient human-to-human transmission. For many, the SARS episode thus represented a warning of what could happen if a renewed flu pandemic ravaged the human population in the twenty-first century.

Influenza pandemic

There were three such human flu pandemics in the twentieth century alone—in 1918, 1957, and 1968. The first of these was particularly severe, breaking out within the harsh conditions of the First World War and leading to the deaths of tens of millions of people around the world. Policy-makers at the World Health Organizations and in several national governments remain concerned today that the H5N1 strand of avian flu has the potential to evolve eventually into such a renewed pandemic, and are framing avian flu as a threat to national security. Writing in the *New York Times* in 2005, Senators Barack Obama and Richard Lugar argued:

> " When we think of the major threats to our national security, the first to come to mind are nuclear proliferation, rogue states and global terrorism. But another kind of threat lurks beyond our shores, one from nature, not humans – an avian flu pandemic. An outbreak could cause millions of deaths, destabilize Southeast Asia (its likely place of origin), and threaten the security of governments around the world "

Obama and Lugar (2005).

The US *National Security Strategy* (2006) thus also points to the dangers posed by 'public health challenges like pandemics (HIV/AIDS, avian influenza) that recognize no borders', arguing that 'the risks to social order are so great that traditional public health approaches may be inadequate, necessitating new strategies and responses' (White House 2006: 47). *The National Security Strategy of the United Kingdom* (2008) similarly cites pandemics alongside terrorism and weapons of mass destruction as part of a 'diverse but interconnected set of threats and risks, which affect the United Kingdom directly and also have the potential to undermine wider international stability' (Cabinet Office 2008: 3).

The scenario that policy-makers are particularly concerned about is that of a zoonic (animal-to-human) transmission of H5N1 that subsequently recombines or mutates to achieve efficient human-to-human transmission. If such a virus emerges, it will in all likelihood be spread through coughing and sneezing, and people will probably become infectious before they actually become aware of any symptoms. This latter fact is crucial and would make a future flu pandemic much more difficult to contain than SARS, where people mostly became infectious only after developing symptoms. The first step in this chain—the zoonic 'leap' from the animal to human populations—was already documented in 1997 in Hong Kong. Officials sought to deal with this danger quickly and at great costs to the animal population by ordering virtually the entire poultry population of Hong Kong (some 1.5 million birds) to be destroyed. Although these measures appeared successful, there was a further outbreak in February of 2003, again in Hong Kong. By June 2008, there had been 385 confirmed cases of bird flu according to the World Health Organization, of which 243 died. The fatality rate for human cases of avian influenza is thus much higher than in the case of SARS, with more than 60 per cent of infected persons dying. Again the region most seriously affected is Asia, with China, Indonesia, Thailand, and Vietnam (but also Egypt) accounting for the majority of cases. On rare occasions it has also been possible for H5N1 to become transmitted between people, but usually only in situations of very close contact with this person during the acute phase of the illness, and even when this spread has occurred it has not gone beyond one generation of close contacts. Despite the anxieties that these developments generate, it is worth bearing in mind that, given the wide geographic spread of the virus in birds, as well as the high number of cases of infection in poultry, the numbers of human infections are at the moment comparatively 'low', which indicates that the virus does not 'jump' the species barrier that easily. If it does, the estimates used by the World Health Organization and the Centers for Disease Control and Prevention (CDC) in the United States indicate that there could be between 2 million and 7.4 million deaths worldwide, with many more becoming ill and requiring hospitalization. There is currently no vaccine, and the seasonal flu jabs administered to elderly populations and health-care workers will not work. Policy-makers have therefore focused their efforts on stockpiling antiviral medicines, and drawing up lists of who should receive priority access to such medicines in the case of a renewed pandemic. Many questions still remain, however, about the efficacy of these drugs, and governments are therefore also trying to increase the worldwide capacity for producing vaccines so that, once the latter is developed, more doses can be manufactured and distributed more quickly.

KEY POINTS

- Since the turn of the century many policy-makers have also come to view newly emerging infectious diseases as threats to their national security.

- The SARS outbreak of 2002–3 confirmed many of these fears, showing how a new infectious disease can rapidly spread across the globe, causing widespread fear amongst populations and generating serious economic consequences.

- Although the SARS outbreak was contained, strong concerns remain about the spectre of a more lethal and infectious flu pandemic emerging in the future.

Health and bio-security

Health issues have also acquired a greater security salience because terrorists or other political groups might attempt a mass casualty attack by deliberately releasing a disease-inducing biological agent. Such agents could enter the bodies of civilians through inhalation if the agent is successfully transformed into an aerosol form. Alternatively, it could enter the body by means of ingestion if, for example, food or water supplies are contaminated with such an agent. Two events have raised the concern of governments about such a scenario. First, the attacks of 9/11 showed that terrorists—if capable—might not shy away from using such weapons. Indeed, from the perspective of a terrorist group, many characteristics of a biological agent may be deemed advantageous. First, several of these agents are naturally occurring and can thus be more readily acquired. Second, they would require only small quantities to have substantial effects. Third, these agents are not perceptible to the human eye; once released, they would initially evade the human senses of smell, taste, and so on, and would therefore allow a potential terrorist time to escape undetected. Finally, the very same quality that has long made biological weapons of dubious military use—namely, their inability to differentiate between civilians and combatants—are unlikely to deter would-be terrorists. However, these advantages also need to be balanced with some disadvantages associated with the use of biological agents, including the risk that the terrorist might become infected as well, the technical difficulty involved in successfully stabilizing and weaponizing these agents, and the fact that attacks with biological agents are heavily susceptible to weather conditions such as wind, levels of cloud cover, and so on (Ryan and Glarum 2008: 35). Expert opinion thus still remains divided as to how probable such an attack actually is.

One event that substantially increased anxieties about the possibility of such a scenario materializing was the discovery that anthrax letters were being sent in the United States in 2001—a time when the country was still reeling from the attacks of 9/11. There were probably two separate batches of anthrax letters sent from mail boxes in Princeton, New Jersey. The first batch, thought to consist of approximately five letters, was sent around 18 September 2001 to media offices, including American Media Incorporated, broadcasters and editors in New York City, and to a tabloid publisher in Boca Raton, Florida. These letters were initially dismissed as hate mail and/or left unopened. A second batch of letters was then mailed on 8 October 2001, two of which went to Democratic senators in Washington, DC. The first of these was opened on the morning of 15 October in the Hart office building of the Senate majority leader Tom Daschle. It would take a week before it was established that these second round of infections had come from letters, by which time many more had become exposed. It was later also discovered that the anthrax used was of the Ames strain, which had been used for several years in the US biological weapons programme (Guillemin 2005: 173–6).

Although the attacks of 9/11 and the letters laced with anthrax were a crucial catalyst in terms of placing the combat of terrorism at the heart of the international security agenda, anxieties about such a biological attack actually pre-date 2001. In 1995 the Aum Shinrikyo cult in Japan had already released Sarin nerve gas in the Tokyo subway. The attack was not very sophisticated, relying on the use of an umbrella to poke holes into plastic bags. The attack killed twelve people and hospitalized a thousand, with thousands more seeking medical care. Less well known is the fact that this was not the first time the cult had struck. A similar attack had occurred in the town of Matsumoto eight months earlier, which killed seven people. In fact, this cult had funding of an estimated US$20 million and was operating internationally, with contacts in post-Soviet Russia, Australia, Germany, Taiwan, and the former Yugoslavia; it even had an office in New York City (Guillemin 2005: 158–9). After being arrested, the head of their germ development programme, Seiichi Endo, revealed that between 1990 and 1993 the cult had also released aerosolized anthrax and botulinum

toxin on several occasions at Japan's legislature (the Diet), the Imperial Palace, as well as several other places in Tokyo and even at the US military base of Yokusaka. Fortunately for those involved, nobody became infected, probably because the strain used was similar to that used in animal vaccination, which is of little danger to humans and has low virulence (Zubay et al. 2005: 134–5).

All these events contributed to a climate in which it was felt that more concerted efforts needed to be undertaken to protect populations in the event of such an attack. In the United States, the Centers for Disease Control and Prevention were charged with drawing up a list of the biological agents that might be used in such an attack. Its list consists of Category A agents, which are highly infectious, have high mortality rates, can be easily disseminated, and are difficult to treat medically. They would thus have a highly disruptive effect if used in a biological attack. Examples of such agents are anthrax, botulism, plague, smallpox, tularemia, and viral hemorrhagic fevers (for example, Ebola, Marburg, Lassa, Machupo). Category B agents, in turn, comprise those agents that cause lower mortality rates, have moderate morbidity rates, and can be treated more readily. They include brucellosis, epsilon toxin of Clostridium perfringens, food-safety threats (for example, salmonella species, Escherichia coli O157:H7, Shigella), glanders, melioidosis, psittacosis, Q fever, Ricin toxin, Staphylococcal enterotoxin B, typhus fever, and viralencephalitis (for example, Venezuelan equine encephalitis, eastern equine encephalitis, western equine encephalitis), and water-safety threats (for example, Vibrio cholerae, Cryptosporidium parvum). Finally, Category C agents refer to emerging pathogens with potential for future weaponization, such as Nipah virus and hantavirus.

In the United States two new initiatives were also launched to respond to potential attacks with these agents: projects BioWatch and BioShield. BioWatch consists of a network of sensors (or stations) in thirty-one cities that analyse particles in the air through a filter system. These filters are collected daily and analysed at the CDC for traces of six agents: anthrax, brucellosis, glanders, meliodosis, plague, smallpox, and turlremia. This process has a turnaround time of at least thirty-six hours (Ryan and Glarum 2008: 262). Project BioShield, in turn, was designed to increase the 'medical defences' of the United States against a range of possible pathogens. At a cost of around US$5.6 billion over a ten-year period, Project BioShield included the purchasing and storing of significant stockpiles of medicines as well as vaccines. It also seeks to fund research into developing new medicines and vaccines to protect populations against such agents. Both programmes have ultimately proved controversial and have encountered significant difficulties in meeting their objectives.

KEY POINTS

- Since the late 1990s many policy-makers have focused on disease-causing biological agents within the context of their efforts to combat domestic and international terrorism.

- The activities of Aum Shinrikyo in Japan, as well as the person(s) responsible for sending letters laced with anthrax in the United States, highlighted a perceived lack of preparedness amongst many countries to deal with the effects of a terrorist attack using such an agent.

- Some governments have launched costly programmes to increase the speed with which such an outbreak could be detected, and respond to such an attack.

Conclusion

This chapter outlined the ways in which health issues have acquired a greater security salience in the context of three competing security frameworks: human security, national security, and bio-security. How is this merging of health and security to be conceptualized? Many analysts have followed the broad tenets of securitization theory (see Buzan et al. 1998) and have identified this emerging health–security nexus as the 'securitization' of health. In this view, health issues have now become the latest in a long line of wider social issues—such as drugs, migration, the environment, and so on—to become securitized—that is, framed as existential threats requiring the adoption of emergency measures. This, however, is not the only way in which the emerging health–security nexus can be conceptualized. It can also be understood from the opposite perspective.

For years scholars outside the discipline of security studies, most notably in sociology, have also been tracing the progressive 'medicalization' of societies, whereby more and more social problems are considered and responded to as medical problems, and where the medical professions (along with pharmaceutical companies) have seen substantial material benefits as well as enjoying an enhanced social position (Conrad 2007). Viewed from this perspective, the recent merging of health and security could be understood not just as the securitization of health, but also as a wider manifestation of the medicalization of security. Put differently, these three debates on health and security are also sites in contemporary world politics where security is itself becomes partially redefined in medical terms requiring the greater involvement of the medical professions. The deeper question that the emerging health–security nexus gives rise to, therefore, is whether it is best understood as the securitization of health, or as the medicalization of security?

QUESTIONS

1. What is relationship between health and human security?

2. What are the implications of HIV/AIDS for human security?

3. To what extent are infectious diseases also a threat to national security?

4. What can be done to reduce the spread of infectious diseases in the context of rapid international travel?

5. What, if anything, is gained by referring to diseases as security issues, rather than as health or medical issues?

6. What lessons can be learned from the securitization of health for securitization theory?

7. What lessons can be learned from the SARS outbreak of 2002 – 3?

8. Are the threats of a bioterrorism and an influenza pandemic exaggerated?

9. Do non-infectious diseases have security implications as well?

10. Is the health – security nexus a manifestation of the securitization of health, or of the medicalization of security?

 FURTHER READING

■ Chen, Lincoln, Leaning, Jennifer, and Narasimhan, Vasant (2003) (eds.), *Global Health Challenges for Human Security*, Cambridge, MA: Harvard University Press. This volume contains a range or chapters covering the concept of human security and how it relates to several contemporary global health issues.

■ de Waal, Alex (2006), *AIDS and Power: Why there is no Political Crisis—Yet*, London: Zed Books. This book presents a useful overview of what is known about the links between AIDS and security, and also questions many widespread assumptions about the security implications of HIV/AIDS.

■ Fidler, David (2004), *SARS: Governance and the Globalization of Disease*, New York: Palgrave. This book analyses the implications of the SARS crisis for the global governance of health and contemporary world politics. Many of the insights are also relevant to the governance of infectious diseases more generally.

■ Fidler, David, and Gostin, Lawrence (2008), *Biosecurity in the Global Age: Biological Weapons, Public Health and the Rule of Law*, Stanford. CA: Stanford University Press. A recent book analysing the security threat posed jointly by the spread of infectious diseases and biological weapons.

■ Guillemin, Jeanne (2005), *Biological Weapons: From the Invention of State-Sponsored Programs to Contemporary Bioterrorism*, New York: Columbia University Press. This book offers a comprehensive account of the historical evolution of biological weapons, including the challenges involved in responding to the threat of bio-terrorism.

■ Lee, Kelley, and McInnes, Colin (2003), 'Health, Foreign Policy & Security: A Discussion Paper', UK Global Health Programme, London: Nuffield Trust, http://nuffieldtrust.org.uk/ecomm/files/Health_Foreign_Policy.pdf. Offers a comprehensive overview of the links between health and security, and how they are related to wider issues of trade and the environment.

■ Price-Smith, Andrew (2001), *The Health of Nations: Infectious Disease, Environmental Change, and their Effects on National Security and Development*. Cambridge, MA: MIT Press. One of the first books systematically to set out the relationships between health issues and national security.

IMPORTANT WEBSITES

● http://www.globalhealth.org   The website of the Global Health Council; has information on global health issues and recent developments in global health.

● http://www.who.int   The website of the World Health Organization; has information on most of the diseases discussed in this chapter.

● http://www.upmc-biosecurity.org   The website of the Center for Biosecurity at the University of Pittsburgh Medical Center (UPMC).

● http://www.rand.org/health/centers/healthsecurity   The website of the Rand Center for Domestic and International Health Security.

Visit the Online Resource Centre that accompanies this book for lots of interesting additional material: www.oxfordtextbooks.co.uk/orc/collins2e/

25

Transnational Crime

JEANNE GIRALDO AND HAROLD TRINKUNAS

 Chapter Contents

- Introduction
- Definitions and key concepts
- The increase in transnational crime
- Transnational crime and terrorism
- Assessing the threat
- Government responses
- Conclusion

Reader's Guide

This chapter explains why many governments have increasingly come to consider trans-national crime as a threat to national security. It explores both the reasons for and the nature of the increase in transnational crime since the end of the Cold War. It also considers what we know about how transnational crime is organized and finds that our understanding is quite limited. The chapter also explores debates over the strength and nature of the 'nexus' between transnational crime and terrorism. It concludes by discussing how the government response to transnational crime has evolved over time.

Introduction

With the end of the Cold War, the popular media, academic journal articles, and 'threat assessments' produced by **think tanks** and governmental organizations shifted their attention from traditional security threats and began to trumpet the dangers posed by **transnational crime**. A 1994 conference organized by a leading Washington think tank, the Center for Strategic and International Studies, labelled transnational crime the 'new empire of evil.' A 1996 UN Report asserted that transnational crime had become the 'new form of geopolitics'. The US National Security Strategy released in 1996 presented this phenomenon as a major national security threat. Governments no longer looked at transnational crime merely as a threat to individuals or society, but as a threat to the very state itself. Looking back, has transnational crime lived up to its billing? Does it represent a major international security threat today?

The growth of transnational crime since the 1980s is indisputable, but its impact varies considerably across the globe. While **organized crime** has always been with us, new trends in the international system, particularly globalization, have made it increasingly possible for criminal enterprises to cross borders. As the rate of globalization of trade, finances, and travel accelerates, we should expect crime to become even more transnational in the future and increasingly to adopt flexible network forms of organization. This means that more countries will be exposed to the effect of transnational crime on individual security, societies, and the rule of law at a time when the phenomenon is becoming more difficult to address and contain. The persistence of poorly governed or essentially ungoverned spaces around the globe, which provide fertile home bases for transnational crime, means that even states with strong law enforcement are vulnerable to spillover effects.

Thinking about transnational crime is difficult from a traditional international security perspective, which typically focuses on questions of war and peace, conflict and cooperation, often with a state-centric perspective. The threat posed by transnational crime has both international and sub-national dimensions, and, as we will see in this chapter, it has implications for national security, public safety, and even the stability of regimes. Its ability to transcend borders and commit crimes far from its origins, its covert nature, and its ability to corrupt and subvert government agents makes it challenging for states to anticipate threats and prepare their defences. It is even more difficult for governments to think about whether this type of threat can be countered with traditional security instruments, although there have been controversial calls for a greater use of military and intelligence assets to counter transnational crime. For this reason, the theoretical lenses used in this chapter to understand the problem have less to do with our traditional interpretations of international relations and draw more heavily on theories about organizational forms and domestic politics.

This chapter examines the emergence of transnational crime as an international security threat. We provide an overview of how transnational crime changed with increasing globalization and the weakening of state authority in the aftermath of the Cold War. We discuss the debates over how transnational crime is organized, which range from those who view it as highly hierarchical to those who argue it is closer to a decentralized market, and the implications of each model for our understanding of the severity of the threat and how to counter it. This includes an assessment of the latest arguments concerning the potential links that may develop between transnational crime and terrorism. We conclude by analysing government responses to transnational crime.

KEY POINTS

- Transnational crime is perceived as a major international security threat by governments and scholars, but traditional theories of international relations are less useful for understanding the threat.

- International trends such as globalization may have the unintended consequence of opening new spaces for the development of transnational crime.

- The threat posed by transnational crime is growing in scope and severity, and it affects even states with strong law-enforcement agencies.

- Using theories about organizational forms and domestic politics provides us with insights about the nature of the threat and how to address it.

Definitions and key concepts

Transnational Crime

Traditionally, transnational crime has referred to criminal activities extending into and violating the laws of two or more countries. In 2000, the United Nations in its Convention against Transnational Organized Crime defined transnational crime even more broadly to encompass any criminal activity that is conducted in more than one state, planned in one state but perpetrated in another, or committed in one state where there are spillover effects into neighbouring jurisdictions (United Nations 2000). Efforts to typify the nature of the activities labelled as transnational crime are similarly encompassing, as is suggested in Background 25.1.

The increasing globalization of economic activity has provided a wider range of activities and opportunities for crime to cross national boundaries than in the past. Criminals, like businesses in the licit economy, seek to match supply and demand and to take advantage of differences in

---

BACKGROUND 25.1

Categories of transnational crime

1. Money laundering
2. Illicit drug trafficking
3. Corruption of public officials
4. Infiltration of legal businesses
5. Fraudulent bankruptcy
6. Insurance fraud
7. Computer crime
8. Theft of intellectual property
9. Illicit traffic in arms
10. Terrorism
11. Aircraft hijacking
12. Piracy
13. Hijacking on land
14. Trafficking in persons
15. Trade in human body parts
16. Theft of art and cultural objects
17. Environmental crime
18. Other illicit smuggling

Fourth United Nations Survey of Crime Trends and Operations of Criminal Justice Systems (1994), cited in Mueller (2001).

profits, regulations, and risk levels between markets. These differences may emerge from the availability of supply in certain regions that can be matched to demand in others, such as the flow of narcotics from Afghanistan and South America into Europe and the United States, respectively. In other cases, criminals may exploit differences in the regulation of activities, as is often the case in **money-laundering** transactions that take advantage of variations in banking secrecy between offshore financial havens and conventional banks. Variations in risk in performing activities may also shape the geographical presence of transnational crime, with criminal enterprises developing their **home bases** in low-risk, poorly governed states, such as Nigeria. Criminal activities are likely to take place in **host nations**, where higher risks are compensated for by the lure of higher profits. Other countries are less important as markets (or hosts) for transnational crime groups, but contribute to the illicit economy as trans-shipment states, through which illicit goods pass, or as **service states** (as in the case of money-laundering havens).

Organized crime

When governments and international organizations refer to transnational crime, they most often mean transnational *organized* crime. For example, the Europol Convention on the European Law Enforcement Organization noted that its objective was to target 'terrorism, unlawful drug trafficking and other serious forms of international crime *where there are factual indications that an organized criminal structure is involved*' (EU 1995; emphasis added); in 2000 the United Nations issued the Convention against Transnational *Organized* Crime. This raises the question of what the qualifier 'organized' adds to our understanding of transnational crime.

As the UN definition in Key Quotes 25.1 indicates, organized crime is differentiated from other crime in that it is *profit-driven* and *ongoing* (that

---

> ### KEY QUOTES 25.1
>
> ### United Nations definition of organized crime
>
> Organized crime is defined as any 'structured group of three or more persons existing for a period of time and acting in concert with the aim of committing one or more serious crimes or offenses . . . in order to obtain, directly, or indirectly, a financial or other material benefit'.
>
> A structured group is one that is 'not randomly formed for the immediate commission of an offence and that does not need to have formally defined roles for its members, continuity of its membership or a developed structure'.
>
> Article 2, UN Convention against Transnational Organized Crime (United Nations 2000).

is, a one-time offence would not be included).[1] While everyone can agree on these two dimensions, a more encompassing definition of organized crime has proved elusive. Originally, the term 'organized crime' was used to refer to hierarchical crime groups that were believed to monopolize the criminal market in a given area; to deploy violence and corruption systematically in pursuit of their illicit activities; and to perceive abnormally high profit levels that allowed them to threaten political and economic structures. When applied to transnational crime, this view lent itself to notions of a centrally orchestrated conspiracy by leaders of organized crime groups to carve up the world into their own individual fiefdoms. While most analysts no longer believe in notions of monopolistic control, many still see systemic violence and corruption as the essence of organized crime. Transnational organized crime is often (mistakenly) thought to refer to complex and sophisticated organizations with a centralized leadership directing cross-border operations.

---

[1] Note that hijacking and terrorism from the original UN list of transnational crime (see Background 25.1) would be excluded by this definition.

Other analysts put a great deal of emphasis on the network form of organization as the defining characteristic of transnational crime since the 1990s, highlighting the entrepreneurial flair, scale, sophistication, flexibility, efficiency, and resilience of this form of organization.[2] Networks (defined simply by their parts—the component entities or 'nodes' and the relationships or 'links' between them) are a decentralized, 'flat' organizational form said to enable criminals to maximize their profits while minimizing their risk from law enforcement. Collaboration between individuals is often ad hoc and transitory, with the networks being formed and disbanded as circumstances warrant (Williams 2001). Under these conditions, many analysts feel it is more appropriate to talk about criminal 'structures' or 'enterprises' rather than 'groups' (which implies a clearly defined membership, UN definition notwithstanding).

Finally, a key group of scholars argues that it is more important to think of transnational crime as a marketplace rather than a network of groups (Naylor 2002; Beare 2003). The need to minimize risk (that is, to avoid law enforcement) and other limits imposed by the illicit marketplace means criminal organizations will tend to be small, vulnerable, and competitive—a far cry from the monopolies or collusive oligarchies stressed in the traditional, hierarchical vision of organized crime. While network theorists point to the adaptability and sophistication of criminal networks as a key source of their resilience in the face of law-enforcement efforts, the market scholars note that the 'great majority of crime is the province of small-time losers' (Naylor 2002: 10). From this perspective, the resilience of transnational crime can be attributed to the inexorable logic of the marketplace—supply rising to meet demand—rather than the sophistication or entrepreneurial flair of networks.

How can these competing visions be reconciled? Most observers agree that transnational crime groups vary greatly in their size, organization, and modes of operation and that hierarchies, networks, and markets coexist. The challenge for organized-crime theorists and law-enforcement practitioners is to determine which organizational logics operate in any given situation and determine empirically (rather than assume)

KEY POINTS

- Transnational crime involves ongoing profit-driven criminal activity that crosses national boundaries.

- Not all organized crime is transnational, but there are growing incentives for criminal enterprises to operate across national borders because of differences in the supply and demand for illegal goods and services among countries.

- Most observers agree that transnational crime groups vary greatly in their size, organization, and modes of operation.

- Proponents of a hierarchical view of organized crime view these groups as wealthy, powerful, violent, and under the control of a small number of individuals.

- Others argue that most transnational crime operates through networks of individuals and small groups who operate on a transitory or ad hoc basis to minimize the risk from law enforcement.

- Critics argue that organized crime is in fact highly disorganized, and resembles more a market for illicit goods and services than an organization. Proponents of this view minimize the threat posed by organized criminals to states and societies.

---

[2] Although it is commonly believed that it is easier for law enforcement to dismantle hierarchical organizations than networks, it is not clear whether this is the case because networks are more flexible and sophisticated or simply because police agencies tend to focus more on hierarchical organizations and have more information about them (Kenney 2007).

whether the logics are correlated with other factors such as types of crime, patterns of cooperation with other groups, linkages to the legal world, different threat levels, and vulnerability to law enforcement or other interventions.

The increase in transnational crime

Transnational crime is not a new phenomenon. Organized crime groups have operated transnationally for decades, if not centuries. How then can we account for the widespread alarm over transnational crime beginning in the 1990s and intensifying with the terrorist attacks of 9/11? Many observers argue that much of the initial concern was generated by the military, intelligence, and broader national security communities, which needed a new justification for their relevance (and budgets) in the post-Cold War era (Beare 2003). Although there is some truth to this, there is also a consensus that a very real increase in the scale and scope of transnational crime occurred in the 1980s and 1990s.

Transnational crime has become global in scale and is no longer exclusive to certain geographical areas or ethnic groups. There has been a marked increase in the number and size of illegal markets, the number of groups involved, the number of countries affected, and the overall amount of illicit trade. Whereas illegal markets were small and isolated in the past, today illicit markets tend to be interrelated, mutually supporting, and more embedded in the legal economy than ever. The 'democratization' of crime has been matched by an increasing reliance on decentralized, network forms of organization.

The increased scale and scope of transnational crime and its changing nature can be explained in large part by two developments. First, the increased transnational flow of people, goods, and money in the second half of the twentieth century (a process often referred to as 'globalization') has contributed to the growth of both licit and illicit economies that operate across national boundaries. Second, a wave of 'dual transitions' (away from closed economies and authoritarian political regimes) and an increase in civil unrest with the end of the Cold War have undermined state authority in a number of countries, providing a home base for crime groups or otherwise facilitating the operation of transnational criminal networks.

Globalization

The increased transnational flow of people, goods, and money that occurred during the second half of the twentieth century was greatly facilitated by advances in communications and transportation technologies, such as the advent of inexpensive passenger air travel, the personal computer, the Internet, and cellular communications. However, the process of globalization, properly understood, is not just a matter of technological innovation but is even more fundamentally linked to the economic and political reforms that reduced the restrictions on the international movement of goods, people, and money in the 1980s and 1990s. Beginning in the 1970s, a wave of market-oriented reforms in the developing and developed world reduced barriers to trade and promoted the development of export-based economies. In addition, a wave of transitions towards democracy, beginning in 1974 in Southern Europe and moving to Latin America in the 1980s and on to Africa, Eastern Europe, and the former Soviet Union following the fall of the Berlin Wall, increased transnational flows. Borders that had been closed shut under authoritarian rule now spilled open.

This largely positive process of economic and political liberalization had a 'dark side'. In an increasingly global marketplace, illicit actors, like their licit counterparts, took advantage of business opportunities wherever they occurred. The growth of global trade and global financial networks provided an infrastructure and cover that illicit actors could exploit. For example, as a result of the creation of the North American Free Trade Area, trade between the United States and Mexico grew from $81.5 billion in 1993 to $247 billion in 2000 and to nearly $347 billion in 2007. This land border is also one of the main routes for the smuggling of illegal goods and aliens into the United States. Burgeoning cross-border traffic increases the opportunities for criminals to hide their activities within the flow of legal commerce, while law enforcement reports ever greater difficulty in monitoring this traffic. Only 2–3 per cent of bulk shipping containers entering the United States by sea undergo physical inspection. The globalization of financial markets has accelerated dramatically since the 1980s, making it easier for criminals to move and store their profits quickly and secretly. The challenge to governments is to find the criminal 'signal' within the 'noise' generated by the large and growing amounts of international trade and finance produced by globalization.

At the same time, globalization increased the importance of 'network' forms of organization for both legal and illegal enterprises. Hierarchical organizations no longer had to recruit personnel with the full range of specialized skill sets necessary for various operations; instead these functions could be 'contracted out'. In the criminal world, fluid and

readily adaptable networks of individuals and organizations could group together and disband as required by the needs of particular illicit ventures. Operations such as money laundering or the manufacturing of false identities could be outsourced to independent specialized contractors, who might very well be part of multiple criminal networks. In short, innovations in technology and the proliferation of illicit markets had the effect of 'democratizing' the criminal underworld, making it easier for individuals to participate in crime without the need for large, hierarchical organizations to provide the infrastructure and necessary social contacts.

This phenomenon was also encouraged by the increased movement of people across borders, and their ability to remain in contact with their homelands long after they had resettled elsewhere. The

---

BACKGROUND 25.2

Sample of prominent transnational criminal 'clusters'

The following are not 'single and interconnected criminal groups in their own right' but are more appropriately thought of as 'clusters' of groups (UNODC 2002: 8). These broad labels are convenient (but potentially misleading) shorthand used by the media and law-enforcement agencies to refer to individuals and groups that share ethnic or social characteristics, and may show some similarities in structure and organizations.

Italian Mafia. In Italy, this is a generic term applied to the Sicilian Mafia, the Neapolitan Camorra, the Calabrian 'Ndrangheta, and the Apulian Sacra Corona Unita. It is known for its connections to other organized crime elements, such as the Colombian drug-trafficking cartels.

Russian organized crime. Based on legacy organized crime groupings that exploited the inefficiency of the Soviet centrally planned economy, these groups are now able to operate more freely in the lax post-Communist Russian state. They include persons from all the former Soviet states, including prominently Russians, Ukrainians, Chechens, Georgians, and Azeris. They are known to have connections to organized crime in the United States and Western Europe.

Chinese Triads. Working predominantly from Hong Kong and Taiwan rather than the Chinese mainland, these groups

are involved with drug trafficking, prostitution, gambling, extortion, and human trafficking. They have developed a global presence throughout the Chinese international diaspora.

Japanese Yakuza (Boryokudan). These Japanese-based gangs engage in some transnational crime, mainly drug trafficking and human smuggling for prostitution. Their activities are concentrated in Japan, South East Asia, and the United States.

Colombian and other Latin American drug cartels. These groups are highly specialized and organized around the various stages of production and transportation of cocaine, heroin, and marijuana from Bolivia, Peru, and Colombia into the United States through Central America, Mexico, and the Caribbean. Insurgent groups in Colombia and Peru have become involved in this type of organized crime as well, and Mexican transnational criminal groupings have become increasingly prominent.

Nigerian organized crime. These transnational organizations take advantage of weak rule of law in their home country and the Nigerian diaspora throughout the world to engage in organized drug trafficking, computer and mail fraud, and various forms of financial fraud.

Williams and Savona (1998); on criminal 'clusters', see UNODC (2002).

end of the Cold War created new opportunities for economic migrants from the former Soviet states, as did the continuing economic disparities between the developing and developed world. The sharp increase in civil conflicts around the globe also created a new generation of refugees. These diasporas have provided the family and ethnic ties that help facilitate a transnational criminal enterprise. Groups such as the Chinese triads operating in Hong Kong, the United States, and Western Europe or Kosovar drug smuggling networks in Western Europe, depend on the links maintained between individuals of similar cultural backgrounds across borders. Unassimilated ethnic minority populations are often vulnerable to exploitation by criminals, yet they are also fearful of cooperation with law enforcement.

Despite the undeniable importance of family and ethnic ties in facilitating collaboration, this element can be overemphasized—and often is, given law enforcement's tendency to focus on these visibly different groups (see Background 25.2). However, of the 40 organized crime groups in 16 countries studied by UNODC, only 13 were based on shared ethnic identities (and another 10 were based on shared social characteristics; the other half had no strong shared identity). Collaboration *between groups* is even less likely to depend on shared identities, being driven instead by opportunism (UNODC 2002)—as was first emphasized with the widely noted alliance between Colombian cartels and the Sicilian mafia in the late 1980s to facilitate the entry of cocaine into Europe. In some cases, a shared position of marginalization within a society can facilitate cooperation between different ethnic groups, as is the case with Vietnamese vendors of smuggled cigarettes and Polish smugglers in East Germany (von Lampe and Johansen 2003).

The undermining of state authority

As noted above, dual transitions toward free-market economies and democracy in the 1980s and 1990s contributed greatly to the increased mobility of people, goods, and money that provided increased opportunities for transnational crime. In many countries these dual transitions have contributed to the spread of transnational crime in another way as well. This section refers to transitions that have gone awry, leaving behind a state that is often unable to assert the rule of law (so-called grey areas) or even to exert control over its territory (creating 'ungoverned areas'). These grey and ungoverned areas have provided the home base for a wide range of groups engaged in transnational criminal activities: from organized criminals to warlords to insurgents.

In some cases, such as Russia and many of the post-Soviet states, organized crime took advantage of the dual transitions to enhance their power and corrupt the state (Shelley 2008). In Russia, economic 'fixers' that had greased the wheels of the pre-1991 command economy and small organized crime groups that survived the Soviet period joined with some discharged elements of the Soviet intelligence and security apparatus and emerging entrepreneurs to take advantage of the poorly regulated transitional economy. Combining inside knowledge of state enterprises and resources, access to intelligence and surveillance files, experience and contacts in the West, and expertise in violence and intimidation, these new organized crime elements were well positioned to exploit the weaknesses of the emerging Russian state to great personal advantage (Finckenauer and Voronin 2001). The efforts of these emerging organized crime groups did much to undermine investor confidence in the Russian economy, driving up the cost of doing business and aggravating a scarcity of legal capital for legitimate business development. They also delegitimized the new Russian democratic regime by calling into question its ability to maintain the rule of law and provide for public safety.

In other cases, such as the Balkans and various countries in Africa, failed transitions to democracy resulted in open warfare, a situation that lends itself to the creation of ties between political elites and criminal elements that persist even when the conflict ends. In the case of the Balkans, the embargo against the warring states created new asymmetries that could be exploited by organized crime through the trafficking of commodities, gasoline, and arms. With the connivance of local authorities, organized crime groups trafficked women into Western Europe and, in some instances, to the peacekeeping forces attempting to reduce the level of conflict. These groups included the highest levels of society within the former Yugoslavia, including the leadership of Serbia, which used these networks to enrich themselves and provide the supplies necessary for their forces to continue the war. Similarly, Kosovar drug traffickers in Western Europe generated funding necessary to support the insurgency of the Kosovo Liberation Army in their home territory. In the wake of the war, these organized crime elements proved to be particularly difficult to control, at one point even participating in the assassination of the Serbian Prime Minister, Zoran Dindic, in 2003. The inclusion of law enforcement, intelligence, and military officials in these transnational crime networks explains their ability to endure beyond the end of the Balkan wars and the advent of democracy in the region (Saponja-Hadzic 2003).

KEY POINTS

- Transnational crime increased in scale and scope by the 1990s, with a jump in the number of groups involved, the range of countries affected, the number and density of illicit markets, and the prevalence of networks.

- The increased globalization of trade, finances, and travel has produced an environment conducive to transnational crime by making it easier for criminals to move illicit profits and illegal goods, provide service, and smuggle persons across state borders.

- Political transitions to democracy and economic transitions to free markets since the 1980s, often simultaneously in the same country, have occasionally gone awry, undermining state capacity to enforce the rule of law and creating new opportunities for organized crime to penetrate societies in transition.

Transnational crime and terrorism

Groups that use terrorist methods have long relied on crime as a means to fund their activities. For example, many Marxist-Leninist terrorist groups of the 1970s and 1980s engaged primarily in domestic crimes—bank robbery, extortion, or kidnapping in the country where they operated—for funds. With the vast increase in opportunities for transnational crime in the 1990s, it is not surprising that transnational terrorist groups (as well as those located in a single country) have increasingly engaged in crime as a source of financing. For example, despite ongoing high levels of state support for Hezbollah, supporters of the group have engaged in various criminal schemes to raise funds, such as cigarette smuggling and coupon fraud in the United States and smuggling and counterfeiting in the largely lawless 'Tri-border' frontier area of Argentina, Brazil, and Paraguay. Similarly, al-Qaeda cells in Western Europe engaged in credit-card fraud in the 1990s. Warlords in Africa have benefited from illicit trade in diamonds; Iraqi insurgents resell hijacked petroleum and traffic in drugs; and guerrillas and paramilitary groups in Colombia (both of whom use terrorist tactics) greatly increased their participation in the cocaine trade in the 1990s.

In short, the same democratizing effects of globalization that increased the opportunities for criminal activity apply to terrorists. The 'ungoverned' areas that have proliferated since the end of the Cold War have been used by terrorists and criminals to take refuge, and the decentralization of transnational crime groups that was evident by the 1990s has contributed to the ability of 'terrorists' to increase their involvement in crime. In addition to engaging in criminal activities to fund their activities (and sometimes cooperating with criminals in illicit trading), terrorists also seek the services provided by criminals for operational reasons—for example, buying weapons from illicit arms traffickers or false identity documents from counterfeiters. One of the greatest fears is that terrorists will be able to procure weapons of mass destruction from criminals.

While no one disputes these connections, there has been a great deal of disagreement over their meaning and the future course of events (for a review of the debate and evidence, see Prefontaine and Dandurand 2004.) The 'criminal–terrorist nexus' *can* be overstated—governments have incentives to discredit terrorists by labelling them as criminals, concerned only with profits, and law enforcement stands to benefit from more resources and powers by invoking the spectre of a 'strategic alliance' between the two. This view assumes that criminals and terrorists share an interest in both money making and destabilizing the state and that the multiplier effect of cooperating to attain their goals will be devastating.

While there is more contact between criminals and terrorists than ever before, collaboration is by no means automatic, nor—with the exception of the smuggling of nuclear materials—is it likely to have the devastating effects that some predict. As the US State Department emphasizes, the two groups share 'methods but not motives', and this tends to limit their collaboration. Criminals interested in profits may at times engage in tactical collaboration with terrorists, particularly where the latter control essential territory or resources (just as multinational corporations acting in conflict zones often do). In contrast, when criminal organizations are strong, they are likely to create barriers to entry for terrorists (and other individuals) interested in criminal activities. Even when collaboration brings monetary benefits, criminals may eschew it so as not to attract unwanted attention from law enforcement.

The different motives of the two groups also mean it is incorrect to predict an inevitable convergence of the two in the future. The ideological motives of terrorists usually persist, despite their participation in criminal activities: 'fighters turned felons' are a relatively rare phenomenon. For example, this label had been applied to the Islamic Movement of Uzbekistan but could not explain why a profit-driven group would fight to the death on behalf of the Taliban in Afghanistan in 2002. A more problematic phenomenon is that of 'felons turned zealots'. There is some evidence that criminals and terrorists who share jail cells also develop shared interests in joint criminal and terrorist ventures upon their release. This has been documented not only in South Asia, but also in the 2004 Madrid bombings, in which a radicalized drug dealer played an instrumental role.

Despite these caveats, it is important for policymakers and law enforcement to develop strategies to address the link between crime and terrorism. The risk of 'catastrophic criminality' requires particular attention to the smuggling of nuclear material. Targeting the criminal activities of terrorists is unlikely to bankrupt any organization, as most groups have diversified funding streams, but it could hinder their ability to fund and arm themselves on the margins. As importantly, identifying the criminal nexus within terrorism can provide an entry point into otherwise hermetic organizations for counterterrorist and intelligence specialists to exploit.

KEY POINTS

- Terrorist groups often rely on crime to fund and carry out their operations.

- There is increasing concern over the connections between terrorism and transnational criminal groups, but in most cases these are episodic 'marriages of convenience'.

- The radicalization of criminals by terrorists during periods when they are in close proximity, such as when they share prison cells, is one way in which criminal expertise is made available to terrorist groups.

Assessing the threat

Transnational criminal groups cause harm to individuals and societies with the profit-driven crimes they carry out. For example, drug trafficking con-

tributes to levels of substance abuse, petty crime, and the spread of HIV/AIDS by intravenous drug-users. Lost productivity, work accidents, and

 THINK POINT 25.1

Human trafficking and transnational crime

Transnational human trafficking has garnered an increasing amount of attention since the end of the Cold War. In 2007, the US State Department estimated that 800,000 persons were trafficked across international borders for the purpose of forced labour or involuntary prostitution. Many millions more suffer this fate within national borders. It is also estimated that 80 per cent of the victims are women or girls, many of whom are trafficked for the purpose of sexual servitude. Approximately half the victims are minors. The Terrorism, Transnational Crime and Corruption Center at George Mason University estimates that the industry generates between US$10 billion and US$40 billion per year.

Transnational criminal organizations play a major role in facilitating and profiting from this modern form of slavery. Victims are lured by scams or false promises made by criminal gangs, or sometimes are simply taken by force. Profits can derive from the smuggling process itself, since criminal gangs are often paid by employers at the destination for the delivery of forced labourers. In the case of integrated transnational networks, criminal organizations benefit directly by exploiting victims' labour in prostitution rings or other illegal ventures once they have reached their destination. Trafficking organizations typically move victims from less-developed to more-developed countries. Most human trafficking takes place in South East Asia, but there are also well-established trafficking networks connecting states of the former Soviet Union to Western Europe, and Latin America to the United States.

Human trafficking is not just another profit centre for transnational criminal organizations, but it is one of the activities these groups undertake that is viewed as a direct and growing threat to human and national security. On an individual level, human trafficking directly attacks a victim's human rights, health, and safety by pressing them into forced labour, exposing them to increased risk of sexually transmitted disease, physical assault, and mental illness, particularly post-traumatic stress disorder. It also degrades communities by breaking up families and

lowering levels of trust among community members, particularly because many victims come first into contact with trafficking networks through acquaintances. However, governments also perceive human trafficking as a threat to national security. In part, this is because trafficking networks are facilitated by official corruption, so they have a corrosive effect on the integrity of security forces. However, governments also worry that these dark networks may be used to traffic more than victims, serving as conduits for terrorist organizations, epidemic disease, or other nefarious threats to the state and its citizens.

Governments have reacted with increasing vigour to this threat, particularly in the developed world. Breaking up human trafficking networks is a classic example of a threat that requires a transnational response, since it crosses borders, but also an inter-agency response within states. In 2000, the United Nations adopted two protocols against the trafficking of women and the trafficking of migrants as part of the Convention against Transnational Organized Crime. In 2008, the Council of Europe Convention on Action against Trafficking in Human Beings came into effect. At the national level, countries such as the United Kingdom have explicitly criminalized trafficking in forced labour. Within the United States, for example, there have been federal efforts since 1998 to develop a national response to human trafficking through horizontal integration among different agencies (forty-two were involved at one count), but also vertical integration between national and local officials, typically taking the form of special task forces operating in urban areas hit particularly hard by this form of crime. However, conflicts between US government agencies over funding, jurisdiction, personnel, and information sharing are often cited as obstacles to effective government action against human trafficking. Similar inter-agency conflicts and lack of cooperation is also reported in many national anti-trafficking efforts. This suggests that there is still a long way to go before states develop effective responses to human trafficking.

Langberg (2008).

increased expenditures on health care are all economic costs associated with drug use. Coca production in South America has led to the deforestation of increasing areas of the Amazon forest and to the pollution of land and waterways with the chemicals used for growing and processing coca. These costs are often cited to justify viewing drug trafficking as a threat to human security or environmental security (see Think Point 25.1).

Often, however, transnational crime is characterized as a *national* security threat, requiring a quantitatively and qualitatively different response from government. This sometimes occurs when the *level* of harm caused by transnational crime reaches epidemic proportions—for example, the increase in the HIV infection rate unleashed by drug use in Russia. Or, if the crime itself is of a serious enough nature—for example, smuggling of nuclear material—the threat posed would be considered a matter for national security experts. Most often, however, the *perpetrators* of transnational crime—rather than the crimes themselves—are seen as the real threats to national security. According to this view, increasingly wealthy and powerful criminals undermine the state, democracy, and the economy through the use of corruption, violence, and reinvestment of their profits in the licit economy.

On a very basic level, the ability of transnational crime enterprises to evade state border controls and provide new avenues for the illicit transportation of goods and persons challenges the state's ability to exercise its core functions as guarantor of national sovereignty, the holder of the monopoly on force, and provider of the common good. In the course of their activities, transnational criminal enterprises corrupt and undermine numerous state agencies, providing mechanisms by which transnational criminal enterprises can affect the very nature of government and state policy in the host countries. At the extremes, transnational criminal enterprises become so powerful as to challenge and replace the state's monopoly on the use of force, as has occurred in some remote areas of the drug-producing regions of Colombia, Peru and Bolivia.

Second, governments view transnational crime as a security threat to the extent that it undermines democratic stability. In many states, transnational criminal enterprises have taken advantage of the instability that accompanied transitions to democracy to become entrenched, using corruption to extend their influence into the upper reaches of the state and thus shield themselves from law enforcement. The corruption of public institutions and the perceived fecklessness of law enforcement in new democracies contribute to undermining public confidence and loyalty to the new regime. In the extreme, popular reaction can lead to the replacement of governments or regimes, sometimes producing a restoration of democracy, as occurred during the Orange Revolution in Ukraine in 2004, but at other times leading to a nostalgia for more authoritarian forms of government, as has arguably occurred in Russia during the Putin presidency. This aspect of the threat posed by transnational crime is of concern to major powers such as the United States and the European Union that have a vested interest in promoting democracy.

Third, transnational crime is seen as a threat to economic development (and therefore national security). Organized crime is perceived as a threat to development in so far as it undermines the rule of law and deters foreign investment by increasing the level of violence and insecurity in host communities. In addition, criminals often reinvest their proceeds in the legal economy as part of its money-laundering efforts, and these criminally affiliated businesses often have an unfair competitive advantage through their access to cheap capital and their ability to intimidate competitors in the market.

While this threat assessment is true for some organized crime structures and countries, it is often incorrectly applied across the board to all instances of 'transnational organized crime'. Recall, however, that the minimalist definition of transnational organized crime used by governments and international organizations means there is a great deal of variation in the size, structure, and activities of these groups. In particular, they vary greatly in the factors that are often considered the 'trademarks' of organized crime; the extent to which they use violence and corruption to facilitate their crimes; and the degree to which they penetrate the legal economy. This variation can help explain the very different threat perceptions of organized crime held by groups of academics who study the topic. In particular, analysts who study criminal markets in advanced industrial democracies are more likely to stress the 'disorganized' nature of criminal networks and downplay the threat posed by these groups. These critics point to misleading and sensationalized media coverage of 'mafia-like' organized crime groups; political rhetoric based on grossly over-inflated official estimates of criminal profits; and undifferentiated threat assessments by law enforcement based on unclear methodological and empirical grounds to argue that the threat is exaggerated (Naylor 2002; van Duyne 2004). In other countries, organized crime lives up to its billing as violent, corrupting, and disruptive of national economies.

The challenge for students of transnational organized crime is to develop empirically grounded theories of the threat transnational crime poses, rather than assuming the threat based on the 'transnational-organized-crime' label (which tends to be most readily applied to ethnic groups

operating at the margins of society). For example, while many observers believe that hierarchical organizations are more wealthy, corrupt, and violent than other criminal structures, there is a lack of empirical information to determine if this is the case.[3] Others have suggested that organized crime groups be categorized not according to their organizational logic but rather in terms of the different ways they are embedded in society (von Lampe 2004). Groups embedded in high-level social and political structures are likely to pose a greater threat (through corruption and penetration of the licit economy) than those that operate at the margins of society.

KEY POINTS

- The crimes committed by transnational criminal groups often harm individuals and societies, posing a threat to human security.

- Transnational crime often comes to be seen as a national security threat because of the added danger posed by the modus operandi of the perpetrators of transnational crime.

- Policy-makers and law-enforcement agencies are particularly concerned with the extent to which wealthy and powerful criminal groups engage in corruption and violence and reinvest their illicit profits in ways that undermine the basic functions of the state, democracy, and the economy. The challenge is to determine which crime groups pose this threat and which are dangerous primarily for the threat they pose to individuals and society.

Government responses

Transnational criminal organizations are not inherently more sophisticated or dangerous than other crime structures, but they do tend to pose greater challenges for governments, which are much more constrained than illicit actors by borders and traditional norms of sovereignty. In an effort to deal with the increasingly transnational and decentralized

nature of criminal networks, governments have globalized their law-enforcement efforts, harmonizing laws to remove loopholes exploited by

---

[3]Though see UNODC (2002), which surveys forty crime groups in sixteen countries and finds that hierarchical groups are more likely to employ violence and corruption than criminal networks.

criminals and creating police networks to facilitate cross-national cooperation. The overwhelming emphasis on transnational crime as a national security threat since the end of the Cold War (and especially after the terrorist attacks of 9/11) has meant increased resources for law enforcement, incursions on civil liberties, increasingly blurred lines between law-enforcement and national security apparatuses (particularly intelligence agencies), and an emphasis on targeting criminal organizations rather than criminal markets.

Global policing trends: increased coordination and securitization

The 'war on drugs', rather than a concern with transnational crime per se, led the United States to place an increased emphasis on both bilateral and multilateral cooperation on law enforcement in the 1980s. The USA used financial sticks and carrots to promote drug-control efforts in producer and transit nations; pushed hard in multilateral circles for the 1988 UN Convention against Illicit Traffic in Narcotic Drugs and Pyschotropic Substances and the G8's establishment of the Financial Action Task Force to promote laws and expertise for countering the money laundering associated with the drug trade; and encouraged sometimes reluctant European law-enforcements agencies to adopt more aggressive and intelligence-based approaches to counter narcotics trafficking.

With the extension of transnational crime to new areas of the globe in the 1990s, increasing numbers of nations began to see transnational crime as a serious problem and were willing to take measures to reduce the asymmetries between countries though harmonization of legislation and increasing police capacity and networking. This trend was reinforced by the emphasis placed on it by a hegemonic USA in the 1990s and by processes of regional integration (such as the creation of the European Union) that created additional incentives and opportunities for law-enforcement cooperation (Andreas and

Nadelmann 2006). One example is the European Police Office (EUROPOL), which was established in 1992 as part of the Maastricht Treaty creating the European Union; its initial focus on fighting drugs soon expanded to other forms of transnational crime, and this broader emphasis was formalized in the 2002 annex to the Europol Convention. The 2000 UN Convention against Transnational Organized Crime and 2003 UN Convention against Corruption are also indicative of increased international cooperation on transnational crime.

The terrorist attacks of 9/11 in the United States and the subsequent emphasis on fighting terrorism on both sides of the Atlantic only deepened already unprecedented levels of cross-national cooperation. The blurring of lines between law-enforcement and national security agencies and missions that had already begun with the emphasis of transnational crime as a national security threat only increased with the fear of 'catastrophic criminality', forcing law-enforcement agencies to engage in the worst-case scenario planning usually reserved for the military and national security apparatus. Despite significant disagreements on how to address terrorism, there was significant transatlantic convergence on the role of law enforcement. Many governments were willing to embrace more drastic responses, devoting additional resources to law enforcement and introducing more draconian legal measures, some of which arguably endangered civil liberties, such as the forfeiture of all assets held by persons participating in organized crime schemes, not just those related to the crime itself. In addition, governments considered how emerging technologies, often derived from military programmes, could be put to use in improving the ability of government to gather information on transnational crime and, in some cases, how the military could be used to attack this threat.

Evaluating government responses

Overwhelmingly, the government response to transnational crime has focused on targeting the individuals and organizations perpetrating the crime rather than the criminal markets themselves. In the case of the drug trade, for instance, leaders or 'critical nodes' of drug-trafficking organizations are targeted (depending upon whether they are hierarchies or networks), as are criminal assets. Less attention is paid to reducing the demand for drugs or the social conditions that contribute to the attractiveness of illicit crop cultivation. Although it is often criticized, this organizational focus may make sense, especially if the targeted criminal organizations are so powerful, violent, and corrupt that they pose an even greater immediate threat to the state and democracy than the drug trafficking itself—as was the case in

Colombia in the late 1980s and early 1990s (see Case Study 25.1).

Law-enforcement approaches that target criminal organizations have had some tactical successes. For example, the Cali and Medellin cartels were dismantled and 50 per cent of the transnational organized crime groups identified in a 1999 UNODC survey were defunct by the time of the study's publication in 2002. However, the overall strategic effectiveness of this approach has been called into question. In the short to medium run, law-enforcement efforts tend to increase corruption (paying off officials is only necessary if criminals have something to fear from law enforcement) and violence (as criminals compete to fill the organizational vacuums left open by

---

CASE STUDY 25.1

Targeting criminal organizations: trade-offs and unintended consequences

The Cali and Medellin drug-trafficking organizations that dominated the drug-trafficking market in Colombia were not 'cartels' in the strict sense of the word (they were *not* monopolistic business corporations that 'cornered' the criminal market, controlling the levels of production of cocaine or its distribution). Despite this, they were large and hierarchical structures that posed a significant threat to political stability in Colombia, each in its own way. Pablo Escobar, head of the Medellin cartel, orchestrated the assassination of police officers and presidential candidates as part of his campaign to avoid extradition to the United States. The Cali cartel, in contrast, threatened democracy not with extraordinary violence but rather through their large-scale penetration of the legal economy and use of corruption (including an alleged US$6 million contribution to the successful presidential campaign of Ernesto Samper in 1994). The threat posed by these groups led to a campaign by the Colombian government (with US assistance) against, first, the Medellin cartel and then the Cali cartel in the early to mid-1990s.

Both campaigns were successful, leading to the dismantling of the cartels and the threat they posed to the state and democracy at the national level. The constituent parts of the cartels remained, however, and these decentralized networks

continue to traffic drugs out of Colombia to the United States and Europe. Some analysts even argue that these decentralized groups are more 'dangerous' than the cartels they replaced: as decentralized groups they are presumably more efficient, and their lower profile and lack of government intelligence on their operations allow them to work more surreptitiously than the cartels had. This view is questionable; the *cartelitos* do not pose the same threat to the state and democracy as the cartels, and it is not clear that the organizational form of their enterprise matters much for the ongoing vitality of the drug trade, which is guaranteed by its profitability.

While the dismantling of the cartels had little effect on the availability and price of illicit drugs, it did have unintended consequences that increased the threat posed to the Colombian state and population. Violent right-wing paramilitary forces and left-wing insurgents were able to expand their participation in the drug trade, stepping into the vacuum left by the cartels. The *cartelitos* were weaker and less able to resist incursions into the drug trade by the well-armed insurgents and paramilitaries; rather than try to protect their market share, the *cartelitos* instead engaged in transactions with the armed groups to a far great extent than did the cartels to produce and traffic drugs. Not only did increased drug money fuel insurgent and paramilitary activities, but turf wars between the two over trafficking routes contributed to massacres of civilians and mass internal refugee movements.

law-enforcement successes). In the medium to long run, tactical successes in one country can lead to the spread of illicit markets to other countries and strengthen new sets of actors, who may pose an even graver threat to the state (see Case Study 25.1)—without having much effect on the price and availability of illicit goods. While these 'unintended consequences' are commonplace and well documented, governments continue to fail to anticipate them when devising enforcement strategies.

While law enforcement is an important part of any strategy to combat transnational crime, the shortcomings identified above have rightly led to calls for a more comprehensive approach that relies on all elements of national power to address crime. To the extent that transnational crime harms individuals and society, public-health ministries, non-governmental organizations (NGOs), and other groups should be involved. For example, devising measures protecting the victim (for example, in the case of trafficking in persons) and minimizing the harm to society should be given more importance than targeting organizations. Given the harm posed to the integrity of public institutions by corruption, collaborators of organized crime groups in the licit sector should be targeted with as much vigour as the 'career' criminals themselves.

Approaches that focus on the general underlying conditions that facilitate illicit markets, such as state failure or corruption, are important, particularly to the extent that they bring into play actors and approaches often neglected in the traditional law-enforcement approach. The World Bank has emphasized building up the capacity of judicial systems as a mechanism to ensure good governance and the rule of law and in addressing corruption. The private sector and NGOs have also contributed, both by setting industry-wide standards designed to combat organized crime, as has been done by the international banking industry, and through civic education designed to help citizens resist the influence of these groups in their lives. NGOs such as Transparency International (founded in 1993) can also play an important role in targeting corruption and in linking transnational crime and a wide range of other important issues on the international agenda such as responses to conflict situations, peacekeeping, promotion of the rule of law, and protection of human rights (Godson and Williams 1998). This brings a new set of groups and agencies to bear on the problem, checks the penetration of government and the private sector by transnational crime, and provides new avenues by which citizens can hold states accountable for this problem.

KEY POINTS

- The US war on drugs largely drove initial state and international responses to transnational crime in the 1980s.

- With the spread of transnational crime in the 1990s, growing US hegemony, and regional integration initiatives, nations increasingly coordinated regional and international responses to crime.

- Governments have come to perceive transnational crime as a national security threat, leading to the temptation to use intelligence assets and the military to supplement law enforcement.

- At the same time, the concern of international financial institutions and non-governmental organizations with corruption and state failure—two issues closely related to transnational crime—holds the promise of more comprehensive national responses to supplement law enforcement.

Conclusion

Transnational crime has expanded aggressively since the late 1980s, particularly since the end of the Cold War opened up new possibilities for criminal enterprises. Globalization has particularly facilitated not only the development of new criminal markets but also new forms of organization. The available evidence suggests that organized crime is becoming more difficult to fight because it has become more adaptable and resistant to available law-enforcement strategies. Even if organized crime networks turn out to be more vulnerable than many analysts believe, the ability for organized crime to form tactical or strategic alliances more easily today should give governments cause for concern.

Ironically, the global trends most welcomed by leaders in developed countries, globalization, democratization and economic liberalization, also have a dark side: the capacity to create new spaces for the spread of transnational crime. Just as these trends promote greater political, economic, and personal freedom, they also facilitate the ability of criminals to transcend national jurisdictions. Even if countries were to decide that costs of globalization outweighed the benefits, these are trends that are largely beyond the control of any single government. The question becomes one of how to contain this phenomenon and reduce the harm it causes.

This is particularly true if we consider that organized crime not only targets individuals but undermines societies, particularly those in transition to democracy and free markets. The threat that transnational crime poses to whole regions, be it the Horn of Africa or the Balkans, means that even governments with relatively robust law-enforcement capabilities and well-established rule of law are faced with the spillover effects of transnational crime based in poorly governed areas of the globe.

Does this rise to the level of a national security threat justify the use of intelligence and military assets, and, perhaps, even a certain level of expediency in the pursuit of justice? Not all governments or societies will concur. Those countries where law enforcement and judiciaries are highly capable and adapt sufficiently quickly to contain transnational crime are unlikely to face such a choice. However, in countries where voters believe that the rule of law and personal safety is disappearing, pressure will develop for politicians to seek more draconian solutions. This is particularly true where a link is established, correctly or not, between transnational crime and terrorism. In extreme cases, it can lead to support for more authoritarian forms of government and restrictions on free markets, as has arguably occurred in Putin's Russia.

The question is therefore what can governments, the private sector, and civil society do to reduce the harm caused by transnational crime before they are driven to extreme measures? Clearly, there is room for solutions short of militarization. One approach suggests greater cooperation between law-enforcement and national intelligence assets to address threats that cross borders. Others have suggested greater attention to preventive measures, particularly by those developed states with the greatest stake in the success of the emerging international system. To the extent that the United States, Western Europe, Australia, and Japan value democracy and free markets, then it makes sense for them to engage in capacity-building processes designed to strengthen the rule of law and law-enforcement agencies, particularly in countries that are experiencing so-called dual transitions. Given what we also know about the consequences of civil war for the proliferation of transnational crime, this also suggests another arena for anticipatory measures.

QUESTIONS

1. What factors enabled the expansion of transnational crime during the 1990s?

2. What is new about transnational crime today?

3. Does it matter if transnational crime is organized as hierarchies, as networks, or as markets?

4. Is transnational organized crime a greater threat than other forms of illicit activity?

5. What factors affect the extent to which terrorist groups and transnational criminal groups cooperate?

6. What indicators should we consider in deciding whether transnational crime has become a national-security threat?

7. Why are governments tempted to use military and intelligence assets to address transnational crime? What problems might arise from such a response to this threat?

FURTHER READING

- Andreas, Peter, and Nadelmann, Ethan (2006), *Policing the Globe: Criminalization and Crime Control in International Relations*, New York: Oxford University Press. Description and analysis of the internationalization of crime control, from the 1800s through 2005.

- Naylor, R. T. (2002), *Wages of Crime: Black Markets, Illegal Finances, and the Wages of Crime*, Cornell, NY: Cornell University Press. This book presents a critique of the view of organized crime as a powerful hierarchical organization and a threat to national security.

- Prefontaine, D. C, and Dandurand, Yvon (2004), 'Terrorism and Organized Crime: Reflections on an Illusive Link and its Implications for Criminal Law Reform', paper prepared for the annual meeting of the International Society for Criminal Law Reform, Montreal, Aug., www.icclr.law.ubc.ca/Publications/Reports/International%20 Society%20Paper%20of%20Terrorism.pdf. Based on a United Nations survey of dozens of countries and a review of the literature, this paper provides a critical assessment of the argument that terrorism and transnational criminal organizations are converging and may begin to cooperate to a greater extent.

- United Nations Office on Drugs and Crime, Global Programme against Transnational Organized Crime (2002), 'Results of a Pilot Survey of Forty Selected Organized Criminal Groups in Sixteen Countries', Sept., www.unodc. org/pdf/crime/publications/Pilot_survey.pdf. Reports the findings from a 1999 survey of law-enforcement and academic experts on organized crime and presents a typology of organized crime groups.

- Williams, Phil (2001), 'Transnational Criminal Networks', in J. Arquilla and D. Ronfeldt (eds.), *Networks and Netwars: The Future of Terror, Crime and Militancy*, Santa Monica, CA: RAND Corporation, 61–97; www.rand. org/publications/MR/MR1382/MR1382.ch3.pdf. This RAND study uses network theory to explain the organization of transnational crime and argues that networked criminal organizations are more flexible and robust than the governments that target them.

IMPORTANT WEBSITES

- http://www.organized-crime.de Klaus von Lampe Organized Crime Research. Although the geographical focus of this website is the USA and Germany, its social-science perspective and collection of organized crime definitions, papers, book reviews, and web links makes it an essential resource.

- http://www.ojp.usdoj.gov/nij/publications/annual-reports.htm   National Institute of Justice, US Department of Justice. This webpage provides a comprehensive collection of official reports and commissioned research publications that provide an overview of the US perspective on organized crime.

- http://policy-traccc.gmu.edu Transnational Crime and Corruption Center, George Mason University. This center brings together a large collection of academic and policy research on transnational crime (with a focus on Russia and former Soviet states), as well as providing a comprehensive set of links to other online resources on this subject.

- http://www.unodc.org United Nations Office on Drugs and Crime (UNODC). The UNODC is one of the leading international agencies focused on assisting states in developing international efforts to fight drug trafficking, terrorism, and organized crime.

 Visit the Online Resource Centre that accompanies this book for lots of interesting additional material: www.oxfordtextbooks.co.uk/orc/collins2e/

26

Child Soldiers

HELEN BROCKLEHURST

Chapter Contents

- Introduction
- Children and war: a brief history
- Rough guide to contemporary child soldiers
- Responses to child soldiers
- Critical issues
- Conclusion

Reader's Guide

This chapter explores the issue area of child soldiers and considers how and why young people have taken up roles in armed conflict. Using examples from historical and contemporary conflicts, the chapter outlines the reasons for children's recruitment and the impact that war has on them. Voluntary and forced conscription, armed and unarmed roles, gendered practices and post-conflict rehabilitation are considered. The chapter then goes on to look at the attention given to this area by the international community and policies and legislation designed to curb the use of child soldiers. The final section looks at some of the more critical security issues associated with research into child soldiers, including stereotypes in popular culture, Western practices of militarization and cadetship, and the ethical and methodological challenges to researching this area. The chapter begins by looking at the meanings and importance attached to childhood and the changing ideas and values associated with child soldiers.

Introduction

Child soldiers are now regarded as one of the most challenging issues of today's modern wars. Indeed the presence of an estimated 300,000 child soldiers has created substantially more attention than millions of civilian children killed and affected by war. Even though child soldiers' needs and rights did not feature in peace agreements until 1996, this issue area can now be said to be a global one; and the response to them in part forms an international regime. The United Nations and a proliferation of international organizations have sought to raise awareness of 'war affected children' and an increasing number of international agreements and legislation call for an end to the use of child soldiers and for children's protection in war. The organization Coalition to Stop the Use of Child Soldiers (2009) estimates that the number of conflicts *directly* involving child soldiers dropped from 27 in 2004 to 17 by 2008. However, this downward trend is thought to be more the result of conflicts ending than the impact of initiatives to end child-soldier recruitment and use. Further, it observes:

> The military recruitment of children (under-18s) and their use in hostilities is a much larger phenomenon, that still takes place in one form or another in at least 86 countries and territories worldwide. This includes unlawful recruitment by armed groups, forcible recruitment by government forces, recruitment or use of children into militias or other groups associated with armed forces, their use as spies, as well as legal recruitment into peacetime armies.

Coalition to Stop the Use of Child Soldiers (2009).

A United Nations report by the Special Representative for Children and Armed Conflict acknowledged that,

despite 'clear and strong children and armed conflict protection standards, and important concrete initiatives, particularly at the international level', atrocities against children and impunity for violators continue largely unabated on the ground' (United Nations 20005c). It has also been observed by many NGOs that in the last decade pre-teen child soldiers have become far more prevalent. These facts about their use may reflect the unchanging economy of child soldiers—in short, they are abundant, cheap, and extremely useful to military groups. It is also likely that many child soldiers are not simply forcibly recruited but are choosing an armed role in exchange for freedom from want and even freedom from fear. We rarely think about child soldiers as being relatively safe in their roles. Indeed, their protection in a militia or regular army may be the primary reason for them enlisting. As Wessells (2006: 23) notes, 'children's vulnerability in war zones sets the stage for them becoming soldiers' (see Background 26.1).

Global efforts to curb child soldiers, however futile, also represent the desire to recognize and address a collective of 'child soldiers'. However, as this chapter will illustrate, child soldiers are not new in the sense of young people's participation in war; moreover, child soldiers are not a consequence of particular and recent kinds of conflict. Child soldiers are indeed symptomatic of complex emergencies, but it is worth considering the label of child soldier carefully when thinking about their roles in war and their recognition in understandings of security. Rosen (2007: 304) notes 'this child-soldier "crisis" is also a modern political crisis, which has little to do with whether there are more or fewer children in wars today'.

Children and war: a brief history

Although child soldiering is frequently described as a modern phenomenon, children have often been trained and engaged in warfare in the past. Children

under the age of 15, for example, have been present in wars since they have been recorded—many successfully or famously so, including leaders such as Alexander the Great, Joan of Arc, the mythic children's crusaders, and captains of 'nursery' ships under Napoleon. Rosen (2005: 4) even describes the American civil war as 'a boys' war'. Conservative estimates are of 250,000–420,000 boys, many in their early teens, serving in the Union and Confederate armies and celebrated for doing so. Avery Brown, for example, was aged 8, but convinced his recruiters that he was aged 12 (Rosen 2005: 4). Evidence of such labour in terms of their individual heroics survives but recognition of their wider participation generally has not. For an issue that has emerged within the last twenty years of the so-called information age, a little knowledge has gone a long way. In the past century children have swelled the ranks of armies of both world wars and more recently the Cold War. Child soldiers fought against Russian soldiers in Afghanistan in the 1980s and have gone on to remain in insurgent forces as adults. More recently, the Taliban in Afghanistan has recruited an estimated 8,000 children into its ranks, and Tajik and Uzbek boys have been recruited as their adversaries (Wessells and Kostelny 2002). Interestingly, a number of authors now draw attention to vast numbers of children who fought in colonial wars of independence, some of whom have gone on to hold positions of leadership, and who have not generated the attention afforded to today's child soldiers. Indeed, as we shall see from the section below, the arrival of the pejorative label 'child soldier' does not indicate the beginnings of the practice of soldiering by children, but marks the point at which a society's conception of childhood became incommensurable when harnessed to its practices of warfare.

Childhoods

There is no single agreed definition of a child that is in use worldwide for any purpose. Neither is there agreement on the question of how long childhood is or what it is that makes childhood unique, special, or a time of 'innocence'. The generally accepted definition in development studies and enshrined in

international law is that a child is a person under the age of 18. But childhood is also a social construct. Its duration and dimensions can be made and un-made, and this flexibility is partly where its power lies for those who deploy children and childhoods in the service of war. For example, in the USA the minimum age for marriage with parental consent ranges from 14 to 18 for males, and from 12 to 18 for females. In Palestine, Military Orders subject children over 16 to adult treatment, including incarceration. Their Israeli counterparts are allowed to remain children, and therefore free from adult imprisonment, until they are 18. Childhoods vary dramatically around the globe in terms of duration and responsibilities. Child soldiers are most commonly recruited around the ages of 13–15, and in many of their communities they may already be regarded as youths or adults once they have reached the age of 14 (Wessells 2006: 8). The definition of a child as a person under the age of 18 may not be accepted by child soldiers themselves or those who recruit them. In addition, young people often equate the experience of exercising power (especially through criminal, violent, or military activity) with the crossing of the threshold into adulthood (Marks 2001). In this way war automatically generates both child soldiers and new 'adults'. This is well documented in conflicts and public protests from Northern Ireland to Gaza and South Africa.

Definitions and understandings matter here in other ways. Definitions mirror priorities, shape policies, and direct resources towards the assistance of child soldiers. Some researchers theorize that part of the brain associated with risk does not reach its full development until the age of 20. This could have crucial implications for how we assess young people's drive to participate in political violence. The academic study of childhood studies that includes their development and its socio-economic and political context is still relatively new. Attention on children's moral and even political *capacity* is also extremely recent, despite evidence of their long-standing political roles throughout history. There is now a notable paradigm shift underway in childhood studies that suggests that Western conceptions of childhood may have held back understandings of children's agency. Consequently we are late in recognizing the multiple forms in which children yield power and exercise responsibilities and rights. As Wyness, Harrison, and Buchanan (2004: 81) state:

> Children are seen as 'presocial', unable to articulate a set of coherent political views (Sears and Valentino 1997). The social science community has thus treated children's political participation as a contradiction in terms. A political community has an exclusive adult membership with children unable to provide qualifications for entry.... these research assumptions connect with broader social forces of convention. For many the very essence of childhood, at least in contemporary western terms, prohibits political participation such that the 'political child' is seen as the 'unchild', a counter-stereotypical image of children that does not fit with the way we commonly view childhood.

(Stainton-Rogers and Stainton-Rogers 1992: 32 – 3)

Children in military roles playing out their own ethical dilemmas very much challenge the idea that they are non-political beings. The latest research on children in peaceful environments suggests that they can engage with moral issues from the ages of 4 or 5 and reach adult levels of understanding from the age of 12 (indeed it has been noted that 12 is the age at which many child migrants make their decision to flee). Ongoing debates, therefore, about children's understandings of identity, violence, and power have many serious implications for how we assist child soldiers and respond to children in any political roles. As we shall see in the later examples of child soldier rehabilitation, efforts to have equal partnerships with children in order to further facilitate their contribution to society are still lacking.

The shifting debate in the study of children and childhoods is summarized in Think Point 26.1.

THINK POINT 26.1

Changing understandings of childhood

From	To
Children	Children and childhood
Understood	Partially knowable
Male or female	Gendered
Unable/developing	Also 'hyper-enabled'
Innocent and passive	Also actors, consumers, agents
Non-citizens/un-political	Also potentially morally and politically engaged

---

'The child soldier'

The most accepted definition of a child soldier, which was adopted by relief agencies around the world, was created in 1997 through a meeting of academics and non-governmental organizations. Their aim was better to identify child soldiers through a more accurate, less weapon-centric interpretation of soldiering. These conditions, known as 'the Cape Town Principles', include the following definition of a child soldier as

> any person under 18 years of age who is part of any kind of regular or irregular armed force in any capacity, including but not limited to cooks, porters, messengers, and those accompanying such groups, other than purely as family

members. Girls recruited for sexual purposes and forced marriage are included in this definition. It does not therefore only refer to a child who is carrying or has carried arms. 🙶🙶

UNICEF (1997: 1).

It may still not be clear from this accepted definition who exactly is a child soldier. The criteria for participation in an armed group are not given, and this leaves out children participating in less organized political violence and those children who are 'armed' using homemade weapons. Rosen (2007: 299) speaks of a 'humanitarian narrative' of childhood and argues that 'its expression in international law is embedded in transnational politics, is not cross-culturally grounded, and is extremely limiting. It is too blunt an instrument, which does not allow for varying solutions to the very real network of social problems it has identified and is trying to address.'

The labelling of child soldiers can indeed raise further practical dilemmas on the ground. In one respect they are part of a broader group of children caught up in war. Wessells noted as early as 1998 that child soldiers may not want to be categorized as child soldiers because further victimization and stigma may ensue. The term used by Wessells in his advocacy work is 'Children (or Minors) Associated with Fighting Forces' or CAFF. He notes that in war-torn communities the term 'underage' soldiers or 'minors' is used alongside the term 'child soldier', suggesting that it is more compatible with local traditions of childhood (Wessells 2006: 8).

KEY POINTS

- Persons under the age of 18 have fought throughout history. The idea of the teenage child soldier as a global concern is new.

- Growing research since the 1990s is indicating that children are capable of thinking about moral and political issues far earlier than we expect.

- Definitions of childhood vary considerably worldwide.

- We do not commonly regard the child as a political child, *least of all* as an *actor* in the international system.

Rough guide to contemporary child soldiers

CASE STUDY 26.1

Children in the Democratic Republic of Congo

'The six-year conflict in the Democratic Republic of Congo (DRC) is the deadliest war on the planet since the Second World War, and the worst ever recorded in Africa. From 1998 to 2004, approximately 3.8 million people died as a result of the crisis. Eighteen months after the signing of a formal peace agreement, people in the DRC continue to die at a rate three times higher than the average for sub-Saharan Africa. The war has led to extreme violence, widespread rape, mass population displacements, and a collapse of public services. Deaths from non-violent causes, such as infectious diseases, are highest in conflict-prone regions where security problems continue to affect access to health care and humanitarian assistance.

All the parties involved in the conflict in the DRC have recruited, abducted, and used child soldiers. Children made up approximately 40 per cent of the members of some armed groups in the eastern DRC in 2003, with at least 30,000 taking an active part in combat. There are thousands more children, mostly girls, attached to these groups who are used for sexual and other services.'

Hobson (2005: 7)

Recruitment and treatment

Until recently the political will has not existed to track the number and extent of the majority of child soldiers. Even the origin of the most quoted statistic on the global number of child soldiers (300,000) remains uncertain and is but a soft estimate. Currently both governments and illegal armed groups use child soldiers. States may recruit children between the ages of 16 and 18 directly into their ranks, including as part of compulsory service. States that have been using children in hostilities in recent years include Chad, the Democratic Republic of the Congo (DRC), Israel, Myanmar (which has the most number of child soldiers), Somalia, Sudan and Southern Sudan, Uganda, Yemen, and the United Kingdom. The youngest ever recorded child soldier was a 5-year-old in Uganda. The youngest ever recorded child terrorist was a 7-year-old in Colombia (Singer 2005).

A majority of child soldiers are estimated to be in non-state armed groups. In 2005, Save the Children estimated that there were 120,000 girls, some as young as 8, who had been forced to become front-line fighters or support armed groups. In Sierra Leone, for example, approximately 48,000 child soldiers were used by the various fighting forces, with 12,000 of these estimated to be girls. The recruitment strategies of armed groups vary widely, but it is thought that the vast majority of child soldiers within these ranks have joined voluntarily. The reality for most children probably lies somewhere in between forced and voluntary recruitment, as neither term depicts the threats that children are under, nor the agency that they can still demonstrate within their predicament. Isolated or orphaned children are not necessarily more at risk of abduction by armed groups (SWAY 2008), though this is a common perception. Similarly, refugee camps are not necessarily recruiting grounds, though they can lead many children to return to child soldiering.

The forced recruitment of children covers a number of means. In the worst cases, children are directly abused, tortured, raped, or forced to participate in this treatment of other children and family members as part of a their initiation. Children may be intimidated through the threat of physical torture (press ganging). There are many children who cannot verify their age with birth certificates because of low or no birth registration in some regions; this also makes it easier for children to be conscripted underage. Child soldiers may be given alcohol or drugs in order to encourage them or confuse them. However, some authors have cautioned that this may not be typical, even though it is widely reported because of its sensationalist impact. Children have been forcibly recruited from schools in Afghanistan, Burma, El Salvador, Ethiopia, and Mozambique. Even so, forced recruitment does not equate to victimhood and incapacity. Such children may be making an active decision to save their own lives.

Children may enlist to gain protection, shelter, food, 'family', and direction. Children may also wish to demonstrate their moral or political allegiance to sides involved in local or state violence, especially if family members are already involved. Children may perceive that a military group offers them education or career advancement, and some rebel groups do provide more schooling and support than children might otherwise receive (Brett and Specht 2004). In all these examples children have been commonly reported to make such decisions at around the age of 12. Excitement is another reason why up to 10 per cent of children in some studies have reported joining an armed group.

Roles and responsibilities

Childhood and soldiering can be extremely compatible, and children's roles in conflict are numerous. Children may be needed simply in the absence of available adult combatants, or because they offer another valued capacity. In this deadly occupation, children may be cheap and efficient, and, in comparison to adults, less demanding and more obedient. Positive aspects of childhood may be relied upon, including dexterity and vitality. Physically, child soldiers may be capable of adult roles using lightweight weapons such as AK47s, although it is arguable whether weapon weight has ever been a deterrent to child soldiers throughout history. Conversely, children's roles or functions may also be based on qualities of weakness or innocence afforded by their status. Child soldiers may be used because of their inferior mental development and their greater susceptibility to manipulation through fear or drugs. Child soldiers may be forced to commit some atrocities that adults do not wish to. If one takes a very broad definition of participation in fighting forces then the following roles can be identified:

- combatants
- camp support roles (portering, cooking, cleaning)
- sex slaves and 'wives' of commanders
- messengers
- logistics
- intelligence gatherers
- minesweepers
- suicide bombers
- distracters on the front line
- recruiters and trainers of other children
- commanders of units of children

In some conflicts girls have been sought out for their ability to carry and porter heavy camp equipment. Other armed groups have created units solely made up of children, such as the Lord's Liberation Army in Uganda and the LTTE's 'Baby Brigade' in Sri Lanka. Children can take on a variety of roles and responsibilities, but this does not, of course, mean that that a child is acting in war knowingly or effectively or with compliance.

Does gender matter?

As UNICEF notes, whilst the term 'child soldier' conjures up images of gun-toting adolescent boys, the reality is very different. A number of the world's child soldiers are actually girls—in some countries up to 40 per cent—and many are as young as 7 or 8

years old. Reports of girls being used within armed groups come from Colombia, East Timor, Pakistan, Uganda, the Philippines, Sri Lanka, and the DRC, to name a few locations. In 2005, in the DRC, there were up to 12,500 girls in armed groups. In Sri Lanka, 43 per cent of the 51,000 children involved in the conflict were girls (Hobson 2005). The UN Department of Peace Keeping Operations (UNDPKO)'s Principles and Guidance also recognize that 'special attention should be devoted to . . . female ex-combatants and child soldiers'.

Although girl soldiers may seek out military roles for their promise of gender equality, one of the biggest issues facing them in the armed forces is sexual violence. Both boys and girls of every age have been routinely raped in war. Child soldiers are not immune from this, and gender-based atrocities have been perpetrated by state and non–state forces. Sexual violence may also be a reason why children flee to armed groups. Investigative reports following the 1994 genocide in Rwanda concluded that nearly every female over the age of 12 who survived the genocide was raped (OAU 2000: 159). In one Save the Children's programme in West Africa, 32 per cent of all girls in an armed group reported having been raped, 38 per cent were treated for sexually transmitted infections, and 66 per cent were single mothers.

However, not *all* groups who use child soldiers use sexual violence on them, though this is widely suggested. Research from the DRC shows a prevailing assumption that girl soldiers are used *always* and *only* as sexual possessions ('wives' of commanders). Though sexual violence against girls is very common, girls here may be provided with weapons in order to protect themselves from male predation. There is also evidence of groups where perpetrators of sexual violence within ranks are punished and evicted. In Columbia, the Philippines, and Sri Lanka even consensual relationships may be prohibited.

In one study, nearly half of the girls in an armed group that used camp 'wives' described their primary role as a 'fighter'. Others listed military duties such as portering, cleaning, providing medical assistance, gathering information, or cooking.

However, girls' participation in armed groups has partly remained hidden because so few have chosen to enrol in formal demobilization processes. In addition, former girl soldiers have typically been presumed to have provided only unarmed support roles and not to be in need of the kind of assistance provided for former boy soldiers.

Attention to specific needs of both boys and girls can be lost if their identities are subsumed under general discourses of childhood. In the context of soldiering, 'children' are often imagined to be boys, and boys themselves can be thought of as older than their years. The word 'youth' might potentially be used for both sexes but is nearly always assumed by Western commentators to describe a male collective. It is also imbued with overtones of strength and violence and is consequently a pejorative description that may incite fear and foster neglect (Kurtenbach 2008). Similarly, researchers have shown that girls are not only a marginalized gender but also a marginalized age group. Women's and older girls' experiences are often conflated, and the particular challenges of being *both* young and female are neglected (McKay and Mazurana

2004). This oversight also reflects the broader gendered position of women in war, whose recognition as agents or targets remains hard earned. In many other aspects of global politics statistics on the plight of women and girls also remain aggregated.

KEY POINTS

- Child soldiers are also caught up in conflict and in this sense can be thought of as both victims and victimizers.
- The constant and unreferenced global estimate of 300,000 child soldiers hides the fact that, because they are constantly dying, the total number used each year is far greater.
- Child soldiers may be forced to act in particular roles while also readily embracing others.
- We may need to think more about gender and stages of childhood and especially girlhood instead of one category of children.
- Within each role, gender plays a part in determining the nature and cost of their participation.

Responses to child soldiers

Engaging child soldiers: military perspectives

It is curious that, despite immense Western (European and American) attention on child soldiers and the roles they are assigned, there has been relatively little preparation by Western militaries in engaging with them. The child has a capacity to provide greater shock to those cultures where use of children is uncommon and child martyrdom not celebrated. In 2003, Germany declined to send troops to the DRC out of concern they would face child soldiers. Hesitation, however momentary, by combatants unprepared for targeting children can lead to fatalities. Singer raised this issue when he cited child soldiers' tactical successes in the ambush or kidnapping of military personnel. In 2000,

a commander of the Royal Irish Regiment refused to fire on 'children armed with AKs'. His squad was subsequently taken hostage by a group of child soldiers in Sierra Leone known as the West Side Boys (Singer 2005). Singer notes that non-lethal weapons are little used, even though evidence suggests that soldiers facing children can benefit from this additional option.

The construction of the child as an essentially innocent being is one such reason why children are tactically useful in these cases. Children are also known to have become suicide bombers. There are related examples of older women, pregnant women, and disabled persons being used in this way, because their perceived incapacity and innocence can render them beyond any military suspicion.

International law on child soldiers

Recruitment and use of children *below the age of 15* in any armed conflict is prohibited by international humanitarian law, international human rights law, labour and criminal laws. *Voluntary* recruitment and use of children above 16 *is*, however, currently permitted by states. Armed groups are not permitted to allow any children under 18 into their ranks. The key international legal instrument is outlined below.

The Optional Protocol to the 1989 UN Convention on the Rights of the Child on the Involvement of Children in Armed Conflict (OP-CRC-CAC, or OP-CRC) was adopted by the UN General Assembly in May 2000 and entered into force in February 2002. It has now been ratified by 120 states and requires state parties to set a minimum age of 18 for compulsory recruitment and participation in hostilities. The protocol raises the minimum age of compulsory enlistment into war to age 18 and the age of volunteer enlistment to above age 15. It also provides that 'armed groups, distinct from the armed forces of a State, should not, under any circumstances, recruit or use in hostilities persons under the age of 18 years' (United Nations 2000: Article 4). Rosen (2007) notes that, since states can recruit children on a voluntary basis from 16 years of age, the Optional Protocol has a double standard, as it permits sovereign states to recruit child soldiers but prevents rebel groups from doing the same.

During these negotiations the incentives for allowing 'older' child soldiers were made clear. Pakistan, for example, stated that 16-year-olds 'voluntarily entered the armed forces because of the job stability, training and educational opportunities offered to them, providing in some cases a livelihood for themselves and their families. Lowering the age could cause severe social dislocation for individuals and families' (Breen 2007: 79). Additionally, the conscription or enlistment of children under the age of 15, or using them to participate actively in hostilities in both international and non-international armed conflict, is also classified as a war crime by the *Rome Statute of the International Criminal Court.* A complicating factor here is whether or not state parties in a conflict have ratified this treaty. In addition, states may indirectly allow child soldiers through their support of armed groups in proxy arrangements (see Background 26.1).

Post-conflict rehabilitation

Child soldiers may be little different from other 'war-affected children' in terms of the impact of war and its physical and psychological impact. Destitution, trauma, motherhood, and sexually transmitted infections are but a few of the issues that confront them. However, child soldiers are arguably vulnerable in further, complex ways when war ends. War may have formed part of their employment and survival, and the military may have been a family, an identity, and a passage to adulthood. Despite vast media and humanitarian attention, there are still limited long-term resources made available to child soldiers as victims of war. Where help is provided, it is often of the wrong sort. Many disarmament, demobilization, and reintegration (DDR) programmes focus only on the younger cohorts of child soldiers—leaving those who were children during the conflict and those considered to be youth without assistance (McEvoy-Levy 2006). The official UN definition of 'youth' refers to young people between the ages of 15 and 24.

In Sierra Leone's DDR programme, the broader definition of 'children associated with armed groups' was initially used—but funding constraints subsequently restricted the programme to only those children who could demonstrate experience in using a weapon. Eligibility by role as armed combatant poses a dilemma for children who did not solely take on this role, especially girls, or those who wish to protect their identity and not draw attention to their past. Some rehabilitation programmes make referrals of children without naming them, so as to protect them from possible spies. Michael Wessells, for example, recounts how in Uganda over 10,000 girl soldiers were overlooked, because they did not wish to attend DDR camps. In Sierra Leone, only 506 girls went through formal DDR programmes

BACKGROUND 26.1

Groups in Sudan using child soldiers and their abuses committed against children

SOUTHERN SUDAN

Parties under the control of the Government of the Sudan

Sudanese Armed Forces (SAF). *This party has been responsible for committing rape and other grave sexual violence against children.*

Parties under the control of the Government of southern Sudan

Sudan People's Liberation Army (SPLA)

Lord's Resistance Army (LRA).

DARFUR

Parties backed by the Government of the Sudan

Chadian opposition groups. *This party has been responsible for the killing and maiming of children.*

Government-supported militias. *This party has been responsible for killing and maiming, committing rape, and other grave sexual violence against children, and attacks on schools.*

Police forces, including the Central Reserve Police. *This party has been responsible for killing and maiming and committing rape and other grave sexual violence against children.*

Sudanese Armed Forces (SAF) *This party has been responsible for killing and maiming, committing rape, and other grave sexual violence against children, and attacks on schools and hospitals.*

Former rebel parties that have accepted the Darfur Peace Agreement

Justice and Equality Movement (Peace Wing)

Movement of Popular Force for Rights and Democracy

Sudan Liberation Army (SLA)/Abu Gasim/Mother Wing

Sudan Liberation Army (SLA)/Free Will

Sudan Liberation Army (SLA)/Minni Minnawi, *This party has been responsible for the killing and maiming of children.*

Sudan Liberation Army (SLA)/Peace Wing

Rebel parties that have rejected the Darfur Peace Agreement

Justice and Equality Movement (JEM). *This party has been responsible for the killing and maiming of children and attacks on schools and hospitals.*

Sudan Liberation Army (SLA)/Abdul Wahid

Sudan Liberation Army (SLA)/Unity. *This party has been responsible for the killing and maiming of children and attacks on schools and hospitals.*

Adapted from United Nations (2009a: annex 1)

KEY POINTS

- Children's smaller bodies and less-developed minds contribute to practices of war. Children holding military and political roles are one example of children at work in the international political system.

- There is yet no official guidance or rules of engagement with child soldiers.

- Children can use light weapons from the age of 6 and be effective soldiers from the age of 10.

- Children can be useful in war, performing roles that adults cannot or will not.

- International legislation permits states to use child soldiers under 18.

- Children are not yet widely consulted in human-rights agreements or post-war rehabilitation programmes. This further curbs their capacity to ameliorate theirs and other children's suffering.

- Survival of children may be linked to the preservation of their families, their emotional intelligence, and their resilience.

compared to 6,052 boys (McKay and Mazurana 2004). Further, children who perceive themselves to be *neither* victims nor combatants, are significant in number yet

rarely traced or consulted in post-conflict reconciliation and integration programmes. Their agency remains unknown. Cultures of childhood mentioned earlier also come into play here. There is little expectation of children's reliance in war: consequently, it is under-researched and potentially untapped. Similarly, children are little able to articulate guilt or partial responsibility for their actions within humanitarian aid programmes that are set around the restoration of their innocence (Schultheis 2008).

Critical issues

Empowered childhood

Children who have been active in political violence have often become newly aware of a political as well as a personal concept of security. Peters and Richards (1998: 183–4) argue that 'military activity offers young people a chance to make their way in the world' and conclude that child soldiers should be seen as 'rational human actors' who have a 'surprisingly mature understanding of their predicament'. Yet, typically, their 'rehabilitation' seeks effectively to depoliticize them. In apartheid South Africa, children and youth acted as social and political agents and defenders of communities. However, in their subsequent portrayal, their enemies exaggerated children's ages, or switched to the term 'youth' and also used criminal descriptors such as 'rioters', as if also to render them politically impotent. After the struggle their political contribution has had little recognition. Their new-found political agency became wasted, and, if recalled or repeated, it redefined them as 'problematic elements', isolating them from the very community they helped to bring about (Marks 2001). Boyden and Levison (2000) have raised the question of whether children are morally developed or advanced by aspects of war. More recently, long-term studies into the impact of child soldiering are starting to reveal that former combatants may make peaceful, civic and political capital from their experiences (Boothby 2006; Peters 2006; Blattman 2008).

Detailed ethnographic work with former child soldiers has revealed girls who have actively sought out the military life for its empowerment. Children in FRELIMO's *Destacemento Feminino* ('Female Detachment') 'saw their participation in combat as empowering and liberating and continue to see it this way as adults. Many interpret their war experiences as freeing them both from colonial rule and from male structures of dominance in "traditional" Mozambique society, and leading to their full citizen participation in the political life of Mozambique' (West 2000, cited in Rosen 2007).

Stereotypes of child soldiers

Much reporting about child soldiers does not mirror the complexity of children's roles but instead reflects concern at their violent and adult-like capacities—a newsworthy contrast to Western norms of childhood as protected, dependent, and innocent. Framed in this way, the issue area of child soldiers simultaneously serves to detract attention from the broader, political, and cultural context of war in which these children are participating. Shepler (2005: 206) notes how the child soldier issue may be deliberately shaped as 'communities organize their self presentation around the idea of "war-affected youth" to gain access to a certain amount of international aid'.

Conversely images and exposures of child soldiers can also become a shorthand diplomacy of condemnation. Reporting may carry further political currency through embedded racial and postcolonial overtones. Distant, different, and deadly child soldiers make the news. Brooten (2008) has shown how, in the USA, media stories on child soldiers in Burma can eclipse or even distort the broader picture behind their participation and not even make clear in whose forces the children are fighting:

> The focus on individual child soldiers, whether the Htoo twins or other children fighting other wars, also diverts attention from the structural issues underlying these wars, as well as any complicity readers may have in the situation. With only a simple understanding of what are always complex

situations, readers can feel comfortable with uncomplicated images (however sensational) of other countries' use of child soldiers. 〞

The reportage on child soldiers that is consumed in the West forms part of a broader humanitarian discourse (Breen 2007; Podder 2008; Macmillan 2009). In order to amplify their plight and signify their unique status, the child soldier is often represented as separate from local social and political networks or even family members. Just as childhood stands in poor relation to the master narrative of adulthood, child soldiers cannot easily challenge assumptions about their experiences. As noted earlier, dominant images of child soldiers have reinforced a sense that they are predominantly armed, male, African, traumatized, and potentially corrupted. The dominant paradigm also dwarfs observations that such young people may also be weak, vulnerable, confused, dependent, caring, moralistic, and providing security or well-being for others.

Anthropologists' field interviews with current and former child soldiers also indicate that the actual experience of many child soldiers has little connection with the depictions offered in the humanitarian literature (Boyden and de Berry 2004). Reports provided by SWAY (2006) indicate that even the most horrific regimes such as the Lords Resistance Army have not used force or torture to the degrees that are widely circulated. Both media and NGO reports have thus contributed to generalizations that distort the child-soldier issue through sensationalizing 'barbaric' and brutal aspects of their lives.

The assumption that such children are a 'lost generation' pervades not only the media but the community that works with former child soldiers (Ochieng 2007). That child soldiers and also child civilians are described as having *lost* their childhood may lead to limited understanding of their resilience or their agency. Most importantly, children may find that after war they do not receive appropriate recognition for the political and military roles they have undertaken or sufficient consultation in their own healing. A related example is that of advocacy groups for war-affected migrant children. They may privately acknowledge the courage and agency that is self-evident in a young child's passage—but concede that victim status

remains instrumental in the subsequent pitch they make for charitable support. Without it there is less sympathy for their cause and less funding is made available[1]. A recognizably robust 'victimhood' is required to legitimize action, thus continuing also to dis-able such children (Brocklehurst 2009).

Western child soldiers: citizens and cadets

Another area of critical concern is military based schooling—from the infamous Suvavov academies in the Russian Federation, which offer places for young orphans—to cadet training across Europe. Military culture and military recruitment via schools are just beginning to be viewed through the child soldier lens, and attention has now turned to Western states. Advocacy groups for the protection of children argue that young people may be harmed by peacetime training for war and manipulated by military institutions at ages before they are able to make judgements about their future and their security—tempted by training, payment, recognition, and the presumed excitement of a military career. In the UK, the Army fan club 'Camouflage' forms a vital part of recruitment strategy and helps to encourage children towards a military career from the age of 9. As the UK Ministry of Defence has admitted, children's academic underperformance might also make them ripe for selection. The appropriateness of recruitment teams and careers advisers from the armed services visiting schools, perhaps under the rubric of citizenship lectures, is still little questioned, and formal education on war and on soldiering does not precede such visits from the military establishment.

Researching child soldiers: ethics and methodology

Researching child soldiers is fraught with difficulty. Child soldiers may not be in a safe position to

---

[1] Confidential interview with NGO personnel.

volunteer information about their roles. It may also be very dangerous and practically difficult to collect reliable data and consistent information for analysis. The presence of researchers may be viewed with suspicion or become harnessed to personal and political goals of participants. Post-war research with children may bring further challenges of secondary trauma and real or imagined risk of recrimination. Cultural and gender sensitivities may also limit the degree to which precise information can be attained. Children may not wish to draw attention to their roles and may endanger themselves by doing so. Shame may prevent many children, especially girls, from revealing the nature of their roles.

The ethical minefield here is also borne out by the circulation of their iconographic portraits in literature about child soldiers. Very few humanitarian agencies digitally obscure the faces or eyes of such children so that future recognition is impossible. Given that hundreds of thousands of these images alone can be found on the Internet today, their potential problem is not insignificant.

Much of the literature about children conflates ages and stages of childhood and youth, prompting calls for more sensitive research and analysis. As Boyden (2006: 5) notes: 'Such disaggregation is especially important in gauging the causes of violence in the young, because it is very likely that significant structural (or generational), experiential and developmental (or life course) differences exist between different age cohorts, these in turn producing different motives and opportunities for fighting in war.'

Information about child soldiers is drawn from a wide variety of sources, not all of which have neutral interests or standpoints. Just as war is a transient process, so too is childhood a passing life phase. Such shifting research sands are further destabilized by stereotypes of childhood and simplifications of war in the popular press and by agencies that seek to draw attention to their plight. As with many issue areas that are about children's capacity, agency, and rights, children themselves may be the last to be considered worthy of consultation. In attempts to rehabilitate sexually abused girl soldiers in Southern Africa, girls were asked by aid agencies how they could better facilitate their integration into society. Unexpectedly, they requested that *male* adults from their community were given central roles in their care, in order to increase awareness of their experiences and respect for its gendered impact. In this case, which proved to be a successful strategy, prior underestimation of these children may have been the biggest challenge to their rehabilitation.

Think Point 26.2 illustrates the transition towards a new, more informed, and critical understanding of child soldiers.

THINK POINT 26.2

Child-soldier paradigms

Context	'Classical' depiction	'Critical' lens
Age/gender	Boys/male youth	All ages/girls
Locations	Africa/failed states	Global (including Western)
Recruitment	Forced	Forced, pressured, voluntary
Impact	Lost childhood	Altered childhood
Role	Combatant	Multiple roles
Means	Brutalized by and like adults	(ab)used 'as children'
Societal impact	Criminalized, lost generation	Disenfranchised

Conclusion

Rosen (2007: 296) talks of the *politics of age* to mean the use of age categories by different international, regional, and local actors to advance particular political and ideological positions.

> The politics of age is central to the competing agendas of humanitarian groups, sovereign states, and the United Nations and its constituent agencies, and it brings them into complex struggles over the recruitment and use of children as soldiers, the ideological and political manipulation of the concept of 'childhood', and the definition of who should be considered a 'child soldier'.

War can reveal roles, practices, manipulation, exploitation, and expectations of childhood that coexist in global politics. Children's bodies and minds, and adults' vulnerability towards particular ideas about children, can function to make children effective weapons. From the Cold War to civil wars, and from total war to totalitarianism, there are many recorded and often parallel uses of children as political currency in some way—as threats, models, investments, instruments, resources, symbols, and icons.

Children's politicization is enabled here because it is also under-represented and underplayed in many other sectors. Sensationalized, posed, isolated, 'humanitarian children' help foster the illusion that children were not prior members of the political sphere but are exceptionally and temporarily drawn into it. Through institutions of the home, school, and military, in propaganda and through policies of health and welfare, children have become an epicentre of security driven practices (Brocklehurst 2006).

Ongoing recognition of the incorporation of children and the family into militarized practices, and the logical corollary of this, the targeting of the (enemy) civilian sphere, dispel the myth that children are simply the protected or only victims. Children and their guardians are a form of security themselves (whether alive or dead) and are clearly treated as such. Terrorism, civil war, and total war are dependent to varying degrees on the manipulation of children, and share similar rationales. As Peterson (1992: 56) notes, 'the dichotomies of protector–protected, direct–indirect violence, and war–peace are inter-woven; denying them as oppositional dichotomies means recognizing the complexity of (inter)dependence, the interrelationship of oppressions, and the uncertainty of security'. And, as Rosen (2007: 300) concludes, to 'understand the experience of child soldiers requires deconstructing the idea of the "child soldier" as a generic archetype of humanitarian discourse to focus concretely on the *conflicts and settings* in which children are more likely to experience extreme brutality and trauma' (emphasis added).

Security and war have been at the heart of the study of international relations since its inception. They have helped to define the discipline and to fix its boundaries. War has been one of the areas on which *critical* social projects have focused a great deal of attention, albeit with an assumption that the victims of war (women, children, refugees, and so on), are easy to identify and 'offer a voice for the silenced'. This now raises difficult questions in terms of using generalized conceptions of children and childhood. It also highlights postmodernist concerns about the dangers of using simplistic categorizations in the analysis of international relations in a world characterized by multiple identities and fluid meanings. Battles that use children's bodies and minds as effective weapons have so far taken place without being recorded in the pages of security textbooks and have remained outside the knowledge of those who accept the typically presented parameters and ontology of security.

Although it is progress that children are thought about at all in security, they are still positioned or represented in ways that reflect wider political contexts. For example, a focus on child soldiers can serve conceptually to separate children from other actors and the broader identity of war-affected children. The identity of 'child soldier' is easily cemented by images of armed and powerful children on their own or surrounded by other child soldiers. These images may attract attention, but they do not help us to remember that many child soldiers may be integrated into multiple networks of family, community, and militia or state. Like adults, they may adopt roles and identities simultaneously; as both guardians and parents, as targets and soldiers, as stakeholders and slaves, peacemakers and labourers. As 'war-affected children', child soldiers face numerous challenges. Our responses to them, however, do not typically accommodate this multiple instrumentality nor their contribution to current and future security.

? QUESTIONS

1. Is the phrase 'child soldier' useful today? What other terms may be more accurate?

2. Why might child soldiers have caught the world's attention since the end of the Cold War?

3. In what way do child soldiers' roles differ from those of adult soldiers?

4. Children are said to volunteer to enlist. Why should we take them seriously? Have their reasons changed over time?

5. Why are there restrictions on rebel recruitment below 18 but not on government recruitment of children?

6. Are there child soldiers in the West?

7. Why do the experiences of girl soldiers need special recognition and attention?

8. Are child soldiers responsible for their actions?

9. Why is international law on child soldiers difficult to enforce?

10. Where do children belong in issues of security?

≋ FURTHER READING

■ Boyden, Jo, and de Berry, Joanna (2004) (eds.), *Children and Youth on the Front Line: Ethnography, Armed Conflict and Displacement*, New York: Berghan Books. This critical and informative text from the field challenges assumptions about children's roles in war.

■ McEvoy-Levy, Siobhan (2006) (ed.), *Troublemakers or Peacemakers? Youth and Post-Accord Peace Building*, The RIREC Project on Post-Accord Peace Building, Notre Dame, IN: University of Notre Dame Press. McEvoy-Levy focuses on the contribution made by youth in post-conflict settings.

■ Rosen, David (2005), *Armies of the Young: Child Soldiers in War and Terrorism*, New Brunswick, NJ: Rutgers University Press. Rosen's provocative text uses three major conflict case studies to explore and critique humanitarian responses to child soldiers.

■ Wessells, M. (2006), *Child Soldiers: From Violence to Protection*, Cambridge, MA: Harvard University Press. Informed by many field interviews, Wessells writes with sensitivity and compassion about child soldiers' experiences and their potential contribution to peace. See also Boothby, Neil, Strang, Alison, and Wessells, Michael. (2006) (eds.), *A World Turned Upside Down: Social Ecological Approaches to Children in War Zones*, Bloomfield, CT: Kumarian Press.

IMPORTANT WEBSITES

● http://www.un.org/children/conflict/english/index.html Office of the Special Representative of the Secretary General for Children and Armed Conflict. After the United Nations Security Council Resolution 1612 (2005), the Office established a comprehensive monitoring and reporting process relating to grave violations against children in situations of armed conflict, in particular the recruitment and use of children as soldiers.

● http://www.sway-uganda.org Survey of War Affected Youth (SWAY). SWAY is a research programme in northern Uganda. Academics and practitioners provide papers dedicated to understanding the scale and nature of war violence and the effects of war on youth.

● http://www.child-soldiers.org/home Coalition to Stop the Use of Child Soldiers (CSC). Founded in 1998, the CSC unites national, regional, and international organizations and networks in Africa, Asia, Europe, Latin America, and the Middle East. Its founding organizations are Amnesty International, Defence for Children International, Human Rights Watch, International Federation Terre des Hommes, International Save the Children Alliance, Jesuit Refugee Service, the Quaker United Nations Office-Geneva, and World Vision International.

Visit the Online Resource Centre that accompanies this book for lots of interesting additional material: www.oxfordtextbooks.co.uk/orc/collins2e/

27

After the Return to Theory: The Past, Present, and Future of Security Studies

OLE WÆVER AND BARRY BUZAN

Chapter Contents

- Introduction
- The origins and institutional structure of security studies
- The Golden Age of security studies
- Institutionalization and stagnation
- Disciplinary questioning and theoretical relaunch
- Conclusion: the powers of theory and the challenges of the future

Reader's Guide

This chapter presents an interpretation of the past and present of security studies with an emphasis on the changing periods of theory production and practical problem solving. The field started out as a distinct US specialty much shaped by the new conditions of the 1940s set by nuclear weapons and a long-term mobilization against the Soviet Union, two factors that created a need for a new kind of civilian expert in defence and strategy. From an American, think-tank based, interdisciplinary field, security studies became institutionalized as a part of one discipline, International Relations (IR), increasingly international and with theory anchored in the universities. Since the 1990s, the field has been in a new period of high theory productivity, but largely in two separate clusters with the USA and Europe as centres of each. This analysis is used as a basis for raising some central questions and predictions about the future of the field.

Introduction

The fact that a book like the present one can be made, indeed had to be made, to present an existing field to people entering it testifies to major change in security studies. Had a similar book been produced in previous decades, it would have looked very different. A 1950s version would have been very short. In the 1960s, it would have been structured with chapters on different kinds of policy questions—strategy, economy of defence, decision making—and in some of these (notably the chapter on strategy) there would have been a lot of theory (deterrence theory), but the theories would not have competed for dealing with the same questions; a division of labour would have kept them in different chapters. The 1970s edition would probably have been thinner on theory and more comprehensive in the thematic chapters—and it would have come with a companion volume (in German) denouncing the whole field as part of the repressive, militarized, Cold War system. The 1980s textbook would have been a reader of texts arguing for and against the continued relevance of the field, its possible widening or even dissolution and merger into wider fields. With developments in the 1990s, the field has come to take a shape as reflected in the structure of this volume: the wideners have succeeded enough for chapters on different sectors of security to be necessary, and a number of theories now compete for tackling the whole field of security. In the first decades of the twenty-first century, this reshaped discipline seems to gain increased attention, generate more undergraduate courses and not least more—often theoretically inclined—Ph.D. projects. This augmented attraction is supported both by the prominence of 'security' in the era of the 'global war on terror' and 'climate security', and by the availability of the family of theories that sprang up during the 1990s.

 KEY IDEAS 27.1

Terminology

The names 'strategic studies' and 'security studies' (or 'international security studies') are used by some authors interchangeably, while others use them systematically on different objects. It is possible to give distinct definitions, typically with security studies being broader, and strategic studies the narrower subset oriented towards military issues (e.g. Buzan 1991a; Betts 1997). However, in a historical overview like the present, it would be anachronistic to use such terminology for the whole period. 'Strategic studies' was the established term from the 1940s into the 1980s, and we use it accordingly, retaining the construction of the time with most often military affairs as the self-evident core of the field and circles around this drawn more or less narrowly. From the 1980s and onwards, this field was in most contexts relabelled as security studies, and only in some places but far from all was the hard-core military part of this field assigned the specific name 'strategic studies'. Therefore, we do not use here a systematic distinction between the two terms, but let them cover the whole area and use mostly strategic studies in the early period and security studies in the later. Today, the name 'strategic studies' seems mostly to linger on because it is institutionalized in outfits like the 'International Institute for Strategic Studies', 'Journal of Strategic Studies' and 'Journal of Military and Strategic Studies'. The dominance of the term 'strategic studies' during the Cold War was in any case more pervasive in the UK than in the US.

Our focus in this chapter is on *security theory*, which we define as theory that aims at the understanding and/or management of security issues. Such theory can at different points in time resemble developments within general IR theory, while at other points there can be less contact. For instance, some major developments in IR theory, such as 1970s interdependence and regime theory, had minimal impact on security studies (at the time, at least), and some security theories were (originally) specific to security studies, such as deterrence theory or the Copenhagen School, not general theories of IR. Other cases of security theory are simultaneously IR and security theory, such as constructivism, feminism, or democratic peace. While distinct from IR theory, security theory is different also from security studies at large, because much work in security studies does not deal explicitly with theory. Thus, security theory is a specific subset of security studies and one whose development has gone through distinctive phases.

One peculiarity of this field is that it is divided more strongly than comparable fields into subsets without mutual recognition, often without even mutual awareness. Especially in European journals, conferences, departments, and research centres, one finds a lively discussion of a number of recent approaches: critical security studies, feminism, the Copenhagen School, the Paris School, and the merits of all these compared to 'the traditional approach'. Go to most departments in the USA or the leading journals, such as *International Security* and *Security Studies*, And most scholars there would say 'who?' and 'what?' about authors intensely discussed by a large number of scholars especially in Europe and parts of the third world (Wæver 2004). In turn, the mostly American main scene has had debates centred on offensive versus defensive realism, the relative importance of ideational variables, and the role of power and institutions in orders (and empires). These debates did not structure the universe for most scholars in the rest of the world.

Therefore, when this concluding chapter attempts an assessment of where we are, where we came from, and not least where we might be going, it needs to follow an asymmetrical structure, where the first part treats the field as homogeneous—a kind of unified centre–periphery structure with the US definition of security studies unrivalled—while the later part

splits into two parallel tracks. The chapter is structured chronologically. The first section looks at the origins and institutional structure of security studies—what and where is it? The second covers the so-called Golden Age, the formative period of strategic studies when most notably deterrence theory was developed and game theory applied to it (and in turn given much original impetus at the level of abstract theory), to assist in the handling of novel challenges from nuclear weapons. The third section is about the immediate post-Golden Age, when strategic studies was consolidated as an integral part of the security establishment, and theory often lost out to 'hectic empiricism' (Buzan 1981, 2000), which might in turn have contributed to the decline of strategic studies as a field. A fourth section deals with the soul-searching debates on widening and (sub)disciplinary identity during the 1980s and 1990s, culminating in various theoretical innovations. The final section looks from the current situation of theoretical wealth into a future where these theories might change their mutual relationships while also becoming involved with the main issues on the policy agenda.

The first and second sections deal overwhelmingly with the USA, because this is where modern strategic studies emerged and found its characteristic shape. When modern-style strategic studies grew elsewhere, even where independent traditions existed, this happened to such a large extent by attempts to copy or import the American experience, that the formative period of American strategic studies became the referent point for the field everywhere. A systematic comparison of American and European strategic studies is therefore presented towards the end of the second section (referring to the status in the early 1970s), and only in the latest phases do distinct trajectories become self-reliant enough that a story of two parallel tracks can explain the above-mentioned peculiarity of debates unrecognizable to each other.

The origins and institutional structure of security studies

War and peace, threats and strategy, as well as welfare and epidemics: issues like these have been on the agenda of thinkers and writers for centuries. However, anything resembling security studies as we now know it did not become a distinct field of study until around the end of the Second World War. As always, *when* a field is established, it is easy to see predecessors and preparatory work done in previous phases, and thus security studies can be projected back into the inter-war period with reference to work done on the causes and prevention of wars (Baldwin 1995).

The novelty in the 1940s, however, was the emergence of a distinct category of work at the intersection of military expertise and university-based social science aimed at delivering policy-relevant knowledge supported by a broad, interdisciplinary academic knowledge base. In large part because of the unprecedented implications of nuclear weapons for war fighting, but also because of the broad-spectrum challenge to the USA posed by the Soviet Union (ideological and economic, as well as military) and the general prestige gained during the Second World War by both natural scientists (new weapons, code breaking) and social scientists (for example, in advising on strategic bombing priorities), civilian experts would now also specialize in military issues under the heading of security. That the leading strategic thinkers should be mainly civilians was what distinguished post-1945 security studies both from what had been done before, and from what continued to be done outside the West.

This institutional innovation happened at the same time as the concept of security moved centre stage, becoming the guiding idea over previously supreme slogans such as defence and national interest (Yergin 1977; Wæver 2006).

General enabling conditions in the USA were: optimism about the usefulness of science, the possibility of rational solutions to societal problems,

novel security issues that seemed not only urgent and primary but very much so (nuclear weapons and the Soviet, communist threat), generous funding for research, and exponential expansion of higher education.

The main key to the emergence of strategic studies around the time of the end of the Second World War and the beginning of the Cold War was the need for civilian experts to balance the military leadership, a need driven certainly by technological developments (nuclear weapons and the rapid rise of war avoidance as the key strategic imperative), but probably also by broader political considerations about the potentially problematic political implications of long-term mobilization.

The military driver is straightforward: gradually, it became clear how radically nuclear weapons would transform the security equations, and the kind of expertise needed differed from the classical military one. At some risk of oversimplification (actual planning was quite a bit more mixed), the problem was that wars should no longer be fought but avoided, and ways should be found so that the possibility/impossibility of war generated by nuclear deployments could be manipulated for political gain. The centre of gravity shifted from the tactical and operational level to true long-term strategy (Brodie 1949), and from the deployment of a given technology to the targeted development of fast-changing technologies for the future. Although at first it seemed that even the games of deterrence could be seen as controlled by the bottom line of what would happen in an actual fight, it gradually became necessary to treat nuclear strategy as a partly independent universe to be analysed in its own right. This demanded a completely different form of knowledge from the one delivered by military experts. As succinctly put by Richard Betts (1997: 13): 'Nuclear war spurred theorizing because it was inherently more theoretical than empirical: none had ever occurred.' Or, in the words of Richard Smoke (1976: 275), the first precondition for the emergence of security studies was a 'complexity dissectible by abstract analysis'.

While this is probably a relatively uncontroversial interpretation of the emergence of security studies, it should also be noticed that the combination of nuclear weapons and the Cold War meant a need to coordinate more closely military and non-military considerations. Already wartime experiences had shown, especially in the US, how challenging it was to coordinate economic, political, and military planning (Etzold 1978: 1–2; Hogan 1998: 25). As it began to be clear that the Cold War could become a drawn-out, all-encompassing, and existential struggle, the idea took hold that one needed a form of integrated understanding, where these different forms of knowledge could become combined, and this was a major part of the reasoning behind the National Security Act of 1947—in addition to closer coordination of the services plus intelligence reform (Stuart 2008).

The specific challenge of the USA, with its 'no-standing-armies' tradition having to organize for long-term mobilization, shaped the emerging civil–military interface in strategic studies. It was a deep-seated argument within American political thought that a permanent military institution would be a threat to democracy because it could be misused by 'a tyrant', an anti-democratic executive (Publius 1787–8; Bailyn 1992; Deudney 1995). Also, it was only during the Second World War that 'the uniformed heads of the US armed services assumed a pivotal and unprecedented role in the formulation of the nation's foreign policies' (Stoler 2000: p. ix). Therefore, when the USA moved towards institutionalizing an unprecedented level of military mobilization, this could not be done purely in terms of 'war' or 'defence'. This is a central part of the explanation for the rise of the term 'security' to cover the mobilization in more inclusive and 'civilian' terms (Wæver 2006, 2008). And it conditioned a particular space for civilian expertise in a military-centred universe. The Cold War mobilization inevitably entailed a tension between American liberalism and military professionalism, and the field of strategic studies emerged as part of the institutional responses to this tension (Lasswell 1950; Huntington 1957).

KEY POINTS

- Security studies as a distinct field of study was born in the 1940s in the USA.

- Nuclear weapons created a strategic challenge not covered by traditional military expertise.

- Long-term, broad-based mobilization collided with an American wariness of 'standing armies'. Where the USA had traditionally kept war and peace more distinct than other states, the new situation called for a new cover term (security) and new experts (security studies) in order not to end up in permanent war and at the mercy of the military—or the enemy.

The Golden Age of security studies

The period of the 1950s and 1960s is widely celebrated as one where the field was simultaneously productive, influential, and relatively coherent. Although the field contained a wide variety of other kinds of work (to which we return shortly), the central and defining area was game theory and nuclear strategy. We pay particular attention to this period for two reasons. First, it was the formative period of the new discipline, and therefore developments in the so-called Golden Age are not just episodes equal to many others; they defined how security studies was perceived: for good and bad these developments were the quintessential work of security studies. Second, this marked a (first) high point of theorization, and we want to point to the pattern of ebb and flow of theory making within security studies.

The work on game theory and deterrence theory was a rare instance of an intellectual development that scores high in terms of theoretical creativity and sophistication, and simultaneously policy relevance. Very often this is seen as a trade-off—policy relevance/utility versus theoretical abstraction/ sophistication (cf. Hill 1994; Lepgold and Nincic 2001)—but when nuclear weapons created a novel challenge of understanding a situation that was hypothetical and speculative through-and-through and open to swift and dramatic developments, a very sophisticated theoretical boom gained centrality politically. At the same time, this development became highly influential within the academic world, because the nature of the object allowed for a high degree of abstraction and formalization that scored well on the criteria of the day for a new, more 'scientific' form of International Relations. Under a Cold War situation with a booming US economy, a mood of technological optimism and a willingness to support social science as part of the solution to social challenges (including not only the Cold War struggle but social problems of all kinds), the reward was high for new approaches that seemed to move IR in the direction of the use of scientific methods and tools, ranging from coding of events data allowing for computerized data processing, through cybernetic models and experimental psychology, to game theory. Deterrence theory became a success story in this context for two reasons. On the one hand, it produced a seemingly productive ('progressive') research programme where theoretical work produced ever new and more complex problems that could in turn be dealt with by new theoretical moves. On the other hand, all this seemed highly useful because the theories actually produced their own reality of abstractions, the world of 'secure

second strike capability', 'extended deterrence', and 'escalation dominance'.

This was reflected in the critique from peace research and critical theory that the whole 'Golden Age' idea is a self-glorifying construction of academics whose real accomplishment was to make morally corrupt government policies (MAD, Vietnam) look respectable and/or inevitable.

Some critics said that this whole literature produced validating smokescreens for what the politicians and the military wanted to do anyway: build up a huge nuclear force and promote military Keynesianism (Green 1966, 1968; Senghaas 1969). Although undoubtedly true that these theories legitimized deterrence and nuclear weapons as such, it is not fair to conclude that their 'influence' on policy was illusory. Theories of deterrence shaped the whole way of making sense of nuclear weapons, and thereby influenced the shape if not necessarily the size of investments. The relative merits and roles of bombers, missiles, submarines, the uses and non-uses of tactical nuclear weapons, and how to avoid vulnerability of systems (the famous basing study by Wohlstetter et al. in 1954)—for all such policies, there was a clear link from theorists to policymakers. But, in relation to targeting, there was a major slippage where Strategic Air Command largely continued with its own roughly 'first-strike'-oriented policy (Rosenberg 1983). If one counterfactually imagined that the civilian experts had not existed at all, it seems much more probable that the whole nuclear build-up would have been shaped by an old-fashioned military logic of maximizing 'fire power' without much concern for overall stability and the political possibilities for signalling and manœuvring. Nuclear *quantity* was probably a product of semi-independent dynamics having to do with the military industrial complex and the overall politics of sizing the defence budget, but it should be beyond doubt that Golden Age theorizing produced a different mix of nuclear weapons with different qualities and locations, and a different role in policy, from what would otherwise have happened. For better or worse, this story of the Golden Age and deterrence theory became the heart of the discipline—its founding myth somewhat similar to the way the first great debate operates in IR theory.

What is most unique about this particular episode is, however, the degree to which policy-oriented work made significant contributions to general theory. This was not just application of work done elsewhere to policy questions or transfer of knowledge to the political world, as we have come to expect it of think tanks. Neither was it, as with the most recent think tanks, primarily about lobbying for specific policies, although the work of RAND clearly served the general interests of the air force and had built-in biases towards a distrustful policy vis-à-vis the Soviet Union (Green 1968). This did not prevent lasting contributions to game theory. Even a mathematician prefacing the sixtieth anniversary edition of von Neumann and Morgenstern's foundational *Theory of Games and Economic Behavior* (Kuhn 2004: p. x) posits that 'many observers agree' that RAND was one of two centres in which game theory flourished in the first post-war decade (see also Dimond and Dimond 1996: 142–3). One need just mention the 1950 invention at RAND of the prisoner's dilemma (Poundstone 1992: 103) and the late 1950s bargaining twist given to game theory by Thomas Schelling (1960b). It is quite easy to see how these developments grew out of specific challenges relating especially to the nuclear situation. Noticeably, these were also major contributions to basic science at the same time.

The second biggest example from the Golden Age of policy-relevant work that simultaneously constituted general theory was systems analysis, a method for solving problems of force structure and resource allocation that drew on economic theory as well as operations research developed by natural scientists, engineers, and economists during the Second World War (Stern 1967; Smoke 1976 290–3). Several pioneering RAND studies were implemented into policy, notably the famous 'air-bases' study by Wohlstetter et al. (1954). Several of the leading representatives entered the Kennedy administration—McNamara's 'whiz kids' (Brodie 1965; Kaplan 1983). From there, this method and related RAND techniques like the 'Planning-Programming-Budgeting-System' 'spread through most of the federal government' (Smoke 1976: 292). It is generally underestimated today how much of early strategic studies was not only inspired by the *discipline* of economics (Hitch 1960; Schelling 1960a) but was actually *about* economics. A typical early course or 1960s–1970s textbook in strategic studies had strategy and deterrence as the biggest sub-field, but the second biggest would usually be 'the economics of defence'—not so puzzling given the size of the American defence budget! (See Knorr and Trager 1977 for a broader treatment of 'economic issues and national security'.) The image nowadays is often that Cold War strategic studies was obsessed with military questions, and this is partly true—it was mostly the economics of *defence* planning—but strategy was closely followed by economics as a key concern.

Many other things happened in strategic studies around this nexus, but the identity and nature of the field were shaped by the Golden Age episode. Beyond nuclear strategy, important areas within strategic studies were systems analysis (planning, organization), arms control, alliance politics, counter-insurgency, and organization of government institutions and decision making (Smoke 1976). In the late 1960s and early 1970s were added area studies and internal developments (bureaucratic politics; decision making). Later in the 1970s came perceptions, arms-race theory, proliferation of nuclear weapons, proliferation of advanced military technology, utility of force, strategic intelligence, conventional strategy, and self-reflections of the field (Bull 1968; Gray 1977; Howard 1979).

Many of the new developments (notably perceptions and decision making) were reactions to the difficulties that the classical form of security studies ran into. The overly rational game theory became complemented by theories of 'irrationality' like bureaucratic politics, and this, along with the Vietnam War, became a turning point towards the next phase. The USA entered the war with all the instruments of strategic studies in high esteem. The Kennedy administration and McNamara's time as Secretary of Defense marked a high point in the belief in the social-scientific vision of security knowledge (Morgenthau 1962). But, in the words of Colin Gray (1982: 90), the strategists knew 'next to nothing' about 'peasant nationalism in Southeast Asia or about the mechanics of a counter-revolutionary war'.

KEY POINTS

● The defining moment—or founding myth—for security studies was the development of deterrence theory, which both spurred general theory of a 'basic science' nature (game theory) and simultaneously fed directly into policy.

● The economics of defence was the second biggest field in early security studies.

Institutionalization and stagnation

The crisis for security studies—or what Baldwin (1995) dubs the move into a phase of 'decline'—was, however, not only about external challenges to an otherwise perfect theoretical construction. The previous period had already witnessed some 'internal weakening' of the mainstream strategy scholarship. Even in the core area of nuclear (and other forms of military) strategy, the highly theoretical and academic scholarship of the earlier period had succumbed to 'hectic empiricism' (Buzan 2000). The task of security scholarship was to keep up with fast-changing technologies and the twists and turns of political developments. Increasing amounts of effort therefore went into ever-more detailed work on technical specificities and narrow perfection of isolated bits of knowledge.

The corrupting influence of policy was, however, not the only explanation. During the 1970s and 1980s, the very abstraction of deterrence logic more or less broke down under the weight of its own complexity (ex post/ex ante, limited nuclear war, rationality debates), causing an exhausted drift towards general or existential deterrence (Morgan 1983; Freedman 1988). The Golden Age lost its lustre also because the internal logic of its key contribution broke down.

A further complication of the policy–academe interaction has to do with an aspect that is very often ignored in the debates these days, especially within the more critical and/or European forms of security studies: in the post-Golden Age period, the field was marked by a gradual IR'ification of security studies. It moved from interdisciplinarity into becoming one of IR's two pillars, paralleling

International Political Economy (IPE). Not only did this mean that IR became almost formalized as consisting of these two components (in the USA symbolized by two lead journals, *International Security* and *International Organization*); more importantly in the present context—seen from the angle of security studies itself—it meant that IR became the main disciplinary context for security studies theorizing, in striking contrast to the early Golden Age situation. Then, the leading scholars came from a variety of backgrounds—sociology, mathematics, psychology, natural sciences, political science, and quite a lot of economists. Increasingly, one discipline came to dominate: political science.

Since the late 1960s, 'strategic studies' became the subject for specific courses as part of general IR/political science departments (Smoke 1976: 292; Gray 1982: 86) and not least in specific, specialized institutes, often with government support, such as SAIS at Johns Hopkins, the Saltzman Institute at Columbia, and Harvard's 'John M. Olin Institute'. The military academies and (especially in the USA) the 'war schools' of each service became another arena for systematic teaching of courses in security studies. Particularly in the USA, scholars—with military or civilian background—in these latter institutions have been natural participants in the 'international security studies'/'international security and arms control' sections of ISA and APSA that were set up in the 1980s. 'Security *theory*' almost only develops within the civilian, university-based part—no longer in the think tanks. This is important as background for understanding the current situation regarding security theory, because the field is now closely intertwined with the (sub)discipline of IR in universities.

The potential problem for policy in this academicized development has been compensated by a gradual modification of the role of think tanks in the USA. In the early period, the leading think tanks—notably the pioneering RAND Corporation—housed (within their social-science sections) heavy theory work and large innovative projects. Today theory has moved to the universities, and think tanks have come under strong competitive pressure for delivering fast, usable policy guidance. Some think tanks have been politicized and operate not only from a political angle but as a key element in political strategies for (neo-)conservatives or liberals; others are still loosely tied to the services, but follow the policy agenda closely (Rich 2004; Buzan and Hansen 2009). It has become much rarer to find theory even explicitly discussed in think-tank work, but it is clearly drawn upon. The result is a chain construct, where academe, think tanks, and policy-makers are distinct and each purifies its role. Persons might travel between the categories—move from think tank to university or to policy, or vice versa—but, as institutions, they are distinct. This is, as we will return to in the next section, much less clearly the case outside the USA (probably because of weaker competitive pressures on the intellectual market).

Structural observation about the different kinds of intellectual institutions in strategic studies is also the ideal context for characterizing the difference between the USA and Western Europe during the early decades, a comparison that should be introduced here because the contrast will carry increasing weight as our story unfolds. In Europe, even in the UK, think tanks from the beginning mostly had the with which they are associated today: to influence policy in a specific direction, to mobilize the public behind policy, and at best to digest, popularize, and apply academic work done elsewhere into a more useful format for policy-makers (Abelson 2002; Haas 2002; Parmar 2004). In the area of foreign and security affairs, most policy-oriented work took place in 'foreign-policy institutes', which rarely engaged in more theoretical efforts. One partial exception was in the early decades of the International Institute for Strategic Studies (IISS), in London, where the series of *Adelphi Papers* especially included serious research, often by scholars from around the world who were resident at the Institute for a period. But generally, during the Cold War Europeans characteristically conducted their political arguments over political and military strategy—often against the USA—on the basis of theories made in the United States.

The most important non-American contributions to strategic studies were probably Hedley Bull's foundational work on arms control (1961) and the continuous interaction of American social-science scholarship with a tradition of British work steeped in classical military strategy (Basil Liddell Hart, Michael Howard, Lawrence Freedman, and P. M. S. Blackett). The US–European contrast is clearly expressed in the way France's leading IR scholar, Raymond Aron, wrote repeatedly about Clausewitz, and France's main entries in the history of post-war strategic thought are two generals involved with the argument behind France's independent nuclear force. This in contrast to the centrality in the USA of a kind of strategy rooted in modern social science and relatively independent of classical military strategy. In hindsight, it can be seen that Pierre Hassner (1997), throughout the Cold War and after, produced a unique series of analyses of the political dimension of security anchored in political theory, but this did not take off as a style or approach establishing itself as a distinct presence in security studies, and most of his work during the Cold War appeared in policy-oriented anthologies on current challenges as 'the French chapter', rarely recognized for the theory work they constituted (Gloannec and Smolar 2003).

The distinct phenomenon of strategic studies emerged in Europe clearly as an imported American speciality. A most revealing testimony to the asymmetrical relationship is the incredibly condescending tone in Wohlstetter and Wohlstetter's 1963 report on the state of strategic studies in Europe. They give marks to the different national research communities (good to Sweden, not so good England, hope for Germany, and so on). Security studies was not born simultaneously in two places, and developments cannot be compared as independent phenomena. It emerged in the USA and was exported to Europe. Since European security studies mostly took shape in the late 1960s and early 1970s, it became the post-Golden, institutionalized, theory-has-already-been-done kind of work that struggled to keep up with the newest technological developments to assess optimal Western military policy vis-à-vis the Soviet Union.

Strategic studies beyond the NATO area (Japan, third world, Israel, and so on) has been almost solely of the kind resembling political argumentation with a bit of factual, technical expertise—never 'basic conceptual analysis' (Wohlstetter and Wohlstetter 1966). An interesting parallel to the US case was the Soviet one, where think-tank-like 'institutes' gained a distinct niche producing research with a different theoretical orientation than the (Marxist-Leninist) one in the dominant academic institutions. It is far beyond the remit of this chapter to include a detailed and nuanced coverage of this development, but, in striking parallel to the USA, real-world challenges formed the basis for innovative work in an institutional setting with a creative tension between two creative tensions: combining a bond with a distance to high academe and a similar duality in relation to policy itself. Comparable developments were not found to the same extent in Europe.

Nowhere beyond the USA occurred, within an independent field of strategic studies, something similar to 'RAND's ability to produce systematic, long-range, "creative" research rather than to engage in mere short-range tinkering with other peoples' ideas' (Green 1968: 304). If one chooses anachronistically to project the history of security studies back into the inter-war period, it can be noted that the think tanks of the day (the first such) produced policy-oriented work that simultaneously was theoretically innovative and entered the annals of IR-theory history. This happened in think tanks such as the 'Institute for Government Research'

(Later Brookings), Carnegie, the Council on Foreign Relations, and the Hoover Institution, plus Chatham House in Britain. They contributed to the formulation of plans for the international order in the inter-war period, and much of the thinking recorded in IR theory's history as 'idealism' was produced in connection to these.

Thus, the simultaneity of policy and theory work in universities and especially in separate institutions characterized both the inter-war and the first post-war periods in the USA, but this changed towards the end of the 1960s. 'Having played a central role in the development of deterrence theory, economists were by [the 1970s] found hardly anywhere in the academic study of military affairs. RAND had also evolved into a bureaucratized contract research organization as much as a think tank and was no longer the hothouse of theoretical ferment it had been in the 1950s' (Betts 1997: 16).

A final element to cover regarding this phase is the parallel track constituted by peace research in relation to security studies. These two tracks merge only during the 1980s and 1990s, and, despite some overlaps of subject matter (arms racing, arms control, war), generally treated each other as political rivals divided by the acceptability, or not, of the whole structure of nuclear deterrence specifically, and the role of war in human relations generally (Buzan and Hansen 2009). Sometimes peace research would be treated as 'left-wing' security studies, and on other occasions as something (very much) other than security studies. Most often, peace research repaid the latter favour by seeing itself as certainly not 'security studies'. Early peace research ironically emerged in forms reminiscent of strategic studies—as a scientific alternative to mainstream IR. Much inter-war IR had been programmatically constructed as aiming for the production of peace, and thus the history of peace research can quite easily be anchored in inter-war (and immediate post-war) classics such as Quincy Wright's *A Study of War* (1942) and Lewis Fry Richardson's books, *Generalized Foreign Politics* (1939), *Arms and Insecurity* (1949), and *Statistics of Deadly Quarrels* (1950). After 1945, the

UNESCO-sponsored attempt to form a social-science-based study of war was dismissed by the emerging discipline of International Relations (Aron 1957; Waltz 1959), and consequently peace research formed with roots mostly in the 'softer' or more humanistic social sciences such as sociology and psychology, with pioneers like Herbert Kelman and Johan Galtung. The irony of this is that the same impulse towards 'scientific' approaches spurred the development of strategic studies mostly anchored in game theory and thus economics. Especially in Europe, peace research went through a radicalization in the late 1960s and early 1970s, and so-called critical peace research with strongholds in Germany, the Netherlands, and Scandinavia, came to see strategic studies as part of the problem.

Especially in analyses like Dieter Senghaas's critique of deterrence theory (Senghaas 1969) and Johan Galtung's work on violence (Galtung 1969), mainstream theories were understood as part of the balance of terror, bipolar, Cold War system of militarization, superpower dominance, and exploitation of the third world. Critical peace research was usually not seen as part of strategic studies or even security studies, either by the main stream or by the critics themselves. The critics did not write in the name of security, but more often in the name of *peace* depicting 'security' as a destructive pursuit (Jahn et al. , 1987; Wæver 2008). Peace and security were symbols of the opposing sides during the Cold War (Buzan 1984; Wæver 2008).

The period 1965–80 has been seen by many observers as less successful, and by Baldwin (1995) it was even labelled 'decline'. Already in the 1970s, however, some new developments had begun that came into clearer focus in the 1980s. Critics of the traditional approach had started to make the case for inclusion of security challenges in, for example, the economic and environmental sectors (Brandt et al. 1980; Palme et al. 1982; Buzan 1983; Ullmann 1983; Nye and Lynn-Jones 1988; Mathews 1989).

KEY POINTS

- 1965–80 marked a period both of stagnation for security studies in terms of theory development, and of institutionalization in textbooks, courses, and organizations.

- Security studies went from being interdisciplinary to being mostly understood as political science, often as one of International Relations' two pillars (IPE being the other).

- Security studies, invented in the USA, was copied—often with direct American assistance—in Western Europe and in the rest of the world, especially among allies.

- The think tanks gradually stopped being innovative, interdisciplinary places for thinking and became increasingly routinized producers of more narrow, technical problem solving.

- Peace research developed on a parallel but so far separate track, and especially its most distinct, critical branch was seen neither by its representatives nor by security studies as part of the latter.

Disciplinary questioning and theoretical relaunch

There is no need here to rehash the familiar story of the wide/narrow debate of the 1970s and especially 1980s. The debate as such is covered well elsewhere—within and beyond (Buzan and Hansen 2009) the present volume—but for the present purpose of this chapter it is necessary to understand the way the field developed theoretically in the 1980s and 1990s, not so much the debate as such, but the theoretical approaches that emerged out of this debate.

Of particular interest is the parallel turn to increasingly abstract and ambitious theorizing on both sides of the Atlantic—on separate tracks. The US mainstream of security studies focused on debates over offensive and defensive realism, some discussion of constructivism, democratic peace, and an emerging debate on power versus institutions in empire/order building—all shaped by a quest for empirically validated generalizations about cause–effect relationships. A specific form of knowledge is hegemonic: cause–effect statements backed up either by statistical data or more often by historical case studies (Walt 1999; Wæver 2004). In Europe, a debate emerged between a number of more or less critical theories: Critical Security Studies, feminism, Copenhagen School, Paris School and poststructuralism.

The different form of knowledge in Europe relates to a conflicting conception of the relationship to policy: less inclined to search for cause–effect generalizations to assist policy-makers in calculating policy, more partaking in political reflections—that is, more the role of public 'intellectual' than 'expert'. It is striking, however, that, parallel to both these theoretical clusters, lots of specific 'technical expertise' developed on both sides, and they were often less different than the theories: knowledge about AIDS as security problem, health security, or missile defence. On top of this practical, empirical knowledge, two *different* clusters of theorization have developed. This general split partly reflects a more 'problem-solving' tradition in US social science versus a more critical one in Europe, but recent developments are more extreme than the usual pattern, and security studies was largely coherent across the Atlantic during the Cold War, with the deep split developing only during the 1980s and especially after the end of the Cold War (see Think Point 27.1).

While it would probably be wrong to *explain* this difference by policy needs (that is, an externalist sociology of science), the pattern is clearly reinforced by the pattern of world power at the beginning of the twenty-first century. In a world that might be described as consisting of one superpower

THINK POINT 27.1

Places, persons, and paradigms

When we talk in broad terms about 'European' and 'US' theories, this should not be taken as statements generalizing about scholars in Europe and the USA respectively, but as a reference to distinct arenas of theoretical discussions. Some scholars located in the USA draw from and contribute to debates that mostly take place in Europe and—more clearly—many scholars in Europe work from theories made in the USA and aim their publications at American colleagues. In the discipline of International Relations, there is a US-centred, global discipline that overlaps and intersects with weaker independent traditions like the English School, French IR, and non-Western contributions. We do not want to deny the importance of 'American-style' work done by Europeans and vice versa, but we want to point out how disconnected different sets of theoretical debate are, and these tend to have their main institutional anchorage (journals, research institutions, organizations) in different continents.

and four great powers ('1+4' according to Buzan and Wæver 2003; Buzan 2004b) or uni-multipolar (Huntington 1999) with the USA seeing and handling it as unipolar and the other great powers acting according to multipolar logic, the different angles of watching the world point to different *forms* of knowledge (Wæver 2004): US decision-makers and academics see the USA as the actor that shapes the world and accordingly they need knowledge about cause–effect relationships in order to understand how to work the material they act upon (the world).

From a European perspective, in contrast, it is more common to see the main voice of security as an external factor to deal with (the USA) and therefore to be in a tension-ridden relationship to security as such. Calls for action in the name of security can be seen as part of the US attempts to organize the world—recently especially under the slogan of a global war on terror (Buzan and Wæver 2003: 297, 300, 303, 2009; Wæver 2005; Buzan 2006), and therefore 'Europe' takes a position vis-à-vis security where it is possible to problematize pronouncements about what is a security issue (that is, de-securitize) and insist on a wider concept of security—for example, an interpretation of terror and terror fighting that emphasizes economic and political mechanisms. Therefore, the whole question of what should and should not count as security issues and how to conceptualize security is much closer to the European policy agenda than to the US one.

The difference also expresses a general meta-theoretical divide—with the USA the more rationalist, Europe the more reflectivist (Tickner and Wæver 2009)—but this is far from the whole story. At least two other elements need to be taken into account (Wæver 2004): one is the different relationship to the *concept of security*. In Europe, the debate on this has stayed part of the field. It is seen as part of the ongoing practice of being a security analyst, to reflect on and problematize the concept—in order to understand and unveil the practices by practitioners in the name of security, but also as the politico-ethical self-reflection of a scholar who inevitably 'does security' when working in the name of security. In the USA, the question of the concept of security is seen as at most a necessary 'define your terms' operation in order to delineate what is counted in and out. When done with, one knows what is security or not, and the concept is not interesting in itself any more.

The other element is the exact form of knowledge that is valued. In contrast to the situation in general IR, where the USA has been dominated especially in the 1990s by rational choice, the US security studies field is absolutely *not* hard-core rational choice. The leading security theory journals, *International Security* and *Security Studies*, publish rather little formalized rational choice, and even soft rational choice that draws on economic theory or organizational theory is far from valued in the way it is in journals such as *International Organization* or *International Studies Quarterly* (Wæver 1998, 2007; Brown 2000). The typical article in *International Security* uses historical case studies—maybe one in-depth historical case study—to examine a hypothesis framed as cause–effect relationships and very often tied into general debates that are, on the one hand, of sweeping magnitude, and, on the other hand, boiled down to the measurement of one or a few variables, such as offensive versus defensive motivations (do states maximize power or security), the importance of ideational variables, or whether international order builds on pure power or also on institutions and legitimacy. Although each of these debates could easily be phrased as broad philosophical issues (as predecessors of each were in previous decades) or as ethical dilemmas, the American security literature constructs these questions as part of a tight, causal machinery, where a single, crucial question of how the logic unfolds is to be settled by empirical knowledge.

The most focused and sustained debate is probably offensive versus defensive realism, where a number of monographs (some major ones reviewed in Rose 1998) tried to use historical case studies to settle big, causal questions (see also Mearsheimer 2001). Similarly, the challenge from constructivism, which in Europe turned into major self-reflective debates on the conditions and responsibility of scholarship, became in US security studies mostly a question of testing the influence of ideational variables in the big causal picture (Desch 1998; Tannenwald and Wohlforth 2005).

The top-level policy debate on American grand strategy under presumed unipolarity was academically addressed mainly in terms of the proper expectations regarding the balancing behaviour of others (Brooks and Wohlforth 2005), which again hinges mostly on the general questions from the offensive–defensive realism debate, and second on the power of institutions. The latter question generated a very focused debate easily stylized (and taught) as Ikenberry versus Wohlforth (Ikenberry 2002). Realism traditionally took unipolarity to be impossible, and the strictest of neorealists—Waltz himself—actually predicted that it *would* not last long. Those who wanted to argue that some kind of preponderance could endure faced the challenge of *explaining* its relative stability. The major competing explanations emphasized, on the one hand, the USA's uniquely reassuring liberal form of hegemony partly derived from attributes of the US state, partly built into US policy of institution building and self-binding, and, on the other hand, the purely power-based stability of a situation where the USA is *so* superior that balancing becomes impossible. (The debate is collected in Ikenberry 2002; see also Mearsheimer 2001; Buzan and Wæver 2003; Buzan 2004b; Brooks and Wohlforth 2005; Deudney 2006.) The debate clearly has immediate implications for optimizing American grand strategy. But it is conducted less in terms of a future-oriented, purposive, and partly ethical debate about what future to aim for, and almost solely as (if it was) a theoretical-empirical debate over what theory can explain the past record. During the presidency of Bill Clinton, the debate on democratic peace had much the same status: the seemingly most relevant knowledge for security studies to supply to policy-makers is whether there is or is not a reliable causal connection between democracy and peace (Lepgold and Nincic 2001: ch. 5).

The common denominator tying together these differences is diverging understandings of the *role* of security studies, their function vis-à-vis policy. In the USA, this is most clearly understood as theory uncovering causal laws about the workings of world politics, which enables policy-makers to make the right choices when facing situations where these relationships are relevant. This in turn reflects a situation of an *acting* power, one that has to decide about how to shape world affairs, and it reflects a clear division of labour between politics, policy advice, and academic research.

In circles more clearly anchored on the European side, the trend was towards critical theories of various kinds that reflected on the practices of policy and problematized the nature of security making. This goes for Aberystwyth-style critical security studies, the Bourdieu-inspired work around Didier Bigo as well as the Copenhagen School, feminists and radical postmodernists such as Dillon, Constantinou, and Der Derian. Here, the concept of security has stayed part of the ongoing debate, and the form of knowledge differs from the one in the American mainstream, and is closer to that of a critical intellectual reflecting openly about one's own

political responsibility—who argues about one's analytical and theoretical choices in terms of their political implications (Booth 1997; Wyn Jones 1999; Bigo 1996, 2002a, b; Huysmans 2002, 2006; Buzan et al. 1998; Buzan and Hansen 2009).

A part of this story is the role of peace research and its change during the 1980s. With the new peace movement, peace research suddenly gained a new practical relevance. What Håkan Wiberg (1988) has called 'the peace research movement' had to fulfil its function as the natural intellectual adviser (more or less asked for) to the peace movement (Jahn 1984). This led in much of North European peace research to a new 'realism'. Peace research became pro-security and pro-Europe (where previously it had been anti-security in the name of peace and anti-Europe in the name of the third world). Even defence was reappropriated as alternative defence (non-offensive defence) (Møller 1991).

Security became during this period a meeting ground for strategic studies, which had until then operated more with *power* as the guiding concept and peace research having obviously *peace* as the key concept. In the 1980s, *security* emerged as a more constructive analytical concept (Buzan 1984; Jahn et al. 1987). Power thinking is a national concern and sees anarchy as inescapable and the end of the story—peace is cosmopolitan and claims that anarchy has to go before anything good can be achieved. In contrast, security is a relational concept (that is, in-between national and cosmopolitan), and sees anarchy as a spectrum, where conditions can be improved in the direction of a mature anarchy (Buzan 1984). In this sense, security became the middle ground and increasingly explicit as the basis for much IR work from the 1980s and onwards.

Peace research institutes especially in the 1980s were often in a position somewhat parallel to that of think tanks during Golden Age strategic studies. The link to policy was very different—not official advisers to policy-makers—but European security studies gained political relevance (in a broader sense) because of the politicization of security issues during the period defined by the peace movement, Reagan, and Gorbachev. The setting was—as in the

1950s—simultaneously interdisciplinary and connected to current developments in theory in the different disciplines. Peace research in contrast to university IR was under pressure to deal with relevant issues, but there was no expectation of immediate delivery of policy answers. At RAND in the 1950s, the theorists were given extraordinary leeway to pursue highly abstract, idiosyncratic theoretical tracks, which clearly could not be justified in terms of guaranteed pay-off vis-à-vis products to be delivered to policy-makers (Stern 1967). Exactly, therefore, publications often ended up being innovative solutions to policy questions. Similarly peace research was interdisciplinary, politically oriented, but with a distance both to immediate policy responsibility and to the major powers of the academic system. It is less clear whether there were policy effects, but our main point here is the impact of political involvement on theory. As rightly noted by Betts (1997: 32) in relation to traditional strategic studies: 'Ironically, in the past quarter century, policy experience has enriched academic research more than the reverse.' The same might be said about the 1980s and the birth of critical, European theories. A volatile political situation, a sense of importance and relevance, and engagement in heated political debates clearly contributed to the birth of these theories, and, in a few cases, theorists probably had some role as intellectuals of or for social movements such as the peace movements and Pugwash as well as some, mostly oppositional, political parties, but in general the effect of practice on theory was probably larger than vice versa.

Several observers (and observer participants) have noted that the debates among the new critical schools of security studies—to some extent seen as a 'European' development—have become surprisingly productive and generated theory of broader relevance and inspiration to the field of IR in general (Huysmans 1998; Eriksson 1999; Williams 2003). Security studies in the USA largely works with theories that are developed within IR and then tested and refined within security studies on security cases—neo-realism, soft constructivism, and so on (Wæver 2004). The most monumental

illustration of this is the nature of constructivism in American security studies. The main work here is the big Katzenstein volume on *The Culture of National Security* (Katzenstein 1996b). This was mainly manned by scholars who did not have a long-term involvement with security affairs. They were IR scholars who had taken part in the theory wars on the constructivist side, and it seemed the right move at the time to prove constructivism on the home ground of materialist approaches: security. Quite visibly this is a foray by general IR theorists into security studies for the sake of making a point within IR theory debates. The new 'European' schools, in contrast, did not develop deductively from the guiding symbolic positions within the theory debates (and therefore they are often hard to pin down—is the Copenhagen School constructivist, neorealist, postmodernist, or all of the above?); they emerged as part of the engagements on a distinct security scene, and the theoretical innovations *have become* part of the theory landscape in IR theory. For instance, one can find discussions of securitization theory in general IR journals (Williams 2003; Balzacq 2005) in ways that constitute the main investigations of the potential for IR of drawing on speech-act theory in general. Similarly, debates within the discipline (at least in Europe) of the political role of researchers have been conducted with security theory as the platform (Eriksson 1999; Huysmans 2002). The fate of Frankfurt-style 'Critical Theory' in IR has also been decisively influenced by security studies. The attempts in the 'fourth debate' in the 1980s to launch Critical Theory were largely abortive, and postmodern approaches came to structure the meta-theoretical scene to a much larger extent. But gradually Critical Theory gained a position in the general IR landscape mainly because of the success of Ken Booth and others in showing its value within the area of security (Wyn Jones 1999; Booth 2005b, 2007).

One might ask now whether these lively debates in and among the new schools still qualify as 'security studies'. Have they simply become IR and lost the in-between position that defines security studies? Where the first-generation representatives of

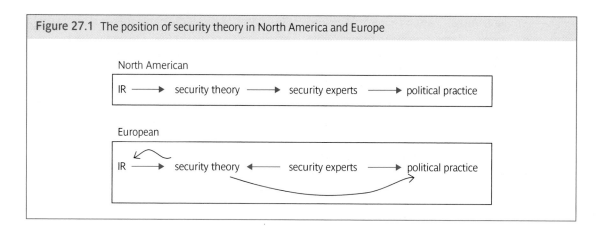

Figure 27.1 The position of security theory in North America and Europe

the different schools—Booth, Bigo, Buzan, Wæver—had developed their arguments in engagements with policy questions and in direct interaction with policy-makers and think tanks, the next generation would be more clearly academically defined and develop these arguments in a more isolated academic setting. However, the set-up continues to be one where security theory is located between the IR discipline as such and technical experts and practitioners, only with the arrows somewhat different from the North American ones (see Figure 27.1).

The place of security experts here underlines the point that much work in European and North American research institutes is quite similar: detailed technical work on AIDS as an epidemic, on the proliferation of missile technology, on the efficiency of various counterterrorist strategies. Most of what goes on in foreign-policy institutes as well as the IISS in Europe and in American think tanks is of this nature, delivering on the demand of politicians for factual knowledge here-and-now on a question that came up yesterday and needs an answer tomorrow (maybe with the main difference that in the USA this is often structured more as a partisan advocacy for a specific policy, and in Europe as seemingly neutral, technical background knowledge). The point here is that, as soon as this is reflected on in terms of theory—when an interaction emerges between, on the one hand, technical experts in say European foreign-policy institutes or Washington think tanks,

and, on the other, in university circles, for instance through Ph.D. students who do work that is simultaneously part of their university-based Ph.D. and part of the research institute—the theoretical context differs. In the USA, this will usually be the discussions reflected in *International Security*, whereas in parts of Europe, the young scholars will relate to and draw inspiration from the new theories that emerged in European research institutes and now mainly thrive in European universities.

On both sides, it is essential to the particular nature of security theory that there is a distinct category of 'policy knowledge' that functions as expertise supporting policy—a form of knowledge that security theory in the USA wants to assist, while security theory in Europe (to draw the contrast sharply) treats it as a main empirical source for critical analysis. Critics of current policy in the USA will aim to obtain a policy change by presenting theoretical generalizations based on empirical data that give scientific credentials to a different policy as more likely to achieve the aims aspired to. Critics working with the theories here associated with European security studies are more likely to criticize politically and ethically the current policy for its aims and effects and to expose the involved 'policy knowledge' as a part of policy making, structurally complicit and produced from the policy-maker's perspective, rather than criticizing it for being scientifically wrong and up for revision.

Conclusion: the powers of theory and the challenges of the future

Security studies in the first decades of the twenty-first century is in a strong position. It has been through a second decade of theoretical productivity. Strangely, this has happened to roughly parallel degrees in Europe and the USA, despite the very minimal connections between these two sets of theoretical developments. Now it is well equipped with a battery of theories and the field is simultaneously seen as generally important, so it attracts bright students, and increasingly, funding. What kind of development will this lead to?

It is quite plausible that the new 'European' security studies does not remain structured by separate 'schools' (Wæver 2004). There is a tendency in the fast-growing and very active trans-European community of Ph.D. students to move among and across these schools. Thereby they become treated more as *theories*, where one has to understand their distinct character—they do not blend into one synthesized European security theory—but they can be drawn upon in individual projects as inspiration and instruments. While it is still possible to find contributions (e.g. Booth 2005b) that try to cultivate a situation of competition and theory construction through caricaturing others, it is clearly more common among the emerging generation of scholars to see the combined field of 'New European Security Theories' (NEST) as a joint debate where the different theories are developed and applied through their interaction (Büger and Stritzel 2005).

The future of security theory in the USA should be assessed in a different manner, because the theories there are less security specific than the European theories and more closely integrated into the main constellation of IR theories. The future of these security theories is therefore inseparable from the general prospects for IR theory. As often noticed (e.g. Goldmann 1988), US theory debates within IR tend to be about general theories—frameworks potentially explaining everything or at least a major part of every important question. The main theories in the security field are expressed in such general terms that, if valid, they would be overarching frameworks for our general understanding of international relations. Therefore, their fate as security theories hinges on their ability to prevail in the general debates in the discipline of IR, and these are at the moment quite inconclusive and somewhat unfocused (Wæver 2007). The only strong candidate for a kind of hegemony is rational choice as meta-theory, and this is exactly the theory that is comparatively weak within security studies even in the USA. Therefore, it is unlikely that the internal dynamics of the theory debate will be decided by a general prevalence of one of the current candidates.

More important for the future development of each theory in both Europe and the USA is probably how it handles some of the current issues on the political agenda. The two sets of theories will be working on partly overlapping sets of questions, as indicated in many chapters of this book. Probably, it will mostly be the European theories that try to make sense out of environmental security, health security, identity issues and gender, while the US theories will be most active in areas such as proliferation of weapons of mass destruction and global military stability. Both will work on terror and its counterpart, the US-centred international order, and, where the first waves after 9/11 mainly came from the USA, it has become a main object of analysis to European scholars, not only think tanks and the terrorism experts, but also from the theory-inclined academics. Conversely, both will work on migration and the tension between security and liberty, including the logic of exceptionalism, although at least at present the theoretical side of this is far more developed in the debate among the European schools, where in the USA this is mostly policy work disconnected from the main theories but with some notable exceptions (like Andreas and Biersteker 2003). Both will be working on the role and nature of technology, globalization, risk society, and international economic order. This quick picture shows that there will actually be a lot of points of contact between the currently disconnected fields of theory. A major question is, therefore: will they merge again—not in agreement but in debate? Will there be more exchange between the different research environments? Some signs in this direction can be found in the acceptance of a somewhat widened security agenda in American textbooks, while—as always—all major American theories are read in Europe. The particularly heavy-handed usage of security justifications under the administration of George W. Bush (2001–8), seems to have created an increased interest among American scholars in the European theories, not least securitization theory. As the polarization of IR's '4th debate' (rationalism-versus-reflectivism) wears off, there are also signs of European critical scholars reintegrating arguments about power and polarity; maybe they too were motivated by the Bush administration.

What will happen when the theories meet trans-Atlantically on issues of common concern? Will they try to learn from contrasting insights from different kinds of theories? The most obvious current joint issue is *terror and order*, the one that tops the American agenda and is still high enough on the European one for contributions to come from there too. Fast-rising concerns over environmental/climate security could easily provide another big linking issue, but it seems less likely that the rise of China will work in this way. Because the rise of China threatens US unipolar status, this is much more likely to be a central concern of US security studies than of European.

With or without such a meeting, this will be a time when theory is central to security studies. What can be envisaged here is not a 'new great debate' between clusters of security theories—rather a new encounter between different debates in which the theories to some extent represent a division of labour brought to bear on common problems. The theories of the 1990s will have to prove themselves in a dual challenge. The first question is do they have the inner vitality to become a dynamic research programme that continues to evolve? This depends largely on the constellation of key concepts—is this at once tight enough to be operational and open enough to generate puzzles and research problems? So far the signs here are quite promising. The second challenge is to be able to take up in interesting ways the political challenges of the day. In that regard, and particularly in relation to how it deals with terrorism and the environment, and state responses to these, security studies will continue to grapple with the problem noted long ago by Waltz (1979: 112): 'States, like people, are insecure in proportion to the extent of their freedom. If freedom is wanted, insecurity must be accepted.'

KEY POINTS

- Security studies is in the advantageous position of housing much theoretical productivity and issues high on the public agenda, attracting therefore both funding and talent. Whether this opportunity will be used to produce better theories is yet to be seen.

- The different new 'schools' in Europe increasingly intersect and form a field with opportunities for a new generation to combine and innovate across the theories.

- In the USA, the development of security theory is tied up with the general trends of the IR discipline.

- Both families of theories as well as their interaction will be much influenced by their ability to engage in relevant ways with the main issues on the policy agenda.

 QUESTIONS

1. Why was it primarily in the USA that strategic studies formed as a separate field?

2. Why did the Vietnam War not become the generator of new waves of theorization to deliver on this new policy challenge?

3. On the basis of the previous chapters in this book as well as this chapter, to what extent does 'security studies' appear to be one integrated field, or is it more appropriately seen as two or more arenas sharing a name but separated by either geographical or meta-theoretical distance?

4. Would you explain the increasing distance between security theorizing in Europe and the USA mainly by differences in foreign policy, general philosophical orientations, institutional differences within the academic world, or other factors?

5. Why does constructivism lead to such different kinds of work in the USA and Europe?

6. What is different between the form of knowledge in US and European work?

7. What institutional reforms regarding universities, think tanks, policy institutes, or policy making would be most conducive to better security theory and better security policy?

8. What are the most important questions on the policy agenda to get a better understanding of, and why do these not become the most active areas of research?

9. Do the current policy challenges point to a need for new interdisciplinary configurations?

10. Is a close connection between theory and policy conducive or disruptive for good theory?

 FURTHER READING

- Brown, Michael E. (2000) (ed.), *Rational Choice and Security Studies: Stephen Walt and his Critics*, Cambridge, MA: MIT Press. Stephen Walt's attack on rational-choice approaches to security is both interesting as an exploration of the pros and cons of this approach, and as a clarification of how security studies, International Security style, defines itself methodologically and meta-theoretically.

- Buzan, Barry (1983), *People, States and Fear: The National Security Problem in International Relations*, Brighton: Wheatsheaf (2nd edn subtitled *An Agenda for International Security Studies in the Post Cold War Era*, Boulder CO: Lynne Rienner 2001; re-issued with new introduction as ECPR classic 2007). A defining work from the second productive period, which both summarizes the preceding reflections on the concept of security and puts forward an original synthesis that made one of the first coherent cases for widening.

■ Buzan, Barry, and Lene Hansen (2009), *The Evolution of International Security Studies*, Cambridge: Cambridge University Press. Surveys the history of security studies, traditional as well as critical forms, and offers an explanation in terms of driving forces that shaped debates in ISS.

■ Buzan, Barry, Wæver, Ole, and de Wilde, Jaap (1998), *Security: A New Framework for Analysis*, Boulder, CO: Lynne Rienner (Chinese translation 2004; follow-on edition in 2010 entitled *The Politics of Security*). The main theoretical statement from the Copenhagen School. While its world analysis is more fully elaborated in a later book, the defining categories of the theory are put forward here: securitization and sectors.

■ Croft, Stuart, and Terriff, Terry (2000) (eds.), *Critical Reflections on Security and Change*, London: Frank Cass. Combines reflections on more traditional security studies—realism, liberalism, etc.—with the new debates.

■ Gray, Colin (1982), *Strategic Studies and Public Policy: The American Experience*, Lexington, KY: University Press of Kentucky. A critical history of early strategic studies, which combines observations about institutions, politics, and theory.

■ Guzzini, Stefano, and Jung, Dietrich (2004) (eds.), *Contemporary Security Analysis and Copenhagen Peace Research*, London: Routledge. Explores the role of peace research (especially in Northern Europe) in furthering the emergence of the new European security theories.

■ Ikenberry, G. John (2002) (ed.), *American Unrivaled: The Future of the Balance of Power*, Ithaca, NY: Cornell. Includes a number of powerful contributions that represent the main American debates over both offensive/defensive realism and international orders built on power/institutions.

■ Jervis, Robert (1976), *Perception and Misperception in International Politics*, Princeton: Princeton University Press. One of the main books (together with Allison's *Essence of Decision*) to open up the psychological and decision-making approaches to strategic thinking in opposition to rational actor models.

■ Krause, Keith, and Williams, Michael C. (1997) (eds.), *Critical Security Studies: Concepts and Cases*, Minneapolis: University of Minnesota Press. The defining work from Critical Security Studies, which includes sufficient diversity to represent much of the new work in general, not only one narrowly defined school, and paradoxically thereby produces the ideal manifesto for CSS.

■ Schelling, Thomas C. (1960), *The Strategy of Conflict*, Cambridge, MA: Harvard University Press. One of the most original works from the (first) Golden Age, produced at RAND, eventually earning the author a 2005 Nobel Prize in economy (or in security studies, if one reads closely the justification from The Royal Swedish Academy of Sciences). Even fun to read.

IMPORTANT WEBSITES

● http://www.isn.ethz.ch   International Relations and Security Network, Center for Security Studies, ETH, Zurich, Switzerland. A good collection of links to both current security issues and centres of research. From here one can get to the institutes, journals, and organizations, of which there are too many to list individually here.

● http://www.casecollective.org   Open Working Group on Critical Approaches to Security in Europe. A good road especially to the younger generation of scholars working with the new European approaches.

● http://www.intlsecurity.org   Joint webpage for the International Security Studies Section (ISSS) of International Studies Association (ISA) and the International Security and Arms Control (ISAC) section of the American Political Science Association (APSA).

● http://www.mitpressjournals.org/is   *International Security*, the leading mainstream journal.

- http://www.tandf.co.uk/journals/titles/09636412.asp   *Security Studies*, another high-ranking journal mostly publishing American mainstream research, but often more open to deep theoretical debate than International Security.

- http://ejt.sagepub.com   *European Journal of International Relations*. Much of the debate over the new European theories has taken place in general IR journals such as EJIR, Review of International Studies, and Millennium.

- http://sdi.sagepub.com   *Security Dialogue* has recently developed into one of the leading places for discussion on 'human security', 'risk/security', 'gender and security', and the new European theories, while also relatively strong on policy articles.

 Visit the Online Resource Centre that accompanies this book for lots of interesting additional material: www.oxfordtextbooks.co.uk/orc/collins2e/

Glossary

There is no single correct or agreed-upon definition of any of these terms, as you will no doubt have noticed already. This can be unsettling if you are used to the idea that there is a 'right answer' or the 'right definition'. The definitions offered below indicate how they have been used in this book. The important thing is for you to be clear about how your sources use these terms and be clear about how you are using them yourself.

1925 Geneva Protocol for the Prohibition of the Use in War of Asphyxiating, Poisonous, or Other Gases, and of Bacteriological Methods of Warfare: Outlawed the use in war of asphyxiating, poisonous gases and liquids

1972 Anti-Ballistic Missile Treaty: The treaty banned the United States and the Soviet Union from constructing national missile defences. After giving the six months' notice called for by the Treaty, the United States withdrew from the agreement in June 2002, citing the Treaty's fundamental obsolescence. Critics decried the move, but the deployment of extremely modest US missile defences have failed to generate an appreciable international response.

1972 Biological and Toxin Weapons Convention (BWC): Opened for signature on April 1972. Parties agreed not to acquire stockpile biological weapons and toxins. In 1996, the fourth review conference failed to reach an agreement on verification procedures to strengthen the 1972 agreement. Although signatories continue to abide by the agreement, the treaty has not entered into force.

2002 Moscow Treaty: Agreement between the United States and Russia to cut deployed offensive strategic nuclear warheads to between 1,700 and 2,200 by 31 December 2012. Unlike previous arms control treaties between the superpowers, this treaty leaves it up to the parties to determine the pace of reductions and exact composition of its forces on New Year's Eve 2012.

9/11: A widely accepted shorthand way of referring to the 11 September 2001 al-Qaeda attack on the two towers of the World Trade Center in New York City, the Pentagon in Washington DC, and the failed attempt to crash a fourth aircraft into the White House.

Action–reaction model of the arms dynamic: The idea that actors increase the quantity or quality of their military forces in response to increases on the part of a potential adversary.

Agency–structure debate: This refers to whether the structure of the international system directs the behaviour and actions of its parts. A neorealist view of this debate is that the structure of anarchy conditions the behaviour of states. The opposite view would be that actors construct the structure. Constructivists argue that both structures and actors influence each other.

Agenda for Peace: A report to the UN Secretary General in January 1992 advocating peacekeeping, peacemaking, and conflict prevention as priorities for avoiding military confrontations.

AIDS: Acquired Immunodeficiency Syndrome or Acquired Immune Deficiency Syndrome; it refers to a host of symptoms and illnesses caused by the weakening of the human immune system due to infection with the human immunodeficiency virus.

AIDS-related illnesses: Illnesses such as pneumocystis pneumonia (a lung infection) and Kaposi's sarcoma (a skin cancer) that accompany the onset of AIDS; strictly speaking people do not die of AIDS, but of AIDS-related illnesses.

Alienation: In historical materialist thought: the lack of control by most people of their labour in a context in which this is represented as natural and inevitable, with people often feeling this alienation emotionally, as they spend most of their lives doing work they do not believe in just to survive.

Al-Qaeda (The Base): A network of extremist Muslim groups, initially organized by Osama bin Laden, which seeks to drive Western ideas and influence out of Muslim countries.

Alliance: The coming-together of a group of states with a formal agreement to work together to accomplish a particular military security objective.

Anarchy: In the field of international politics, a term for the absence of any ultimate power and authority over states. In short, the absence of a world or regional government, or binding international law, that is superior to states; it does not mean that international relations are chaotic.

Anthrax: Disease caused by the *Bacillus anthracis* bacterium that forms in spores. The infection in humans can occur in the skin, lungs, and digestive tract and is often contracted from infected animals (e.g. sheep). It is not contagious, but, because humans can be infected by coming into contact with anthrax spores, it is considered to be a good candidate for weaponization.

Arlington National Cemetery: Home to the Women in Military Service for America Memorial; this was dedicated on 18 October 1997.

Arms control: Represents 'restraint internationally exercised upon armaments policy, whether in respect of the level of armaments, their character, deployment or use'.

Arms dynamic: Is best understood as the various factors that lead actors such as states or other significant political entities to acquire armed forces and change the quantity and/or quality of those forces they already maintain.

Assassins: An unorthodox sect of Shia Muslims who used assassination to protect themselves from the surrounding rulers who adhered to the Sunni majority views.

Audience: It consists of a group (public opinion, politicians, military officers, or other elites) that needs to be convinced that a referent object is existentially threatened.

Aum Shinriyko: A Japanese religious cult that released sarin gas in the Tokyo subway system in an effort to kill thousands.

Autonomy: Being free from any higher power or authority, or, inside a state, being free within a specified geographical area or sphere of activity from such authority. In international politics states claim autonomy on a scale unmatched by, accorded to, or exercised by any other political actor.

Balance of power: In international politics, a term used primarily in three ways. First, to refer to an existing distribution of power among members of an international system. Second, to refer to a distribution of power in which—among the major members—power is distributed so that the members balance each other's power and therefore constrain each other. Third, to label a strategy for state security that is preoccupied with creating or maintaining a distribution of power in the system that is considered beneficial in terms of maintaining security and stability.

Balancing: The options available to a state for increasing its military capabilities and ability to defend. There are two key types of balancing. External balancing refers to forming alliances with other states, thereby enabling the state to draw on other states' resources. When people think about balancing, this is the type they usually imagine. There is, however, a second key type of balancing—internal balancing: a state's internal efforts to increase its own economic capability and to build larger and/or better military forces.

Bandwagoning: When the response by a government to the rise of an increasingly powerful state is to associate or ally itself with it. This is in contrast to a strategy of opposing or balancing—trying to offset the power of—such a powerful state.

Berlin Air Lift: A crisis between June 1948 and May 1949 when the Soviet Union blocked the ground routes to Berlin, and the USA, UK and other Western states responded with a massive airlift of supplies to the city.

Biopolitics: In his later writings, Michel Foucault turned to the analysis of contemporary political life, and argued that since the middle of the nineteenth century the state has been basing claims to legitimacy on its capacity to make populations live. That is, the state has increasingly come into the business of providing for the health, education, and well-being of its people, which has in turn underpinned the state's claim to the right to continue. This notion of the biopolitical states is in contrast to the traditional sovereign state, which based its legitimacy on the basis of its ability to kill.

Bipolar: The label for a power distribution in an international system in which two states are roughly equal in power and are each much more powerful than any of the other members. As a result, the power of each balances that of the other, and each has a number of states associated or allied with it. The relations between the two giants and between the two blocs dominate the politics of the system.

Bretton Woods system: The institutional arrangements created by the USA and the UK for managing the post-Second World War international economic system, including the International Monetary Fund, the International Bank for Reconstruction and Development (now the World Bank), and the General Agreements on Tariffs and Trade as the primary institutions.

Brute/full-scale force: Use of force to impose compliance on the adversary or settle the dispute at hand.

Cambridge Five: The popular name for a ring of British citizens recruited by Soviet intelligence before and during the Second World War. It consisted of Guy Burgess, Donald Maclean, Harold (Kim) Philby, Anthony Blunt, and John Cairncross. As more information was released during the 1990s, it appears that several others were also involved.

Cape Town Principles: Cape Town principles and best practice on the prevention of recruitment of children into the armed forces and demobilization and social reintegration of child soldiers in Africa. Adopted by the participants in the Symposium on the Prevention of Recruitment of Children into the Armed Forces and Demobilization and Social Reintegration of Child Soldiers in Africa, organized by UNICEF in cooperation with the NGO sub-group of the NGO Working Group on the Convention on the Rights of the Child, Cape Town, 30 April 1997.

Capitalism: A mode of production characterized by private property, the profit motive, competition, and freedom of contract with this system guaranteed by the state and norms that are embedded in the habits and practices of states and international organizations. Historical materialists disagree with the liberal position that this is a free, just, mutually beneficial system in tune with human nature. The representation of aspects of economics by realism and liberalism as somehow non-political and private is regarded by historical materialists as serving the interests of capitalists (by allowing them to retain unelected and for the most part unaccountable control).

Capitalists (capitalist ruling class): Those who own and control the means of production of goods and services in capitalism.

Causality: The relationship between cause and effect.

Chemical Weapons Convention: An agreement by which state parties agree never, under any circumstances, to acquire, stockpile, or transfer chemical weapons, to use chemical weapons, to prepare to use chemical weapons, or to induce others to engage in activity prohibited by the Convention. The Convention entered into force on 29 April 1997. The Organization for the Prohibition of Chemical Weapons in The Hague, Netherlands, is responsible for implementing the Chemical Weapons Convention.

Civil society: (1) The totality of all individuals and groups in a society who are not acting as participants in any government institutions, or (2) all individuals and groups who are neither participants in government nor acting in the interests of commercial companies. The two meanings are incompatible and contested. There is a third meaning: the network of social institutions and practices (economic relationships, family and kinship groups, religious, and other social affiliations) that underlie strictly political institutions.

Class: In historical materialist terms class refers to one's position in relation to ownership or control of the physical and financial assets necessary for production (at this stage in history mostly capitalist production). Hence there are in capitalist society two basic classes—a ruling class of capitalists, which retains as profit some of the value produced by labour, and a ruled class of workers compelled to sell their labour to capitalists in order to survive—but also managers, etc. In contrast, social class refers to perceived and objective stratifications of society whereas elites are composed of those with concentrations of power of any kind. Classes and elites may overlap, may be united on some things and divided on others, and their unity or division may be perceptual or objective.

Codes and ciphers: Nations communicate to their representatives abroad not in plain text that could be read by anyone, but in encoded or enciphered text that cannot be read by those who do not know how the plain text was encrypted or transformed into secret writing. Other nations who desire that information try to collect it and then to decode or decipher it—that is, to turn it back into plain text. Encryption refers to the act of turning plain text into a code or a cipher and decryption refers to the process of attempting to turn the secret writing back into plain text.

Coercive diplomacy: Use of threats and limited force to influence the adversary to stop or undo something it has already embarked upon.

Cold War: The global competition from 1945 to 1989 (when the wall dividing West and East Germany came down) between capitalist and Communist states in which the United States and Soviet Union did not fight each other directly but backed local rivals in armed conflicts. At its peak in the early 1980s, the two alliances (NATO and the Warsaw Pact) deployed over 60,000 nuclear weapons and spent $1,000 billion a year (2006 prices) on the military.

Commodification: Turning previously non-monetary social relations into monetary relations.

Common security: Joint action by a number of states to address shared problems that cannot be solved by the actions of any single state.

Compellence: Use of threats and limited force to influence the adversary to do something.

Comprehensive Test Ban Treaty: A disarmament measure, this treaty bans nuclear testing, thereby disrupting the development of human capital and technology needed to create and maintain a nuclear arsenal. Over 148 countries have signed the CTBT. The United States Senate failed to ratify the treaty in December 1999. The United States and the rest of the world, however, have maintained a nuclear-test moratorium so far in the twenty-first century.

Conflict management: Concerns the amelioration of conflict between one or more parties.

Constructivism: General 'school' within IR theory that rose during the late 1980s–early 1990s to become the leading alternative to the dominant rationalist theories of neorealism and neoliberalism. Constructivists emphasize the importance of ideational factors such as culture, beliefs, norms, ideas, and identity. Constructivism covers a wide spectrum from the borderland to poststructuralism/postmodernism to 'soft constructivists', who share the postivism and state-centrism of mainstream approaches.

Containment: The creation of strategic alliances in order to check the expansion of a hostile power or to force it to negotiate peacefully.

Copenhagen School: Emerged at the Conflict and Peace Research Institute (COPRI) of Copenhagen and represented by the writings of Barry Buzan, Ole Wæver, Jaap de Wilde, and others. It is partly about widening the threats and referent objects, especially societal/identity, partly about paying more attention to the regional level, but mainly about focusing on securitization—the social processes by which groups of people construct something as a threat—thus offering a constructivist counterpoint to the materialist threat analysis of traditional strategic studies.

Critical realism: The philosophical position that there are social structures independent of discourses about them, which have the capacity to have particular effects and which have more potential to change in some ways than in others.

Critical security studies: Based partly on a critique of the state-centric paradigm and partly on the prescription for emancipatory action. See Chapter 6 in this volume.

Cuban Missile Crisis: One of the most dangerous crises of the Cold War, when in October 1962 the United States blocked Soviet installation of medium-range nuclear-armed missiles in Cuba.

Cultural autonomy: The granting of rights in relation to the means of cultural reproduction, such as autonomy over educational and religious institutions.

Cultural cleansing: The deliberate destruction of symbols, signs, and institutions, such as schools, museums, and places of worship of one ethnic group by another.

Cultural nationalism: A movement/project designed to generate strong feelings of self-identification, emphasizing various commonalities such as language, religion, and history.

Defence sale: This is a broad term that can refer to the sale of either a complete weapons system such as a tank or a fighter plane but can also include the sale of components, training, spares, and other defence services. The term can also encapsulate commercial arrangements such as the leasing of defence equipment. Payment for such sales can be made either in cash or in kind (e.g. through the provision of other goods such as oil) or through some combination of the two. Defence sales, it should be noted, are rarely perfect examples of free-market competition, with factors such as price and quality often taking second place to considerations such as prestige or security of supply as well as the effectiveness of suppliers in lobbying decision-makers, a process that may well extend to the provision of bribes.

Democratic peace theory: A theory claiming that democratic states do not go to war with each other, with variants of the theory differing as to what it is about democracies—as democracies—that produces this behaviour.

Desecuritization: Refers to a process that reintroduces a securitized matter into the standard political domain.

Deterrence: Use of threats and specific actions to discourage the adversary from doing something in the first place.

Development: Extensive enhancement of a society's basic capabilities and resources. This is of great interest to many governments because they can tap the additional capabilities and resources for their own purposes and can cite them to build political popularity and legitimacy with citizens.

Dialogical: Relating to and in the form of dialogue.

Discourse: In its most loose usage of the term by adherents of objectivism, a discourse is simply a way of describing or labelling a real phenomenon. In contrast, for constructivists, discourses are practices (words and other actions) that play an active role by giving phenomena meaning, by being inherently normative (that is, having inbuilt ideas of right and wrong), and by silencing (that is, making it more difficult to understand the phenomenon in other ways).

Dismal science: An early version of economics claimed that population growth would always match or exceed economic growth so that poverty was inevitable, which led to economics being labelled a dismal science.

Domestic factor models of the arms dynamic: The idea that domestic military expenditure and weapons procurement decisions are not strongly linked to the external actions of other states. Instead, emphasis is placed on a variety of *domestic* bureaucratic, political, or economic explanations. For example, it is sometimes argued that the need to maintain a defence industrial base creates a 'follow-on' imperative under which governments place orders simply to keep companies and skilled workers rather than as a function of any immediate military necessity.

Domestic procurement: This is the term used to describe the acquisition of defence goods from a firm within the country of a purchasing government.

Doublecross system: An elaborate deception operation began in 1939 when a Welsh electrical engineer who had been reported to British intelligence about his business trips to pre-war Germany decided to spy instead for Germany. He later changed his mind and became a double agent for the British, sending deceptive information back to Germany. This led to a large ring of German agents being rounded up in Britain and given the choice of being executed or being used to send additional false information back to Germany. It was called the Doublecross system because, as a pun, the British intelligence committee that ran the system was called the Twenty (XX) Committee.

Dual-use technology: Refers to equipment or technology that has both military and civilian applications.

Dutch disease: A phenomenon that marks many of those economies heavily reliant upon the exploitation of natural resources (such as oil and gas). Vast quantities of revenue and foreign direct investment into an economy work to drive up the exchange rate. In turn, this higher rate reduces the competitive nature of other domestic sectors (primarily industrial), thus 'hollowing out' the economy and increasing reliance on resource 'rents'. This has consequences for the responsiveness of governments, as those dependent on income generated from rents rather than taxes are not driven to ensure political legitimacy to the same extent.

Economic security: Safeguarding the structural integrity and prosperity-generating capabilities and interests of a politico-economic entity in the context of various externalized risks and threats that confront it in the international economic system.

Economics-security nexus: The linkages between economic policy and traditional or politico-military security policy.

ECOWAS monitoring group (ECOMOG): A multinational armed force that was established in West Africa by the Economic Community of West African States (ECOWAS); it is not a standing army, but rather an agreement for cooperation between several militaries in the region to work together when necessary.

Elite accommodation: The process of managing or accommodating the threat by powerful elites, including strongmen, to the security of the regime, usually through various forms of power-sharing, patronage, or graft.

Emancipation: Emancipation refers to the freeing of people from the structures of oppression or domination in which they find themselves. Various forms of critical theory are driven by a political commitment to emancipation from different structures of oppression and domination. Generally, post-Marxist Critical Theory will speak of emancipation in the singular, emphasizing its belief that the political economy is the root of all oppression; poststructural critical theories are more likely to speak of emancipations in the plural, emphasizing the multiple forms of domination, or the multiple means of subjection.

Empirical: Relating to facts as opposed to abstractions such as theories or values.

'End of history': The German philosopher Hegel saw history as an evolution through repeated struggles towards a perfect society. Francis Fukuyama, in 1992, suggested that, with the collapse of communism and the triumph of democracy and capitalism, this evolution was now coming to an end.

Endogenous: Having internal origin; associated with a referent such as 'inside the state'.

Energy diversification: High levels of energy security depend upon ensuring a diversified set of energy sources. In this context, diversification can refer to meeting needs through a range of energy *types* (such as oil, solar, nuclear), or to meeting needs through a range of sources of one particular energy type. By diversifying oil production away from the Persian Gulf, the USA and other key consumers hope to improve their energy security, by making their economies less reliant on the unstable Middle East.

Enigma: A German electrical enciphering machine used by Germany during the Second World War. With help from French intelligence and some Polish mathematicians, British code-breakers at Bletchley Park, using a prototype computer, deciphered the code. The intelligence gained from this feat was critical for victory in the war.

Environment: That part of the Earth's surface that includes living organisms, the remains of living organisms, and the physical and chemical components of the total system necessary for, or involved in the process of, life (Boyden et al. 1990: 314).

Environmental change: Short- and long-term changes in biological, physical, and chemical components and systems resulting from both human activities and natural processes.

Environmental security: The assurance that individuals and groups have that they can avoid or adapt to environmental change without critical adverse effects.

Epidemic: An usually large or rapid outbreak of a contagious disease that exceeds the normal level in a particular population at a given time.

Epistemology: Epistemology is the *study* of the way we know. Within a theory or approach, the epistemology refers to the set of assumptions about how knowledge is generated that inform that theory or approach. All forms of scholarship must make assumptions about knowledge; therefore they must have an epistemology.

Ethnic cleansing: The deliberate killing, use of violence, or deportation of members of one ethnic group by another.

Euzkadi ta Askatasuna (ETA): The Basque dissident group that has used terrorism for over twenty-five years in an effort to achieve independence.

Excess production capacity: The amount of spare production potential that is not currently being used. Acts as a cushion for international energy markets, where in times of crisis additional capacity can be brought online to stabilize prices. Saudi excess capacity is vast, and has been used at many points in history (such as during the 1991 Gulf War) to stabilize markets.

Existential threat: Threats to the continued existence of a referent object. Individuals face an existential threat when they are threatened with death; states face an existential threat when, among other things, they are threatened with external invasion and conquest. Existential threats are the most serious threats a referent object can face, and thus are seen to justify the most extensive measures to secure against them.

Exogenous: Having external origin; often associated with a referent such as 'outside the state'.

Exploitation: In historical materialism this refers to the fact that workers are paid less than the value of their labour: this surplus value, as it is called by historical materialists, goes to the capitalist as profit. Hence the concept of exploitation is used here both to describe something and also to make a negative value judgement on it.

Extraordinary measures: Such measures go beyond rules ordinarily abided by and are thus located outside the bounds of political procedures and practices. Their adoption involves the identification and classification of some issue as an existential threat.

Failed state: A state that is incapable of and/or unwilling to meet the basic needs of its population, provide domestic order, and represent national interests externally. This term is often used in the context of assumptions that the lack of performance is mainly due to factors internal to that state and that external intervention or occupation is therefore legitimate and necessary. Hence it can have ideological functions, with the role of global capitalism or the actions of external actors in undermining that state capacity or preventing its establishment obscured.

Fascists (Italy): The right-wing party that used violence and terrorism to help Benito Mussolini take power in Italy in 1922.

Fatah: The major faction in the Palestinian Liberation Organization when it was opposed to Israel has reappeared in the West Bank and Gaza in opposition to Hamas.

Femininity/Feminism: The advocacy of women's rights based upon ideas of equality between men and women. Note, though, that there are many variations of feminism. These include liberal, radical, and Marxist categories.

Force multipliers: The term refers to factors, usually understood as technological development, that significantly increase the combat effectiveness of militaries.

Foreign direct investment (FDI): Investment carried out with the aim of acquiring a lasting interest in an enterprise operating in an economy other than that of the investor, the investor's purpose being to have an effective voice in the management of the enterprise.

Foreign economic policy (FEP) power: Typically nation states or some other state form and can include sub-state units (e.g. states within a federated union such as the US), supranational or inter-governmental units (e.g. the EU), city-states (e.g. Singapore) or quasi-states (e.g. Taiwan).

Foreign economic policy (FEP): May be broadly thought of as having two main dimensions. The 'policy-technical' dimension comprises the technical operation of trade policy, international finance policy, foreign-direct-investment policy, overseas development assistance policy, and so on. The second 'economic diplomacy' dimension concerns how FEP powers (e.g. nation states) manage their economic relations with other powers and agencies within the international system.

Free ride: Obtaining something valuable by relying on the efforts of others to supply it while doing little oneself to obtain it. For example, a country in a strategically vital location may remain safe while doing little to protect itself if it has a powerful ally (a good example is Japan).

Free-trade agreement: An agreement among a limited number of states to remove all or nearly all the barriers between them on trade, flows of money, and other economic activities—in contrast to an arrangement to do this that is open to all members of the international system who wish to join.

Gamma radiation: Also known as penetrating radiation because dense shielding is needed to protect individuals from its effects. Gamma radiation is high-energy ionizing radiation, which is one of the first effects produced by a nuclear detonation. Because it can penetrate the body, it is usually the primary cause of radiation sickness.

Gender: Refers not just to the biological differences between men and women but to a set of culturally shaped and defined characteristics, which underpin the notion of what it is to be a man or a woman.

Geneva Conventions: There are four Geneva Conventions, signed 12 August 1949, and the two additional Protocols of 8 June 1977. In addition, there are many other international treaties that govern the conduct of war or establish human rights standards.

Genocide: Usually refers to the deliberate killing of civilians with the intention of destroying an ethnic, national, religious, or other group in whole or in part.

Globalization: A term for the process, and the effects, of a sharp increase in the interactions among societies in recent decades in economic matters, population shifts, cultural interactions, information flows, and other areas. Often seen as revolutionizing international politics and the world; often criticized as grievously harmful.

Global jihad: The term for a loose network of Muslim extremist groups seeking to fight Western influence in Muslim countries and in some cases to establish a new caliphate for all Muslims.

Global North: The section of humanity that is deeply integrated into advanced capitalism, wealthy and on behalf of which the global South is contained and securitised. The global North has a major presence in Southern states via those elites that are part of the global North.

Global South: The section of humanity that consumes minimally and that is marginalized, uninsured, policed, and repressed. Northern states have substantial parts of their population that are part of the global South.

Global War on Terror: A general term used by President George W. Bush of the United States to cover the vigorous US response to the 9/11 attacks in New York and Washington.

Greenham Common: Site of a US airbase. From 1981 through until 1999 tens of thousands of women either lived at or visited the Greenham Common airbase in the UK. The women protested against the decision made by NATO to site cruise missiles at the base. It was the site of a number of high-profile protests. In December 1982, for example, 30,000 women joined hands to 'embrace the base'. In March 1991 the United States removed the cruise missiles under the terms of the 1987 INF (Intermediate Nuclear Forces) agreement.

Group of 77:   The unofficial term for the bloc of southern states attempting to negotiate trade reform in their relations with northern industrial states, especially in the 1960s and 1970s.

Guantanamo Naval Base: US naval base in Cuba that has served as a prison for suspected terrorists.

Guerrilla: Someone fighting for primarily political purposes, usually against a state, as part of a group that is not as rigidly hierarchically organized as a regular army. Literally someone fighting a small war.

Hamas: (acronym in Arabic for Islamic Resistance Movement) Islamic group in the Gaza Strip and West Bank that seeks to create an Islamic Palestinian state encompassing both the Occupied Territories and Israel and that has relied on suicide attacks.

Hegemon: A state or coalition much more powerful than any other state or likely coalition and thus able to dominate an international system.

Hegemonic stability theory: The theoretical claim that a hegemonic state may provide favourable circumstances for the emergence of an extended period of stability in an international system. This is because the hegemon is strong enough to deter any challenges by force to the status quo, to prevent disruptions to the system, and to encourage considerable management of the system. Within these conditions rivalries among other states can relax and cooperation can increase.

Historical materialism: Human history, politics and subjectivity are influnced by particular forms of the ownership and control of the production of goods and services and associated class conflict. At its most useful, HM sees the economic and the political as inseparable, does not assert that economics determines everything else, considers the possibility that human subjectivity (thoughts and feelings) play a significant role, produces historically-specific analyses rather than supposedly universal generalisations and draws on the insights of other theoretical perspectives.

HIV: The human immunodeficiency virus that causes AIDS. It is transmitted through sexual contact with an infected person, by sharing needles with someone who is infected, from mother to child during or after birth, and through transfusions with infected blood.

Home bases: Used to designate countries where organized crime groups originate, often because the rule of law is weak and law enforcement is ineffective.

Horizontal competition: Where groups must change their ways because of the overriding linguistic and cultural influences of others.

Host nations: Term used to designate countries that are the main targets of transnational crime organizations.

Human security: Emphasizes the safety and well-being of individuals, groups, and communities as opposed to prioritizing the state and its interests.

Humanitarian intervention: Article 24(1) Chapter VII of the UN Charter gives the Security Council the power to 'restore international peace and stability' if a threat, including a humanitarian disaster, is imminent and if there is consensus in the Council. The intervention in the Kosovo crisis, however, was undertaken without the Security Council's approval.

IGOs: Intergovernmental organizations; organizations with governments as the members.

Imperialism: Relations of domination and subordination across societies. In historical materialist thought, imperialism connects the global order to particular forms of state–society relations in class terms that are themselves expressions of particular modes of production.

Independent and dependent variable: Controversial terms used in the social sciences usually to describe the relationship between two entities: the dependent variable is the entity under observation or the effect, and the independent variable is the entity that affects it or the cause.

Indo-China War: Fought between the French and Viet Minh insurgents, 1946–54, ending in defeat for the French.

Insecurity dilemma: The unique situation in which a state's primary threats originate from the internal rather than external sphere, and where efforts by the ruling elite to increase regime security creates further insecurity for the regime, the state, and society.

Insecurity: The risk of something bad happening to a thing that is valued.

Insurgent: A guerrilla seeking to overthrow a state. This term has fewer connotations of legitimacy than guerrilla, and even fewer than the term 'resistance' member.

International Atomic Energy Agency (IAEA): An agency of the United Nations, the IAEA was created as part of the Eisenhower administration's 'Atoms for Peace' initiative to allow the civilian application of nuclear power to generate electricity. The IAEA is charged with monitoring the civilian application of nuclear technology to guarantee that nuclear materials and know-how are not diverted into clandestine programmes to develop nuclear weapons.

International civil society: The label for the efforts of myriads of non-governmental organizations active in international politics in pressuring and lobbying governments, in calling attention to issues, problems, and developments, and in taking direct action to deal with them. These efforts are seen by some analysts as evidence of, and a major contribution to, the development of a global community.

International Criminal Court: The first ever permanent, treaty-based, international criminal court established to promote the rule of law and to ensure that the gravest international crimes do not go unpunished. The Court is complementary to national criminal jurisdictions. The jurisdiction and functioning of the Court are governed by the provisions of the Rome Statute. The Rome Statute of the International Criminal Court was established on 17 July 1998 and entered into force on 1 July 2002.

International regimes: Clusters of norms and patterns of behaviour, sometimes codified in international agreements and managed through international organizations, that have been developed to manage the interactions among states and other entities in specific areas of activity. Examples include the regimes on the conduct and treatment of diplomatic personnel, on nuclear non-proliferation, and on proper reactions to the outbreak of highly contagious and lethal diseases.

International relations: An interdisciplinary area of study, also called international politics, which at its core examines interactions between states but with the inclusion of world politics now canvasses a broader array of interactions, issues, and actors.

Intersubjectivity: Refers to the fact that ideas and concepts are held in common by a group.

Intra-state war: The primary form of international conflict today, in which organized and sustained political violence takes place between armed groups representing the state and one or more non-state groups. It takes place primarily within the borders of a single state, but usually has significant international dimensions and a tendency to spill over into bordering states.

IRA (Irish Republican Army): Group that has used terrorism and violence in its efforts to achieve the union of Northern Ireland with the Republic of Ireland.

Irish National Liberation Army (INLA): Dissident group in Northern Ireland that has combined nationalist with a Marxist-Leninist leftist ideology to justify its attacks.

Iron Curtain: A term made famous by Winston Churchill in a speech in Fulton, Missouri, in 1946. It was used to describe the barrier to the exchange of ideas and goods created by Soviet policies of secrecy and repression.

Islamic Jihad: Small group in the Gaza Strip and West Bank that has sought to create an Islamic Palestinian state and that has relied on suicide attacks.

Italian–Turkish War: A war in 1911 and 1912 in which Italy seized some territories (the Dodecanese and Tripoli) from the Ottoman Empire.

Just War Theory: An ancient notion drawn principally from the Christian tradition but with some contribution from Islamic thought that assumes that states occasionally need to go to war with one another but that attempts to minimize war's dire consequences by spelling out both the conditions that must exist before the war is initiated (*jus ad bellum*) and what states can and cannot do during the conflict (*jus in bello*).

Korean War: One of the worst East–West confrontations of the Cold War era, the Korean War (1950–3) initially involved a North Korean invasion of South Korea

in June 1953 but was fought principally between the Chinese and a UN force headed by the United States.

Ku Klux Klan (KKK): American racist and right-wing group that first appeared after the Civil War and that was active in the 1920s, 1960s, and 1970s.

Kurds: Ethnic group in Turkey (and Iraq and Iran) that has been involved in terrorist campaigns directed towards creating an independent state.

Leaderless resistance: Term used to describe loose organizations where the leadership suggests courses of action or identifies possible targets but avoids issuing direct orders to avoid arrest or prosecution.

Liberal/liberalism: A school of thought in the study of international politics emphasizing the existence of an international society with common habits and practices that enable growing cooperation and collective management of international politics. Liberals tend to believe that world politics is basically evolving towards tolerance and peace because these cooperative developments lead to reducing conflict, insecurity, and warfare without sacrificing national sovereignty.

Macro-level economic security: Concerned with FEP powers (e.g. nation states) and their engagement in the international economic system (see 'economic security' above).

Malaria: A life-threatening parasitic disease transmitted by mosquitoes; it is characterized by fever and influenza-like symptoms, including chills, headache, and malaise.

Manhattan Project: Codename given to the British–American effort to build a fission bomb during the Second World War.

Mass atrocities: Usually used as shorthand for the widespread and systematic use of war crimes, ethnic cleansing, and crimes against humanity. Such crimes include the deliberate killing of civilians without genocidal intent and the forced displacement of populations.

Q-Fever: Fever caused by the bacterium *Coxiella burneti*. Only about half of the people infected by the bacteria show symptoms. Because the bacterium is resistant to heat and drying, it would make a suitable agent for aerosol delivery. Although it is lethal in only about 2 per cent of cases, people who suffer Q-Fever can remain sick for months and require intensive medical treatment to counteract secondary infections (pneumonia and hepatitis).

Marketed energy: Those sources bought and sold commercially, traditionally involving a producer and a consumer, linked together by some form of transmission network (e.g. pipeline). Examples include fossil fuels (oil, gas, coal), nuclear energy, and the range of renewable sources. Non-marketed energy sources include local firewood and waste products.

Marxism: An influential school of thought in international politics derived from the ideas of Karl Marx, Lenin, and others. It stresses the role of dominant classes and the dynamics of international capitalism in shaping the behaviour of governments, and of dominant states and societies in maintaining a very unequal, and exploitative, international system.

Masculinity: Those qualities that are considered appropriate to a man, usually associated with strength and bravery.

Micro-level economic security: Concerns the economic security of 'localized' agents such as individuals, households, and local communities, and is primarily concerned with safeguarding their livelihoods.

Migration: The movement of people from one place to settle in another, especially a foreign country. The host society, through a shift in the composition of the population, might be changed by the influx of those from outside.

Militarization: The process by which some aspect of social relations is integrated into the organization of physical violence and threats of violence for political purposes (cf. militarism).

Militarism: The prevalence of military sentiments among people and the idea that military efficiency or military preparedness is the highest duty of the state.

Military Malthusianism: This is a term used to describe the idea that the defence budgets of states are unable to keep up with constant real-terms increase in the cost of defence equipment, thereby creating a situation in which states are faced with purchasing fewer or lower-quality weapons.

Misogyny: A dislike, perhaps even a deep-seated dislike, for women or characteristics traditionally associated with women.

Mode of production: A way of producing, distributing, and exchanging goods and services, including the wider social relations associated with that, such as ideas about the meaning of freedom, individuality, and so on.

Money laundering: Process by which money derived from illegal activities is made to appear as if proceeding from legitimate business enterprises.

Morbidity: The number of people in a given population afflicted with a disease.

Multinational enterprise (MNE): A company that controls and operates assets over two or more countries.

Multipolar: A power distribution in an international system in which three or more major states are much more powerful than any others and roughly equivalent in power among themselves. Shifting patterns of collusion and rivalry among these states, reflecting their preoccupation with the distribution of power among them, dominate the politics of the system.

National Organization for Women (NOW): A charitable organization designed to secure equality and fair treatment for women in all aspects of American life.

Necessary but not sufficient: The best way to explain this concept is to use an analogy—sunlight is necessary for a flower to grow but it is not sufficient because the flower also requires water and probably good soil. Together, sunlight, water, and soil are the necessary and sufficient conditions for flowers to grow. In the same way, when conceptualizing security, it can be argued that the realist state-centric argument is a necessary but not sufficient argument, and likewise human security.

Neoliberal/competition political economy: Competitiveness is promoted through business deregulation and incentives, privatization, reduced state spending, manipulation of the welfare system, and multi-levelled governance.

Neorealism—Structural Realism: A variant of the realist theoretical perspective that emphasizes anarchy and the distribution of power among the major states (the system structure) as the key factors shaping the behaviour of governments, as opposed to the domestic characteristics of states—leadership, nature of political system, national culture, etc. This was the dominant approach in the field in the 1970s and 1980s.

Networks: A series of nodes that are connected.

Neutrality: The adoption by a state of a particular legal stance, recognized by the other states in the international community, that forbids it from being a member of a military alliance, or of pursuing policies that clearly identify it with such an alliance.

NGOs: Non-governmental organizations of individuals or groups, across or above national boundaries, that do not include governments.

Nodes: The elements that make up a network. These may be individuals or organizations. Law enforcement attempts to identify the nodes that are most critical to the functioning of the network and strike at these.

Non-politicized issue: An issue is said to be non-politicized when it is not a matter for state action and is not included in public debate.

Non-Proliferation Treaty: One of the key arms-control treaties of the Cold War era, the NPT was open for signature in 1968 and allows countries to develop civil nuclear power under international inspection, but not nuclear weapons. By 2006, 187 countries had signed.

Non-interference: An important principle of international society that holds that states should not interfere in the domestic affairs of other states. This principle in enshrined in Article 2(7) of the UN Charter.

Non-state actor: A term widely used to mean any actor that is not a government. Ambiguity is best avoided by referring separately to categories, transnational actors, and international organizations.

Non-traditional security: This category of security studies focuses on non-military challenges to security. It incorporates the state but also includes other referent objects.

Norms: Concern the moral and ethical dimensions of international affairs, such as rules, beliefs, and ideas.

Objective/Objectivism: The view that we can know what is real and what has been distorted by misrepresentation in ideology, propaganda, or, in its loosest sense, discourse.

Ontology: Ontology is the *study* of being. Within a theory or approach, the ontology refers to the set of assumptions about the nature of being in the world that inform that theory or approach. All forms of social investigation must make assumptions about the nature of the world they investigate (what kinds of thing populate that world, what sorts of relationship exist among those things); therefore they must have an ontology.

Open Skies Proposal: A proposal made by American President Eisenhower to Soviet First Secretary Nikita Khrushchev during their 1955 Geneva Summit. The proposal called for both nations to allow aerial surveillance of their territory in order to allow verification of the existence of weapons systems and to reduce international tensions. Khrushchev vetoed the proposal and, in response, Eisenhower initiated clandestine overflights of the Soviet Union using the then secret American spy plane, the U-2.

Organized crime: Profit-driven crime committed by any 'structured group of three or more persons existing for a period of time and acting in concert'.

Oslo Accords: Agreement in 1993 between Israel and the PLO that provided for increasing degrees of self-governance for the Palestinians in parts of the West Bank and the Gaza Strip but that collapsed in the face of attacks by extremists on both sides.

Ottawa Treaty: A convention on the prohibition of the use, stockpiling, and transfer of anti-personnel mines and their destruction that became international law on 1 March 1999.

Pandemic: The outbreak of infectious disease across a geographically extensive area; a regional or global epidemic.

Paramilitary: Someone fighting for primarily political purposes, usually on behalf of a state, as part of a group that is not as rigidly hierarchically organized as a regular army.

Paris School: Draws especially on the theories of Pierre Bourdieu and Michel Foucault to establish an approach that studies the discursive and non-discursive practices through which especially bureaucratic agencies construct insecurity and unease in their competition for tasks and control. Technologies of surveillance and control are much emphasized, especially in the study of issues such as migration and terrorism.

Patriot Act (United States): Legislation passed after 9/11 providing the government with greater surveillance opportunities and greater freedom to deal with suspected terrorists.

Peace building: Actions that support political, economic, social, and military measures and structures, aiming to strengthen and solidify political settlements in order to redress the causes of conflict.

PLO (Palestinian Liberation Organization): Umbrella liberation organization representing a variety of secular and nationalist Palestinian groups.

Pluralistic security community: A concept developed by Karl Deutsch of a group of independent and sovereign states so harmonious in their relations that they have no inclination to go to war with each other and thus do not fear each other. It was first applied to the states in the North Atlantic region associated with NATO and the West in the 1950s.

Policy community: All the actors that inform and participate in the process of formulating policy, which can include politicians, members of the judiciary, public servants, academics, members of the private sector, think tanks, civil society groups, and policy analysts.

Political (ethnic) autonomy: As with cultural nationalism, the granting of rights in relation to the means of cultural reproduction, but where this involves territorially defined self-government along a wider range of issues, such as autonomous policing and finance.

Political (ethnic) nationalism: As with cultural nationalism, a movement/project designed to generate feelings of self-identification, but where this carries with it an explicit territorial element.

Politicized issue: An issue becomes politicized when it is part of public policy and managed within the standard political system.

Popular Front for the Liberation of Palestine (PFLP): Palestinian group that combined nationalism with Marxist-Leninist views and that was frequently at odds with the PLO leadership.

Post-Marxism: Claims to draw on but also to have transcended Marxism, mainly by having Marxist ideas playing a secondary and adapted role within an approach mainly drawing on other theorizing.

Post-Marxism can be so 'post' that it is for all practical purposes non-Marxist.

Post-positivism: Post-positivism is a generic term to refer to those theories and approaches that reject positivism as an adequate epistemology for the investigation of social life. Most forms of critical social theory are post-positivist in their epistemologies.

Poststructuralist/structuralism: This is the most thoroughgoing version of constructivism and places even more emphasis on the analysis of discourse.

Power: The resources available to a state for building military forces. Key elements of power include a state's wealth, population, and technological sophistication. In this context, power does not refer to the ability to influence other states; instead, it refers narrowly to a state's potential to build military forces and the assets required effectively to command them.

Prevalence rate: An epidemiological term referring to the proportion of those suffering from a disease in a particular population; it is usually cited in percentages.

Prevention of Terrorism Acts (United Kingdom): Series of acts giving the British government increased powers and discretion to deal first with suspected IRA terrorists and then with terrorists in general.

Primary arms dynamic: Refers to the set of pressures to acquire armed forces experienced by those states that possess the capacity independently to produce all or most of their defence equipment.

Prisoners of War (POW): Prisoners of War are combatants captured by the opposing side in war. They are imprisoned, usually until the end of conflict, but may be traded. Historically, few rules have governed the treatment of POWs until the Geneva and Hague Conference and the conventions of 1864, 1899, and 1907, which declared that POWs should be treated humanely.

Private military companies (PMCs): Corporate bodies that specialize in the provision of services associated with security and the use of force. There exist a huge number of such companies, providing a wide range of services, from static security of infrastructure to logistical support for state militaries, and from bodyguards to high-end military training and operations.

States such as the USA have become increasingly reliant on these firms, which make up a rising proportion of personnel in any military campaign.

Pugwash: The Pugwash Conferences on Science and World Affairs is an international organization facilitating international dialogue among scholars and political practitioners to handle global security threats. A manifesto by Bertrand Russell and Albert Einstein in 1955 called for scientists to face the dangers of nuclear weapons, and a conference was held in Pugwash, Nova Scotia, in 1957. During the Cold War, the organization was often an important back channel between US and Soviet experts and intellectuals. Pugwash and its co-founder, Joseph Rotblat, received the Nobel Peace Prize in 1995 for their work for nuclear disarmament.

Punjab: Indian province where Sikh dissidents used guerrilla warfare and terrorism in an effort to gain autonomy or independence for their religious group.

RAND: RAND Corporation was set up in 1946 by the US Air Force under contract to the Douglas Aircraft Company. In 1948 it became an independent non-profit organization and during the 1950s it formed the model for the modern think tank, famous enough for it to feature in the film *Dr Strangelove* as 'the BLAND Corporation'. In addition to research in engineering, health policy, and many other fields, inter-disciplinary work between especially mathematics, economics, and political science pioneered game theory and deterrence theory.

Rape/genocidal rape: The forcing of women to have sex without their consent. Genocidal rape refers to the use of sex as an instrument of war used deliberately to humiliate women of a certain ethnicity or identity.

Rational choice: Theories that focus on strategic, instrumental calculation and draw on economics in establishing models, where actors and their incentives are given, while often sophisticated calculations drawn from game theory explain behaviour, outcomes, and the effects of institutions and other conditions.

Rationalism: One side of the main theoretical debate in IR theory during the 1980s and 1990s—the position, which adopts from rational-choice theory the general premise that theory should start from actors with given identities and interests, is that a specified rationality assumption explains behaviour (without necessarily including the more technical instruments of rational-choice theory). Neorealism and neoliberal institutionalism have been the main representatives of rationalist IR theory. (The terminology of rationalism versus reflectionism was introduced by Robert Keohane in 1988.)

Realist/realism: The view that world politics is anarchic (in the sense of there being no overall authority, not chaos), the key actors are states, the key element of power is military power, and the moral duty of the decision-maker is to serve the national interest. Realists assert that they see world politics as it really is, that world politics changes but does not progress, and it is the inherent sense of state insecurity that is critical in understanding the dynamics of international politics.

Realpolitik: Politics based on practical rather than moral or ideological considerations.

Red Army Faction (also often referred to as the Baader-Meinhof Gang): Small group of West German terrorists that mounted attacks against the state, and capitalism in general, in the 1970s and 1980s.

Red Brigades: Large Italian leftist group that launched a major terrorist campaign that at times disrupted the Italian state and that took years for the state to defeat.

Referent object (of security): Common to most notions of security is the *protection* of some thing from a threat of some kind. The thing to be protected is the referent object. In conventional security studies, the referent object is generally considered to be the state. Other approaches to security consider other referent objects: for example, individuals, societies, economies, or the environment.

Reflectivism: The counter-position to rationalism, where constructivists, feminists, poststructuralists, critical theorists, and moral theorists, among others, argue that state identities and interests are not given or stable but produced and reproduced continuously. Norms and identity shape policy as much as material interests. Often reflectivist theories will posit understanding rather than science-like explanation as the aim of research. (The terminology of rationalism versus reflectionism was introduced by Robert Keohane in 1988.)

Regimes: The most widely used definition is formal or informal institutional arrangements consisting of 'sets of implicit or explicit principles, norms, rules, and decision-making procedures around which actors' expectations converge in a given area of international relations' (Krasner 1983: 2) The idea is that the participants in a regime understand and accept the proper ways of behaving on the matters to which a regime pertains, much like a code of etiquette in a culture works.

Regime security: A condition where the governing elite is secure from the threat of forced removal from office and can generally rule without major challenges to its authority.

Responsibility to Protect (R2P): A commitment made by all UN Member States in 2005 that they have a responsibility to protect their populations from genocide, war crimes, ethnic cleansing, and crimes against humanity and that the international community has a duty to take timely and decisive action in situations where the state manifestly fails in its responsibility.

Revolutionary Armed Forces of Colombia (FARC): Leftist group that has joined with Colombian drug cartels to prevent government control of significant areas of the country and has threatened the stability of the government.

Rule: Effective control over a specified territory and the people who reside there by exercising the powers of a government.

Safety: One of the main components of security for states and their societies. Most emphasis is normally placed on being safe from deliberate efforts by outsiders, or disaffected insiders, to inflict harm. But under various circumstances this can extend to seeking to ensure safety from a number of other kinds of harm as well.

Sarin: A chemical weapon, originally developed in Germany as a pesticide in the 1930s, Sarin is a colourless, odourless, and tasteless liquid at room temperature. It interferes with the nervous system by impeding the proper function of the neurotransmitter acetylcholine. Exposure to Sarin causes neurons to be continuously stimulated by acetylcholine, leading to convulsions, coma, and suffocation.

Satellite: For intelligence-gathering purposes, a satellite is a man-made object that either orbits the earth or remains geo-synchronous above a specific spot on the earth while it collects all kinds of electronic transmissions or even takes digital photographs of designated places on the earth. All the collection information is used for intelligence purposes.

Secondary arms dynamic: Refers to the set of pressures to acquire armed forces experienced by those states that have limited or no capacity for independent production of defence equipment and that are therefore reliant on the import of defence technology.

Securitize: A so-called speech act that elevates an issue with the objective of making it critically important.

Securitization: Refers to the accepted classification of certain and not other phenomena, persons, or entities as existential threats requiring emergency measures. Through an act of securitization, a concern is framed as a security issue and moved from the politicized to the securitized.

Securitized issue: An issue is securitized when it requires emergency actions beyond the state's standard political procedures.

Securitizing actor: Refers to an actor who initiates a move of securitization through a speech act. Securitizing actors can be policy-makers or bureaucracies but also transnational actors and individuals.

Security dilemma: The situation that arises when one state, in seeking to be more secure, expands its military capabilities but, in doing so, increases fears in other states about their security so that they also build up their military capabilities. The dilemma is that states end up no more secure, perhaps even less, in spite of and because of their individual efforts to make themselves safe.

Security: The assurance people have that they will continue to enjoy those things that are most important to their survival and well-being.

Service states: Used to designate countries where transnational criminal organizations can easily access services designed to provide cover for their activities, such as false identities, or launder the proceeds of their activities.

Shadow of the future: When the expectation of future benefits from cooperation makes it easier in the present to get that cooperation. Cooperation is easier when it, and the benefits it can provide, are not a one-shot deal.

Sikhs: Religious group in India that includes extremists who attempt to achieve autonomy or independence to maintain the group vis-à-vis the majority Hindu population.

Social science: This approach assumes that fact and value can be separated sufficiently to generate theoretically grounded hypotheses that can be tested against evidence. In other words, description (what is), explanation (why it is), and prescription (what should be) are treated as separable.

Societal identity: The self-identification by members of the community as constituting 'us'; that is to say, a shared sense of belonging to the same collectivity, most often ethno-national and religious groups.

Societal security dilemma: Where the actions of one society, in trying to increase its security (strengthen its identity), causes a reaction in a second, which, in the end, causes a decrease in its own security (weakens its identity).

Soft security: Emphasizes mechanisms other than military ones that enhance the safety and well being of states or other actors.

Southern African Development Community (SADC): An international organization promoting regional cooperation in economic development in southern Africa.

Sovereignty: The legal status of having effective control over a specified territory and the people who reside there, and recognized by other sovereign states as having such control and being entitled to be regarded as sovereign. Being sovereign entitles a state, and its government, to be free, under most circumstances, of responsibility to any higher authority and of interference from outside in its internal affairs.

Speech act: Consists of a discursive representation of a certain issue as an existential threat to security.

Speech-act theory: Speech is commonly considered to refer to objects and actions outside itself; speech-act theory examines those instances in which actions are performed *by virtue* of their being spoken. Naming, marrying, and promising are notable examples of speech acts. Securitization treats security as a speech act.

Stand-off missiles: These are missiles capable of being launched outside a theatre of operation and then guided to a distant target.

State collapse: A condition where the main state institutions and governing processes completely fail and cease to function in any meaningful sense, through either internal processes of mismanagement or overwhelming challenges to state authority. The most visible signal of state collapse is the total breakdown of law and order. State collapse creates a power vacuum that is then filled by alternative forms of power and governance.

State security: A condition where the institutions, processes, and structures of the state are able to continue functioning without the threat of collapse or significant opposition, despite threats to the current regime or changes to the make-up of the ruling elite.

State-centric: A term that is used loosely, often to describe the realist paradigm that is said to give priority to protection of the state above all else. See Chapter 2.

Strategic culture: Those 'beliefs and assumptions that frame … choices about international military behaviour, particularly those concerning decisions to go to war, preferences for offensive, expansionist or defensive modes of warfare, and levels of wartime casualties that would be acceptable' (Rosen 1995: 12).

Strongmen: A term used to describe individuals or groups who possess a degree of coercive power in their own right and who pose a challenge to weak state rulers. Typically, they include local politicians or tribal leaders with private armies, warlords and criminal gangs, well-armed and organized ethnic or religious groups, and various private militia.

Structural violence: Deaths and suffering caused by the way society is organized so that huge numbers of people lack the means necessary to avoid starvation, preventable illness and so on.

Taliban: Extreme Islamic government formerly in power in Afghanistan that provided support to Osama bin Laden and al-Qaeda until overthrown by domestic groups and foreign troops after 9/11.

Tamil Tigers (Liberation Front of Tamil Eelam): Group in Sri Lanka that has used guerrilla warfare and terrorist attacks (including many suicide attacks) in an effort to achieve an independent Tamil state on the island.

Technological imperative explanations of the arms dynamic: The constant modernization of defence equipment as a function of an imperative to update equipment that is created as a consequence either of the institutionalization of military R&D or as a by-product of a process of permanent technological change in the civil sector.

Terrorism: The use of force or the threat of force by organized groups too weak to use other methods in an effort to achieve political goals with attacks directed towards a target audience that involves non-governmental actors.

Think tank: A research institute or other organization providing advice and ideas for policy-makers or business leaders. Around 1960 the term came to be used primarily to describe RAND and other institutions assisting the armed forces and defence planners. The number and partisan affiliation of think tanks in the USA accelerated during the 1980s and 1990s, leading to a decline in their status as independent advisers and an increase in their role as producers of ideological munition. Foreign-policy institutes and to some extent peace research institutes have fulfilled parallel functions in Europe and elsewhere, where, however, American-style think tanks have begun to expand as well.

Traditional security: Security is defined in geopolitical terms, encompassing aspects such as deterrence, power balancing, and military strategy. The state, and especially its defence from external military attacks, is the exclusive focus of study.

Transaction costs: The concept that putting together a serious, complicated agreement, particularly between governments, is not free. Time, effort, compromises, political capital concessions, and so on are all costly, so if there is a way significantly to ease these costs, cooperation becomes much easier to undertake.

Transnational crime: Criminal activity that is conducted in more than one state, planned in one state but perpetrated in another, or committed in one state where there are spillover effects into neighbouring jurisdictions. The phrase is often used more specifically to refer to transnational *organized* crime—crimes that cross national borders, are profit driven, and are committed by a group organized for that purpose.

Tuberculosis: A bacterial disease that usually attacks the lungs, but can also affect the kidney, spine, or brain. Like the common cold, it is contagious and spreads through the air from person to person. If left untreated, tuberculosis is fatal. More recently, some strains of tuberculosis resistant to all medicines have also emerged.

Tularemia: Disease caused by bacterium *Francisella tularensis* often found in animals (e.g. rodents). The vector (means of transmission) to humans in naturally occurring disease is the flea. As a weapon, the bacterium is highly infectious and would probably be distributed as an aerosol that would produce a severe respiratory illness.

UAV: A remote-controlled unmanned aerial vehicle used for both intelligence collection (imagery) and, more recently, for the delivery of missiles.

UN Conference on the Human Environment (UNCHE): Also known as the Stockholm Environment Conference, this was held in May 1972 and was the first major international meeting on global environmental issues.

UN Conference on Trade and Development (UNCTAD): A UN agency set up specifically to improve the trading position of third world states. It met for the first time in Geneva in 1964.

Unipolar: The term for the structure of an international system that has a hegemon—the one dominant state provides a single pole of concentrated power, and this structure dominates the politics of the system.

United Nations Charter: The Charter is the legal regime that created the United Nations as the world's only 'supranational' organization. It is the key legal document limiting the use of force to instances of self-defence and collective peace enforcement endorsed by the United Nations Security Council.

Universal Declaration of Human Rights: Established on 10 December 1948 by the General Assembly of the United Nations. It recognizes the inherent dignity and equal and inalienable rights of all members of the human family as the foundation of freedom, justice, and peace in the world.

Uranium-235: A key ingredient of a nuclear weapon. It is called a 'fissile' material because an atom of uranium-235 can be split into roughly two equal-mass pieces when struck by a neutron. If a large enough mass of uranium-235 is brought together, a self-sustaining chain reaction results after the first fission occurs. If large amounts of U-235 are brought together quickly, a supercritical reaction occurs, which is the basis of both fission and fusion nuclear weapons.

Venezuelan equine encephalitis: A mosquito-borne viral illness that causes flu-like symptoms, which can progress to encephalitis in a relatively small number of cases. Because it is a virus, observers fear that it could be subject to genetic manipulation to infect and incapacitate thousands of people quickly.

VENONA: A code word used to characterize the intelligence gathered by the USA and the UK (code-named BRIDE in the UK) from intercepted Soviet classified communications during the last two years of the Second World War. Though the enciphered texts were not decoded until late 1948, the intelligence derived from them revealed massive Soviet penetration into the highest decision bodies in the USA, the UK, and other countries.

Vertical competition: Where groups are pushed towards either narrower or wider societal identities because of integration or disintegration.

Veteran: A term used to describe people who have served in national armed forces. This term is usually associated with those who have served in the US military.

Vietnam War: Fought between the Viet Cong guerrillas and the North Vietnamese Army, on the one hand, and the South Vietnam Army and the United States, on the other. US involvement was principally between 1965 and its final withdrawal in 1973. North and South Vietnam were ultimately unified under the control of the North.

Warlord: A military leader who exercises civil power in a region, such as collecting taxes, providing a semblance of law and order and engaging in commerce, either in alliance with or in defiance of the central state. The warlord commands the personal loyalty of a private army and rules by virtue of his war-making ability.

Weak states: States possessing one or more of the following characteristics: infrastructural incapacity, evidenced by weak institutions and the inability to penetrate and control society effectively or enforce state policies; lack of coercive power and a failure to achieve or maintain a monopoly on the instruments of violence; and the lack of national identity and social and political consensus on the idea of the state.

Weathermen: Radical leftist group in the United States that used terrorist tactics in their opposition to the government and the war in Vietnam but never achieved the notoriety or gained the support that some West European leftist groups did.

Westphalia: A general settlement in 1648 ended the Thirty Years War and in doing so laid the basis for the European state system, particularly with respect to the sovereignty and autonomy of the states. Hence the international system, with sovereign states as the members, is still referred to as the Westphalian system.

Wilsonian internationalism: A powerful component of American thinking and preferences in foreign policy since early in the twentieth century, which received its initial elaboration in President Woodrow Wilson's efforts after the First World War to use American leadership to reorder the international system along liberalist lines so as to eliminate major wars.

Xenophobic: Term used to describe those who are violently opposed to foreigners or foreign ideas and cultures.

Zimmerman Telegraph: A diplomatic message of 16 January 1917 from the German Foreign Minister (Arthur Zimmerman) to the German ambassador in Mexico offering Mexico support in reclaiming 'lost' territory in Texas, New Mexico, and Arizona in return for Mexican support if the United States should enter the war against Germany. British naval intelligence intercepted and decoded the note and provided it to US President Woodrow Wilson to help bring America into the war on the British side. It worked, as it was actually more important than the sinking of the Lusitania or unrestricted U-boat warfare in getting America into the war.

References

Abelson, Donald E. (2002), *Do Think Tanks Matter? Assessing the Impact of Public Policy Institutes*, Kingston, Ontario: McGill-Queen's University Press.

Adams, G. (1982), *The Politics of Defence Contracting: The Iron Triangle*, New Brunswick, NJ: Transaction Books.

Adler, E. (1992), 'The Emergence of Cooperation: National Epistemic Communities and the International Evolution of the Idea of Nuclear Arms Control', *International Organization*, 46/1: 101–45.

Adler, E. (1997), 'Seizing the Middle Ground: Constructivism in World Politics', *European Journal of International Relations*, 3/3: 319–59.

Adler, E. (2008), 'The Spread of Security Communities: Communities of Practice, Self-Restraint, and NATO's Post–Cold War Transformation', *European Journal of International Relations*, 14/2: 195–230.

Adler, E., and Barnett, M. (1998), 'Security Communities in Theoretical Perspective', in E. Adler and M. Barnett (eds.), *Security Communities*, Cambridge: Cambridge University Press, 3–28.

Agence France Presse (2003), 'Thailand Set to Declare Victory in Drugs War', 2 Dec.

Aggestan, L., and Hyde-Price, A. (2000) (eds.), *Security and Identity in Europe*, London: Macmillan.

Agius, C. (2006), *The Social Construction of Swedish Neutrality: Challenges to Swedish Identity and Sovereignty*, Manchester: Manchester University Press.

Air Force Technology (2006), 'Gripen Multirole Fighter Aircraft, Sweden', airforce-technology.com, www.airforce-technology.com/projects/gripen

Albert, M. (1993), *Capitalism against Capitalism*, London: Wiley Blackwell.

Albright, D., and Hinderstein, C. (2005), 'Unraveling the A. Q. Khan and Future Proliferation Networks', *Washington Quarterly*, 28/2: 111–28.

Aldrich R. J. (2002), 'America Used Islamists to Arm the Bosnian Muslims', *Guardian*, 22 Apr., www.guardian.co.uk/print/0,3858,4398721-103677,00.html

Alibek, K. (2000), *Biohazard*, New York: Random House.

Alkiri, S. (2004), 'A Vital Core that must be Treated with the Same Gravitas as Traditional Security Threats', *Security Dialogue*, 35/3: 359–60.

Allan, J. (2002), *The Middle East Water Question: Hydropolitics and the Global Economy*, London: I. B. Taurus Publishers.

Allison, G. (1971), *Essence of Decision: Explaining the Cuban Missile Crisis*, Boston: Little, Brown and Co.

Alonso, Harriet Hyman (1993), *Peace as a Woman's Issue: History of the US Movement for World Peace and Women's Rights*, New York: Syracuse University Press.

Amsden, A., and Hikino, T. (2000), 'The Bark is Worse than the Bite: New WTO Law and Late Industrialization', *Annals of American Political and Social Science*, 570 (July), 104–14.

Anderson, Guy (2005), 'US Defense Budget Will Equal ROW Combined within 12 Months', *Jane's Defence Industry*, 4 May, www.janes.com/defence/news/jdi/jdi050504_1_n.shtml

Andreas, P. and Biersteker, T. J. (2003), *The Rebordering of North America; Integration and Exclusion in a New Security Context*, London: Routledge.

Andreas, P., and Nadelmann, E. (2006), *Policing the Globe: Criminalization and Crime Control in International Relations*, New York: Oxford University Press.

Andrew, C. (1987), *Her Majesty's Secret Service: The Making of the British Intelligence Community*, London: Penguin Books.

Andrew, C., and Gordievsky, O. (1991), *KGB: The Inside Story*, New York: HarperCollins Publishers.

Annan, K. (1999), 'Annual Report of the Secretary-General to the United Nations General Assembly', 20 Sept., www.un.org/News/ossg/sg/stories/statments_search_full.asp?statID=28

Anthony, M., Emmers, R., and Acharya, A. (2006) (eds.), *Non-Traditional Security in Asia: Dilemmas in Securitization*, London: Ashgate Publishing.

Arend, A. C., and Beck, R. J. (1993), *International Law and the Use of Force: Beyond the UN Charter Paradigm*, London: Routledge.

Aron, R. (1957), 'Conflict and War from the Viewpoint of Historical Sociology', in *The Nature of Conflict*, Paris: UNESCO, 177–203.

Art, R. J. (1980), 'To What Ends Military Power?', *International Security* (Spring), 3–35.

Art, R. J. (2003), 'Introduction', in R. J. Art and P. M. Cronin (eds.), *The United States and Coercive Diplomacy*, Washington: United States Institute of Peace, 3–20.

Ash, T. G. (2003), 'Is There a Good Terrorist?', in Charles W. Kegley, Jr. (ed.), *The New Global Terrorism: Characteristics, Causes, Controls*, Upper Saddle River, NJ: Prentice Hall, 60–70.

Asia Foundation (2007), 'Afghanistan in 2007: A Survey of the Afghan People', Kabul Office, http://asiafoundation.org/pdf/AG-survey07.pdf

Asia Foundation (2008), *'Afghanistan in 2008: A Survey of the Afghan People'*, Kabul Office, http://asiafoundation.org/country/afghanistan/2008-poll.php

Asia-Pacific Centre for the Responsibility to Protect (2008), 'Cyclone Nargis and the Responsibility to Protect', 16 May, at www.r2pasiapacific.org/images/stories/food/cyclone%20nargis%20and%20the%20responsibility%20to%20protect.pdf (accessed 26 Nov. 2008).

Aydelott, D. (1993), 'Mass Rape during War: Prosecuting Bosnian Rapists under International Law', *Emory Law Review*, 7/2 (Fall), 585–631.

Ayoob, M. (1995), *The Third World Security Predicament: State Making, Regional Conflict, and the International System*, Boulder, CO: Lynne Rienner.

Ayoob, M. (1997), 'Defining Security: A Subaltern Realist Perspective', in K. Krause and M. C. Williams (eds.), *Critical Security Studies: Concepts and Cases*, Minneapolis: University of Minnesota Press, 121–46.

Bacevich, A. J. (2006), *The New American Militarism: How Americans Are Seduced by War*, Oxford: Oxford University Press.

Baechler, G. (1999), *Violence through Environmental Discrimination: Causes, Rwanda Arena, and Conflict Model*, Dordrecht: Kluwer.

Bailyn, B. (1992), *The Ideological Origins of the American Revolution*, Cambridge, MA, and London: Belknap Press and Harvard University Press.

Bal, I., and Laciner, S. (2001), 'The Challenge of Revolutionary Terrorism to Turkish Democracy, 1960–1980,' *Terrorism and Political Violence*, 14/4: 90–115.

Baldwin, D. (1995), 'Security Studies and the End of the Cold War', *World Politics*, 48/1: 117–41.

Baldwin, D. A. (1997), 'The Concept of Security', *Review of International Studies*, 23: 5–26.

Balzacq, T. (2005), 'The Three Faces of Securitization: Political Agency, Audience and Context', *European Journal of International Relations*, 11/2: 171–201.

Ban Ki-moon (2008), 'Responsible Sovereigns', address of the UN Secretary-General, SG/SM/11701, 15 July.

Baran, P. A., and Sweezy, P. M. (1966), *Monopoly Capital*, New York: Monthly Review Press.

Barcelona Report (2004), *A Human Security Doctrine for Europe: The Barcelona Report of the Study Group on Europe's Security Capabilities*, Barcelona: EU.

Barkawi, T. (2005), *Globalization and War*, London: Rowman & Littlefield.

Barkawi, T., and Laffey, M. (2006), 'The Postcolonial Moment in Security Studies', *Review of International Studies*, 32/4: 329–52.

Barnett, J. (2001), *The Meaning of Environmental Security: Ecological Politics and Policy in the New Security Era*, London: Zed Books.

Barnett, J., and Adger, N. (2003), 'Climate Dangers and Atoll Countries', *Climatic Change*, 61/3: 321–37.

Barnett, M. (2002), *Eyewitness to a Genocide: The United Nations and Rwanda*, Ithaca, NY: Cornell University Press.

Barnett, T., and Whiteside, A. (2006), *AIDS in the Twenty-First Century: Disease and Globalization*, 2nd edn., Basingstoke: Palgrave.

Bazergan, R. (2002), *HIV/AIDS & Peacekeeping: A Field Study of the Policies of the United Nations Mission in Sierra Leone*, London: International Policy Institute.

BBC News (2003), 'Thais Swear to Stay Drug-Free', 1 Apr., http://news.bbc.co.uk/1/hi/world/asia-pacific/2895383.stm

BBC News (2004). Michael Howard's speech on immigration and asylum, http://news.bbc.co.uk/1/hi/uk_politics/3679618 (accessed July 2009).

BBC News (2006a), 'Saudis "Foil Oil Facility Attack"', 24 Feb., http://news.bbc.co.uk/1/hi/world/middle_east/4747488.stm

BBC News (2006b), 'Shell Evacuates Nigeria Workers', 16 Jan., http://news.bbc.co.uk/1/hi/world/africa/4615890.stm (accessed July 2009).

Beare, M. E. (2003) (ed.), *Critical Reflections on Transnational Organized Crime, Money Laundering, and Corruption*, Toronto: University of Toronto Press.

Beevor, A. (2002), *Berlin: The Downfall 1945*, London: Penguin.

Behnke, A. (2007), 'Presence and Creation: A Few (Meta-) Critical Comments on the C.A.S.E. Manifesto', *Security Dialogue*, 38/1: 105–11.

Beier, M. (2001), 'Postcards from the Outskirts of Security: Defence Professionals, Semiotics, and the NMD Initiative', *Canadian Foreign Policy*, 8/2: 39–49.

Bellamy, A. J. (2004), 'Ethics and Intervention: The "Humanitarian Exception" and the Problem of Abuse in the Case of Iraq', *Journal of Peace Research*, 41/2: 131–47.

Bellamy, A. J. (2006), 'Whither the Responsibility to Protect? Humanitarian Intervention and the 2005 World Summit', *Ethics and International Affairs*, 20/2: 143–69.

Bellamy, Ian (1981), 'Towards a Theory of International Security', *Political Studies*, 29/1 (1981), 100–5.

Berger, P., and Luckmann, T. (1991), *The Social Construction of Reality: A Treatise in the Sociology of Knowledge*, London: Penguin.

Berger, T. U. (1996), 'Norms, Identity, and National Security in Germany and Japan', in P. J. Katzenstein (ed.), *The Culture of National Security. Norms and Identity in World Politics*, New York: Columbia University Press, 317–56.

Betts, R. (1997), 'Should Strategic Studies Survive', *World Politics*,. 50/1 (Oct.), 7–33.

Bigo, D. (1996), *Polices en réseaux, l'expérience européenne*, Paris: Presses de Sciences Po.

Bigo, D. (2002a), 'To Reassure and Protect, after September 11', in Social Science Research Council, 'After September 11', www.ssrc.org/sept11/essays/bigo.htm

Bigo, D. (2002b), 'Security and Immigration: Toward a Critique of the Governmentality of Unease', *Alternatives*, 27 (Feb., suppl.), 63–92.

Bilgin, P., and Morton, A. D. (2002), 'Historicizing Representations of "Failed States": Beyond the Cold War Annexation of the Social Sciences?', *Third World Quarterly*, 23/1: 55–80.

Bill, J. (1988), *The Eagle and the Lion: The Tragedy of American–Iranian Relations*, London: Yale University Press.

Bitzinger, R. A. (2003), *Towards a Brave New Arms Industry?* Adelphi Paper 356, London: International Institute for Strategic Studies.

Blair, T. (1999), 'Doctrine of the International Community', speech to the Economic Club of Chicago, Hilton Hotel, Chicago, 22 Apr.

Blair, T. (2000), 'Speech by the Prime Minister at Warwick University', 14 Dec., www2.warwick.ac.uk/services/communications/archive/clinton/blairsspeech (accessed 10 Nov. 2008).

Blakeley, R. (2009), *State Terrorism and Neoliberalism: The North in the South*, London: Routledge.

Blattman, C. (2008), 'From Violence to Voting: War and Political Participation in Uganda', *American Political Science Review*, Working Paper Number 138, Jan.

Boeles, Jan (1990), 'EU Monitor Mission to the Former Yugoslavia', quoted in Robert Fisk, 'Waging War on History', *Independent*, 20 June 1994.

Böge, V. (1999), 'Mining, Environmental Degradation and War: The Bougainville Case', in M. Suliman (ed.), *Ecology, Politics and Violent Conflict*, London: Zed Books, 211–27.

Bolton, J. (2007), *Surrender is Not an Option: Defending America at the United Nations and Abroad*, New York: Threshold Editions.

Booth, K. (1975), 'Disarmament and Arms Control', in John Baylis, Ken Booth, John Garnett, and Phil Williams, *Contemporary Strategy: Theories and Policies*, London: Croom Helm.

Booth, K. (1991), 'Security and Emancipation', *Review of International Studies*, 17/4: 313–26.

Booth, K. (1997), 'Security and Self: Reflections of a Fallen Realist', in Keith Krause and Michael C. Williams (eds.), *Critical Security Studies: Concepts and Cases*, Minneapolis: University of Minnesota Press, 83–119.

Booth, K. (2005a), 'Beyond Critical Security Studies', in Booth (ed.), *Critical Security Studies and World Politics*, Boulder, CO: Lynne Rienner, 259–78.

Booth, K. (2005b) (ed.), *Critical Security Studies and World Politics*, Boulder, CO: Lynne Rienner.

Booth, K. (2007), *Theory of World Security*, Cambridge: Cambridge University Press.

Boothby, N., Strang, Alison, and Wessells, Michael (2006) (eds.), *A World Turned Upside Down: Social Ecological Approaches to Children in War Zones*, Bloomfield, CT: Kumarian Press.

Booysen, F., and Bachmann, M. (2002), 'HIV/AIDS, Poverty and Growth: Evidence from a Household Impact Study Conducted in the Free State Province, South Africa', paper presented at the Annual Conference of the Centre for the Study of African Economies, Oxford, Mar.

Born, H., Johnson, L., and Leigh, I. (2005) (eds.), *Who's Watching the Spies: Establishing Intelligence Service Accountability*, Dulles, VA: Potomac Books.

Boureston, J. (2002), 'Assessing Al Qaeda's WMD Capabilities', 2 Sept., www.ccc.nps.navy.mil/rsepResources/si/sept02/wmd.asp

Boyden J. (2006), 'Children, War and World Disorder in the 21st Century: A Review of the Theories and the Literature on Children's Contributions to Armed Violence', Working Paper 138, Queen Elizabeth House Working Paper Series, Oxford University.

Boyden, J., and de Berry, J. (2004) (eds.), *Children and Youth on the Front Line: Ethnography, Armed Conflict and Displacement*, New York: Berghan Books.

Boyden, J., and Levison, D. (2000), 'Children as Economic and Social Actors in the Development Process', Working Paper 1, Expert Group on Development Issues, Ministry for Foreign Affairs.

Boyden, S., Dovers, S., and Shirlow, M. (1990), *Our Biosphere under Threat: Ecological Realities and Australia's Opportunities*, Melbourne: Oxford University Press.

Brandt, W., et al. (1980), *North–South: A Programme for Survival: Report of the Independent Commission on International Development Issues* ('Brandt Report'), Cambridge, MA: MIT Press.

Braun C., and Chyba, C. F. (2004), 'Proliferation Rings: New Challenges to the Nuclear Nonproliferation Regime', *International Security*, 29/2: 5–49.

Breen, C. (2007), 'When Is a Child not a Child? Child Soldiers in International Law', *Human Rights Review*, 8/2: 71–103

Brett, R., and Specht, I. (2004), *Young Soldiers: Why they Choose to Fight*, Boulder, CO: Lynne Rienner.

British Offset, 'Opportunities through Economic Cooperation in Saudi Arabia', www.britishoffset.com/pages/content/index.asp?PageID=10 (accessed 14 Jan. 2006).

Broad, R., and Cavanagh, J. (2009), *Development Redefined: How the Market Met its Match*, Boulder, CO: Paradigm.

Brocklehurst, H. (2006), *Who's Afraid of Children? Children, Conflict and International Relations*, Aldershot: Ashgate.

Brocklehurst, H. (2009), 'Will the Real Child Soldier Please Stand up?' in Jennifer Gunning and Søren Holm (eds.), *Ethics and Law Review*, Aldershot: Ashgate.

Brodie, B. (1946) (ed.), *The Absolute Weapon: Atomic Power and World Order*, New York: Harcourt, Brace & Co.

Brodie, B. (1949), 'Strategy as a Science', *World Politics*, 1/4: 467–88.

Brodie, B. (1959), *Strategy in the Missile Age*, Princeton: Princeton University Press.

Brodie, B. (1965), 'The McNamara Phenomenon', *World Politics*, 17/4: 672–86.

Brooks, E. (1974), 'The Implications of Ecological Limits to Development in Terms of Expectations and Aspirations in Developed and Less Developed Countries', in Anthony Vann and Paul Rogers (eds.), *Human Ecology and World Development*, London and New York: Plenum Press.

Brooks, S. G., and Wohlforth, W. C. (2005), 'Hard Times for Soft Balancing', *International Security*, 30/1: 72–108.

Brooten, L. (2008), 'The "Pint-Sized Terrorists" of God's Army', *Journal of Children and Media*, 2/3: 219–34

Brown, L. (1977), 'Redefining National Security', Worldwatch Paper No. 14, Washington: Worldwatch Institute.

Brown, M. E. (2000) (ed.), *Rational Choice and Security Studies: Stephen Walt and his Critics*, Cambridge, MA: MIT Press.

Brown, M., Lynn-Jones, S., and Miller, S. (1996) (eds.), *Debating the Democratic Peace*, Cambridge, MA: MIT Press, 301–34.

Brownlie, I. (1974), 'Humanitarian Intervention', in John N. Moore (ed.), *Law and Civil War in the Modern World*, Baltimore: Johns Hopkins University Press, 217–21.

Brownmiller, S. (1975), *Against our Will: Men, Women and Rape*, New York: Simon and Schuster.

Brzezinski, Z. (2003–4). 'Hegemonic Quicksand', *National Interest*, 74:. 5–16.

Buckley, Mary (1989), *Women and Ideology in the Soviet Union*, London: Harvester Wheatsheaf.

Büger, C., and Stritzel, H. (2005), 'New European Security Theory: Zur Emergenz eines neuen europäischen Forschungsprogramms—Tagungsbericht: Critical Approaches to Security in Europe, Rencontres doctorales Européennes sur le thème de la Sécurité, Paris 2004', in *Zeitschrift für Internationale Beziehungen*, 12/2: 437–46.

Bukovansky, M. (1997), 'American Identity and Neutral Rights from Independence to the War of 1812', *International Organization*, 51/2: 209–43.

Bull, H. (1961), *The Control of the Arms Race*, London: Weidenfeld and Nicolson.

Bull, H. (1968), 'Strategic Studies and its Critics', *World Politics*, 20/4: 599–600.

Burr, W. (2008), 'Prevent the Re-emergence of a New Rival', The Making of the Cheney Regional Defense Strategy, 1991–1992, National Security Archive, Electronic Briefing Book 255, 26 Feb.

Bush, G. W. (2001), 'Address to a Joint Session of Congress and the American People', 20 Sept., www.whitehouse.gov/news/releases/2001/09/20010920-8.html (accessed 23 Nov. 2008).

Bush, G. W. (2007). *State of the Union Address 2007*, 23 Jan.

Buzan, B. (1981), 'Change and Insecurity: A Critique of Security Studies', in Barry Buzan and R. J. Barry Jones (eds.), *Change and the Study of International Relations: The Evaded Dimension*, London: Pinter, 155–72.

Buzan, B. (1983), *People, States and Fear: The National Security Problem in International Relations*, Brighton: Wheatsheaf Books.

Buzan, B. (1984), 'Peace, Power, and Security: Contending Concepts in the Study of International Relations', *Journal of Peace Research*, 21/2: 109–25.

Buzan, B. (1991a), *People, States and Fear: An Agenda for International Security in the Post-Cold War Era*, 2nd edn., London: Harvester Wheatsheaf.

Buzan, B. (1991b) 'Is International Security Possible?', in K. Booth, *New Thinking about Strategy and International Security*, London: Harper Collins, 31–55.

Buzan, B. (1993) 'Societal Security, State Security, and Internationalisation', in O. Wæver, B. Buzan, M. Kelstrup and P. Lemaitre (eds.), *Identity, Migration and the New Security Agenda in Europe*, London: Pinter, 41–58.

Buzan, B. (2000) ' "Change and Insecurity" Reconsidered', in Stuart Croft and Terry Terriff (eds.), *Critical Reflections on Security and Change*, London: Frank Cass, 1–17.

Buzan, B. (2004a), 'What is Human Security? A Reductionist Idealistic Notion that Adds Little Analytical Value', *Security Dialogue*, 35/3: 369–70.

Buzan, B. (2004b), *United States and the Great Powers*, Cambridge: Polity.

Buzan, B. (2006), 'Will the "Global War on Terrorism" be the New Cold War?', *International Affairs*, 82/6: 1101–18.

Buzan, B., and Hansen, L. (2009), *The Evolution of International Security Studies*, Cambridge: Cambridge University Press.

Buzan, B., and Herring, E. (1998), *The Arms Dynamic in World Politics*, Boulder, CO: Lynne Rienner.

Buzan, B., and Sen, G. (1990), 'The Impact of Military Research and Development Priorities on the Evolution of the Civil Economy in Capitalist States', *Review of International Studies*, 16/4: 321–39.

Buzan, B., and Wæver, O. (1997), 'Slippery? Contradictory? Sociologically Untenable? The Copenhagen School Replies', *Review of International Studies*, 23: 241–50.

Buzan, B., and Wæver, O. (2003), *Regions and Power: The Structure of International Society*, Cambridge: Cambridge University Press.

Buzan, B., and Wæver, O. (2009), 'Macrosecuritization and Security Constellations: Reconsidering Scale in Securitization Theory', *Review of International Studies*, 35/2: 253–76.

Buzan, B., Wæver, O., and de Wilde, J. (1998), *Security: A New Framework for Analysis*, Boulder, CO: Lynne Rienner.

Byers, M. (2005), 'High Ground Lost', *Winnipeg Free Press*, 18 Sept., p. B3.

Byman, D. Waxman, M., and Larson, E. (1999), *Air Power as a Coercive Instrument*, Santa Monica, CA: RAND, MR-1061-AF.

CAAT (2005), Campaign Against the Arms Trade, *Who Calls The Shots? How Corporate-Government Collusion Drives Arms Exports*, London: CAAT.

Caballero-Anthony, M., Emmers R., and Acharya, A. (2006), *Non-Traditional Security in Asia: Dilemmas of Securitization*, Aldershot: Ashgate.

Cabinet Office (2008), *The National Security Strategy of the United Kingdom: Security in an Interdependent World*, London: The Stationery Office.

Cammack, P. (2006), 'The Politics of Global Competitiveness', Papers in the Politics of Global Competitiveness, No. 1, Institute for Global Studies, Manchester Metropolitan University, e-space Open Repository.

Cammack, P. (2007a), 'Forget the Transnational State', Papers in the Politics of Global Competitiveness, No. 3, Institute for Global Studies, Manchester Metropolitan University, e-space Open Repository.

Cammack, P. (2007b), 'RIP IPE', Papers in the Politics of Global Competitiveness, No. 7, Institute for Global Studies, Manchester Metropolitan University, e-space Open Repository.

Campbell, D. (1992), *Writing Security: United States Foreign Policy and the Politics of Identity*, Manchester: Manchester University Press.

Campbell, D. (1998a), *Writing Security: United States Foreign Policy and the Politics of Identity*, rev. edn., Minneapolis: University of Minnesota Press.

Campbell, D. (1998b), *National Deconstruction: Violence, Identity, and Justice in Bosnia*, Minneapolis: University of Minnesota Press.

Caney, S. (1997), 'Human Rights and the Rights of States: Terry Nardin on Non-Intervention', *International Political Science Review*, 18/1: 27–37.

Carnegie Commission (1997), *Preventing Deadly Conflict—Final Report*, Washington: Carnegie Commission on Preventing Deadly Conflict.

Carr, E. H. (1981), *The Twenty Years' Crisis 1919–1939: An Introduction to the Study of International Relations*, Houndmills: Macmillan.

Carson, R. (1962), *Silent Spring*, Boston: Houghton Mifflin.

CASE Collective (2006), 'Critical Approaches to Security in Europe: A Networked Manifesto', *Security Dialogue*, 37/4: 443–87.

CASE Collective (2007), 'Europe, Knowledge, Politics: Engaging the Limits: The CASE Collective Responds', *Security Dialogue*, 38/4: 559–76.

Ceyhan, A., and Tsoukala, A. (2002), 'The Securitization of Migration in Western Societies: Ambivalent Discourses and Policies', *Alternatives*, 27 (Feb., suppl.), 21–40.

Chalk, P. (1996), *West European Terrorism and Counterterrorism: The Evolving Dynamic*, Houndsmills: Macmillan.

Chalmers, D. M. (1965), *Hooded Americanism: The History of the Ku Klux Klan*, New York: Quadrangle Books.

Chandler, D. (2005), 'The Responsibility to Protect: Imposing the Liberal Peace', in Alex J. Bellamy and Paul D. Williams (eds.), *Peace Operations and Global Order*, London: Routledge, 59–82.

Cheluget, B. K., Ngare, C., Wahiu, J., Mwikya, L., Kinoti, S., and Ndyanabangi. B. (2003), 'Impact of HIV/AIDS on Public Health Sector Personnel in Kenya', Presentation to the ECSA Regional Health Ministers' Conference in Livingstone, Zambia, 17–21 Nov.

Chesterman, S. (2001), *Just War or Just Peace? Humanitarian Intervention and International Law*, Oxford: Oxford University Press.

Chomsky, N. (1973), *For Reasons of State*, London: Fontana Collins.

Chomsky, N., and Herman, E. S. (1979), *The Washington Connection and Third World Fascism: The Political Economy of Human Rights*, i, Boston: South End Press.

Chossudovsky, M. (1996), *The Globalization of Poverty: Impacts of IMF and World Bank Reforms*, Penang: Third World Network.

Clary, C. (2004), 'A. Q. Khan and the Limits of the Non-Proliferation Regime', *Disarmament Forum*, 4: 33–42.

Claude, I. (1964), *Swords into Ploughshares: The Problems and Progress of International Organization*, New York: Random House.

Clemens, M. (2004), 'The Long Walk to School: International Education Goals in Historical Perspective', CGD Working Paper, No. 37, Washington: Centre for Global Development.

CNA Corporation (2007) *National Security and the Threat of Climate Change*, Alexandria, VI: CNA Corporation.

CNN (2008), 'Iraq Signs $3 Billion Oil Deal with China', 30 Aug., www.cnn.com/2008/BUSINESS/08/30/iraq.china.oil.deal/index.html

Coalition to Stop the Use of Child Soldiers (2009), 'Child Soldiers: Some Facts', www.child-soldiers.org/childsoldiers/some-facts (accessed 8 Feb. 2009.

Cochrane, J. (2003), 'Blood in Bangkok Streets', *Newsweek*, 10 Mar.

Coebergh, J. (2005), 'Sudan: The Genocide has Killed More than the Tsunami', *Parliamentary Brief*, 7/9 (Feb.), 5–7.

Coker, C. (2002), *Globalization and Insecurity in the Twenty-first Century: NATO and the Management of Risk*, Adelphi Paper No. 345, Oxford: Oxford University Press.

Collier, P. (2000), *Economic Causes of Civil Conflict and their Implications for Policy*, Washington: World Bank.

Collins, A. (2003), *Security and Southeast Asia: Domestic, Regional and Global Issues*, Boulder, CO: Lynne Rienner.

Collins, A. (2005), 'Securitization, Frankenstein's Monster and Malaysian Education', *Pacific Review*, 18/4: 565–86.

Commission on Human Security (2003), *Human Security Now*, www.humansecurity-chs.org/finalreport/FinalReport.pdf

Conca, K. (1997), *Manufacturing Insecurity: The Rise and Fall of Brazil's Military–Industrial Complex*, London: Lynne Rienner.

Conka, K. (2002), 'The Case for Environmental Peacemaking', in K. Conka and G. Dabelko (eds.), *Environmental Peacemaking*, Baltimore: Johns Hopkins University Press, 1–22.

Conka, K., and Dabelko, G. (2002) (eds.), *Environmental Peacemaking*, Baltimore: John Hopkins University Press.

Conrad, P. (2007), *The Medicalization of Society: On the Transformation of Human Conditions into Treatable Disorders*, Baltimore: Johns Hopkins University Press.

Cooper, N. (1997), *The Business of Death: Britain's Arms Trade at Home and Abroad*, London: I. B. Tauris.

Cooper, N. (2000), 'The Pariah Agenda and New Labour's Ethical Arms Sales Policy', in Richard Little and Mark Wickham-Jones (eds.), *New Labour's Foreign Policy: A New Moral Crusade?*, Manchester: Manchester University Press, 147–67.

Copeland, D. (2000), *The Origins of Major War*, Ithaca, NY: Cornell University Press.

Copeland, D. C. (2006), 'The Constructivist Challenge to Structural Realism: A Review Essay', in S. Guzzini and A. Leander (eds.), *Constructivism and International Relations: Alexander Wendt and his Critics*, Abingdon and New York: Routledge, 1–20.

Cordesman, A., and Al-Rodhan, K. (2005), *The Changing Risks in Global Oil Supply and Demand: Crisis or Evolving Solutions?*, Washington: Center for Strategic and International Studies.

Cox, C. (1996), Chairman, 'Iran–Bosnia Credibility Gap', House Republican Policy Committee, Policy Perspective 26, www.fas.org/irp/news/1996/hrpc_irancred.htm

Cox, R. (1985), 'Social Forces, States and World Orders: Beyond International Relations Theory', in Robert O. Keohane (ed.), *Neorealism and its Critics*, New York: Columbia University Press, 204–54.

Cragin, K., and Hoffman, B. (2003), *Arms Trafficking and Colombia*, Santa Monica, CA: RAND.

Crenshaw, M. (1998), 'Questions to be Answered, Research to be Done, Knowledge to be Applied', in Walter Reich (ed.), *Origins of Terrorism: Psychologies, Ideologies, Theologies, States of Mind*, Washington: Woodrow Wilson Center Press, 247–60.

Crenshaw, M. (2003), 'Coercive Diplomacy and the Response to Terrorism', in R. J. Art and P. M. Cronin (eds.), *The United States and Coercive Diplomacy*, Washington: United States Institute of Peace, 305–57.

Cruickshank, J. W. (2007) (ed.), *Critical Realism: The Difference It Makes*, London: Routledge.

Daalder, I. H. (1993) (ed.), *Rethinking the Unthinkable: New Directions for Nuclear Arms Control*, London: Routledge.

Dalby, S. (1990), *Creating the Second Cold War: The Discourse of Politics*, New York: Guilford Press.

Dalby, S. (1992a), 'Ecopolitical Discourse: "Environmental Security" and Political Geography', *Progress in Human Geography*, 16/4: 503–22.

Dalby, S. (1992b), 'Security, Modernity, Ecology: The Dilemmas of Post-Cold War Security Discourse', *Alternatives*, 17: 95–134.

Dalby, S. (2002), *Environmental Security*, Minneapolis: University of Minnesota Press.

Dalby, S., and Ó Tuathail, G. (1998), *Rethinking Geopolitics*, London: Routledge.

Dauphinée, E. (2008), *The Ethics of Researching War: Looking for Bosnia*, Manchester: University of Manchester Press.

Dauvergne, P. (1998), 'Weak States, Strong States: A State-in-Society Perspective,' in P. Dauvergne (ed.), *Weak and Strong States in Asia-Pacific Societies*, Australia: Allen and Unwin.

Davie, M. R. (1929), *The Evolution of War: A Study of its Role in Early Societies*, Dover Publications; repr. 2003.

Davis, M. (2006), *Planet of Slums*, London: Verso.

Dawson, D. (1996), *The Origins of Western Warfare*, Boulder, CO: Westview.

de Soysa, I. (2000), 'The Resource Curse: Are Civil Wars Driven by Rapacity or Paucity?', in M. Berdal and D. Malone (eds.), *Greed and Grievance: Economic Agendas and Civil Wars*, Boulder, CO: Lynne Rienner, 113–36.

de Waal, A. (2002), 'New-Variant' Famine: How Aids Has Changed the Hunger Equation', 20 Nov., http://allafrica.com/stories/200211200471.html

de Waal, A. (2006), *AIDS and Power: Why There is no Political Crisis—Yet*, London: Zed Books.

de Waal, A. (2007), 'No Such Thing as Humanitarian Intervention: Why We Need to Rethink how to Realize the "Responsibility to Protect" in Wartime', *Harvard International Review*, 21: 1–7.

Defense News (1999), 'Project Source Codes', Editorial, 18 Oct., p. 56.

Defense Security Cooperation Agency (2005), 'Saudi Arabia: Continued Assistance in the Modernization of the SANG', news release, transmittal no. 06-05, 3 Oct.

Deng, F. M., Kimaro, S., Lyons, T., Rothchild, D., and Zartman, W. (1996), *Sovereignty as Responsibility: Conflict Management in Africa*, Washington: Brookings Institution.

Dent, C. M. (2001), 'The Eurasian Economic Axis: Its Significance for East Asia', *Journal of Asian Studies*, 60/3: 731–59.

Dent, C. M. (2002), *The Foreign Economic Policies of Singapore, South Korea and Taiwan*, Cheltenham: Edward Elgar.

Department of Defense (2007), *Transforming the Way DoD Looks at Energy: An Approach to Establishing an Energy Strategy*, Report FT602T1, Apr.

Der Derian, James (1995), 'The Value of Security: Hobbes, Marx, Nietzsche, and Baudrillard', in Ronnie D. Lipschutz (ed.), *On Security*, New York: Columbia University Press, 24–45.

Der Derian, J. (2001), *Virtuous War: Mapping the Military–Industrial–Media–Entertainment Network*, Boulder, CO: Westview.

Desch, M. C. (1998), 'Culture Clash: Assessing the Importance of Ideas in Security Studies', *International Security*, 23/1: 141–70.

Destler, I. M. (1977), 'National Security Advice to US Presidents: Some Lessons from Thirty Years', *World Politics*, 29/2: 143–76.

Deudney, D. (1990), 'The Case against Linking Environmental Degradation and National Security', *Millennium: Journal of International Studies*, 19/3: 461–76.

Deudney, D. H (1995), 'The Philadelphian System: Sovereignty, Arms Control, and Balance of Power in the American States-Union, circa 1787–1861', *International Organization*, 49/2, 191–228.

Deudney, D. (2006), *Bounding Power: Republican Security Theory from the Polis to the Global Village*, Princeton: Princeton University Press.

Deutsch, K. (1957), *Political Community and the North Atlantic Area*, New York: Greenwood Press.

Devine, K. M. (2006), 'The Myth of "The Myth of Irish Neutrality": Deconstructing Concepts of Irish Neutrality Using International Relations Theories', *Irish Studies in International Affairs*, 17: 115–39.

Dillon, M. (1996), *Politics of Security: Towards a Political Philosophy of Continental Thought*, London: Routledge.

Dillon, M. (2006), *Governing Terror,* London: Palgrave Macmillan.

Dillon, M., and Neal, A. W. (2008) (eds.), *Foucault on Politics, Security and War*, Basingstoke: Palgrave Macmillan.

Dillon, M., and Lobo-Guerrero, L. (2008), 'Biopolitics of Security in the 21st Century: An Introduction', *Review of International Studies*, 34/2: 265–92.

Dimand, M. A., and Dimand, R. W. (1996), *The History of Game Theory, Volume I: From the Beginnings to 1945*, London: Routledge.

Dingley, J., and Kirk-Smith, M. (2002), 'Symbolism and Sacrifice in Terrorism', *Small Wars and Insurgencies*, 13/1: 102–28.

Dishman, C. (2005), 'The Leaderless Nexus: When Crime and Terror Converge', *Studies in Conflict and Terrorism*, 28/3: 237–52.

Dixon, N. (1976), *On the Psychology of Military Incompetence*, London: Basic Books.

Donnelly, J. (1998), *International Human Rights*, 2nd edn., Boulder, CO: Westview.

Doty, R. L. (1996), *Imperial Encounters*, Minneapolis: University of Minneapolis Press.

Downs, E. (2000), *China's Quest for Energy Security*, Santa Monica, CA: RAND.

Draguhn, W., and Ash, R. (1999) (eds.), *China's Economic Security*, London: Curzon Press.

Drimie, S. (2003), 'HIV/AIDS and Land: Case Studies from Kenya, Lesotho and South Africa', *Development Southern Africa*, 20/5: 647–58.

Duffield, M. (2001), *Global Governance and the New Wars: The Merging of Development and Security*, London: Zed Books.

Duffield, M. (2007), *Development, Security and Unending War: Governing the World of Peoples*, Cambridge: Polity.

Dunne, T., Kurki, M., and Smith, S. (2007) (eds.), *International Relations Theories: Discipline and Diversity*, Oxford: Oxford University Press.

Dycus, S. (1996), *National Defense and the Environment*, Hanover, NH: University Press of New England.

Edkins, J. (2003), *Trauma and the Memory of Politics*, Cambridge: Cambridge University Press.

Edwards, R. D. (1999), *The Faithful Tribe*, London: Harper Collins

Elshtain, J. B. (1987), *Women and War*, New York: Basic Books.

Elshtain, J. B. (1992) (ed.), *Just War Theory*, Oxford, Basil Blackwell.

Elshtain, J. B., and Tobias, S. (1990) (eds.), *Women, Militarism and War*, Savage, MD: Rowman & Littlefield.

Emmers, R. (2004), *Non-Traditional Security in the Asia-Pacific: The Dynamics of Securitisation*, Singapore: Eastern Universities Press.

Enders, W., and Sandler, T. (2006), *The Political Economy of Terrorism*, Cambridge: Cambridge University Press.

Energy Information Administration (2007), 'Country Analysis Briefs: Persian Gulf Region', June update, www.eia. doe.gov

Energy Information Administration (2008), 'International Energy Outlook 2008', Sept., www.eia.doe.gov

Enloe, C. (1993), *The Morning After: Sexual Politics at the End of the Cold War*, London: University of California Press.

Eriksson, J. (1999), 'Observers or Advocates? On the Political Role of Security Analysts', *Cooperation and Conflict*, 34/3: 311–30.

Escobar, A. (1995), *Encountering Development: The Making and Unmaking of the Third World*, Princeton: Princeton University Press.

Esty, D., Goldstone, J., Gurr, T., Harff, B., Levy, M., Dabelko, G., Surko, P., and Unger, A. (1999), 'State Failure Task Force Report: Phase II Findings', *Environmental Change and Security Project Report*, 5: 49–72.

Etzold, T. H. (1978), 'American Organization for National Security 1945–50', in Thomas H. Etzold and John Lewis Gaddis (eds.), *Containment: Documents on American Policy and Strategy, 1945–50*, New York: Columbia University Press, 1–23.

EU (1995), European Union, The Europol Convention, Article 2, www.europol.europa.eu/index.asp?page=legalconv (accessed July 2009).

Evans, G. (2008), *The Responsibility to Protect: Ending Mass Atrocity Crimes Once and for All*, Washington: Brookings Institution.

Falk, R. (1971), *This Endangered Planet: Prospects and Proposals for Human Survival*, New York: Random House.

Falk, R. (2003), 'Humanitarian Intervention: A Forum', *Nation*, 14 July.

FAO (2003), *HIV/AIDS and Agriculture: Impacts and Responses—Case Studies from Namibia, Uganda and Zambia*, Rome: Food and Agricultural Organization, Dec.

Farrell, T. (1996), 'Figuring out Fighting Organisations: The New Organisational Analysis in Strategic Studies', *Journal of Strategic Studies*, 19/1: 128–42.

Farrell, T. (1997), *Weapons without a Cause: The Politics of Weapons Acquisition in the United States*, London: Macmillan.

Farrell, T. (2002), 'Constructivist Security Studies: Portrait of a Research Program', *International Studies Review*, 7/3: 49–72.

Fearson, J., and Laitin, D. (2003), 'Ethnicity, Insurgency, and Civil War', *American Political Science Review*, 97/1: 75–90.

Fehl, C. (2004), 'Explaining the International Criminal Court: A "Practice Test" for Rationalist and Constructivist Approaches', *European Journal of International Relations*, 10/3: 357–94.

Feinstein, L. (2007), 'Darfur and Beyond: What is Needed to Prevent Mass Atrocities', *Council on Foreign Relations Special Report*, Washington: Council on Foreign Relations Press.

Finckenauer, O., and Voronin, Y. A. (2001), 'The Threat of Russian Organized Crime', *National Institute of Justice*, NCJ 187085, June.

Fidler, D., and Gostin, L. (2008), *Biosecurity in the Global Age: Biological Weapons, Public Health and the Rule of Law*, Stanford, CA: Stanford University Press.

Fierke, K. M. (2001), 'Critical Methodology and Constructivism', in K. M. Fierke and K. E. Jørgensen (eds.), *Constructing International Relations: The Next Generation*, New York: M. E. Sharpe, 115–35.

Fierke, K. M. (2002), 'Links across the Abyss: Language and Logic in International Relations', *International Studies Quarterly*, 46/3: 331–54.

Fierke, K. M. (2007), *Critical Approaches to International Security*, Cambridge: Polity.

Fierke, K. M., and Jørgensen, K. E. (2001) (eds.), *Constructing International Relations: The Next Generation*, New York: M. E. Sharpe.

Fierke, K. M., and Wiener, A. (1999), 'Constructing Institutional Interests: EU and NATO Enlargement', *Journal of European Public Policy*, 6/5: 721–42.

Findlay, T. (2002), *The Use of Force in UN Peace Operations*, Oxford: Oxford University Press for SIPRI.

Finnemore, M. (1996), 'Constructing Norms of Humanitarian Intervention', in P. J. Katzenstein (ed.), *The Culture of National Security: Norms and Identity in World Politics* (New York: Columbia University Press), 153–85.

Finnemore, M. (2003), *The Purpose of Intervention: Changing Beliefs about the Use of Force*, Ithaca, NY: Cornell University Press.

Finnemore, M. (2008), 'Paradoxes in Humanitarian Intervention', in Richard M. Price (ed.), *Moral Limit and Possibility in World Politics*, Cambridge: Cambridge University Press, 197–224.

Finnemore, M., and Sikkink, K. (1998), 'International Norm Dynamics and Political Change', *International Organization*, 52/4: 887–917.

Finnemore, M., and Sikkink, K. (2001), 'Taking Stock: The Constructivist Research Program in International Relations and Comparative Politics', *Annual Review of Political Science*, 4: 371–416.

Flight International (1994), 'UK C-130 Hercules for Sale', 4 Oct.

Flint, J., and de Waal, A. (2008), *Darfur: A New History of a Long War*, rev. and updated edn., London: Zed Books.

Fortna, V. P. (2008), *Does Peacekeeping Work? Shaping Belligerents' Choices after Civil Wars*, Princeton: Princeton University Press.

Franck, T., and Rodley, N. (1973), 'After Bangladesh: The Law of Humanitarian Intervention by Military Force', *American Journal of International Law*, 67/2: 275–305

Frederking, B. (2003), 'Constructing Post-Cold War Collective Security', *American Political Science Review*, 97/3: 363–78.

Freedman, L. (1988), 'I Exist; Therefore I Deter', *International Security*, 13/1: 177–95.

Freedman, L. (1992), 'The Concept of Security', in Mary Hawksworth and Maurice Kogan (eds.), *Encyclopaedia of Government and Politics*, 2nd edn., London: Routledge, ii. 752–61.

Freedman, L. (1998), 'International Security: Changing Targets', *Foreign Policy*, 110 (Spring), 48–63.

Fukuyama, F. (1992), *The End of History and the Last Man*, New York: Free Press.

Galtung, J. (1969), 'Violence, Peace and Peace Research', *Journal of Peace Research*, 6/3: 167–91.

Gates, R. (1987–8), 'The CIA and Foreign Policy', *Foreign Affairs*, 66: 215–30.

GCR2P (2008), Global Centre for the Responsibility to Protect, 'The Georgia–Russia Crisis and the Responsibility to Protect: A Background Note', www.globalr2p.org/pdf/related/GeorgiaRussia.pdf (accessed 25 Nov. 2008).

Geertz, C. (1973), *The Interpretation of Cultures*, New York: Basic Books.

George, A. L., and Simons, W. E. (1994) (eds.), *The Limits of Coercive Diplomacy*, 2nd rev. edn., Boulder, CO: Westview.

Gheciu, A. (2005a), 'Security Institutions as Agents of Socialization? NATO and the "New Europe"', *International Organization*, 59/4: 970–1012.

Gheciu, A. (2005b), *NATO in the New Europe: The Politics of Socialization after the Cold War*, Stanford, CA: Stanford University Press.

Gheciu, A. (2008), *Securing Civilization: The EU, NATO, and the OSCE in the Post-9/11 World*, Oxford: Oxford University Press.

Giddens, A. (1985), *The Nation-State and Violence: Volume Two of a Contemporary Critique of Historical Materialism*, Cambridge: Cambridge University Press in association with Basil Blackwell, Oxford.

Giddens, A. (1990), *The Consequences of Modernity*, Cambridge: Polity.

Gillespie, S. (2006) (ed.), *AIDS, Poverty, and Hunger: Challenges and Responses*, Washington: International Food Policy Research Institute.

Gilpin, R. (1981), *War and Change in World Politics*, Cambridge: Cambridge University Press.

Glaser, C. (1997), 'The Security Dilemma Revisited', *World Politics*, 50/1: 171–201.

Glaser, C. (1994–5), 'Realists as Optimists: Cooperation as Self-Help', *International Security*, 19/3: 50–90.

Gleditsch, N. (1998), 'Armed Conflict and the Environment: A Critique of the Literature', *Journal of Peace Research*, 35/3: 381–400.

Gleick, P. (1991), 'Environment and Security: The Clear Connections', *Bulletin of the Atomic Scientists*, 47/3: 17–21.

Gloannec, A.-M. Le, and Smolar, A. (2003) (eds.), *Entre Kant et Kosovo: Études offertes à Pierre Hassner* (Paris: Presses de Sciences Po).

Godson, R., and Williams, P. (1998), 'Strengthening Cooperation against Transnational Crime', *Survival*, 40/3 (Autumn).

Goetschel, L. (1999), 'Neutrality: A Really Dead Concept?', *Cooperation and Conflict*, 34/2: 115–39.

Goldmann, K. (1988), *Change and Stability in Foreign Policy: The Problems and Possibilities of Detente*, Princeton: Princeton University Press.

Graham, D.T. (2000), 'The People Paradox: Human Movements and Human Security in a Globalising World', in D.T. Graham and N.K. Poku (eds.), *Migration, Globalisation and Human Security*, London: Routledge, 192–9.

Gray, C. (1971), 'What RAND Hath Wrought', *Foreign Policy*, 4: 111–29.

Gray, C. S. (1977), 'Across the Nuclear Divide: Strategic Studies Past and Present', *International Security*, 2/1: 24-46.

Gray, C. (1982), *Strategic Studies and Public Policy: The American Experience*, Lexington, KY: University Press of Kentucky.

Gray, C. (1996), 'Arms Races and Other Pathetic Fallacies: A Case for Deconstruction', *Review of International Studies*, 22/3: 323–35.

Grayson, K. (2003), 'Securitization and the Boomerang Debate: A Rejoinder to Liotta and Smith-Windsor', *Security Dialogue*, 34/3.

Grayson, K. (2008), *Chasing Dragons: Security, Identity, and Illicit Drugs in Canada*, Toronto: University of Toronto Press.

Green, E. M. (1996), *Economic Security and High Technology Competition in an Age of Transition*, Westport: Praeger.

Green, P. (1966), *Deadly Logic: The Theory of Nuclear Deterrence*, Columbus, OH: Ohio State University Press.

Green, P. (1968), 'Science, Government, and the Case of RAND: A Singular Pluralism', *World Politics*, 20/2 (Jan.), 301–26.

Gruffydd Jones, B. (2008), 'The Global Political Economy of Social Crisis: Towards a Critique of the "Failed State" Ideology', *Review of International Political Economy*, 15/2: 18–205.

Guardian (2005), 'Eurofighter Sale to Saudi Arabia Agreed', *Guardian Unlimited*, 21 Dec., http://politics.guardian.co.uk/foreignaffairs/story/0,11538,1672166,00.html

Guillemin, J. (2005), *Biological Weapons: From the Invention of State-Sponsored Programs to Contemporary Bioterrorism*, New York: Columbia University Press.

Gulf Industry (2004), 'Glaxo SA to Enlarge Product Range: Reader Inquiry No. 23', *Gulf Industry Online Edition*, 13/5 (Sept.–Oct. 2004), www.gulfindustryworldwide.com

Gunder Frank, A. (1971), *Capitalism and Underdevelopment in Latin America: Historical Sketches of Chile and Brazil*, Harmondsworth: Penguin.

Gurr, T. R. (1993), *Minorities at Risk*, Washington: United States Institute of Peace Press.

Gurr, T. (2000), *People versus States: Minorities at Risk in the New Century*, Washington: United States Institute of Peace Press.

Gusterson, H. (1998), *Nuclear Rites: A Weapons Laboratory at the End of the Cold War*, Berkeley and Los Angeles: University of California Press.

Guy, Jess (1989), 'Illegal Trafficking of Arms by Small Time Operators', in Peter Unsinger (ed.), *The International Legal and Illegal Trafficking of Arms*, (Springfield, IL: C. C. Thomas).

Guzzini, S., and Jung, D (2004) (eds.), *Contemporary Security Analysis and Copenhagen Peace Research*, London: Routledge.

Haas, R. N. (2002), 'Think Tanks and US Foreign Policy: A Policy-Maker's Perspective', *US Foreign Policy Agenda*, 7/3 (Nov.), usinfo.state.gov/journals/itps/1101/ijpe/pj73toc.htm

Hammond, G. T. (1993), *Plowshares into Swords: Arms Races in International Politics, 1840–1991*, Colombia, SC: University of South Carolina Press.

Hansen, C. (1988). *US Nuclear Weapons: The Secret History*, New York: Orion Books.

Hansen, L. (2000), 'The Little Mermaid's Silent Security Dilemma and the Absence of Gender in the Copenhagen School', *Millennium: Journal of International Studies*, 29/2: 285–306.

Hansen, L. (2006), *Security as Practice: Discourse Analysis and the Bosnian War*, London: Routledge.

Harris, S., and Mack, A. (1997), 'Security and Economics in East Asia', in S. Harris and A. Mack (eds.), *Asia-Pacific Security: The Economics–Politics Nexus*, Pymble, NSW, Australia: Allen and Unwin, 1–29.

Hartley, T., and Russet, B. (1992), 'Public Opinion and the Common Defense: Who Governs Military Spending in the United States', *American Political Science Review*, 86/4: 905–15.

Hartung, William D. (1996), *Welfare for Weapons Dealers: The Hidden Costs of the Arms Trade*, World Policy Papers, New York: World Policy Institute.

Harvey, D. (1989), *The Urban Experience*, Oxford: Basil Blackwell

Harvey, D. (2005), *A Brief History of Neoliberalism*, Oxford: Oxford University Press.

Hassner, P. (1993), 'Beyond Nationalism and Internationalism: Ethnicity and World Order', *Survival*, 35/2: 49–65.

Hassner, P. (1997) *Violence and Peace: From the Atomic Bomb to Ethnic Cleansing*, trans. Jane Brenton, Budapest: Central European University Press.

Haubrick, D. (2003), 'September 11, Anti-Terror Laws and Civil Liberties: Britain, France and Germany Compared', *Government and Opposition*, 38/1: 3–28.

Hayden, R. (1996), 'Imagined Communities and Real Victims: Self-Determination and Ethnic Cleansing in Yugoslavia', *American Ethnologist*, 23/4: 273–96.

Heininen, L. (1994), 'The Military and the Environment: An Arctic Case', in J. Kakonen (ed.), *Green Security or Militarized Environment*, Aldershot: Dartmouth, 155–67.

Held, D., and Goldblatt, David, Perraton, Jonathan, and McGrew, Anthony (1999), *Global Transformations: Politics, Economics and Culture*, Cambridge: Polity.

Hellman, C., and Sharp, T. (2008), 'The FY 2009 Pentagon Spending Request: Global Military Spending', Center for Arms Control and Non-Proliferation, 22 Feb., www.armscontrolcenter.org/policy/securityspending/articles/fy09_dod_request_global/

Herd, G. P., and Lofgren J. (2001), ' "Societal Security" in the Baltic States and EU Integration', *Cooperation and Conflict*, 36/3: 273–96.

Herz, J. H. (1950), 'Idealist Internationalism and the Security Dilemma', *World Politics*, 2/2: 157–80.

Hicks Stiehm, J. (1983) (ed.), *Women and Men's Wars*, Oxford: Pergamon Press.

Hicks Stiehm, J. (1989), *Arms and the Enlisted Woman*, Philadelphia: Temple.

Hill, C. (1994), 'Academic International Relations: The Siren Song of Policy Relevance', in Christopher Hill and Pamela Beshoff (eds.), *Two Worlds of International Relations: Academics, Practitioners and the Trade in Ideas*, London: Routledge, 3–25.

Hitch, C. J. (1960), *The Uses of Economics*, P-2179-RC, Santa Monica: Rand Corporation.

Hobson, M. (2005), *Forgotten Casualties of War: Girls in Armed Conflict*, Save the Children Fund (SCF), www.savethechildren.org.ukk

Hocking, J. (2003), 'Counter-Terrorism and the Criminalisation of Politics: Australia's New Security Powers of Detention, Proscription and Control', *Australian Journal of Politics and History*, 49/3: 355–71.

Hofstader, R. (1970), 'Reflections on Violence in the United States', in R. Hofstader and M. Wallace (eds.), *American Violence: A Documentary History*, New York: Alfred A. Knopf, 3–43.

Hogan, M. J. (1998), *A Cross of Iron: Harry S. Truman and the Origins of the National Security State, 1945–1954*, Cambridge: Cambridge University Press.

Hollingdale, R. J. (1977) (trans.) *A Nietzsche Reader*, London: Penguin.

Holsti, K. (1996), *The State, War, and the State of War*, Cambridge: Cambridge University Press.

Holt, V. K., and Berkman, T. C. (2006), *The Impossible Mandate? Military Preparedness, The Responsibility to Protect and Modern Peace Operations*, Washington: Henry L. Stimson Center.

Homer-Dixon, T. (1991), 'On the Threshold: Environmental Changes as Causes of Acute Conflict', *International Security*, 16/2: 76–116.

Homer-Dixon, T. (1999), *Environment, Scarcity, and Violence*, Princeton: Princeton University Press.

Hooks, B. (1995), 'Feminism and Militarism: A Comment', *Woman's Studies Quarterly*, 3–4: 58–64.

Hope, Christopher (2005), '£20bn Jets Deal Will Secure 14,000 Jobs', *Daily Telegraph*, 22 Dec., http://portal.telegraph.co.uk/news/main.jhtml?xml=/news/2005/12/22/nbae22.xml&sSheet=/portal/2005/12/22/ixportal.html

Hopf, T. (1998), 'The Promise of Constructivism in International Relations Theory', *International Security*, 23/1: 171–200.

Hough, Peter (2004), *Understanding Global Security*, London: Routledge.

Howard, Michael (1979), 'The Forgotten Dimensions of Strategy', *Foreign Affairs*, 57/5: 975–86.

Hoyle, Craig (2005), 'Saudi Arabia Commits to Eurofighter Typhoon Deal', *Flight International*, 21 Dec., www.flightinternational.com/Articles/2005/12/21/Navigation/177/203773/Saudi+Arabia+commits+to+Eurofighter+Typhoon+deal.html

Hubert, D. (2004), 'An Idea that Works in Practice', *Security Dialogue*, 35/3: 351–2.

Hülsse, R. (2008), 'The Metaphor of Terror: Terrorism Studies and the Constructivist Turn', *Security Dialogue*, 39/6: 571–92.

Human Rights Watch (1999), 'World Report, Violence against Women', www.hrw.org/hrw/world report 99.

Human Rights Watch (2007), 'Saudi Arabia: Events of 2006', *World Report 2007,* New York: Human Rights Watch.

Human Security News, www.hsrgroup.org

Human Security Brief 2005, www.humansecurityreport.info

Human Security Brief 2006, www.humansecuritybrief.info/2006/index.html

Human Security Brief 2007, www.humansecuritybrief.info

Human Security Centre (2005a), 'Human Security News', www.hsc.list@ubc.ca

Human Security Centre (2005b), *Human Security Report 2005*, www.hsrgroup.org

Human Security Centre (2006), *Human Security Report 2006*, Vancouver: The University of British Columbia, www.hsrgroup.org ,

Huntington, S. P. (1957), *The Soldier and the State: The Theory and Politics of Civil–Military Relations*, Cambridge, MA: Harvard University Press.

Hutchinson, J. (1994), 'Cultural Nationalism and Moral Regeneration', in J. Hutchinson and A. D. Smith (eds.), *Nationalism*, Oxford: Oxford University Press, 122–31.

Huysmans, J. (1995), 'Migrants as a Security Issue: The Dangers of "Securitizing" Societal Issues', in R. Miles and D. Thranhardt (eds.), *Migration and European Security: The Dynamics of Inclusion and Exclusion*, London: Pinter, 53–72.

Huysmans, J. (1998), 'Revisiting Copenhagen: Or, On the Creative Development of a Security Studies Agenda in Europe', *European Journal of International Relations*, 4/4: 479–506.

Huysmans, J. (2002), 'Defining Social Constructivism in Security Studies: The Normative Dilemma of Writing Security', *Alternatives*, 27 (suppl.), 41–62.

Huysmans, J. (2006), *The Politics of Insecurity: Security, Migration and Asylum in the EU*, London: Routledge.

ICISS (2001), International Commission on Intervention and State Sovereignty, *The Responsibility to Protect*, Ottawa: IDRC.

Ignatieff, M. (1993), *Blood and Belonging: Journeys into the New Nationalism*, London: Vintage.

Ijaw Youth Council (1998), *Kaiama Declaration*, 11 Dec., www.ijawcenter.com/kaiama_declaration.html

Ikegami-Andersson, Masako (1992), *The Military–Industrial Complex: The Cases of Sweden and Japan*, Dartmouth: Dartmouth Press.

Ikenberry, G. J. (2001), *After Victory*, Princeton: Princeton University Press.

Ikenberry, G. J. (2002) (ed.), *American Unrivaled: The Future of the Balance of Power*, Ithaca, NY: Cornell University Press.

IMF/World Bank (2009), 'Heavily Indebted Poor Countries Initiative: Status of Implementation', Washington: World Bank.

Ingram, Paul, and Davis, Ian (2001), *The Subsidy Trap: British Government Financial Support for Arms Exports and the Defence Industry*, Oxford and London: Oxford Research Group and Saferworld.

International Crisis Group (2006a), 'The Swamps of Insurgency: Nigeria's Delta Unrest', Africa Report No. 115, Aug.

International Crisis Group (2006b), 'Fuelling the Niger Delta Crisis', Africa Report No. 118, 28 Sept.

Isaksson E. (1988) (ed.), *Women and the Military System*, Basingstoke: Palgrave Macmillan.

Jackson, Richard (2005), *Writing the War on Terrorism: Language, Politics and Counter-Terrorism*, Manchester: Manchester University Press.

Jackson, Robert H. (1990), *Quasi-States: Sovereignty, International Relations, and the Third World*, New York: Cambridge University Press.

Jackson, Robert H. (2002), *The Global Covenant: Human Conduct in a World of States*, Oxford: Oxford University Press.

Jahn, E. (1984), 'Zum Verhältnis von Friedensforschung, Friedenspolitik und Friedensbewegung', *Dialog*, 1/1: 21–31.

Jahn, E., Lemaitre, P., and Wæver, O. (1987), *European Security: Problems of Research on Non-Military Aspects*, Copenhagen Papers 1, Copenhagen: Copenhagen Peace Research Institute.

Jakobsen, P. V. (1998), *Western Use of Coercive Diplomacy after the Cold War: A Challenge for Theory and Practice*, London: Macmillan Press.

Jakobson, M. (1961), *The Diplomacy of the Winter War: An Account of the Russo-Finnish Conflict, 1939–1940*, Cambridge, MA: Harvard University Press.

Jervis, R. (1970), *The Logic of Images in International Relations*, Princeton: Princeton University Press.

Jervis, R. (1976), *Perception and Misperception in International Politics*, Princeton: Princeton University Press.

Jervis, R. (1978), 'Cooperation under the Security Dilemma', *World Politics*, 30/1: 167–214.

Jervis, R. (1989), *The Meaning of the Nuclear Revolution*, Ithaca, NY: Cornell University Press.

Jervis, R. (1991), 'The Spiral of International Security', in Richard Little and Michael Smith (eds.), *Perspectives on World Politics*, 2nd edn., London: Routledge, 91–101.

Jessop, B. (2004), 'Critical Semiotic Analysis and Cultural Political Economy', Cultural Political Economy Research Cluster, Working Paper 1, University of Lancaster; pre-print from *Critical Discourse Studies*, 1/1: 1–16.

Job, B. A. (1992) (ed.), *The Insecurity Dilemma: National Security of Third World States*, Boulder, CO: Lynne Rienner.

Joenniemi, P. (1988), 'Models of Neutrality: The Traditional and the Modern', *Cooperation and Conflict*, 23/1: 53–67.

Johnson, C. (2006), *Nemesis: The Last Days of the American Republic*, New York: Metropolitan Books.

Jones, R. W. (1999), *Security, Strategy, and Critical Theory*, Boulder, CO: Lynne Rienner 1999, 145–68.

Joosse, P. (2007), 'Leaderless Resistance and Ideological Inclusion: The Case of the Earth Liberation Front', *Terrorism and Political Violence*, 19/3: 351–68.

Jung, D., and Schlichte, K. (1999), 'From Inter-State War to Warlordism: Changing Forms of Collective Violence in the International System', in H. Wiberg and C. Scherrer (eds.), *Ethnicity and Intra-State Conflict: Types, Causes and Peace Strategies*, Aldershot: Ashgate.

Kahl, C. (2006), *States, Scarcity, and Civil Strife in the Developing World*, Princeton: Princeton University Press.

Kahler, M. (2004), 'Economic Security in an Era of Globalization: Definition and Provision, *Pacific Review*, 17/4: 485–502.

Kaldor, M. (1982), *The Baroque Arsenal*, London: André Deutsch.

Kaldor, M. (1999), *New and Old Wars: Organised Violence in a Global Era*, Cambridge: Polity.

Kanbur, Ravi (2002), 'Conceptual Challenges in Poverty and Inequality: One Development Economist's View', Apr., www.arts.cornell.edu/poverty/kanbur/CCPI.pdf

Kaplan, F. (1983), *Wizards of Armageddon*, Stanford, CA: Stanford University Press.

Kapstein, E. B. (1992), *The Political Economy of National Security*, New York: McGraw-Hill.

Katzenstein, P. J. (1996a), 'Introduction: Alternative Perspectives on National Security', in P. J. Katzenstein (ed.), *The Culture of National Security: Norms and Identity in World Politics*, New York: Columbia University Press, 1–32.

Katzenstein, P. (1996b) (ed.), *The Culture of National Security: Norms and Identity in World Politics*, New York: Columbia University Press.

Keegan, J. (1998), *War and our World*, London: Pimlico.

Keegan, J. (2003), *Intelligence in War: Knowledge of the Enemy from Napoleon to Al-Qaeda*, London: Hutchinson.

Kegley, C., Jr. (1995), 'The Neorealist Challenge to Realist Theories of World Politics: An Introduction', in C. Kegley (ed.), *Controversies in International Relations Theory*, New York: St Martins Press, 1–24.

Kegley, C. W., and Raymond, G.A. (1982), 'Alliance Norms and War: A New Piece in an Old Puzzle', *International Studies Quarterly*, 26: 572–95.

Kennedy, R. F. (1969), *Thirteen Days*, New York: Norton

Kennedy-Pipe, Caroline (2004), 'Whose Security? State-Building and the "Emancipation" of Women in Central Asia', *International Relations*, 18/1: 91–107.

Kenney, M. (2007), *From Pablo to Osama: Trafficking and Terrorist Networks, Government Bureaucracies, and Competitive Advantage*, University Park, PA: Pennsylvania State University Press.

Keohane, R. (1988), 'International Institutions: Two Approaches', *International Studies Quarterly*, 32/4: 379–96.

Keohane, R. O. (2000), 'Ideas Part-Way Down', *Review of International Studies*, 26/1: 125–30.

Keohane, R.O., and Nye, J.S. (1977), *Power and Interdependence*, Boston: Little Brown.

Kerr, P. (2003), 'The Evolving Dialectic between State-Centric and Human-Centric Security', Working Paper 2003/4, Department of International Relations, Australian National University, Canberra, 1–34.

Kerr, P., Tow, W. T., and Hanson, M. (2003), 'The Utility of the Human Security Agenda for Policy-Makers', *Asian Journal of Political Science*, 11/2: 89–114.

Kingham, A. (2006) (ed.), *Inventory of Environmental Security Policies and Practices: An Overview of Strategies and Initiatives of Selected Governments, International Organisations and Inter-Governmental Organisations*, The Hague: Institute for Environmental Security.

Kissinger, H. (1956), 'Force and Diplomacy in the Nuclear Age', *Foreign Affairs*, 34: 349–66.

Klare, M. (2004), *Blood and Oil: How America's Thirst for Petrol is Killing us*, London: Penguin.

Klare, M. (2008), *Rising Powers Shrinking Planet: The New Geopolitics of Energy*, New York: Metropolitan Books.

Klein, B. (1994), *Strategic Studies and World Order*, Cambridge: Cambridge University Press.

Klotz, A. (1995), 'Norms Reconstituting Interests: Global Racial Equality and US Sanctions against South Africa', *International Organization*, 49/5: 451–78.

Knightley, P. (1986), *The Second Oldest Profession: Spies and Spying in the Twentieth Century*, London: Penguin Books.

Knorr, K, (1970), 'The International Purposes of Military Power', in J. Garnet (ed.), *Theories of Peace and Security*, London: Macmillan.

Knorr, K. (1977), 'Economic Interdependence and National Security', in K. Knorr and F. N. Trager (eds.), *Economic Issues and National Security*, Lawrence, KA: Regents Press.

Knorr, K., and Trager, F. N. (1977), *Economic Issues and National Security*, published for the National Security Education Program by the Regents Press of Kansas.

Kober, K., and van Damme, W. (2006), 'Public Sector Nurses in Swaziland: Can the Downturn be Reversed?', *Human Resources for Health*, 4/13: 1–11.

Kolodziej, Edward A. (2005), *Security and International Relations*, Cambridge: Cambridge University Press.

Kowert, P. (2001), 'The Peril and Promise of Constructivist Theory', *Ritsumeikan Kokusai Kenkyu (Ritsumeikan Journal of International Studies)*, 13/3: 157–70.

Krasner, S. D. (1983) (ed.), *International Regimes*, Ithaca, NY: Cornell University Press.

Krasner, S. D. (1999) (ed.), *Sovereignty: Organized Hypocrisy*, Princeton: Princeton University Press.

Krasner, S. D. (2000), 'Wars, Hotel Fires, and Plane Crashes', *Review of International Studies*, 26: 131–6.

Kratochwil, F. (1991), *Rules, Norms, and Decisions: On the Conditions of Practical and Legal Reasoning in International Relations and Domestic Affairs*, Cambridge: Cambridge University Press.

Kratochwil, F. V. (2001), 'Constructivism as an Approach to Interdisciplinary Study', in K. M. Fierke and K. E. Jørgensen (eds.), *Constructing International Relations: The Next Generation*, New York: M. E. Sharpe, 13–35.

Krause, K. (1992), *Arms and the State: Patterns of Military Production and Trade*, Cambridge: Cambridge University Press.

Krause, K. (1998), 'Critical Theory and Security Studies: The Research Programme of "Critical Security Studies"', *Cooperation and Conflict*, 33/3: 298–333.

Krause, K. (2007), 'Towards a Practical Human Security Agenda', *Policy Paper* (26), Geneva: Geneva Centre for the Democratic Control of Armed Forces, 1–20.

Krause, K., and Williams, M. C. (1997a), 'From Strategy to Security: Foundations of Critical Security Studies', in K. Krause and M. C. Williams (eds.) *Critical Security Studies: Concepts and Cases*, Minneapolis: University of Minnesota Press, 33–59.

Krause, K., and Williams, M. C. (1997b) (eds.), *Critical Security Studies: Concepts and Cases*, Minneapolis: University of Minnesota Press.

Krepon, M. (1984), *Strategic Stalemate: Nuclear Weapons and Arms Control in American Politics*, London: Macmillan.

Kuhn, H. W. (2004), 'Introduction', in John von Neumann and Oskar Morgenstern, *Theory of Games and Economic Behavior*, Sixtieth Anniversary Edition, Princeton: Princeton University Press, pp. vii–xiv.

Kuperman, A. J. (2008), 'The Moral Hazard of Humanitarian Intervention: Lessons from the Balkans', *International Studies Quarterly*, 52/1: 49–80.

Kurtenbach, S. (2008), 'Youth Violence as a Scapegoat: Youth in Post-War Guatemala', Project Working Paper No. 5, Social and Political Fractures after Wars: Youth Violence in Cambodia and Guatemala, German Foundation for Peace Research.

Kydd, A. (1997), 'Sheep in Sheep's Clothing: Why Security Seekers Do Not Fight Each Other', *Security Studies*, 7/1: 115–54.

Kydd, A. (2005), *Trust and Mistrust in International Relations*, Princeton: Princeton University Press.

Kymlicka, W. (2001), 'Justice and Security in the Accommodation of Minority Nationalism: Comparing East and West', Working Paper, Central European University.

Laffey, M., and Dean, K. (2002), 'A Flexible Marxism for Flexible Times: Globalization and Historical Materialism', in Mark Rupert and Hazel Smith (eds.), *Historical Materialism and Globalization*, London: Routledge, 90–109.

Lamb, W. (2007), *What Would Military Security Look Like through a Human Security Lens*, Oxford, Oxford Research Group.

Langberg, D. R. (2008), 'US Government Response to Human Trafficking in the Twenty-First Century', in Richard Weitz (ed.), *Project on National Security Reform: Case Studies (Volume I)*, Washington: Center for the Study of the Presidency.

Laqueur, W. (2001), *A History of Terrorism*, New Brunswick, NJ: Transaction Publishers.

Larsen, J. (2002) (ed.), *Arms Control: Cooperative Security in a Changing Environment*, Boulder, CO: Lynne Rienner.

Lasswell, H. D. (1950), *National Security and Individual Freedom*, New York, Toronto, and London: McGraw-Hill.

Laville, Helen (1997), 'The Committee of Correspondence: CIA Funding of Women's Groups 1952–1967', in Rhodri Jeffreys-Jones and Christopher Andrew (eds.), *Eternal Vigilance? 50 Years of the CIA*, London: Frank Cass.

Lavoy, P. R., Sagan, S. D., and Wirtz, J. J. (2000) (eds.), *Planning the Unthinkable: How New Powers will Use Nuclear, Chemical and Biological Weapons*, Ithaca, NY: Cornell University Press.

Lawler, P (1995), *A Question Of Values: Johan Galtung's Peace Research*, Boulder, CO: Lynne Rienner Publishers)

Layne, C. (2006), *The Peace of Illusions: American Grand Strategy from 1940 to the Present*, Ithaca, NY: Cornell University Press.

Lederberg, J., Shope, R. S., and Oaks, S. C., Jr. (1992) (eds.), *Emerging Infections: Microbial Threats to Health in the United States*, Committee on Emerging Microbial Threats to Health, Institute of Medicine, Washington: National Academy Press.

Lee, C. (1999), 'On Economic Security', in G. Wilson-Roberts (ed.), *An Asia-Pacific Security Crisis?: New Challenges to Regional Stability*, Wellington, New Zealand: Centre for Strategic Studies.

Lefever, E. W. (1962) (ed.), *Arms and Arms Control*, New York: Praeger.

Leitzel, J. (1993) (ed.), *Economics and National Security*, Boulder, CO: Westview Press.

Lemkin, R. (1944), *Axis Rule in Occupied Europe*, Washington: Carnegie Endowment.

Lens, S. (1970), *The Military Industrial Complex*, Philadelphia, PA: Pilgrim Press.

Lepard, B. (2002), *Rethinking Humanitarian Intervention: A Fresh Legal Approach Based on Fundamental Ethical Principles in International Law and World Religions*, University Park, PA: Pennsylvania State University Press.

Lepgold, J., and Nincic, M. (2001) *Beyond the Ivory Tower: International Relations Theory and the Issue of Policy Relevance*, New York: Columbia University Press.

Libiszewski, S. (1997), 'Integrating Political and Technical Approaches: Lessons from the Israeli–Jordanian Water Negotiations', in N. Gleditsch (ed.), *Conflict and the Environment*, Dordrecht: Kluwer, 385–402.

Lieblich, A. (1997), 'The POW Wife—Another Perspective on Heroism', *Women's Studies International Forum*, 20 (Sept.–Dec.), 621–30.

Liew, L. (2000), 'Human Security and Economic Security: Is There a Nexus?', in W. Tow, R. Thakur, and I. T. Hyun (eds.), *Asia's Emerging Regional Order: Reconciling Traditional and Human Security*, New York: United Nations University Press.

Lindberg, T. (2005), 'Protect the People', *Washington Post*, 27 Sept.

Lindsay, J. M. (1991), *Congress and Nuclear Weapons*, Baltimore: Johns Hopkins University Press.

Lindholm, Helena (1993), 'Introduction: A Conceptual Discussion', in Lindholm (ed.) *Ethnicity and Nationalism: Foundation of Identity and Dynamics of Conflict in the 1990s*, Gothenburg: Nordnes.

Linklater, A. (1986), 'Realism, Marxism and Critical International Theory', *Review of International Studies*, 12: 301–12.

Lippman, W. (1943), *US Foreign Policy: Shield of the Republic*, Boston: Little, Brown and Co.

Lock, P. (1998), 'Military Downsizing and Growth in the Security Industry in Sub-Saharan Africa', *Strategic Analysis*, 22/9 (Dec.), 1393–1426.

Lodgaard, S. (2000), 'Human Security: Concept and Operationisation', Paper presented at the Expert Seminar on Human Rights, Palaise Wilson, Geneva, 8–9 Dec., 1–25, www.hsph.harvard.edu/hpcr/events/hswokshop/lodgaarrd.pdf

Lonergan, S. (1997), 'Water Resources and Conflict: Examples from the Middle East', in N. Gleditsch (ed.), *Conflict and the Environment*, Dordrecht: Kluwer, 375–84.

Lowenthal, M. (2003), *Intelligence: From Secrets to Policy*, 2nd edn., Washington: CQ Press.

Luciani, Giacomo (1989), 'The Economic Content of Security', *Journal of Public Policy*, 8/2: 151–73.

Luck, E. (2008), 'The United Nations and the Responsibility to Protect', *Policy Analysis Brief* (Aug.), The Standley Foundation, pp. 1–11.

Luttwak, E. N. (1995), 'Toward Post Heroic Warfare', *Foreign Affairs* (May–June), 109–22.

Luttwak, E. N. (1999), 'Give War a Chance', *Foreign Affairs*, 78/4: 36–44.

Lutz, B. J., Lutz, J. M., and Ulmschneider, G. W. (2002), 'British Trials of Irish Nationalist Defendants: The Quality of Justice Strained,' *Studies in Conflict and Terrorism*, 25/4: 227–44.

Lutz, J. M., and Lutz, B. J. (2005), *Terrorism: Origins and Evolution*, New York: Palgrave.

Lutz, J. M., and Lutz, B. J. (2008), *Global Terrorism*, 2nd edn., London: Routledge.

McCurry, Justin (2000), 'Games Machine "Poses Military Threat"', *Guardian*, 17 Apr., p. 10.

McEvoy-Levy, S. (2006) (ed.), *Troublemakers or Peacemakers? Youth and Post-Accord Peace Building*, The RIREC Project on Post-Accord Peace Building, Notre Dame, IN: University of Notre Dame Press.

McGuire, M. (1986), 'The Insidious Dogma of Deterrence', *Bulletin of the Atomic Scientists* (Dec.), pp. 24–9.

Mack, A. (2004), 'A Signifier of Shared Values', *Security Dialogue*, 35/3: 366–7.

McKay, S., and Mazurana, D. (2004), *Where are the Girls? Girls in Fighting Forces in Northern Uganda, Sierra Leone, and Mozambique: Their Lives during and after War.* Montreal: International Centre for Human Rights and Democratic Development.

Mackenzie, D. (1990), *Inventing Accuracy: A Historical Sociology of Nuclear Missile Guidance*, Cambridge, MA: MIT Press.

Macmillan, L. (2009), 'The Child Soldier in North–South Relations', *International Political Sociology*, 3/1: 36–52.

McSweeney, B. (1996), 'Identity and Security: Buzan and the Copenhagen School', *Review of International Studies*, 22/1: 81–93.

McSweeney, B. (1999), *Security, Identity and Interests: A Sociology of International Relations*, Cambridge: Cambridge University Press.

Mansfield, E. D., and Snyder, J. (1989), 'Democratization and the Danger of War', in J. Mueller (ed.), *Retreat from Doomsday: The Growing Obsolescence of Major War*, New York: Basic Books.

Marks, M. (2001), *Young Warriors: Youth Politics, Identity and Violence in South Africa*, Johannesburg: Witwatersrand University Press.

Markusen, A. (1999), 'The Rise of World Weapons', *Foreign Policy*, 114 (Spring), 40–51.

Marx, K. (1859), *A Contribution to the Critique of Political Economy*, www.marxists.org/archive/marx/works/1859/critique-pol-economy

Marx, K. (1875), *Critique of the Gotha Program*, www.marxists.org/archive/marx/works/1875/gotha

Mastanduno, M. (1998), 'Economics and Security in Statecraft and Scholarship', *International Organization*, 52/4: 825–54.

Mathews, J. T. (1989), 'Redefining Security', *Foreign Affairs*, 68/2: 162–77.

Mayer, K. R. (1991), *The Political Economy of Defense Contracting*, New Haven: Yale University Press.

Mayhew, E. (2005), 'A Dead Giveaway: A Critical Analysis of New Labour's Rationale for Supporting Military Exports', *Contemporary Security Policy*, 26/1: 62–83.

Maynes, C. (1995), 'Relearning Intervention', *Foreign Policy*, 98 (Spring), 96–113

Mearsheimer, J. (2001), *The Tragedy of Great Power Politics*, New York: Norton.

Mearsheimer, J. (2005), 'Hans Morgenthau and the Iraq War: Realism versus NeoConservatism', OpenDemocracy.net, 19 May.

Melman, S. (1970), *Pentagon Capitalism*, New York: McGraw-Hill.

Melman, S. (1974), *The Permanent War Economy: American Capitalism in Decline*, New York: Simon & Schuster.

Melman, S. (2003), 'In the Grip of a Permanent War Economy', *CounterPunch*, 15 Mar.

Mertus, J. (2000), 'The Legality of Humanitarian Intervention: Lessons from Kosovo', *William and Mary Law Review*, 41/4: 1743–87.

Migdal, J. (1988), *Strong Societies and Weak States: State–Society Relations and State Capabilities in the Third World*, Princeton: Princeton University Press.

Milliken, J. (2001), *The Social Construction of the Korean War: Conflict and its Possibilities*, Manchester: Manchester University Press.

Mills, C. Wright (1956), *The Power Elite*, Oxford: Oxford University Press.

Milner, H. (1992), 'International Theories of Co-operation among Nations: Strengths and Weaknesses', *World Politics*, 44 (Apr.), 466–96.

Møller, B. (1991), *Resolving the Security Dilemma in Europe: The German Debate on Non-Offensive Defence*, London: Brassey's Defence Publishers.

Monbiot, G. (2008) 'At Last, a Date', *Guardian*, 15 Dec.

Moran, D., and Russell, D. (2008), 'The Militarization of Energy Security', *Strategic Insights*, 7/1 (Feb.).

Moravcsik, A. (2001), 'Constructivism and European Integrations: A Critique', in T. Christiansen, K. E. Jørgensen, and A. Wiener (eds.), *The Social Construction of Europe*, London: Sage, 176–88.

Morgan, P. M. (1983), *Deterrence: A Conceptual Analysis*, 2nd edn., Beverley Hills, CA: Sage.

Morgenthau, H. J. (1962), 'The Trouble with Kennedy', *Commentary*, 33/1: 51–5.

Morgenthau, H. J. (1978), *Politics among Nations: The Struggle for Power and Peace*, New York: Alfred A. Knopf.

Morris, J. (1995), 'Force and Democracy: The US/UN Intervention in Haiti', *International Peacekeeping*, 2/3: 391–412.

Morris, J., and Wheeler, N. J. (2006), 'Justifying Iraq as a Humanitarian Intervention: The Cure Is Worse than the Disease', in W. P. S. Sidhu and Ramesh Thakur (eds.), *The Iraq Crisis and World Order: Structural and Normative Challenges*, Tokyo: United Nations University Press.

MOSOP (1990), 'Ogoni Bill of Rights', Oct., www.mosop.org/ogoni_bill_of_rights_text.html

Mueller, G. O. W. (2001), 'Transnational Crime: Definitions and Concepts', in Phil Williams and Dimitri Vlassos (eds.), *Combating Transnational Crime: Concepts, Activities and Responses*, London: Frank Cass Publishers, 13–21.

Mueller, J. (1989), *Retreat from Doomsday: The Growing Obsolescence of Major War*, New York: Basic Books.

Muggah, R., and Gainsbury, S. (2003), 'Holding up Development: The Effects of Small Arms and Light Weapons in Developing Countries', *id21 media*, www.id21.org/id21-media/arms.html (accessed 18 Sept. 2005).

Münkler, H. (2005), *The New Wars*, Cambridge: Polity.

Mutimer, David (2000), *The Weapons State: Proliferation and the Framing of Security*, Boulder, CO: Lynne Rienner.

Myers, N. (1986), 'The Environmental Dimension to Security Issues', *Environmentalist*, 6/4: 251–7.

Myers, N. (1987), 'Population, Environment, and Conflict', *Environmental Conservation*, 14/1: 15–22.

Naff, T. (1992), 'Water Scarcity, Resource Management, and Conflict in the Middle East', in E. Kirk (ed.), *Environmental Dimensions of Security: Proceedings from an AAAS Annual Meeting Symposium*, Washington: American Association for the Advancement of Science, 25–30.

Nantais, C., and Lee, M. F. (1999), 'Women in the United States Military: Protectors or Protected? The Case of Prisoner of War, Melissa Rathburn-Nealy', *Journal of Gender Studies*, 8/2: 181–90.

Nation (2004), 'Thaksin Issues Warning to Police', *Nation (Thailand)*, 5 Oct.

National Energy Policy Development Group (2001), *National Energy Policy*, May.

National Intelligence Council (2000), 'The Global Infectious Disease Threat and its Implications for the US', Washington: National Intelligence Council, www.cia.gov/cia/reports/nie/report/nie99-17d.html

National Intelligence Council (2003), 'SARS: Down but Still a Threat', Washington: National Intelligence Council, www.dni.gov/nic/PDF_GIF_otherprod/sarsthreat/56797book.pdf

NATO (2007), 'The Protection of Critical Infrastructures', *Committee Report*, 162 CDS 07 E rev 1, NATO Parliamentary Assembly.

Naylor, R. T. (2002), *Wages of Crime: Black Markets, Illegal Finance, and the Underworld Economy*, Cornell, NY: Cornell University Press.

Nedoroscik, J. A. (2002), 'Extremist Groups in Egypt', *Terrorism and Political Violence*, 14/4: 47–76.

Nef, Jorge (1999), *Human Security and Mutual Vulnerability*, 2nd edn., Ottawa: IDRC.

Newman, E. (2001), 'Human Security and Constructivism', *International Studies Perspectives*, 2/3: 239–51.

Newshour (1996), 'Gun Running', Public Broadcasting Service transcript, *Online Newshour*, 24 Apr., www.pbs.org/newshour/bb/bosnia/iran_4-24.html

Nicarchos, Catherine (1995), 'Women, War and Rape: Challenges Facing the International Tribunal for the Former Yugoslavia', *Human Rights*, 17: 668–71.

Nincic, M. (1982), *The Arms Race: The Political Economy of Military Growth*, New York: Praeger.

Nun, J. (2000), 'The End of Work and the "Marginal Mass" Thesis', *Latin American Perspectives*, 27/1: 6–32.

Nye, J., and Lynn-Jones, S. (1988), 'International Security Studies: A Report of a Conference on the State of the Field', *International Security*, 12/4: 5–27.

Nye, Jr., J. S. (2008), *Understanding International Conflicts: An Introduction to Theory and History*, 7th edn., London: Pearson Longman.

OAU (2000), Organization of African Unity, 'Rwanda: The Preventable Genocide, Report of the International Panel of Eminent Personalities to Investigate the 1994 Genocide in Rwanda and Surrounding Events', May.

Obama, B., and Lugar, R. (2005), 'Grounding a Pandemic', *New York Times*, 6 June.

O'Brien, K. (2006), 'Are We Missing the Point? Global Environmental Change as an Issue of Human Security', *Global Environmental Change*, 16/1: 1–3.

Ochieng, Z. (2007), 'Child Soldiers not a Lost Generation', *East African* (Nairobi), 18 Sept.

O'Connor, P. (2002), 'Australia to Ask Neighbors to Join Struggle against People Smuggling', *Associated Press*, 23 Feb.

OECD (2006), EUROSTAT-OECD Methodological Manual on Purchasing Power Parities (PPPs), Paris: OECD, www.oecd.org/dataoecd/59/10/37984252.pdf

OECD (2008), *The DAC Guidelines Poverty Reduction*, Paris: OECD.

OECD (2009), *OECD Factbook 2009: FDI Flows and Stocks*, Paris: OECD, http://caliban.sourceoecd.org/pdf/factbook2009/302009011e-03-02-01.pdf

Onuf, N. (1989), *World of our Making: Rules and Rule in Social Theory and International Relations*, Columbia, SC: University of South Carolina Press.

Onuf, N. (1998), 'Constructivism: A User's Manual', in V. Kubláková, N. Onuf, and P. Kowert (eds.), *International Relations in a Constructed World*, New York: M. E. Sharpe, 58–78.

Onuf, N. (2002), 'Worlds of our Making: The Strange Career of Constructivism in International Relations', in D. J. Puchala (ed.), *Visions of International Relations: Assessing an Academic Field*, Columbia, SC: University of South Carolina Press, 119–41.

Osgood, R. E. (1968), *Alliances and American Foreign Policy*, Baltimore: Johns Hopkins University Press.

O'Tuathail, G. (1996), *Critical Geopolitics*, London: Routledge.

Owen, W. (1995), *The Collected War Poems*, New York: Norton.

Oye, K. A. (1986) (ed.), *Cooperation under Anarchy*, Princeton: Princeton University Press.

Palan, R. (2000), 'A World of their Making: An Evaluation of the Constructivist Critique in International Relations', *Review of International Studies*, 26/4: . 575–98.

Palme, O., et al. (1982), *Common Security: A Blueprint for Survival: Report of the Independent Commission on Disarmament and Security Issues* [Palme Report], New York: Simon and Schuster.

Parekh, B. (1997), 'Rethinking Humanitarian Intervention', *International Political Science Review*, 18/1: 49–69.

Paris, R. (2001), 'Human Security: Paradigm Shift or Hot Air?', *International Security*, 26: 2.

Paris, R. (2004), 'Still an Inscrutable Concept', *Security Dialogue*, 35/3: 370–1.

Parmar, I. (2004), 'Institutes of International Affairs: Their Roles in Foreign Policy-Making, Opinion Mobilization and Unofficial Diplomacy', in Diane Stone and Andrew Denham (eds.), *Think Tank Traditions: Policy Research and the Politics of Ideas*, Manchester: Manchester University Press, 19–33.

Paul, T. V., Harknett, R. J., and Wirtz, J. J. (1998) (eds.), *The Absolute Weapon Revisited: Nuclear Arms and the Emerging International Order*, Ann Arbor: University of Michigan Press.

Peluso, N., and Harwell, E. (2001), 'Territory, Custom, and the Cultural Politics of Ethnic War in West Kalimantan, Indonesia', in N. Peluso and M. Watts (eds.), *Violent Environments*, Ithaca, NY: Cornell University Press, 83–116.

Peluso, N., and Watts, M. (2001) (eds.), *Violent Environments*, Ithaca, NY: Cornell University Press.

Peters, K. (2006), 'Footpaths to Integration: Armed Conflict, Youth and the Rural Crisis in Sierra Leone', thesis, Wageningen University.

Peters, K., and Richards, P. (1998), 'Why we Fight: Voices of Under-Age Youth Combatants in Sierra Leone', *Africa*, 68/2: 183–210.

Peterson, V. S. (1992), *Gendered States: Feminist (Re)Visions of International Relations Theory*, Boulder, CO: Lynne Rienner.

Pick, Daniel (1993), *War Machine: The Rationalisation of Slaughter in the Modern Age*, New Haven and London: Yale University Press.

Pillar, P. R. (2001), *Terrorism and US Foreign Policy*, Washington: Brookings Institution.

Piot, P. (2001), 'AIDS and Human Security', speech delivered at the United Nations University, Tokyo, 2 Oct., www.unaids.org/html/pub/media/speeches01/piot_tokyo_02oct01_en_doc.htm

Podder, S. (2008), 'Doctrinal Challenges, Nation Building, Terror Tactics and the Power of the Child: A Tale of Three "Sites"', *Strategic Analysis*, 3/1: 147–59.

Poku, N. K. (2006), *The Politics of Africa's AIDS Crisis*. Cambridge: Polity.

Poland, J. M. (2005), *Understanding Terrorism: Groups, Strategies, and Responses*, 2nd edn., Upper Saddle River, NJ: Prentice Hall.

Poundstone, W. (1992), *Prisoner's Dilemma*, New York: Doubleday.

Prefontaine, D. C., and Dandurand, Y. (2004), 'Terrorism and Organized Crime: Reflections on an Illusive Link and its Implications for Criminal Law Reform', paper prepared for the annual meeting of the International Society for Criminal Law Reform, Montreal, Aug., www.icclr.law.ubc.ca/Publications/Reports/International%20Society%20Paper%20of%20Terrorism.pdf

Prins, G. (1993) (ed.), *Threats without Enemies: Facing Environmental Insecurity*, London: Earthscan.

Publius (1787–8), Alexander Hamilton, James Madison, and John Jay, *The Federalist*, www.constitution.org/fed/federa00.htm

Radu, M. (2002), 'Terrorism after the Cold War,' *Orbis*, 46/2: 363–79.

Ramakrishna, K., and Tan, A. (2003), 'The New Terrorism: Diagnosis and Prescriptions', in Andrew Tan (ed.), *The New Terrorism: Anatomy, Trends and Counter-Strategies*, Singapore: Eastern Universities Press, 3–29.

Ramsbotham, O., Woodhouse, T., and Miall, H. (2005), *Contemporary Conflict Resolution*, 2nd edn., Cambridge and Malden, MA: Polity.

Ramsey, P. (2002), *The Just War: Force and Political Responsibility*, Lanham, MD: Rowman & Littlefield.

Rengger, Nicholas (1999), *International Relations, Political Theory and the Problem of Order: Beyond International Relations Theory?* London: Routledge.

Renner, M. (1991), 'Assessing the Military's War on the Environment', in L. Brown (ed.), *State of the World 1991*, New York: W. W. Norton, 132–52.

Reno, W. (1998), *Warlord Politics and African States*, Boulder, CO: Lynne Rienner.

Reus-Smit, C. (1992), 'Realist and Resistance Utopia's: Community, Security and Political Action in the New Europe', *Millennium: Journal of International Studies*, 21: 1–28.

Reus-Smit, C. (1996), 'The Constructivist Turn: Critical Theory after the Cold War', Research School of Pacific and Asian Studies, Australian National University, Department of International Relations, Canberra, Working Paper No. 4.

Rich, A. (2004), *Think Tanks, Public Policy, and the Politics of Expertise*, Cambridge: Cambridge University Press.

Richardson, L. F. (1960), *Statistics of Deadly Quarrels*, Pittsburgh: Boxwood Press.

Richelson, J. (1995), *A Century of Spies: Intelligence in the Twentieth Century*, Oxford: Oxford University Press.

Rind, David (1995), 'Drying Out the Tropics', *New Scientist*, 6 May.

Risse-Kappen, T. (1994), 'Ideas do not Float Freely: Transnational Coalitions, Domestic Structures, and the End of the Cold War', *International Organization*, 48/2: 185–214.

Risse-Kappen, T. (1996), 'Collective Identity in a Democratic Community: The Case of NATO', in P. J. Katzenstein (ed.), *The Culture of National Security: Norms and Identity in World Politics*, New York: Columbia University Press, 357–99.

Roberts, A. (1993), 'Humanitarian War: Military Intervention and Human Rights', *International Affairs*, 69/3: 429–49.

Robinson, W. I. (2004), *A Theory of Global Capitalism: Production, Class, and State in a Transnational World*, Baltimore: Johns Hopkins University Press.

Rodríguez-Garavito, C., Barrett, P., and Chavez, D. (2008), *The New Latin American Left: Utopia Reborn*, London: Pluto.

Roe, P. (2001), 'Misperception and Minority Rights: Romania's Security Dilemma', *European Yearbook of Minority Issues, Volume 1, 2001/2*, Bozen/Bolzano: European Centre for Minority Issue, 349–71.

Roe, P. (2002), 'Misperception and Ethnic Conflict: Transylvania's Societal Security Dilemma', *Review of International Studies*, 28/1: 57–74.

Roe, P. (2004), 'Securitization and Minority Rights: Conditions of Desecuritization', *Security Dialogue*, 35/3: 279–94.

Roe, P. (2005), *Ethnic Violence and the Societal Security Dilemma*, London: Routledge.

Rogers, K. (1997), 'Ecological Security and Multinational Corporations', *Environmental Change and Security Project Report*, 3: 29–36.

Rogers, P. (2010), *Losing Control: Global Security in the 21st Century*, 3rd edn., London: Pluto Press.

Rogers, P., and Ramsbotham, O. (1999), 'Then and Now: Peace Research – Past and Future', *Political Studies*, XLVII, pp. 740–54.

Rosato, S. (2003), 'The Flawed Logic of Democratic Peace Theory', *American Political Science Review*, 94/4 (Nov.), 585–602.

Rose, G. (1998), 'Neoclassical Realism and Theories of Foreign Policy', *World Politics*, 51/1 (Oct.), 144–72.

Rosen, S. P. (1995), 'Military Effectiveness: Why Society Matters', *International Security*, 19/4: 5–31.

Rosen, D. (2005), *Armies of the Young: Child Soldiers in War and Terrorism*, New Brunswick, NJ: Rutgers University Press.

Rosen, D. (2007), 'Child Soldiers, International Humanitarian Law, and the Globalization of Childhood', *American Anthropologist*, 109/2: 296–306.

Rosenberg, D. A. (1983), 'The Origins of Overkill', *International Security*, 7/4 (Spring), 3–71.

Ruggie, J. G. (2006), 'Interim Report of the Special Representative of the Secretary-General on the Issue of Human Rights and Transnational Corporations and Other Business Enterprises', UN Doc. E/CN.4/2006/97, Feb.

Ruggie, J. G. (1998), 'What Makes the World Hang Together? Neo-Utilitarianism and the Social Constructivist Challenge', *International Organization*, 52/4: 855–85.

Rummel, R. J. (1994), *Death by Government*, London: Transaction Press.

Rupert, M. (2007), 'Marxism and Critical Theory', in Tim Dunne, Milja Kurki, and Steve Smith (eds.), *International Relations Theories: Discipline and Diversity*, Oxford: Oxford University Press, 148–65.

Rupert, M., and Smith, H. (2002) (eds.), *Historical Materialism and Globalization*, London: Routledge.

Rupert, M., and Solomon, S. (2006), *Globalization and International Political Economy*, Lanham, MD: Rowman & Littlefield.

Russett, B. (1971), 'An Empirical Typology of International Military Alliances', *Midwest Journal of Political Science*, 15: 262–89.

Rutledge, I. (2006), *Addicted to Oil: America's Relentless Drive for Energy Security*, London: I. B. Tauris.

Ryan, J., and Glarum, J. (2008), *Biosecurity and Bioterrorism: Containing and Preventing Biological Threats*, New York: Elsevier.

Sachs, Jeffrey (2009), 'Resolving the Debt Crisis for Low-income Countries', Brookings Papers on Economic Activity.

Saferworld (2007), *The Good, the Bad and the Ugly: A Decade of Labour's Arms Exports*, London: Saferworld.

Sagan, S., and Waltz, K. (2003), *The Spread of Nuclear Weapons: A Debate Renewed*, 2nd edn., New York: Norton.

Salter, M. (2007), 'On Exactitude in Disciplinary Science: A Response to the Network Manifesto', *Security Dialogue*, 38/1: 113–22.

Saponja-Hadzic, M. (2003), 'Serbia after Djindjic: The Maelstrom of its own Crimes', *World Press Review*, 50/6, www. worldpress.org/Europe/1082.cfm#down

Sasse, G. (2005), 'Securitization or Securing Rights? Exploring the Conceptual Foundations of Policies towards Minorities and Migrants in Europe', *Journal of Common Market Studies*, 43/4: 673–93.

Sayer, A. (2005), *The Moral Significance of Class*, Cambridge: Cambridge University Press.

Scheetz, Thomas (2004), 'The Argentine Defense Industry: An Evaluation', in Jurgen Brauer and J. Paul Dunne, *Arms Trade and Economic Development: Theory, Policy and Cases in Arms Trade Offsets*, London: Routledge, 205–16.

Scheffer, D. J. (1992), 'Towards a Modern Doctrine of Humanitarian Intervention', *University of Toledo Law Review*, 23/2: 253–93.

Schelling, T. C. (1960a), 'The Role of Theory in the Study of Conflict', RAND Research Memorandum 2515 (abridged version published in *Midwest Journal of Political Science*, May 1960 and as Schelling 1960b: ch. 1).

Schelling, T. C. (1960b), *The Strategy of Conflict*, Cambridge, MA: Harvard University Press.

Schelling, T. C. (1966), *Arms and Influence*, New Haven: Yale University Press.

Schelling T. C. (1985–6), 'What Went Wrong with Arms Control?', *Foreign Affairs*, 64/2 (Winter), 219–33.

Schelling, T. C., and Halperin, M. H. (1961), *Strategy and Arms Control*, New York: Twentieth Century Fund.

Schimmelfennig, F. (1998), 'NATO Enlargement: A Constructivist Explanation', *Security Studies*, 8/2–3: 198–234.

Schmid, H (1968), 'Politics and Peace Research', *Journal of Peace Research*, 3: 217–32.

Schmidt, J. (2000), *Disciplined Minds*, Lanham, MD: Rowman & Littlefield, http://disciplined-minds.com

Schultheis, A. (2008), 'African Child Soldiers and Humanitarian Consumption', *Peace Review*, 20: 1, 31–40.

Schweller, R. (1998), *Deadly Imbalances: Tripolarity and Hitler's Strategy of World Conquest*, New York: Columbia University Press.

Seager, J. (1993), *Earth Follies*, New York: Routledge.

Sederberg, P. C. (2003), 'Global Terrorism: Problems of Challenge and Response', in Charles W. Kegley, Jr. (ed.), *The New Global Terrorism: Characteristics, Causes, Controls*, Upper Saddle River, NJ: Prentice Hall, 267–84.

Sen, A. (1999), *Development as Freedom*, New York: Anchor Books.

Senghaas, D. (1969), *Abschreckung und Frieden: Studien zur Kritik organisierter Friedlosigkeit*, Frankfurt/M.: Suhrkamp.

Shah, M. K., Osborne, N., Mbilizi, T., and Vilili, G. (2002), *Impact of HIV/AIDS on Agriculture Productivity and Rural Livelihoods in the Central Region of Malawi*, Lilongwe, Malawi: Care International.

Shaw, M. (1984) (ed.), *War, State and Society*, London: Macmillan Press.

Shearer, David (1999), 'Private Military Force and Challenges for the Future', *Cambridge Review of International Affairs*, 8/1 (Autumn–Winter), 84.

Sheehan, Michael (2005), *International Security: An Analytical Survey*, Boulder, CO: Lynne Rienner.

Shelley, L. (2008), 'The Divergent Organized Crime of Eastern Europe and the Soviet Successor States', *HEUNI Papers*, 28: 51–70.

Shepler, S. (2005), 'The Rites of the Child: Global Discourses of Youth and Reintegrating Child Soldiers in Sierra Leone', *Journal of Human Rights*, 4/2: 197–211.

Sher, Hanan (1995), 'Flying with the Russians', *Jerusalem Report*, 27 July, p. 40.

Sherry, M. S. (1995), *In the Shadow of War: The United States since the 1930s*, New Haven: Yale University Press.

Shinawatra, T. (2003), 'Keynote Address', Willard Hotel, Washington, 10 June, www.us-asean.org/Thailand/ thaksin-visit03/speech.asp

Shisana, O., Hall, E., Maluleke, K. R., Stoker, D. J., Shwabe, C., Colvin, M., Chauveau, J., Botha, C., Gumede, T., Fomundam, H., Shaikh, N., Rehle, T., Udjo, E., and Grisselquist, D. (2003), *The Impact of HIV/AIDS on the Health Sector: National Survey of Health Personnel, Ambulatory and Hospitalized Patients and Health Facilities*, Pretoria: Human Sciences Research Council and the Medical Research Council.

Sims, Brendan (2001), *Unfinest Hour: Britain and the Destruction of Bosnia*, London: Alan Lane.

Singer, P. (2003), *Corporate Warriors: The Rise of the Privatized Military Industry*, Ithaca, NY: Cornell University Press.

Singer, P. (2005), *Children at War*, New York: Pantheon Books.

SIPRI (2008a), Stockholm International Peace Research Institute, *SIPRI Yearbook 2008: Armaments, Disarmament and International Security*, Oxford: Oxford University Press.

SIPRI (2008b), *Background Paper on SIPRI Arms Transfer Data*, www.sipri.org/contents/armstrad/at_db.html

Skjelsbaek, I. (2001), 'Sexual Violence and War: Mapping out a Complex Relationship', *European Journal of International Relations*, 7/2: 211–37.

Slijper, F. (2005), *The Emerging EU Military–Industrial Complex: Arms Industry Lobbying in Brussels*, Amsterdam: Transnational Institute.

Slim, H. (2008), *Killing Civilians: Method, Madness and Morality in War*, New York: Columbia University Press.

Small, M., and Singer, D. (1982), *Resort to Arms: International and Civil Wars, 1816–1980*, Beverly Hills, CA: Sage.

Smith, A. D. (1993), 'The Ethnic Sources of Nationalism', *Survival*, 35/1: 48–62.

Smith, M. (1986), *Realist Thought from Weber to Kissinger*, Baton Rouge, LA: Louisiana State University Press.

Smith, M. (2005), 'Iraq Battle Stress Worse than WWII', *Sunday Times*, 7 Nov.

Smith, R. (2005), 'Typhoon in Saudi Arabia: BAE Systems Wins a Huge Arms Sale', *Motley Fool*, 22 Dec., http://msnbc.msn.com/id/10573979

Smith, S. (1996), 'Positivism and Beyond', in K. Booth, S. Smith, and M. Zalewski (eds.), *International Theory: Positivism and Beyond*, Cambridge: Cambridge University Press, 11–44.

Smith, S. (2005), 'The Contested Concept of Security', in K. Booth (ed.), *Critical Security Studies and World Politics*, Boulder, CO: Lynne Rienner, 27–62.

Smoke, R. (1976), 'National Security Affairs', in F. I. Greenstein and N. W. Polsby (eds.), *Handbook of Political Science*, 8, Reading, MA: Addison-Wesley, 247–361.

Snow, D. M. (1991), *National Security*, 2nd edn, New York: St Martins Press.

Snyder, G. H. (1984), 'The Security Dilemma in Alliance Politics', *World Politics*, 36/4: 461–95.

Snyder, G. H, (1997), *Alliance Politics*, Ithaca, NY: Cornell University Press.

Snyder, J. (1991), *Myths of Empire: Domestic Politics and International Ambition*, Ithaca, NY: Cornell University Press.

Snyder, J. (1998), *The Myths of Empire: Domestic Politics and International Ambition*, Ithaca, NY: Cornell University Press.

Soeya, Y. (1997), 'Japan's Economic Security', in S. Harris and A. Mack (eds.), *Asia-Pacific Security: The Economics-Politics Nexus*, Pymble, NSW, Australia: Allen and Unwin.

Solingen, E. (1998), *Regional Orders at Century's Dawn: Global and Domestic Influences on Grand Strategy*, Princeton: Princeton University Press.

Solingen, E. (2007), *Nuclear Logics: Contrasting Paths in East Asia and the Middle East*, Princeton: Princeton University Press.

Sorenson, B. R. (1999), 'Recovering from Conflict: Does Gender Make a Difference?', *UN Chronicle*, 2: 26–7.

Sorokin, P. (1937), *Social and Cultural Dynamics*, New York: American Books.

Soroos, M. (1994), 'Global Change, Environmental Security, and the Prisoner's Dilemma', *Journal of Peace Research*, 39/3: 317–32.

Soroos, M. (1997), *The Endangered Atmosphere: Preserving a Global Commons*, Columbia, SC: University of South Carolina Press.

Sperling, J., Malik, Y., and Louscher, D. (1998) (eds.), *Zones of Amity, Zones of Enmity: The Prospects for Economic and Military Security in Asia*, Leiden: Brill.

Sprout, H., and Sprout, M. (1971), *Toward a Politics of Planet Earth*, New York: Von Norstrand Reinhold.

Start (2007), The Study of Terrorism and the Responses to Terrorism, 'Global Terrorism Database', University of Maryland, www.start.umd.edu/data/gtd

Stavrianakis, A. (2005a), '(Big) Business as Usual: Sustainable Development, NGOs and UK Arms Export Policy', *Conflict, Security and Development*, 5/1: 45–67.

Stavrianakis, A. (2005b), 'UK Arms Exports and Military Globalisation', paper presented at the British International Studies Association Conference, St Andrews.

Stavrianakis, A. (2006), 'Call to Arms: The University as a Site of Militarised Capitalism and a Site of Struggle', *Millennium: Journal of International Studies*, 35/1: 139–54.

Steans, J. (1998), *Gender and International Relations. An Introduction*, Cambridge: Polity.

Stern, J. (2000), *The Ultimate Terrorists*, Cambridge, MA: Harvard University Press.

Stern, S. (1967), 'Who Thinks in a Think Tank', *New York Times Magazine*, 16 Apr.

Stewart, F. (2008) (ed.), *Horizontal Inequalities and Conflict: Understanding Group Violence in Multiethnic Societies*, London: Palgrave Macmillan.

Stiglitz, J. (2003), 'Foreword', in Svetlana Tsalik, *Caspian Oil Windfalls: Who Will Benefit?*, New York: Caspian Revenue Watch, Open Society Institute.

Stiglmayer, Alexandra (1994) (ed.), *The War against Women in Bosnia-Herzegovina*, London: University of Nebraska.

Stiles, K. W. (1995), *Case Histories in International Politics*, New York: HarperCollins.

Stokes, D. (2005), *America's Other War: Terrorizing Colombia*, London: Zed Books.

Stoler, M. A. (2000), *Allies and Adversaries: The Joint Chiefs of Staff, the Grand Alliance, and US Strategy in World War II*, Chapel Hill, NC: University of North Carolina Press.

Stremlau, J. (1994), 'Clinton's Dollar Diplomacy', *Foreign Policy*, 97: 18–35.

Stuart, D. T. (2008), *Creating the National Security State: A History of the Law that Transformed America*, Princeton: Princeton University Press.

Suhrke, A. (2004), 'A Stalled Initiative', *Security Dialogue*, 35/3: 365.

Sum, Ngai-Ling (n.d.), 'From "Integral State" to "Integral World Economic Order": Towards a Neo-Gramscian Cultural International Political Economy', Cultural Political Economy Research Cluster, Working Paper 7, University of Lancaster.

SWAY (2006), *Survey of War Affected Youth*, www.sway-uganda.org

SWAY (2008), *The State of Female Youth in Northern Uganda: Findings from the Survey of War Affected Youth*, www.sway-uganda.org

Sylvester, C. (1996), 'The Contributions of Feminist Theory to International Relations', in Steve Smith, Ken Booth, and Maryisa Zalewski (eds.), *International Theory: Positivism and Beyond*, Cambridge: Cambridge University Press.

Sylvester, C. (2007), 'Anatomy of a Footnote', *Security Dialogue*, 38/4: 547–58.

Tan, A. T. H. (2006), *The Politics of Terrorism: A Survey*, London: Routledge.

Tannenwald, N. (1999), 'The Nuclear Taboo: The United States and the Normative Basis of Nuclear Non-Use', *International Organization*, 53/3: 433–68.

Tannenwald, N., and Wohlforth, W. C. (2005) (eds.), Special issue on 'The Role of Ideas and the End of the Cold War', *Journal of Cold War Studies*, 7/2 (Spring), 3–12

Tarzi, S. M. (2005), 'Coercive Diplomacy and an "Irrational" Regime: Understanding the American Confrontation with the Taliban', *International Studies*, 42/1: 21–41.

Taylor, S., and Goldman, D. (2004), 'Intelligence Reform: Will More Agencies, Money, and Personnel Help?', *Intelligence and National Security*, 19/3: 416–35.

Tesón, F. R. (1997), *Humanitarian Intervention: An Inquiry into Law and Morality*, 2nd edn., New York: Transnational Publishers.

Tesón, F. R. (1998), *A Philosophy of International Law*, Boulder, CO: Westview Press.

Tesón, F. R. (2003), 'The Liberal Case for Humanitarian Intervention', in J. L. Holzgrefe and Robert O. Keohane (eds.), *Humanitarian Intervention: Ethical, Legal and Political Dilemmas*, Cambridge: Cambridge University Press.

Thakur, R. (2004a), 'A Political Worldview', *Security Dialogue*, 35/3: 347.

Thakur, R. (2004b), 'Iraq and the Responsibility to Protect', *Behind the Headlines*, 62/1: 1–16.

Thee, M. (1986), *Military Technology, Military Strategy and the Arms Race*, London: Croom Helm.

Theiler, T. (2003), 'Societal Security and Social Psychology', *Review of International Studies*, 29/2: 249–68.

Therborn, G. (2008), *From Marxism to Post-Marxism?*, London: Verso.

Thomas, C. (1987), *In Search of Security: The Third World in International Relations*, Boulder, CO: Lynne Rienner.

Thomas, C. (2004), 'A Bridge between the Interconnected Challenges Confronting the World', *Security Dialogue*, 35/3: 353–4.

Thurow, L. (1992), *Head to Head: The Coming Economic Battle among Japan, Europe and America*, London: Nicholas Brealey.

Tickner, J. A. (1992), *Gender in International Relations: Feminist Perspectives on Achieving Global Security*, New York: Columbia University Press.

Tickner, Arlene B. and Wæver, Ole (eds.) (2009) *International Relations Scholarship Around the World*, Book series: Worlding Beyond the West, vol.1, London: Routledge.

Tilly, C. (1990), *Big Structures, Large Processes, Huge Comparisons*, New York: Russell Sage Foundation.

Time (1975), 'The Executive Mercenaries', 24 Feb.

Tow, W. T. (2001), 'Alternative Security Models: Implications for ASEAN', in A. Tan and K. Boutin (eds.), *Non-Traditional Security Issues in Southeast Asia*, Singapore: Institute of Defence and Strategic Studies, 257–85.

Trachtenberg, M. (1991), *History and Strategy*, Princeton: Princeton University Press.

Tuchman Mathews, J. (1989), 'Redefining Security', *Foreign Affairs*, 68/2: 162–77.

Tucker, R. K. (1991), *The Dragon and the Cross: The Rise and Fall of the Ku Klux Klan in Middle America*, Hamden, CT: Archon Books.

Tunyasiri, Y. (2003), 'War on Drugs—Seize More Assets, Thakshin Urges Police', *Bangkok Post*, 23 Mar.

Turco, R. P., Toon, O. B., Ackerman, T. P., Pollack, J. B., and Sagan, C. (1990), 'Climate and Smoke: An Appraisal of Nuclear Winter', *Science*, 247: 166–76.

Turner, M. (2005), 'UN "must never again be found wanting on genocide"', *Financial Times*, 16 Sept.

Tusa, F. (1994), 'Old but Fit: Bargains Galore in the Secondhand Ship Market', *Armed Forces Journal International* (Nov.), 30–1.

Tyler, Patrick E. (1992), 'Pentagon Drops Goal of Blocking New Superpowers', *New York Times*, 23 May, p. A1.

Ullman, R. (1983), 'Redefining Security', *International Security*, 8/1: 129–53.

UNAIDS (2007), *AIDS Epidemic Update*, Dec., Geneva: Joint United Nations Programme on HIV/AIDS (UNAIDS) and World Health Organization (WHO)

UNCTAD (2009), *United Nations Conference on Trade and Development, The Least Developed Countries' Report: Escaping the Poverty Trap*, Geneva: United Nations.

UNDP (1994), United Nations Development Program, *Human Development Report 1994*, New York: Oxford University Press.

UNDP (1998), United Nations Development Program, *Human Development Report 1998*, New York: Oxford University Press.

UNDP (2005), United Nations Development Programme, *UNDP Human Development Report 2005*, Oxford: Oxford University Press.

UNDP (2008), United Nations Development Program, *Making Global Trade Work for People* (London: Earthscan), www.undp.org/mainundp/propoor/docs.trade-jan2003.pdf

UNDP (2009), United Nations Development Program, *Human Development Report 2009* (Oxford: Oxford University Press)

UNEP (2002), United Nations Environment Program, *Vital Water Graphics: An Overview of the State of the World's Fresh and Marine Waters* (Nairobi: UNEP).

UNEP (2003), United Nations Environment Program, *Global Environmental Outlook 3*, London: Earthscan.

UNEP (2005), United Nations Environment Program, *One Planet, Many People: Atlas of Our Changing Environment*, Nairobi: UNEP.

UNESCO (2008), United Nations Educational, Scientific and Cultural Organization, *Trends and Projections of Enrolment, 1960–2025*, Paris: United Nations.

UNESCO (2009), 'MDG Attainment Database', Paris: UNESCO, www.uis.unesco.org /v.php?URL_ID=5261&URL_DO=DO_ TOPIC&URL_SECTION=201 (accessed 28 Mar. 2009).

UNICEF (1997), *Cape Town Principles and Best Practice on the Prevention of Recruitment of Children into the Armed Forces and on Demobilization and Social Reintegration of Child Soldiers in Africa*, New York: UNICEF.

United Nations (2000), 'United Nations Convention against Transnational Crime', www.unodc.org/unodc/en/crime_cicp_convention.html

United Nations (2004), *A More Secure World: Our Shared Responsibility*, Report of the Secretary's General's High-Level Panel on Threats, Challenges and Change, New York: United Nations, www.un.org/secureworld

United Nations (2005a), 'Draft Outcome Document, 2005 World Summit', 13 Sept., 27–8, www.un.org/apps/news/story.asp?NewsID=15853&Cr=world&Cr1=summit

United Nations (2005b), 'In Larger Freedom', Report of the Secretary-General of the United Nations for Decision by Heads of State and Government in September 2005, New York: United Nations, www.un.org/largerfreedom

United Nations (2005c), Agenda Item 101: Promotion and Protection of the Rights of Children: Children and Armed Conflict, Report of the Secretary-General, UNICEF, 15A/59/695S/2005/72.

United Nations (2005d), World Summit Outcome, A/RES/60/1, 24 Oct.

United Nations (2009a), *Children and Armed Conflict*, Report of the Secretary-General, 26 Mar., A/63/785–S/2009/158.

United Nations (2009b), *Globalization and its Full Impact on the Enjoyment of Human Rights*, New York: United Nations Publications.

United Nations (2009c), 'MDG Indicators Database', UN Statistics Division, New York: United Nations Publications, http://millenniumindicators.un.org (accessed 27 Feb. 2006).

United Nations Security Council (2004), 'Meeting on the Situation in Sudan', S/PV.4988, 11 June.

United Nations Statistics Unit (2009), *World Economic and Social Survey 2009*, New York: UN Department of Economic and Social Affairs.

United States Congress (1979), *The Effects of Nuclear War*, Washington: Congress of the US, Office of Technology Assessment, US Government Printing Office.

UNODC (2002), United Nations Office on Drugs and Crime, Global Programme against Transnational Organized Crime, *Results of a Pilot Survey of Forty Selected Organized Criminal Groups in Sixteen Countries*, Sept., www.unodc.org/pdf/crime/publications/Pilot_survey.pdf

US Council on Competitiveness (1994), *Economic Security: The Dollars and Sense of US Foreign Policy*, Washington: US Council on Competitiveness.

Van Crevald, M. (2001), *Men, Women and War: Do Women Belong in the Front Line?* London: Cassell.

van Duyne, P. C. (2004), 'The Creation of a Threat Image: Media, Policy Making and Organized Crime', in P. C. van Duyne, M. Jager, K. von Lampe, and J. L. Newell (eds.), *Threats and Phantoms of Organised Crime, Corruption and*

Terrorism: Critical European Perspectives, papers presented at the Fourth Colloquium on Cross-Border Crime, The Netherlands: Wolf Legal Publishers.

Van Evera, S. (1999), *Causes of War: Power and the Roots of Conflict*, Ithaca, NY: Cornell University Press.

Van Niekerk, P. (2002), 'Making a Killing: The Business of War', *The Center for Public Integrity*, 28 Oct., www.icij.org/bow/default.aspx (accessed 18 Sept. 2005).

von Lampe, K. (2004), 'Measuring Organised Crime: A Critique of Current Approaches', in P. C. van Duyne, M. Jager, K. von Lampe, and J. L. Newell (eds.), *Threats and Phantoms of Organised Crime, Corruption and Terrorism: Critical European Perspectives*, papers presented at the Fourth Colloquium on Cross-Border Crime, The Netherlands: Wolf Legal Publishers.

von Lampe, K., and Johansen, P. O. (2003), 'Criminal Networks and Trust', paper presented at the 3rd Annual Meeting of the European Society of Criminology. Helsinki, Finland, 29 Aug.

Wæver, O. (1993), 'Societal Security: The Concept', in O. Wæver, B. Buzan, M. Kelstrup, and P. Lemaitre (eds.), *Identity, Migration and the New Security Agenda in Europe*, London: Pinter, 17–40.

Wæver, O. (1994), 'Insecurity and Identity Unlimited', Working Paper No. XI, Copenhagen: Copenhagen Peace Research Institute.

Wæver, O. (1995), 'Securitization and Desecuritization', in R. Lipschutz (ed.), *On Security*, New York: Columbia University Press, 46–86.

Wæver, O. (1998), 'The Sociology of a Not So International Discipline: American and European Developments in International Relations', *International Organization*, 52/4 (Oct.), 687–727.

Wæver, O. (1999), 'Securitizing Sectors: Reply to Eriksson', *Cooperation and Conflict*, 34/3: 334–40.

Wæver, O. (2004), 'Aberystwyth, Paris, Copenhagen: New "Schools" in Security Theory and their Origins between Core and Periphery', paper for ISA in Montreal, Mar.; rev. version forthcoming in Arlene B. Tickner and Ole Wæver, *Thinking the International Differently*, London: Routledge.

Wæver, O. (2005), 'The Constellation of Securities in Europe', in Ersel Aydinli and James N. Rosenau (eds.), *Globalization, Security, and the Nation-State: Paradigms in Transition*, New York: State University of New York Press, 151–74.

Wæver, O. (2006), 'Security: A Conceptual History for International Relations', manuscript in preparation, www.cast.ku.dk (accessed July 2009).

Wæver, O. (2007), 'Still a Discipline after all these Debates?', in T. Dunne, M. Kurki, and S. Smith (eds.), *International Relations Theories: Discipline and Diversity*, Oxford: Oxford University Press, 288–308.

Wæver, O. (2008), 'Peace and Security: Two Evolving Concepts and their Changing Relationship', in H. G. Brauch, U. O.

Spring, C. Mesjasz, J. Grin, P. Dunay, N. C. Behera, B. Chourou, P. Kameri-Mbote, and P. H. Liotta (eds.), *Globalisation and Environmental Challenges: Reconceptualising Security in the 21st Century,* Heidelberg: Springer Verlag, 99–112.

Wæver, O., Buzan, B., Kelstrup, M., and Lemaitre, P. (1993) (eds.), *Identity, Migration and the New Security Agenda in Europe*, London: Pinter.

Walker R. B. J. (1993), *Inside/Outside*, Cambridge: Cambridge University Press.

Walker, R. B. J. (1997), 'The Subject of Security', in K. Krause and M. C. Williams (eds.), *Critical Security Studies: Concepts and Cases*, Minneapolis: University of Minnesota Press, 61–81.

Wallerstein, I. (2004), *World-Systems Analysis: An Introduction*, Durham, NC: Duke University Press.

Walt, S. (1987), *The Origin of Alliances*, Ithaca, NY: Cornell University Press.

Walt, S. (1991), 'The Renaissance of Security Studies', *International Studies Quarterly*, 35/2.

Walt, S. (1999), 'Rigor or Rigor Mortis? Rational Choice and Security Studies', *International Security*, 23/4 (Spring), 5–48.

Waltz, K. N. (1959), *Man, the State, and War*, New York: Columbia University Press.

Waltz, K. N. (1979), *Theory of International Politics*, New York: McGraw-Hill.

Waltz, K. (1989), 'The Origins of War in Neorealist Theory', in R. I. Rotberg and T. K. Robb (eds.), *The Origin and Prevention of Major Wars*, Cambridge: Cambridge University Press.

Warren, B. (1980), *Imperialism: Pioneer of Capitalism*, London: Verso.

Watts, M. (2001), 'Petro-Violence: Community, Extraction, and Political Ecology of a Mythic Commodity', in N. Peluso and M. Watts (eds.), *Violent Environments*, Ithaca, NY: Cornell University Press, 189–212.

Way, Debra, and Polglaze, Karen, (2001), 'Fed: Strip Search Powers for Guards Severe but Justified', *AAP Newsfeed*, 6 Apr.

WCED (1987), World Commission on Environment and Development, *Our Common Future*, Oxford: Oxford University Press.

Weber, C. (1999), 'IR: The Resurrection or New Frontiers of Incorporation', *European Journal of International Relations*, 5/4: 435–50.

Weiss, T. G. (2004), 'The Sunset of Humanitarian Intervention? The Responsibility to Protect in a Unipolar Era', *Security Dialogue*, 35/2.: 135–53.

Weldes, J. (1999a), 'The Cultural Production of Crises: US Identity and Missiles in Cuba', in J. Weldes, M. Laffey, H. Gusterson, and R. Duvall (eds.), *Cultures of Insecurity: States, Communities, and the Production of Danger*, Minneapolis: University of Minnesota Press, 35–62.

Weldes, J. (1999b), *Constructing National Interests: The United States and the Cuban Missile Crisis*, Minneapolis: University of Minnesota Press.

Weldes, J., Laffey, M., Gusterson, H., and Duvall, R. (1999) (eds.), *Cultures of Insecurity: States, Communities and the Production of Danger*, Minneapolis: University of Minneapolis Press.

Wells, J., Meyers J., and Mulvihill, M. (2001), 'US Ties to Saudi Elite May Be Hurting War on Terrorism', *Boston Herald*, 10 Dec.

Welsh, J. (2004), 'Conclusion', in J. Welsh (ed.), *Humanitarian Intervention and International Relations*, Oxford: Oxford University Press.

Wendt, A. (1992), 'Anarchy is what States Make of it: The Social Construction of Power Politics', *International Organization*, 46/2: 391–425.

Wendt, A. (1994), 'Collective Identity Formation and the International State', *American Political Science Review*, 88: 384–96.

Wendt, A. (1996), 'Identity and Structural Change in International Politics', in Y. Lapid and F. Kratochwil (eds.), *The Return of Culture and Identity in IR Theory*, Boulder, CO: Lynne Rienner, 47–64.

Wendt, A. (1999), *Social Theory of International Politics*, Cambridge: Cambridge University Press.

Wendt, A., and Barnett, M. (1993), 'Dependent State Formation and Third World Militarization', *Review of International Studies*, 19/4: 321–47.

Wessells, M. (1998), 'Children, Armed Conflict and Peace', *Journal of Peace Research*, 35/5: 635–46.

Wessells, M. (2006), *Child Soldiers: From Violence to Protection*, Cambridge, MA: Harvard University Press.

Wessells, M., and Kostelny, K. (2002), *After the Taliban: A Child-Focused Assessment in the Northern Afghan Provinces of Kunduz, Takhar, and Badakshan*, Richmond, VA: CCF International.

West, H. (2000), 'Girls with Guns: Narrating the Experience of War of Frelimo's "Female Detachment"', *Anthropological Quarterly*, 73/4: 180–94.

Westing, A. (1986), 'An Expanded Concept of International Security', in A. Westing (ed.), *Global Resources and International Conflict: Environmental Factors in Strategic Policy and Action*, Oxford: Oxford University Press, 183–200.

Wheeler, N. J. (2000), *Saving Strangers: Humanitarian Intervention in International Society*, Oxford: Oxford University Press.

Wheeler, N. J., and Booth, K. (1992), 'The Security Dilemma', in John Baylis and Nicholas J. Rengger (eds.), *Dilemmas of World Politics: International Issues in a Changing World*, Oxford: Oxford University Press, 29–60.

White House (1998), *The National Security Strategy of the United States of America*, Washington: White House, www.au.af.mil/au/awc/awcgate/nss/nssr-1098.pdf

White House (2002), *The National Security Strategy of the United States of America*, Washington: White House, http://georgewbush-whitehouse.archives.gov/nsc/nss/2002/nss.pdf

White House (2006), *The National Security Strategy of the United States of America*, Washington: White House, www.strategicstudiesinstitute.army.mil/pdffiles/nss.pdf

WHO (2002), World Health Organization, *The World Health Report 2002*, Geneva: WHO.

Wiberg, H. (1988), 'The Peace Research Movement', in Peter Wallensteen (ed.), *Peace Research: Achievements and Challenges*, Boulder, CO, and London: Westview Press, 30–53.

Wiebes, Cees (2003), *Intelligence and the War in Bosnia, 1992–1995*, Edison, NJ: Transaction Publishers.

Williams, M. C. (1998), 'Modernity, Identity and Security: A Comment on the "Copenhagen Controversy"', *Review of International Studies*, 24/3: 435–9.

Williams, M. C. (2003), 'Words, Images, Enemies: Securitization and International Politics', *International Studies Quarterly*, 47/4: 511–31.

Williams, M. C., and Krause, K. (1997), 'Preface: Toward Critical Security Studies', in K. Krause and M. C. Williams (eds.), *Critical Security Studies: Concepts and Cases*, Minneapolis: University of Minnesota Press, pp. vii–xxi.

Williams, M. C., and Neumann, I. B. (2000), 'From Alliance to Security Community: NATO, Russia, and the Power of Identity', *Millennium*, 29/2: 357–87.

Williams, P. (2001), 'Transnational Criminal Networks', in J. Arquilla and D. Ronfeldt (eds.), *Networks and Netwars: The Future of Terror, Crime and Militancy*, Santa Monica, CA: RAND Corporation, 61–97; www.rand.org/publications/MR/MR1382/MR1382.ch3.pdf

Williams, P., and Savona, E. U. (1998) (eds.), *The United Nations and Transnational Organized Crime*, London: Frank Cass.

Williams, P. D. (2006), 'Military Responses to Mass Killing: The African Union Mission in Sudan', *International Peacekeeping*, 13/2: 168–83.

Williams, P. D., and Bellamy, A. J. (2005), 'The Responsibility to Protect and the Crisis in Darfur', *Security Dialogue*, 36/1: 27–47.

Wohlstetter, A. J., and Wohlstetter, R. (1963), 'The State of Strategic studies in Europe', report prepared for the Ford Foundation.

Wohlstetter, Albert J., and Wohlstetter, R. (1966), 'The State of Strategic Studies in Japan, India, Israel', report prepared for the Carnegie Endowment for International Peace.

Wohlstetter, A. J., Hoffman, F. S., Lutz, R. J., and Rowen, H. S. (1954), *Selection and Use of Strategic Air Bases*, R-266, Santa Monica, CA: RAND Corporation.

Wolf, A. (1999), 'Water Wars and Water Reality: Conflict and Cooperation along International Waterways', in S. Lonergan (ed.), *Environmental Change, Adaptation, and Security*, Dordrecht: Kluwer, 251–65.

Wolfers, A. (1952), 'National Security as an Ambiguous Symbol', *Political Science Quarterly*, 67/4: 481–502; repr. in A. Wolfers, *Discord and Collaboration: Essays on International Politics*, Baltimore and London: Johns Hopkins University Press, 1962, 147–66.

Wolfers, A. (1962), *Discord and Collaboration: Essays on International Politics*, Baltimore and London: Johns Hopkins University Press.

Woodward, B. (2001), 'Bin Laden Said to "Own" the Taliban: Bush Is Told He Gave Regime $100 Million', *Washington Post*, 11 Oct., A01.

Woodward, B. (2007), 'Greenspan: Ouster of Hussein Crucial for Oil Security', *Washington Post*, 17 Sept.

World Bank (1998), *Development and Human Rights: The Role of the World Bank*, Washington: World Bank.

World Bank (2006), *Adjustment in Africa: Reform, Results, and the Road Ahead, World Bank*, Washington: World Bank.

World Bank (2008a), Poverty Data: A Supplement to World Development Indicators 2008, Washington: World Bank, http://siteresources.worldbank.org/DATASTATISTICS/Resources/WDI08supplement1216.pdf

World Bank (2008b), *World Development Indicators: Viewing the World at Purchasing Power Parity*, Washington: World Bank, http://siteresources.worldbank.org/DATASTATISTICS/Resources/WDI08_section1_intro.pdf

World Bank (2008c), *Adjustment Lending and Economic Performance in Sub-Saharan Africa in the 1980s and 1990s: A Comparison with Other Low-Income Countries*, Washington: World Bank.

World Bank (2009a), 'World Bank Estimates Costs of Millennium Development Goals', 21 Feb.

World Bank (2009b), *Heavily Indebted Poor Countries Initiative: Status of Implementation*, Washington: World Bank.

World Bank (2009c), *World Development Report 2009: Reshaping Economic Geography*. Washington: World Bank.

World Social Forum (2002), 'Note from the Organizing Committee on the Principles that Guide the WSF', www.forumsocialmundial.org.br/main.php?id_menu=4_2&cd_language=2

Wright, E. O. (1997), *Class Counts*, Cambridge: Cambridge University Press.

Wright, Q. (1942), *A Study of War*, Chicago: University of Chicago Press.

Wright, Q. (1965), *A Study of War*, 2nd edn., Chicago: University of Chicago Press.

Wyn Jones, R. (1996), 'Travel without Maps: Thinking about Security after the Cold War', in M. J. Davis (ed.), *Security Issues in the Post-Cold War World*, Cheltenham: Edward Elgar, 196–218.

Wyn Jones, R. (1999), *Security, Strategy, and Critical Theory*, Boulder, CO: Lynne Rienner.

Wyness, M., Harrison, L., and Buchanan, I. (2004), 'Childhood, Politics and Ambiguity: Towards an Agenda for Children's Political Inclusion', *Sociology*, 38/1: 81–99.

Xinuha (2000), News Agency, 16 Nov.

Yergin, D. (1977), *Shattered Peace: The Origins of the Cold War and the National Security State*, Boston: Houghton Mifflin Company.

Young, O. (1968), *The Politics of Force: Bargaining during Superpower Crises*, Princeton: Princeton University Press.

Zalewski, D. A. (2005), 'Economic Security and the Myth of the Efficiency/Equity Trade-Off', *Journal of Economic Issues*, 39/2: 383–90.

Zehfuss, M. (2002), *Constructivism in International Relations: The Politics of Reality*, Cambridge: Cambridge University Press.

Zeldin, T. (1998), *An Intimate History of Humanity*, London: Vintage.

Zinni, Anthony (1998), 'Avoid a Military Showdown with Iraq', *Middle East Quarterly*, Sept., www.meforum.org/408/anthony-zinni-avoid-a-military-showdown-with-iraq

Zubay, G., et al. (2005), *Agents of Bioterrorism: Pathogens and their Weaponization*, New York: Columbia University Press.

Index